LIFE INSURANCE:
A Financial Planning Approach
Second Edition

Mark S. Dorfman
University of Arkansas at Little Rock

Saul W. Adelman
Miami University (Ohio)

Dearborn Financial Publishing, Inc.

While a great deal of care has been taken to provide accurate and current information, the ideas, suggestions, general principles and conclusions presented in this text are subject to local, state and federal laws and regulations, court cases and any revisions of same. The reader is thus urged to consult legal counsel regarding any points of law—this publication should not be used as a substitute for competent legal advice.

Publisher: Carol Luitjens
Editorial Assistant: Elizabeth Ireland
Manager, Editorial Production: Gayle Sperando
Cover Design: Lucy Jenkins
Copy Editor: Christine Benton

© 1992 by Dearborn Financial Publishing, Inc.

Published by Dearborn Financial Publishing, Inc.

All rights reserved. The text of this publication, or any part thereof, may not be reproduced in any manner whatsoever without written permission from the publisher.

Printed in the United States of America.

92 93 94 10 9 8 7 6 5 4 3 2 1

Library of Congress Cataloging-in-Publication Data

Dorfman, Mark S., 1945–
  Life insurance : a financial planning approach / Mark S. Dorfman, Saul W. Adelman — 2nd ed.
     p.   cm.
  Rev. ed. of: Life Insurance and financial planning. 1986.
  Includes bibliographical references and index.
  ISBN 0-79310-199-9
     1. Insurance, Life—Unied States.   I. Adelman, Saul W.
II. Dorfman, Mark S., 1945–   Life Insurance and financial planning.
III. Title.
HG8951.D67 1992   91-32234
368.3′2′00973—dc20   CIP

To my outstanding teachers, students and friends from whom I've learned so much.

M.S.D.

To my mother, Dorothy C. Adelman, and my sister, Arlene G. Mandel.

S.W.A.

Contents

Preface — vii

Part One: Introduction to Life Insurance

1. Introduction: Life Insurance — 1
2. The Motivation to Purchase Life Insurance — 14
3. Traditional Life Insurance Products — 36
4. Nontraditional Life Insurance Products — 64
5. Annuities — 86
6. Life Insurance—Costs and Comparisons — 108

Part Two: Introduction to Health Insurance

7. Medical Expense and Disability Insurance — 131
8. Health Insurance for an Aging and Uninsured Population — 161

Part Three: Law and the Life Insurance Contract

9. The Legal Framework of Life Insurance — 181
10. Life Insurance Policy Provisions — 202

Part Four: Taxation and Investments

11. The Federal Income Tax — 230
12. The Federal Gift and Estate Tax — 245
13. Financial Mathematics and Investments — 262

Part Five: Financial Planning

14. Social Security — 282
15. Financial Planning: The Early Adult Years — 304
16. Financial Planning: The Middle Years — 342
17. Financial Planning: The Later Adult Years — 374

Part Six — Employee Benefits and Business Life Insurance

18.	Employee Benefits: Group Insurance	**397**
19.	Employee Benefits: Pension Plans	**417**
20.	Business Uses of Life and Disability Insurance	**438**

Part Seven — The Mathematics of Life Insurance

21.	The Net Single Premium	**465**
22.	Leveling the Net Single Premium	**489**
23.	Reserves, Nonforfeiture Values and Gross Premiums	**509**

Part Eight — Company Operations and Regulation

24.	Life Insurance Operations: Organization, Underwriting, Marketing and Reinsurance	**535**
25.	Life Insurance Operations: Regulation, Financial Operations and Taxation	**555**

Appendix A: Formula for Compound Interest Tables — **579**

Glossary — **581**

Index — **597**

Preface

Since publication of our first edition, the life insurance market has changed extensively. The life insurance industry's movement toward one-stop financial planning reached high tide and receded. As a result this edition has been almost totally rewritten, to focus more on life insurance fundamentals while still providing a financial planning perspective.

All the chapters retained from the first edition provide greater depth of coverage. We have added new chapters on income and estate taxation (Chapters 11 and 12), employee benefits (Chapters 18 and 19) and health insurance (Chapter 8). Chapter 2, "The Motivation to Purchase Life Insurance," provides a broad overview of demographic data, economic and psychological theory and several short case studies to explain why people make the life insurance transaction.

Special Features

This edition includes enhanced computer exhibits and improved practice cases for Chapter 15 on life insurance planning for the early adult years, Chapter 16 on preretirement financial planning and Chapter 17 on estate planning. The heart of the text remains the three annotated case studies appearing in these three chapters. Each of these chapters contains two practice cases requiring student solutions using personal computers and electronic spreadsheets. The emphasis on problem solving will be familiar to students who have completed basic accounting and managerial finance courses. The problem-solving requirement also differentiates this book from other life insurance textbooks.

The book contains several learning aids to help students focus on main ideas. Each chapter begins with specific learning objectives and ends with review questions. Clarity of explanations and general readability remain our overriding concern. In most chapters we include illustrative applications to make the theory clearer. In many chapters we focus the reader's attention on several interesting summary questions, with a section titled "Financial Planning Issues." For example, "Should workers eligible for Social Security take early, normal or delayed retirement?" (Chapter 14), "Is cash value life insurance a competitive savings medium?" (Chapter 3), "Should wealth be transferred by gift during the owner's lifetime or should wealth be transferred at death?" (Chapter 17).

An Integrated Framework

Explaining the life insurance transaction requires authors and readers to consider several related topics, many of which are the subject of other business school courses. While our primary focus is the life insurance transaction, we often discuss closely related topics to explain, illustrate and illuminate the life insurance transaction. Our reference to other areas of the business curriculum helps integrate knowledge from these areas with the study of life insurance. In cases where the reader may feel the need for more background information, we suggest books and articles in chapter-ending bibliographies.

We explain life insurance in the context of the following closely related topics, each of which could be the subject of a book or a business school course:

- Federal taxation, both income and estate
- Investment alternatives
- Employee benefits
- Financial mathematics
- Retirement planning
- Estate planning

After studying this text, the reader should be keenly aware of the broad scope of the topic of life insurance and should appreciate the depth of "collateral" information needed to keep current on this subject. For readers with background in these areas, this text should serve as a useful review of previously learned concepts, but from a new perspective. For readers without background in these subjects, the material contained here may stimulate interest in additional course work in one or more of these areas.

Societal Issues

This text provides a foundation for understanding some of the most important individual and societal problems faced by our aging, democratic and industrialized society. Gerontological issues are found in several chapters—financing retirement (Chapter 16), financing long-term care (Chapter 8) and defining the role of Social Security in future retirement plans (Chapters 14 and 16).

Moral and ethical issues also concern us. Access to adequate health care (Chapter 7) and financing of universal health care (Chapters 7 and 8) are addressed. Chapters 18 and 19 pose questions such as "Should substantial tax advantages be given to employers and employees to encourage the provision of retirement and other employee benefits?" Chapter 25 explores whether sensitive regulatory information concerning company solvency should be available for public consumption and possible misinterpretation.

Without question, the life insurance transaction affects the lives of most adult Americans. Therefore, society has a great stake in determining how the life insurance transaction is regulated. The immense problems associated with the weakness and failures in the savings and loan industry would pale in comparison to the problems arising *if* life insurer solvency were threatened on a similar scale. As this book is being written, a few large insurers have been placed in receivership, causing short-term and perhaps long-term financial hardships for their policyholders. The quality ratings of several other large, well-known life insurance companies have been lowered by Moody's Investors Services. The impact on insurance consumers of these failures and quality deteriorations has yet to be measured or fully felt. Because of the integral role life insurance plays for individuals, families and business firms, increasingly intelligent choices must be made by consumers, regulators and industry employees. To make these choices, accurate technical information is critical. Much of that needed information is found throughout this text.

Audience

We have written this book for college students, practitioners, regulators and all others interested in the life insurance transaction. We have not avoided controversy, but we have tried diligently to present a balanced account of the many controversial issues raised. The reader, upon completing this text, will not have all the answers, but at least the questions should be clear.

Acknowledgments

Many people shared their talents and ideas with us as we developed this edition. However, we retained the right to make the final changes and therefore remain responsible for any real or perceived shortcomings.

We are pleased to recognize significant contributions from the following readers:

Khurshid Ahmad
Thomas Baxley
Donald Bender
Pamela Carr
Stephen D'Arcy
Edward Graves
Harry Johnson
Robert J. Myers
James R. Newell

Jim P. Rohr
Barry Schweig
Ralph Shull
David Sinow
Wayne Staton
A. Frank Thompson
Michael Watts
Frank L. Whitbeck

Some special people require special mention. The entire manuscript was reviewed and constructively criticized by the following people. We are most grateful for their suggestions.

Nancy Sutton-Bell, Florida State University
Larry Cox, University of Georgia
Robert Drennen, Temple University
Donald Hardigree, University of Nevada–Las Vegas

Many people contributed to the first edition of this text, and we remain grateful for their efforts. Among them are Thomas Aiuppa, Joseph Belth, James Jensen, Barry Schweig and A. Frank Thompson.

A. Frank Thompson and Arthur Cox of the University of Northern Iowa have prepared the Instructor's Manual for this book. Their work on that project is most appreciated.

Our editor, Carol Luitjens, has shown great enthusiasm and support for this revision. She met with us on several occasions, both advising us and listening to our ideas. More important, she provided valuable suggestions for improvement throughout the book.

Marcia T. Dorfman, former Head Science Librarian at Miami University, was involved in this project every step of the way. She proofread Professor Dorfman's share of the manuscript, reading rough drafts and page proofs. She researched many issues in the University of Arkansas at Little Rock library and greatly aided in developing many end-of-chapter bibliographies.

One source of regular stimulation, inspiration and ideas is the students to whom we presented this material during development, sometimes in lectures and sometimes as rough drafts of chapters. We gratefully acknowledge the help of these students, some of whom made very incisive observations.

Finally, each co-author would like to acknowledge the friendship, skill, ingenuity and trust of the other. We have worked together on books and research projects for almost 15 years. We are still learning from each other and still enjoying the experience.

Mark S. Dorfman
University of Arkansas at Little Rock

Saul W. Adelman
Miami University (Ohio)

Chapter 1 Introduction: Life Insurance

Chapter Objectives

- Introduce basic terminology and concepts
- Categorize life insurance as a branch of contract law and its products by contract type and marketing method
- Provide an overview of the book's structure

Introduction

Life insurance is a contractual arrangement in which an insurer agrees to pay a predetermined sum to a beneficiary in the event of the insured's death. While this statement correctly defines the life insurance transaction, it does not convey the complexity, subtlety or financial importance of this contract today. Monumental changes are occurring in the life insurance marketplace, including:

- introduction of new products and services;
- increased potential for interindustry and intraindustry competition; and
- adoption of a "financial services" philosophy by the members of an industry originally founded on individual products.

Concurrently, the life insurance marketplace is undergoing an exciting metamorphosis stimulated in part by external factors. As we near the end of the 20th century, the life span of the average American is increasing, meaning an extended retirement period for most. This trend has also urged us to look more closely at the federal government's role in providing financial security for its citizens, with an eye to reducing the role of Social Security and other public programs in the future. Simultaneously, the need to solve some of society's complex problems—how to efficiently provide medical care to the entire population and how to provide for long-term care for an aging population—has become more urgent. Surrounding all of these issues is the continuing evolution of social philosophies addressing the roles of men, women, families and work patterns.

All of these changes are affecting how life insurance, which continues to be a major force in the financial planning process, is bought, sold, distributed and priced. This book is intended to help readers understand not only how life insurance is changing but also its precise present and future role in financial planning. Additionally, of course, the book will clarify many technical aspects of the complex market. Toward that last goal, this chapter presents the fundamentals that readers must grasp before they can master the more complex details of this dynamic subject. For some this will be an introduction; for others it will be a review.

The chapter begins by defining the life insurance product—first in terms of what is actually bought and sold, then in the context of the law that governs the product and finally in marketing terms, according to the types of products offered and how they are distributed. Then the chapter explains the structure and design of this book and how it comprehensively addresses the timely topic of life insurance as an integral part of the financial planning process.

Life Insurance Defined

To provide a common body of knowledge for use in the remainder of this text a concise review of fundamental insurance principles and terminology follows. Many readers will have taken a basic insurance course or have some insurance industry experience or both; for those who have neither background, this section is not meant to replace an introductory insurance course or text.[1]

Basic Terminology and Principles

Insurance is a contractual agreement between two parties. The first party (called the *insurer* or *insurance company*) agrees to pay the second party (called the *insured*) at the occurrence of a specified event. In **life insurance** the insured is the person whose death causes the policy to mature in the form of a claim payment made by the insurer. The *owner* is the person who may exercise the policy rights, such as designating the beneficiary or using the life insurance policy as collateral for a loan. The insured and the owner may be, and frequently are, the same person. The **beneficiary** is the party (individual, trust, charitable organization or company) receiving the proceeds when the insured dies. The insured may not be the beneficiary, but the insured's estate may, by design or default, receive the proceeds. The owner and the beneficiary may be the same person. In exchange for the insurer's promise, the insured pays a specified sum, called a *premium*.

This definition raises several points that characterize the **insurance** transaction. First, the insured gives up a predetermined, known amount, while the insurer makes only a contingent promise to pay an unknown amount ranging from nothing to a maximum known as the policy **face amount,** which is the initial amount scheduled to be paid. That is, if the specified event (called a **loss**) occurs, the insurer potentially could pay an amount much greater than the premium it has collected. If no covered loss occurs, the insurer pays nothing. The inherently unequal exchange between the parties to an insurance contract makes the contract **aleatory**, as opposed to an equal-exchange, or commutative, contract.

A second element of the insurance transaction suggested by this definition is the willingness of the insured to pay a relatively small, certain amount (the premium usually is small relative to the dollar value of the exposure) to avoid the consequences of a relatively large, uncertain financial loss (the insured event generally will produce a large loss relative to the insured's financial assets).

A third element of the insurance transaction conveyed by this definition is pooling. Insurance works most efficiently as a money transfer mechanism, where the premiums from all insureds (most of whom experience no loss) are transferred to the relatively few insureds experiencing loss. In life insurance, as in all other forms of insurance, it is not the insurer who pays for the losses. Despite writing the check when a claim is paid, only in a most restrictive sense does the insurer pay claims; the insurer is merely transferring pooled funds—the premium payments of all the insureds—to the beneficiary. The insurance company earns interest on the premiums collected from insureds and thus derives its income from this flow of cash, just as does a financial institution that operates checking accounts.

The essence of insurance is **indemnity**. In theory, the person who has been indemnified by an insurance payment is placed in the same financial position after the loss as before the loss occurred; that is, he or she has neither profited nor been disadvantaged by the covered loss. In practice, however, insureds commonly receive less from the insurer than the amount of damage sustained. And although the principle that insurance is a contract of indemnity is well established, many life insurance authorities are reluctant to put life insurance in this indemnity framework because the exact amount of financial loss associated with a person's death cannot be established in the same way as it can be measured in property insurance. Nevertheless, the life insurance transaction does honor the principle of indemnity.

Scientific estimates of the damage associated with premature death are routinely made in wrongful death litigation. Accurate estimates of the need for funds in the event of a person's death should be made prior to the occurrence of such a loss. Each of these analyses provides a basis for determining human economic value and an estimate of the economic damage associated with a premature death. Moreover, no life insurance company would deliberately provide insurance in an amount clearly exceeding the estimated economic value of the covered life. Limiting the amount of life insurance sold to reflect economic value gives explicit recognition to the rule of indemnity.

Life insurance companies recognize the rule of indemnity in two ways. First, as just mentioned, the amount of life insurance purchased must bear a reasonable relation to the amount of potential loss. Second, only the person or persons exposed to the potential loss may legitimately own the insurance covering the insured's life. This doctrine of **insurable interest** keeps life insurance from being used for gambling or antisocial purposes such as promoting or inducing murder.

Life Insurance and the Law

In a democracy the law reflects the rules and principles that those governed accept as standards for behavior, regulating their relationships with each other and controlling their relationships with the government. The law reflects society's

Figure 1.1
The Law and the Life Insurance Contract

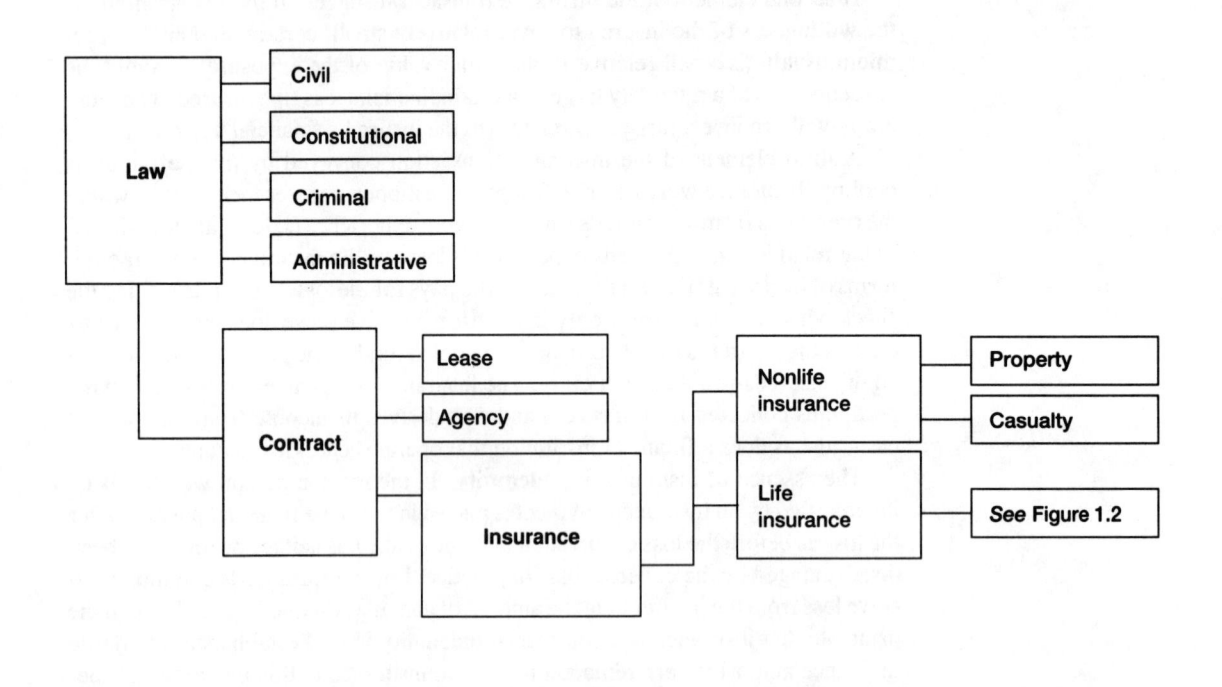

morality, ethics and beliefs. American law has several clearly identifiable branches, including civil, constitutional, criminal, administrative, patent, tort and contract law. Because every life insurance policy is a legal document, specifically a contract, life insurance transactions are governed by contract law. Figure 1.1 shows how this marketplace fits into the American legal system.

Contract law covers the relationships arising when two or more parties agree to enter into a commercial transaction, typically resulting in exchanges of money, goods, services or promises. Several types of these contractual relationships are shown in Figure 1.1. Insurance transactions make up a unique category of contract law. Chapters 9 and 10 describe specific applications of contract law to insurance transactions.

Every insurance purchase may be categorized as either a life or a nonlife transaction. Nonlife insurance covers direct and indirect property losses associated with such perils as fire, theft, and windstorm. (Direct losses occur when there is actual destruction of property; indirect losses occur when financial losses result from the property's "loss of use.") Casualty (including workers' compensation claims, legal liability from negligence and bonding transactions) is another distinct area of nonlife insurance. Life insurance transactions help fund losses caused by adverse human life contingencies: death, accident and illness, and length of survival. The distinction between life and nonlife insurance is blurred in the area

Figure 1.2
Life Insurance Products

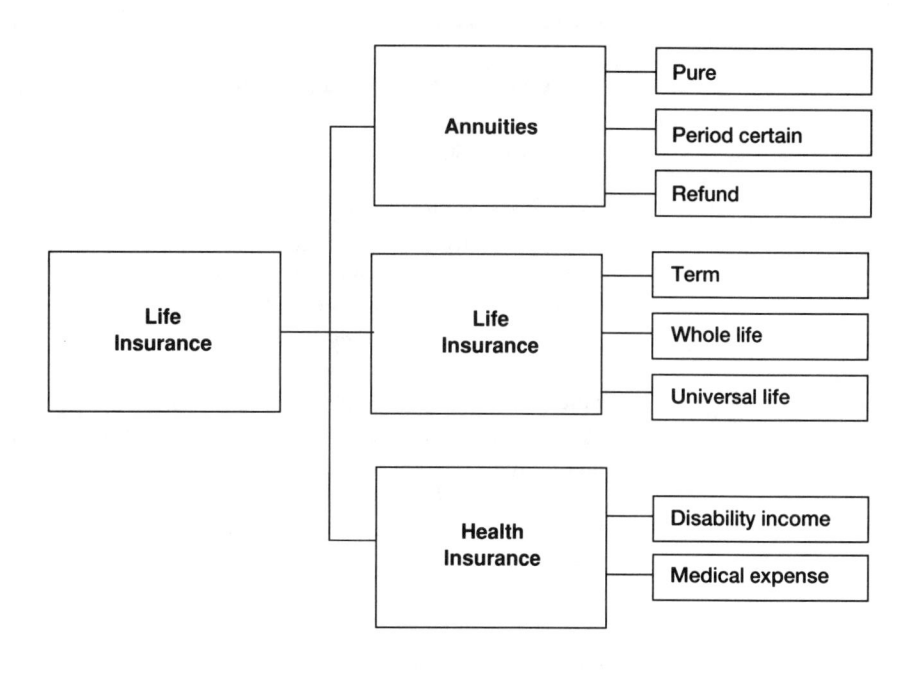

```
                                    ┌─── Pure
                         ┌ Annuities ├─── Period certain
                         │          └─── Refund
                         │
                         │           ┌─── Term
          Life Insurance ┼ Life      ├─── Whole life
                         │ Insurance └─── Universal life
                         │
                         │ Health    ┌─── Disability income
                         └ Insurance └─── Medical expense
```

of accident coverage. Accident coverage includes industrial accidents (which fall under workers' compensation, a nonlife insurance coverage) and nonindustrial accidents (covered by both life and nonlife insurers). In the latter the nonlife insurance companies provide accident insurance and the life insurance companies provide health insurance. Otherwise, the distinction between life and nonlife insurance is clear.

Types of Life Insurance Products

Three distinct categories of contracts are offered by life insurers: annuities, health insurance and life insurance (*see* Figure 1.2).

Annuities

While some forms of life insurance have living benefits and some forms of annuities have death benefits, basically life insurance contracts are designed to pay in the event of death, while annuities pay in the event of survival. Annuities are designed to preclude the possibility of people outliving their income or consuming their assets before death. The annuity contract allocates lifetime consumption scientifically by combining many lives exposed to the same chance of loss. Those who die relatively soon release their unconsumed assets to those who enjoy extended lives. Since nobody knows the length of his or her life at the outset of the annuity period, many people willingly enter such an arrangement. Most pension benefits are based on this annuity arrangement.

The New York Insurance Code, which is often used as a model because most insurance companies are licensed in New York, defines **annuities** as follows:

> "Annuities" [means] all agreements to make periodical payments where the making or continuance of all or some of a series of such payments, or the amount of any such payment, is dependent upon the continuance of human life.[2]

Americans' increasing life spans and their associated lengthy retirement periods, generally without employment income, combined with relatively favorable federal income tax treatment, have made the annuity an increasingly important life insurance offering in recent years.

Annuity contracts may be categorized in several ways. One of the clearest methods involves the guarantees provided by the different types of annuities. The most fundamental annuity guarantee is called the **pure annuity**, or **straight life annuity**, in which the insurer agrees to make payments only so long as the annuitant is alive. If death occurs after the first payment is received, the insurer's obligation ends. A *life annuity, period certain*, guarantees payment for life or for at least a specified minimum number of years, such as five or ten years. Thus a life annuity with five years certain would pay until the annuitant's death or for five years, whichever period is longer. A **refund annuity** guarantees that the total amount of payments received by an annuitant will never be less than the premium paid, but the total can exceed the premium payment in the event of long life. If an annuitant dies relatively early in the annuity period, the insurer makes payment to a beneficiary in an amount equal to the difference between the annuity payments received by the annuitant and the premium paid. For example, if $50,000 were paid for an annuity and $30,000 were received by the annuitant, at the annuitant's death $20,000 would be paid to a beneficiary. Chapter 5 describes annuities in depth.

Health Insurance

When a person becomes ill or has an accident, the consequences may include medical expenses, lost income or the need to replace the services ordinarily provided by the healthy person. (The health insurance industry is also involved in supplying custodial care for the aged through long-term care [LTC] policies. LTC policy design and pricing are in their infancy. Some life insurance companies also allow the use of a portion of the death benefits before death if the insured is certified as terminally ill.) Insurance logically may be used to transfer the costs associated with these problems, and insurance companies offer several kinds of contracts to cover this exposure to loss. (Health insurance contracts also are offered by Blue Cross and Blue Shield plans, a distinction explained in Chapter 7.)

The New York Insurance Code defines **health insurance** as follows:

> "Accident and health insurance" [means] (a) Insurance against death or personal injury by accident or by any specified kind or kinds of accident and insur-

ance against sickness, ailment, or bodily injury, . . . and noncancelable disability insurance, meaning insurance against disability resulting from sickness, ailment, or bodily injury (but not including insurance solely against accidental injury) under any contract which does not give the insurer the option to cancel or otherwise terminate the contract at or after one year from its effective date or renewal date.
(para. 3)

Disability income contracts—either separate policies or riders attached to life insurance policies—indemnify the insured if an accident or illness prevents earning an income by providing spendable cash. Disability income coverage is often associated with employment and is usually provided by the employer; however, this type of contract can also be purchased by individuals.

Medical expense insurance contracts provide payment for health care costs such as hospital and doctor charges associated with an accident or illness. Different health insurance contracts provide for the first dollar of loss or for larger expenses associated with "catastrophic" illness. Some contracts cover both classes of expenses. Some policies reimburse the insured directly, while other policies provide for payments made directly to health care providers. As with disability income policies, most of these contracts are associated with employment. However, individuals purchase a significant number of medical expense insurance policies.

The serious financial problems caused by accident or illness are a national concern, and the methods used to share the burden of these costs transcend the private insurance transaction. Chapter 7 describes the details of private health insurance coverage, while other aspects of health insurance as a part of Social Security are covered in Chapter 8.

Life Insurance

Life insurance contracts promise to pay sums of dollars when a contractually specified event occurs. In life insurance the event is death; in disability insurance it is a defined disability; in medical expense insurance it is incurring eligible medical expenses. Here is the definition of **life insurance** given by the New York Insurance Code:

> "Life insurance" [means] every insurance upon the lives of human beings and every insurance appertaining thereto. The business of life insurance shall be deemed to include the granting of endowment benefits; additional benefits in the event of death by accident or accidental means; additional benefits operating to safeguard the contract from lapse, or to provide a special surrender value, in the event of total and permanent disability of the insured; and optional modes of settlement of proceeds.
> (para. 1)

Recent years have seen the creation of nontraditional, investment-oriented life insurance contracts that emphasize the savings element, raising the question of whether these contracts qualified for income tax treatment as life insurance. Therefore, the Deficit Reduction Act of 1984 defined *life insurance* for federal income tax purposes. To qualify as a life insurance contract under the 1984 law, the policy must pass two tests throughout its life. According to the *cash value accumulation test,* the cash surrender value of the policy cannot exceed the net single premium that would be required to fund the future benefits of the policy. The *guideline premium/cash value corridor test* requires the face amount to be at least a multiple of the contract's cash value. (These two tests and their rationale are explained more thoroughly in Chapter 4. The exact provisions of these complex texts can be found in the Internal Revenue Code, Section 7702.) These tests are important to understanding the structure of the nontraditional life insurance products.

As shown in Figure 1.2, life insurance falls into three basic categories: term and whole life, classified as "traditional" contracts (*see* Chapter 3), and universal life insurance contracts, categorized as "nontraditional" (*see* Chapter 4). (Endowment life insurance is another "traditional" form of life insurance. Endowment contracts promise to pay the face amount if the insured dies during the policy's term. If the insured survives the policy's term, the face amount is paid to the policy owner. Endowments are not currently sold because they violate the tests for life insurance under the Deficit Reduction Act of 1984.) Combinations of term, whole life and endowment policies regularly have been sold to create the appearance of numerous types of life insurance contracts. Nevertheless, for more than 200 years, term, whole life and endowment contracts have been the basis of the life insurance industry.

Term Life Insurance Contracts. In **term insurance** the insurer is bound to pay the face amount of the contract only if the insured's death occurs within a specific time period—the term of the contract. Many term contracts are renewable for additional periods. However, since the premium is based on age at renewal, the payment may become prohibitive.

Whole Life Insurance Contracts. In **whole life insurance** death claims will be paid at any age, so long as the contract is supported by current or previous premium payments. Whole life insurance has both death and living contractual benefits. The living benefits result from a premium payment schedule in which the initial premiums exceed the insurance (mortality) costs during the first years of the contract and the (mortality) expenses exceed the premium payments in the later period. The difference between the premium payments and the mortality and administrative costs earns interest and gives rise to the cash surrender value. The cash surrender value can be withdrawn if the contract is terminated. The "leveling process" provides affordable coverage for the insured's life. The level-premium plan of paying for whole life insurance is illustrated in Figure 1.3.

Endowment Life Insurance Contracts. In **endowment life insurance** the insurer agrees to pay death claims during the term of the contract or to pay a survivor claim if the insured survives the endowment period. This contract does not appear in Figure 1.2 since very few endowment policies are currently sold due to the

Figure 1.3
Level-Premium Whole Life Insurance

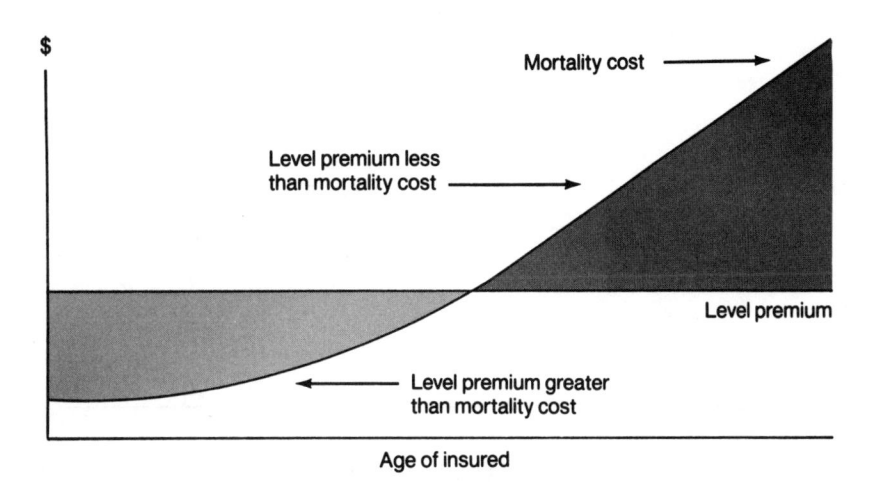

[Figure 1.3: Graph showing Mortality cost as an increasing curve vs. Age of insured, with a horizontal Level premium line. The area where level premium is greater than mortality cost is shown at younger ages, and level premium less than mortality cost at older ages.]

problems of not being able to meet the current IRS technical definition of a life insurance contract for tax purposes.

Universal Life Insurance Contracts. Nontraditional contracts typically allow the insured to determine, at each payment date, the premium payment amount, which in turn determines whether a particular contract has the characteristics of a term or whole life policy. The terms **universal life, variable life,** and **variable universal life** identify types of contracts that provide flexibility in one or more of the following areas: premium payment pattern, face amount, investment portfolios for cash value amounts and withdrawal of funds from the cash value. These contracts are permanent contracts because death benefits are paid whenever death occurs as long as current or prior premiums (and investment income) are sufficient to support the policy charges. Chapter 4 describes these nontraditional contracts in detail and how they meet the IRS's definition of life insurance.

Methods of Life Insurance Distribution

Five distinct and separate markets exist for distributing life insurance products (*see* Figure 1.4):

1. Individual life insurance
2. Business life insurance
3. Group life insurance
4. Credit life insurance
5. Industrial life insurance

Figure 1.4
Life Insurance Marketing Channels

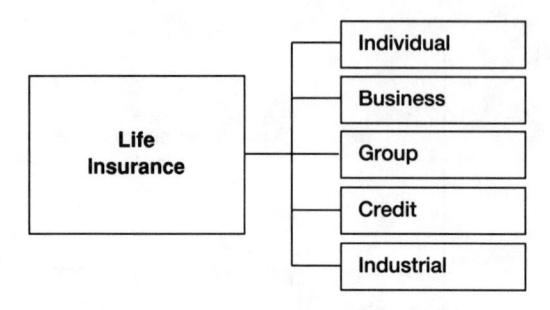

```
                    ┌── Individual
                    ├── Business
   Life Insurance ──┼── Group
                    ├── Credit
                    └── Industrial
```

Individual Life Insurance

In **individual life insurance**, a separate policy is used for each purchase. The insurance generally is issued only after the applicant passes a medical examination, though significant numbers of "nonmedical policies" (those that do not require medical examinations) are sold. The minimum policy amount typically is $10,000, and multimillion-dollar policies are sometimes sold, though the latter are restricted to young and presumably healthy people. Premiums may be paid annually, semiannually, quarterly or monthly, by mail or by direct deposits from the insured's to the insurer's bank. Policies written on an individual basis include term, whole life, endowment and universal life insurance contracts. Health insurance is also sold on an individual basis.

Business Life Insurance

Business life insurance is sold to enterprises seeking solutions to income losses associated with an owner's or key employee's premature death or disability. Business insurance may be purchased to fund a continuation plan, allowing an enterprise to continue after the owner's death. Business life insurance is purchased regularly as part of a fringe benefit package including deferred compensation programs. The contracts used in a business life insurance program are the same ones used in individual life insurance; the provisions relating to medical examinations, policy size and premium payment are similar as well. Chapter 20 describes business life insurance.

Group Life and Health Insurance

Business enterprises frequently purchase **group insurance,** whereby one policy (a master contract) is issued to a group of individuals. The group must have been formed for a purpose other than securing insurance. Each covered member is issued a certificate of participation rather than an individual contract. Usually no medical examination is required for participation, but employers may require such an examination for employment. Small groups tend to be underwritten on a medical basis. The amount of life insurance for each participant generally is determined by a formula, such as the same dollar amount for all employees or one year's wages for all covered employees. The employer administers the program and pays the premiums, although some plans require employees to contribute. While the contractual arrangement is quite different from that of individual or business life insurance, group life insurance is most often term life insurance. Chapter 18 covers group life insurance in more detail.

Credit Life Insurance

Credit life insurance, which may be viewed as a special type of group life insurance usually treated as a separate category, is provided to all debtors of a particular creditor. The debtors use life insurance proceeds to repay any outstanding loans in the event of premature death. The master contract is written with the lender (such as a bank, department store or credit union), and each debtor pays for and receives an amount of coverage related to the size of the outstanding debt. Typically the cost of the life insurance is added to the individual's debt repayment program. The policy type is term life insurance.

Credit disability insurance is offered by the same institutions and in a similar fashion. Credit disability insurance pays the debtor's normal payment during a defined disability.

Industrial life Insurance

Industrial life insurance, also known as **debit life insurance, burial life insurance** or, more recently, **home service life insurance**, is typified by a relatively small contract size (often $1,000 or less) and a premium payment/collection method involving regular (sometimes weekly) visits to the insured's home. The policies are comparable to whole life insurance. The product has a long history in this country and is still purchased in modest amounts, especially in the South and some large cities.

The Structure of This Book

As mentioned in the preface, this book addresses the subjects of life insurance and financial planning by explaining the life insurance product in detail and describing how the life insurance product can solve personal and business financial planning problems. Individual topics are discussed as follows.

Chapter 2 describes the economic and social environment in which Americans make financial decisions. The chapter presents psychological motivating and economic explanations for much financial behavior. Life and health insurance products are discussed in Chapters 3–8. Legal aspects of life insurance contracts are described in Chapters 9 and 10. The tax aspects of financial planning are the subject of Chapters 11 and 12. Chapter 13 describes investment-related topics, including alternatives to cash value life insurance.

Financial planning material, including a description of Social Security benefits, is found in Chapters 14–17. The latter three chapters bring together all of the preceding material with the presentation of extended and annotated case studies. Chapter 15 emphasizes planning for premature death and other problems typically associated with the young adult years. Chapter 16 stresses saving for retirement and other aspects of financial planning associated with the middle adult years. Chapter 17 presents plans that are appropriate for the last trimester of adult life. This process is usually called *estate planning*.

A discussion of the business applications of life insurance products is found in Chapters 18–20, including a description of employee benefits, pension benefits and business uses of life insurance. The mathematics underlying life insurance transactions are analyzed in Chapters 21–23. The institutional aspects of life insurance companies are described in Chapters 24 and 25.

Because life insurance products are inextricably entwined with the financial planning process, the interaction of life insurance with the financial planning process is illustrated throughout the text. Several chapters include a section on financial planning issues that summarizes in an unbiased manner material about which experts disagree. Readers may be surprised to learn how controversial some aspects of the life insurance transaction are and should form their own opinions after reviewing the material carefully. Over the years, vociferous arguments have been raised by life insurance companies selling one or another type of contract they claim to be the "best." Other controversy arises from interindustry bias, pitting insurance companies and their agents against banks or security brokerage firms and their salespeople. Various government agencies and congressional committees have made frequent contributions to this public debate about life and health insurance.

Experts disagree about such issues as what the actual cost of life insurance is, which financial product is most useful in a given situation, which tax strategy is most evident and whether a person should retire early with reduced pension and Social Security benefits. Sometimes expert opinion is a function of financial self-interest or industry propaganda. Sometimes differences of opinion are based on superior analysis or superior results in practice. In most cases simple solutions do not apply universally to the complex financial problems faced by individual Americans. Therefore the financial planning issues sections are intended to alert readers to some of the areas in which honest, intelligent people disagree.

Review Questions

1. Discuss the statement "Life insurance is a branch of contract law."
2. How does disability income insurance differ from medical expense insurance? What do they have in common?

3. What are the important characteristics of individual life insurance? How does individual life insurance differ from group life insurance?
4. What is meant by indemnity? Is the life insurance contract an indemnity contract? Why or why not?
5. Distinguish between life insurance, annuities and health insurance. What is the purpose of each?
6. What are the five distinct markets for insurance distribution? Why do you think these five markets evolved?
7. What is meant by a "nonmedical" policy? What requirements help protect insurers from insureds with medical problems seeking coverage?

Endnotes

[1] The authors recommend *Introduction to Risk Management and Insurance*, 4th ed., by Mark S. Dorfman (Englewood Cliffs, N.J.: Prentice-Hall, 1991). Other introductory texts also cover this material well.

[2] New York Insurance Code Section 1113(2). This and all subsequent references in this book to the New York Insurance Code are taken from *McKinney's Consolidated Laws of New York (annotated, revised, 1984)*, (St. Paul, Minn.: West Publishing, 1984).

Bibliography

Belth, Joseph M. "Credit Life Insurance Prices." *Journal of Risk and Insurance* 40, No. 1, March 1973, p. 115.

Cooper, Robert W., and Richard M. Ulivi. "Comprehensive Personal Financial Planning: A Survey of Consumer Opinions." *CLU Journal* 37, No. 2, April 1983, p. 40.

Johnson, Dale S. "Comprehensive Financial Planning: A Survey Process and the Professionals." *CLU Journal* 37, No. 4, October 1983, p. 40.

_____. "The Need for Comprehensive Financial Planning." *CLU Journal* 37, No. 3, July 1983, p. 40.

McLean, Ephraim R. "An Appraisal of Computerized Life Insurance Estate Planning." *Journal of Risk and Insurance* 41, No. 3, September 1974, p. 497.

Chapter 2: The Motivation to Purchase Life Insurance

Chapter Objectives

- Explain the needs-based purchase of life insurance
- Define permanent, temporary and savings needs for life insurance
- Illustrate the usefulness of life insurance in solving personal financial problems
- Describe the impact of American demographic changes on the use of life insurance products and services
- Explain the interrelationship between life insurance and theories of consumption, human capital and human life value
- Explain the interrelationship between life insurance and psychological theories relating to stress, death and motivation

Introduction

Many factors, often intertwined and overlapping, come into play in the life insurance purchase decision. Some factors are external—demographic, economic and other societal forces—and are always evolving in their influences on individuals and families. Some factors are internal—psychological and behavioral patterns—influencing how people perceive the need to save money and to protect themselves and their families from financial misfortune. The role of life insurance in the lives of today's Americans cannot be understood fully without knowledge of these motivational forces.

The most fundamental motivation for buying life insurance is need. Therefore, this chapter begins by describing the needs-based purchase of life insurance. Purchasing an amount of life insurance appropriate to meet a carefully quantified need is logical. This section explores the capability of life insurance to satisfy permanent, temporary and savings needs.

This discussion is followed by case studies designed to illustrate specific instances where the life insurance transaction is useful. Because the usefulness of the life insurance transaction depends on the age composition, marital status and other demographic characteristics of our society, this section also includes facts regarding and projections of American demographic trends.

Economic theories explaining the lifetime allocation of consumption and the role of savings over a financial life cycle also may help explain the motivation to purchase life insurance; these theories of economic behavior are addressed next. The life insurance purchase decision is not, however, based solely on logical thought processes. Inextricably involved in the transaction are issues such as the person's attitude toward death, stress and motivation. Thus some psychological explanations of human motivation are explored briefly. Every insurance agent is likely to be aware of cases in which logic and the needs-based formula clearly indicate the purchase of life insurance and yet the person exposed to this potential loss fails to act. The underlying explanation for this inaction may well be psychological rather than economic.

The Needs-Based Purchase of Life Insurance

Logically used, life insurance answers the financial needs caused by a premature death. In the needs-based financial analysis, **death is always assumed to be immediate**. Plans based on the subject's surviving for a number of years or even months could prove catastrophic to survivors, because even young adults can become uninsurable or die in accidents, leaving unmet financial needs. The needs-based purchase of life insurance argues that the right time to purchase life insurance is when an immediate death would cause financial problems. (Note that disability income continuation insurance and health medical expense reimbursement coverage also can be purchased in adequate amounts only after a needs-based analysis is completed.)

The **needs-based approach** is a three-step process:

1. Calculate all financial needs caused by an immediate death.
2. Subtract any assets available to fund financial needs after death.
3. Purchase life insurance in the amount adequate to fill all gaps between needs and available assets.

The needs that life insurance can satisfy are categorized as permanent, temporary and savings. **Permanent needs** are not a function of time. These needs, such as the need for cash to pay for funeral arrangements, are present despite the insured's age at death. Permanent needs are met with permanent life insurance contracts, those designed to remain in effect until death, including whole life and universal life insurance.

Temporary needs diminish over time and ultimately disappear. For example, the need to repay a loan ends once the loan has been repaid. Temporary needs may be met with term life insurance. These contracts have no cash values and typically are unavailable after the insured reaches age 65 or 70.

Savings usually are needed to provide for retirement, fund a college education or save for another long-term purpose, and these needs are often best met by cash value life insurance contracts, such as whole life or universal life insurance and annuities.

Permanent Needs

Death Fund

Typical funeral and burial costs range from $3,000 to $10,000. Cash also is needed to probate the decedent's estate. **Probate** is the legal process needed to transfer property to the decedent's heirs. The estates of people dying with or without a will must go through the probate process. Sometimes unpaid expenses associated with a final illness exist or other outstanding bills must be paid. Life insurance provides the decedent's estate with cash, often called **liquidity**, to meet these immediate needs.

Readjustment Fund

Often survivors of a deceased wage earner need time to readjust their standard of living, sell a house, acquire or reacquire marketable job skills or find suitable employment. The amount needed for these purposes varies. The need may increase or decrease over time, but it usually is not a function of the insured's age at death, especially if death occurs before age 65.

Emergency Fund

The best financial plans allow for the unplanned event—the uninsured theft, the need for a new roof or a new car. While the size of the need is unknown in advance, a cash cushion can make the effect of "outrageous fortune" tolerable. These needs are not a function of the insured's age.

Permanent Dependent(s)

Some people are responsible for the care and financial support of a permanently disabled child, spouse or parent. The serious financial problems caused by the death of the caregiver during the disabled person's life can often be met with life insurance. When the disabilities are permanent, the life insurance also should be permanent.

Some families plan for one spouse to remain at home for his or her lifetime should the other spouse die prematurely, with the survivor supported by life insurance proceeds. Such a plan requires permanent life insurance. However, the amount of life insurance decreases as the person gets older, because it takes a greater total sum of money to support a 45-year-old than it does to support the survivor at age 65. Also, at later ages family savings may be sufficient to provide income for the surviving spouse.

Estate Planning

Estates exceeding $600,000 may need cash to pay the administrative costs of estate transfer, pay federal and state death (inheritance) taxes or provide funds for equalizing bequests among heirs. When estate plans are funded with life insurance, the event creating the need for cash—death—is also the event providing the cash.

Temporary Needs

Mortgage Fund

Some needs for life insurance, such as the need to repay outstanding loans mentioned earlier, diminish over time, and some end. At one spouse's death it is often desirable to relieve the survivor of the need to make monthly mortgage payments. Mortgages are not legally payable in lump sum at the mortgagee's death. However, if no income is available to make the monthly mortgage payments as they fall due and the family wants to continue living in the house, the home loan should be retired. Outstanding balances on home loans steadily diminish over time. The amount of life insurance needed to repay the outstanding balance also declines steadily. When the mortgage is repaid, usually 20 or 30 years after the loan is made, this need for life insurance ends. In circumstances involving a lower interest rate on the home loan than available investment returns, it may be preferable to invest the life insurance proceeds at market rates and use the income stream from the investment to make loan payments.

Dependents' Support

In a pattern similar to the mortgage redemption fund, the amount of funds needed to support dependent children generally declines over time. Assuming that the dependency period ends at age 21, it will obviously take a greater total sum of money to support a 3-year-old than to support a 16-year-old. Each year the wage earner survives, a year's less income is needed to support a dependent and a year's less life insurance proceeds are needed, until the need ends altogether when the child reaches age 21.

With each passing year, the need to provide funds allowing a surviving spouse to remain at home during the child-rearing years also declines. If the need is for a limited period—for example, until the youngest child reaches age ten—then the need is classified as temporary. As noted, if the surviving spouse plans to remain at home until death, then the need is classified as permanent.

Education Fund

The need to provide funds for a college, private elementary or private secondary school education diminishes with time and ultimately ends once the child completes the education. If the wage earner dies before paying for any of the education, the need is greater than if one or more years of tuition already have been paid. If funds have been set aside for this purpose or if a regular savings program is begun while the child is young, then the need for life insurance diminishes with the increase in the educational savings fund. (*See* Chapter 15 for a description of alternative financial strategies for funding private educations.)

Savings Needs

The need to save exists in most family situations and in large part is unrelated to the need for life insurance. Most individuals and families need to save during their working years to maintain their standard of living during their retirement years. People need to save to handle emergencies and to give themselves peace of mind. Traditionally, many people have chosen to save using cash value life insurance.

Several arguments can be made for using cash value life insurance for savings:

- Historically it has proven safe.
- It is a compulsory plan, providing the discipline many savers require.
- The life insurance company provides investment management.
- Cash value life insurance provides liquidity, the ability to realize cash quickly without suffering a decline in asset value.
- Cash value life insurance and annuities enjoy federal income tax advantages.
- Cash value life insurance generally is safe from creditors' claims in the event of the insured's bankruptcy or death.

Cash value life insurance, however, has several drawbacks as an investment:

- Inflation has a corrosive effect on all fixed-dollar investments, such as the cash value of whole life insurance.
- The marketing cost of the life insurance delivery system significantly reduces the amount of money accumulated during the early policy years.
- The yield, or rate of return, while guaranteed, is less than many available market rates. Also, the yield has proven uncompetitive in times of rapid inflation.

More than half of all life insurance sold in the United States in recent years involved cash value policies, leading to the conclusion that many people found the advantages of saving with life insurance to outweigh the disadvantages. These purchasers preferred the combination of insurance and savings to the pure protection provided by term life insurance or to the combination of term insurance and an outside savings program.

Life Insurance and American Demographic Trends

The following case studies may present some challenge for readers lacking any exposure to life insurance either in practice or in an introductory risk management and insurance course. The specific policy types mentioned are described fully in Chapters 3, 4 and 5. These case studies are part of the foundation being laid for those three chapters and other material found later in the text.

Demographic Observations: Stone Case

The Stone family case illustrates several aspects of American demographics that have undergone great change since the 1960s. The Stones got married, remained married and reared and educated two children; Beth Stone remained at home after her children were born. This is the type of environment in which life insurance is most useful. As the case illustrates, several purchases of relatively large amounts of life insurance were employed appropriately in the Stone case.

The **Life Insurance Marketing and Research Association (LIMRA)** reports that, despite undergoing statistical decline, the traditional family market remains

Case Study: The Stone Family

Facts and Data

Greg and Beth Stone were married in 1960, when Greg was 24 and Beth was 25. Greg graduated from a large southern state university with a degree in English. For several years he worked as an editor at a well-known sports magazine. In 1970 he left the magazine to work in his father's flourishing chain of retail sporting goods stores. Greg's father planned to transfer management and ultimately ownership of the firm to Greg if Greg decided he wanted to continue the firm and if his dad was satisfied that Greg was capable of doing so.

Beth earned an undergraduate degree in history from a well-known eastern university and a master's degree in business administration from a leading university in Illinois. She met Greg while working for a Philadelphia advertising firm. After seven years of marriage the Stones had a child, Kay Lynn. Five years later they adopted a second child. While Beth planned to return to work after both children were in their teens, she never did. Instead she was elected to the local school board and became heavily involved in local politics. Both of the Stones' children have graduated from college, and both are now married.

Greg Stone's dad incorporated the business and gave Greg, his only child, half the shares of stock. At the time of the gift, in 1982, the firm was worth $1 million. Today the firm is estimated by an accountant to have a fair market value of $8 million. Greg's mother died in 1987, and Greg's father's will names Greg as sole heir.

The Stones' Use of Life Insurance

Neither Greg nor Beth Stone owned life insurance before marriage. After their marriage, a neighbor, who was a life insurance agent, tried to sell them each a policy. They did not make the purchase because their income was limited, they had no children or debts and they were saving for a down payment on a house. At the birth of Kay Lynn, Greg purchased a $100,000 whole life insurance policy. Greg was 31, and the annual premium was about $1,400. At the time, Greg was earning $22,000 a year at the magazine. The life insurance policy was the Stones' only savings program. The Stones purchased a house the year Kay Lynn was born, which was at the same time Beth left her advertising job. The life insurance purchase was not the result of a careful calculation of needs but represented the amount the Stones felt they could afford to pay in premiums (a common, if not always the best, approach).

The year the Stones adopted their second child, Greg went to work for his dad. He earned $50,000 that year. They also purchased a larger house and asked their life insurance agent to recommend an appropriate amount of life insurance for Greg. Considering the costs of educating two children, repaying the mortgage on the new home and providing a sum for Beth to live on if Greg died prematurely, the agent recommended the purchase of $100,000 in decreasing term insurance combined with an additional $50,000 of whole life. The program provided Greg with $250,000 of life insurance: $150,000 of whole life and $100,000 of term. The annual premium was about $2,800, but because the whole life policies were participating contracts paying annual dividends, the net cost of the whole life insurance was less than the annual $2,800 premium.

After several years of working for his father, Greg clearly was willing and able to operate the business. The business prospered, and Greg was earning about $100,000 by his late 40s. At that time he was investing in common stocks and U.S. Treasury securities. He also began purchasing a series of single-premium deferred annuities to fund his retirement. Beginning at age 47, Greg put about $15,000 each year into his annuity. After six years and $90,000 in payments, the annuity had a value of $110,000. Greg estimated that if the payments were continued in this fashion, the annuity would be worth about $560,000 at the time of his retirement at age 65.

Greg and his father set up several insured employee benefit plans. The group life insurance and health insurance plans included Greg, his father and all their employees. The pension plan involved the purchase of a group annuity for Greg, his father and the employees.

By age 54, because the business had prospered greatly, Greg and his dad, who was 78, conferred with their attorney to draft an estate plan. Without planning, because Greg's father was widowed and his entire estate was to pass to Greg, the attorney estimated a tax liability of about $2 million at Greg's father's death. With planning, including the use of a life insurance trust, the transfer costs could be lowered to less than $1 million. (See Chapter 17 for a discussion of estate planning, including the use of life insurance trusts.) Because Greg was married, his estate planning possibilities were greater. The whole life insurance policies Greg purchased when he was younger were relied on to provide needed cash at Greg's death.

The Stones were excellent life insurance clients. Both Greg and Beth understood the need for the purchase, and neither had problems discussing the possibility of death. Because of Greg's business experience and his concern for his family's future, their insurance agent did not have to overcome procrastination or compete with extra demands to maximize current consumption of tangible goods.

---

the largest market for life insurance in the 1990s. LIMRA reports that about a quarter of young married couples between the ages of 25 and 34 are childless. However, about half of all married couples have children under the age of 18. Other LIMRA data show that adult males account for 48 percent of policies sold and 69 percent of premium volume. Females account for 38 percent of policies sold and 27 percent of premium volume. The remaining 14 percent of life insurance policies sold insure juveniles.[1]

Census Bureau data for 1988 portray a changing picture of American family life. In 1988 there were 91 million American households. Each household had 2.64 persons. The number of households headed by people under age 25 declined by 20 percent since 1980. The number of one-parent households increased 25 percent since 1980 to 9.4 million.[2]

The data in Table 2.1 highlight some changes that have occurred in American family life in the past 30 years, including the quadrupling of the percentage of divorced people. Part 2 of the table reveals a dramatic reduction of the American birthrate over this period. The lower birthrate and the increasing number of never-married people and of childless couples can be expected to have a dramatic impact on both the amount and type of life insurance products and services sold in the future.

Demographic Observations: Scott Case

The case of Louis Scott illustrates several current population trends. Like a growing percentage of our population, Louis never married. He lacked family responsibilities justifying the life insurance purchase. However, Louis needed significant amounts of life insurance for business purposes. Also, his responsibility for aging parents required the purchase of life insurance. The need of middle-aged and old people to care for very old parents will be an ever-increasing phenomenon in coming decades. In fact some researchers believe the typical adult will spend more years with aged parents than with children under age 18.

Table 2.2 clearly reveals the aging of American society over the preceding three decades. The percentage of children under age 14 has decreased by almost the same percentage as the number of people older than age 65 has

Case Study: Louis Scott

Facts and Data

Louis Scott is 45. He has never married. Louis began but never completed college. He ended his education in his junior year at age 20, when he had the opportunity to purchase an interest in a local greenhouse and nursery. He had worked at the greenhouse since he was a teenager. For the past 25 years Louis has worked about 60 hours a week. Louis is now half owner of the business. The current owner, Bob Adams, plans to sell his interest in the firm to Louis when he retires sometime in the next 10 years. The transaction is likely to occur sooner than the partners originally planned, because Bob's health has been declining.

Louis Scott's Use of Life Insurance

When he was 21, Louis Scott borrowed $85,000 from the bank to purchase his interest in the business. His parents cosigned the loan. At the time of the loan Louis purchased a $100,000, 25-year decreasing term life insurance policy, naming his parents as beneficiaries. Louis had no savings except his equity in the business until he was 35.

When Louis reached age 35, his father retired. Because he was frequently laid off during his working years, his father had no pension and had never accumulated any savings. Louis's parents' only source of income was Social Security. Louis realized at some point that he and his two sisters would be responsible for their parents' care, and he converted the remaining $65,000 of term insurance into a whole life insurance policy. Louis kept his parents as beneficiaries of the whole life insurance policy. He felt if he predeceased his parents the proceeds would be his contribution to his parents' care.

The greenhouse and nursery were moderately successful, providing Louis and Bob each an annual before-tax income ranging from $20,000 to $30,000. After working together as partners for ten years, Louis and Bob each took out a $50,000 life insurance policy on the other partner's life. The policies were intended to allow a surviving partner to purchase the other's interest in the business if one partner died prematurely. The fair market value of the firm has been about $100,000 for the past five years. These policies also contained a modest disability rider that provides a disabled partner with $500 a month income if he becomes permanently disabled. No disability insurance policies were purchased to allow a partner to fund the purchase of a disabled partner's share of the business. Such a purchase, in retrospect, would have been wise, because Bob Adams's failing health is leading to permanent disability.

At first the reason neither partner purchased life insurance or adequate disability insurance to protect his business interest involved an indifference to the risk. A mutual friend, Tony Stein, pointed out the business continuation problem to Louis and Bob. Tony, a CPA, recommended they consult with Bill Levy, an agent for a large mutual life insurance company. Because they were both working 60 hours a week, and because buying life insurance did not seem necessary when they were young, the business life insurance purchase was postponed for ten years, and the disability insurance purchase was never made. If Bill Levy had not persisted in reminding the partners of their insurance need, it is doubtful any business life insurance would be in place.

Table 2.1
American Demographics

Part 1	Marital Status of U.S. Population (Percent)			
	1960	1970	1980	1986
Single	22.0	16.0	20.0	21.8
Married	67.0	72.0	66.0	62.9
Widowed	8.0	9.0	8.0	7.5
Divorced	2.0	3.0	6.0	7.8
Part 2	**American Birthrates**			
Birthrate/1,000 women	118	87.9	68.4	65.4

Source: U.S. Bureau of the Census, *Statistical Abstract of the United States, 1989*, 109th ed. (Washington, D.C.: U.S. Government Printing Office, 1989).

increased. While the percentage of people over age 65 is expected to double from 1960 to 2030, the number of people over age 85 is expected to quadruple during the same period.[3] The aging of American society will have profound effects on the life insurance industry. The need for annuities, health insurance and disability insurance will increase while the likelihood of premature death decreases. However, the need for life insurance covering adult children responsible for their parents will increase. Such caregivers should maintain adequate amounts of life insurance to replace their services in the event they predecease their parents.

Demographic Observations: Logan Case

Accurate data on handicapped children are not widely available:

> Available national survey samples are too small to yield reliable estimates of the prevalence of particular types of most disabling conditions. However, it can be estimated that 4.2 percent of all children under age 21 had a chronic activity limitation (i.e., a limitation in the amount or kind of activities in which they could engage) in 1981. . . . The percentage of children reporting activity limitations has doubled from 1966 to 1981.[4]

The Logan family example is, unfortunately, not unusual. Many families undoubtedly are coping with the problem of permanently dependent children. In such circumstances an adequately funded life and disability insurance program is essential to guarantee the financial future of the children. If the parents were to die or become disabled themselves, large amounts of financial resources would be needed to maintain the family. Also, guardianships and trusteeships would be necessary in many cases to guarantee desired financial and caregiving results.

The Logan case also illustrates the role business life insurance can play in allowing estates to be settled fairly and promptly in the event of premature deaths. In this case, where no heirs can assume responsibility for a valuable ongoing enterprise, life insurance allows the preservation of business values and provides financial security for the heirs.

Case Study:
The Logan Family

Facts and Data

Todd Logan is severely mentally handicapped. His problem is congenital. Todd's parents greatly love their son, and because they are in their early 70s, they are concerned about Todd's future care. He is 29 years old, lives at home and will never be independent. His parents, Carl and Louise, own and operate a plumbing supply company in a large California city.

The business is a proprietorship owned by Carl. Louise is an employee. The business is successful; gross revenue in recent years has exceeded $250,000. The Logans have a housekeeper caring for Todd during the days while the Logans are working. The Logans have no other children.

The Logans' Use of Life Insurance

After the severity of Todd's problem became apparent, the Logans purchased $300,000 of life insurance, naming a trust as owner and beneficiary. The amount of life insurance purchased was determined by consultation with a life insurance agent and a private care facility that agreed to accept Todd if the Logans died or otherwise were incapable of caring for Todd. A whole life insurance policy was purchased because it was clear that Todd's handicap was permanent. The Logans used a trust because they were concerned about the possibility of their simultaneous deaths leaving Todd without resources or a guardian.

For the past ten years the Logans have had a buy-and-sell agreement with a key employee to purchase the business when Carl Logan retires or if he dies before retirement. This agreement is funded with a life insurance policy on Carl's life. The insurance policy is a participating whole life policy for the fair market value of the business, which was $2 million when the buy-and-sell agreement was made. In the past ten years the participating dividends have been used to purchase more whole life insurance, allowing the policy to increase in value as the value of the business increased. Carl gave the purchaser-employee, Randy Wyle, a $15,000 annual raise to provide the funds needed for the insurance premium. The increased salary was a deductible business expense to Carl and provided several benefits, including taking the uncertainty out of the estate settlement aspect of selling the business and maintaining Randy Wyle's commitment to the firm during Carl's lifetime.

The Logans plan to sell the business to Wyle and retire within three years. If the business is sold before their deaths, the sale will be financed with the cash value of the life insurance and bank financing. If Carl Logan dies before retiring, the business will be sold to Randy Wyle, and the proceeds will support Louise. At Louise's death the business proceeds will be added to the trust for Todd. At Todd's death the remaining business and life insurance proceeds will be given to three different charities.

Todd Logan's problems proved to be quite stressful for his parents at first. They sought and received very effective counseling. Subsequently the opportunity to meet Todd's special needs made the Logans very confident parents. Carl Logan was able to redirect much of his attention from his business, which had been his consuming interest before Todd's birth, to his family. Thus the initial stress had ultimately positive results for the Logans.

Economic Theory and Life Insurance

While everyone would like it otherwise, generally people make economic choices without complete information. They purchase a particular product, follow a particular career path or invest their savings without having all the information needed to

Table 2.2
Age Cohorts as a Percent of U.S. Population

Age	1960	1970	1980	1987	% Change 1960–1987
Under 5	11.3	8.4	7.2	7.5	(34)
5–14	19.8	19.9	15.3	14.0	(29)
15–19	7.4	9.4	9.3	7.6	3
20–24	6.2	8.4	8.5	8.2	32
25–34	12.7	12.3	16.5	17.9	41
35–44	13.4	11.3	11.4	14.1	5
45–54	11.4	11.4	10.0	9.6	(16)
55–64	8.6	9.1	9.6	9.1	6
65 & over	9.2	9.8	11.3	12.2	33

Source: U.S. Bureau of the Census, *Statistical Abstract of the United States, 1969,* 109th ed. (Washington, D.C.: U.S. Government Printing Office, 1989).

make a perfect choice. One of the most difficult choices people face is the task of allocating their total lifetime income over their total lifetime, because the total amount of income and the length of the lifetime are both unknowns until an individual's death. Yet people continue to make these choices because they are inescapable—deciding what percentage of current income will be consumed, whether to borrow or to save to match current consumption with current income and whether to purchase life insurance.

Economists and financiers have long observed the percentage of annual income people consume, how they hold their savings and when they repay their loans. Different economic theories of individual financial behavior may be seen, in a simplified fashion, as different endings to the phrase "In general, the amount of annual consumption is determined by. . . ." Some completions of this sentence have proved to be more accurate than others, and many such theories have a direct bearing on how and when life insurance is purchased.

Economic Consumption Theories and the Purchase of Life Insurance

Life insurance in the broad economic context can be viewed as a transaction made to add certainty to a lifetime consumption pattern. The payment of a relatively small, certain premium is designed to remove many uncertain financial consequences of a premature death. Savings represent a redistribution of the consumption pattern. Both the purchase of life insurance and the decision to save are related directly to the consumption decision. This section of the chapter draws insights from consumption theory to explain the life insurance purchase.

Keynesian Theory

One of the simplest theories of savings behavior comes from one of the most profound and influential economic thinkers of the 20th century, John Maynard Keynes. In at least one instance Keynes identified savings as a residual left after one's consumption needs were satisfied. He stated, "A man's habitual standard of life usually has the first claim on his income."[5] Such a "residual savings" theory implies that current consumption is the individual's dominant concern, that the individual might be indifferent to the possibility that the future income stream will be reduced or eliminated by such circumstances as death, disability, unemployment and retirement. However, Keynes later points out that the individual's propensity to save is in large part a function of the level of current income. The purchase of life insurance requires reduction of current consumption to add certainty to the future income stream. That is, the person purchasing life insurance willingly reduces current consumption to eliminate the possibility of future consumption being drastically reduced for beneficiaries.

Keynes, of course, recognized that business firms and individuals did save more than a residual amount. He identified four reasons for business firms doing so, including the "rainy day" motive of providing a cash cushion for emergencies. Such a savings motive also provides an explanation for the individual purchase of term life insurance. The purchase of term life insurance does not involve savings, but the common thread between saving and term life insurance is that both require the reduction of current consumption to add certainty to future consumption.

The relationship between the purchase of cash value life insurance and other savings decisions is clear. With cash value life insurance the savings and insurance decisions are combined.

The Life-Cycle Hypothesis

The life-cycle hypothesis was postulated by Franco Modigliani (winner of the 1985 Nobel Prize in economics) and his associates Richard Brumberg and Albert Ando. The life-cycle hypothesis takes a multiperiod approach to explaining financial behavior. "The rate of consumption in any given period is a facet of a plan which extends over the balance of the individual's life, while the income accruing within the same period is but one element which contributes to the shaping of such a plan."[6]

The life-cycle hypothesis states that savings are made as a part of a plan to allocate lifetime consumption. In a perhaps overly simple view, savings are seen as a function of age. During the early part of the life cycle, the family-dependency years, savings are negative (the family incurs debt), as income is relatively low and spending relatively high. During the post-family-dependency period savings are positive, as income is relatively high and expenses are relatively low. During the retirement period, in the absence of a bequest motive (and such an absence was a tenet of the early life-cycle hypothesis), families again return to dissaving. The essence of the life-cycle hypothesis is that, subject to the constraint of current financial resources and current income, consumption will be distributed over a lifetime to maximize lifetime (as opposed to current-period) utility. The purchase of life insurance is a critical part of a lifetime financial plan.

The person with a lifetime financial plan makes allowances for unfavorable human life contingencies. People insure against the possibility of income loss due to death or disability during the family-dependency years, allowing the plan to be followed in the absence of the family wage earner(s). In the event of a premature death during the family-dependency period, life insurance proceeds can be used to repay past borrowing as well as allow future consumption to continue as planned.

The life-cycle hypothesis provides a good theoretical basis for understanding lifetime financial planning. Using home computers or the services of a financial planner, many families make and update lifetime financial plans with reasonable accuracy. Such potential was not available when the life-cycle hypothesis was postulated; yet observation and reason led to its formulation.

The Purchase of Life Insurance

Economic theories of consumption put the purchase of life insurance in a broad perspective. The purchase becomes a part of the economic goal of allocating consumption over a lifetime. Purchasing life insurance is a part of the decision as to how much current income will be consumed immediately. Like savings, the purchase of life insurance requires a lower level of current consumption of tangible goods. The same factors that explain a person's willingness to postpone some amount of current consumption to save for future consumption may explain a willingness to postpone or eliminate some amount of current consumption to ensure future consumption.

Human Capital and Human Life Values

The Keynesian theory of savings and the life-cycle hypothesis both suggest that people take a multiperiod, long-run view of their consumption and saving alternatives. That is, people do not behave by simply adjusting their current consumption to whatever their current income happens to be. Also, people taking a long-run view of their consumption possibilities often are willing to forgo current consumption so that total future consumption possibilities are enhanced. Forgoing current consumption to enhance future consumption describes exactly what people do when they postpone working and pursue an undergraduate degree or pursue a master's degree after getting an undergraduate degree.

Human Capital

Human capital represents the investment people make in themselves to acquire the marketable skills, knowledge and experience necessary for greater future productivity. An investment in human capital is seen clearly in the acquisition of a college education. No prudent business investor would make a substantial capital investment and then expose the investment to an uninsured loss by fire or other common peril. Likewise, the prudent investor in human capital (whether the investment is in a college education or in work experience) requires protection from uncertainty and from loss caused by the common perils of premature death or disability.

Human Life Value

Many current life insurance practitioners and many life insurance educators have used the **human life value** concept as a way of explaining the individual motivation to purchase life insurance. This concept is firmly associated with an outstanding American educator, S. S. Huebner. Huebner used the human life value concept as a measure of the economic value of the loss a family would suffer if a wage earner were to die prematurely.

In contrast to human capital, which is the productive potential of an individual, the basic human life value is a measure of the actual future earnings or service of an individual, that is, the capitalized value of an individual's net future earnings after subtracting self-maintenance costs.[7]

The Purchase of Life Insurance

Both the human capital and the human life value concepts provide a logical explanation for the motive to purchase life insurance. However, neither provides a logical answer to the question of how much life insurance should be purchased in a particular case.

The human life value approach requires estimating a person's entire earnings during a working career, from which total the money used to support the wage earner is subtracted. The remainder represents the net loss to the family if the wage earner were to die prematurely. Such a long-range estimate made in the early years is not likely to be accurate. Human life value represents a rough estimate of the damage sustained from a premature death. However, the purchase of such an amount of life insurance could create a moral hazard and an insurance premium disproportionately large relative to disposable income.

The human capital approach also has shortcomings, such as ignoring the time value of money and failing to incorporate a risk factor. Nevertheless, Huebner's contribution retains merit because it gives a person a sense of the dollar amount of damage that would be sustained by the survivors in the event of a premature death. If this sense of the magnitude of the exposure to loss provides a motivation to purchase an adequate amount of life insurance, then the value of Huebner's work is established.

Homeowners willingly spend $700 or more each year to protect against $100,000 in property loss potential, yet many do not spend an equal amount to acquire a $200,000 estate for their family in the event of their premature death. One of many explanations for this phenomenon is that the property loss is easier to see and understand than is the loss of future income. Huebner's analysis brings this latter loss potential into clear view.

Psychological Theories and Life Insurance

While economic theories expose some potential motives explaining the life insurance transaction, they should not be isolated from the equally relevant psychological theories. Psychologists try to understand and explain why people behave in characteristic ways. They reach conclusions and formulate theories through either controlled experiments, survey research or statistical analysis of observed human behavior. It would be impossible to understand life insurance completely without some understanding of the psychological aspects of the transaction. Despite the difficulties a nonpsychologist may have in attempting to resolve numerous apparently inconsistent and incomplete theories, the student of life insurance can learn much from this literature.

The purchase of life insurance touches on at least three areas of study of concern to psychologists:

1. Stress
2. Motivation
3. Reactions to death

Stress

Stress is a term used in both psychology and physics to define an excessive external force acting on a person or a material structure. The result of stress is strain. Excessive strain can cause structures to crack and break, and analogous results can be identified in humans. Psychological theories of behavior under stress might be useful in explaining why some people purchase life insurance while others do not. They also might explain why some people require more sales motivation than others.

Many events occurring during a person's lifetime can produce stress. One researcher developed a scale to measure the different degrees of stress associated with many different life events. A partial listing of the results appears as Table 2.3. The events in the table were selected because they are most closely related to life insurance.

The single most stressful event Richard Rahe measured was the death of a spouse. Divorce, death of a close family member, personal injury or illness and retirement were also among the ten most stressful items measured. Financial planners working with people to solve these problems should never forget that even the contemplation of these events can produce discomfort defined as anxiety. Anxiety is the fear, dread or foreboding arising from the contemplation of a threat, even though the threat is not present and actually may be a remote possibility.

Human reactions to stress and anxiety differ greatly. In general there is some kind of complex reaction designed to protect the body and remove the source of the stress. Some typical reactions to stress include:

- denial, including irrational denial of a present danger;
- stunned immobility, including an inability to communicate adequately;
- apathy and depression;
- docile dependency, with some people becoming very susceptible to outside influences; and
- aggressive irritability, including hostility that would not occur in non-stressful situations.

None of these five reactions is particularly healthy. In fact such unhealthy mental conditions may be forerunners of serious mental and physical illness. On the other hand, for some people a limited amount of stress becomes a source of motivation to take positive action. For such people stress impels greater efforts at problem solving and corrective action. For example, the death of a spouse may incapacitate some people, while it may cause others to pay greater attention to the parenting of surviving children. Likewise, the contemplation of a relatively large financial transaction may cause some people to procrastinate (become apathetic), while others may enjoy making important decisions. The point of the examples is that the type of reaction to stress or anxiety is a peculiar characteristic of each individual; one person's stumbling block may be another's stepping stone.

Table 2.3
Stress Values of Life Changes: Holmes-Rahe Scale

Score		
1.	Death of spouse	100
2.	Divorce	73
5.	Death of close family member	63
6.	Personal injury or illness	53
10.	Retirement	45
11.	Change in health of family member	44
14.	Gain of new family member	39
15.	Change in financial state	38
16.	Death of a close friend	37
39.	Minor violation of the law	11

Source: Richard H. Rahe, "Life Change and Subsequent Illness Reports," in *Life Stress and Illness*, E. Gunderson and R. Rahe, eds. (Springfield, Ill.: Charles C. Thomas, 1974), pp. 60–61.

Individual reaction to stress may well play a role in the purchase of life insurance. The mutual reaction to stress experienced by husband and wife when jointly contemplating their financial future or their deaths should also be considered a possible explanation for the purchase of life insurance. The contemplation of death or one's spouse's death produces anxiety for some people. This anxiety may cause the negative results of apathy or denial, but it may also prove to be a goad to take steps to remove or at least mitigate the source of the problem. The purchase of life insurance does not alter the chance of death, but it may lower the level of anxiety about adverse financial consequences. It is not being suggested that the purchase of life insurance can eliminate the emotional trauma associated with death, but the anxiety associated with the contemplation of death may seem less awful when accompanied by the knowledge that the event will not cause the survivor's impoverishment. The purchase of life insurance to lessen such stress and anxiety probably is the main reason some people make the purchase.

Providing support for the hypothesis that life insurance is purchased to relieve stress and anxiety is an old industry adage that to motivate some people to buy life insurance the salesperson must "back up the hearse and let 'em smell the roses." That is, one must first cause stress and anxiety, then provide an action—the purchase of life insurance—allowing the reduction of the stress and anxiety.

However, life insurance agents assume considerable risk in employing this strategy. Pointing out a real and serious problem, even if it produces stress, is a desirable action in many cases. But not all reactions to stress are positive. The results of an agent's sales efforts or of advertising showing "angels accompanying a newly departed person on the escalator to heaven" may be the previously described counterproductive, negative reactions to stress: denial, apathy or irritability. Motivating people, given the uniqueness of human beings, is a delicate skill, which may, in part, explain the high failure rate of new insurance agents.

Motivation

Personality is a term used by psychologists to categorize types of people. Among the less desirable personality types identified are moody, anxious, rigid, aggressive and impulsive. Among the more positive types are careful, reliable, responsive and peaceful.[8] There is consensus on these categorizations by psychologists, but there is little agreement on the causes of personality development or on the most effective ways to motivate different personalities.

Freud stressed the development of personality based on internal reactions to events occurring very early in life. He identified the id, ego and superego as the elements of a personality. The id represents the individual reacting internally, seeking immediate gratification of instinctual impulses. The desire to reduce or eliminate stressful situations is motivated by the id. The ego represents the individual responding to the external world. The ego protects the individual from harm. "What would people think of me if I died and left my family impoverished?" is an ego-derived question. The superego, in Freudian terminology, describes the development of conscience or the mechanism by which an individual internalizes society's morals and norms.

The Freudian approach to personality development would explain the purchase of life insurance as the satisfaction of needs associated with the id, ego and superego—needs that often cannot even be articulated by the individual making the purchase, ranging from relieving a sense of guilt to expressing love.

Another view of personality development comes from psychologists who view behavior as a reaction to external stimuli. Such a view is associated with Pavlov and B. F. Skinner. Given continual conditioning by the environment, people learn which responses produce successful results and which do not. In the vocabulary of these psychologists, stable and successful personalities learn correct responses more quickly and accurately than do unstable personalities. For this school of thought the purchase of life insurance may be a conditioned response to such external events as the birth of a child, a sales presentation or marriage. That is, those who learn through observation of relatives or peers that "successful" people purchase life insurance when a specific event occurs will imitate that behavior, trying to follow the pattern of success.

Another psychologist, Abraham Maslow, provides a framework different from those emphasizing internal or external factors as explanations for personality development. Maslow viewed behavior as the result of the individual attempting to satisfy different types of needs, which he ranked in ascending order as physiological, safety, love, esteem and self-actualization. One implication from Maslow's work is that life insurance can provide a sense of safety (from financial harm, not from death) and thus can satisfy a very basic need for most people.

However, explanations stopping at this point are far too simple considering the richness of Maslow's work. Life insurance also can be an expression of love for one's spouse and family and also may satisfy a need for esteem. ("My family is fully protected by one of the largest, best, fastest-growing, most advanced life insurance companies in the country!") Used in this way, Maslow's work provides psychological clues that help explain the purchase of life insurance.

The study of personality and motivation can shed light on the decision to purchase life insurance. Those characteristics identified as positive, however they are developed, are probably compatible with the purchase of life insurance. That is, some personality types are probably going to purchase life insurance and feel more satisfied with the decision than are other types of personalities, though research is needed to prove this assertion.

Death

Life insurance is a euphemism for *death insurance*. The need for such a euphemism is deeply rooted in one basic reaction to death: denial. Our many taboos preclude even the mention of death in many contexts. The human reaction to death, the pervasive fear of death, cross-cultural differences in attitudes toward death and the understanding of these and other complex problems presented by death occupy much space in the literature of psychology and other social sciences such as sociology, anthropology and religion. The purchase of life insurance must by its very nature be put within the framework of what is known about the human reaction to death.

The relationship between the study of life insurance and the study of death finds a focus in one question: Does the person purchasing life insurance really acknowledge the possibility of immediate death? Freud's analysis suggests a negative response.

> At heart one doesn't feel that he will die, he only feels sorry for the man next to him. Freud's explanation for this was that the unconscious does not know death or time: in man's physiochemical, inner organic recesses he feels immortal.[9]

There is a paradoxical problem for purchasers of life insurance who believe in immortality: to those who have not accepted the possibility of their own death, life insurance makes no sense. But it cannot be reasonably concluded that every purchaser of life insurance has accepted the possibility of death. Perhaps different levels of consciousness are simultaneously maintaining two antagonistic positions, the acceptance and the denial of death. Using Freud's terminology, it is possible that the recognition of death given at the conscious level may be suppressed at the unconscious or subconscious level of thought.

Research suggests that reactions to death and change over time are a function of age. That is, reactions to death are assumed to be different among the child, the adolescent, the adult and the aged. Reaction to death may be a function of internal or external experience. The child confronted early by the death of a parent may develop fears and reactions absent in children not thinking about death. Yet no one universally predictable reaction to the need to confront death, especially one's own, exists. Likewise, research on the effects of a joint consideration of death in a financial planning context would be useful, as the dynamics of this situation might be different from people contemplating only their own deaths.

The way people react to death, the thought of their own or another's, may be a function of their culture and society as well as a function of their age. The American view of death is hardly shared by other societies and is typified by denial of death and isolation of the dying, with the hospice, nursing home and funeral home being the chief means to our societal ends. In *The American Way of Death*, Jessica

Mitford noted the peculiarly American approach to the problems death presents: the great reliance on funeral directors rather than family to see to the details of burial, the use of makeup on the corpse to eliminate the picture of death to the greatest extent possible, and, in general, the isolation of the process of death from the ongoing business of life.[10]

Mitford's analysis of the American attitude toward death is somewhat dated but remains valid for large numbers of people. It is possible that the current generation's attitudes toward death, at least the component of the attitude that is shaped by society, will undergo significant change due to education.

The implication for life insurance companies is that life insurance may be easier to discuss with the current generation than with previous generations. However, such an assumption should be supported by scientific research before it is generally accepted, because some component of an individual's attitude toward death may not be affected by the social environment or education.

Some researchers believe that humans have an inherent fear of death that serves the very healthy purpose of making them cautious about exposing themselves to harm. Whether such a trait is inherent or learned or even exists in some or all cases is, of course, debated by psychologists. In a Pulitzer Prize-winning book, *The Denial of Death*, Ernest Becker suggests that the terror of death pervades every aspect of our lives.

> The first thing we have to do with heroism is to lay bare its underside, show what gives human heroics its specific nature and impetus. Here we introduce directly one of the great rediscoveries of modern thought: that of all things that move man, one of the principal ones is his terror of death. . . . We admire most the courage to face death; we give such valor our highest and most constant adoration; it moves us deeply in our hearts because we have doubts about how brave we ourselves would be. When we see a man bravely facing his own extinction we rehearse the greatest victory we can imagine.[11]

Another researcher reinforces Becker's conclusion and sums up the matter:

> Whatever the disagreements between philosophers and psychologists on the status of death anxiety, there is somewhat greater agreement about how the human species deals with this anxiety: by elaborate attempts to deny the reality and ultimacy of death.[12]

The purpose of this brief treatment of the concept of death is to alert the reader to one possibly very important explanation for why the life insurance transaction is made or why often it is not made. The contemplation of the reality of their own death may be more than some people can tolerate. It may be a conviction of immortality, a terror of death, a repression of the subject or another psychological mechanism that inhibits the completion of the life insurance transaction. However, like the study of stress and personality theories, the psychological theories of death can cut two ways. Perhaps the fear of death, the ever-present knowledge of its likelihood, will serve as a stimulus to action, as a prod to purchase life insurance as an ironic and morbid gamble to cash in on one's greatest fear. Or life insurance may be viewed as a heroic purchase (in Becker's vocabulary), allowing one to continue to do good even after death. Surely some life insurance is purchased because people are convinced that ancestors leaving significant bequests are remembered better than those that do not do so.

> Most of all, it [money] can be accumulated and passed on, and so radiates its powers even after one's death, giving one a semblance of immortality as he lives in the vicarious enjoyments of his heirs that his money continues to buy, or in the magnificence of the art works that he commissioned, or in the statues of himself and the majesty of his own mausoleum.[13]

In summary, the student of life insurance should realize that the life insurance transaction involves one of the most complex of human reactions. For that reason decisions not appearing logical or rational from an economic or financial standpoint may be more easily explained and understood from a psychological standpoint. Still, psychological explanations of the life insurance transaction need a great deal more investigation and thought before any theories or hypotheses are accepted as proven conclusions.

Review Questions

1. Explain the differences among permanent, temporary and savings needs for life insurance. Give two examples of each category.
2. Describe the arguments for and against saving with cash value life insurance.
3. What evidence suggests a decline in the numbers of "traditional" American families? What effects might such a decline have on the sale of life insurance?
4. List some uses for life insurance outside the traditional family structure.
5. Explain the statement "Life insurance adds certainty to the lifetime consumption pattern."
6. What is the life-cycle hypothesis, and what is its relevance to life insurance?
7. Describe the difference between human capital and human life value.
8. Explain some human reactions to stress. Can stress ever be useful?
9. Motivating people is a difficult challenge. List some reasons why there are no simple explanations for human behavior.
10. How does society shape its members' views of death? How might a person's attitude toward death explain the purchase of life insurance?

11. Why is the needs-based purchase of life insurance based on the assumption of immediate death?
12. Explain the concept of "permanent" dependents.
13. Describe a circumstance when life insurance proceeds should *not* be used to repay a mortgage after the main wage earner's death.
14. Describe some financial planning problems faced by parents with handicapped children. Explain how life insurance can help solve some of these financial problems.

Endnotes

[1] *Life Association News*, February 1990, p. 29; March 1990, p. 32.

[2] U.S. Bureau of the Census, Current Population Reports, Series P-20, #437: *Household and Family Characteristics: March 1988*, p. 1.

[3] Alan Pifer and Lydia Bronte, *Our Aging Society* (New York: W. W. Norton, 1986), p. 4.

[4] Human Services Research Institute, *Summary of Data on Handicapped Children and Youth*, U.S. Department of Education, December 1985.

[5] John Maynard Keynes, *The General Theory of Employment, Interest and Money* (New York: Harcourt Brace Jovanovich, 1936), p. 96.

[6] Franco Modigliani and Richard Brumberg, "Utility Analysis and the Consumption Function: An Interpretation of Cross-Section Data," in *Post Keynesian Economics*, Kenneth Kurthara, ed. (Brunswick, N.J.: Rutgers University Press, 1954), p. 391.

[7] S. S. Huebner and Kenneth Black, Jr., *Life Insurance*, 10th ed. (Englewood Cliffs, N.J.: Prentice-Hall, 1982), p. 15.

[8] Some personality types are neither wholly positive nor negative. See James B. Weitzul, "Selling to the Overachiever: Be Cool, Concise and Careful," *Life Association News*, January 1985, pp. 143–149.

[9] Ernest Becker, *The Denial of Death* (New York: Free Press, 1973), p. 2.

[10] Jessica Mitford, *The American Way of Death* (Greenwich, Conn.: Fawcett, 1963).

[11] Becker, *Denial of Death*, p. 11.

[12] Richard Momeyer, *Confronting Death* (Bloomington, Ind.: Indiana University Press, 1988), p. 3.

[13] Ernest Becker, *Escape from Evil* (New York: Free Press, 1975), p. 81.

Bibliography

Atchley, Robert C. *Social Forces and Aging*, 6th ed. Belmont, Calif.: Wadsworth Publishing Co., 1990.

Becker, Ernest. *The Denial of Death*. New York: Free Press, 1973.

Dorfman, Mark S., and Charles P. Flynn. "Immortality-Striving, Heroism, and Power: Psychological Contributions to Life Insurance Marketing." *Journal of the American Society of CLU & ChFC* 41, March 1987, pp. 56–60.

Hochschild, Richard. "Biological Age as a Measure of Risk." *Journal of the American Society of CLU & ChFC* 42, September 1988, pp. 60–66.

Holdren, Don P. "Financial Planning for the Unique Needs of the Handicapped." *Journal of the American Society of CLU & ChFC* 40, September 1986, pp. 40–46.

Leimberg, Stephan R., and Herbert D. Hinkle. "Financial and Estate Planning for Parents of the Disabled." *Journal of the American Society of CLU & ChFC* 43, May 1989, pp. 38–50.

Leming, Michael R., and George E. Dickinson. *Understanding Dying, Death and Bereavement*, 2nd ed. Troy, Mo.: Holt, Rinehart & Winston, 1990.

Phillips, Michael. *Baby Boom Two: Projections for the 1990s*, 2nd ed. San Francisco: Clear Glass, 1988.

Schott, Francis H. "The Financial Position of the U.S. Households and the Life Insurance Industry." *Journal of the American Society of CLU & ChFC* 41, September 1987, pp. 50–55.

Chapter 3 Traditional Life Insurance Products

Chapter Objectives

- Explain the building of all life insurance policies
- Describe the nature and uses of term life insurance
- Describe the nature and uses of whole life insurance
- Explain the advantages and disadvantages of saving with whole life insurance
- Describe three different payment patterns for whole life insurance
- Explain the flexibility inherent in the traditional whole life insurance contract

Introduction

A life insurance contract, stripped to its barest essentials, is an agreement between an insurer and a policy owner to pay a beneficiary if the insured dies during the contract period. The insurer receives a premium, and in return the owner receives a promise of payment contingent on the insured's death. The simplest life insurance contract lasts for one year, typically requires one premium payment, is called *annual renewable term life insurance (ART)* or *yearly renewable term life insurance (YRT)* and does not solve very many financial problems.

People often need more complex life insurance contracts, many lasting for a lifetime instead of one year, for several reasons. First, as discussed in Chapter 2, many life insurance needs are permanent. ART cannot be relied on for such needs, because the insured may outlive the policy's term. Second, ART rates increase with age because the likelihood of death increases with age. The ever-increasing rates lead to unaffordable premiums and to adverse selection. **Adverse selection** describes the tendency of people who believe they are most likely to experience a loss to try to buy insurance at average rates. With respect to renewing term life insurance, when rates increase dramatically after age 60, the most likely buyers are those most likely to die. A principle of insurance states that when only those most likely to experience loss purchase coverage, the insurance system will fail.[1] Third, ART does not provide the financial flexibility required in many cases.

To answer the needs unmet by ART, insurers have developed products that offer savings and long-term affordable insurance coverage while minimizing the effect of adverse selection. Called *cash value life insurance,* these ingenious financial transactions are legally, financially and actuarially complex. Basically, however, they all feature a **cash surrender value**—the amount of savings available to policy owners voluntarily ending their policies before death.

Traditionally, insurers called cash value life insurance *whole life insurance* or *ordinary life insurance*. In recent decades insurers have developed nontraditional cash value life insurance forms categorized as universal, variable or variable universal life insurance. Both traditional and nontraditional policies feature premium payments in excess of insurer charges and contractual rights extending longer than one year. The nontraditional policies differ significantly from the traditional policies as to their flexibility in changing premiums and death benefits, more varied underlying investment media and the "transparency" of insurer charges and investment earnings. This chapter describes traditional term and whole life insurance; nontraditional life insurance is addressed in Chapter 4.

The Building Blocks of Life Insurance Policies

Chapters 21, 22 and 23 present the mathematics of life insurance premium construction. This section describes premium construction without actuarial explanations.[2]

The apparent variety of life insurance policies is astounding. A thousand different insurers, some selling as few as a dozen different policy types and some selling many dozens of different forms, comprise the market. While some companies simply use the fundamental terms *universal* and *term* life insurance to name their products, many insurers use distinct names such as *executive estate builder, golden accumulator* and *extraordinary heritage protector*. The frequency, size and certainty of the amounts vary among policy types, but actuarial science requires all policies to be built of the same charges and credits.

The following items are the basic building blocks of all life insurance policies:

- A charge for mortality
- A charge for acquisition expense
- A charge for ongoing administration expense
- A credit for premiums paid
- A credit for investment earnings
- A survivorship benefit

Mortality Charge

Every life insurance rate begins with a **mortality charge.** The rate is the cost per thousand dollars of insurance. The premium is that rate multiplied by the number of thousand dollars of life insurance purchased. The premium, collected in advance from each insured, causes all insureds to bear their mathematically fair share of the death payments. This charge reflects the probability of death derived from an actuarially appropriate mortality table. The actuarial tables used to calculate premiums differ significantly from those used for the purpose of calculating legal reserves such as the 1980 Commissioners Standard Ordinary (CSO) mortality table. (Chapter 21 describes mortality table construction.) The mortality tables reflect age, gender, health factors and other characteristics. After receiving the insurance application, the underwriter categorizes each applicant based on the same factors the actuary used in constructing the mortality tables. The result is a premium fairly reflecting expected losses.

☐ **Example**

Tom, Dick and Harry are all age 35. Each applies for $100,000 of whole life insurance. Tom is a nonsmoker who exercises regularly and is in excellent health, a "preferred risk." His premium is $1,442. Dick is significantly overweight. The underwriter uses "Table 2," charging Dick 150 percent of the standard mortality cost. His premium is $2,138. Harry's health is seriously impaired. Because the underwriter used "Table 6" to calculate his premium, he pays 250 percent of the standard mortality rate. His premium is $3,530. The mortality charge for each man is based on the expected mortality of the group in which he is placed by the underwriter. (Details of underwriting and rate making are presented in Chapter 23.)

You can see that Dick's premium is only about 50 percent greater than Tom's despite the mortality charge being 150 percent of the standard charge. The increased mortality charge is only one portion of the premium, and the other components, which we describe shortly, do not reflect the increased health risk. That is, the acquisition expenses and other charges are not increased for impaired health.

Acquisition Expenses   The costs incurred in placing a life insurance policy in force can include some or all of the following items:

- Advertising and promotion expense
- Commissions and fees paid to agents, brokers, general agents or other distributors
- Expenses of medical selection and of information services
- Home office processing costs, policy printing and related fees
- An addition to the insurer's reserves, surplus or profits
- Premium taxes

Each insurer has considerable latitude in incurring most of these expenses. New York State places a limit on total acquisition expenses and limits first-year commissions paid to agents to 55 percent of the first year's premium. However, not all insurers operate in New York or are subject to its rules. Thus, non–New York companies without similarly stringent expense limitations can pay agents and brokers 110 percent of the first year's premium and incur additional first-year expenses. A simple rule of economics applies to acquisition expenses: the greater the costs incurred, the higher the rate that must be charged to cover the costs.

Insurers recover acquisition expenses in two ways. Traditionally they subtracted substantial *front-end loads* from premiums paid by all insureds for the first year or two. The front-end load decreases the cash value in the policy's early years. The second approach is the *rear-end load* or *surrender charge*, applied only to policies surrendered in the early years. Some companies combine front-end and rear-end loads in their policies.

Rear-end loads often diminish gradually over time, eventually disappearing between the eighth and tenth policy anniversary. For example, one company applies a 16 percent charge against the cash value of policies surrendered in the first year. Each succeeding year the surrender charge drops by 2 percent. After the eighth year there is no surrender charge. The disappearing rear-end load is associated with newer policy types.

Because it applies only to those dropping policies, the rear-end load shifts more of the unrecovered acquisition costs to those incurring them, lowering the cost to insureds that persist. The rear-end load transfers the risk of early policy termination, called *lapsation,* from the insurer back to those insureds lapsing their policies.

Administration Expenses

Each year a life insurance policy remains in force, the insurer incurs costs that can include some or all of the following:

- Costs of collecting premiums and distributing dividends
- Costs of continuing producer remuneration
- Investment costs
- Home office overhead costs
- Premium and other taxes
- Additions to surplus, reserves or profits

Each insurer has some control over continuing expenses, though premium taxes and some home office costs are fixed. Any costs the insurer incurs must be recovered, either explicitly in renewal premium charges or indirectly in reduced investment credits.

Premiums Paid

Each in-force life insurance policy requires an initial premium payment. To remain in force, most policies require subsequent annual (or more frequent) payments. The premium must offset all the expenses. If the premium is greater than the incurred expenses, the policy builds a cash value. With the exception of long-term contracts, which do build a limited cash value and a reserve designed to disappear before the policy terminates, term life insurance accumulates no cash value because premiums equal expenses and charges. Contracts providing flexibility in determining the amount of annual premium, called *universal* and *flexible-premium variable life insurance*, also can be continued without accumulating cash value if the policyholder pays the minimum premium. Typically, however, these policy types accumulate cash value because the insured pays a "suggested" premium in excess of the minimum premium.

Permanent, or cash value, life insurance contracts provide for premiums in excess of expense charges during the first half of the contract's expected duration.

**Figure 3.1
Level-Premium Whole Life Insurance**

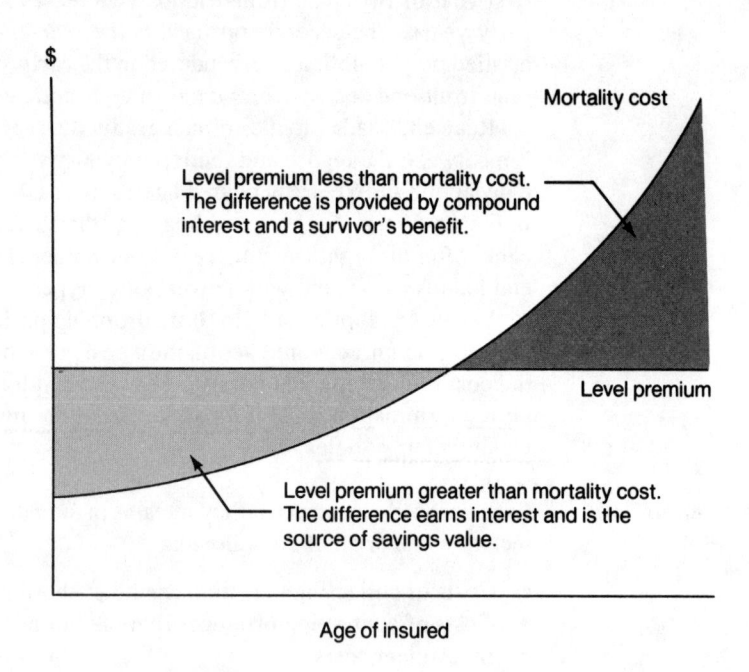

```
$
                                              Mortality cost

        Level premium less than mortality cost.
        The difference is provided by compound
        interest and a survivor's benefit.

                                              Level premium

        Level premium greater than mortality cost.
        The difference earns interest and is the
        source of savings value.

                  Age of insured
```

These policies develop a cash surrender value after the insurer recovers most of the acquisition expenses from the first year or two's premiums. Figure 3.1 illustrates this concept through level-premium insurance.

Investment Earnings Insurers invest the cash value generated by a surplus over premiums and credit the insureds based on the *new money rate* or on its *portfolio rate*. The new money rate reflects recent investment returns, while the portfolio rate reflects the insurer's overall investment return. During periods of rising investment returns, new insureds benefit from new money rates; the opposite is true when investment results are declining significantly. If policies are held for long periods, both methods should produce about the same result.

Policies based on accumulating cash value incorporate the time value of money (compound interest) in their premium assumptions. These policies guarantee a minimum investment return. With most policies currently sold, if the insurer's investment results exceed the guaranteed minimum, policy owners benefit either from participating dividends or from the crediting of excess interest to the cash value. Insurers' operating results benefit from any investment earnings not transferred to policy owners.

Table 3.1
Cash Value and Amount at Risk

The face amount *always* equals $1,000.

Policy Year	Cash Value	Amount at Risk
1	$ 0	$1,000
5	125	875
10	250	750
15	500	500

Survivorship Benefits With cash value life insurance insureds who do not die or surrender their policies receive a benefit identified as a **survivorship benefit.** Traditional cash value policies promise to pay the face amount as the death benefit. They do not pay the face amount plus accumulated cash value. The funds used for payment of the death benefit come from the mortality charge assessed each insured, including those insureds dying. As Table 3.1 shows, the cash value total increases each year the policy remains in force. The death benefit remains constant. At death the insurer distributes the cash value in the deceased insureds' policies to the living insureds. The distributed amounts produce the survivorship benefit.[3]

A second approach to viewing the cash value life insurance death benefit is to assume the beneficiary receives the increasing cash value plus a declining amount of life insurance called the **amount at risk.** Since the beneficiary is presumed to receive the insured's cash value combined with the amount at risk in the death claim, no cash value remains to distribute as a survivor's benefit. The sum of the cash value and the amount at risk always equals the policy face amount. This view is different from the survivorship view, which holds that the amount at risk is always the face amount.

☐ **Example**

Using the data in Table 3.1, the survivorship approach assumes an assessment of $2.50 for $1,000 of life insurance in year five, when the policy has a cash value of $125. This approach also assumes a $.50 credit to each survivor as a survivor benefit. The mortality cost and the credit produce a net mortality charge of $2 for the year.

The "amount at risk" viewpoint suggests that the insurer charges $2 in the fifth year for $875 of life insurance protection. The $1,000 death benefit is comprised of $875 in protection and $125 in cash value.

While mathematically both views end with the same result, payment of the face amount, the difference between them is more than academic. If a court considers the death proceeds in part a return of the policy's cash value, then creditors of the deceased's estate would have a legitimate claim against that portion. If, on the contrary, a court considers the death proceeds entirely insurance, creditors' claims would not apply. (The various district tax courts have ruled both ways on this issue when the creditor was the U.S. Treasury.)

Table 3.2
T-Account for Life Insurance Charges and Credits

Inflows	Outflows
1. Premiums paid	1. Mortality charge
2. Investment returns	2. Acquisition charge
3. Survivorship benefit	3. Administrative charge

The T-Account   Because insurance requires application of the law of large numbers, insurers do not keep individual accounts as banks do. Instead, insurers treat all similarly situated insureds as a "block" of business. The insurer applies the charges and credits to the entire block of policies. Table 3.2 illustrates the various policy credits and charges using the familiar T-account format.

History of Life Insurance Purchases in the United States[4]

Before delving into the examination of traditional life insurance products in this chapter and nontraditional products in Chapter 4, readers should understand that the popularity of the different policy types changes over time. Just as specific products answer the changing needs of individuals, particular products are better suited than others for certain economic conditions.

For the first 100 years of American life insurance sales, term, whole life and endowment policies comprised the great majority of all policies sold. Almost no new products were developed by the life insurance industry from 1850 to 1950.[5] In 1975, when various types of term and whole life together held almost 90 percent of new life insurance sales, new products began to appear. The two most significant new products were variable life insurance and universal life insurance.

Table 3.3 presents sales data for the years 1979, 1984 and 1989. Figure 3.2 presents the data graphically. In 1979 neither of the two new policy types was sold in sufficient amount to appear in the table. By 1984 these new products represented more than 30 percent of sales. In 1989, the most recent year for which data are available, nontraditional policies have declined to 24 percent of sales. The decline is thought to be related to the decline in interest rates, because the products' returns are interest sensitive.

Term Life Insurance

A term life insurance contract promises a death benefit to a beneficiary if the insured dies during a specified period (term). If the insured survives the period, the insurer's contractual obligation ends. Term insurance is the least complicated life insurance contract. It may be purchased as a separate contract or in conjunction with cash value products, in which case it is called a *term rider*.

Chapter 3 Traditional Life Insurance Products

Table 3.3
Analysis of Ordinary Life Insurance Purchases in the United States
(Percentage of amount of annual purchases)

Year	Whole Life	Term	Nontraditional	All Other	Total
1979	36	48	0	16	100
1984	19	35	32	14	100
1989	26	42	24	8	100

Term life insurance contracts are either short-term or long-term. Short-term policies include annual and five-year policies. Long-term policies remain in force until the insured reaches a specified age, such as 55 or 65. The typical pattern of pricing term insurance is for the rate for each $1,000 of insurance to rise at each renewal. Sometimes the face amount of insurance decreases while the premium remains constant. Either of these approaches recognizes that it is more expensive to purchase life insurance as a person gets older.

Reentry Term Life Insurance

Reentry term life insurance, a relatively new form of this policy type, requires insureds to pass regular medical examinations to qualify for lower rates. This pol-

Figure 3.2
Life Insurance Purchases
(By percent)

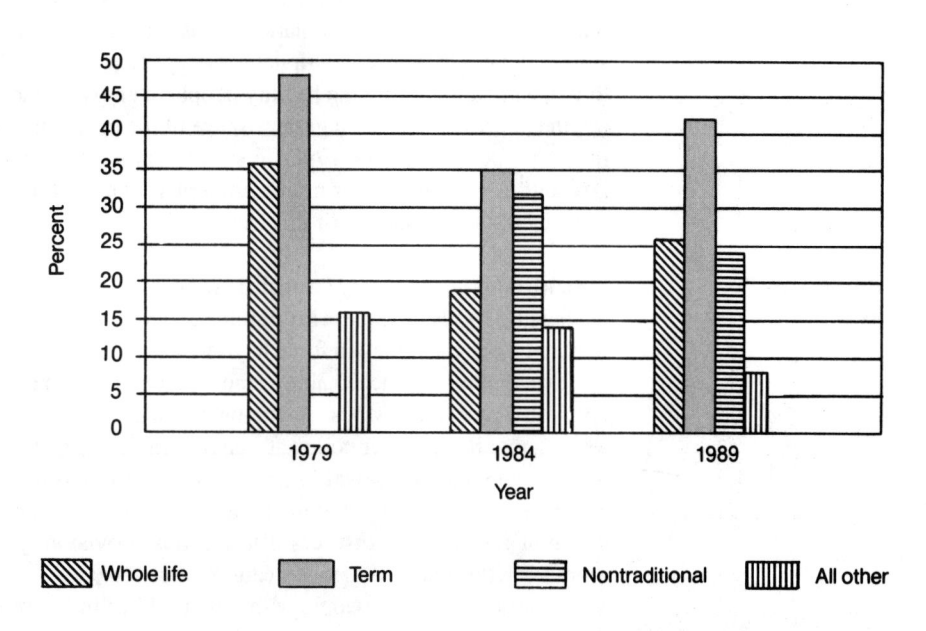

icy clarifies several fundamental points about term insurance, such as rates increasing with age and the effect of medical selection. Table 3.4, a typical sales presentation, presents one company's reentry term insurance rates.

Richard L. Hart, is a 25-year-old male nonsmoker. Separating smokers from nonsmokers allows the insurer to offer more competitive rates to better risks. The face amount of insurance is $500,000 because this is the minimum policy size this company will sell at these preferred rates. This policy is five-year, level term insurance. The face amount remains constant. The reentry premiums increase at five-year intervals, which is why the table shows the same premiums both in year 16 and year 20.

The table shows two sets of premiums. Premium #1 is called the *reentry premium*. Hart must establish evidence of insurability, including good health, at each fifth anniversary of the policy issue. If he remains insurable, the premiums follow the pattern illustrated. Premium #2 is the guaranteed rate, which is available if the insured fails to qualify for the reentry rate. The guaranteed premiums increase at a growing rate after age 38 because more insureds are in impaired health after this age. Because they have a right to retain the insurance, death claims will be greater than in the group including only those passing the medical examination. This illustration shows that no difference exists between the reentry rates and the guaranteed rates before age 35, because people are unlikely to become uninsurable before this age.

The reentry approach transfers some risk traditionally borne by the insurer to the insureds. Specifically, the insureds purchasing reentry term life insurance bear the risk of impaired health. Historically, insurers have aggregated mortality costs, administering medical examinations only when the policy begins. Relying only on initial medical examinations causes insureds remaining in good health to subsidize people whose health deteriorates. Repeated medical examinations end this subsidization, allowing healthy people to enjoy lower premiums, while causing the unhealthy to bear a greater share of the cost.[6] In the competitive environment of the 1980s and 1990s insurers tended to remove previously given guarantees in exchange for more competitively priced policies. Reentry term life insurance is one evidence of this trend.

Renewable Term Insurance

Policies other than reentry term also allow insureds to continue their coverage for extended periods. People who purchase annual or five-year term policies often intend to keep the policy in force beyond the initial period. When they are in good health and otherwise acceptable to the insurer, they can purchase subsequent policies. However, those whose health becomes seriously impaired during a covered term cannot buy another policy at standard rates and may not be able to purchase a policy at any rate. **Renewable term insurance** avoids this problem by containing a contractual provision guaranteeing renewability at standard rates without evidence of insurability. Insurers offering this provision typically specify a maximum age after which the policy cannot be renewed.

Because a group of people with impaired health has more death claims than a group of people in average health, insurers charge an additional sum for the renewability provision. Some, but certainly not all, people renewing their policies

Table 3.4
Reentry Term Insurance Ledger Sheet

Illustration for Richard L. Hart
Age 25, Nonsmoker
Death Benefit = $500,000

Year	Age	Premium #1	Premium #2
1	25	$400	$ 400
6	30	425	425
11	35	500	580
16	40	750	2,585
20	44	750	2,585

Premium #1 assumes evidence of insurability shown at each renewal.
Premium #2 is the guaranteed rate.

will be in impaired health. Some, but certainly not all, people in impaired health will die sooner than people in average health. Yet all insureds having policies with guaranteed renewability pay standard premiums at renewal. Therefore, the amount charged for the renewal privilege must provide the funds for the above-normal death claims. By paying for the renewability guarantee, all insureds bear a portion of the increased death costs of insureds with deteriorating health. This result is the opposite of that occurring with reentry term life insurance, where only insureds with impaired health pay the increased cost.

Convertible Term

Convertible term insurance provides the insured with the option of converting the term contract to permanent life insurance at standard rates without evidence of insurability. In general, when an insured converts a term policy to a permanent contract, the insurer determines the premium by the insured's age at the time of conversion. Insurers call this an *attained-age conversion*. Insurers call the alternative an *original-age conversion*, which requires the insured to pay a conversion premium equal to the difference between the premiums paid on the term policy and what would have been paid if the permanent policy had been begun initially.

☐ **Example**

Attained-Age Conversion: Thelma Ann, age 30, converts her term policy to whole life insurance. She purchased the term policy at age 25. Thelma pays the standard premium on the whole life policy appropriate for a 30-year-old.

Original-Age Conversion: On conversion, at age 30, Thelma pays $5,000, the difference in premium between her term policy and a whole life policy purchased at age 25. Thereafter, she pays the whole life premium appropriate for a 25-year-old.

The conversion privilege is useful for people who want cash value life insurance but initially cannot afford it. If their health deteriorates after beginning the term policy, they may not be eligible for a standard-rate cash value policy without the conversion feature. Before making a decision, people in normal health, of course, should always make comparisons between beginning a new cash value policy and converting an existing term policy. Convertible term insurance is one method of guaranteeing the availability of insurance for a lifetime at a relatively low initial cost. In long-term policies, the conversion privilege generally ends before the maximum length of the contract. For example, conversion may be allowed only in the first ten years.

☐ **Example**

Betty Brinkley is a single parent of twins aged eight. She purchased a $250,000 convertible term policy to provide funds for her children's education if she dies prematurely. Because she needs such a large amount of coverage, the term premium is all she can afford presently. Betty's income should rise significantly in the next ten years as her paint manufacturing firm continues its rapid growth. Betty intends to convert the term insurance to whole life insurance as soon as her income allows. She wants the permanent coverage to avoid the ever-increasing term premiums and to begin a savings program.

Level, Decreasing or Increasing Face Amounts

Insurers write term life insurance with level or decreasing face amounts. Increasing term insurance is found only as a rider on cash value life insurance.

Level Term Life Insurance

Level term life insurance has a level death benefit and a premium that increases with age. The reentry term illustration in Table 3.4 illustrates this pattern. Popular policy types in this category include *yearly renewable term* (also known as *annual renewable term*) and *five-year renewable term* life insurance.

Decreasing Term Life Insurance

Because premiums remain constant, decreasing term policies provide a declining death benefit as the insured ages. Each premium buys less insurance because the mortality charge increases with age. The pattern of level premiums and decreasing insurance is useful when the need for funds at the insured's death diminishes over time.

☐ **Example**

The Knudsen family wants to repay its home mortgage if Bill Knudsen dies prematurely. Decreasing term insurance can be arranged to follow closely the declining balance of the mortgage. In such cases insurers call the policy *mortgage protection insurance.*

Other needs also diminish over time. The need to provide funds for dependent children diminishes, though inflation affects the rate of decrease. Each year a parent survives and provides a dependent's support, one less year's funds are needed if the parent dies before the child's independence. The child's financial independence ends the need for life insurance proceeds to support the child. Thus the need to support children can be met with decreasing term insurance.

If the decrease in the term insurance is offset by an increase in an investment fund, the total amount of cash available at death remains constant. This is the plan of the buy-term-and-invest-the-difference argument. The sum of the term insurance death benefit and the investment fund is supposed to meet the individual's or family's need for postdeath funds. Chapter 6 presents more details on the buy-term argument.

Increasing Term Insurance

Some life insurance companies sell riders on cash value policies called **cost-of-living** riders, **return of cash value** riders or **return of premium** riders. These riders are increasing term insurance. Each annual premium for any increasing term rider is a function of the insured's attained age at the time of purchase and the amount of coverage purchased.

Cost-of-living riders provide an increased amount of insurance in direct relation to increases in the U.S. Department of Labor's consumer price index (CPI). Return-of-premium or return-of-cash-value forms provide increased coverage each year the policy remains in force. These increases in coverage are unrelated to changes in the CPI. Thus only the cost-of-living riders are designed to maintain constant purchasing power.

☐ **Example**

As of 1990, cost-of-living riders on policies begun in 1977 had more than doubled the original death proceeds. That is, a cost-of-living rider attached to a $50,000 term or whole life policy now provides more than $50,000 of coverage in addition to the original death benefit.

Uses of Term Life Insurance

Term life insurance is used most advantageously to meet temporary needs, those ending at a definite time. Funding mortgage repayments and providing postdeath dependent child support are examples of this type of need. Term insurance is also appropriate where life insurance premium dollars are limited and the need for protection is great, as is often the case with young families. For a given amount of initial premium, term insurance always provides the greatest amount of protection.

Term insurance policies are, however, limited in meeting some financial goals:

- Term policies do not involve cash value. Many people benefit from the savings feature of cash value life insurance.
- Term life mortality charges increase with age. The increased cost of the policies may make insurance unaffordable while the insured still needs coverage.
- Term life insurance policies are generally unavailable after age 70. Some people still need life insurance protection at later ages. While insurers do

not issue new term policies after age 70, some existing policies continue past this age.

Some critics of term life insurance claim this policy type is generally inappropriate for most people because the data show that relatively few term policies mature as a death claim.[7] This reasoning is faulty. First, term insurance policies result in few death claims because term policies do not cover the period after age 70, when death is most likely. Second, many people convert their term policies to cash value policies. Third, most Americans survive past their 50th birthday. By age 50 mortgages are often repaid and children are independent. Therefore, many people allow their term life insurance policies covering these temporary needs to expire.

Whole Life Insurance

Whole life insurance contracts require an insurer to pay a beneficiary at the insured's death or to pay insureds living to age 100. (Whole life contracts may cover more than one life. This chapter describes only single life contracts. Chapter 17 describes a contract used in estate planning cases covering two lives, called *second death* or *survivor life insurance*.) In addition to death benefits, these policies provide cash value or savings benefits during the insured's lifetime.

Traditional whole life insurance policies have fixed premiums and fixed death benefits. Nontraditional policies, described in the next chapter, give policy owners greater flexibility, including the ability to change annual premiums and total death benefits. The increase in contractual flexibility comes at the price of reduced guarantees or the shifting of some risk from the insurer to the policyholder.

The Decision to Save   As already explained, whole life insurance policies inevitably involve a cash surrender value. This savings feature historically has stimulated much debate. One group argues that the cash values are an end in themselves, that whole life insurance is a savings program guaranteed of completion even if the owner dies. For these people the savings justify the policy's purchase. Actuaries, on the other hand, argue that the cash value is merely a by-product of a financial plan to keep the premium level and affordable for life. Debate over whole life's desirability often centers on whether the contract offers savings *and* protection or savings *or* protection. Is the contract divisible into its component parts (savings and protection)? Regardless of the legal, actuarial, economic or practical sides of these arguments, whole life insurance cannot be purchased without saving, so it is reasonable to view an *informed* decision to purchase this policy as partially a decision to save and partially a decision to insure.

Now, is this approach that combines savings with insurance appropriate to meet savings goals? To determine whether whole life insurance is an appropriate purchase in a given circumstance, both the need to save and the need to insure must be evaluated. If either need is absent, whole life likely is not an economically efficient purchase. Some critics of cash value life insurance maintain that whole life provides few contractual rights that cannot be duplicated with a combination of term insurance and a savings medium. Supporters of whole life insurance argue that the contract's flexibility, protection from creditor's claims and tax advantages make cash value life insurance very difficult to duplicate.

Whole life insurance involves a compulsory, long-term savings program. It can be used efficiently for many long-term savings goals, including leveling term premiums or funding retirement income. Because of relatively high transaction costs, however, it performs poorly as a short-term savings medium.

Advantages of Saving with Whole Life Insurance

Safety

Because of close regulatory supervision of insurer solvency, savings in life insurance policies historically have proven safe. The safety record of life insurance companies compares favorably to that of banks and savings and loan associations. Even during the Depression life insurance proved to be a safe investment. Insureds of the few life insurance companies regulators felt were operating imprudently were transferred to stable companies.

In early 1991 critics were questioning the financial stability of several life insurance companies, including a few large ones. These critics note that life insurance policy owners do not benefit from federal regulation and do not have a federal insurance guarantee if insurers fail. In April 1991 California state insurance regulators took control of First Executive Corporation, a $15 billion insurance holding company. The company's assets included $9 billion (face amount) of junk bonds, one-quarter of which were in default at the time of the regulatory action. In June 1991, New Jersey regulators interceded to protect policyholders of Mutual Benefit Life Insurance Company, one of the 20 largest life insurers in the United States.

Investment Management

As financial intermediaries, life insurers receive funds from millions of savers and then purchase corporate and government securities, finance real estate transactions and invest in other quality assets. The choice of investments is a complicated process requiring expert judgment and timing. Because of the scale of their investment operations, insurers get timely information and forecasts, hire investment specialists and investigate more alternatives than smaller-scale investors. Furthermore, because of the large sums available for investment, life insurers often secure better terms than smaller investors. On the other hand, because of their size, large insurers may find it hard to move quickly when market conditions change. Overall, life insurance companies provide skilled investment management and broadly diversified investment portfolios earning competitive rates of return.

Liquidity

While saving with a whole life insurance policy is basically a long-term commitment, the cash value can be obtained quickly by the policyholder with no sacrifice in investment value. Contractually the policy owner may use the cash value by

(1) borrowing from the insurer, (2) surrendering the policy for cash or (3) assigning the policy to a bank or other lender as collateral for a secured loan.

Protection from Creditors

Because the law and the courts recognize that society benefits if bankrupt debtors are not stripped of all their assets, an exemption from creditors' claims exists for certain amounts and types of assets. The amounts and types of assets differ among the various states and between the state laws and federal law. Typically these various laws provide that life insurance proceeds are exempt from a deceased insured's creditors, especially if a surviving spouse or dependent child receives the proceeds. Sometimes the cash values also are protected from the policy owner's creditors' claims during the insured's lifetime. Chapter 9 presents details of the relevant state laws; suffice it to say here that protection from creditors' claims is a possible advantage of saving with cash value life insurance.

Favorable Tax Treatment

Tax treatment is a relative matter depending on changing individual circumstances, tax laws and investment alternatives. It is risky to generalize about the relative tax treatment of different investments. Life insurance contracts have two significant tax advantages. First, the beneficiary's gross income does not include proceeds paid at death. Second, during the insured's lifetime, taxes are deferred on investment income credited to the policy. (Chapter 11 covers the taxation of life insurance transactions more completely. The taxation of business life insurance cannot be summarized simply.)

Regular Saving

Another advantage for people saving with whole life insurance is convenience and the compulsory nature of the program. Because the premium payment includes the amount needed to increase the cash value and the insurer sends premium notices regularly, many insureds are more likely to save than they would be in the absence of a regular bill. Most Americans die without accumulating any significant wealth beyond the equity in their home, so insurers logically argue that people benefit from a compulsory savings program.

Disadvantages of Saving with Whole Life Insurance

Saving with whole life insurance presents three potential disadvantages. First, the program is a fixed-dollar savings medium and is subject to erosion of purchasing power caused by inflation. Second, the transaction costs associated with whole life insurance are high relative to those of other investments. Such relatively large costs, especially front-end loads, lower the rate of return compared to that provided by other investments. Third, the investment rate of return of traditional whole life insurance may not be competitive with that of other alternatives. However, comparisons of rates of return among investment alternatives are meaningless unless safety and liquidity are comparable to those of whole life insurance.

Distributing Investment Earnings: Premiums versus Cost

Traditionally life insurance companies sold participating (par) or nonparticipating (nonpar) policies. Participating policies require a larger advance premium than nonpar policies but pay a nontaxable year-end dividend. Nonparticipating life in-

Table 3.5
Traditional Continuous-Premium Whole Life Insurance Participating Policy with Illustrated Dividends
(Policy issued to a male, age 35, $250,000 face amount, nonsmoker)

Policy Year	Annual Premium	Cash Value (end of year)	Illustrated Dividend
1	$3,560	$ 0	$ 0
2	3,560	750	485
3	3,560	4,000	680
4	3,560	7,250	890
5	3,560	10,750	1,100
10	3,560	28,750	2,260
15	3,560	49,250	3,617
20	3,560	71,250	5,155

surance requires a lower initial premium, pays no dividends and guarantees all results. With results guaranteed for periods over 60 years, only very conservative interest and mortality assumptions are appropriate.

Insurers still sell many participating policies, but traditional nonpar policies are much less common because they became much harder to price in the volatile investment environment of the 1970s and 1980s. Because there was no way to pass favorable operating results to policy owners, nonpar insurance became an increasingly poor bargain for consumers. Many companies selling nonparticipating policies changed their pricing methods and now sell interest-sensitive products, which allow policy owners to earn additional interest based on company results.

Participating policies are associated with mutual insurers, though some stock companies also sell par policies. These carriers are owned, operated for the benefit of and in theory controlled by current policy owners. The policy owners bear the favorable or unfavorable results of current operations. Insurers price participating policies using even more conservative mortality and investment assumptions than for nonpar policies. Actuaries assume about 20 percent more deaths than data actually predict. Insurers assume interest earnings of 4 to 5 percent despite higher prevailing market rates. When these conservative assumptions prove inaccurate, the company, usually with considerable fanfare, declares a dividend.

Insurers do not guarantee payment of participating dividends, but in the absence of a health or investment catastrophe they pay dividends annually. Insurers build in dividends by using unrealistically high mortality and unrealistically low interest assumptions. (*See* Chapter 21 for a mathematical explanation.) If insurers used a realistic interest assumption of 8 percent, for example, to discount future premium obligations instead of the conservative 5 percent, the difference in annual premiums would be substantial. But the insurer would be contractually bound to the 8 percent return, and over a 50- to 85-year period this guarantee would be an imprudent commitment. Thus there is logic in making a minimum investment guarantee and crediting dividends when earnings allow it.

During sales presentations agents illustrate participating dividends. Table 3.5 shows such an illustration. The insurer bases its illustrations on current perfor-

Table 3.6
Actual versus Illustrated Dividends,
20-Year History of Policy Issued in 1966

Year	Policy Year	Illustrated	Actual
1971	5	$4.28	$4.46
1976	10	7.90	8.23
1981	15	9.56	12.77
1986	20	11.28	22.28

mance. That is, the insurer is indicating that if the insured pays the premiums and the investment, mortality and expense results equal current results, the insurer will pay the illustrated dividends.

People recognize that future results will not coincide with current results. During many years of the 1970s and 1980s mortality and investment outcomes were far better than initially predicted. Thus participating dividends exceeded initial estimates. Table 3.6 shows the illustrated and actual dividend history for the same company and policy used as the basis for Table 3.5.

Abnormally high dividend illustrations concern industry critics. If current investment returns represent a peak performance, unrealistically high dividend illustrations would be projected. Unrealistically high dividend projections could lead to considerable disappointment or policy surrender when illustrated results are not realized.

Table 3.7 is based on a commonly used sales illustration. It is for a nonpar, "excess interest," limited payment, whole life policy, with premium payments ending after the first eight years. The policy assumes a 9 percent return on the cash values, while guaranteeing a 5.5 percent rate. The careful reader will have already noticed that the cash and surrender values differ for the policy's first 15 years, indicating a steadily diminishing rear-end load. More surprisingly, the guaranteed

Table 3.7
Nonparticipating Policy with Guaranteed and Excess Interest

Ledger Illustration
Male, Age 25, nonsmoking
Annual Premium = $2,945
Face Amount = $500,000
Interest Assumption = 9%, Guaranteed Rate = 5.5%

			Assumed		Guaranteed	
Year	Age	Total Outlay*	Cash Value	Surrender Value	Cash Value	Surrender Value
5	30	$14,725	$ 13,465	$ 5,315	$ 12,489	$ 4,339
10	35	23,560	26,871	20,041	28,829	21,999
15	40	23,560	34,402	33,267	49,386	48,251
20	45	23,560	46,051	46,051	74,644	74,644
40	65	23,560	152,856	152,856	232,997	232,997

*Total outlay remains constant after 8 years for "Assumed" data. "Guaranteed" data assume continuous $2,945 annual outlay.

Chapter 3 Traditional Life Insurance Products

values, earning 5.5 percent, exceed the assumed rates, earning 9 percent. The explanation for this anomaly is that premiums end ("disappear") after eight years in the assumed columns but are paid continuously in the guaranteed columns. The summary shows premiums remaining constant after the tenth year (premium payments actually end in the eighth year), but the cash values continue to grow because of the investment returns.

Both participating dividends and excess interest credits reduce the policy owner's outlay. Thus a comparison of annual premium payments without netting dividends or investment credits serves little purpose. The cost of life insurance can be measured logically in different ways; simply comparing annual premiums is not one of them. (Chapter 6 explains some logical life insurance cost comparisons.)

Premium Payment Patterns

Insurers classify whole life insurance policies based on the number of scheduled premium payments. Most policies sold fall into these three categories:

- Single-premium policies
- Continuous-premium policies
- Limited-payment policies

Single-Premium Policies

Single-premium whole life policies require only one premium. In exchange, the insurer promises to pay the policy face amount whenever death occurs. Because the single premium is large, these whole life policies create immediate cash values.

Insureds needing large amounts of life insurance protection seldom purchase single-premium whole life insurance.

☐ **Example**

If the single premium for $1,000 of whole life insurance is $350 for a man aged 25, then $100,000 of insurance costs $35,000. Most young men could not afford this payment. The annual premium for the same amount of term life insurance would be about $150.

After the **Tax Reform Act of 1986** the sales of single-premium whole life insurance soared. Because of a loophole in the tax law, this policy became a desirable investment. The interest earned on the single-premium deposit escaped annual taxation because it was earned as the "inside buildup" on a life insurance policy. Insurers gave people access to the investment earnings through interest-free loans. In 1988 Congress closed this loophole by defining certain products, including the abusive single-premium policies, as **modified endowment contracts (MECs).** Any life insurance policy failing a "seven-pay" test is now considered a MEC. To avoid being labeled a MEC and losing the advantage of tax-free policy loans, premiums cannot be paid more rapidly than necessary to provide the paid-up death benefits that seven level annual payments can purchase. (*See* Chapter 11 for technical details of MECs.) **Paid-up policies** remain in force and earn dividends, and the cash value increases without requiring additional premium payments. Single premium policies are paid up after one payment.

Single-premium whole life insurance is no longer the attractive short-term investment it once was, but it is still being sold. Some agents recommend it in some gift and estate planning cases or as an alternative to single-premium deferred annuities as a retirement funding vehicle. Single-premium whole life insurance produces a larger death benefit than the single-premium deferred annuity, and in some cases the larger death benefit may be desirable. On the other hand, the life insurance product may involve larger transaction costs and a lower rate of return than the annuity, so careful consideration must be given to all factors and to any differential tax consequences before either choice is implemented.

Continous-Premium Policies

Continuous-premium whole life insurance is the most popular form of whole life. These policies require insureds to pay the same annual premium until they die or reach age 100. After the policy develops a savings value, policyholders may discontinue premium payments and take available benefits under a nonforfeiture option (*See* Chapter 10). Insurers also call these policies **ordinary life, level-premium whole life** and **straight life.** Scheduled premiums mathematically reflect both compound interest and the probability of the insured's death. An insured's death means the insurer must make a claim payment. It also means an insured will no longer make premium payments to the insurer. (Chapter 22 presents the mathematical calculation of level premiums.) Table 3.5 presented data for a continuous-premium whole life insurance policy.

Limited-Payment Policies

Limited-payment whole life policies fall somewhere between single-premium and continuous-premium policies. In all three cases, because the policies are whole life insurance, the protection continues until the insured dies. With limited-payment policies the insured pays premiums only for a limited number of years, with ten or fewer annual payments being most popular. After the insured makes the prescribed number of payments, the policy is paid up. Though the grammar is incorrect, agents describe paying up the policy as "disappearing" or "vanishing the premium." Other limited-payment policies require premiums until a specified age is reached, such as age 60 or 65. Agents call these policies "whole life, paid up at 65."

The size of each premium payment depends on the number of times it will be paid. The fewer the payments, the larger each payment must be. Thus, for a man age 35 annual premiums for a 10-payment whole life policy are larger than those of a whole life policy paid up at age 65, where 30 payments are presumed. However, at age 45 the premiums for a 20-payment whole life policy are the same as a whole life policy paid up at age 65. Table 3.8 shows this result.

Insureds who want lifetime death protection but do not want to continue paying life insurance premiums after their wages and salaries end purchase limited-payment whole life insurance. Insureds also use these policies in business continuation and estate planning cases because they provide permanent protection without an extended premium payment period.

Table 3.8
Limited-Payment Life Insurance
(Annual premiums for $1,000 of insurance)

Age	20-Pay Life	Paid Up at 65
25	$17.75	$12.44
35	23.55	18.91
45	32.18	32.18
55	45.62	68.44

Limited-payment whole life policies build larger cash values sooner than comparable continuous-premium policies. The secret of the limited-payment policy is that it earns greater compound interest than continuous premium policies. The increased interest earnings result from the greater difference between the premium and the mortality charges and other loadings compared to continuous-premium whole life. Figure 3.3 illustrates the cash value buildup of single-premium, continuous-premium and limited-payment whole life insurance.

Modified Whole Life and Combination Policies

Two other types of payment plans for whole life insurance deserve brief mention. **Modified whole life insurance policies** have level premiums rising in stair steps. The first step is below that of continuous-premium whole life, while the last step is above the comparable level premium. A typical modified whole life program has three or fewer steps. See Figure 3.4.

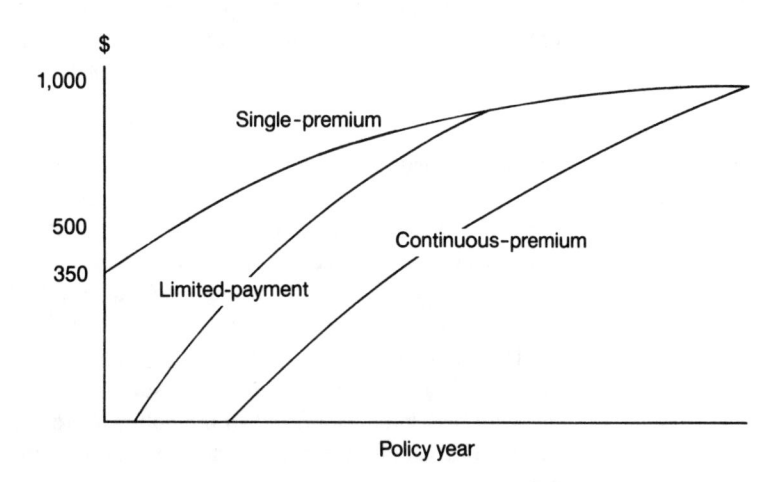

Modified whole life policies allow people who desire whole life insurance to make the purchase even though their current income cannot support the whole life

Figure 3.3
Cash Value Buildup for the Three Premium Payment Patterns

**Figure 3.4
Modified Whole Life Program**

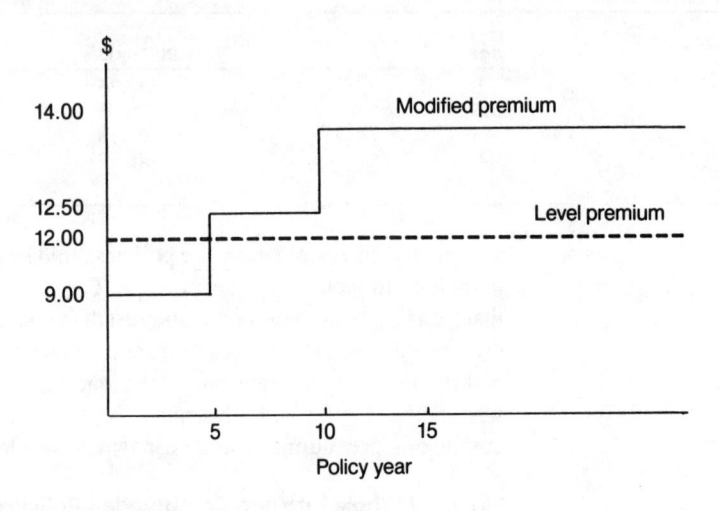

[Graph showing Modified premium starting at $9.00 for years 1-5, rising to $12.50 for years 5-10, then to $14.00 after year 10; Level premium shown as dashed line at $12.00. X-axis: Policy year (5, 10, 15).]

premium. In later years, when income levels are presumed to be greater, the slightly increased modified premium is supposed to prove no burden. Agents often recommend this premium payment format for medical students.

Combination whole life policies combine decreasing term insurance with a participating whole life policy. The contract requires reinvesting the annual dividends in the policy. The dividends purchase amounts of paid-up whole life insurance exactly offsetting the decreasing term portion of the contract. Thus the face amount of the insurance remains constant. This premium payment pattern leaves the insured with only whole life insurance after the paid-up additions entirely replace the term portion. Table 3.9 shows a sales illustration for a combination policy.

Uses of Whole Life Insurance

Whole life insurance meets the permanent needs for life insurance described in Chapter 2—typically the need for burial funds, the need to provide income to a permanently dependent spouse or child and the need to provide funds to pay federal and state death taxes. Many business continuation and estate planning problems also require whole life insurance. (Chapters 17 and 20 cover estate planning and business insurance problems respectively.)

Traditional whole life insurance contracts provide the insured many opportunities to modify the contract after the insurer issues the policy. This inherent flexibility increases the usefulness of the policy. Some options increase the proceeds received by beneficiaries. Some decrease the amounts paid to beneficiaries. Others affect the size of premium payments. The following descriptions briefly summarize material presented in greater detail in Chapter 10.

Table 3.9
Combination Policy Illustration
(Male, age 35, data per $1,000 coverage, $100,000 minimum, dividends assume no loans)

Policy Year	Annual Premium	Cash Value	Dividend*
1	$8.93	$ 0	$ .01
2	8.93	6	.73
3	8.93	13	1.19
4	8.93	20	1.69
5	8.93	27	2.24
10	8.93	68	6.54
15	8.93	118	13.92
20	8.93	177	25.07

*Dividends must be used to purchase paid-up additions of whole life insurance.

Policyholder Loans

A policyowner may borrow the contract's cash surrender value from the life insurance company. The policyholder loan can be arranged quickly, and the insurer cannot refuse the request even if the policyowner is in poor financial condition. The insurer charges interest on the loan as prescribed by the policy. This interest is no longer deductible by individuals.

The amount of the loan outstanding reduces the proceeds received at the insured's death. Interest charges can be added to the loan balance as long as the policy's cash values and future returns (participating dividends or excess interest credits) support the total loan outstanding.

☐ Example

Edward Byron began a $150,000 whole life insurance policy at age 23, when his daughter Karen was born. If he had died prematurely, part of the proceeds would have been used to provide funds for Karen's education. Edward survived well past Karen's college years, but when Karen was 18 he borrowed $39,000 from the insurance policy to pay her college expenses. The $39,000 loan and accumulated interest reduced the available proceeds at Edward's death. Because they had already paid for Karen's college education, the reduction did not upset the Byrons' financial plans.

Nonforfeiture Options and Reinstatement

Nonforfeiture options provide the policyholder with continuing benefits even if premium payments stop. The nonforfeiture options give the insured limited control over the amount and timing of premium payments, because payments may be stopped without sacrificing all contractual rights. These rights are available only if a policy has a cash surrender value. Many whole life policies show no cash value in the first year and have low rates of increase until the insurer recovers the policy's acquisition costs.

The three nonforfeiture options are a lump-sum cash payment of the surrender value that ends the contract, a reduced amount of paid-up whole life insurance and term insurance equaling the original face amount but for a limited period. The insurer determines the period by the amount of the cash surrender value and the insured's age when the option is chosen. Outstanding policyholder loan balances reduce both the death benefits and the duration of the term coverage.

☐ **Example**

Cindy Jones began a $100,000 whole life policy 15 years ago. It now has a $35,000 cash surrender value. If Cindy surrenders the policy to the insurer, she is entitled to a cash payment of $35,000. She also may choose a $55,000 paid-up whole life policy. A third alternative would be to continue $100,000 of insurance for 17 years and 4 months.

The latter two nonforfeiture options, when combined with the **reinstatement provision,** add control over the premium payments. The reinstatement provision typically gives a two-year (or longer) period to return to the original contract. Reinstatement requires repayment of all past-due premiums (with interest), repayment of all outstanding loans (with interest) and evidence of insurability. Reinstatement provisions vary by company, and state laws specify minimum requirements.

The reinstatement option allows the insured to make premium payments for only a few years and retain the insurance on a term or whole life basis as just described. Assuming continuing insurability and available funding, the original contract, including its cash values, subsequently may be resumed. The reinstatement procedure is cumbersome compared to the premium flexibility found in universal life insurance contracts. Reinstatement also involves the risk of the insured's becoming uninsurable while the policy is under a nonforfeiture option.

Guaranteed Insurability, Waiver of Premium and Accelerated Benefits

Whole life insurance policies contain many contractual provisions giving the policy owner increased protection or continuing control over the contract after it is written. These features allow whole life insurance policies to accommodate changing financial plans. Options providing the policyholder added flexibility include settlement options, dividend options (on participating policies), guaranteed insurability options and waiver-of-premium options. Some insurers also provide cost-of-living riders, which is increasing term insurance.

Briefly, the **guaranteed insurability** option allows insureds a limited number of opportunities to increase the amount of insurance in force, even if they are in poor health. Opportunities for increasing the amount of insurance occur at predetermined policy anniversaries and at the occurrence of specified events, typically at the birth of a child. The exercise of this option increases future premium payments because of the increased face amount of coverage. The insurer charges the standard cost per $1,000 of coverage appropriate for the insured's age when the purchase is made, even if the insured has impaired health.

The **waiver-of-premium** option relieves insureds of the obligation to pay future premiums if they become permanently disabled after the policy is in force. This option is a form of disability insurance because the omitted premiums do not reduce the scheduled increases in cash values or receipt of policy dividends. (Chapter 10 explains both of these options more fully.)

Accelerated benefits policies or riders pay all or part of the policy's death benefit if the insured is diagnosed as having a specified dread disease (e.g., stroke, heart attack or cancer) or is medically certified as terminally ill with death imminent. This feature appeared in the United States in 1987, when a few insurers voluntarily began to prepay a portion of the death claims of AIDS patients. The insurers felt the proceeds would help their insureds cover some of their nursing home and medical expenses. At the time some noninsurance parties were offering for a fee to advance funds to AIDS-afflicted people if they would assign their death benefits to the lenders.

As of 1991 about three dozen companies were offering policies providing accelerated benefits.[8] In September 1990 the National Association of Insurance Commissioners (NAIC) issued an exposure draft of guidelines covering accelerated benefits policies and riders. The IRS had not, as of 1991, ruled on the tax consequences of a premature distribution of death benefits under this provision. Briefly, benefits paid at death generally are excluded from the beneficiary's taxable income. Benefits received by the owner during his or her lifetime are taxable if they exceed the owner's cost basis. Because insurers pay accelerated death benefits during the insured's lifetime, the IRS must develop some guidelines. Until the IRS resolves the tax issues and until the NAIC develops final standards for the contractual terms, accelerated benefits contractual provisions will probably continue to evolve slowly.

Financial Planning Issues

Identifying the most appropriate policy choice in a particular case can be controversial. All life insurance policies provide payment at the insured's death. Some policies provide living benefits such as cash surrender values, loan privileges and disability benefits. Policy choice should occur only after financial needs have been analyzed carefully. If the need is temporary or the need is for maximum protection, term insurance is implied. If the need is for a combination of living and death benefits, cash value life insurance is appropriate. If the need is solely for savings, no life insurance policy may be needed, and investment alternatives should be considered.

Whether cash value life insurance is a competitive savings medium is another matter for argument. Logic demands that, to the extent possible, alternatives should have comparable characteristics. Points of comparison include risk level, liquidity, tax treatment and safety. By presenting a mathematical framework for comparisons of life insurance rates of return and costs, Chapter 6 shows that, when compared to logical alternatives, cash value life insurance can be a competitive financial choice.

From a financial planning perspective, life insurance contracts have certain unique characteristics. In a world characterized by uncertainty about the time of death, the potential for permanent disability or the possibility of reaching retirement without accumulated savings, life insurance contracts guarantee results. While unfavorable life contingencies affect all other savings and investment strategies, life insurance allows the continuation of consumption plans despite the unfortunate occurrence. As noted in Chapter 2, life insurance requires the reallocation of consumption patterns; some current consumption is given up so future consumption can be guaranteed.

Table 3.10 provides a review of some of the policy comparison highlights presented in this chapter.

Table 3.10
Policy Comparison

	Level Term	Decreasing Term	Level-Premium Whole Life	Limited-Payment Whole Life
Premiums	increasing	level	level	level, greater than whole life
Death Benefit	level	decreasing	level, can be increased by dividends, decreased by policyholder loan	level, can be increased by dividends, decreased by policyholder loan
Savings	no	no	yes	yes, greater than whole life
Uses	1. temporary needs; family dependency period 2. insure completion of separate savings plan 3. maximize coverage with initial premium	1. temporary needs; family dependency period 2. insure completion of separate savings plan 3. maximize coverage with initial premium	1. combination savings and insurance plan 2. lowest-cost permanent plan 3. permanent needs; burial fund, emergency fund, permanent dependents	1. combination savings and insurance plan 2. premium payments end at predetermined date 3. business continuation, estate planning and savings uses
Disadvantages	1. insurance may end, needs may not 2. no savings 3. premiums may become unaffordable	1. insurance may end, needs may not 2. no savings	1. adversely affected by inflation 2. high acquisition costs	1. adversely affected by inflation 2. high acquisition costs
Useful Options	1. renewability 2. convertibility	1. renewability 2. convertibility	1. guaranteed insurability 2. disability income	1. guaranteed insurability 2. disability income

Appendix
Additional Policy Types

Endowment Life Insurance

Endowment life insurance is a contractual agreement to pay insureds living to a specified date (e.g., until their 65th birthday or on the tenth anniversary of the policy's issue date) or dying before this date. Insureds are sure of collecting the face amount whether they live or die. Since all endowments result in a claim for the face amount, the premiums are high relative to other forms of life insurance. These contracts also place a heavy emphasis on savings.

Before the 1970s endowment life insurance sales accounted for about 10 percent of the life insurance sold in the United States. Since the 1970s sales of endowment insurance have declined. In recent years endowment sales have been less than .5 percent of all individual life insurance sold.[9] Sales of endowments have declined because of changes in tax laws and because changes in the financial environment produced more efficient alternatives from both life insurers and other financial organizations.

After the Deficit Reduction Act of 1984 (DEFRA) endowments maturing as living benefits lost favorable tax treatment. Under current law, when an endowment matures as a living benefit, the owner must include as ordinary income any excess between the amount received and the net premiums paid. Net premiums are the total premiums paid to the insurer less any dividends paid by the insurer.

☐ **Example**

Daniel Webb purchases a 20-year endowment in 1986. He pays 20 premiums of $1,000 each. He receives $5,000 in policy dividends. His net premium is $15,000. In 2006 he receives the endowment benefit of $30,000. If current tax law prevails, Daniel will report $15,000 in taxable income.

Industrial, Debit, Home Service or Burial Life Insurance

Typically these types of life insurance have face amounts less than $5,000 and weekly or monthly premium payments that are often collected at the insured's home. The high cost of these policies results from the large expenses associated with frequent premium collection and other administrative expenses and from the above-average number of death claims. The high mortality cost results because people with lower incomes frequently purchase this type of life insurance. Lower incomes often result in less access to health care and poorer diets, thus, poor longevity. Because of the high cost and small face amounts, most financial planners will not recommend purchase of these policies.

Family Policies

Some insurers provide package policies in which purchase of insurance on one spouse allows purchase of smaller amounts of (usually term) insurance on the other spouse and children. Because the collateral coverage may be unrelated to any need for life insurance, planners usually will not recommend purchase of these policies.

Juvenile Life Insurance

Some life insurance companies design specific policies for children. In a needs-based purchase analysis, it is usually difficult to justify the purchase of **juvenile life insurance**, though the provision of a burial fund could justify the purchase of a small amount of coverage.

Jumping juvenile policies provide for the face of the policy to increase, often to five times the initial amount, upon the child's 18th birthday. Agents selling this coverage argue that this provision protects the child's future insurability. Because life insurers accept about 95 percent of applicants younger than age 40, the worth of this feature is questionable.

Review Questions

1. Very few term life insurance policies result in death claims. Is this outcome to be expected? Does this result mean term life insurance is rarely the right policy to purchase?
2. What arguments favor adding the renewable and convertible feature to a term life insurance policy?
3. List several uses for decreasing term insurance.
4. Describe some of the features that make traditional whole life such a flexible contract.
5. What are the advantages and disadvantages of saving with whole life insurance?
6. Participating whole life insurance does not penalize policy owners even though insurers use conservative interest assumptions. Explain.
7. What is the purpose of modified whole life insurance?
8. In combination whole life policies the policy face amount stays level despite a decreasing term component. How is this result achieved?
9. Explain how explicit surrender charges or rear-end loads cause a different expense distribution from exclusive reliance on front-end loads to recover all expected insurer acquisition costs.
10. Why do life insurance companies guarantee interest rates well below prevailing market rates? How does the guaranteed rate affect premium size? Should consumers rely on the guaranteed rate when comparing purchase alternatives?
11. List some financial planning needs best met by term life insurance. List some financial planning needs best met by whole life insurance.
12. Explain the difference between reentry term life insurance and renewable term life insurance.

Endnotes

[1] Mark S. Dorfman, *Introduction to Risk Management and Insurance,* 4th ed. (Englewood Cliffs, N.J.: Prentice-Hall, 1991), p. 25.

[2] *See* Kiri Parankirinathan, "Large Corporations and Sophisticated Life Insurance Products," *Journal of the American Society of CLU & ChFC,* May 1991, pp. 38–42.

[3] *See* Robert I. Mehr and Sandra G. Gustavson, *Life Insurance: Theory and Practice,* 4th ed. (Plano, Tex.: Business Publications, Inc., 1987), pp. 39–43.

[4] The data in this section come from the annual *Life Insurance Fact Book* (Washington, D.C.: American Council of Life Insurance).

[5] Mark S. Dorfman, "The Product Performance of the Life Insurance Industry," unpublished PhD dissertation, University of Illinois, 1970.

[6] For an extended discussion of subsidization in insurance pools, *see* Dorfman, *Introduction to Risk Management and Insurance,* pp. 26, 27.

[7] One 25-year study reported that fewer than 2 percent of the term life insurance policies resulted in death claims, 31 percent were lapsed and more than 50 percent were converted to cash value policies. *See* Arthur L. Williams, "Some Empirical Observations on Term Life Insurance: Revisited," *Journal of Insurance Issues and Practices,* January 1984, pp. 52–62.

[8] "Living Benefits Policies/Riders as Life Insurance Products," *Employee Benefit Practices,* Fourth Quarter, 1990 (Brookfield, Wis.: International Foundation of Employee Benefit Plans).

[9] *1990 Life Insurance Fact Book,* p.12.

Bibliography

Adney, John T., and Mark E. Griffin. "The Great Single Premium Life Insurance Controversy: Past and Prologue—Part 1." *Journal of the American Society of CLU & ChFC* 43, May 1989, pp. 64–74.

Broverman, Samuel. "The Rate of Return on Life Insurance and Annuities." *Journal of Risk and Insurance* 53, September 1986, pp. 419–434.

Budnitz, Emil A., Jr. "The Evolution of Split Dollar Life Insurance." *Journal of the American Society of CLU & ChFC* 43, September 1989, pp. 46-51.

Friedman, Douglas I. "Section 1035 Exchanges and Modified Endowment Contracts." *Journal of the American Society of CLU & ChFC* 43, July 1989, pp. 62–67.

Gallagher, Hillery James. "Simplified Split Dollar." *Journal of the American Society of CLU & ChFC* 43, March 1989, pp. 74–77.

Parankirinathan, Kiri. "Large Corporations and Sophisticated Life Insurance Products." *Journal of the American Society of CLU & ChFC* 45, May 1991, pp. 38–42.

Seher, Alan R. "Reverse Split Dollar Insurance: A Conservative Perspective." *Journal of the American Society of CLU & ChFC* 43, July 1989, pp. 40–45.

Stoeber, Edward A. "Modified Endowment Contracts—A New Level of Complexity." *Journal of the American Society of CLU & ChFC* 43, May 1989, pp. 42–49.

Warshawsky, Mark. "Life Insurance Savings and the After-Tax Life Insurance Rate of Return." *Journal of Risk and Insurance* 52, December 1985, pp. 585–606.

Chapter 4 Nontraditional Life Insurance Products

Chapter Objectives

- Review the impact of inflation and an unstable economic environment on traditional life insurance products
- Describe the financial environment leading to the development of the nontraditional products
- Explore the basic features of universal life insurance, variable life insurance and variable universal life insurance

Introduction

The traditional life insurance polices described in Chapter 3 were the basic products sold for the first 200 years of the life insurance industry in the United States. Because of the unstable economic conditions in the second half of the 1900s, however, consumers became more sophisticated in their purchases of financial assets, including life insurance. The "nontraditional" policies discussed in this chapter evolved out of consumers' increased sophistication, their need for better and more competitive products and the influences of the economic and tax environment. The nontraditional life insurance products, designed to overcome some perceived disadvantages of traditional life insurance, include variable life, universal life and variable universal life insurance. Variable-universal life insurance is also known as *flexible-premium variable life insurance*. This chapter will explain how these newer policies solve several problems caused by the fixed face amount and guaranteed cash value featured in the traditional products.

The Evolution of the Nontraditional Products

As mentioned in Chapter 3, traditional life insurance policies have several shortcomings, especially in an inflationary and unstable economic environment. During such periods, a traditional cash value policy owner faces:

- a substantial erosion of the purchasing power of the face amount and cash value, especially over long periods of time;
- a higher level of risk or uncertainty in predicting the amount of funds needed at death or retirement because of a lower ability to predict values; and
- the likelihood of noncompetitive investment performance of the cash value policy compared to other investments.

Policyholders facing these eventualities understandably tend to question the value of life insurance in providing the long-term economic and financial security promised by the insurer. To overcome such problems consumers could increase their amount of coverage (if insurable), borrow the cash value and reinvest it at higher rates (**disintermediation**), purchase term insurance and invest in other assets or surrender the contract.

The same environment is troubling for the insurer with outstanding or in-force traditional cash value life insurance contracts. The erosion of the purchasing power of the face amount, especially over long periods of time, makes it difficult for insurers to:

- provide long-term economic and financial security to the public;
- provide reasonable rates of return on savings compared to other investments;
- retain the amount of life insurance in force in a competitive environment; and
- maintain their investment portfolio, because of policy owner loans and surrenders due to disintermediation.

The inflationary and unstable environment of the 1970s contributed to increased sales of term insurance. In 1970, 28.5 percent of in-force life insurance was term. By 1981 term policies accounted for 38.5 percent. And by 1989, 48.4 percent of life insurance in force was term.[1] Responding to economic and competitive forces, insurers sought ways to enhance the value of permanent life insurance. In the process they developed policies providing the policy owner flexibility in making premium payments, withdrawing cash value, selecting investment options and picking the style and amount of the death benefit pattern. Table 4.1 shows that *variable life insurance (VLI)* was introduced in 1976 and *universal life insurance (ULI)* in 1979, both in response to the then-prevailing economic conditions. Flexible-premium variable life insurance products, known as *variable universal life insurance (VULI)*, followed in 1984. Table 4.1 shows that the in-force face amounts of the three products have grown substantially. However, with respect to the numbers of individual life insurance policies sold, sales of the nontraditional products peaked at 26 percent in 1987. By 1989 the number fell to 18 percent.[2]

Two other insurance products that evolved for competitive and economic reasons are *indeterminate-premium whole life* and *current-assumption whole life*. Indeterminate-premium whole life insurance is offered by many stock insurance companies to help compete against participating contracts sold by mutual companies. A maximum premium is quoted for the policy, but the actual initial premium paid is significantly lower than the maximum. After the first year, the discount changes based on expected investment and mortality experience.

Table 4.1
Variable, Universal and Flexible-Premium Variable Life Insurance in Force ($000s)

Year	Variable	Universal	Flexible-Premium Variable
1976	$ 46,541		
1977	168,632		
1978	224,497		
1979	382,716	na	
1980	965,576	na	
1981	3,720,739	$ 4,868,293	
1982	7,636,076	40,439,550	
1983	13,885,000	131,309,000	
1984	21,506,000	319,922,000	+
1985	29,055,000	563,609,000	$ 6,052,000
1986	38,037,000	864,479,000	26,486,000
1987	49,230,000	994,863,000	57,813,000
1988	50,277,000	1,169,892,000	85,911,000
1989	53,949,000	1,390,937,000	107,219,000

na: not available
+ : less than $500,000

Source: *1990 Life Insurance Fact Book* (Washington, D.C.: American Council of Life Insurance), p. 29.

Current-assumption whole life insurance is similar to indeterminate premium whole life except that the cash value amount is "interest-sensitive." Cash value increases are based on the insurer's current payment rate subject to a minimum guarantee.

Universal Life Insurance

In 1989 sales of universal life insurance (ULI) exceeded $1.3 trillion, accounting for more than 15 percent of the total life insurance sales. Such acceptance of a new life insurance policy is unusual, especially considering that only a few large insurers initially sold the product. Because of legal and tax hurdles and the uncertainty of consumer acceptance, insurers were initially hesitant to develop the products.

ULI allowed life insurance companies to offer a product with clearly identified investment features that were competitive with other savings and investment opportunities. (Critics complain about the unrealistically high investment rates of return used to illustrate and market ULI.) ULI is flexible in the amount and timing of premium payments, which some planners thought would help insurers deal with the problem of early lapse. Also, the ULI contracts allowed companies more latitude in their agent compensation schemes and in some aspects of computing insurer federal income tax liabilities.

Insurers are investigating the use of agent compensation schemes that pay a small percentage for the life of the contract instead of a large percentage of the first year's premium. The new pattern encourages agents to provide continuing service to policy owners. Heavy first-year commission patterns encourage agents to replace old policies to the owner's detriment and do not encourage continuing service. Flexibility in computing the insurer's federal income tax stemmed from accounting uncertainty surrounding the new products.

With respect to investments, life insurance companies traditionally invested in low-risk, low-return assets. The new products continue to use these as well as other high-yielding investments, shifting the investment risk and some business risk (through the expense loadings) to the policy owner. Life insurance agents wanted products that combined the benefits of cash value life insurance with competitive investment results to serve their clients. Because of their investment posture or ties to their agency force, many companies, especially those not wedded to traditional policies, had good reasons to promote ULI.

The Building Blocks of Universal Products

There is no standard ULI contract, but federal income tax provisions provide a common denominator for all ULI contract features. Thus such policy components as the computation of cash values, policy expenses, guaranteed and excess interest earnings and the computation of death benefits follow a common pattern among the different companies offering the policy. Figure 4.1 illustrates the basic features of ULI. Within this framework great variation exists among ULI contracts in the marketplace. This discussion, therefore, focuses on the prevailing ULI contractual arrangements. These contract provisions are presented along with an example of how ULI works financially. The impact of the Tax Reform Act of 1984 on ULI product design also is discussed.

Premium Payments

ULI contracts give the policyholder significant flexibility in both the timing and amount of premium payments. Certain minimum restrictions apply. There is a minimum initial premium, and future payments must be sufficient to cover the monthly term insurance charge. If the cash value falls below the amount needed to pay mortality or other charges, the policyholder has a 60-day grace period to make the needed payments, or the policy lapses. There is also a maximum premium amount that can be paid to the insurer. That upper limit is the result of federal income tax laws that impose a complex calculation based on the net single premium for a given amount of insurance. Alternatively, the contract must pass a different premium guideline test developed by the IRS. Under the Tax Reform Act of 1984 life insurance contracts must meet the cash value accumulation test or the guideline premium/cash value corridor test. Between these minimum and maximum premium amounts, the insured determines the size and timing of the premium payments, subject to any administrative restrictions imposed by the insurer. (The purchaser of any life insurance contract should be aware of the tax disadvantages of having the contract classified as a modified endowment contract [MEC] when these limits are violated. MECs are discussed in Chapter 11.) The policyholder may operate the ULI policy as term insurance or as a policy with a heavy emphasis on savings by voluntarily changing the amount and frequency of premium payments.

Many life insurance companies propose or illustrate a vanishing-premium ULI contract. **Vanishing-premium universal life insurance** contracts receive suffi-

Figure 4.1
Basic Features of the ULI Contract

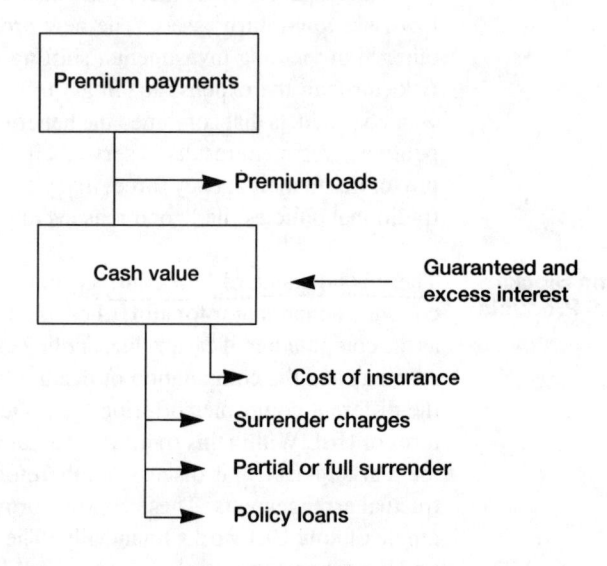

```
              ┌──────────────────┐
              │ Premium payments │
              └────────┬─────────┘
                       │
                       ├──────► Premium loads
                       ▼
              ┌──────────────────┐       Guaranteed and
              │    Cash value    │◄──────  excess interest
              └────────┬─────────┘
                       │
                       ├──────► Cost of insurance
                       ├──────► Surrender charges
                       ├──────► Partial or full surrender
                       └──────► Policy loans
```

cient funds through several large premium payments, allowing the contract to continue for life without any additional infusions of cash. Typically under this approach, the scheduled premium payments are large for the first five to ten years. If the illustrated mortality rates and interest projections are realized, the illustrated pattern of cash values and death benefits results. If mortality charges are higher than illustrated or interest amounts lower, additional premium payments are required to maintain the face amount or cash values at predetermined levels.

Some companies require a minimum premium on each payment date. Without the minimum premium, insurers and insureds find that the premium payment's inherent flexibility may lead to inadequate cash value amounts to maintain insurance at reasonable premium levels for life.

Premium-Related Expenses

The following premium-related expenses or "loads" are associated with ULI insurance:

- A flat dollar amount per month (which usually applies only during the first year)
- A dollar amount per $1,000 of the face amount (which usually applies only during the first year)
- A flat percentage of each premium, paid for the life of the contract

- A surrender charge applied to partial or full surrenders during the first 5 to 15 years of the policy

The first three of the expenses listed above are *front-end loads*, while the fourth is a *rear-end* or *back-end load*. The first and second expense types are intended to cover acquisition costs. The third charge, typically ranging from 5 to 10 percent of each premium payment, covers continuing expenses such as commissions, overhead and transaction costs. (State premium [sales] tax is an additional expense. The amount, as a percentage of premium, varies by state.) The fourth charge is imposed only if the insured partially or fully withdraws (surrenders) the cash value from the contract. Thus ULI predominantly follows the front-end load expense pattern of traditional cash value contracts. The insured is more likely to be aware of the initial charges in a ULI contract than in the traditional whole life insurance policy, because the policy owner receives an annual report showing expense amounts with ULI contracts. Expense factors and amounts are not revealed with traditional policies. Because expenses charged by one are not necessarily consistently lower than the other, purchasers should compare traditional and nontraditional contracts.

Cash Values

Perhaps the greatest distinction between ULI and traditional life insurance contracts is in the treatment of cash values. In traditional life insurance contracts cash value amounts are predetermined and identified in the policy's table of guaranteed policy values. (The table of guaranteed policy values identifies the minimum guaranteed cash value and the nonforfeiture options provided by the contract. Also shown is the amount of extended term insurance and the amount of paid-up insurance as a function of issue age and number of years in force.) In ULI contracts the cash value is a function of the size and timing of each premium payment (over which the insured exercises considerable control) and future investment returns. The cash value of a ULI contract is calculated by a formula in which the amount of cash value depends on the premiums paid, the expenses charged, the cost of term insurance, investment earnings and any partial or full surrenders of cash value. Figure 4.2 presents the formula for calculating the monthly cash value balance in a typical ULI contract.

Each policyholder receives an annual statement based on the calculation shown in Figure 4.2. The statement isolates the part each factor played in the cash value's determination. The transparency of the investment earnings and expense charges allows close comparison with other investment alternatives. The disclosure of all income and expenses is an appealing feature of ULI for those interested in evaluating policy performance.

Guaranteed and Excess Interest

ULI policies have a minimum interest guarantee similar to that of traditional cash value life insurance. (Traditional cash value life insurance policies do not specify an interest rate but schedule the amount of cash value in the table of guaranteed policy values. The fixed nature of the premium payment, as opposed to flexible

Figure 4.2
Formula for Calculating the Cash Value of ULI Contracts

The ending cash value balance from the prior month
+   premiums paid during the current month
−   premium-related loadings
−   other expense loadings (normally only the first year)
+   guaranteed interest and excess interest earnings
−   the monthly cost of insurance (term mortality expense)
−   any partial surrenders and related surrender charges

=   the cash value's monthly ending balance

---

payments in ULI, allows scheduling in this manner.) Besides the *guaranteed interest* payment, the plan of the policy calls for crediting cash values with *excess interest* when earned. The amount of excess interest may be determined arbitrarily by the insurer or may be based on a predetermined formula such as an index linked to the yield on U.S. Treasury securities. It should be noted that sales presentations using above-market interest earnings may project misleadingly high policy values especially over long periods of time, and such projections will prove inaccurate if the insurer earns lower rates of return. Even if high returns are achieved, if prices are inflating simultaneously, the policyholder may fare no better than to maintain stable purchasing power, which in itself is an achievement.

Insurers currently use 4.5 percent for the guaranteed rate. To make the purchase attractive, some insurers guarantee the market rate or a higher rate for the first year of the policy, then reduce the credited rate in subsequent years. Insurers are reluctant to guarantee market rates for long periods. Guaranteeing above-average investment performance without running a substantial amount of financial risk is improbable. (Higher guaranteed rates also require higher deficiency reserves on the balance sheet. The amount approximates the difference between state reserve requirements using a low rate and the rate guaranteed by the company. As states increase the reserve discount rate, deficiency reserves decline.)

When some insurers declare excess interest, it is usually not paid on the first $1,000 of cash value. When found, this scheme effectively proves to be another policy charge occurring at each excess interest payment. Insurance companies also do not pay excess interest on the amount of any policy loan. The unpaid excess interest raises the effective cost of borrowing. As of this writing, the total amount of interest (guaranteed and excess) paid on the cash value of ULI policies ranges from 7 to 9 percent. Note, however, that comparisons between life insurance contracts and investment alternatives must be made with caution due to the difference in promises, risk levels and tax implications.

Death Benefits and the Amount at Risk

ULI contracts allow the insured to select an amount of insurance called a *specified amount* and one of two patterns of death benefits. *Plan A* and *Plan B* or *Type I* and *Type II* are the terms usually used to identify the death benefit patterns.

Plan A provides a level death benefit. The death benefit increases if the cash value exceeds a predetermined level at specified ages. With this calculation the death proceeds are always greater than the cash value by at least some minimum amount. The top illustration in Figure 4.3 illustrates Plan A. The initial amount of insurance equals A − 0, and the minimum amount at risk is A − B. Note that the death benefit does not increase until the cash value equals B − 0. If the cash values never reach or exceed the B − 0 level, the death benefit remains constant. (Since the cash value is increased by interest and is not denominated in a share price similar to a mutual fund, the cash value line increases, but the rate of change may vary each period.) The purpose of the minimum death benefit is to meet the IRS's definition of life insurance and thus retain the income tax benefits traditionally associated with life insurance, including the receipt of death benefits without income taxation.

Plan B provides a death benefit equal to the specified amount (the minimum death benefit) plus the cash value at the time of death. The bottom illustration in Figure 4.3 illustrates this plan. The minimum death benefit equals A − 0. If the cash value goes up or down, the face amount or death benefit changes by the same amount.

Some companies allow a limited amount of switching between Plans A and B after the policy is in effect. Typically, underwriters freely allow a switch to Plan B from Plan A, with a reduction in the death benefit. Insurers are more cautious, however, when the death benefits increase (Plan A to Plan B), and they impose various underwriting rules and standards. With Plan A or B the *amount at risk* equals the difference between the death benefit and the cash value. The amount at risk, in part, determines the charge for the term insurance expense.

Cost of Insurance

A monthly charge for term insurance reduces the ULI cash value. The charge depends on the *amount at risk* and the age, sex and other underwriting characteristics. A schedule or description in the policy specifies the maximum charge for the term insurance, but the actual charge applied is typically significantly less than the maximum. Currently the guaranteed mortality cost is set by the 1958 CSO mortality table. Some companies use the 1980 mortality table, which predicts a lower death rate and in turn produces a lower guaranteed rate. Few insurance companies use select and ultimate rates similar to reentry term insurance (explained in Chapter 3) due to the already complex life insurance product. Once the term insurance rate is set (e.g., $0.10 per $1,000 of face amount per month) based on underwriting considerations, the amount charged for the pure life insurance or the *amount at risk* depends on the insured's choice of the death benefit pattern. The policy owner selects the death benefit plan, which in turn determines the pattern of the amount at risk.

☐ **Example**

Roland Richards owns a ULI contract. For his age, 37, the term rate is $0.10845 per month per $1,000. His policy has a cash value of $6,000 and a specified amount of $100,000.

Figure 4.3
Universal Life Death Benefit

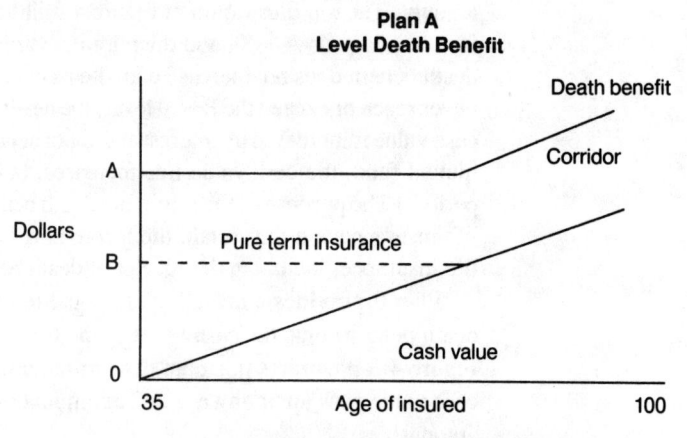

Plan A
Level Death Benefit

A – B = Minimum amount at risk. Death benefit does not rise until the cash value equals B – 0.

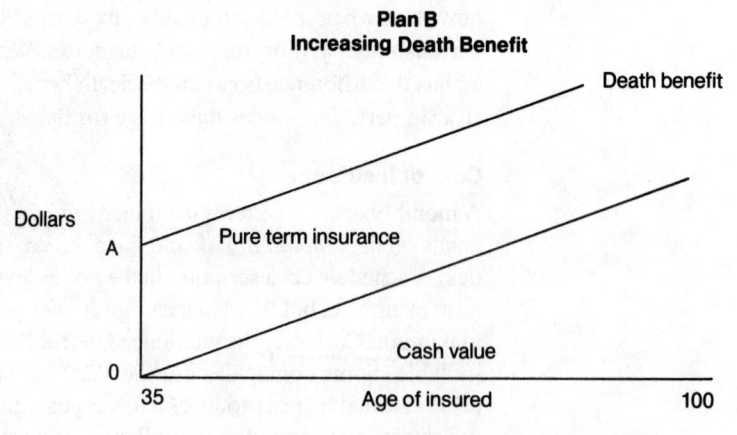

Plan B
Increasing Death Benefit

A – 0 = Amount at risk and minimum death benefit.

Under Plan A the amount of risk is $94,000, and the monthly mortality cost is $10.19 ($94,000 ÷ 1,000 × 0.10845).

Under Plan B the amount of risk is $100,000, and the monthly mortality cost is $10.85 ($100,000 / 1,000 × 0.10845).

Even though the total mortality charge is different under both plans, the rate per $1,000 of coverage is the same. In both plans the basis for the mortality calculation is the net amount at risk (Plan A, $94,000; Plan B, $100,000).

Chapter 4 Nontraditional Life Insurance Products   73

A Sample ULI Annual Statement

Table 4.2 shows the assumptions and the projected financial statements for the first three years of a $100,000 ULI contract issued to a male nonsmoker, aged 33. The policy owner has a specified amount of $100,000 under Plan B (death benefit equals $100,000 plus the cash value). Credits for excess interest are earned on cash value amounts exceeding $1,000, and charges for two of the expense loadings apply in the first year. In this example the excess interest amount remains the same. In reality the excess interest amount changes based on the calculation method used by the insurer and prevailing economic conditions.

If the policy owner selected Plan A (a constant death benefit), computation of the term cost would be based on the difference between the specified amount and the cash value, as illustrated in the preceding example.

The Tax Reform Act of 1984

Table 4.1 showed that there was a significant increase in the sales of interest-sensitive life insurance in the early 1980s. Due to the design of the newly created products, the industry's marketing tactics and application of then-current tax law, the distinction between life insurance and investment products blurred. Life insurance has been and is used as an investment partly because of the tax-advantaged nature of the inside buildup of cash values. In addition, life insurance pays beneficiaries death benefits free from income tax, the owner can use before-tax earnings on the cash value to pay for much of the product's cost and the policyholder can borrow funds at relatively low interest rates. The perceived abuses of these products led to temporary rules for flexible-premium life insurance contracts under the Tax Equity and Fiscal Responsibility Act (TEFRA) in 1982.

The temporary rules under TEFRA provided tests to separate life insurance from investment products. Insurers quickly modified outstanding and current products to meet the standards imposed by the tax code. The rules required a sufficient amount of insurance protection to exist relative to the cash value, thus limiting the product's use solely as a tax-deferred investment.

The Tax Reform Act of 1984 (TRA '84) replaced the temporary rules installed by TEFRA. The rules under TRA '84 are more restrictive and apply to *all* life insurance products. Two rules must be met under TRA '84 to escape loss of the favorable tax treatment of life insurance:

1. The life insurance product must meet the definition of life insurance under applicable state laws.
2. The life insurance product must meet either
   - a cash value accumulation test *or*
   - a guideline premium/cash value corridor test.

It is not sufficient to meet these tests once. The product must continue to meet the standards throughout its existence. If at any time the product fails the tests, it will be split into its insurance and savings portions and will lose several tax advantages afforded the life insurance product.

Figure 4.4 shows part of the tax impact of failing to meet these tests under IRC Sec. 7702(g) (1) (B). Under IRC Sec. 7702 (g) (1) (C), income from the contract for all prior years is included in gross income in the year the policy fails to meet the

Table 4.2
Universal Life Insurance Annual Report

Assumptions:
  Specified amount $100,000
  Plan B, male, 33, nonsmoker
  Death benefit equals $100,000 plus cash value

  Premium $70.00 monthly
  Guaranteed interest   4.5% annual
  Excess interest*   5.3% annual

  Annual term cost:
      Age 33 $1.86
      Age 34   1.92
      Age 35   1.96

  Loadings:
      Per policy (first year) $120.00 annual
      Per $1,000 (first year) $ 2.50 annual
      Percent of each premium   7.00%

Policy Financials:

	Year 1	Year 2	Year 3
Premium	$840.00	$ 840.00	$ 840.00
Less loading (7%)	58.80	58.80	58.80
Net premium	781.20	781.20	781.20
Beginning cash value	0.00	260.35	898.63
Total invested funds	781.20	1,041.55	1,679.83
Interest:			
Guaranteed	35.15	46.87	75.59
Excess	0.00	2.20	36.03
Other deductions:			
Policy loading	120.00	0.00	0.00
Per $1,000 loading	250.00	0.00	0.00
Term cost	186.00	192.00	196.00
Ending cash value	$260.35	$ 898.63	$1,595.45

*Paid on funds over $1,000
Note: The excess interest amount is constant in this example. In reality the excess interest amount fluctuates based on prevailing economic conditions and the method of calculation. Insurers make these computations monthly.

test. The tax law treats the pure life insurance amount and the investment portion differently.

If a policy fails the IRS guidelines at death, any amounts paid in excess of the death benefit minus the cash value is treated as a tax-free payment. Effectively, the cash value amount is not exempt from income taxation when paid to a beneficiary.

☐ **Example**

Assume this policy does *not* meet the IRS guidelines.

Specified amount = $100,000
Cash value = $42,000
This year's increase in net surrender value = $5,000

Figure 4.4
Computation of Taxable Amount upon Failure of TRA '84 Rules

Increase in the year's net surrender value
+   the term cost of the pure life insurance provided
+   dividends received by the policy owner
−   premiums paid

=   the year's taxable income

Cost of life insurance = $220
Dividends = $0
Premiums paid = $1,500

$5,000	year's increase in net surrender value
+ 220	term cost of life insurance
+ 0	dividends
−1,500	premiums paid
$3,720	year's taxable income

If the life insurance matured as a death benefit, $42,000, the amount of the cash value, would be a taxable death benefit.

This example illustrates why insurance companies very closely monitor cash value amounts to ensure compliance with the following IRS guidelines to continue the policy's favorable tax status.

The cash value accumulation test requires the cash value not to exceed the net single premium needed to pay all future benefits under the contract. (*See* Chapter 21 for a fuller explanation of the mathematics involved.) The net single premium is the amount of money the insurer must have on hand (discounted for the time value of money and other factors) to allow the policy owner to stop paying premiums while still obligating the insurer to pay all contractual benefits. If the cash value exceeds this amount during the life of the contract, more money exists than is necessary to fund the payment of the death claim. If the cash value exceeds the line labeled *net single premium* in Figure 4.5 for the attained age of the insured, the policy fails the cash value accumulation test.

The guideline premium/cash value corridor test is a two-part test, both of which must be satisfied if used under TRA '84 to prove a life insurance contract exists. The *guideline premium* section requires that the sum of all premiums paid not exceed the guideline single premium or the sum of the guideline level premiums at any time. The guideline single premium amount equals the one-time premium paid by the policy owner to fund all future benefits under the contract—similar to the net single premium, except that the mortality and interest assumptions are different and the guideline single premium includes the insurer's operating expense loadings. The guideline level premium is a periodic amount that funds the benefits under the contract until at least age 95. This amount is similar to the level premium paid on the limited-payment plans discussed in Chapter 3.

Figure 4.5
Cash Value Accumulation Test

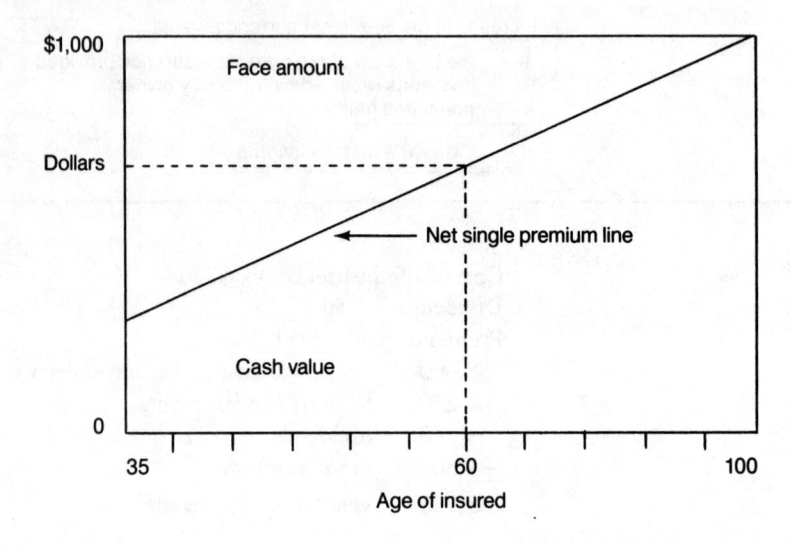

[Figure 4.5: Graph showing Face amount line rising from age 35 to $1,000 at age 100, with Net single premium line intersecting at age 60, and Cash value shown below. Y-axis: Dollars; X-axis: Age of insured]

Passing the *cash value corridor test* means the death benefit always exceeds a multiple of the cash value based on the insured's age. Table 4.3 provides selected multiples for meeting the cash value corridor test.

This discussion is intended to explain why the death benefit increases when the cash value exceeds a minimum amount (IRC Sec. 7702). In Plan A of Figure 4.3, the death benefit must increase given the level of cash value, or the contract fails the life insurance test and loses the favorable tax treatment afforded life insurance contracts.

Taxation of ULI

The taxation of ULI has been a subject of considerable attention from the IRS and from competitors inside and outside the life insurance industry. Several

Table 4.3
Selected Multiples for the Cash Value Corridor Test

Age	Multiple
0–40	250%
45	215
50	185
55	150
60	130
65	120
70	115
75–90	105
95 and over	100

guidelines, private letter rulings and recent changes in the tax law combine to produce the result that, if the policies maintain the minimum life insurance characteristics, the contracts will be taxed in a manner comparable to traditional cash value life insurance contracts. That is, death benefits will pass to the beneficiary free of federal income tax, and federal income taxes will be deferred on investment gains until they are withdrawn by the policyholder during the insured's lifetime.

Other Provisions for Flexibility

ULI contracts provide the policy owner with additional rights that increase the owner's flexibility in tailoring the policy to meet changing financial plans. For example, having provided evidence of insurability allows the insured to increase the amount of insurance without starting another policy each time life insurance needs increase.

ULI contracts provide for partial withdrawal of cash value amounts, though a charge for each withdrawal may apply, and the number of withdrawals allowed each year may be limited by the insurer. Also, a partial or full surrender may produce taxable income if the amount withdrawn exceeds the cost basis of the contract, unless it qualifies as a tax-free policy exchange. For small frequent withdrawals, these surrender charges may be a large percentage of the amount withdrawn, discouraging the use of the policy as a typical short-term savings account.

ULI contracts allow the owner to request a loan secured by the cash value (as with whole life insurance). Some insurers pay the guaranteed rate but not excess interest on borrowed amounts. The loan interest rate is either a fixed rate or a rate set by a formula linked to an index.

ULI contracts have other features in common with traditional cash value contracts, including the following options:

- *Accidental death benefits*—This rider provides a multiple of the death proceeds if the cause of death is a covered type of accidental event.
- *Guaranteed insurability*—This rider allows the purchase of limited amounts of additional insurance at standard rates at specific points in time irrespective of the insured's current health and without new evidence of insurability. (Some ULI contracts allow the insured to add more insurance coverage at any time upon presentation of evidence of insurability.)
- *Waiver of premiums*—The monthly term insurance charge is forgiven if the insured becomes permanently disabled. Definitions of disability vary, and the mortality charge continues if the insured recovers.
- *Disability income rider*—Spendable cash is provided if the insured becomes disabled. Definitions of disability, waiting periods and length of the benefit period vary.
- *Family term coverage option*—Other members of the family can be included as insureds for limited amounts of term coverage.

The ULI contract has all the usual flexibility of traditional policies, provides more flexibility in premium payment schedules, offers participation in investment gains (and risk) and gives the insured a more complete picture of the various cost and savings components comprising the policy.

Variable Life Insurance

Variable life insurance is a fixed-premium product providing a minimum death benefit. The actual death benefit depends on the performance of the underlying investment portfolio. Today no one standard VLI contract exists, but the contracts sold as variable life insurance have common features.

VLI did not sell well in the United States immediately after its 1976 introduction. (The product was available in both Europe and Canada for several years earlier.) Only in the mid-1980s have significant sales occurred (*see* Table 4.1). The slow initial sales level is attributed to various causes, the following of which are among the more important:

- Regulation of the product by the Securities and Exchange Commission (SEC). (SEC rules regarding sales charges and prospectus requirements were stricter than prevailing rules governing the sales of other life insurance products.)
- A requirement that those selling VLI contracts be registered members of the National Association of Security Dealers (NASD). (Life insurance agents generally require a Series 6 or Series 7 NASD license to sell VLI. A Series 6 license allows the sale of variable contracts, mutual funds and investment company products. A Series 7 license allows the sale of variable contracts, stocks, bonds, mutual funds and municipal securities.)
- A steep decline in the stock market after the product's 1976 introduction caused it to perform poorly.

Only one large company devoted much attention to promoting VLI in its early years of product development. Today many large companies currently offer the product.

Basic Features of Variable Life Insurance

With VLI, the guaranteed minimum death benefit is also the initial face amount of variable life insurance. The fixed VLI premium payments are made annually, in one lump sum (single-premium VLI) or even monthly, quarterly or semiannually. Typically, the single-premium VLI contracts allow for "pour-ins" or additional contributions to the cash value. Features shared with traditional whole life insurance include the fixed-level premium and the minimum death benefit guarantees. However, unlike the traditional contracts, the VLI contracts provide for cash values that vary as a direct function of an underlying portfolio of investments, with no minimum guarantee provided for cash values. If the investment portfolio—also known as the *separate account(s)*—performs well, both the cash value and the death benefit amounts increase. If the investment performance is poor, the cash value may be zero, but the death benefit can never go below the guaranteed minimum. Thus the insured bears the entire investment risk with respect to the cash value. With respect to the death benefit, the insured bears investment risk only if the death benefit rises above the guaranteed minimum.

Figure 4.6 illustrates the operation of the VLI contract. The insurer deducts charges for administration, mortality expenses and state premium taxes from the premium. The remaining sum goes into the investment accounts selected by the

Figure 4.6
Variable Life Insurance
Premium and Cash Value Accounts

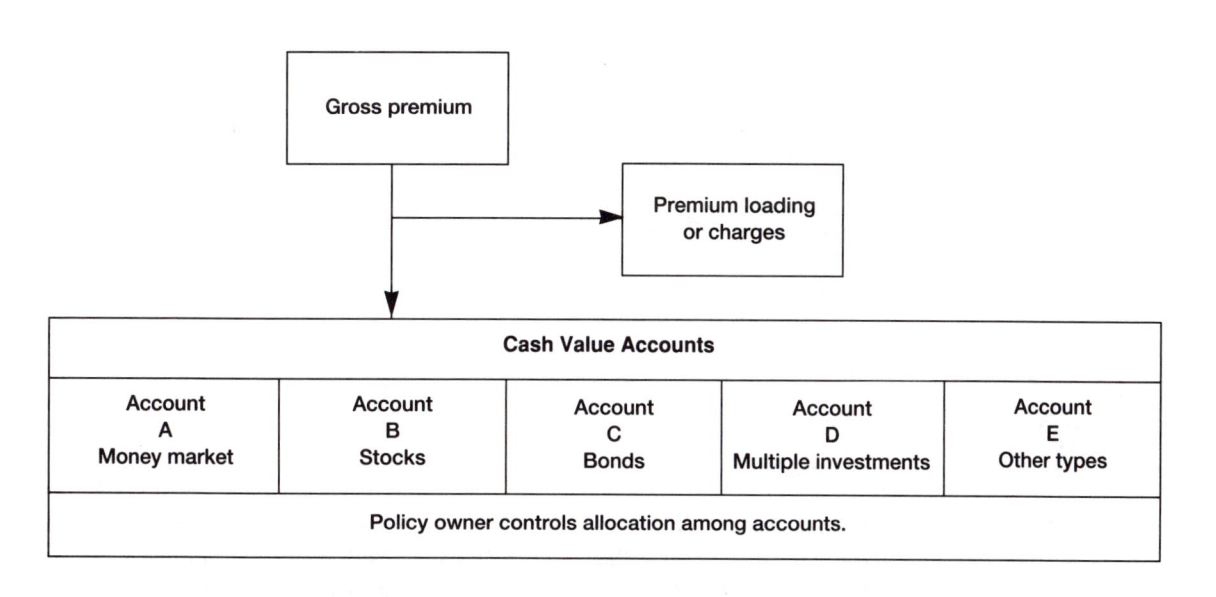

```
                    ┌─────────────────┐
                    │  Gross premium  │
                    └────────┬────────┘
                             │      ┌──────────────────┐
                             ├─────▶│ Premium loading  │
                             │      │   or charges     │
                             ▼      └──────────────────┘
┌─────────────────────────────────────────────────────────────────┐
│                      Cash Value Accounts                         │
├──────────┬──────────┬──────────┬──────────────┬─────────────────┤
│ Account  │ Account  │ Account  │   Account    │    Account      │
│    A     │    B     │    C     │      D       │       E         │
│  Money   │  Stocks  │  Bonds   │  Multiple    │  Other types    │
│  market  │          │          │ investments  │                 │
├──────────┴──────────┴──────────┴──────────────┴─────────────────┤
│         Policy owner controls allocation among accounts.         │
└─────────────────────────────────────────────────────────────────┘
```

policy owner. These accounts, by law, must be segregated from other assets of the insurer. Many insurers use established mutual funds for VLI contracts. Portfolio management fees (which are typically less than 1 percent of assets managed) pay for the fund's administration charges.

Most companies offering VLI contracts allow policy owners to allocate premiums and cash value amounts among at least three different underlying investment portfolios, including a stock fund, a bond fund and a money market fund. Many companies offer a multiple-investment fund, where the professional managers switch investments freely, depending on economic conditions. The insured determines how the premium, after charges, is split among the funds. The number of times a person may switch may be limited, and a fee may be imposed for each switch. The policyholder receives an annual statement detailing cash value results, the amount of available death benefits and mortality and policy charges.

Figure 4.7 shows the relationship between the cash value as generated in the various portfolios and the guaranteed minimum death benefit. If the cash value equals zero at death, the beneficiary receives the minimum guaranteed death benefit amount. If the cash value is greater than zero, the death benefit increases, equaling the sum of the cash value and the minimum guaranteed amount.

VLI policies provide many of the traditional extra cost contract options, including family term benefits, accidental death benefits, the waiver-of-premium rider, the disability income rider, and the guaranteed insurability option. The one traditional contract feature that does not follow the usual pattern is the policyholder loan

**Figure 4.7
Variable Life Insurance
Relation of Cash Value to Death Benefit in VLI**

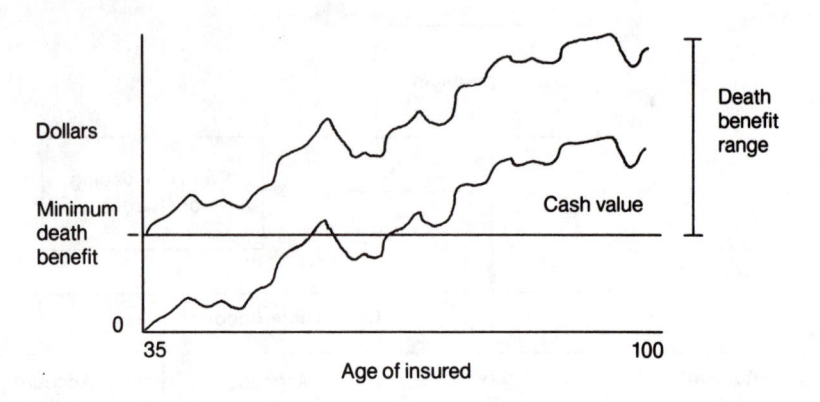

provision. Because VLI cash values fluctuate daily, a loan of the entire cash value could leave the insurer without security for some portion of the debt if the value of the underlying portfolio declined subsequent to making the loan. Thus loans are limited to some percentage of the cash value, such as 75 percent, whereas whole life loans may be limited to as much as 92 percent. Amounts equal to the loan and accrued interest are credited with a percent specified in the contract or a stipulated reduction of the investment rate instead of the full portfolio investment rate.

☐ **Example**

Harry Welford borrows $10,000 from the insurer using the assets in a stock fund as security. The insurer credits his contract using a 5 percent rate (for example) on the $10,000 plus accrued interest, not the 12 percent current earnings on the stock portfolio.

The taxation of VLI follows the traditional pattern: the beneficiary can exclude death proceeds from federal taxable income. No tax applies to the earnings on the cash value until the surrender of the policy. (A section 1035 tax-free exchange for another life insurance contract is possible upon surrender.) The excess of the cash surrender value over the owner's cost basis is taxed as ordinary income upon surrender.

Variable Universal Life

Variable universal life insurance (VULI) is a combination of the universal and variable life insurance contracts. VULI allows flexibility in premium payments, death benefit pattern and investment alternatives. It can be configured as a term insurance contract or a cash value life insurance contract, depending on the level and frequency of premium payments.

The flexibility of the VULI product stems from these features:

- The ability to move cash value amounts among the various accounts maintained by the insurer
- The ability to increase death benefit amounts (within limits without evidence of insurability)
- The ability to change the death benefit plan (fixed face amount or cash value plus specified amount) as financial needs change subject to company restrictions and insurability requirements
- The ability to increase, decrease or suspend premium payments as long as there is sufficient cash value to support policy changes

One major difference between ULI and VULI contracts is in the underlying investment media. The insurer selects and manages the portfolio in ULI. Excess interest earnings are usually based on an index or formula approach typically linked to the rate paid on U.S. Treasury securities. VULI contracts allow the insured some choice in the underlying separate account of the insurer (*see* Figure 4.6), and the policy owner bears the consequences of the good or bad performance of the investment portfolio(s) selected. Some VULI designs allow the policy owner to select a target interest rate above which returns are treated as excess earnings.

Figure 4.8 illustrates the death benefit options when the cash value depends on an underlying portfolio of investments. These options are equivalent to Plans A and B discussed for ULI (*see* Figure 4.3), except the cash value depends on the fund's share value as opposed to the credits of guaranteed and excess interest.

The features of the cash value, policy loans and surrenders are similar to the VLI policy discussed earlier. In addition, VULI contracts typically have an *exchange privilege*, and all life insurance policies typically have a *free-look provision*.

The exchange privilege allows the policy owner to exchange the variable universal life contract for a traditional form within 24 months of the issue date. The replacement contract assumes the same age, date and underwriting classification as the original policy. The free-look provision allows the policy owner to return the policy for a full refund of premiums within a short period (usually the earliest of 10 days after the policy is delivered, 10 days after the free-look notice is received or 45 days after the application is signed; some insurers use a 30-day free-look provision).

Like VLI, VULI is subject to dual regulation from the states as an insurance product and the SEC (federal) as an investment product. The National Association of Insurance Commissioners (NAIC) has developed a model bill for the various states to adopt to regulate VULI. The NAIC model bill eliminates the need for the insurer to provide a minimum death benefit, and it also specifies that the grace period begins on any policy day when the cash value of the policy is less than the amount charged to keep the policy in force. At this point the insurer

**Figure 4.8
Variable Universal Life**

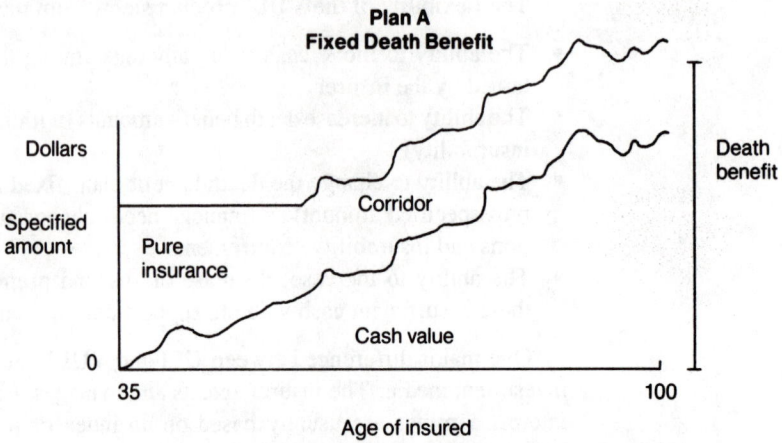

**Plan A
Fixed Death Benefit**

Dollars

Specified amount

Corridor

Pure insurance

Cash value

Death benefit

0

35 — Age of insured — 100

Actual cash value amount is a function of investment performance.

**Plan B
Variable Death Benefit**

Dollars

Cash value amount

Specified amount

Death benefit

0

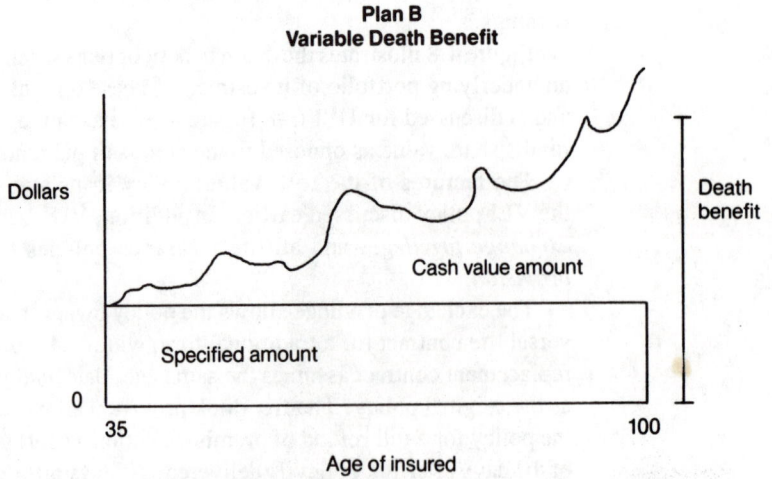

35 — Age of insured — 100

Actual cash value amount is a function of investment performance.
Death benefit equals specified amount plus cash value.

must send the insured a notice of the amount needed to keep the policy in force. Both requirements differ from traditional life insurance contract regulations in that there is no schedule for the amount or timing of premium payments in a VULI contract.

Chapter 4 Nontraditional Life Insurance Products

Table 4.4
Comparison of Life Insurance Products

	Term	Whole Life	Variable	Universal	Variable Universal
Premiums	Fixed for term and increasing at renewal	Leveled and fixed	Leveled and fixed	Flexible, owner controls	Flexible, owner controls
Face Amount Death Benefit	Leveled, fixed amount, decreasing, increasing	Leveled and fixed	Minimum guaranteed, actual based on investment performance	Guaranteed minimum or fixed face	Guaranteed minimum or fixed face
Cash Value	None	Fixed, dividends may increase	No guarantees, function of investment performance	Minimum guaranteed interest, excess interest paid if earned, also function of premium and face amount	No guarantees, function of investment performance, also function of premium and face amount
Investment	None	No control by owner	Allocation by owner among separate accounts	No control by owner	Allocation by owner among separate accounts
Policy Information	Expense and investment information undisclosed	Expense and investment information undisclosed	Expense, mortality and investment information disclosed at least annually, prospectus	Expense, mortality and investment information disclosed at least annually	Expense, mortality and investment information disclosed at least annually, prospectus

Table 4.4 summarizes the features of term, whole life, variable life, universal life and variable universal life insurance contracts as described in this chapter.

Uses of Nontraditional Policies

The descriptions of ULI, VLI and VULI have stressed that these contracts have most of the advantages of the traditional cash value contracts but place greater emphasis on the investment element and provide a clearer picture of the amounts going to insurer charges and the cash value. In the case of VLI and VULI there is a greater element of investment management and concomitant risk to the policyholder; there is also the potential for greater investment gains.

These new policies should prove most valuable in an inflationary environment, in which short-term and long-term yields on debt instruments and long-term returns on common stocks should increase. Even if the investment generated increases the cash values and death benefits, such increases will likely be partially offset by price increases. The net result allows the insured a better chance of maintaining a constant amount of purchasing power.

The nontraditional contracts exemplify what whole life insurance contracts have always been, a combination of a savings plan and life insurance protection. By giving the policyholder some additional measure of control over the amount and timing of premium payments, by giving a better accounting of the policy expenses and the cost of insurance, these contracts more closely approach noninsurance investment opportunities. The contracts should appeal to those who need permanent insurance protection but also want to save for medium-range to long-range goals. These people also benefit by using the investment services provided by life insurance companies and by taking advantage of the favorable features traditionally associated with whole life insurance products.

Review Questions

1. Describe the economic environment leading to the development of nontraditional products.
2. What are the financial and economic problems encountered by a *purchaser* of a traditional cash value life insurance contract in an inflationary and unstable environment?
3. What problems are faced by *insurers* when issuing traditional cash value life insurance contracts in an inflationary and unstable environment?
4. Distinguish between guaranteed and excess interest in a ULI contract.
5. What kind of control does a policy owner have over the premium payments in a ULI contract? What is a *vanishing premium*? Explain how the policy owner makes the premium vanish.
6. What is the difference between a rear-end and a front-end load? What are the premium-related and surrender-related expenses? Explain. Classify them as rear-end or front-end load.
7. Explain the difference between the amount of risk in a ULI contract under Plan A and under Plan B. What happens to the specified amount and the cash value when death occurs in both plans?
8. Explain why it is important for life insurance policies to meet certain tests under TRA '84 to retain the life insurance contract status. Describe the tests.

9. What are the major differences between a ULI and a VLI contract? What is a pour-in?
10. What options for investing the cash value exist in the variable and the variable universal life contracts? Explain.
11. Describe the variable universal life insurance contract. What are the advantages of VULI over traditional cash value life insurance policies?
12. Why is it necessary to increase the death benefit amount of the nontraditional life insurance products when the cash value amount exceeds certain levels?
13. What are the differences in taking a policy owner loan from a traditional cash value life insurance contract, a ULI, VLI or a VULI contract?
14. Describe the tax aspects of (a) partial or full surrenders exceeding the policy's cost basis, (b) death benefits paid to a beneficiary, (c) the tax deductibility of premiums and (d) the taxability of cash value increases.
15. Who regulates ULI, VLI and VULI policies? Explain.

Endnotes

[1] *1990 Life Insurance Fact Book* (Washington, D.C.: American Council of Life Insurance), p. 27.

[2] *1990 Life Insurance Fact Book*, p. 11.

Bibliography

Advanced Underwriting Service. Chicago: Dearborn Financial Publishing, Inc.

Miller, Walter N. "Variable Life Insurance Product Design." *Journal of Risk and Insurance* 38, No. 4, December 1971, pp. 527–542.

Fitzhugh, Gilbert. "VUL: A Blend of the Best." *Best's Review (Life/Health Ed.)*, February 1987, p. 40.

Lynch, Timothy J. "A Guide to the Life Insurance Provisions of the 1988 Tax Law." *Journal of the American Society of CLU & ChFC*, November 1989, p. 58.

Rainaldi, Frank L. "Variable Life: An Investment Oriented Life Insurance Product with a Non-Investment Alternative." *Journal of the American Society of CLU* 34, No. 1, January 1985, pp. 34–37.

Tegeler, Jeffrey W., and Dan W. Smith. "Life Insurance Tax and Planning Considerations." *Journal of the American Society of CLU & ChFC*, November 1989, p. 48.

Chapter 5   Annuities

Chapter Objectives

- Provide examples of logical uses of annuities
- Explain annuity terminology
- Explain the use of the annuity as an investment alternative
- Explain the determination of annuity benefits
- Describe the variable annuity's unique characteristics

Introduction

In the 1990s both trade journals for the life insurance industry and consumer publications began to recognize the growing popularity of the annuity in financial planning. Crediting the demand for "safe investments with a tax break," *Life Association News* called annuities "the hottest products of the 1990s, much as mutual funds were in the 1980s."[1] *Consumer Reports* summed up the annuity's virtues this way:

> The fixed-dollar deferred annuity offers safety of principal and, often, outstanding long-term guaranteed rates that could be very valuable over 15 or 20 years, should market-interest rates go down. (If market-interest rates go up, the insurance company would probably credit higher rates.) And it is the only investment that can provide, at your option, the security of a monthly payment for life, regardless of how long you live. These features make annuities a good way to save for retirement.[2]

An **annuity** contract commits an insurer to make a regular stream of payments to an annuitant, the person receiving the payments. (Terms such as *fixed-dollar deferred annuity* will be defined later in the chapter.) The payments made to an annuitant usually are contingent on survival, but this need not be the case. Because they cannot outlive the income stream, people use annuities to fund their retirement. Experts predict that, as our population ages, annuities will become increasingly popular with more people using them to provide retirement income. As the quotes suggest (*see also* Table 5.1), such a trend has already begun.

From a consumption theory standpoint annuity deposits are analogous to annual cash value life insurance premium payments. Life insurance premiums require reducing current consumption to add certainty to the lifetime consumption pattern, while annuity deposits reallocate consumption from the employment period to the retirement period. During the working years people make annuity deposits with insurers, until the retirement years when the annuity is liquidated. Because of tax deferral on the investment earnings, annuities often allow the annuitant to accomplish the reallocation on a tax-advantaged basis. However, as this chapter points out, making withdrawals from annuities before age 59 1/2 exposes the annuitant to a potential tax disadvantage.

Besides providing a guaranteed retirement income stream, annuities can be used to guarantee lifetime income so remainders of estates can be gifted and bequests left to contingent beneficiaries. Annuities scientifically liquidate accumulated wealth using the insurance principle of pooling loss exposures. Because annuities allow the liquidation of principal, they can provide larger income streams than produced by investment income streams (dividends or interest) alone. These features of annuities will be explored in depth as the chapter addresses the various applications of the products.

The Rise in Annuity Sales

Table 5.1 shows that total payments for annuities have overtaken life insurance premiums as a percentage of disposable personal income. While the ratio of life insurance premiums to disposable personal income remained about constant during the period, annuity considerations (payments) grew by more than 50 percent. The Life Insurance Marketing and Research Association reports that from 1975 to 1990 life insurance premiums dropped from 70 percent to 25 percent of total industry premium; annuity deposits increased from 8 percent to more than 50 percent of this total.[3] Note that the increase in payments has been rapid for both individual and group annuities. (The latter are purchased by employers to fund pension obligations.) Between 1985 and 1989 individual annuity payments grew by 133 percent while group annuity payments grew by 100 percent. This entire trend may be explained in part by increasing longevity, as premature death becomes less of a problem for most people than funding an extended retirement period.

How Annuities Are Acquired

Annuities can be acquired:

- as a pension benefit;
- by individual purchase;

Table 5.1
Life Insurance and Annuity Data
(000,000s)

	1985	1986	1987	1988	1989
Life Insurance Premiums					
Ordinary	$46,096	$51,618	$62,134	$ 58,017	$ 57,558
Group	11,041	11,826	11,779	12,712	13,120
Industrial	905	787	724	696	616
Credit	2,085	1,982	2,100	2,106	1,996
Total	$60,127	$66,213	$76,737	$ 73,531	$ 73,290
Annuity Considerations					
Individual	$20,891	$26,117	$33,764	$ 43,784	$ 49,407
Group	33,008	57,595	54,913	59,494	65,590
Total	$53,899	$83,712	$88,677	$103,278	$114,997
Ratio of Premiums to Disposable Personal Income					
Life Insurance	1.92	2.12	2.20	2.39	1.94
Annuities	1.90	2.78	2.77	2.97	3.04

Source: *1990 Life Insurance Fact Book* (Washington, D.C.: American Council of Life Insurance), pp. 69–72.

- by conversion of cash value life insurance; or
- as private annuities.

Pension Benefit

Retired employees receiving a stream of income from their employer are getting an annuity benefit. Employers with fewer than 50 employees often fund their pension plans by purchasing group annuities for their employees during their working years. Larger employers often operate their own annuity pool, using a trust fund to hold investment assets and dispense benefits. (Chapter 19 presents a description of pension plans, including alternative methods of funding pension benefits.)

Individual Purchase

Two demographic trends, increased longevity and early retirement, may be contributing to the rapid increase in the purchase of annuities by individuals. Some experts expect the 20-year-old trend toward early retirement to continue or even accelerate.[4] People retiring before age 65 should begin to fund their retirements earlier because mortality probability indicates they will have longer retirement periods than people retiring after age 65. A longer retirement period requires greater initial funding. Other explanations for the growth in individual purchases include the annuity's tax advantages, the insurer's professional investment management, the plan's somewhat compulsory savings features and the lifetime guarantee of income. These attractive features will ensure an increasingly important role for annuities in financial plans.

Life Insurance Conversion

Sometimes, when they no longer need life insurance protection, insureds exchange whole life insurance policies with significant cash values for annuities.

Example

James Monroe purchased $250,000 of whole life insurance when his children were young. The policy's purpose was to provide funds if James died prematurely, but like most Americans, he lived past age 55. James is now age 65 and has just retired. His main financial goal is to maximize his retirement income. His children are no longer dependent; he has repaid his mortgage loan and has accumulated a reasonable amount of savings. The cash surrender value of his life insurance policy is $145,000. James may convert his life insurance to an annuity at rates guaranteed when he began the life insurance policy. Longevity increased significantly during the period James owned the life insurance policy, so he receives more income than a current annuity purchaser. The insurer has no charge when James makes the conversion.

A second conversion of life insurance to an annuity can occur when policies mature as a death claim. The beneficiary has the option of taking a lump sum of cash or choosing an equivalent promise of lifetime income, an annuity.

Example

James Monroe's wife dies after having named James the beneficiary of $100,000 of life insurance. Rather than taking the lump sum of cash and facing the task of investing this sum, James takes a lifetime income settlement option, which provides greater cash flow than any alternative of similar risk and has certain tax advantages.

Private Annuities

Private annuities involve a series of payments made by one person to another in exchange for something of value. Among the most important of the IRS's many rules governing private annuities is the requirement that the present value of the annuity equal the fair market value of the property for which it is being offered; otherwise the property owner is considered to be making a taxable gift equal to the difference.[5] Private annuities typically involve the transfer of assets among family members.

Example

A father, age 70, wants to transfer his interest in a farm to a son in exchange for the promise from the son to make regular monthly payments to the father as long as the father is alive. The father's interest in the farm has a fair market value of $500,000. The son agrees to pay his father $31,500 each year that his father survives in exchange for ownership of the property. The son's tax attorney calculated the $31,500 using the appropriate IRS tables, and no gift is involved in this transaction. Since the father's basis in the land is $100,000, he realizes a $400,000 capital gain.

A life insurance policy on the son's life with the father as beneficiary might be purchased in this case to provide security for the father in the event the son predeceases the father. If the son purchased the life insurance policy to guarantee the annuity payments, the arrangement would be called an *insured private annuity*.

Annuities and the Insurance Principle

In all insurance operations insurers pool funds from parties exposed to loss and ultimately transfer funds to parties experiencing loss. In an annuity contract the loss is survival. The probability of survival is the reciprocal of the probability of death, and actuaries know both sets of probabilities well. (The use of mathematics and probabilities in calculating annuity premium rates is described in Chapter 21.) Using accurate predictions of how many survivors there will be in a given group of annuitants for a given period, the insurer can calculate in advance the amount of funds needed to make the required annuity payments. The insurer charges a premium sufficiently large, when combined with investment earnings, to make all the anticipated payments.

From the annuitant's standpoint each annuity payment received may be thought of as containing three components: a portion of liquidated principal, a portion of investment earnings and a survivor benefit. The survivor benefit arises when the insurer transfers funds from nonsurvivors to survivors. People who die release funds because they no longer have a legal claim on the insurer. Over time the survivor benefit increases as more annuitants die and their funds are distributed to ever fewer survivors.

☐ **Example**

Mr. Red pays $70,000 as an annuity premium in exchange for a promise of $500 a month for life. If death occurs shortly after the contract is effective, a substantial sum is available for transfer to Mr. Blue and all other survivors of the annuity pool. The portion of Mr. Blue's (and other survivors') future annuity receipts coming from Mr. Red's (and other decedents') forfeiture is the survivor benefit.

Classification of Annuities

Annuities can be categorized according to premium payments, benefit calculations and whether the payout is fixed or variable.

Premium Payments and Timing of Receipts

Immediate Annuity

Annuities may be purchased through a single payment or a series of payments. When the annuitant makes a single deposit just before the beginning of benefits, the contract is called an **immediate annuity**. The immediate annuity involves a short delay, typically one period, between the premium payment and the initial benefit receipt. (An annuity due describes a time-value-of-money concept. *See* Chapter 13.)

☐ **Example**

Mom and Pop, both age 65, sell the Peaceful Rest Motel to a large chain operation. They receive $1 million after taxes. They use $500,000 to purchase an immediate annuity guaranteeing retirement income until both die. Annuity receipts begin one month after the annuity purchase.

They invest the remaining $500,000. Mom and Pop plan to begin a program of gift-giving to their children, secure in the guarantee of a lifetime income.

Single-Premium Deferred Annuity

When a single premium is paid more than one period before the initial receipt of benefits, the contract is called a *single-premium deferred annuity (SPDA) contract*. Deposits earn compound interest at a minimum guaranteed rate, and this interest accrues on a tax-deferred basis until liquidation. In liquidation only the interest portion of each annuity receipt is taxed. The deferral period is referred to as the *accumulation phase* and the benefit period as the *liquidation phase* of the annuity contract.

☐ **Example**

Scott Roberts pays a single premium of $5,000 on his 50th birthday. His insurer guarantees he will earn 6 percent on this deposit. When he begins liquidating his annuity at age 65, his deposit has grown to about $12,000. Figure 5.1 illustrates these data.

If life insurance company interest earnings exceed the minimum guaranteed in the single-premium deferred annuity contract, the company increases the earnings by crediting excess interest to the account. In recent years the minimum guaranteed rate has been almost meaningless because the excess rates have been far greater than the minimum guaranteed. However, if the insurer's investment earnings decline, the annuitant's accumulation period earnings will never be less than the minimum guaranteed.

Typically insurers guarantee SPDA current interest rates for one year. In 1991 a competitive current rate might be 8.5 percent, with a guaranteed rate of 4.5 percent. On the first anniversary date the insurer notifies the policy owner of the current interest rate for the second year. Similar notification takes place on each anniversary date after that. If the carrier drops the current rate to an unacceptable level—6 percent, for example—the policy owner may surrender the contract, incurring surrender charges if applicable, and pay the federal income tax and penalty for early withdrawal. A (Internal Revenue Code Section) 1035 exchange to another carrier is also possible if the policyholder finds a better alternative. The 1035 exchange, while tax-free, might still involve surrender charges.

Figure 5.1
Single-Premium Deferred Annuity

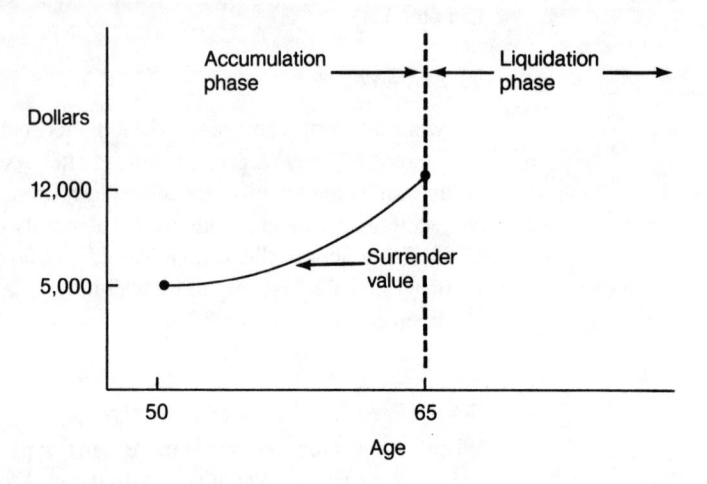

Some carriers offer slightly lower current rates but guarantee this rate for up to five years. This approach gives the policy owner more protection, and after the guarantee period the surrender penalty is so small the owner could transfer (Section 1035) or surrender the policy without as much economic harm as a first-year surrender would involve.

SPDAs are usually a "no-load" contract with rear-end surrender charges that typically decline and finally disappear over a six- to ten-year period. The surrender charge allows the carrier to recover the acquisition costs if policyholders withdraw in the years immediately after the contracts begin.

Flexible-Premium Deferred Annuity

Often people plan to accumulate the sum needed to purchase an annuity at retirement by purchasing a series of single-premium deferred annuities. Because insurance companies have minimum deposit requirements of about $5,000 for SPDAs, another contract, the **flexible-premium deferred annuity (FPDA)**, must be used for deposits of smaller amounts. The FPDA does not require the annuitant to make an even series of level payments. The annuitant determines the contributions within minimum amount (typically $25) and maximum frequency (typically monthly) limits established by the insurer. Because of the flexibility in premium payment possibilities, insurers have greater administrative charges for these contracts than for SPDAs. Some FPDA contracts provide for the deduction of an expense charge from each premium payment (a front-end load). Other contracts provide for surrender charges (a back-end load). Still other insurers impose both front- and back-end loads. Often insurers reduce surrender charges on a straight-line basis over time. For example, a company may assess an 8 percent charge for

Table 5.2
Flexible-Premium Deferred Annuity Ledger

		8% Current Rate		3.5% Guaranteed Rate	
Year	Annual Premium	Cash Value	Current Surrender Value	Cash Value	Guaranteed Surrender Value
1	$1,000	$ 1,083	$ 909	$ 1,035	$ 869
2	1,000	2,255	1,962	2,106	1,832
3	1,000	3,523	3,171	3,215	2,893
4	1,000	4,897	4,554	4,362	4,057
5	1,000	6,384	6,129	5,550	5,328
10	1,000	15,878	15,878	12,142	12,142
30	1,000	128,645	128,645	53,429	53,429

surrender within the first year and reduce this charge by 1 percent each year until it disappears by the ninth year.

Like the SPDA, FPDA contracts have minimum guaranteed interest rates that are well under current market rates. They also have a provision for crediting excess earnings when available. For example, the guaranteed accumulation rate might be 3.5 percent, but the carrier may actually declare a rate of 8.5 percent for the first year. On each policy anniversary the insurer declares an excess interest rate in keeping with the prevailing investment climate.

Table 5.2 illustrates a ledger for an FPDA contract. The ledger statement assumes the annuitant makes annual deposits of $1,000. Level annual deposits are not necessary. In some years, no deposit might be made; in others, a sum much greater than $1,000 might be deposited. The table also shows the difference between the current rate the insurer is illustrating, about 8 percent, and the rate the insurer guarantees, 3.5 percent. This insurer imposes a 16 percent surrender charge on withdrawals during the first year. The insurer then reduces the surrender charge by 3 percent each year until no surrender charge remains after the fifth year.

Benefit Calculations Annuity benefits are a function of five factors:

1. Amount of premium paid
2. Annuitant's age when liquidation begins
3. Annuitant's gender
4. Number of lives covered by the contract
5. Any minimum guarantees purchased

Premium Size

The greater the amount of money on hand when the liquidation period begins, the greater the regular installments will be. If an insurer promises to provide $7 monthly for each $1,000 paid for an annuity, an annuitant depositing $100,000 receives $700 each month. Reworking the problem from the opposite direction, an

Table 5.3
Effect of Age and Gender on Annuity Payments

	Monthly payments per $1,000 of deposit: pure annuity	
Age	Male	Female
55	$ 7.78	$7.35
60	8.29	7.73
65	9.06	8.29
70	10.19	9.12

annuitant who wants monthly income of $900 must deposit $128,571 (or $900/7 × $1,000). Typically the annuitant receives monthly payments, but quarterly, semiannual and annual benefits can be arranged.

Age

For a given deposit older people receive larger installments than younger people once payments begin. Because life expectancy of a large group of older people is less than that for a comparable group of younger people, principal can be liquidated more rapidly for the older group. Also, with greater mortality each year, the survivor benefit is greater for older annuitants. Table 5.3 illustrates the effect of age on monthly installments using data from one large life insurance company. Once begun, liquidation payments remain constant. The insurer establishes the size of the monthly payments at the age liquidation begins.

Gender

At any age women as a group have a greater life expectancy than men. Because of this indisputable fact, men get greater monthly annuity payments than women when insurers calculate benefits using gender-distinct mortality tables such as Table 5.3. For example, the table shows a 65-year-old male receiving $9.06 per month per $1,000 of premium while a 65-year-old female receives $8.29.

Some life insurance companies use a "set-back" approach to calculate female annuity installments. That is, insurers calculate female annuity installments by using male tables and subtracting four or five years from the female's age to find the appropriate male rate. For example, a female aged 65 would be treated as a male aged 60 for rating purposes.

The U.S. Supreme Court has forbidden the use of gender-distinct (or set-back) mortality tables in the calculation of annuity benefits arising from private pension plans. The Court held that gender-based payment schemes violate the Civil Rights Act of 1964[6]. Insurers still can legally use gender-distinct mortality tables for individually purchased annuities, though some companies voluntarily use gender-neutral mortality tables.

Number of Lives

An annuity may be written contingent on the expiration of one, two or more lives. If the benefits end at the first death when multiple lives are covered, the contract is called a *joint-life annuity*. In many situations it is more useful to have benefits continue until the last death among the covered lives. If the annuity continues until the last death when two or more lives are covered, the contract is called a **joint-and-last-survivor annuity**.

Holding other factors constant, adding more covered lives on a joint-and-last survivor basis reduces monthly payments because the insurer predicts payments will continue for a longer time. The mathematical explanation for the adjustment is that the compound probability of death is less than the single-life probability; thus the insurer is more likely to make a payment to a surviving annuitant. Consider the probability of payment when an annuity covers two lives, each having a .08 chance of dying in a given year. The chance of both lives ending in this year is .0064 (.08 × .08). If other factors are not held constant, adding a young life to a joint-and-last-survivor annuity reduces benefits more than adding an older life. Also, if gender-distinct tables are used, adding a female life reduces benefits more than adding a male life of the same age.

Insurers write contracts calling either for installment payments to continue at the same level following the first death or for fractional payments to be made after the first death. That is, payments under a joint-and-last-survivor contract continue to surviving annuitants at the same rate, while a *joint-and-one-half-survivor* annuity provides for payments to survivors at one-half the amount being paid before the first death. Insurers also sell joint-and-two-thirds and joint-and-three-quarter-survivor contracts.

☐ **Example**

Charles and Mary Baxley are about to retire. Both are in good health. They have accumulated $200,000 and plan to purchase an annuity. The insurer offers them two choices for contracts paying until the second spouse dies. The joint-and-last-survivor alternative pays $1,400 each month as long as either Baxley survives. The joint-and-one-half-survivor annuity pays $1,800 a month as long as both Charles and Mary are alive. Payments drop to $900 a month after the first spouse dies. The Baxleys prefer the joint-and-one-half-survivor option because they prefer greater income when both spouses are alive and assume expenses will drop after one spouse dies.

Minimum Guarantees

An annuity that pays until the end of the annuitant's lifetime, with no other contingencies controlling the payment period, is called a *pure annuity, straight life annuity* or *life income annuity*. With this contract payments may last for only one installment or for decades.

An annuity may be purchased in which the insurer agrees to make a specific number of payments whether the annuitant lives or dies. This arrangement is called an *annuity certain*, and the contract involves no life contingencies. Thus a ten-year annuity certain commits the insurer to pay the annuitant or a contingent beneficiary for ten years.

A *temporary life annuity* is an annuity arrangement in which payments from the insurer end at the death of the annuitant or at the end of the designated period,

Table 5.4
Nonparticipating Monthly Annuity Rates
(Per $1,000 of premium, male rates)

Age	Straight Life	10 Years Certain	20 Years Certain	Cash Refund
55	$ 7.78	$5.14	$4.79	$4.85
60	8.29	5.68	5.10	5.30
65	9.06	6.35	5.38	5.88
70	10.19	7.00	5.56	6.65
75	12.85	8.07	5.72	7.68

whichever event occurs *first*. For example, a ten-year temporary life annuity pays annuitants for ten years only if they live ten or more years. This contract pays for the whole period of survival only if it is less than ten years.

Many people, either because they dislike risk or for other psychological reasons, cannot accept the possibility of making a substantial annuity premium payment in exchange for receipt of one or a few payments before death. Sometimes the annuitant's concern about an early death centers on leaving a dependent without support. The joint-and-last-survivor annuity addresses this need. For other people the problem is simply the disutility associated with the possibility of "losing" a relatively large amount of money. This latter concern is addressed by purchasing an annuity contract with a minimum-payout guarantee. The available guarantees may be separated into two categories: a minimum number of payments or a full refund of premium paid.

Annuity, with Period Certain. An annuity, with period certain guarantees regular installment payments for the annuitant's lifetime or for a minimum number of years, whichever is longer. Thus a life annuity ten years certain, will involve no fewer than ten years of payments made to the annuitant or one or more contingent beneficiaries if the annuitant fails to survive the ten-year period. If the annuitant lives more than ten years, payments continue until death. The longer the period certain chosen by the annuitant, the lower the installment payments are for a given amount of premium. The actuarial explanation for the reduction is that the survivor benefit component of each installment received is less than would be the case in a pure annuity. Table 5.4 illustrates sample annuity rates from one nonparticipating life insurance company.

☐ **Example**

Howard Humphrey, a widower aged 70, plans to deposit $100,000 for an annuity. Using the data in Table 5.4, if he chooses a life annuity 10 years certain, his monthly installment is $700. If he chooses a life annuity 20 years certain, his monthly installment is $556. Adding 10 years to the guarantee period lowers monthly installments about 21 percent. In both cases payments last for Howard's lifetime, no matter how long. Howard must balance his need for current income against his need to provide income to contingent beneficiaries in choosing whether to extend the guarantee period from 10 to 20 years.

Refund Annuity. Insurers also write *refund annuity* contracts guaranteeing minimum payments equal to the entire premium paid for the contract, with regular payments continuing for the lifetime of the annuitant in any case. For example, if the policy owner deposits $100,000 for a refund annuity paying $10,000 a year, the insurer pays a refund if the annuitant does not survive for ten years. If the annuitant survives for ten or more years, payments continue to the original annuitant for life.

If the annuitant does not survive for ten years, the refund of the difference between the premium paid and the sum received by the original annuitant may be made in a lump sum or by continuing the stream of regular installments to a contingent beneficiary. If the contract calls for a lump sum refund, it is called a *cash refund annuity*. If the regular installments continue to contingent beneficiaries until they receive the guaranteed minimum (the premium paid), the contract is called an *installment refund annuity*.

☐ **Example**

Assume Elton Smith paid a $100,000 premium and received 60 monthly installments of $500 before death. If the contract calls for a cash refund, the contingent beneficiary receives $70,000 in a lump sum ($100,000 − [60 × $500] = $70,000). If the contract calls for an installment refund, monthly payments of $500 continue for 140 months, until Elton and his contingent beneficiary receive a total of $100,000.

Refund annuity contracts involve substantially smaller amounts of survivor benefits than do pure annuities. Thus the purchase of a refund annuity lowers the liquidation receipts for a given amount of premium. Table 5.4 shows this result.

Participating Annuities. Table 5.4 illustrates nonparticipating annuity rates, which were chosen because they are predetermined and do not change over the life of the contract. Most companies follow a different pattern. They recognize the impossibility of forecasting interest rates over the life of an annuity contract. They guarantee a minimum interest rate but allow contract owners to participate in excess earnings when the insurer's portfolio produces greater returns than those guaranteed. Deferred annuity contracts accrue excess earnings during both the accumulation and liquidation periods.

During liquidation annuitants benefit from excess earnings if insurers pay rates in excess of those guaranteed. For example, an insurer may guarantee a new policy owner, now age 40, that at liquidation at age 65 the company will pay $6.65 for each $1,000 on deposit. Then, 25 years later when the annuitant is ready to retire, he finds the prevailing rate is $8.50 per $1,000. Thus, assuming $100,000 is on deposit, instead of the guaranteed $665 per month, the annuitant receives $850 per month. Moreover, the $850 is guaranteed for the remainder of the annuitant's life. It is not recomputed annually as excess interest is during the accumulation period.

Fixed or Variable Benefits

A fourth way to categorize annuities is by fixed or variable benefits. All the annuities described so far in this chapter are **fixed-benefit annuities**. With these contracts, once the annuitant begins the liquidation phase of the annuity, the guaranteed amount of the liquidation payments does not change. Such an arrangement can prove a hardship in an inflationary economy, because the purchasing power of each monthly payment is less than that of the preceding month. In the early 1950s, because some insurers recognized the serious implications of inflation on fixed annuity benefits, they designed a contract to provide constant purchasing power. They called this arrangement the **variable annuity**.

Maintaining constant purchasing power in an inflationary environment means the annuitant must be supplied with an increasing number of dollars. It means that if annuitants can purchase a particular market basket of goods and services at retirement, they should be able to make the same purchase 20 years after retirement. Guaranteeing such results is too great a risk for a private insurer to assume. So the variable annuity does not guarantee purchasing power; rather, it arranges to deliver payments based on the performance of an underlying portfolio of equity investments. If the investments perform well, the annuitant's monthly payments increase. The opposite result also is possible.

The following sequence is a simple representation of the economic and financial theory on which the variable annuity is based:

1. Inflation implies rising prices to consumers.
2. Inflation implies inflated profits to producers.
3. Inflated profits produce inflated reports of earnings per share.
4. Inflated earnings per share lead to inflated market values of securities and inflated dividends.
5. Inflated dividends yield a larger cash stream from which annuity installments can be paid.

If this theoretical sequence occurs, the variable annuity recipient can be paid inflated monthly installments from the inflated market value of the underlying portfolio (capital gains realized by the insurer) and from the inflated dividends received by the insurer.

The essence of this argument is that the same engine driving up consumer prices can be harnessed to drive up annuity payments, using an investment in common stock to achieve this result. Of course theory and practice have not necessarily coincided. Experience with variable annuities over 30 years leads to the conclusion that the theory seems valid in the long run, especially in periods of inflation less than 6 percent. In the short run, however, government efforts to stem rapid inflation using high interest rates have led to falling stock prices during inflationary periods. In such periods underlying equity investments have decreased in price while the prices of consumer goods simultaneously were increasing. This situation is disadvantageous for the variable annuity recipient, because it means the annuity payments are reduced during a period of rising prices. The phenomenon of decreasing stock prices and rising consumer prices has occurred when inflation has exceeded about 9 percent annually.

An Alternative

Before delving into the mechanics of the variable annuity, consider an alternative to dealing with the erosion of purchasing power. The **increasing-benefit annuity**

**Figure 5.2
The Increasing-Benefit Annuity**

involves liquidation payments in the early years that are smaller than the actuarially determined amount. Starting from the reduced base, liquidation payments increase in each successive period. Figure 5.2 illustrates this process. Those grasping the "under-over payment" principle on which the whole life insurance contract is based will immediately perceive the same approach in action in the increasing-benefit annuity. The forgone payments in the early years, when allowed to grow by compound interest, provide the basis for the increasing payments in later years. Mortality and survivorship benefits also may be used to increase subsequent benefits, depending on the contractual arrangement chosen. The main drawback to using this approach is that in many situations the scheduled increases in benefits will be insufficient to maintain constant purchasing power if the inflation rate exceeds the growth rate in monthly installments. The greater the difference between the two growth rates, the less adequate the purchasing power. Also, the increasing-benefit annuity arrangement may provide an initial monthly payment insufficient for individual needs.[7]

Mechanics of the Variable Annuity

Insurers sell the variable annuity only on a deferred basis, which means the annuitant makes a series of accumulation payments before the liquidation phase begins. During the deferral period the insurer invests accumulation payments in a portfolio of stocks, bonds or money market investments. The closing stock prices of the securities in the portfolio at a given time determine the value of the portfolio (for example, $10 million). The value of the portfolio divided by the number of issued accumulation units determines the price of an accumulation unit and the purchase price at the particular time under consideration. (For example, $10 million/1 million issued units = $10 accumulation unit value.) When an annuitant deposits a premium payment during the accumulation period, the premium payment is divided by the accumulation unit value to determine the number of units credited to the annuitant's account. (For example, a $500 deposit divided by $10 per unit means 50 units are credited.) This arrangement is similar to that of the mutual fund arrangement. The purchaser of the variable annuity purchases accumulation units, while the purchaser of a mutual fund acquires shares. The mathematics of both purchases are the same.

During the liquidation phase the variable annuity loses its resemblance to the mutual fund and takes on the characteristics usually associated with the life insurance guarantee. That is, the insurer agrees to provide a stream of income the annuitant cannot outlive. A mutual fund cannot make this commitment.

An interesting change occurs when the accumulation period of the variable annuity ends and the liquidation phase begins. Accumulation units are transformed into liquidation units using the appropriate annuity mortality tables consistent with the contractual promises made by the insurer. At the point of transformation the total market value of the accumulation units is considered a single-premium purchase of a traditional fixed-benefit annuity.

Once the value of the monthly liquidation payment of a fixed-benefit annuity is determined, the insurer refers to the current payout of the variable annuity units and determines the number of units needed to equal the income generated by the fixed-benefit annuity. This number of annuity units is the exact number credited to the annuitant. It never changes. Only at the point of transformation will the annuitant receiving variable annuity installments receive an income of necessity equal to that of the fixed-benefit annuitant. After that the variable annuity recipient's income fluctuates, while the fixed-benefit annuity installments remain constant.

☐ **Example**

Assume Mary Stewart is now 65 and owns 5,000 variable annuity accumulation units. She purchased the accumulation units at various prices on a monthly basis over the 20 years preceding her retirement. Mary decided to take her annuity income on a straight life basis.

At the date of the transformation from the accumulation to the liquidation phase, the market value of one accumulation unit is $15 and the value of Mary's 5,000 units equals $75,000 ($15 × 5,000). Mary's insurer pays $5.98 per month per $1,000 of premium for a 65-year-old woman taking an annuity on a straight life basis. Thus, if Mary had chosen a fixed-benefit annuity, her monthly income would be $448.50 (75 × $5.98). The variable annuity liquidation unit pays $54 per month at the time Mary begins her annuity liquidation. Mary is credited with 8.31 ($448.50/$54) liquidation units, and this number never changes.

The regular monthly payments received from each liquidation unit are determined by the underlying value of the liquidation investment portfolio. If, for

Figure 5.3
Classification of Annuities

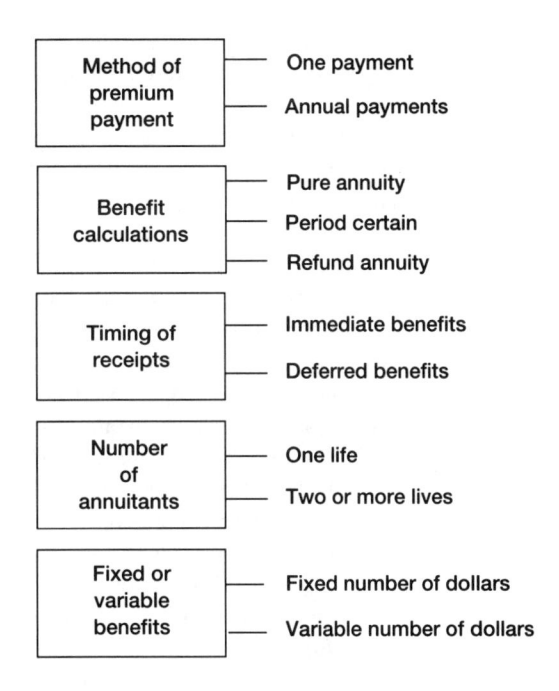

Method of premium payment	One payment; Annual payments
Benefit calculations	Pure annuity; Period certain; Refund annuity
Timing of receipts	Immediate benefits; Deferred benefits
Number of annuitants	One life; Two or more lives
Fixed or variable benefits	Fixed number of dollars; Variable number of dollars

example, the insurer raises the payout from the liquidation unit to $60 per unit, Mary receives $498.60 (8.31 × $60). If the insurer lowers the payout to $50 per unit, Mary receives $415.50 (8.31 × $50).

The theory underlying the variable annuity suggests that Mary's income should increase if prices increase, and her purchasing power should remain stable. Historically the theory has not always proved correct in the short run. In the long run insurers believe that a well-managed portfolio of equity investments will allow them to provide benefits enabling the annuitant to maintain a fairly constant standard of living throughout the retirement period, especially in a mildly inflationary environment.

Figure 5.3 presents a diagram summarizing the different ways annuities can be classified.

Annuities as Investment Alternatives

In many respects annuities should be viewed as an alternative to an investment program: an alternative with more guarantees, less risk and less flexibility than other investments. In both cases income is redistributed from an initial period when income exceeds consumption to a subsequent period when savings are used to generate an income stream. The differences or similarities between annuities and other investment programs are a function of the features chosen in the annuity contract. Some modern annuities allow the owner to obtain investment flexibility by giving up some traditional guarantees. Some annuity contracts have mortality guarantees during the accumulation period, providing some protection against adverse market results. (Some companies guarantee to pay an amount equal to premiums paid, sometimes with minimum interest, if an annuitant dies and the underlying investment has had such poor results that it is smaller than this guaranteed amount.) The most fundamental difference between the annuity and other investments is that life annuity contracts guarantee that liquidation income streams will not end during the insured's lifetime.

In comparing annuities to other investments, the investor must find alternatives with comparable risk characteristics. Both the income stream and the residual funds at death should be considered. If one investment alternative of equivalent risk produces a higher income stream and a higher residual amount, it is the more efficient alternative. If one alternative produces the higher income stream while the other leaves the higher residual, then the individual must place a relative value on both components to make a decision.

One main factor determining an annuity's cash flow is the annuitant's age. That is, for a given amount of premium the annuity will provide more cash per year for an older than for a younger investor. The reason for this assertion is twofold. First, at later ages each annuity receipt includes a greater proportion of principal, because the principal is always liquidated over the life expectancy. The shorter the life expectancy, the greater the amount of principal liquidated. Second, at later ages each annuity payment has a greater proportion of survivor benefits, as more deaths occur each succeeding year. (As the number of deaths increases, the amount of principal released by those dying increases. The increased principal released is spread over progressively fewer survivors. Thus the amount of survivor's benefits increases with age.)

The taxation of the annuity is often favorable compared to most other investments.[8] No tax applies to the amount of each liquidation payment classified as a return of premium. (The material presented here applies to nonqualified annuities, not to qualified annuities, which are also known as *tax-deferred annuities*. People purchase qualified annuities with before-tax dollars as part of an Internal Revenue Code–approved retirement plan such as a 403[b] plan or Keogh plan. Chapter 16 describes these tax-advantaged retirement plans.) Taxes on investment earnings are deferred until received. Thus tax deferral allows annuitants to earn investment income on money that otherwise would be paid in taxes. The greater the annuitant's marginal tax bracket, the more valuable are the tax advantages. Annuities, however, have one significant tax disadvantage compared to other investment alternatives. A 10 percent penalty tax applies to withdrawals before age 59 1/2. The penalty applies to all amounts included in income. Chapter 11 presents the rules covering annuity taxation in detail, including an example of this calculation.

For at least three reasons it must be assumed that an investment being considered as an alternative cannot be liquidated. First, liquidation may leave the investor without income or wealth if the liquidation proceeds too rapidly. Second, liquidation of principal results in a diminishing income stream. Third, liquidation of small regular amounts may not be possible or may involve high transaction costs. None of these restraints applies to the annuity.

The annuity also has drawbacks. At younger ages both the amount of principal and the survivor benefits included in the annuity are small and do not enhance the cash flow much compared to alternative investments. Guaranteeing results combined with regulatory constraints on the insurer's investment opportunities places annuities in the low risk and low to moderate return category. Finally, the greater the refund or period certain guarantees chosen with the annuity, the lower the monthly income.

Table 5.5, which appears on page 105, presents data comparing the income stream and residual investment of two alternatives, an annuity and a comparable investment in government securities. The annuity involves the purchase of a nonparticipating straight life annuity contract from a financially strong life insurance company. The other alternative involves the purchase of 25-year U.S. Treasury bonds yielding 6 or 9 percent annual interest.

In both cases $100,000 is invested, and the investor's marginal tax bracket is 28 percent. The focus of the table is the liquidation period. The $100,000 initial deposit could be accumulated either within or outside the annuity transaction. Whether the annuity is a desirable accumulation vehicle is a separate issue from whether it is a desirable liquidation plan. (Some insurers pay higher rates for individuals using the annuity to accumulate and liquidate as opposed to merely liquidating deposited sums.)

The table would have to be modified if other investments were chosen for comparison. For example, tax-free municipal securities provide a lower investment return than federal securities, but no federal income taxes apply, making the taxable equivalent return a function of the investor's marginal tax bracket. However, not all municipal bonds are in the same risk class as an annuity from a strong insurer. If a mutual fund or common stock investment alternative is considered, an ever-increasing income stream estimate may be used for the illustration. Again, differences in risk class using an appropriate discounting technique must be employed to make the comparison logically conclusive. (With all nonannuity investment alternatives, including government securities and municipal bonds, the market value of the investment fluctuates with changes in interest rates and other market forces. The annuity results are guaranteed.)

The net income stream produced by the annuity begins with the payment promised by the insurer (column 2), which is guaranteed for life. (Remember that the rates used are from one insurer and are not an industry average.) Column 3 provides the appropriate multiple from the IRS "Ordinary Life Annuities—One Life—Expected Return Multiples" table (*see* Table 11.2). The exclusion ratio (column 4) is determined by multiplying the annual annuity receipt by the IRS multiple and dividing the annuity premium of $100,000 by the result.

At age 60 the exclusion ratio is 24.2 × $8,290 = $200,618 divided into $100,000 = .50.

Column 5 is the taxable portion (nonexcluded cash flow), which is subject to taxation at the investor's marginal tax rate, 28 percent.

At age 60 for this annuity the taxable portion equals the excluded portion because the exclusion ratio is 50 percent. For any other exclusion ratio these portions would not be equal.

The taxes payable on the cash flow are found by multiplying the tax rate by the taxable portion of the annuity cash flow.

At age 60 the taxable portion is $4,145, the tax rate is 28%, so the taxes payable equal $1,161.

The net cash flow (column 6) is the annual annuity receipt less the taxes payable.

At age 60 the net cash flow is $8,290 less the taxes of $1,161, or $7,129.

This annuity provides no amount to heirs or contingent beneficiaries at the annuitant's death. In the case of a minimum guarantee the calculation of the IRS income tax exclusion ratio changes, as does the annual cash flow. Such changes can be incorporated into the decision-making process, but it becomes more difficult to keep the alternatives comparable.

Analyzing the net income stream from the investment in government bonds is less complex than the preceding calculation. The investment yield does not vary with age, nor does the tax rate or the net income stream change. If this alternative is chosen, the principal amount is available for distribution at the investor's death. The market value of the bonds at that time will be a function of the then-prevailing interest rates relative to the coupon rate on the bonds. If interest rates have risen, the market value of the bonds declines, and vice versa.

Estate tax effects on the two alternatives will be different. The pure annuity alternative reduces the gross estate by $100,000, while the market value of the bonds must be added to the taxable estate. Estate taxes, if applicable, will reduce the residual from the bonds.

The rates used for the annuity calculation were actual rates published for a large stock life insurance company. The data show that the securities investment yielding 9 percent is a slightly more efficient investment at age 60. For all other cases the annuity provides a significantly greater income stream than the securities investment. The larger income stream must be weighed against the residual amount provided by the securities and the risk of losing the principal amount in the event the annuitant dies shortly after liquidation begins.

The point of this demonstration is to compare the annuity to other logical investment choices. Intangible psychological factors, protection from creditors'

Table 5.5
Annuity and Federal Securities: Income Streams

Alternative 1: Annuity
Remainder at Death = 0

1 Age	2 Annuity Installment	3 IRS Multiple	4 Exclusion Ratio	5 Taxable Portion	6 Net Cash Flow
60	$ 8,290	24.2	0.50	$4,145	$7,129
65	9,060	20.0	0.55	4,094	7,914
70	10,190	16.0	0.61	3,974	9,077

Annuity terms: straight life, nonparticipating, male life

exclusion ratio = purchase price/expected value = 100,000/Col. 3 × col. 2

Taxable portion = (1 − exclusion ratio) × installment

Net cash flow = annuity installment − (taxable portion × 0.28)

Alternative 2: Federal Securities
Remainder at Death = $100,000

25-year federal securities earning 9%

Age	Investment Income	Tax Rate	Net Cash Flow
60	$9,000	0.28	$6,480
65	9,000	0.28	6,480
70	9,000	0.28	6,480

25-year federal securities earning 6%

Age	Investment Income	Tax Rate	Net Cash Flow
60	$6,000	0.28	$4,320
65	6,000	0.28	4,320
70	6,000	0.28	4,320

claims and the amount of other sources of income all might play a role in choosing the annuity or an alternative investment. A format such as that shown in Table 5.5 can help organize the quantifiable aspects of such a decision so the investor can then weigh them with any nonquantifiable factors involved.

Financial Planning Issues

Annuities can be purchased with many or few options, the choice of which directly affects the price. The simplest annuity agreement commits the insurer to paying the annuitant only as long as the annuitant survives. Insurers can enhance the contract to pay until the second of two lives fails, until a minimum amount of dollars has been received from the contract or until a certain minimum period has expired regardless of the annuitant's survival. Each of these enhanced promises increases the cost of the annuity, and care must be taken to purchase only as much protection as needed if the primary goal is to provide an adequate income stream.

The tax advantages and disadvantages of annuities have been mentioned briefly in this chapter and are addressed in detail in Chapter 11.

Shopping for annuities can prove most worthwhile. Insurers differ widely on guaranteed and excess rates of return during the accumulation and liquidation phases of an annuity. Contractual terms differ among carriers, and insurers vary on surrender charges and other contract costs.

Review Questions

1. What is the difference between an annuity certain and a life annuity period certain?
2. What is the logic behind the choice of a pure annuity to fund retirement? What arguments can be made against this choice?
3. What is a private annuity? What is an insured private annuity?
4. What advantages do annuities have over other investments available to finance retirement? What are the annuities' disadvantages?
5. Calculate the exclusion ratio when the IRS multiple is 20, the annual annuity receipt is $6,000 and the premium is $100,000.
6. What is the logic behind the joint-and-one-half-survivor annuity?
7. What purpose is served when annuities are purchased with minimum guarantees? Is anything given up when such guarantees are purchased?
8. Mark Jefferson is 65. He has $250,000 to invest for his retirement income. He has no other assets and no pension plan. His need is to maximize his income. He is married to Sue, who worked for a major corporation, thereby earning a pension equal to 80 percent of her preretirement income of $40,000. Sue's pension is adequate to support her if Mark dies. Mark is considering purchasing an annuity paying $8 per $1,000 of deposit or investing in 25-year federal securities yielding 7.5 percent. Address the quantifiable aspects of Mark's decision. Assume he invests all the funds in one alternative or the other.
9. Explain the survivor benefit portion of annuity liquidation benefits.
10. Describe some circumstances in which an immediate annuity would be a useful financial planning tool. Describe some circumstances in which a deferred annuity would be a useful financial planning tool.
11. Explain the difference between the cash refund and the installment refund annuity.
12. Describe the theory that allows a variable annuity to increase liquidation payments during periods of inflation.

Endnotes

[1] Joseph C. Razza, Jr., "Annuity Sales Surge as Consumers Weigh Safety and Risk," *Life Association News*, April 1991, p. 37.

[2] "Annuities," *Consumer Reports*, January 1988, p. 41.

[3] Razza, "Annuity Sales Surge," p. 37.

[4] Neal E. Cutler, "Financial Gerontology," *Journal of the American Society of CLU & ChFC*, March 1991, p. 18.

[5] See *Advanced Underwriting Service*, Section 7, page 31.

[6] *City of Los Angeles, Department of Water and Power* v. *Marie Manhart*, 434 U.S. 815 (1978), *Arizona Governing Committee for Tax Deferred Annuity and Deferred Compensation Plans, etc., et al. Petitioners Nathalie Norris etc.*, U.S. Supreme Court, 1982, (No. 82-52).

[7] Francis P. King, "An Increasing Annuity . . . ," *Journal of Risk and Insurance*, December 1984, pp. 624–639.

[8] See J. Mark Poerio, "Everything You Wanted to Know About the Taxation of Annuities," *Life Association News*, April 1991, pp. 50–62.

Bibliography

Commito, Thomas F. "When an 'Annuity' Is a 'Security'—SEC Regulation and Its Implications." *Journal of the American Society of CLU & ChFC* 43, January 1989, pp. 24–29.

Cutler, Neal E. "Financial Gerontology." *Journal of the American Society of CLU & ChFC* 45, March 1991, pp. 18–22.

Gustavson, Sandra G., and James S. Trieschmann. "Universal Life Insurance as an Alternative to the Joint and Survivor Annuity." *Journal of Risk and Insurance* 55, September 1988, pp. 529–538.

Murray, Michael L., and Stuart Klugman. "Impaired Health Life Annuities." *Journal of the American Society of CLU & ChFC* 44, September 1990, pp. 50–58.

Warshawsky, Mark. "Private Annuity Markets in the United States: 1919–1984." *Journal of Risk and Insurance* 55, September 1988, pp. 518–528.

Chapter 6 Life Insurance—Costs and Comparisons

Chapter Objectives

- Explore the life insurance purchase decision
- Discuss the selection of a financially sound life insurance company
- Explore product cost and cost disclosure
- Discuss individual life insurance evaluation techniques
- Discuss the issues concerning replacement of life insurance policies

Introduction

The life insurance consumer is faced with a bewildering array of policies from which to choose. Life insurance policies differ not only by type but also in their provisions. Further, the purchase decision is influenced by the selling technique and persuasiveness of the life insurance agent, the amount and quality of expected service, the financial strength and historical track record of the issuing company and the product's cost. All of these factors (and others) enter into the decision to purchase a particular life insurance policy.

The life insurance purchase decision involves selecting the product and its characteristics; evaluating the company for financial strength, management quality and past and future expected performance; and evaluating the product's cost. The chapter is divided into three main sections, each of which addresses one of these categories of qualitative product consumption issues. (*See* Chapter 2 for a discussion of the psychological motivations for purchasing life insurance.)

Product Selection Issues

Life insurance contracts emphasize savings, protection or a combination of savings and protection. The ratio of savings to protection is a function of the type of insurance and its premium payment schedule. Whole life insurance contracts that are paid up in a short time have a higher cash value (savings) and lower protection (pure insurance) than those paid up over a longer period of time. How dividends are treated—retained to earn interest or used to purchase paid-up additions, buy one-year term insurance, reduce premium payments or pay the contract up sooner than the maximum number of scheduled payments—also influences the level and rate of change in the savings amount. The financial planner/purchaser needs to balance the treatment of savings and protection to meet specific financial goals. For example, term insurance contracts provide death benefits and in only rare cases a small amount of savings. Whole life insurance contracts and universal plans fall between the two in their mix of savings and protection. (Depending on the amount contributed in flexible-premium plans, the universal life type of contract may emulate a term, endowment or whole life plan.)

Term versus Whole Life

The **buy-term-and-invest-the-difference (BTID)** strategy seeks to minimize the cost of providing death protection by purchasing term insurance and accumulating wealth through savings. For example, one life insurance company charges $1,389 for a nonpar ordinary life insurance policy ($100,000 face amount) while charging $285 a year for five-year renewable term insurance. (A nonpar contract is one that does not pay dividends. Policyholders of mutual companies are eligible to receive policyholder dividends, whereas policyholders of stock companies are not.) Investing the premium difference between the two plans can accumulate substantial savings, especially over a long period of time. Proponents of the buy-term-and-invest-the-difference strategy present several compelling arguments against purchasing whole life products:

- Both the term face amount and the side fund are available to meet financial goals. If level term and a side fund are used, the increasing sum (the invested difference) is a possible source of hedging for inflation. If a level amount is required to meet financial goals, the increasing savings fund offsets the reduction in the face amount if decreasing term insurance is used.
- Life insurance needs are not as great during old age. Although assets are necessary to take care of permanent and temporary needs of later years, the savings fund should be sufficient to meet the requirements. (Appropriately designed plans require considering cash needs upon death as well. If assets are invested in nonliquid assets such as business pursuits, loss in value will occur if forced liquidation is necessary to meet cash demands upon death.)
- Earnings in the side fund may be significantly greater than the amounts credited to cash value accumulations. (Risk differentials are not considered here.)
- There is no protection from inflation (the purchasing power risk) with a traditional whole life insurance plan due to the fixed nature of the face amount.

Opponents of the buy-term-and-invest-the-difference strategy also present substantial arguments:

- Individuals may have problems affording term insurance coverage at an advanced age or may become uninsurable due to unanticipated medical problems. When term insurance is purchased, the premium amount increases at each term

period. People may assume that increased income will enable them to handle the higher premiums, but the premiums may increase at a higher rate than income, or the increase in income might not materialize at all.
- Whole life insurance plans force saving. Many people are not capable of saving on a regular basis and benefit from the semicompulsory nature of the whole life plan. Even those who save on a consistent basis must resist liquidating the savings prematurely or using the funds compulsively.
- Regular savers may not be skilled investors. Principal amounts may be lost, and the investment may grow less than in whole life insurance. The investor may not be able to achieve the degree of portfolio diversification provided by whole life.
- Life insurance needs continue beyond the ages for which term insurance is available. This is an important consideration because needs during later years may not be determinable at the time of purchase. By investing outside the policy, the insured gives up some creditor protection and tax sheltering. The rights of creditors in attaching cash value amounts are restricted (*see* Chapter 9). Currently cash value increases are not taxable as current income.

The arguments surrounding the buy-term-and-invest-the-difference strategy have been the source of much controversy in the life insurance industry. Many life insurance producers have sold only whole life insurance, while others sell term insurance and savings plans. A whole industry has developed based on the replacement of whole life insurance products with a combination of term and annuity products, one popular combination being a term policy combined with a tax-advantaged plan such as an IRA or a 403 (b) plan. And, as discussed in Chapter 4, the life insurance industry has developed nontraditional products that effectively combine term insurance and saving, providing competition for the buy-term-and-invest-the-difference strategy.

Electronic Spreadsheet Product Comparison

One way to analyze the buy-term-and-invest-the-difference strategy is to prepare an electronic spreadsheet. Two equations must be solved simultaneously for the comparison:

- The whole life face amount must equal the savings fund at the end of the prior year (zero in the first year) plus the amount of term insurance purchased plus the difference invested in the current year (Formula 6.1).
- The premium for the whole life insurance policy must be equal to the premium for term insurance plus the difference invested (Formula 6.2).

$$WFA_t = SF_{t-1} + TFA_t + D_t \quad \text{and} \quad \text{(Formula 6.1)}$$

$$WP_t = \left(\frac{TFA_t \times R_t}{1{,}000}\right) + D_t \quad \text{(Formula 6.2)}$$

or

$$D_t = WP_t - \left(\frac{TFA_t \times R_t}{1{,}000}\right)$$

Chapter 6 Life Insurance—Costs and Comparisons

where:

t = The year indentifier
WFA = Whole life face amount
D = Difference invested
SF = Savings fund at the end of the year
WP = Whole life premium net of any premiums from the prior year
TFA = Term face amount
R_t = Rate per $1,000 of term insurance in year t

Solving both equations simultaneously results in:

$$WFA_t = SF_{t-1} + TFA_t + WP_t - \left(\frac{TFA_t \times R_t}{1,000}\right)$$

$$WFA_t = SF_{t-1} + WP_t + TFA_t \left[1 - \left(\frac{R_t}{1,000}\right)\right]$$

$$TFA_t \times \left[1 - \frac{(R_t)}{1,000}\right] = WFA_t - SF_{t-1} - WP_t$$

$$\frac{WFA_t - SF_{t-1} - WP_t}{1 - (R_t/1,000)} = TFA_t \qquad \text{(Formula 6.3)}$$

The resulting equation (Formula 6.3) provides the amount of term insurance required based on the other factors.

In the example mentioned earlier, the male insured may purchase a whole life insurance contract for $1,389 or follow the buy-term-and-invest-the-difference strategy. If the alternate term strategy is used, $1,389 is available to buy term insurance and invest the difference. As shown in Table 6.1, in year 1 (at age 35), $98,889 (calculated by Formula 6.3) of term insurance is purchased for $278. The remaining $1,111 is invested in a side fund earning 8 percent after tax. At the beginning of the second year $1,200 is available ($1,111 with interest added). Now only $97,695 of term insurance needs to be purchased to provide $100,000 of death benefits ($97,695 + $1,200 + $1,105) in the second year. This process continues for the length of time desired for the analysis. At the end of the period selected (ten years in this case), the investment fund ($16,580) is compared to the cash value amount ($11,400). In this example the buy-term-and-invest-the-difference strategy is clearly superior to purchasing ordinary life insurance in purely financial terms.

Two additional adjustments not found in Formula 6.3 are incorporated into Table 6.1. The first is an adjustment for participating dividends, and the second is a provision for the waiver-of-premium rider. If a participating policy is studied, the formulas use the *net amount* of premium paid. When the waiver-of-premium rider is attached to the whole life insurance policy, the benefits are counterbalanced by a disability income contract producing an equivalent dollar amount for the alternate strategy.

Table 6.1
Buy Term and Invest the Difference
(Nonpar; male, age 35, for $100,000 face value)

(1) Age	(2) Cash Value	(3) Whole Life Premium	(4) Dividend Amount	(5) Net Premium	(6) Saved	(7) Term Rate	(8) Disability Income Premium	(9) Term Face	(10) Term Prem.	(11) Diff. Invested	(12) Cum. Inv.	(13) Inv. EOY Value
35	$ 0	$1,389	$0	$1,389	$ 0	2.81	$0	$98,889	$278	$1,111	$1,111	$1,200
36	0	1,389	0	1,389	1,200	2.91	0	97,695	284	1,105	2,305	2,489
37	900	1,389	0	1,389	2,489	3.04	0	96,415	293	1,096	3,585	3,872
38		1,389	0	1,389	3,872	3.22	0	95,045	306	1,083	4,955	5,351
39	3,700	1,389	0	1,389	5,351	3.44	0	93,582	322	1,067	6,418	6,932
40		1,389	0	1,389	6,932	3.70	0	92,020	340	1,049	7,980	8,619
41		1,389	0	1,389	8,619	4.00	0	90,354	361	1,028	9,646	10,418
42		1,389	0	1,389	10,418	4.31	0	88,575	382	1,007	11,425	12,339
43		1,389	0	1,389	12,339	4.66	0	86,676	404	985	13,324	14,390
44	11,400	1,389	0	1,389	14,390	5.05	0	84,648	427	962	15,352	16,580

Interest rate = .10; tax rate = .20; after-tax rate = .08
(2) cash value for selected years shown
(5) net premium (3) − (4)
(6) saved (13), prior year
(7) term rate per $1,000
(8) for amount in (3)
(9) [100,000 − (3) + (4) − (6) + (8)] / {1.00 − [(7) / 1,000] }
(10) term premium: (9) / 1,000 × (7)
(11) (5) − (8) − (10)
(12) (13), prior year + (11)
(13) (12) × (1.00 + Rate); Rate = after-tax rate assumed

Temporary versus Permanent Protection

Selecting a product providing temporary protection or permanent protection is an additional consideration. Term life insurance policies are considered temporary products; the insured may outlive the policy period. Whole life products, including universal and indeterminate life, are considered permanent; the product exists until the insured desires to surrender the contract or death occurs. The appropriate product selection should be based on a *matching principle*. The length of the financial need should be matched with the product's length. The reader should recognize that one product may satisfy multiple needs. For example, a universal life policy may satisfy the need for long-term death expense, provide the vehicle for retirement income and handle the short-term dependency period of children. If the only financial problem is short-term dependency (no savings required), the universal life product may be appropriate if minimum contributions are made. (Minimum contributions will increase due to the insured's increase in age, and the product may become unaffordable.) Otherwise, term insurance is appropriate.

The premium payment plan must be decided on after the type of insurance coverage is selected. For example, if whole life insurance is required, the policy owner may pay up the insurance over various lengths of time, including 10 years, 20 years, or at age 65. Annual level premiums may be increased to pay up the policy in a shorter length of time. (The premium calculation of various payment lengths is discussed extensively in Chapter 22.) Present-value techniques may be used to analyze

Chapter 6 Life Insurance—Costs and Comparisons

which payment scheme is the most cost-effective. The applicant could calculate the present value of anticipated payments (discounted for the time value of money and the probability of surviving and paying the premium) and choose the policy payment plan producing the lowest present value. Present value, however, may not be the only consideration. There may be other psychological benefits that may modify the rule of selecting the payment scheme producing the lowest present value. Reasons include higher cash value amounts (more saving), the desire not to pay premiums for all of one's life and the issues surrounding affordability.

Participating versus Nonparticipating

The majority of life insurance in the United States is sold by stock and mutual companies. Many people believe that it is more beneficial to purchase a life insurance policy from a mutual company (participating) than from a stock company, even though the initial premiums tend to be higher with the mutual. In mutual companies policy owners participate in favorable or unfavorable interest earnings, mortality experience and overhead expense. Any dividend returned to the policy owner is not considered new money and therefore is not taxed by the IRS. For many people a steady and increasing dividend payment provides psychological benefits. Individuals like an immediate return on their purchase, and the dividend options mentioned earlier may be exercised to satisfy immediate cash needs or used for anticipated future needs (retirement income).

The participating/nonparticipating issue adds another dimension to the purchase decision. This decision must be made on the basis of expected amount, opportunity costs, use of dividends and the overall cost of the product. Moreover, with the introduction of innovative life insurance products allowing the policy owner to participate in investment performance, the distinction between participating and nonparticipating contracts becomes less clear.

Options

Policy options also need to be considered by the purchaser. Accidental death and disability, disability income, premium waiver and guaranteed insurability riders all contribute to the policy's cost as well as its benefits. Many life insurance companies package these riders so their cost is inseparable from the price of the basic policy. Also, the riders' benefits may apply only until a certain age even though the annual premium remains constant.

Evaluation of Companies

An effective purchase decision demands a purchase from a financially sound insurer. Selecting the "best" insurer from more than 2,300 life insurance companies in the United States would be a formidable, costly and time-consuming task. If found, the "best" life insurance company today may not be so tomorrow. Therefore the consumer should make sure that the company selling the policy has a high rating based on past, current and expected financial data.

Anyone versed in finance and financial ratios could use liquidity, leverage and profitability ratios to analyze the life insurance company's balance sheet and income statement. Interpretation of the numbers, however, might be difficult due to the method of financial reporting. Since 1972 generally accepted accounting principles (GAAP) have been used for the certification of life insurance company financial statements. However, generally available financial statements are based on statutory accounting principles and practices.

Statutory accounting practices paint a conservative picture of the insurer's financial condition. The manner of accounting for expenses, the way reserves and securities are valued and the mandatory security valuation reserve all contribute to the complexity of analyzing the life insurance companies' financial information (*see* Chapter 25).

The buyer should also be aware of any nonguaranteed aspects of life insurance contracts. Mutual insurers pay participating dividends based on the company's good or bad performance. The amount of future dividends reflects the quality of operations and investment performance. Because the future cannot be known, analysis of prior actual versus illustrative dividends may be a good indicator of future expectations. Current-assumption and indeterminate-premium life policies do not guarantee premium levels but set them based on prevailing financial considerations.

Regardless of the arguments of one form of organization being better than another (stock versus mutual), the reader must realize that financial quality cannot be based exclusively on the type of organization. There are good and bad providers of life insurance of all kinds, and the product is only as good as the financial ability of the organization to perform according to the contract.

Sources of Information

One standard source used for life insurance company quality ratings is *Best's Insurance Reports (Life/Health Edition)*, published annually by A. M. Best Company, Inc., Oldwick, New Jersey. *Best's* evaluates life insurance companies yearly based on several criteria that produce an overall rating for the firm. The principal factors used in rating life insurance companies are:

- the quality of underwriting;
- the cost of operations and how well the life insurance company is managed;
- the quality of investments;
- the adequacy of reserves to pay current and future liabilities; and
- the adequacy of net worth and the company's financial strength to absorb financial shock.

Before 1976 A.M. Best gave written recommendations based on the quality of the life insurance company. Starting with the 1976 edition, alphabetical ratings were assigned (as well as a rating based on the company's financial size according to net worth):

- A+ and A: Excellent
- B+ and B: Good
- C+: Fairly Good
- C: Fair

Not all life insurance companies are assigned ratings. When this occurs, the company either does not qualify for at least a C rating, is inactive, has provided incomplete financial data or is not currently eligible for a rating (five years of credible operating results are required). In addition, when a change has occurred to warrant a lower rating, *Best's* assigns a contingent rating. If the trend does not revert to its prior condition, the rating subsequently will be lowered.

Life insurance companies are also categorized into 15 net worth sizes. Net worth, the difference between assets and liabilities, is a measure of policyholders' safety. If reserves are undervalued or assets shrink due to security market conditions, the net worth provides a cushion of safety before liabilities exceed assets and insolvency occurs. Net worth is classified from Group I ($250,000 of policyholders surplus or less) to Group XV ($100 million or more of policyholders' surplus).

When selecting a financially sound life insurance company, the buyer should select one that not only is currently rated high but also has historically been rated in the A and A+ category. The excellent, long track record provides evidence of the long-run stability and quality of operations. A larger net worth position may not be as important as the overall quality of operations in selecting a life insurance company. Many financially sound small to medium-sized life insurance companies provide reasonably priced and competitive products.

Besides *Best's, Standard & Poor's, Moody's* and *Duff & Phelps*, among others, rate insurers' financial condition and claim-paying ability. Their rating systems are different from *Best's*. Consumers are becoming aware of the rating differences and are consulting multiple sources to get other views of a company's financial condition. Some consumers and financial planners are concerned about *Best's* close ties to and dependency on the life insurance industry and insurers' ability to influence the publication of their financial rating.

Costs and Cost Disclosure

Life insurance cost disclosure is a sensitive and controversial issue among academics and practitioners in the life insurance industry. Most people agree that there should be complete cost disclosure. However, because the life insurance contract is sold for a variety of reasons, and the "true cost" can be calculated only after the insured dies or the policy has been surrendered, the best that can be hoped for in presale cost disclosure is an index or an estimate of cost assuming a specific event, such as death or surrender, occurs. The intent of an index or rate of return is to provide a guide to compare similar policies so a low-cost product can be identified, but because the event chosen is unlikely to occur, the policy may not produce the lowest cost under all circumstances. Indexes purporting to measure the rate of return of the cash value component of the life insurance policy are misleading, because the product's main purpose is to pay a death benefit.

When the many other reasons life insurance is purchased are taken into account, and when the psychological benefits and the contribution of the life insurance product to an overall financial plan are considered, it becomes obvious that there are factors of great value that cannot be measured directly. Cost and benefit disclosure thus can occur only in a financial sense and cannot measure the nonfinancial benefits of the product.

Many individuals erroneously equate the premium paid to the cost of the life insurance product. The cost of life insurance is normally not equal to the premium payment, because other cash flows are associated with the purchase. With participating policies, dividends result from favorable expense, mortality and investment experience. Dividends are not guaranteed and may be higher or lower than illustrated during the sales process. In addition, *terminal dividends* may be available when a participating contract is surrendered. Terminal dividends are accrued dividends not currently paid but held for future disbursement.

All cash value life insurance products promise other benefits in addition to paying a death claim. Nonforfeiture values allow the insured to borrow against the cash value buildup or change the policy to the extended term or paid-up insurance options. (Withdrawal privileges are also found in newer forms of life insurance.) Some individuals borrow or withdraw cash value to invest the amount at a higher interest rate than charged on policy loans, increasing the value of the life insurance contract by using leverage.

The annual premium of some new life insurance products changes based on economic conditions (current-assumption life or indeterminate-premium life), and some products allow policy owners to choose the premium payment level at inception (the minimum payment), with any excess amounts invested in a side fund. Many of these products allow the policy owner to self-direct the investments and bear the risk of investment performance. Moreover, variable life insurance products provide a changing face amount based on an underlying portfolio of securities.

As a result of all of these changes in the life insurance industry, determining the true cost of life insurance products is becoming more elusive and difficult to calculate. Retrospectively one might evaluate the cash flows after the occurrence of a certain event, such as death of the insured or the surrender of the contract. These methods are called *event-specific*, because the cost calculation is based on an event at an assumed point in time. However, the use of event-specific techniques still leaves the true cost of the product unknown, because the assumed event is unlikely to occur. Techniques using mortality assumptions and/or lapse rates are called *group-average techniques*. The costs calculated by these methods are also not accurate, because the number calculated will be representative of only a fictitious average member of the group.

Cost comparison techniques developed for consumer use should be relatively easy to calculate from available information or they must be available from a reliable source and generally understandable. The cost comparison techniques developed for consumer use have been predominantly event-specific. Two policies are used through the remainder of this chapter to illustrate the various cost comparison techniques. Both policies are issued to a male, age 25, for $25,000. However, one policy is participating (par) and the other is not (nonpar). Table 6.2 provides the data for these policies.

The Traditional Net Cost Approach

The **traditional net cost (NC) approach**, even though forbidden in many states as a sales cost comparison technique, illustrates how cost can be presented. The NC

Table 6.2
Life Insurance Contract Data for $25,000 Policies Issued to Males Age 25

	Nonpar Policy*				Par Policy†					
	Cash Value Per		Dividends Per		Cash Value Per		Sum of Total Dividends Paid Per		Terminal Dividends End of Year Per	
Year	$1,000	$25,000	$1,000	$25,000	$1,000	$25,000	$1,000	$25,000	$1,000	$25,000
1	$0	$0	$0	$0	0	0				
2	0	0	2.56	64.00	0	0				
3	0	0	2.87	71.75	3	75				
4	8	200	3.18	79.50	16	400				
5	17	425	3.49	87.25	24	600				
6	23	575	3.89	97.25	33	825				
7	34	850	3.95	98.75	45	1,125				
8	46	1,150	4.45	111.25	56	1,400				
9	58	1,450	4.74	118.50	68	1,700				
10	70	1,750	5.03	125.75	80	2,000	34.16	854.00	10.00	250.00
11	82	2,050	5.39	134.75	91	2,275				
12	93	2,325	5.79	144.75	105	2,625				
13	105	2,625	6.04	151.00	117	2,925				
14	118	2,950	6.53	163.25	132	3,300				
15	133	3,325	6.83	170.75	145	3,625				
16	145	3,625	7.01	175.25	159	3,975				
17	159	3,975	7.49	187.25	173	4,325				
18	173	4,325	8.25	206.25	189	4,725				
19	186	4,650	8.56	214.00	203	5,075				
20	204	5,100	8.98	224.50	219	5,475	105.03	2,625.75	18.00	450.00
Age 60	451	11,275	15.29	382.25	455	11,375				
Age 65	535	13,375	17.07	426.75	539	13,475				

*Policy Fee = $15.00; premium = $250.75 ($9.43 per $1,000); Loan Rate = 6 %; Average = $10.03 per $1,000.
†Premium = $341.50 ($13.66 per $1,000); loan rate = 8 %.

approach is event-specific in that the policy owner is assumed to live a certain number of years and then surrender the contract. The NC is usually calculated at the end of the 10th and 20th policy years and is equal to the difference between all premiums paid and all cash flows returned to the policy owner. Thus the NC is calculated by taking these steps:

1. Add the premiums paid over the analysis period.
2. Subtract the following amounts from the total:
   a. all dividends paid;
   b. any terminal dividend; and
   c. ending cash value.

The remainder equals the net cost. The NC then can be divided by the number of years in the analysis to provide an annual level cost per year, and this result can be divided by the number of thousands of face amount to provide a net cost for each $1,000 per year. Table 6.3 provides the NC analysis of the two sample policies. Notice that when the NC analysis is made for longer periods of time the policy appears to pay for itself and produce a positive cash flow. This analysis implies that life insurance is costless. However, the NC approach is flawed, because it ignores the

Table 6.3
Traditional Net Cost Analysis, $25,000 Basis*

	Nonpar Policy 10 Years	Nonpar Policy 20 Years	Par Policy 10 Years	Par Policy 20 Years
Total premiums paid	$2,507.50	$5,015.00	$3,415.00	$6,830.00
Less: Total dividends paid	0.00	0.00	854.00	2,625.75
Terminal dividend	0.00	0.00	250.00	450.00
Cash value, end of year	1,750.00	5,100.00	2,000.00	5,475.00
Net cost: All years	$757.50	($85.00)	$311.00	($1,720.75)
Per year	75.75	(4.25)	31.10	(86.04)
Per year/per thousand	3.03	(0.17)	1.24	(3.44)

*Columns may not sum correctly because only two decimal places are shown.

time value of money. In other words, it is assumed that the policy owner and the insurance company are indifferent to paying (receiving) the premiums today or in 10 or 20 years and that the timing of dividend distributions is irrelevant. Ignoring the time value of money distorts costs dramatically. The opportunity cost of money is important, especially if the analysis extends over long periods of time. Failing to consider the time value of money generally produces the negative or low cost in the NC approach.

Interest-Adjusted Methods

Interest-adjusted methods are used to calculate an index that eliminates the major flaw of the NC approach. This chapter discusses several of the event-specific interest-adjusted cost comparison techniques.

The Surrender Cost Index

The **surrender cost index (SCI)** assumes that the policy owner surrenders the contract at the end of the analysis period. The SCI index provides an interest-adjusted yearly level cost of providing death protection. The mechanics of the SCI are to accumulate to the end of the analysis period (usually 10 and 20 years) all values adjusted for the time value of money so as to calculate the total interest-adjusted cost. Referring to Table 6.4, the total interest-adjusted cost (TIAC) is equal to all accumulated premiums minus all accumulated dividends, the terminal dividend and the final cash value. The TIAC is then divided by the appropriate future value of an annuity due factor and then divided by the number of thousands of face amount. The result provides a yearly level amount that, if paid at the beginning of each year and accumulated at the assumed interest rate, will be equal to the total interest-adjusted cost at the end of the analysis period for each $1,000 of coverage. A three-year TIAC and SCI are calculated as follows:

$$TIAC = [\, P_1(1+i)^3 + P_2(1+i)^2 + P_3(1+i)^1 \,] \\ - [\, D_1(1+i)^2 + D_2(1+i)^1 + D_3 + TD + CV_3 \,]$$

$$SCI = \frac{TIAC}{FVA_d \times F}$$

where:

P_n = Premium in year n
D_n = Dividend in year n
TD = Terminal dividend
F = Number of thousands of face amount
CV = Cash value, end of analysis period
i = Assumed interest rate
FVA_d = Future value, annuity due factor
    20 years = 34.7193 (5%)
    10 years = 13.2068 (5%)

The TIAC calculates the difference between the future value of the cash inflows and outflows if the policy is surrendered at the end of the analysis period. When the TIAC (per thousand of face) is divided by the future value of the annuity due factor, the TIAC is leveled such that the index when accumulated at the i rate equals the TIAC (per $1,000 of face amount) as follows:

$$\frac{TIAC}{F} = SCI(1+i)^3 + SCI(1+i)^2 + SCI(1+i)^1$$

The calculation of the SCI for the two hypothetical life insurance contracts is presented in Table 6.4. Each expected dividend is multiplied by a dividend interest factor. Since dividends are paid at the end of the year, the first dividend grows for 19 years. Each premium payment is multiplied by a premium interest factor. In this case, premiums are paid at the beginning of the year so the first premium grows for 20 years. For each successive year the compounding period reduces by one. The resulting totals are the accumulated interest-adjusted premiums and dividends. The SCI is calculated as described above for the 20-year period for both the participating and the nonparticipating policies. A lower SCI is generally better, however, small differences may not be significant.

The Net Payments Cost Index

Instead of assuming that the policy owner surrenders the contract at the end of the analysis period, as in the SCI, the **net payments cost index (NPI)** assumes that the insured dies at the end of the analysis period. The NPI is calculated in the same manner as the SCI, except the terminal dividend (TD) and the cash value (CV) at the end of the analysis period are not considered. These values (cash flows) are not available if the policy terminates because of a death claim. Thus TD and CV will always be equal to zero when the NPI is calculated. Table 6.5 shows the calculations for the NPI.

The NPI and the SCI indexes are similar in that a lower number means a relatively lower cost. Because the terminal dividend and the cash value are not considered in the NPI procedure, the SCI index will be equal to or lower than the NPI when the analysis is made on the same contract. When there are no dividends and no cash value (e.g., nonparticipating term insurance), the indexes are equal for the same contract.

Table 6.4
Surrender Cost Index Method, 5 Percent: 20-Year Analysis*

	Par Contract†					Nonpar Contract‡				
Year	Dividend	Interest Factor Dividend	Interest Factor Premium	Accumulated Premium	Accumulated Dividend	Dividend	Interest Factor Dividend	Interest Factor Premium	Accumulated Premium	Accumulated Dividend
1	$0.00	2.53	2.65	$ 36.24	$ 0.00	0.00	2.53	2.65	$ 26.61	$0.00
2	2.56	2.41	2.53	34.52	6.16	0.00	2.41	2.53	25.35	0.00
3	2.87	2.29	2.41	32.87	6.58	0.00	2.29	2.41	24.14	0.00
4	3.18	2.18	2.29	31.31	6.94	0.00	2.18	2.29	22.99	0.00
5	3.49	2.08	2.18	29.82	7.26	0.00	2.08	2.18	21.89	0.00
6	3.89	1.98	2.08	28.40	7.70	0.00	1.98	2.08	20.85	0.00
7	3.95	1.89	1.98	27.05	7.45	0.00	1.89	1.98	19.86	0.00
8	4.45	1.80	1.89	25.76	7.99	0.00	1.80	1.89	18.91	0.00
9	4.74	1.71	1.80	24.53	8.11	0.00	1.71	1.80	18.01	0.00
10	5.03	1.63	1.71	23.36	8.19	0.00	1.63	1.71	17.15	0.00
11	5.39	1.55	1.63	22.25	8.36	0.00	1.55	1.63	16.34	0.00
12	5.79	1.48	1.55	21.19	8.55	0.00	1.48	1.55	15.56	0.00
13	6.04	1.41	1.48	20.18	8.50	0.00	1.41	1.48	14.82	0.00
14	6.53	1.34	1.41	19.22	8.75	0.00	1.34	1.41	14.11	0.00
15	6.83	1.28	1.34	18.31	8.72	0.00	1.28	1.34	13.44	0.00
16	7.01	1.22	1.28	17.43	8.52	0.00	1.22	1.28	12.80	0.00
17	7.49	1.16	1.22	16.60	8.67	0.00	1.16	1.22	12.19	0.00
18	8.25	1.10	1.16	15.81	9.10	0.00	1.10	1.16	11.61	0.00
19	8.56	1.05	1.10	15.06	8.99	0.00	1.05	1.10	11.06	0.00
20	8.98	1.00	1.05	14.34	8.98	0.00	1.00	1.05	10.53	0.00
Total				$474.26	$153.52				$348.23	$0.00

	Par Contract	Nonpar Contract
Surrender Cost Index (20 years) =		
Premiums accumulated at interest	$474.26	$348.23
Less: Dividends accumulated	153.52	0.00
Terminal dividend	18.00	0.00
Cash value, end of analysis year	219.00	204.00
TIAC	$ 83.75	$144.23
Divided by future value, annuity due factor§	34.7193	34.7193
Surrender Cost Index	2.41	4.15

*Columns may not sum correctly because only two decimal places are shown.
†Premium = $13.66; $1,000 basis.
‡Premium = $10.03; $1,000 basis.
§For 10 years, divide by 13.2068.

The Equivalent Level Annual Dividend

The **equivalent level annual dividend (ELAD)** provides a measure of the importance of participating dividends in the SCI or NPI calculation. Specifically, when the ELAD is added to the SCI or NPI, the resulting index number reflects the relative cost of the participating policy if no dividends are paid during the analysis period. Illustrated dividends are accumulated to the end of the analysis period, and the sum is divided by the appropriate future value of an annuity due factor times the number of thousands of face amount. A three-year ELAD would be calculated as follows:

$$\text{ELAD} = \frac{D_1 (1+i)^2 + D_2 (1+i)^1 + D_3}{FVA_d \times F}$$

Table 6.5
Net Payments Cost Index Method, 5 Percent: 20-Year Analysis*

	Par Contract†	Nonpar Contract‡
Net Payments Cost Index (20 years) =		
Premiums accumulated at interest	$474.26	$348.23
Less: Dividends accumulated	153.52	0.00
Terminal dividend	0.00	0.00
Cash value, end of analysis year	0.00	0.00
TIAC	$320.74	$348.23
Divided by future value, annuity due factor§	34.7193	34.7193
Net Payments Cost Index	9.24	10.03

*Columns may not sum correctly because only two decimal places are shown.
†Premium = $13.66; $1,000 basis.
‡Premium = $10.03; $1,000 basis.
§For 10 years, divide by 13.2068.

The 20-year ELAD calculation is provided in Table 6.6. If no dividends are paid, the cost represented by the SCI or NPI index would understate the relative cost of the product. Thus, when the ELAD is added to the SCI or NPI indexes, a cost index is calculated based on the assumption that no dividends will be paid. The same results could be calculated by using zero for the dividend amount in the participating NPI or SCI calculations. Note that the ELAD calculation is equivalent to determining the interest-adjusted dividend amount in the SCI and NPI calculations.

Even though the SCI, NPI, and ELAD indexes are relatively easy to calculate and understand, these interest-adjusted methods have several theoretical flaws. First, because the NPI, SCI and ELAD indexes are calculated on the values on a certain date (normally 10 or 20 years), policy values may be manipulated by an insurance company to provide an index that is not representative of the entire contract term. Second, when different event-specific indexes are used, conflicting ranks of policies may occur. The NPI focuses on death at the end of the analysis period, while the SCI uses a surrender to terminate the contract. When a conflict occurs, the evaluator must judge whether the payment of a death claim is more important than the accumulation of cash values. If the person does not plan to use the loan nonforfeiture option or surrender the policy, the NPI may be more representative of the cost. Several studies have investigated which cost index provides the best summary of policy values. These studies generally conclude that the choice of index does not matter, because policy costs (measured by indexes) are ranked similarly.

The third criticism of indexes involves the use of nonguaranteed values. Cost comparison techniques do not recognize the difference between guaranteed and nonguaranteed components in the calculation. Illustrated dividends are not guaranteed. In addition, new life insurance products have premiums, face amounts and cash values that are determined by future economic conditions. Thus, as noted, only in retrospect can an accurate cost be calculated.

The fourth criticism involves the use of indexes for comparing dissimilar products. It is debatable whether dissimilar policies can be compared accurately by

Table 6.6
Equivalent Level Annual Dividend, 5 Percent: Analysis of 20-Year Par Contract*

Year	Dividend per Thousand	Interest Factor	Accumulated Dividend
1	$0.00	2.53	$ 0.00
2	2.56	2.41	6.16
3	2.87	2.29	6.58
4	3.18	2.18	6.94
5	3.49	2.08	7.26
6	3.89	1.98	7.70
7	3.95	1.89	7.45
8	4.45	1.80	7.99
9	4.74	1.71	8.11
10	5.03	1.63	8.19
11	5.39	1.55	8.36
12	5.79	1.48	8.55
13	6.04	1.41	8.50
14	6.53	1.34	8.75
15	6.83	1.28	8.72
16	7.01	1.22	8.52
17	7.49	1.16	8.67
18	8.25	1.10	9.10
19	8.56	1.05	8.99
20	8.98	1.00	8.98
			$153.52

Accumulated dividend — $153.52
Divided by annuity due factor† — 34.7193
Equivalent level annual dividend — 4.42

SCI	2.41	NPI	9.24
ELAD	4.42	ELAD	4.42
Cost Index	6.83	Cost Index	13.66

*Columns may not sum correctly because only two decimal places are shown.
†For 10 years, divide by 13.2068.

using these interest-adjusted techniques. For example, it may not be appropriate to compare participating policies with ones that do not pay dividends. If the ELAD is added to the SCI or NPI, a worst-case cost for the participating policy would be compared to a normal situation for the nonparticipating policy. The SCI and NPI are likely to be lower for the nonparticipating policy; but when the ELAD is added, the rankings are likely to switch.

Sources of Index Information

Instead of calculating these indexes by hand, the consumer may refer to published sources of indexes. Two main sources of readily available index information are *Life Rates & Data* published by the National Underwriter Company of Cincinnati, Ohio, and *Best's Flitcraft Compend* published by the A. M. Best Company of Oldwick, New Jersey. Both of these publications are updated annually and report policy information as well as indexes on life insurance plans offered by many companies.

Chapter 6 Life Insurance—Costs and Comparisons

Table 6.7
Benchmarks and Rules for Belth's Single-Year Method

Benchmarks	
Age	Price
Under 30	$ 1.50
30–34	2.00
35–39	3.00
40–44	4.00
45–49	6.50
50–54	10.00
55–59	15.00
60–64	25.00
65–69	35.00
70–74	50.00
75–79	80.00
80–84	125.00

Rules

If:	Relative Cost is:
Price < Benchmark	Very low
Benchmark < Price < 2 × Benchmark	Fairly low
2 × Benchmark < Price < 3 × Benchmark	Fairly high
Price > 3 × Benchmark	Very high

Belth's Single-Year Method

Use of the **Belth single-year method** allows the consumer to determine if life insurance products are priced reasonably.[1] The Belth method calculates a yearly price for the protection provided by the contract. The yearly price is then compared to benchmark figures to determine the relative cost of the policy. Table 6.7 presents the benchmarks and the decision rules.

The following formula is used to calculate Belth's yearly cost of protection for a given policy year t:

$$\text{Cost of protection} = \frac{(P_t + CV_{t-1})(1+i) - (CV_t + D_t)}{(FA_t - CV_t) / 1{,}000}$$

where:

P = Premium
CV = Cash value
D = Dividend
FA = Face amount
i = Assumed interest rate (.06 recommended)

The first term in the numerator $[(P_t + CV_{t-1})(1 + i)]$ in the formula above calculates the wealth at the end of the year, given that the policy owner surrenders the contract at the beginning of the year. The prior end-of-year cash value amount plus the premium amount may be invested at rate i, resulting in a higher future amount. If the policy owner maintains the contract (pays the premium), the wealth position at the end of the year will be $(CV_t + D_t)$, the cash value amount at the end of the year plus any dividend distributions. The difference between these two numbers represents the price paid for the life insurance protection in that year. When the numerator is divided by the thousands of protection [$(FA_t - CV_t) / 1{,}000$], the yearly price for each $1,000 of protection results. The reader should note that the amount of protection is not the face amount but the difference between the face amount and the cash value. For a numerical example, refer to the participating contract in Table 6.2. The price of protection for the tenth year is calculated as follows:

$$\text{Cost of protection} = \frac{(P_{10} + CV_9)(1+.06) - CV_{10} + D_{10}}{(FA_{10} - CV_{10}) / 1{,}000}$$

$$= \frac{(341.50 + 1{,}700)(1.06) - (2{,}000 + 125.75)}{(25{,}000 - 2{,}000) / 1{,}000}$$

$$= \frac{2{,}163.99 - 2{,}125.75}{23} = 1.66$$

The benchmark for under age 30 is $1.50 (from Table 6.7). Because the price of protection for Year 10 is greater than the benchmark but less than two times $1.50 ($3.00), the relative cost is fairly low. Individuals interested in analyzing each policy year may find some policies are more costly than others in their early years and others are more expensive in their later years, thus making the time frame of policy continuation important.

The Linton Yield

The **Linton yield** was developed to compare whole life insurance to the buy-term-and-invest-the-difference strategy.[2] To calculate the Linton yield, the premium on the whole life plan less any annual dividend is assumed to purchase a sufficient amount of term insurance to create an investment fund such that the sum of the two equals the whole life face amount. At any point the separate investment account plus the term insurance equals the whole life face amount. The Linton yield is the rate of return generated on the separate investment account so the accumulated fund's amount will be equal to the cash value of the whole life insurance contract at the end of the analysis period.

The Linton yield can be calculated with the use of an electronic spreadsheet program (*see* Table 6.8). The spreadsheet used to construct Table 6.1 can also be used to calculate the Linton yield. The Linton yield is found by changing the interest rate assumption earned on invested funds until the separate fund approximates the cash value at the end of a selected year (in this case, at the end of the 10th policy year). The Linton yield equals 1.57 percent for the illustration, and any investor could achieve better results. At the end of Year 10 the separate fund is equal to the cash value of the whole life insurance policy ($11,400).

Yearly Rate of Return

The *yearly rate of return* ($YROR_t$) in year t measures the annual holding period return of the "benefits" relative to the "cost" of the cash value policy.

$$YROR_t = \frac{\text{Benefits}}{\text{Costs}} - 1$$

or

Table 6.8
Calculation of Linton Yield
(Nonpar; male, age 35, for $100,000 face value)

(1) Age	(2) Cash Value	(3) Whole Life Premium	(4) Dividend Amount	(5) Net Premium	(6) Saved	(7) Term Rate	(8) Dis. Income Prem.	(9) Term Face	(10) Term Prem.	(11) Diff. Invested	(12) Cum. Inv. EOY	(13) Inv. Value
35	$ 0	$1,389	$0	$1,389	$ 0	$2.81	$0	$98,889	$278	$1,111	$1,111	$1,129
36	0	1,389	0	1,389	1,129	2.91	0	97,767	285	1,104	2,233	2,268
37	900	1,389	0	1,389	2,268	3.04	0	96,637	294	1,095	3,363	3,416
38		1,389	0	1,389	3,416	3.22	0	95,502	308	1,081	4,498	4,568
39	3,700	1,389	0	1,389	4,568	3.44	0	94,367	325	1,064	5,633	5,721
40		1,389	0	1,389	5,721	3.70	0	93,235	345	1,044	6,765	6,871
41		1,389	0	1,389	6,871	4.00	0	92,108	368	1,021	7,892	8,016
42		1,389	0	1,389	8,016	4.31	0	90,987	392	997	9,013	9,154
43		1,389	0	1,389	9,154	4.66	0	89,876	419	970	10,124	10,283
44	11,400	1,389	0	1,389	10,283	5.05	0	88,776	448	941	11,224	11,400

Linton Rate of .0157 is found by trial and error.

(2) cash value for selected years shown
(5) net premium (3) − (4)
(6) saved (13), prior year
(7) term rate per $1,000
(8) for amount in (3)
(9) [100,000 − (3) + (4) − (6) + (8)] / {1.00 − [(7) / 1,000] }
(10) term premium: (9) / 1,000 × (7)
(11) (5) − (8) − (10)
(12) (13), prior year + (11)
(13) (12) × (1.00 + Rate); rate = after-tax rate assumed

$$YROR_t = \frac{CV_t + D_t + [R_t \times (F_t - CV_t) / 1{,}000]}{P_t + CV_{t-1}} - 1$$

where:
CV_t = Illustrated cash − end of policy year t
D_t = Illustrated dividend − end of policy year t
R_t = Mortality charge for $1,000 protection in year t
F_t = Projected death benefit − end of year t
P_t = Beginning of year t

Table 6.9 provides the results of the YROR calculation for the hypothetical participating contract found in Table 6.2. The cost of protection is estimated by a representative low-cost annual renewable term policy. When comparing policies, one may find the YROR for one policy is not consistently higher than the other, and depending on the term rates used as well as the progression of the cash value and dividends, the YROR may not exhibit a consistent pattern.

Equal Outlay

A particularly useful method in analyzing cash value contracts including universal life is the *equal outlay method*. Many agents use variations of this method in their sales presentation due to its ease of use and comprehensibility to consumers. The buy-term-and-invest-the-difference analysis is a variation of the equal outlay method. The method can be used to directly compare any cash value life insurance

Table 6.9
Illustration of Yearly Rate of Return, Male, Age 25

(1) Year	(2) Cash Value $25,000	(3) Illus Div. $25,000	(4) Term Rate	(5)	(6) Premium + Cash Value (BOY)	(7) YROR
1	$ 0	$ 0	$1.11	$ 27.75	$ 341.50	−0.919
2	0	64.00	1.11	91.75	341.50	−0.731
3	75	71.75	1.12	174.67	341.50	−0.489
4	400	79.50	1.13	507.30	416.50	0.218
5	600	87.25	1.14	715.07	741.50	−0.036
6	825	97.25	1.16	950.29	941.50	0.009
7	1,125	98.75	1.19	1,252.16	1,166.50	0.073
8	1,400	111.25	1.22	1,540.04	1,466.50	0.050
9	1,700	118.50	1.27	1,848.09	1,741.50	0.061
10	2,000	125.75	1.32	2,156.11	2,041.50	0.056
11	2,275	134.75	1.40	2,441.57	2,341.50	0.043
12	2,625	144.75	1.47	2,802.64	2,616.50	0.071
13	2,925	151.00	1.58	3,110.88	2,966.50	0.049
14	3,300	163.25	1.68	3,499.71	3,266.50	0.071
15	3,625	170.75	1.80	3,834.22	3,641.50	0.053
16	3,975	175.25	1.94	4,191.04	3,966.50	0.057
17	4,325	187.25	2.08	4,555.25	4,316.50	0.055
18	4,725	206.25	2.24	4,976.67	4,666.50	0.066
19	5,075	214.00	2.43	5,337.42	5,066.50	0.053
20	5,475	224.50	2.65	5,751.24	5,416.50	0.062

(5) $CV_t + D_t + [(R_t) \times (F_t - CV_t) / 1,000]$
(6) $P_t + CV_{t-1}$

policy. There is, however, some difficulty in interpretation when comparing dissimilar policies. Typically the equal outlay method is used to compare a traditional cash value policy with nontraditional ones or two nontraditional policies. In the first case the flexible premium and the face amount of the ULI policy may be set at the traditional policy's level. In the second case a feasible, arbitrary premium and initial face amount may be selected for both policies. (The face amount may change based on projected dividend distributions used to purchase paid-up insurance amounts or to accumulate at interest. Investment results may also change the face amount.)

The equal outlay method assumes the same premium and face amount for the alternative policies. The insurance policy with the highest cash surrender value and death benefits after a specified period of time is estimated to be superior to the other. If there are any distributions such as participating dividends, the amounts may be used to increase the death benefits and the surrender amount. These numbers can be supplied easily by the sales agent.

An additional consideration is the investment performance of the insurer. The investment rate of return should be fixed in the nontraditional contracts to isolate the influence of mortality costs and expenses. (Some practitioners advocate using the guaranteed rate. The guaranteed rate, however, is not representative of the amount likely to be earned.) Presentations may be made based on the guaranteed rate, a historical rate and a projected rate.

Financial Planning Issues: The Replacement Decision

Sometimes it is advantageous for a policy owner to replace an existing life insurance policy with a new one providing essentially the same face amount of coverage, even though the new annual premium will be higher because of the insured's age. When replacement takes place, either the policy owner switches to a similar cash value contract or life insurance can be provided by term insurance. Sales agents who make a living encouraging insureds to replace existing life insurance policies with new ones may mislead policy owners into making a poor decision. Similarly, conservationists—agents who want old life insurance policies to persist—may also persuade the policy owner to make a disadvantageous decision. The consumer must always assess the adequacy of his or her financial plan to determine if the change is warranted. Permanent life insurance may still be required. On the other hand, term insurance may be adequate for one's needs.

Before a replacement occurs, certain factors need to be considered. First, when a life insurance policy is replaced, there are search costs associated with any prospective purchase. The life insurance companies, their contracts and the agent all must be evaluated. In addition, acquisition costs must be paid when a new life insurance contract is purchased. These costs include the agent's commission, policy fees, medical exams, taxes and other overhead expenses. As noted, due to these acquisition costs, cash value life insurance provides low or no cash value amounts during the first few years. However, the removal and investment of the cash value in the original policy may overcome this objection to the low cash value amount. With regard to the incontestable and suicide clauses, the purchaser of a new life insurance contract is subject to the time limits imposed by the new contract. Insurability must also be considered. If the health of the insured is impaired, it may be impossible to replace the old policy, or the increased premium due to poor health may make the replacement financially unattractive. Before surrendering the old contract, the insured should have the new life insurance policy in force. This will preclude the possibility of losing all life insurance coverage when it is not available due to poor health.

Tax considerations are also important.[3] When the old life insurance contract is surrendered, there may be ordinary tax on the excess received over the cost basis. The cost basis is the sum of all premiums paid less any participating dividends and cash value received when surrendered (assuming no loans are outstanding). For example, if all dividends are paid to the policy holder over the 20 years (*see* Table 6.2), the policy owner would pay ordinary tax on $1,720.75, calculated as follows:

Premiums paid	$ 6,830.00
Dividends	−3,075.75
Basis	3,754.25
Basis	3,754.25
Cash value	5,475.00
Excess over basis	$ 1,720.75

Individual policy clauses must also be considered. Besides the incontestability and suicide clauses already mentioned, the nonforfeiture options and settlement options need to be reviewed. The absolute amount of the cash value and any illustrated dividends will be readily available to evaluate. However, the amount of life insurance provided in the paid-up insurance option and the length of insurance provided in the extended term option may differ depending on the mortality tables used. This aspect is difficult to evaluate in that not only is the new policy issued at an older age, but the level of cash value will not allow easy comparison. Even though this aspect of nonforfeiture options is difficult to analyze, loan rates are relatively easy to compare. Newer life insurance policies generally have a higher loan rate than older life insurance contracts.

Interest rates used in settlement clauses vary according to the contract. Higher assumed (sometimes guaranteed) interest rates for the interest, fixed-period, fixed-amount and life income options will increase settlement amounts. Moreover, old life insurance policies may pay higher annuity rent if more deaths were predicted than new contracts when life annuity settlement calculations are made. In this case a switch to a new life insurance contract would provide lower rent payments if a life annuity settlement option is selected.

Review Questions

1. Why does the life insurance premium not reflect the cost of the product?
2. What arguments are used to convince people not to use the buy-term-and-invest-the-difference strategy?
3. What arguments corroborate the buy-term-and-invest-the-difference strategy?
4. Review Table 6.1 and the formulas used in the buy-term-and-invest-the-difference analysis. Does the spreadsheet analysis conform to the requirements that equal dollar amounts are spent regardless of whether whole life insurance is purchased or the buy-term-and-invest-the-difference strategy is used during the period? What about the amount of protection provided by either strategy?
5. What is meant by temporary and permanent protection?
6. How do participating dividends affect the purchase decision? Why are participating dividends not guaranteed?
7. What are the main reasons for the difficulty in analyzing the stability and quality of a life insurance company?
8. When evaluating the financial position of the life insurance company, why is *Best's* concerned about (1) quality of underwriting, (2) overhead and management, (3) investments and (4) reserve adequacy?
9. Why can't the true cost of life insurance be disclosed when the life insurance contract is sold?

Chapter 6 Life Insurance—Costs and Comparisons

10. Distinguish between event-specific and group-average techniques in cost disclosure index calculations.
11. What is wrong with using the traditional net cost approach when disclosing life insurance cost?
12. Cost indexes are based on the assumption that a certain event occurs. What is the event in the surrender cost index and in the net payment cost index?
13. What rationale is used for adding the equivalent level annual dividend to the NPI and the SCI when evaluating participating policies? How does one interpret the resulting number?
14. Compare Belth's single-year method to the NPI and SCI methods for comparing cost. Which method is more accurate? More complicated? Easier to understand? Which provides more information?
15. How is the buy-term-and-invest-the-difference analysis related to the Linton yield?
16. Briefly describe the benefits and costs of replacing a life insurance contract.
17. Calculate the 10-year NPI, SCI and ELAD for the following contract (assume a 5 percent interest rate). Yearly premium (whole life, $50,000) is $1,200 (male, age 45).

Year	Illustrated Dividends
1	0
2	207
3	243
4	280
5	319
6	368
7	417
8	466
9	515
10	564

Terminal dividend = $100 (end of Year 10). Cash value (end of Year 10) = $8,950.

18. Refer to question 17. Perform a buy-term-and-invest-the-difference analysis over the 10-year period. Term insurance rates are as follows:

Year	Age	Rate per $1,000
1	45	$ 3.33
2	46	3.62
3	47	3.94
4	48	4.39
5	49	4.88
6	50	5.45

Year	Age	Rate per $1,000
7	51	6.08
8	52	6.83
9	53	7.67
10	54	8.67

Disability income premium is $43. The rate of return on investments before tax is 10 percent, and the average tax rate is 22 percent.

19. Calculate the Linton yield using the information contained in questions 17 and 18.

Endnotes

[1] Joseph M. Belth, "Is Your Life Insurance Reasonably Priced? How to Evaluate an Existing Life Insurance Policy," *Insurance Forum* 9, No. 6, June 1982, pp. 165–168. *See also* Joseph M. Belth, "How to Buy Cash-Value Life Insurance," *Insurance Forum* 10, No. 10, October 1983, pp. 229–232.

[2] See Albert L. Auxier, "The ABC's of the Linton Method," *CLU Journal*, October 1981, pp. 44–49, for a further explanation of the Linton yield.

[3] The reader should be aware of the possibility of a tax-free exchange. For an excellent discussion, refer to Theodore Paul Manno and Richard T. Nolan, "Internal Revenue Code Section 1035 and the Other Side of Exchange Programs," *Journal of the American Society of CLU* 39, No. 6, November 1985, pp. 66–73.

Bibliography

Cherin, Antony C., and Robert C. Hutchins. "The Rate of Return on Universal Life Insurance." *Journal of Risk and Insurance*, December 1987, p. 691.

Chung, Yosup, and Harold Skipper, Jr. "The Effect of Interest Rates on Surrender Values of Universal Life Policies." *Journal of Risk and Insurance*, June 1987, p. 641.

Goodwin, Dave. "Replacement: A Sin or a Service?" *Best's Review (Life/Health Edition)*, January 1990, p. 48.

King, Carole. "The Fine Art of Comparing Policies." *Best's Review (Life/Health Edition)*, February 1986, p. 42.

Schleef, Harold J. "Whole Life Cost Comparisons Based upon the Year of Required Protection." *Journal of Risk and Insurance*, March 1989, p. 83.

Chapter 7 | Medical Expense and Disability Insurance

Chapter Objectives

- Introduce the economic problems associated with loss of health
- Distinguish between indemnity plans and managed care
- Investigate the sources of health expenditure reimbursement
- Describe individual medical expense contracts and their provisions
- Discuss individual disability income contracts

Introduction

Many people who recognize the need for life insurance to replace lost income do not prepare adequately for the financial consequences of losing their health or becoming disabled. Yet such advance planning is paramount because loss of health can be more financially devastating than death. Death exposes the family to permanent loss of income, but loss of health means continued self-maintenance expenses as well, often along with other services required and large medical bills incurred for long periods of time.

As defined traditionally, health insurance indemnifies or reimburses insureds for necessary medical expenses. However, because the term now includes a wide array of public and private sources that compensate for losses resulting from a decline in health or a short- or long-term disability, this chapter covers a broad range of topics relating to health care delivery, reimbursement and income replacement. No financial plan today is complete without full attention paid to these important topics.

Health Data

Each year the amount spent for health care in the U.S. rises. Health care expenditures in 1988 exceeded $539 billion, accounting for more than 11 percent of the U.S. gross national product. This is the highest percentage of GNP that any nation

Table 7.1
Health Care Expenditures as a Percent of GNP
(Billions of Dollars)

Year	Gross National Product	National Health Expenditures	Percent of GNP
1950	$ 288.3	$ 12.7	4.4
1960	515.0	27.1	5.3
1970	1,016.0	74.4	7.3
1980	2,732.0	249.1	9.1
1987	4,516.0	488.8	10.8
1988	4,874.0	539.9	11.1

Source: *1990 Source Book of Health Insurance Data* (Washington, D.C.: Health Insurance Association of America), p. 58.

spends on health care, yet the U.S. ranks poorly in infant mortality and is far from the top in other measures of health care quality. This increase in national health care expenditures can be attributed to many factors, including a larger population with rising incomes, inflation, the increased demand for more and better health care, excessive hospital capacity, and duplication of hospital facilities, doctor specialization, malpractice litigation and defensive medicine.[1]

Table 7.1 shows expenditure trends in the United States and illustrates the importance of the health care industry to the economy. From 1950 to 1988, expenditures on health care have increased more than 42 times while the gross national product has increased almost 17 times. Although part of the cost increase is due to better quality, much of it is caused by inflation. Figure 7.1 compares price levels for all consumer goods with medical price levels.

Considering these data, the current emphasis on health care cost containment—a concern of individuals, private industry and government—is understandable.

Aggregate national expenditure data reflect the fact that maintaining good health and receiving quality health care can be costly for the individual. Individual statistics[2] reveal that the average hospital stay in the United States is 7.2 days. During that time the patient incurs expenses for room and board and doctors' fees. A semiprivate room in a hospital currently averages $240; intensive care costs more. The average cost per bed, per day is approximately $540, though the actual numbers vary considerably by location. Surgical procedures are expensive. For example, an appendectomy may cost $800 to $2,000, and a heart bypass $10,000 for the surgical procedure alone. Office visits costs $20 to $50, depending on the service provided and how much the doctors charge.

In addition to the direct costs of medical care, loss of income caused by an acute (lasting less than three months) or chronic (longer than three months) condition may result in severe economic hardship. Disability is not a minor problem. The probability of disability is greater at every age than the probability of death, and the financial impact of disability may last for years or for life. As shown in Table 7.2, women tend to have more restricted activity and bed disability days than men. Higher-income families have fewer disability days.

Figure 7.1
Consumer vs. Medical Price Levels

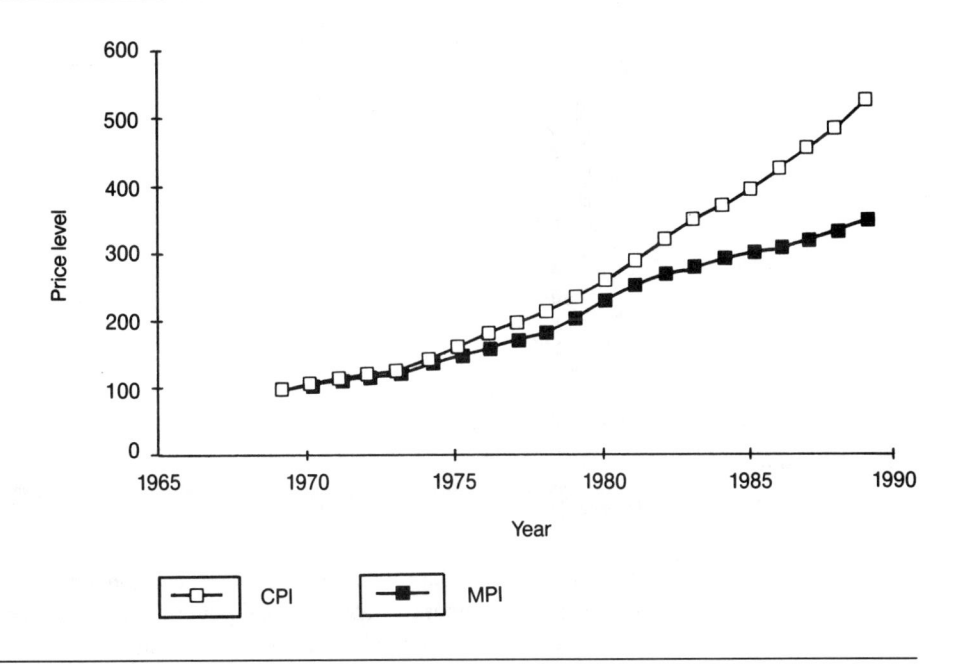

[Line graph showing Price level (0–600) vs. Year (1965–1990), comparing CPI (open squares) and MPI (filled squares). Both indexed near 100 around 1970, with CPI rising to about 530 and MPI to about 350 by 1990.]

Sources of Health Insurance: Public and Private

Health insurance can be classified as group and individual insurance products. In recent years group health insurance has grown in premium volume and the number of people covered. Reasons for this growth include the fact that smaller groups are now eligible, that employer premiums are tax-deductible, and that comparable benefits under nongroup plans are costlier.

The aggregate health care expenditures for 1988 mentioned earlier include private health insurance premiums as well as uninsured expenditures made to pay for a wide array of services, benefits, and activities provided by charity and federal, state, and local governments. Employers provide other health-related benefits, including sick leave, salary continuation plans, vision and dental care reimbursement and drug dependency, prescription drug and wellness programs. Employers and employees must participate in the Social Security program, and employers must comply with workers' compensation laws and with Occupational Safety and Health Administration (OSHA) requirements to provide a safe working environment. Some of these expenses are not included in the aggregate health care expenditure amounts. Government-sponsored health care programs include Medicaid (for low-income and low-resource individuals and families), Medicare (for those over age 65), Aid to Families with Dependent Children, the Civilian Health and Medical Program for the Uniformed Services (CHAMPUS), Veterans

Table 7.2
Average Days of Disability per Person by Sex and Income, 1988

	Restricted Activity	Bed Disability	Work Loss
Male	6.9	2.4	2.7
Female	9.8	3.5	2.7
Family Income:			
Under $10,000	10.0	4.7	3.8
$10,000–19,999	7.7	3.4	na
$20,000–34,999	6.5	2.7	na
$35,000 and over	5.8	2.4	na
Age:			
Under 5 years	9.7	4.9	na
5–17 years	7.2	3.4	na
18–24 years	7.1	3.0	3.5
25–44 years	6.4	2.5	3.2
45–64 years	5.8	2.4	2.5
65 years and older	8.1	3.4	na

na = not available

Source: *1990 Source Book of Health Insurance Data* (Washington, D.C.: Health Insurance Association of America), p. 91.

Administration, Indian Health Services and state and local health programs. Table 7.3 reveals that federal, state and local governments fund approximately 42 percent of the reported national health care expenditure.

Group and Individual Coverage

Individuals, families and employee groups buy health insurance. According to the *1990 Source Book of Health Insurance Data*, in 1988 group insurance premiums

Table 7.3
Public vs. Private Health Care Expenditures in the United States*
(Billions of Dollars)

Year	National Health Expenditure	Private	Public	Federal	State/Local
1970	74.4	46.7	27.7	17.7	9.9
1975	132.9	77.8	55.1	36.4	18.7
1980	249.1	143.9	105.2	72.0	33.2
1985	420.1	245.2	174.9	123.4	51.5
1986	450.5	259.8	190.7	132.8	57.9
1987	488.8	280.5	208.3	144.0	64.3
1988	539.9	312.4	227.5	157.8	69.6

Source: *1990 Source Book of Health Insurance Data* (Washington, D.C.: Health Insurance Association of America), p. 35.
*Numbers may not add exactly due to rounding.

Table 7.4
Percent of Small Businesses Offering Health Insurance Coverage

Number of Employees	Percent
1–9	46
10–24	78
25–99	92
100–499	98

Source: *The Cincinnati Enquirer,* Monday February 18, 1991, p. D1.: Foster and Higgens & Co.; Small Business Administration.

totaled $87.6 billion, while individual and family premiums equaled $10.6 billion. Group plans differ from individual and family plans in that there is no preselection process except employment criteria, and premiums are a function of the coverage provided, the group's loss experience and the distribution of age and gender (the group's census). A single master contract covers the group. Each member receives a certificate and a description of the coverage. Group health coverage often extends beyond the member and covers the member's spouse and dependent children (until a certain age, such as 18). For large groups (typically larger than ten people) insurers do not require evidence of insurability due to the reliance on preemployment screening. (Some small to medium-size groups are written on a medical basis in exchange for lower premiums. Because the credibility of the group is low, however, there is more of a chance of adverse selection against the insurer.) As shown in Table 7.4, the larger the employer-based group, the more likely it is that health insurance is offered. For very large groups with stable and credible experience, self-insurance and experience-rated plans are attractive options. In **self-insurance** the group pays for all of its incurred eligible expenses. Often a third-party administrator (TPA) administers the plan. **Administrative services only (ASO)** contracts are used when the third party is an insurer. Under **experience rating** the plan's cost is a function of the group's past medical experience with an adjustment for expected trends.

Group plans provide approximately 90 percent of private health insurance, and a wide array of organizations form health insurance groups. However, because of adverse selection problems, the group must not be formed for the sole purpose of purchasing insurance.

Group health insurance plans may be paid solely by the group's sponsor, solely by the employee, or by both. Table 7.5 provides data on medical coverage cost during recent years.

People not covered under group plans include workers and their children or spouses who are not eligible under existing group plans, the unemployed and their children and spouses, part-time employees and people working where no group plan exists and people between jobs. Many of these people purchase individual or family plans, the premium for which depends on the scope of coverage. Other underwriting criteria include age, health status, occupation, hobbies and gender. As mentioned earlier, individual plans are more expensive than group plans,

Table 7.5
Employer Health Care Costs: Total Health Plan Cost per Employee

1985	$1,724
1986	1,857
1987	1,985
1988	2,354
1989	2,748
1990	3,217

Costs include employer and employee costs for indemnity plans, HMOs, dental plans and vision/hearing plans.
Source: *The Cincinnati Enquirer*, Monday February 18, 1991, p. D1.: Foster and Higgens & Co., Small Business Administration.

because each individual contract must be sold, serviced and underwritten, and premiums must be collected from each insured.

Private Health Insurance Providers

Currently there are four main sources of private medical insurance:

1. Life and health insurance companies
2. Blue Cross and Blue Shield organizations
3. Health maintenance organizations (HMOs)
4. Preferred provider organizations (PPOs)

In 1988 private insurance companies paid $83 billion in claims payments, Blue Cross and Blue Shield paid $48.2 billion, and the preferred provider (self-insured) and HMO plans jointly paid $62.8 billion.[3] The following paragraphs describe and compare these sources in detail: the difference between indemnity plans and managed care, the difference between cost shifting and cost containment, the traditional differences between indemnity plans and the coverage provided by Blue Cross and Blue Shield organizations and the characteristics of alternative health care delivery provided by HMOs and PPOs.

Indemnity Plans versus Managed Care

Private insurance companies have traditionally sold medical insurance that indemnifies the insured. An **indemnity plan**, as strictly defined, reimburses an insured for eligible expenses. As long as the expense is eligible for payment (subject to policy limits and contract terms), indemnity plans reimburse the insured for the covered services. Insurance companies selling pure indemnity plans find it impossible to control billed expenses to any great extent, and they have no direct say in quality-of-care issues, but the companies are required to pay the bills if they meet the contract's terms. Consequently most current financing arrangements and providers of health care attempt to manage care—that is, to contain costs and ensure the effectiveness of the medical care provided—in a variety of ways.

Managed care is defined as any plan that actively integrates the financing of health-related services and the delivery of health care. Managed care plans, by definition, actively interfere with the doctor-patient relationship in influencing the type of care, the provider of the care, how long the care is available, the amount paid for the care and where the care is to be delivered among other factors. Managed care plans typically are differentiated from pure indemnity plans by these characteristics:

- Financial incentives exist to encourage members to use health care providers identified by the plan and follow its procedures. The incentives greatly influence whom the patient is able to use, which presumably costs the health care provider less money.
- Managed care plans can have a formal and continuous quality assurance plan to monitor the appropriateness and in some cases adjust the type of health care provided.
- When managed care plans restrict their subscribers to a set of health care providers, there is a responsibility to deliver quality care. Therefore, managed care plans actively set specific quality standards for health care providers and monitor their performance.
- Managed care plans can involve contractual arrangements with selected health care providers or the hiring of employees to provide a comprehensive set of benefits to their members.

HMOs and PPOs are clear examples of managed health care. Because of many forces, the traditional notion of a pure indemnity plan is practically nonexistent. All modern organizations involved in financing or providing health care services actively make quality-of-care decisions and adopt their competitors' most effective cost containment, financing and health care delivery procedures to enhance their own effectiveness.

Cost Shifting versus Cost Containment. *Cost-shifting methods* typically do not modify the cost of the health care but redistribute the burden of paying for the services. *Cost-containment* techniques modify or control health care costs by making sure the services delivered are appropriate, effective and cost-efficient. Providers have had various levels of success using cost-containment techniques. Cost-shifting techniques used by providers of health insurance and care include the following:

- *Increasing or decreasing deductibles.* As deductibles increase, the patient must pay a higher amount or wait longer periods before the plan pays eligible expenses thus shifting costs to the insured or subscriber.
- *Changing coinsurance percentages.* As coinsurance or copayment percents increase, the insured or subscriber contributes a larger percent of each eligible dollar, shifting costs to the patient. If coinsurance or copayment percents decrease, a larger proportion shifts to the financing entity.
- *Changing reasonable and customary percentiles.* If insurers decrease the benchmark for reasonable and customary charges for eligible expenses, costs shift to the insured. The opposite is true for an increase in the reasonable and customary benchmark.
- *Changing coordination of benefits priorities.* The priority of payment may be modified by contracts when possible. For example, if an accident hap-

pens and several existing policies or plans exist, paying claims after all other collectible coverage would shift payment to other sources.
- *Changing employee contributions.* Employers may require higher contributions to the plan to shift some or all of the costs of coverage to the employee.
- *Modifying coverage.* Coverage can be modified to exclude expenses otherwise covered. For example, some plans may elect to exclude routine diagnostic tests from coverage, shifting these expenses to the insured.

By changing these health plan features, providers of care and insurance can shift costs and change the responsibility for using health care. Shifting costs, however, may cause the insured or subscriber to delay or forgo preventive or needed health care, which may increase health care costs later. Although cost shifting techniques may modify utilization patterns, they do not change the underlying cost of delivering health care.

Cost-containment techniques include these:

- *Preadmission testing.* Hospital stays are shortened by paying only for required tests before entering the hospital on an outpatient basis.
- *Case management.* A nurse (monitoring for the provider) precertifies treatment for a specified length of hospital stay. The nurse then works with the physician in investigating effective, less expensive procedures and alternatives to the hospital stay. Case management occurs on a prospective basis (before admittance), on a concurrent basis (during treatment) or on a retrospective basis (after the care is provided).
- *Retrospective or utilization review.* After the patient receives care, retrospective review or utilization review is employed to monitor the appropriateness and quality of care to spot unfavorable trends, problem areas and problem doctors. Utilization review may also be used to deny payment for unnecessary or unreasonable care.
- *Second and third opinions.* For some procedures, patients must get a second opinion to validate diagnosis and eliminate unnecessary procedures. Even though a second or third opinion adds to costs, the cost savings due to the reduction in unwarranted procedures may overshadow the expense.
- *Primary care physicians coordinating and managing care.* In this case one physician—the primary care physician—is responsible for the effectiveness of the patient's treatment and rehabilitation, thus focusing responsibility on the doctor.
- *Covering outpatient surgery.* Providing surgery as an outpatient reduces cost by avoiding overnight stays.
- *Home health care, hospice care, extended care, skilled nursing care coverage.* Appropriate care provided in the home, in a **hospice**, in an extended-care facility or in a skilled nursing home is less expensive than providing the care in a hospital.
- *Encouraging the use of generic drugs.* Providers reimburse a higher percentage for the costs of generic drugs compared to name brands. The result reduces the overall cost of prescription medicines.

These cost-containment methods reduce the cost of health care, provide more effective health care or provide similar care at a lower cost.

Blue Cross and Blue Shield Organizations versus Indemnity Plans

Early prepaid hospital plans provided subscribers a limited number of days in the hospital. During the Depression individual hospitals offered this service for a monthly fee to reduce uncollectible bills. The plans expanded geographically in the 1930s because of the influence and control of the American Hospital Association. The American Hospital Association set standards for these **Blue Cross** hospital plans. Based on the success of the Blue Cross plans, physicians, through the American Medical Association, started **Blue Shield** plans. Currently more than 50 Blue Cross and Blue Shield plans exist in the United States. Blue Cross plans provide for eligible hospital services, while Blue Shield plans provide physician services. The need for better organization and coordination among the plans induced a series of mergers resulting in the consolidation of Blue Cross and Blue Shield management in 1982.

Form and Type of Benefits. Health care is said to be provided on a service basis by the Blue Cross and Blue Shield plans. For example, a Blue Cross plan may provide 120 days of hospital room and board. Blue Cross delivers service through contractual arrangements with hospitals and reimburses them for covered services on a predetermined annual basis. If the service's cost increases, the patient receives the service while paying no extra cost. Not all health care providers have a contractual relationship with a Blue Cross plan. If the subscriber uses such services, Blue Cross pays up to the maximum set for nonplan providers. When patients use uncovered services, the patient pays the cost. For example, if the plan pays for only a semiprivate room, the subscriber can pay additional amounts for private accommodations.

Under Blue Shield plans participating physicians are reimbursed for services provided on a *usual, customary, and reasonable (UCR)* basis. Participating physicians agree to accept the UCR payment for full payment. When nonparticipating physicians are used, the patient is responsible for the difference between the amount billed and the UCR amount.

Traditional private insurance companies operating on an indemnity basis reimburse insureds for eligible medical expenses. With private insurance coverage many contracts specify a dollar maximum for services, and the consumer pays the excess. If health costs increase, the insured pays any uncovered expenses. Because of competition and the need for inflation protection in health insurance contracts, many private insurance contracts now pay physicians on a UCR basis.

Regulation and Taxation. Blue Cross and Blue Shield plans are typically incorporated as nonprofit organizations. Some states consider Blue Cross and Blue Shield organizations to be charitable or benevolent because of their community involvement and their method of rating coverage. In these cases no state premium or income taxation applies. Prior to passage of the Tax Reform Act of 1986, Blue Cross and Blue Shield plans paid no federal income tax. Stock and mutual insurance companies argued the Blues enjoyed an unfair cost advantage in providing the coverage. And because of the need to raise revenue on the federal level, part of the Tax Reform Act of 1986 eliminated the federal income tax exemption.

Private insurance companies are also incorporated. Whether they are incorporated as a stock or a mutual company, they pay federal income and state premium and income taxes.

Geographic Territory. Blue Cross and Blue Shield plans are set up primarily to operate in a certain territory. Several plans can be found in a state, and some plans overlap their territories. Blue Cross and Blue Shield plans have procedures to handle services outside the territory. Private insurance companies have no comparable territorial restriction and are thought to have a marketing advantage because they pay eligible expenses wherever the service is provided. (Some territorial restrictions may apply to eliminate worldwide coverage.)

Community Rating versus Experience Rating. A foundation of the prepaid Blue Cross and Blue Shield system is *community rating*. The Blues have traditionally used the community rating approach to setting premiums, which is one reason some states have favored the Blues with the charitable tax status. The community rating scheme results in insuring a large number of people at a standard low cost while ignoring traditional rating differences. The community rating system charges all subscribers the same rate regardless of their health status or whether the coverage is provided through a group or an individual plan.

Private insurance companies use an individual's characteristics, including health status, to rate individual health insurance contracts. Private insurance companies began using *experience rating* for insuring large groups. As mentioned earlier, insurers price the coverage based on the group's loss experience. The higher degree of credibility of larger groups allows insurers to predict more accurately the group's loss experience. Groups within the rating community with better-than-average experience would migrate to private insurers and pay a lower price. Because of this fact, Blue Cross and Blue Shield organizations use experience rating for large employer-based groups. Blue Cross and Blue Shield currently use community rating for individual coverage and smaller groups not having sufficient size to lend sufficient credibility to their experience.

Alternative Sources of Health Care

The increasing cost of delivering health care and the traditional emphasis on cure instead of prevention have led people to seek better health care delivery systems. **Health maintenance organizations (HMOs)** and **preferred provider organizations (PPOs)** provide health care in a nontraditional manner. Table 7.6 illustrates the revolutionary extent of the change. In 1982 the traditional fee-for-service or indemnity plans covered 95 percent of the privately covered population. Estimates indicate they will provide only 16 percent in 1992. In the same period the combined total HMO and PPO share has grown from 4.5 percent to 54 percent. Traditional fee-for-service insurers who have become involved in managing their insureds' health care have grown from zero in 1982 to 31 percent in 1990. The total market for pure fee-for-service insurers is shrinking because the health care community and employers are more proactive in cost-containment measures. A

Table 7.6
Private Insurance Plans—Percent of Population

	1982	1988	1989	1990	1991	1992
HMO	4.5	16.0	18.0	20.0	22.0	23.0
PPO	0.0	17.0	20.5	24.0	27.5	31.0
POS	0.5	0.6	1.6	2.6	4.5	6.6
M-FFS	0.0	30.0	35.0	31.0	26.0	23.0
T-FFS	95.0	36.4	24.9	22.9	19.9	16.4

1990, 1991, 1992 estimated.
HMO = health maintenance organization; POS = point-of-service plan; PPO = preferred provider organization; M-FFS = managed fee for service; T-FFS = traditional fee for service.
Source: Joseph S. Mallory, "Strategies for the 1990s," *Best's Review (Life/Health Edition)*, April 1990, pp. 36ff.

point-of-service (POS) plan, discussed later, can be classified as a type of HMO. In this chapter HMOs and PPOs are examined.

Health Maintenance Organizations. Health maintenance organizations are based on a system of prepaid comprehensive medical care for a certain geographic area. Prepayment of dues to the HMO allows members to use the facilities on an unlimited basis. Usually there is a small fee for each visit to control overutilization. As noted, the concept of prepaying for health-related services is not new and can be traced to the 1930s. The Health Maintenance Act of 1973 (with amendments in 1976) dramatically increased the interest in HMOs. The act authorized federal grants and loans to establish HMOs as long as they met certain benefit requirements. In the early 1980s funding for grants and loans terminated. One mandate of the Health Maintenance Act of 1973 is *dual choice*, and much of the growth of HMOs stems from this requirement. Dual choice requires certain employers to offer an HMO option in addition to their regular health plan if a federally qualified HMO services the employer's geographic area. The dual choice provision of the 1973 HMO act will no longer apply after October 1995.[4]

In 1989 a total of 591 HMOs covered over 34 million members.[5] Many of the HMOs are currently managed by traditional health insurers. Insurers have organized HMOs in an attempt to control costs and provide the pooling process for the funding mechanism. HMOs are typically organized in one of two ways—referred to as a group model or an individual model. Point-of-service plans also exist.

In a *group model*, a physician medical group contracts with the HMO that is responsible for covering subscribers for health care. The group is responsible for providing comprehensive services, and if the service cannot be performed by the group, services are performed at an associated hospital. This plan is typically referred to as a *closed-panel HMO* because the subscribers must use the plan's physicians. In return for the service subscribers prepay a capitation amount for the comprehensive care. Because HMOs receive a fixed capitation payment and expenses are a function of utilization and poor health, the group plan is at risk for any losses the plan incurs. The *staff model* is a variation of the group model. In a staff model the HMO employs salaried physicians to provide the subscribers with health care. A *network model* HMO contracts with more than one independent group to provide health care services to its members.

In the *individual model* the HMO contracts with several independent individual physicians or associations of individual physicians (*independent practice association*). They usually have arrangements with more than one HMO. In these organizations physicians contract with the HMO to provide service at an agreed-on price. Physicians practice out of their own office and serve both HMO and non-HMO patients. Even though the physician is paid on a fee-for-service basis or on a capitation basis (depending on the arrangement), cost control and preventive health care are still emphasized. Because the HMO actually receives the capitation payment, the HMO primarily assumes the risk of poor results.

Point-of-service HMOs (also called *open-ended HMOs*) provide enrollees the option to choose providers outside the HMO plan at the time of the required service. There are various financial incentives to discourage the use of non-HMO providers.

Newer employer group point-of-service plans require the employee to select among various options, including an indemnity plan with high deductibles and co-payments. Financial incentives encourage the use of the HMO plan. Employees must elect annually whether they want the HMO plan or the indemnity plan.

Preferred Provider Organizations. Preferred provider organizations are similar to HMOs. However, PPOs contract with an employer group to provide service at reduced fees. To encourage employees to use the PPO, the employer increases the percent of payment from, say, 80 percent (normal in indemnity contracts) to 100 percent. For example, a PPO might charge $500 and a non-PPO $650 for the same procedure; the employer pays $500 if the PPO is used but only $520 if the non-PPO is used, meaning the insured pays $130 for using the non-PPO.

There is some concern that PPOs will increase utilization to make up for reduced fees. To reduce this fear, PPOs assume some financial risk to control service utilization. Many hospitals set up PPOs to provide health care to employee groups. Premiums are paid to the PPO, the services are provided at the agreed-on price and the PPO (the hospital) is at financial risk if costs increase or there is inefficient health care.

The differences between traditional and nontraditional health care delivery systems are becoming less clear, because each, in an attempt to improve efficiency and reduce cost, borrows effective features from the others. In fact the classical distinctions rarely exist in practice today. Therefore future managed care delivery systems, including traditional indemnity and Blue Cross/Blue Shield plans, may become indistinguishable. Alternative health care delivery probably is here to stay, with more innovations to appear. If HMOs and other nontraditional health care systems provide more of the very expensive services (including 24-hour nursing care and critical care units), newly designed health care delivery methods may provide basic care more economically.

Health Insurance Contracts

Regardless of the number of people covered (individual, group or family), the underwriting criteria used (medical or nonmedical), the benefits and the plan's fi-

Table 7.7
Accidental Death and Dismemberment Schedule

Loss	Amount Paid
Life	Principal Sum
Both hands and feet	Principal Sum
Sight in both eyes	Principal Sum
One hand and one foot	Principal Sum
One hand or one foot and sight in one eye	Principal Sum
One arm or leg	2/3 Principal Sum
One hand or foot	1/2 Principal Sum
Sight in one eye	1/3 Principal Sum

nances, the health insurance contract states that payments will be made or services provided for eligible expenses. However, this simple statement masks the complexity of the health insurance product. Health plans vary depending on the covered losses, the perils covered, the eligible expenses, the amount and level of benefits and the exclusions to the contract among other features.

Covered Losses

Health insurance contracts can cover losses of income, pay for medical expenses or pay predetermined dollar amounts upon certain events. Income can be lost or decreased due to a mental, physical or medical impairment. If such a loss occurs, lost spendable income can be replaced partially or fully by disability income coverage. (Life insurance contracts reimburse income losses by using disability income riders or pay premium payments with the waiver-of-premium rider.)

Expense losses occur when a person incurs necessary medical expenses, typically billed by a hospital or physician. Health insurance contracts typically reimburse people for these expenses as long as they are reasonable and necessary and not otherwise excluded. Deductibles typically apply to reduce the loss amount paid by the insurer.

Health insurance contracts also can make indemnity payments such as payments arising out of accidental death or a dismemberment or by scheduling a set dollar amount per day in a hospital for a maximum number of days. Accidental death and dismemberment riders pay a scheduled amount for an accidental death and for combinations of accidental loss of limbs and sight. The maximum amount paid for the most serious loss (death) is called the *principal sum*. For less serious losses the contract pays part of the principal sum. Some contracts pay a multiple of the principal sum for specified accidental deaths. A typical schedule for an accidental death and dismemberment rider is shown in Table 7.7.

Perils Covered

Health insurance contracts cover either the peril of accident or sickness or both. The peril of accident occurs when an unforeseen event creates or contributes to a sudden injury. Covered amounts differ among contracts. Some accident contracts schedule benefits similar to accidental death and dismemberment riders.

Accident policies also provide loss-of-income payments and may pay for hospital, nursing, surgical or other medical costs up to an aggregate amount or provide an amount per day for a specified number of days. Other sources of accident insurance include travel accident insurance and double-indemnity (multiple) life insurance riders.

The peril of sickness is usually coupled with the peril of accident to provide coverage for both. Even though insurers use the term *comprehensive* to describe a contract covering the perils of accident and sickness, not all illnesses or injuries are covered. Exclusions exist because coverage is available elsewhere, the costs of covering the loss would be prohibitive or certain types of behavior should be discouraged. Accident-only contracts are less expensive than sickness and accident contracts. Because of the wide variation in coverage and provisions, those seeking health insurance coverage should not base their selection on cost alone.

Basic Medical Expense Plans

Basic medical expense plans fall into three categories based on the type of eligible expense—hospital room and board, surgery and doctors' visits. A major medical plan is a comprehensive plan combining all three.

Hospitalization

Hospitalization contracts cover eligible expenses arising out of hospital room and board, nursing care, laboratory fees, pharmaceuticals, supplies and the use of an operating room. Benefit provisions in hospitalization contracts vary. One approach provides payment after a waiting period (deductible) of six or seven days. The contract then pays up to X dollars per day for a maximum of Y days. Shorter waiting periods, higher daily limits or longer benefit periods increase the premium.

☐ **Example**

Sue Smith purchases a policy paying up to $300 per day for a maximum of 120 days after a six-day waiting period. If charges for her stay exceed $300 per day for 12 days, $1,800 [300 × (12 − 6)] is paid by the insurer.

Some contracts provide benefits on a fixed-amount basis and pay a specific dollar amount (for example, $100 per day) regardless of the amount billed. Contracts can provide various benefit periods, including 60, 90 and 120 days after a waiting period. Other contracts provide service instead of indemnity payments. As noted earlier, Blue Cross and Blue Shield plans provide services to their insureds, unlike indemnity plans. Traditional insurance companies provide "reasonable and customary" payments for the care provided; however, dollar limitations may apply.

Surgical Contracts

Surgical contracts provide coverage for the costs of surgical procedures. Some specify a maximum amount of coverage for a representative group of surgical procedures. They typically exclude various types of surgery, including elective or experimental procedures—for example, a mechanical heart implant. (Organ transplants that are not considered experimental are generally covered under health insurance plans. Experimental transplants are generally not covered because the cost of medical research would be borne by the insurers. Transplants having proven effectiveness are considered therapeutic and are paid if the procedure is covered by the contract.) The stated amount is the most the insurer will pay for one procedure. When the patient needs two procedures at the same time, the more expensive required one determines the payment amount. *Surgical schedules* identify a maximum dollar amount for the most difficult procedure and provide a representative list of other procedures and their reimbursement rate. (Some surgical schedules grade the expense of the procedure by using an index.) For example, a $1,000 surgical schedule pays $1,000 for the most difficult operation, and all other procedures are proportionately less. Modern surgical contracts, however, offer coverage on a reasonable-cost basis similar to the newer hospitalization contracts, which provides a measure of inflation-proofing for the insured. Because of the reasonable-cost approach under these surgical contracts, there is no need to schedule representative procedures or maintain different maximum levels of reimbursement.

Regular Medical

Regular medical contracts cover nonsurgical physicians' bills. Specifically these contracts typically pay for physicians' visits wherever furnished. However, some contracts restrict benefits for in-hospital visits. Many variations of benefit payments exist. The contract can pay a maximum amount per visit, pay for visits after a specific number (a deductible) or limit the number of visits per period.

Major Medical

Major medical contracts pay for almost all necessary medical treatment, such as hospital charges, surgical and doctors' bills, laboratory fees, nursing care and pharmaceuticals. The broad definition of an eligible medical expense makes the major medical contract attractive to the buyer. This coverage is written with high policy limits ranging from $250,000 to $1 million. Very few internal limits exist, and the policy usually pays on a reasonable and customary-care basis. **Deductibles** and participation payments encourage the responsible use of the major medical contract. These provisions eliminate the cost of paying small claims and try to control overutilization of medical services.

The major medical deductible usually applies on a calendar year or on a contract year basis. Some major medical contracts charge one deductible for each illness or accident. If the deductible is on a calendar or contract year basis, the insured may pay multiple deductibles for the same accident or illness.

☐ **Example**

If Roger Walton becomes ill one month before the contract's anniversary, Roger will pay the deductible (the policy has a contract year deductible) for the last month of the year and then will pay the deductible again for the new contract year. If the policy has a per-case deductible, Roger will pay the deductible only once for each accident or illness.

Participation clauses in medical expense contracts require the insurer to pay 75 to 80 percent of all eligible expenses after meeting the deductible. This means the insured pays the remaining balance of all costs. Many insurance companies put a cap on the participation provision. They recognize that 20 percent of a $50,000 medical bill, for example, can be financially ruinous (0.20 × $50,000 = $10,000). Participation caps can be on a case, calendar year or contract year basis. A contract may state that after the insured pays $1,000 ("out of pocket") the contract will pay 100 percent of all eligible expenses. Currently the most common copayment percentage is 80 percent. However, as medical costs increase, the percentage will decline, shifting more of the medical cost to the insured. Major medical plans can be combined with the basic medical plans to provide various levels of medical reimbursement for the insured.

☐ **Example**

If a comprehensive medical expense plan paying 80 percent of all covered expenses after a $1,000 deductible is combined with a hospitalization plan paying $100 per day after a six-day waiting period, some of the expense not paid under the comprehensive plan is paid by the hospitalization plan. Consider the combination of the two plans while incurring $6,000 of medical bills in a nine-day hospital stay.

Comprehensive Plan

Medical Charges	$6,000
Deductible	1,000
	$5,000

$5,000 × .8 = $4,000 insurer pays
$5,000 × .2 = $1,000 insured pays

Hospitalization Plan
$100 per day is paid for three days after six-day waiting period, totaling $300.

Insured Pays in Total:

Deductible	$1,000
Participation	1,000
Hospital Plan	−300
Total	$1,700

Other Health Care Products

Many insurance companies market products for either a certain segment of society or to pay for expenses normally excluded under traditional products. These products include vision care, dental care, prescription drug reimbursement, nursing home and hospice care and Medicare gap filler coverage.

Vision contracts pay for eye examinations and glasses but do not pay for injury to eyes by accident or disease that impairs vision. These costs are covered under accident and sickness contracts.

Dental plans pay for preventive and other forms of dental care. These plans typically have a low yearly expense limit and encourage preventive maintenance (e.g., two cleanings per year) by not imposing deductibles and participation percents for routine treatment. For other forms of treatment the plans pay 65 to 80 percent of the cost. Some plans include payment for limited amounts of orthodontia.

Prescription drug plans pay the cost of drugs prescribed by a physician. The insured usually pays a small fee when filling each prescription. The need for the plan is rationalized by the fact that conventional plans do not cover all drug costs. Hospitalization plans pay drug costs when the insured is hospitalized. Major medical plans pay for drug costs in or out of the hospital. However, if deductibles or participation clauses apply, recovery may be limited.

Nursing home care and hospice care are being provided more frequently under individual and group health insurance plans. Nursing care provides coverage during periods of convalescence. It is less expensive to provide nursing care during this period than to allow the patient to remain in the hospital. Hospice care is medical care for the terminally ill. Hospitals and institutions have begun to provide hospice care in an environment designed to allow the terminally ill to live out their final days with dignity and provide coverage for pain and symptom management. Many health care insurance providers recognize this need and find it is less expensive to provide hospice rather than hospital care.

Medicare gap filler policies pay for selected medical expenses not covered by Medicare. A more complete analysis of coverage under the Medicare program and a more complete discussion of Medicare gap filler contracts are found in Chapter 8.

Mental health contracts place severe restrictions on the amount and type of coverage. These restrictions often involve higher and separate deductibles, fewer eligible outpatient and inpatient days and lower lifetime benefit maximums.

Long-term care (LTC) policies provide benefits when a person no longer is able to perform the activities of daily living. There is much concern over the cost of partial or full custodial services for the young and old alike. Long-term care contracts are new, and therefore the quality of coverage and the prices vary considerably. Because of the growing size of the older population and the importance of long-term care to our society, LTC coverage is discussed in detail in Chapter 8.

Cancellation and Renewability

A major and important feature of a health insurance contract, other than the coverage provided, is the contract's renewability feature. Depending on the contract's renewability clause, the insured may have no right to continue the contract. On the other hand, the insured may have the contract's renewal and price guaranteed regardless of health status. The provisions controlling renewability can be classified as cancelable, guaranteed renewable and noncancelable. (Term health insurance contracts also exist and pay claims during a stated period of time with no provision for the insured to continue the contract. These contracts are not used in the ordinary course of holistic financial planning. One example is travel accident insurance.

A **cancelable** health insurance contract may be canceled at any time by the insured or insurer. The insurance company can change the policy coverage or its price by canceling the contract and subsequently offering a new contract. This clause offers no guarantees for the insured. If the insured's health becomes seriously impaired before cancellation, new insurance will be expensive or unavailable, and any preexisting conditions already treated or diagnosed may be eliminated from future coverage.

A variation of the cancelable contract allows the insurance company to withhold renewal upon the policy's anniversary but does not allow changes during the policy period. This is an **optionally renewable** contract. A second variation of this is a **conditionally renewable** contract in which the insured may renew until a stated date. However, the insurer may decline to renew based on any conditions stated in the contract. Because many people are critical of the health insurance industry's right to cancel or not renew a health insurance policy, many states restrict that right. In such states valid reasons for cancellation include fraud, discontinuance of a whole insurance class and overinsurance (moral hazard).

With a **guaranteed renewable** contract insurers must renew if the insured pays the premium. These contracts guarantee renewability typically until age 65. Other ages apply, including renewal for life. While renewal is guaranteed in these contracts, the premium is not. However, the premium for an individual may not be changed unless the premium for the whole insured class changes. In other words, individual insureds may not be medically underwritten at anniversaries.

A **noncancelable** contract guarantees both renewal and premiums. The insurer must renew if the premium is paid, and the amount of the premium cannot change. The guarantee usually extends only until a certain age (for example, age 65). However, noncancelable contracts do not protect the insured from all changes. If the insured lapses and reinstates a contract, contract conditions and premiums may be changed. Due to the inability to predict accurately future increases in medical expenses, premiums are higher than for contracts with stricter renewability clauses. Consequently some professionals recommend the purchase of a health insurance contract with the guaranteed renewable feature; coverage is guaranteed, and the prices more accurately reflect health care costs. Others would argue that a noncancelable contract is better because the risk of any cost increase rests with the insurer.

Regardless of the level of guarantee (and effectively the cancellation clause), most states require at least a ten-day examination or inspection period. An insured who does not want to keep the contract after having a chance to review the policy's terms will receive a full refund.

Common Uniform Contract Provisions

The *Uniform Individual Accident and Sickness Policy Provisions* (referred to as the *uniform provisions*) were drafted by the National Association of Insurance Commissioners (NAIC) and have continually evolved since 1911. The uniform provisions apply to individual accident and sickness policies, and all states require them with some variation. The uniform provisions do *not* apply to life insurance, workers' compensation, reinsurance, group coverage and disability income or waiver-of-premium riders.

Entire Contract and Changes

This provision states that the written policy, its application and its endorsements constitute the entire agreement. No other documents or unattached applications may be incorporated by reference to modify the contract's terms. In addition, any changes must be written and are valid only if the company agrees to them. Agents may not waive or modify the terms of the written contract.

Grace Period

The grace period allows the policy to remain in force for a certain period while the premium is past due. Typically states impose a minimum of 7 days for weekly premium policies, 10 days for monthly, and 31 days for annual premium policies. If the premium remains unpaid after the grace period expires (and proper notification has occurred), the policy terminates. In a cancelable or an optionally renewable contract, the law balances the insurer's right to cancel with the insured's need and right for proper notification.

Reinstatement

If the policy lapses after the grace period, the insured may reinstate the contract under certain conditions. Typically the insured must submit an application with the past-due premium. The insurer then issues a conditional receipt pending a reinstatement decision by the company's underwriters. Under the uniform provisions reinstatement is automatically assumed if the insurer fails to respond within 45 days. Reinstatement also effectively occurs if the insurer accepts the missed premiums with no other requirements. Restrictions usually apply to the reinstated coverage. The contract provides coverage for accidents occurring after the reinstatement and to any sickness after a waiting period such as ten days.

Time Limit on Certain Defenses or Incontestable Clause

Health insurance contracts contain either a time limit on certain defenses or an incontestable clause limiting an insurer's right to contest the contract. A **time limit on certain defenses** clause provides a two- or three-year period after the contract starts in which the contract cannot be contested except for fraudulent misstatements. If an **incontestable clause** exists in the contract, claims are paid after the indicated time even if there were fraudulent misstatements at the time of the application. (Some insurers eliminate the contestable period while the insured is disabled.)

Claims

The insured must file a claim notice within a certain time. There are also time limits for the insurer to supply claim forms, for the insured to submit proof of loss and for the insurer to pay the claim. Written notice of the claim usually must be filed with the insurer or agent within 20 days of the loss or "as soon as practical." Claim forms must be supplied within 15 days of request. Proof of a disability loss must be submitted within 90 days after a benefit period begins. These time limits are, however, modified based on ability, competency and reasonableness of the requirement. Insurers pay claims soon after proof of loss is submitted, with an allowance for proper investigation and validation of the claim.

Physical Exam and Autopsy

Insurers retain the right to examine an insured as often as necessary to determine the claim's legitimacy. Insurers cannot, however, use this clause to harass the insured during the claim investigation process. In the case of death claims insurers may require an autopsy to settle cause-of-loss disputes.

Legal Actions

By contract legal action against the insurer cannot begin earlier than 60 days or later than three years after the insured submits the proof of loss. This provision provides sufficient time for the insurer to process and investigate the claim and for the insured to commence legal action.

Change of Beneficiary

Written notification to the insurer must be made to change a beneficiary identified in the contract. Similar rules apply to the beneficiary designation found in life insurance contracts, discussed in Chapter 10.

Optional Contract Provisions

Health insurance contracts may contain any of the following optional provisions, varying by state. As in the uniform provisions, clauses considered optional must conform to the minimum intent of state law. Provisions may be broadened to benefit the consumer.

Change in Occupation and Illegal Occupation

Benefits can be reduced if the insured is injured or becomes sick after assuming a more hazardous occupation than declared on the application. Premiums may be lowered if the insured changes to a less hazardous occupation. Benefits are not paid when an insured is injured while engaged in an illegal occupation or during the commission of a felony.

Misstatement of Age

If the insured misstates his or her age, benefit amounts change according to the method used in life insurance. Benefits are adjusted upward if the true age is overstated and downward if understated. The time limit on certain defenses and the incontestable clause do not bar this benefit adjustment even after the indicated time period.

Intoxication and Narcotics

Claims resulting from or attributed to the use of narcotics or intoxicants will result in denial. This provision does not apply to prescription medicines taken at the direction of a physician.

Unpaid Premiums

If premiums are due at the time of a claim, benefits equal to the amount owed may be withheld.

Chapter 7   Medical Expense and Disability Insurance

Cancellation

As noted earlier, the insurer's right to cancel may be restricted by the type of coverage purchased. When cancelable, five days' notice of cancellation is typically required. Premiums are returned pro rata if the insurer cancels. If the insured cancels, premiums are returned on a short-rate basis. (On a pro rata basis the proportionate unearned premium is returned. For example, if the premium is $100 and 3 months' premium is earned, $75 [9/12 × $100] is returned on a pro rata basis. On a short-rate basis 85 to 90 percent of $75 will be returned, depending on state law and company practice.)

Common Medical Expense Contract Exclusions

Medical expense contracts do not cover all possible medical expenses. Exclusions may limit the extent of coverage or the types of eligible expenses. The most common exclusion eliminates care or treatment arising out of **preexisting conditions**—those diagnosed or treated before the inception of the contract. When an insured discloses a preexisting condition, companies choose to offer the contract with or without an exclusion and at an increased price. When expenses for that condition are excluded, selection against the insurance company is reduced. Typically, insurers pay for preexisting conditions if the insured has not been treated within 6 to 12 months before the start of the policy. People should not benefit when they buy insurance to cover expected losses.

Also commonly excluded are medical expenses insured by other sources such as workers' compensation benefits, veteran or armed forces benefits. Insurers exclude self-inflicted intentional injury, elective cosmetic surgery, experimental surgery, dental and vision care, extended and nursing home care and chemical substance abuse. Insurers cover some of these in other special contracts.

Tax Treatment of Individual Health Insurance

Individual health insurance premiums and unreimbursed losses are deductible if the taxpayer itemizes deductions. Currently only amounts in excess of 7.5 percent of adjusted gross income reduce taxable income, but be aware that tax law changes frequently.

Disability Income

Disability income contracts replace income if a person cannot perform the duties of his or her occupation. Providers of disability income coverage include private insurers, the federal government, state and local governments, employers, trade associations and union groups. Some individual coverage arises from riders attached to life insurance contracts, including the *waiver-of-premium rider* and the *disability income rider* (*see* Chapters 3 and 4). Disability income provided under Social Security is discussed in Chapter 14. Business uses of disability income products (key employee life and disability, business continuation, overhead disability coverage and salary continuation plans) are discussed in Chapter 20. This chapter focuses on individual disability income contracts purchased from private insurers.

Table 7.8
Probability of One Person Being Disabled Prior to Age 65 (Percent)

Age	Size of Group		
	One	Two	Three
25	27%	60%	79%
30	25	59	77
35	24	57	75
40	23	54	73
45	21	51	69
50	18	46	64
55	15	38	55

Source: 1985 Commissioner's Disability Table. Unisex rates. Disability lasting at least 90 days. Includes all occupation classes.

Disability Data

Table 7.8 shows the probability of one person becoming disabled out of a group of one, two or three people. The likelihood that a disabled person will remain disabled for various periods is presented in Table 7.9. For example, out of a group of three people age 45, the probability of one person becoming disabled prior to age 65 for at least 90 days is 69 percent. Note that, as the age of initial disability increases, so does the probability of experiencing a longer disability.

The loss of earned income caused by a disability can be large. Consider a person earning $30,000 in a year. If a disability that stops all earned income occurs, $150,000 will be lost in five years. This calculation does not include time value of money considerations, taxes, missed increases in salary or any expense increases due to medical, rehabilitative or other support expenses. Potentially the disability can be lifelong.

Individual Disability Income Products

No standard disability income contract exists, and purchasers will find wide variations in contract terms, definitions and coverage. Disability income contracts are more complex than life insurance contracts, and for many people they are more difficult to understand. Individual disability income products vary according to the perils covered, the renewal guarantee, the length of the waiting period, the definition of disability and the benefit amount among other factors.

Table 7.9
Probability of Remaining Disabled After a 90-Day Disability (Percent)

Age When Disabled	One Additional Year	Two Additional Years	Five Additional Years
25	18%	6%	5%
30	20	8	7
35	20	11	9
40	22	14	12
45	27	17	15
50	30	22	17
55	35	26	20

Source: 1985 Commissioner's Disability Table. Unisex Rates. Includes all occupation classes.

Perils Covered

All insurance contracts identify a set of insured perils to define precisely when losses must be paid. In life insurance contracts the peril is death. Disability income contracts cover the perils of accident or accident and sickness combined. The perils covered and their definition are one factor that determines the quality of coverage. Definitions of accident and sickness in disability income contracts can provide severe interpretation problems compared to the definition of death in life insurance contracts. An *accident* is an unusual, unexpected and unforeseen event. However, some disability insurance contracts specify the peril either as bodily injury by **accidental means** or as **accidental bodily injury**—an important distinction. Under an accidental means insuring agreement, disability income pays benefits when the *means* to the incident were totally unforeseen and unexpected. If the injury is a *result* of intentionally doing something, then the injury is not compensable. This is opposite of the accidental injury insuring agreement, where payment is made for an injury resulting from an intentional act.

☐ **Example**

> Harvey Walker professionally races cars. Loss of income arising from a racing accident would not be paid under an *accidental means* contract because the means to the injury was intentional. However, disability income would be paid under the *accidental injury* definition because the injury (result), even though foreseeable and possible, was unintentional.

Because of the legal doctrine of *reasonable expectations* and the difficulty of separating and interpreting accidental means from accidental injury definitions, many courts have broadened the definition of accidental means to include accidental injury. Most modern contracts, because of court interpretation and competition, provide accidental injury coverage, which avoids these complications.

When the contract is issued for accidental disability only, insurers typically require the accident to be independent of any other cause. For example, if Jessica Upson has a heart attack and falls down a flight of stairs and is physically injured as a result of the fall, disability income will not be paid because the contributing factor is medical. Regardless of whether the injury was unintentional, the peril insured (sickness or heart attack) is not covered. Following is an example of a very broad insuring agreement found in a disability income contract covering disability income caused by the perils of accident and sickness. (This and other contracts quoted use the term *he* to mean both he and she):

Benefits are provided for the insured's total or partial disability only if:

- the insured becomes disabled while this policy is in force;
- the insured is under the care of a licensed physician other than himself during the time he is disabled;
- the disability results from an accident or sickness; and
- the disability is not excluded.

When sickness coverage exists, disability benefits are paid if the sickness starts during the policy period. This requirement excludes already existing or preexisting conditions. Many times insurers impose a probationary period during which no sickness-related disability benefits are paid (a presumption of no prior illness). If the insured is not treated for the sickness during this probationary period, subsequent disabilities arising from the untreated ailments are covered. This period is intended to reduce adverse selection. People who feel they will become sick will tend to seek coverage, and the probationary period reduces the claims that are likely to occur. This requirement can cause considerable controversy when a sickness or disease manifests itself after the policy inception, but the condition actually existed prior to that date. As long as there is no actual deception by the insured, the disability should be paid. Following is an example of a provision found in a disability income contract that excludes undisclosed causes of disability that occurred two years before the date of issue. Underwriters decide at inception if disclosed accidents and sickness will be excluded or covered by the contract.

> There will be no benefits for a disability or loss that: (1) starts within two years after the Date of Issue; and (2) results from an accident that occurred or from a sickness that appeared within two years before the Date of Issue and was not disclosed in the application. A sickness is considered to have appeared if it would have caused a prudent person to seek medical attention.

Renewal Guarantees

Disability income contracts use essentially the same levels of renewal guarantees found in the medical expense contracts discussed earlier. The following clause illustrates a noncancelable guarantee until age 65. The contract is renewed as long as the insured pays the premium until the anniversary date after the insured's 65th birthday. The terms of the contract and its premium cannot be changed by the company during that period.

> This disability income policy is guaranteed renewable upon timely payment of the premiums to the first policy anniversary after the Insured's 65th birthday and, during that period, can neither be canceled nor have its terms or premium changed by the Company.

Following the anniversary date after the insured turns age 65, this particular policy is conditionally renewable to age 75. The terms of the contract and the premium may be changed, and renewal is conditional on the terms of the contract.

Waiting Periods

Disability income contracts impose a waiting period between the occurrence of a covered disability and the receipt of benefits. Common waiting periods are 60, 120 and 181 days or longer. Waiting periods reduce costs by eliminating payment for short-term disabilities that would otherwise be payable by the contract. The waiting period also reduces the moral hazard exhibited by people who exaggerate impairments to receive coverage. Employers frequently cover short-term disabilities (during the waiting period) through salary continuation or sick leave plans and other short-term disability income coverage or occupational injury benefits.

Definition of Disability

Defining the term *disability* is extremely important in delineating available coverage. Disability may be defined generously or quite narrowly. Many versions of the definition of *disability* exist, but only a few are presented here to illustrate the wide variation found in disability income contracts. First, however, note that some disability income contracts pay only for nonoccupational causes. Other contracts pay for both occupational and nonoccupational disability but reduce benefits by the recovery from other sources such as workers' compensation, Social Security or occupational disease laws.

The "inability to perform all duties of the insured's own occupation" is a generous definition of disability. Under these terms, if the insured cannot perform *every* duty of his or her *own* occupation, a total disability exists. A second level of disability provides for disability payments if a person is unable to perform "the principal duties in his or her own occupation." A stricter definition refers to the "inability to perform any occupation the insured is reasonably fitted for by education, training and experience." This means, for example, if a surgeon loses the ability to operate because of a nervous disorder but can engage in other occupations such as consulting or teaching, total disability does not exist. A fourth definition is the "inability to perform the duties of any gainful employment." Literally interpreted, if a disabled surgeon could solicit products over the phone, no total disability exists. The following is an example of the definition of disability using the "own occupation" wording:

> The Insured is totally disabled when he is unable to perform the principal duties of his occupation. After the initial period, the Insured is totally disabled when he is unable to perform the principal duties of his occupation and not gainfully employed in any occupation.

By this definition, after the initial period defined by the contract, insureds remain disabled if they still cannot perform the principal duties of their occupation *and are not gainfully employed*. Under this definition insureds can actually choose not to work in another occupation if able. Contrast this definition to the "inability to perform any occupation the insured is reasonably fitted for by education, training and experience." Under this definition, if the insured is able to work, no disability payments are made.

Because of competitive pressures and the need for a more suitable product, many insurance companies use a combination of these two definitions. For example, insurers may define disability as the "inability to engage in (all or principal) duties of one's own occupation" and then after a certain period of years redefine the disability as the "inability to engage in an occupation that the insured is reasonably fit for by training, education and experience." Other combinations are possible.

Presumptive Total Disability

Many disability income contracts assume a total disability exists if the insured loses the use of limbs, vision or mobility (paralysis). Contracts requiring "severance of limbs" as evidence of presumptive total disability are more restrictive than versions requiring "loss of use" of limbs. This is an example of a presumptive disability benefit found in one disability income contract:

> Even if the Insured is able to work, he will be considered totally disabled if he incurs the total and irrecoverable loss of sight in both eyes; use of both hands; use of both feet; use of one hand and one foot; speech; or hearing in both ears.

Partial Disability

Not all disabilities eliminate wage income entirely. Therefore many disability income contracts include a reduced payment (for example, 50 percent) for partial disability or a proportionate benefit. Note that some disability income contracts pay only for *total* disabilities and do not cover partial ones. Partial disability being the inability to engage in a portion of one's occupation. The test and definition, however, are sometimes difficult to apply when a person claims partial disability but there is little evidence of work reduction or impairment. For example, when a forklift operator injures his back in an auto accident, the pain, increased difficulty of operation and reduction in productivity are often hard to measure. Here is an example of a definition of partial disability based on the number of principal duties the insured is unable to perform:

> The Insured is partially disabled when (1) he is unable to perform one or more of the principal duties of his occupation or to spend as much time at his occupation as he did before the disability started and (2) he has at least 20 percent loss of income.

Insurers determine the amount of the benefit for a partial disability in various ways. Some methods focus on the amount of *time lost*. The more modern methods focus on the amount of *earned income lost*, which is more consistent with the intent and purpose of the disability income contract. Instead of providing a set percentage of the total disability amount, the new contracts focus on providing *proportionate benefits*. The proportionate benefit compensates for the loss of earned income caused by a covered disability. The following formula determines the benefit on a monthly basis. The term **residual disability benefit** is commonly used to describe a partial disability payment.

The amount of each monthly benefit is the full benefit multiplied by the Insured's loss of earned income and divided by his base earned income. Thus the proportionate benefit equals:

$$\text{Full Benefit} \times \frac{\text{Loss of Earned Income}}{\text{Base Earned Income}}$$

However, if the insured has at least 80 percent loss of earned income, the proportionate benefit amount will be 100 percent of the full benefit. In no event will the amount payable be more than 100 percent of the full benefit.

Recurrent Disability

If an insured's disability returns after a period of time, benefit payments may be affected. An unrelated disability is usually treated as a separate event. Including a waiting period for recurrent disabilities separates a new benefit period with the restoration of full benefits from a continuance of an old benefit period. Usually, after a six-month waiting period, the insured has available all benefits, subject to any lifetime maximum. However, if a disability recurs from the same set of causes within the waiting period, prior disability benefits resume. Many variations exist. Following is an example of a clause in a disability income contract distinguishing between a new benefit period and the continuation of an old benefit period:

> Each separate time the Insured is disabled, a new Initial Period, Beginning Date and Maximum Benefit Period start. A disability is separate and not a continuation of one that started earlier, if (1) the cause of the later disability is not medically related to the cause of the earlier one, and the Insured had resumed on a full-time basis the principal duties of an occupation for at least 30 consecutive days; or (2) the cause of the later disability is related to the cause of the earlier one, and the later disability starts at least 6 months after the end of the earlier one.

Benefit Period and Amount

Disability contracts also vary according to the length of each benefit period and the amount of each monthly benefit. Benefits may be paid for any practical length of time, including life. However, insurers often terminate or modify benefits at age 65 to integrate the plan with Social Security retirement benefits. In general, the longer the potential benefits for a covered disability, the more expensive is the contract.

Insurers restrict the amount of the benefit to 60 or 70 percent of the insured's gross wage (earned income) for total disability benefits. Some insurers use an average monthly wage (defined by the contract) to determine benefit limitations. The percentage set by underwriters is typically a function of the absolute level of wage income and the taxation of the benefits. The reduced benefit is necessary to promote rehabilitation and to reduce malingering. The wage replacement percent typically declines for higher-income earners. For example, a professional earning $500,000 per year may be allowed only a 40 percent replacement rate by the underwriters. The $200,000 (.40 × $500,000) earned income replacement may be considered sufficient income to cover expenses but will also encourage rehabilitation. If the disability income benefits are taxable, the replacement ratio increases because the insured also must pay the taxes on the benefit.

Inflation Adjustments

Some companies include in their long-term disability income contracts a cost-of-living adjustment (COLA), which attempts to stabilize the purchasing power of the income stream during the period of disability. Following is a formula used by one insurer to adjust the insured's average monthly earned income (the basis for the disability benefit) for a reduction in purchasing power:

$$\text{Average monthly earned income} \times \frac{\text{Consumer price index for the current year of disability}}{\text{Consumer price index for the year disability started}}$$

Other Features

Many contracts waive the premium during disability and rehabilitation. Waiver-of-premium clauses remove the burden of paying the premium while totally disabled. However, premiums resume if the insured recovers. Many premium waiver provisions require 60 or 90 days of disability before premiums are waived. In addition, some premium waiver clauses have retroactive refund features providing a refund of any premiums paid during the disability. If an insured discontinues paying the premium after a disability covered by the contract, without the premium waiver provision, future disabilities will not be paid.

Many plans also include **rehabilitation** benefits. Rehabilitation is for the insured's benefit and also reduces the insurer's ultimate claim cost. Insurers providing this benefit design and enter into a rehabilitation plan with the insured. The plan may pay partial or full benefits during the process of returning the insured to work. And in some cases the insurer may pay for the costs of rehabilitation. Payments terminate when the insured returns to full productive capacity.

Transition benefits also may exist. After the insured returns to work, the insurer may continue partial benefits to ease the transition to full-time work. Even though the insured is working full-time, earned income may not be equal to the predisability amount, and the loss of earned income may be paid for a period such as one year.

The *additional purchase rider* is similar to the guaranteed insurability rider in life insurance. These riders provide opportunities for the insured to purchase additional amounts of insurance without providing any evidence of insurability, usually on the policy's anniversary dates. As the insured's earned income increases, the additional purchase benefit or rider allows the insured to increase the maximum monthly disability benefit subject to the underwriting guidelines of the company. The maximum amount of the increase can be limited per option. The number of options may be limited until a certain age (such as age 50 or 55). And, if the premium is waived due to a disability, the premium also may be waived for the incremental benefit allowed by the underwriters.

Exclusions

Common exclusions in disability income contracts include the following causes of loss:

- Disability from pregnancy (some companies exclude disability from *normal* pregnancy)
- Self-inflicted intentional injuries
- War or military duty
- Injury in illegal occupations or when committing a crime
- Air transportation (except when a passenger of a commercial airline)
- Disability arising out of the use of chemical substances when not under the supervision of a physician

Taxation of Disability Income Benefits

As noted, the income taxation of disability benefits depends on the premium's tax deductibility. If the premium payment is deductible, disability income benefits are taxable, as may be the case with employer-sponsored disability income plans. With individually purchased disability income coverage premiums are not deductible, and therefore benefits received by the insured are not taxable.

Review Questions

1. Discuss the extent of concern and involvement of the federal, state and local governments in the delivery of health care.
2. What are some stated reasons for the rapid rise in health care costs?
3. What are the differences between a group and an individual plan? Why do these differences exist?
4. Explain the difference between managed care and indemnity plans.
5. What is the difference between a cost-containment and cost-shifting technique? Provide some examples of cost-containment methods and cost-shifting methods.
6. How do Blue Cross and Blue Shield plans differ from private health insurance companies in paying for health care?
7. What are the major differences between a health maintenance organization (HMO) and a preferred provider organization (PPO)?
8. Define the perils of "accident," "sickness," "accidental means" and "accidental injury." How does the definition of the peril affect the price and coverage of the health care policy? Why is it important for a purchaser of

disability insurance to inspect the definition of *disability*? Give examples of strict and liberal definitions of disability.

9. List several injuries commonly excluded from health care reimbursement and disability income coverage. Why are they excluded?
10. Describe the expense categories generally covered under a hospitalization contract, a surgical contract, a regular medical contract and a major medical contract.
11. What contract provisions are used in medical expense and disability income contracts to control overuse of health care reimbursement plans?
12. What are the differences among a cancelable, a guaranteed renewable and a noncancelable health insurance contract?
13. Why do most disability income contracts restrict income to a portion of a person's average wage?

Endnotes

[1] An editorial on medical costs and procedures reported that Dr. Louis Sullivan, secretary of health and human services, stated in a speech presented at the University of Chicago Medical Center that "40 percent of procedures used to treat certain diseases are inappropriate" and "for many medical treatments, 'we' don't know what works or what doesn't work." Tony Lang, *The Cincinnati Enquirer*, May 16, 1991, p. A-11.

[2] *1990 Source Book of Health Insurance Data* (Washington, D.C.: Health Insurance Association of America).

[3] *1990 Source Book of Health Insurance Data* (Washington, D.C.: Health Insurance Association of America), p. 26.

[4] Health Maintenance Organization Amendments of 1988.

[5] *1990 Source Book of Health Insurance Information* p. 32.

Bibliography

Beam, Burton T., and John J. McFadden. *Employee Benefits*, 3rd ed. Chicago: Dearborn Financial Publishing, Inc., 1992.

Cornaccia, Harold J., and Stephen Barrett. *Consumer Health: A Guide to Intelligent Decisions*, 4th ed. St. Louis, Mo.: Times Mirror/Mosby College Publishers, 1989.

Cox, Larry A. "Disability Income Insurance and the Individual." *Financial Services Review* 1, No. 1, May 1991.

Frech, H. E. III. *Health Care in America: The Political Economy of Hospitals and Health Insurance*. San Francisco: Pacific Research Institute, 1988.

Jones, Chuck. "4th Annual Long-Term Care Survey." *Life Association News*, May 1990, pp. 106–127.

The Medicare Handbook 1990. Baltimore: U.S. Department of Health and Human Services, Health Care Financing Administration.

Ravlin, Alice M., et al. *Caring for the Disabled Elderly: Who Will Pay?* Washington, D.C.: Brookings Institution, 1988.

Rosenbloom, Jerry S. and Victor Hallman. *Employee Benefit Planning*, 3rd ed. Englewood Cliffs, N.J.: Prentice-Hall, 1991.

Chapter 8 | Health Insurance for an Aging and Uninsured Population

Chapter Objectives

- Explore the role of Medicare in providing medical expense coverage for the aged
- Discuss Medicare gap filler coverage
- Explain how some elderly use Medicaid for long-term care needs
- Describe long-term care (LTC) insurance
- Discuss the problems of the medically uninsured population
- Discuss national health insurance (NHI) and describe several NHI proposals

Introduction

Two major problems relating to medical care face American society, and both must be resolved in the near future. The first problem is how to provide and pay for adequate medical care for an aging population. The second is how to assure access to quality medical care for the entire population. This chapter primarily focuses on these issues as well as a related problem identified in Chapter 7, cost containment. In the U.S. a patchwork of different public programs and private insurance contracts exists to provide medical care for aging citizens. Medicare, the primary source of medical care reimbursement for the elderly, is the foundation of medical coverage for people over age 65. The hospital and medical insurance parts of Medicare provide a wide range of services and benefits, but not all medical and custodial expenses are covered. The private insurance industry provides medigap or Medicare gap filler coverage to augment Medicare. Medigap typically pays deductibles and copayments on eligible expenses not paid by Medicare.

Medicaid, part of Social Security enacted in 1965, is a joint federal and state program providing a wide array of services and medical benefits for people with minimal assets and income. It is considered a welfare program, providing a "safety net" of last resort. Unfortunately, many elderly find themselves dependent on this program, and they often lose control over their housing, health care and quality of life.

Long-term care (LTC) insurance is a relatively new product provided by the private insurance industry. LTC insurance provides funding for different levels of medical and custodial care typically not covered by Medicare program or medigap insurance coverage.

Most people agree that a moral obligation exists to provide medical care for the uninsured population. The major problems in meeting this societal responsibility are how to distribute the service, pay for its cost and distribute the financial burden. Historically, Congress has considered many proposals for national health insurance. This chapter ends by presenting several current proposals to illustrate the issues surrounding national health insurance and the compromises that must be made to implement a plan in the United States.

Medicare

Social Security **Medicare** provides hospital and physician benefits for fully insured retired workers. (*See* Chapter 14 for a discussion of the quarters of coverage required to be fully insured under Social Security.) Enacted in 1965 and put into effect in 1966 after many years of debate, Medicare remains controversial. The current benefits are the result of regular debate and legislation. From 1968 to 1988 enrollment in the Medicare program rose from 20 million people to 33 million people. This 65 percent increase in enrollment reflects several demographic trends, including increases in longevity and an increase in the proportion of people over age 65. Because of Medicare's complexity, the following discussion covers only its basic features.

Medicare has two major parts. *Hospital Insurance (Part A)* provides benefits similar to a hospitalization contract from a commercial insurance company. *Medical Insurance (Part B)* covers physicians' and certain other charges. Eligible people rely on Parts A and B of Medicare for much of their health care. *Medicaid*, discussed later in this chapter, provides health care to low-income Americans; it also became effective in 1966 under Title 19 of the Social Security Act. Medicaid provides medical care for low-income people regardless of age. People must exhaust most of their assets to meet the Medicaid program's eligibility requirements.

Medicare Eligibility

Because eligibility for Medicare benefits is not determined by financial need, it is not considered a welfare program. To be eligible for hospital insurance benefits under Medicare (Part A), a person must be at least 65 and eligible for benefits under the Social Security Act or the Railroad Retirement Act. People under age 65 receiving disability benefits and those with chronic kidney disease also may be eligible. People lacking the required number of covered quarters for Social Security benefits can purchase both the hospital and medical parts. In 1991 the premium for Part A was $177 per month for those not eligible automatically to receive benefits.

Participation in Part B (Medical Insurance) is voluntary. Retired workers over age 65 may choose to participate in the program. Under Part A enrollment is automatic if the person qualifies for retirement benefits. People not entitled to hospital benefits (Part A) because they are not entitled to retirement benefits under Social Security must enroll during their initial enrollment period or during a general enrollment period within three years of their initial enrollment date. The initial enrollment period is the seven months straddling the month of the individual's 65th birthday. As of 1991, Part B cost $29.90 per month for all those enrolled. The monthly premium is deducted from the worker's monthly retirement benefit.

☐ **Example**

George's 65th birthday is April 7, and the months January through July constitute this initial enrollment period. The general enrollment period is January 1 to March 31 of each year. If a person terminates coverage, one reenrollment is permitted during the general enrollment period within three years after the termination date.

The financing of the two parts differs. Financing for Part A, Hospital Insurance, comes from the Social Security tax paid by employers, employees and the self-employed. The cost of Part B, Medical Insurance, is shared equally by retired workers and the federal government.

Hospital Insurance Benefits

Part A, Hospital Insurance, provides four types of care. Payments are made for the following expenses if they are deemed *medically necessary*:

- Inpatient hospital care
- Care provided in a skilled nursing facility
- Home health care
- Hospice care

Inpatient hospital care includes costs of a semiprivate room, board, nursing services, supplies, drugs and diagnostic and therapeutic services in an approved hospital. Specifically excluded are medical, surgical or other services supplied by physicians or interns. Part B, Medical Insurance, covers these excluded expenses. The costs of private-duty nursing and private rooms are excluded if medically unnecessary.

If a patient requires post-hospital services in an extended-care facility (skilled nursing home), Medicare provides services similar to inpatient hospital benefits. However, to receive these services the patient must have been hospitalized for at least three days and must be admitted to the extended-care facility within 30 days after hospital discharge. Custodial care is not provided. An extended-care facility provides medically necessary treatment that does not have to be performed in a hospital but cannot be performed at home.

Part A provides post-hospital home health care after discharge from the hospital or an extended-care facility. The services provided include intermittent nursing and home aid services; physical, occupational or speech therapy;

and medical supplies other than drugs. Providing these medically related services in the home reduces the overall cost of providing benefits compared to providing them in a hospital or in a nursing facility. Post-hospital home health care under Medicare specifically does not cover *full-time* nursing care at home, medicine, homemaker services or personal care, housekeeping needs or meals delivered to the home.

Part A also provides hospice and respite care. A **hospice** helps terminally ill patients with pain relief, symptom management and other supportive services. **Respite care** under the hospice program provides temporary relief to a person regularly assisting with home care. Hospice benefits are provided if a doctor certifies the patient as terminally ill and the patient elects this benefit over the other benefits provided by Medicare. A Medicare-certified hospice program must provide the care.

Benefit Limitations

Participation provisions, deductibles and time limitations apply to benefits under the Hospital Plan. A *spell of illness* is defined as the length of time from which the patient enters the hospital until the patient has been discharged and out of the hospital for 60 days. Once the spell of illness ends, a new spell of illness can start. If the person is readmitted to the hospital before the spell of illness ends, only the remaining unused benefits are available.

When an eligible person uses inpatient hospital services, the first 60 days are subject to a $628 (1991) deductible. For each additional day up to 30 days, a $157 (1991) participation payment or daily copayment applies. All expenses beyond the 90 days must be paid by the patient unless the patient uses one or more of his or her 60 lifetime reserve days. Lifetime reserve days may be used only once and are available only after the 90 days are exhausted. Each reserve day costs $314 (1991).

☐ **Example**

Mary Cunningham stays in a hospital for 95 days in 1991 during one spell of illness. Medicare does not pay $6,908 as shown.

	Medicare does not pay	Basis for charge
First 60 days	$ 628	Deductible
61st to 90th day	4,710	30 days × $157/day
5 reserve days (if used)	1,570	5 days × $314/day
	$6,908	

A limited number of days and participation payments also apply to a stay in a skilled nursing facility. One hundred total days are available for each spell of illness following a minimum three-day hospital stay. After the first 20 days a $78.50 (1991) payment per day applies from the 21st through the 100th day.

Limits also apply to home health services provided by a certified home health care agency. If the patient is confined to the home, is under the care of a physician and requires intermittent skilled nursing care, Medicare provides 21 consecutive

Table 8.1
Medicare Hospital Benefits (Part A)*

Service	Medicare Benefits Paid	Medicare Does Not Pay
Hospitalization	Full cost after deductible Day 1–60 Full cost after copayment Day 61–90 If used, 60 lifetime reserve days If not used, pays $0 after 90th day	$628 per benefit period $157 per day copayment $314 per day copayment Full cost
Certified skilled nursing facility	First 20 days approved each year after a 3-day hospital stay Full cost after copayment for Day 21–100 Past Day 100—$0	$0 $78.50 per day copayment Full cost
Immediate and custodial care	$0	Full cost
Intermittent home health care	Full cost of medically necessary services	$0
	80% of approved amount for durable medical equipment	20% of approved amount
Hospice	210 days	Full cost over 210 days
Blood	Full cost after first 3 pints	First 3 pints

*As of 1991

days of part-time care in the home. No participation or deductible amount applies to home health services. (If durable medical equipment is required, 20 percent of the amount is paid by the patient.)

Hospice coverage pays for two 90-day periods and one 30-day period. No deductible or coinsurance applies to hospice care. However, the patient pays 5 percent of the cost of outpatient drugs or $5 toward each prescription, whichever is less. Under respite care the patient pays 5 percent of the allowed rate per day.

Table 8.1 summarizes the benefits provided by Medicare Hospital Insurance (Part A).

The Prospective Payment System

Payments made to hospitals under the Hospital Insurance coverage of Medicare are paid under the **prospective payment system (PPS)**. Under the prospective payment system hospital payments are based on the principal diagnosis for each stay in the hospital. Payment categories are called **diagnosis related groups (DRGs)**. In some cases when the DRG payment is made, the hospital is overpaid for its services; in other cases the hospital is underpaid. Under the PPS system the patient may not be charged additional amounts except for items not covered by Medicare. Also, the hospital must accept the payment for the DRG as full payment for the covered services received except for applicable deductibles and copayment amounts.

The PPS started in 1983 in an attempt to control ever-increasing health care costs. Prior to 1983 reimbursement for medical services was based on the reasonableness of the charge. If the amount was reasonable relative to the services provided, Social Security paid the billed amount. Because these amounts were reimbursed after providing the service, the provider had no incentive to be efficient. Under the PPS the approximately 500 DRGs have an assigned reimbursement amount and an approved number of days for the service. The Social Security Administration adjusts the amounts annually using a medical price index. The hospital assigns a DRG to the patient's condition upon admission. The hospital therefore knows how much will be paid for the patient's care and knows the number of hospital days Medicare will approve. Because of this preapproval, many critics charge, hospitals are discharging their patients "quicker and sicker." In addition, because the patient spends fewer days under hospital care and supervision, there is more reliance on post-hospitalization care at home or in a skilled medical care facility.

Medical Insurance Benefits

Part B of Medicare provides Medical Insurance coverage for physicians' and surgeons' services. These services do not have to be provided in a hospital. They may be provided in the home, at a clinic, in a hospital or in a doctor's office. Covered services under part B include:

- services and supplies commonly rendered by a physician;
- durable medical equipment;
- diagnostic tests, including X-ray and laboratory tests;
- surgical dressings, splints and casts;
- radiation therapy;
- necessary ambulance services; and
- prosthetic devices and braces.

Benefit Limitations

The benefits under the medical insurance plan are limited by a calendar year deductible and participation (copayment) on any excess eligible expenses. For expenses arising out of physicians' and surgeons' services and other health and medical services (such as rental of equipment, artificial limbs and braces, surgical dressings and casts), a $100 (1991) calendar year deductible applies, and 20 percent of all excess eligible expenses must be paid by the patient. Thus the plan pays 80 percent of all *eligible* expenses over the $100 calendar year deductible. Table 8.2 summarizes the benefits provided under Part B of Medicare.

The Assignment Payment Method

Many doctors and service suppliers agree to take **assignment of Medicare payments** under Part B. If the doctor or supplier accepts assignment, the provider is listed in the *Medicare-Participating Physician/Supplier Directory* and agrees to accept as full payment the Medicare-approved charge for the eligible services or supplies. The patient is responsible only for the deductible and the copayment amount. If assignment is not accepted by the doctor or the supplier, the patient is responsible for any excess charges. Therefore, it is important for the patient to know whether the physician or supplier accepts assignment prior to incurring the service.

Table 8.2
Medical Insurance (Part B)*

Service	Medicare Benefits Paid	Medicare Does Not Pay
Physician and other services	80% of approved charges exceeding the $100 annual deductible	$100 deductible annually plus 20% of approved charges plus any additional charges by doctors not accepting assignment
Home health care	Full cost of medically necessary services 80% of approved amount for durable medical equipment	$0 for services 20% of approved amount for durable medical equipment
Blood (outpatient)	80% of approved amount after the first 3 pints	First 3 pints plus 20% of approved amount
Pap smear (cervical cancer screening began 7/1/90)	80% of approved amount (one routine checkup every three years)	20% copayment

*As of 1991.

☐ **Example**

A doctor accepts assignment of a $350 charge with the Medicare-approved charge equal to $280 (the $100 deductible has already been met by the patient). Medicare pays $224 (.80 × $280), and the patient pays $56 (.20 × $280). If the doctor does not accept assignment, Medicare pays the same amount ($224), but the remainder ($126) is owed by the patient.

A new reimbursement system for Part B started in 1992. Physicians are now compensated based on a *resource-based relative value scale*. Under this system a numerical value is assigned to a service based on the actual work of the physician, the expenses of the practice (including an adjustment for rural versus urban areas) and medical malpractice insurance costs. Payment for the service will be based on the numerical value multiplied by a monetary conversion factor. The conversion factor will be determined by Congress each year and is intended to compensate the physician reasonable amounts based on the actual work and costs involved in providing the service. The annual adjustment of the conversion factor will adjust the reimbursement amount for inflationary factors.

Medicare Exclusions

Even though the services provided under Parts A and B seem complete when combined, important benefit exclusions and limitations exist that many people do not recognize. Readers must understand these gaps to appreciate the role of other private insurance coverage. Medicare does *not* cover:

- care that is *not reasonable* and *medically necessary;*
- physicians' charges greater than Medicare's approved amount;
- intermediate and long-term custodial nursing care;
- skilled nursing care in unapproved facilities;[1]
- care where there is no legal obligation to pay (including workers' compensation claims or charges made by relatives);

- personal comfort items;
- prescription drugs not provided in a hospital;
- private-duty nursing care;
- routine examinations and checkups (including dental care), immunizations, routine foot care;
- eyeglasses and hearing aids;
- cosmetic surgery except for accidental injury; and
- experimental surgery.

Coordination with Group and Individual Health Insurance

Often individual and group health insurance covers a person who is eligible to receive Medicare benefits. This is especially true after the passage of the *Tax Equity and Fiscal Responsibility Act of 1982* (TEFRA). Before TEFRA was passed, when an employee became eligible for Medicare at age 65 the employer would typically eliminate any health care benefits that duplicated the benefits provided by Medicare. In addition, the employer could offer a supplementary plan covering services not provided by Medicare. In either case, Medicare was the primary provider and payer of health care expenses and would pay all eligible costs before any other group or supplementary benefit. Under TEFRA employers with 20 or more employees must allow the employee and spouse to remain under their current health care plan. If the employee elects to remain insured under the group plan, even though eligible for Medicare, the group plan pays all expenses first, before Medicare is billed for any uncovered and eligible expenses. Depending on the group plan's benefits, it may be more advantageous for the employee to remain in the group and use Medicare benefits as a supplement.

Individual health insurance contracts usually terminate or change benefits at age 65 to coordinate benefits with Medicare. Many insurers offer to exchange the original contract for a Medicare supplement policy (discussed in the following section) that is designed to pay for eligible expenses not paid by Medicare, including the deductibles and copayments under Parts A and B. There are advantages to converting the original policy compared to purchasing a supplemental plan from another insurer, including immediate continuation of coverage and immediate coverage for preexisting conditions.

Medicare Gap Filler Coverage

Because of the deductibles and copayments in Medicare's coverage, private insurance companies offer Medicare gap filler coverage, commonly called **medigap** policies. Approximately 70 percent of the 33 million enrolled under Medicare, or 23 million people, supplement their coverage with some form of Medicare gap-filling coverage.[2] Premiums for medigap coverage are based on the insured's age at inception and the coverage provided. No insurability requirements apply; however, expenses for preexisting conditions (within 6 to 12 months prior to the date of coverage) are not covered. (Because of the perceived abuse of the elderly, federal laws make it a federal offense to knowingly sell a policy that duplicates Medicare or other existing health insurance coverage. People misrepresenting themselves as agents of the government, using the mail in a state where the coverage is not authorized and misrepresenting the product are subject to civil and criminal penalties.)

Medigap policies are designed principally to pay Medicare deductibles and copayments. These expenses are found in Tables 8.1 and 8.2. Many of the exclusions applying to Medicare's eligible expenses also apply to medigap coverage sold by the private industry. Therefore, expenses for services such as care that is not reasonable and medically unnecessary, physicians' charges greater than Medicare's approved amount and intermediate and long-term custodial care typically are not covered.

Because of the historic lack of standards for medigap coverage, the documented abuse of the elderly and the unlimited number of coverage choices available in the private insurance market, laws were passed to create standardization. The *Omnibus Budget Reconciliation Act* passed by Congress and signed by President Bush in November 1990 authorized the **National Association of Insurance Commissioners (NAIC)** to develop up to ten standard medigap policies with each covering a "core group" of minimum benefits. Under the law, if standards were not developed by the NAIC, the secretary of health and human services would be responsible for developing the standard set of medigap policies. States would then be encouraged to approve the model legislation developed either by the NAIC or the secretary of health and human services. If the various states fail to approve the standard set of Medicare supplemental policies, any company desiring to sell medigap policies in the state will require approval by the U.S. Department of Health and Human Services. The law imposes a $25,000 fine for anyone selling contracts not meeting the standards.

As of this writing, the NAIC has developed ten standard policies providing a broad range of choices for consumers.[3] The ten standard medigap policies labeled A through J are found in Table 8.3. Every policy provides a basic level or "core" of benefits not covered by Medicare. The core benefit package includes paying for the 20 percent copayment for physician services under Part B and the copayment for a hospital stay between the 61st and 90th day ($157 per day in 1991) under Part A. In addition, the core benefits pay the patient's contribution for blood, and there are some benefits for hospital stays after the 90th day. Nine of the ten policies cover the $628 deductible for each spell of illness, and three of the policies cover the $100 annual deductible under Part B. In addition, there is a wide variety of options, including home health care, prescription drugs, preventive diagnostic care and emergency care while a Medicare participant is traveling in a foreign country. As the deductibles and copayments change under Medicare, the benefits under the Medicare supplemental plans will also change.

Medicaid

Medicaid is a joint federal and state program that provides a last-resort safety net for people requiring medical and other assistance under Title 19 of the Social Security Act of 1965. Even though it is not part of the normal financial planning

Table 8.3
NAIC Medicare Supplement Standard Contracts

	A	B	C	D	E	F	G	H	I	J
Core	X	X	X	X	X	X	X	X	X	X
Skilled nursing care ($78.50 per day, 1991)			X	X	X	X	X	X	X	X
Annual hospital deductible ($628, 1991)		X	X	X	X	X	X	X	X	X
Doctor deductible ($100, 1991)			X					X		X
Excess doctor charges						Pays 80%		Pays 100%	Pays 100%	Pays 100%
Foreign travel Medical emergencies			X	X	X	X	X	X	X	X
At home recovery				X		X			X	X
Prescription Drugs					Basic				Basic	Extended
Preventative screening							X			X

X = coverage provided
Basic has a maximum benefit of $1,250.
Extended has a maximum benefit of $3,000.
Preventative screening includes flu shots, diphtheria and tetanus boosters, tests for colorectal cancer, hearing disorders, diabetes and thyroid functioning.
At-home recovery pays eight weeks beyond Medicare benefits.

process, it is used by people who find themselves uninsured or without sufficient assets or income to pay for their medical services.

The services provided by Medicaid must be medically necessary or certified by a physician. Though they vary from state to state, typically they include:

- inpatient and outpatient hospital services, including ambulance services;
- services of doctors, dentists, optometrists, podiatrists and other licensed specialists;
- nursing home care and home health care;
- care provided by clinics;
- certain prescription drugs, medical supplies and equipment;
- X-ray and laboratory services;
- eyeglasses, hearing aids and dentures;
- artificial limbs and braces;
- physical therapy;
- psychological services and special services for the mentally ill or those who suffer from retardation; and
- family planning services.

Large numbers of people are eligible to receive benefits under the Medicaid program if they meet certain needs tests. As a welfare program, Medicaid is generally available to families who are currently receiving Aid to Families with Dependent Children or Supplemental Social Security (SSI); people who are aged, are aged, blind or disabled and whose income and financial resources are below certain levels; and people in nursing homes without the resources to pay for their care.

Because nursing home care is becoming more expensive and people are living longer, more people are relying on Medicaid to provide a bare subsistence of housing (nursing home care) and medical care. Because one spouse has a legal responsibility to take care of and pay for health care and other expenses of the other spouse, couples were essentially impoverished before they were able to meet the needs test under Medicaid. The *Medicare Catastrophic Coverage Act of 1988* (parts that were not subsequently repealed) requires states to adopt spousal impoverishment rules allowing a nursing home resident and a spouse to retain some of their life savings and still qualify under Medicaid. That is, they may retain approximately $2,000 in liquid assets and retain a home for the spouse. The spouse living at home may also earn 150 percent of the federal income poverty level and still qualify. If the spouse living in the home dies, the home will be sold to pay for services until the nursing home resident exhausts the proceeds and is again eligible under Medicaid. An unmarried person in a nursing home may have only about $2,000 of liquid assets to be eligible under Medicaid. These figures vary by state.

One strategy used to qualify individuals for Medicaid is to transfer assets to another person (typically a family member) or to a **Medicaid qualifying trust.**[4] When either transfer occurs, there is a 30-month waiting period before the person is eligible for Medicaid benefits. This strategy presents several problems: Any funds or assets transferred to a spouse are still considered owned by the transferor, and the couple will not meet Medicaid's needs test. Medicaid deems a transfer to family members or relatives of assets used to pay for medical expenses, an asset transfer to provide medical care, which disqualifies the person for Medicaid. In either case, when assets are transferred, legal control of the assets is lost, and more important, the person gives up control of important decisions such as the level of health care, life-style and living arrangements to others. There are additional problems:

- The assets become the legal property of the donee and can be spent, gifted or lost to creditors and be subject to divorce proceedings.
- The gift tax provisions apply to the transfer, which might require the payment of gift taxes.
- The transferred property is received with the original cost basis as opposed to a stepped-up basis if transferred at death.
- Income-producing property may be taxed at a higher tax bracket than the donor's.
- The donee may predecease the donor, and the property may be disposed of in a manner inconsistent with the intent of the transfer.

If property is gifted to a Medicaid qualifying trust, the trust must meet the following requirements:

- The trust must be irrevocable and unchangeable.
- The person establishing the trust and the spouse can have no access to the principal.

- Neither the person establishing the trust nor the spouse may be a trustee.
- Trust income can be distributed on a discretionary basis by the trustee as long as the money is not spent on any costs paid for by the Medicaid program.

Under a Medicaid qualifying trust the donor loses control of trust assets. Some financial planners are suggesting the combination of a Medicaid qualifying trust and the purchase of a 30-month long-term insurance policy (discussed in the next section) to handle the possible need for long-term care while waiting the 30 months to qualify under Medicaid.[5] As long as the level of care is certified by a medical doctor as required, Medicaid usually will pay for the expense.

Long-Term Care

Financing long-term care (LTC) is a severe financial problem to be faced by an ever-increasing number of Americans. By the year 2030, 22 percent of the American population, about 65 million people, will have reached age 65. Because of the historical lack of coverage for long-term custodial care from the private and public sectors, the aging population, the public's demand for an insurance product and a search for new products and markets by the life insurance industry, LTC insurance continues to receive much attention.

In 1991 no standard LTC insurance product existed. The National Association of Insurance Commissioners (NAIC) has suggested a model law to regulate LTC products to protect consumers against abuses including incomplete descriptions, cancellations and postclaim underwriting. Many insurers have introduced new products in the past decade, and some insurers have eliminated their products from the insurance marketplace. Some companies feel long-term care will be included in a national health insurance scheme and are uncertain about the role the private insurance industry will play in financing or delivering medical and long-term care. Others feel the inability to price correctly, and the prospect of government intervention and regulation are too overwhelming to make this insurance profitable. Some life insurance companies provide the benefit as a rider to whole life or universal life insurance contracts. As described in Chapter 3, many life insurance companies are adding "living benefits" to their life insurance contracts. This option allows people to borrow a percentage of the face amount of coverage to meet medical or other expenses as a premature death benefit. Life insurance companies generally require a physician to certify that the insured is terminally ill. Others sell separate contracts. Competition is shaping and molding the product. And because of its recent development, some uncertainty exists about the actuarial soundness of the product's price.

Long-term care policies pay for various levels of benefits, including skilled, intermediate or custodial care in a nursing home. **Skilled care** refers to around-the-clock supervision and treatment by a registered nurse under the supervision of a physician. **Intermediate care** refers to occasional nursing and rehabilitative care under the supervision of skilled medical personnel. **Custodial care** refers to care that meets purely personal daily care needs such as bathing and eating. Custodial care may be provided by a person with no medical training. LTC insurance contracts frequently cover home-based custodial care.

Because the product is currently changing and continued evolution of LTC insurance is certain, readers should be aware that the following outline of LTC insurance and its variations focuses on the *1991* product.

Group and Individual Coverage

Long-term care insurance is available both on an individual and a group basis. Because of the current uncertainty of the tax status of long-term care insurance coverage as an employee benefit and the potential for escalating costs, most coverage provided on a group basis is paid for by the employee exclusively.

Age Limitations

Individuals can purchase LTC coverage from private insurance companies as early as age 40 and as late as age 84. The most common age range is 50 to 84. Presumably insurers restrict the age of purchase because there is little demand from the lower age group and because they want to protect against adverse selection from the higher age group.

Benefit Amounts

Benefit amounts are set by a daily limit such as $75 or $100. Currently daily limits are found as high as $250. Total benefits are limited by a number of years (e.g., two to five years) or by a dollar maximum, or benefits may be provided for life. Predictably, the higher the daily limit, the longer the benefit period and the higher the dollar maximum, the higher is the premium. Few current policies contain a cost-of-living rider, but cost-of-living adjustment provisions are becoming more common with a concurrent adjustment in the premium. Insurance contracts may be *retained for life*, but very few contracts provide *benefits for life*. Benefits are payable starting at any age. But if a benefit period begins, LTC insurance will not pay benefits longer than agreed in the contract.

Elimination Periods

Elimination periods, similar to those found in disability coverage, exclude short-term care and reduce cost. Benefits start once covered LTC benefits have been provided for a specific number of days. Elimination periods may be stated per spell of illness or on a cumulative basis. Usually each spell of illness is separated by at least 60 days without the need for LTC. On a cumulative basis, once the elimination period is accumulated regardless of the number of LTC episodes, the deductible is satisfied.

☐ **Example**

Emma Jones has an LTC contract, and she requires the following pattern of care:

January 1 to February 19	50 days	LTC needed
February 20 to May 10	80 days	LTC not needed
May 11 to June 9	30 days	LTC needed

If the LTC contract has a 60-day elimination period for each spell of illness, nothing is paid. If the elimination period is determined on a cumulative basis, the last 20 days (during May 11 to June 9) are compensable.

Renewability

Once the policy is issued, LTC policies generally are guaranteed renewable for the insured's life. That is, the insurer must continue the contract as long as the premium is paid. Few individual policies are conditionally renewable (renewable to a stated date or renewable based on conditions stated in the contract).

Premiums

The initial premium is based on the insured's age and the benefits provided when the contract begins. The premium generally remains level for the life of the contract except for adjustments in premium based on any cost-of-living adjustments. Some insurers increase the daily limit at a rate of 5 percent for the first five to ten years of the contract. Some newer LTC contracts provide for a compounded 5 percent increase in the daily benefit annually for the life of the contract and charge a level premium. Some insurers adjust premiums annually based on age and make an adjustment in the daily rate based on the consumer price index. Most LTC insurers sell the contract based on a level premium amount similar to multiple-year life insurance contracts. Many insurers provide spousal discounts for insuring the second person to recognize the fact that a spouse can provide much of the home-based care without triggering the payment of benefits.

Waiver of Premium

Most LTC contracts waive any premium payment while long-term benefits are being paid. Premiums can be waived after the elimination period and an additional number of days. For example, if a contract contains an elimination period of 100 days and has a 90-day waiver of premium, the premium is waived after 190 days have elapsed during an LTC benefit period.

Admission and Benefit Requirements

Insurance companies impose different standards for receiving benefits under LTC contracts. Some insurers consider the insured eligible for LTC coverage if the insured cannot perform a set number (such as two out of five) of a list of activities of daily living (ADLs). Commonly this list includes bathing, dressing, eating, transferring (moving from a bed to a chair), getting around outside, using the toilet, being continent and being able to take medications.

Purchasers of LTC products must be careful to select a contract that defines the ADLs in a responsible manner. For example, consider the definition of *feeding* found in one LTC contract: "Feeding is the ability to feed or nourish one's body in any way, even if you . . . must use a tube or catheter." In this case being fed by tubes is considered a normal activity of living, and an insured who must be nourished this way would not qualify for coverage.[6]

Most of the newer LTC contracts rely on a physician's certification, provide for all levels of care (skilled, intermediate and custodial) and adjust the daily payment amount based on the type of care required. A few insurers engage in post-claim underwriting and determine eligibility based on individual circumstances. Contracts using this later technique should be avoided. Newly issued LTC contracts cover Alzheimer's disease and organically based mental illness and do not require a stay in a hospital before qualifying for benefits. Nor do the newer contracts require entry into a nursing home within a certain number of days after being discharged from a hospital.

Table 8.4
Insured and Uninsured Population 1988 (millions)

Total population	243.1
Number insured	201.5
Number uninsured	31.5
Percent uninsured	**13.0**
Under Age 65	214.3
Number insured	182.9
Number uninsured	31.4
Percent uninsured	**14.7**

Source: *1990 Source Book of Health Insurance Data* (Washington, D.C.: Health Insurance Association of America), p. 13.

In the early stages of certain diseases such as Alzheimer's or Parkinson's and during senility, people usually can perform all ADLs and would not trigger benefits under an LTC contract that uses ADLs alone to trigger coverage. These people may need a minimal level of custodial care. Because of this, some LTC contracts provide benefits for cognitive impairment, the deterioration of intellectual capacity exhibited by loss of memory, orientation or reasoning ability.

Preexisting Conditions

Generally the insured must not have been treated within six months before the application for medical conditions resulting in the need for LTC coverage. If the insured is free from treatment for a period of six months after the application, benefits are paid.

The Uninsured Population

The number of people with access to health insurance has grown over the past several years. Unfortunately, the number of people not having adequate health insurance coverage also has grown rapidly, causing much concern for those people and public policy makers. Estimates of the number of people without health insurance increased from 28 million in 1979 to 31 million in 1988, an increase of about 25 percent (*see* Table 8.4). Among the insured population, not all people have equally good benefits. Some of these people have minimal benefits and are considered underinsured for catastrophic health care costs. Factors increasing the number of uninsured people include inflation during the 1980s, more low-paying jobs without medical benefits, reductions in Medicaid eligibility, and the subsequent increase in health insurance costs, forcing many people and small employers to drop their coverage.

People mistakenly believe the uninsured population exists only in low-income groups. Out of the nonelderly uninsured population in 1989 it is estimated that 61.3 percent had incomes below $20,000, 16.5 percent had incomes between $20,000 and $30,000, and 22.2 percent had incomes greater than $30,000. Thus, the uninsured exist among all income levels. Of the 31 million people who are uninsured, it is estimated that 15 percent are children under age 18 and 66 percent of the uninsured children are older than six years old.[7]

Funding and providing health care for the entire population is controversial. Among the immediate problems caused by the lack of a universal health insurance system in the U.S. (aside from the psychological burdens of the uninsured, especially people with sick children or AIDS) are these:

- Access to health care is difficult or denied to the uninsured. Without health insurance coverage, or other guarantee of payment, some doctors and hospitals are unwilling to provide services.
- When care is provided, it can be costly, untimely and inadequate. Because of the inability to pay, many people do not seek health care when they initially need it. Because of the lack of early intervention, more expensive treatment often is required later.
- Unpaid care is borne indirectly by providers or other insureds through cost shifting. When health care bills remain unpaid, providers write the expense off as uncollectible. Unpaid bills increase the costs to other patients, and "cost shifting" occurs.

National Health Insurance

Dorothea Dix discussed **national health insurance (NHI)** in the United States as early as the mid-1800s in the form of a national mental health bill. Congress passed the bill, but it was subsequently vetoed by President Franklin Pierce. At issue was the federal government's right to interfere with the health of its citizens. Since then the United States has periodically debated the advantages and disadvantages of NHI. Although no NHI bill has passed for the whole population, large segments of the U.S. population are recipients of government-supplied health care services or payment for health care.[8]

Proponents of NHI present five basic arguments:

1. Health care access, especially for the poor, is not satisfactory.
2. The quality and amount of health care delivered to the wealthy is greater than that delivered to the poor.
3. A properly constructed NHI program will reduce the pressure on costs and eliminate much of the administrative cost of our current piecemeal system.
4. Many Americans cannot afford to pay for health insurance or medical care. It should be paid by the public because poor health increases dependency on other governmental programs.
5. NHI is needed to provide health care benefits to the unemployed.

Opponents of NHI make the following arguments:

1. The health of the American population has never been better. Infant mortality rates are declining, and people are living longer.
2. Over 90 percent of the population already is covered by some form of private or governmental program, and the remaining portion is composed of

individuals who are uninsurable, who are not old enough to qualify for governmental programs or who cannot afford coverage.
3. Family use of medical services for the lower-income groups is more frequent than use by higher-income groups, and with the programs already in place there are very few financial barriers to health care access.
4. If an NHI plan is passed, the government would control and affect a large portion of our economy (currently exceeding 11 percent of GNP). The government would have to define good health, determine how to ration the product, price and distribute it, pay the providers of health care and determine the direction of research and development.
5. There are no guarantees that the cost of providing health care would not grow out of control, as with many other government-sponsored programs.

Many NHI proposals were introduced in the last decade, but none has passed. NHI could be implemented in different ways, and the following three proposals have received recent attention.

The Pepper Commission

In April 1990 the Pepper Commission delivered its report on health care to Congress.[9] The report suggests ways of providing health care coverage for all Americans. The committee's report may be an important step toward an NHI plan. However, the committee failed to set up a plan for financing its $66 billion cost. These were the Pepper Commission's recommendations:

- Employers with 100 or more employees would have to provide a health care plan meeting minimum standards for employees and dependents or pay a new payroll tax, which presumably would exceed the cost of the health care plan.
- Small employers with fewer than 100 employees would have to phase in health care coverage by certain dates or pay the new payroll tax.
- Medicaid would be replaced with a new health care plan to cover individuals not covered by employer-sponsored plans, including the self-employed. Premiums for the self-employed and unemployed would be based on income.
- A long-term care plan for the chronically disabled costing $42.8 billion would establish a new nursing home benefit program.

AMA Proposal

The proposal of the American Medical Association (AMA) makes many suggestions with an eye to maintaining the private health care system.[10] The AMA proposal would:

- mandate that employers provide health care coverage;
- allow a 100 percent tax deduction for health care premiums and expenses for the self-employed;

- create state risk pools for people who cannot obtain health insurance because of cost or poor health and for the unemployed with incomes less than 150 percent of the poverty level;
- expand Medicaid to cover people below the poverty level;
- provide tax incentives for expanding long-term care coverage; and
- reform medical malpractice laws to reduce legal liability costs and malpractice insurance premiums.

Health Insurance Industry Proposal

The plan of the Health Insurance Association of America (HIAA) for providing all Americans with health insurance coverage emphasizes the use of the current health care financing industry for a solution.[11] HIAA's plan includes the following points:

- A guarantee that groups with fewer than 25 employees will not be denied health care coverage and that coverage will continue even though one or more in the group are considered uninsurable or high risk
- Elimination of the preexisting condition exclusion for workers or employers changing insurers
- Expansion of Medicaid to cover all people below the federal poverty income level
- State risk pools for the uninsurable
- A "buy-in" to Medicaid for people not having access to health insurance through employment

Other NHI Plans

Other NHI plans that have been suggested include giving tax benefits to employers who offer a choice among health care plans and allowing people to make limited tax-deductible contributions to a fund to pay for future health care needs (similar to an individual retirement account). Whether one plan or a combination of plans is enacted will be a function of the political environment and the public's desire to pay the cost.

Review Questions

1. Are health benefits under Medicare considered a welfare program or an insurance program? Explain.
2. How does one become eligible for Medicare benefits? If one is not automatically eligible, how can one receive the benefits?
3. What kinds of benefits are provided under Part A of Medicare—Hospital Insurance benefits? What are some of the important exclusions to coverage?
4. What is the purpose of the prospective payment system under Medicare Part A? How does it work?

5. What services are provided under Part B of Medicare? Explain the purpose of the assignment payment system under Part B of Medicare. How does it work? What is the purpose of a resource-based relative value scale in compensating for doctors' services?

6. Explain how Medicare benefits coordinate with individual and group health insurance coverage.

7. What kinds of benefits are usually found in medigap insurance contracts? What are some of the important exclusions and limitations of the coverage?

8. What role does Medicaid play in providing medical and custodial care for the aged?

9. Why is LTC insurance needed when Medicare and Medicaid exist?

10. Explain some of the difficulties in developing long-term care (LTC) insurance. What demographic, economic and competitive forces are stimulating the development of LTC coverage?

11. Why are people becoming more concerned about the lack of medical insurance coverage for a segment of the U.S. population?

12. List the main arguments for and against a national health insurance (NHI) plan.

13. Do you feel a national health care plan is necessary to provide comprehensive medical care for the U.S. population?

Endnotes

[1] It is estimated that only one-third of skilled nursing homes are approved by Medicare in the United States. See *The Consumer's Guide to Medicare Supplement Insurance* (Washington, D.C.: Health Insurance Association of America, 1990), p. 9.

[2] *1990 Source Book of Health Insurance Data*. (Washington, D.C.: Health Insurance Association of America), p. 3.

[3] Hilary Stout, "Ten Standard 'Medigap' Plans Devised," *The Wall Street Journal*, May 7, 1991, p. B1.

[4] Armond D. Budish, "Helping Clients Face the LTC Threat," *Best's Review (Life/Health Edition)*, November 1990, pp. 68, 70, 116.

[5] Budish, "Helping Clients Face the LTC Threat," pp. 68, 70, 116.

[6] Peggy Pannke, "LTC under the Surface," *Best's Review (Life/Health Edition)*, April 1991, p. 33.

[7] *1990 Source Book of Health Insurance Data*, p. 14. The federal poverty level for a family of four in 1989 was $12,091.

[8] For an excellent treatment of the economic and political problems facing NHI, *see* Frech, H. E. III, *Health Care in America: The Political Economy of Hospitals and Health Insurance*. San Francisco: Pacific Research Institute, 1988.

[9] The U.S. Bipartisan Commission on Comprehensive Health Care is known as the Pepper Commission.

[10] Alain Enthoven and Richard Kronick, "A Consumer Choice Health Plan for the 1990s: Universal Health Insurance in a System Designed to Promote Quality and Economy," *The New England Journal of Medicine*, January 1989 (first of two parts).

[11]Mary Jane Fisher, "Kinder, Gentler HIAA Plan Expands Medicaid Eligibility," *National Underwriter (Life/Health Edition)*, April 3, 1989, p. 3.

Bibliography

Cornaccia, Harold J., and Stephen Barrett. *Consumer Health: A Guide to Intelligent Decisions*, (4th ed). St. Louis, Mo.: Times Mirror/Mosby College Publishers, 1989.

Frech, H. E. III. *Health Care in America: The Political Economy of Hospitals and Health Insurance*. San Francisco: Pacific Research Institute, 1988.

Himmelstein, David U., and Steffie Woolhandler. "A National Health Program for the United States." *The New England Journal of Medicine*, January 12, 1989, pp. 102–108.

Jones, Chuck. "4th Annual Long-Term Care Survey." *Life Association News*, May 1990, pp. 106–127.

The Medicare Handbook 1990, Baltimore, Md.: U.S. Department of Health and Human Services, Health Care Financing Administration.

Pannke, Peggy. "LTC under the Surface." *Best's Review (Life/Health Edition)*, April 1991, pp. 30–33, 98–99.

Ravlin, Alice M., et al. *Caring for the Disabled Elderly: Who Will Pay?* Washington, D.C.: Brookings Institution, 1988.

Rejda, George E. *Social Insurance & Economic Security*, 4th ed. Englewood Cliffs, N.J.: Prentice-Hall, 1991.

Chapter 9 | The Legal Framework of Life Insurance

Chapter Objectives

- Explore the necessary requirements of a valid life insurance contract
- Differentiate normal business contracts from life insurance contracts
- Demonstrate the importance of the principal-agent relationship in product distribution
- Discuss creditors' rights in life insurance

Introduction

Life insurance may be viewed both as a pooling transaction, where many individuals contribute to a pool to fund death benefits, and as a contractual agreement between two parties, where the issuer contracts to pay a death claim when the insured dies. Implied in both definitions is the legal obligation of one party to another. Because the life insurance contract must conform to certain legal requirements, an introduction to the law that shapes and molds the transaction is essential to its understanding. This chapter explores a variety of topics concerning the legal nature of the life insurance contract.

First the chapter examines the requirements for starting a life insurance contract and the customary form of those requirements. Purchasing a life insurance contract is considered by many to be different from entering a contract to purchase goods; thus the law must deal with several special problems to determine if all requirements of a valid contract exist.

The second subject covered in this chapter is the legal characteristics of the life insurance contract. Life insurance contracts are different from typical business contracts in many respects. For example, a life insurance contract need be performed by only one party, the negotiating power is not equal and all parties to the contract rely on the accuracy of information provided by the others. An analysis of life insurance contract characteristics sheds light on the courts' treatment of controversies surrounding these transactions.

Third, life insurance contracts are sold by individuals (or by using vending machines) for an artificial being (a corporation or an association), so individuals must be given the power to transact business on its behalf. The laws creating and controlling the principal-agent relationship must be examined with respect to (1) the rights and duties of the principal agent, (2) how the agent receives the authority to perform for the principal and (3) extensions and or limitations to that authority.

The final topic in this chapter is creditors' rights. Creditors are individuals who are owed value. Because life insurance contracts can be a source of money for creditors, their ability to attach any proceeds before or after a debtor's death is an important consideration in any financial plan.

Contracts

A **contract** is "a promissory agreement between two or more persons that creates, modifies or destroys a legal relation."[1] One party acts or makes a promise to act in return for something of value—an act or promise from the other person. As introduced in Chapter 1, the life insurance contract conforms to this definition: In return for paying the premium and making other considerations, an individual is promised payment of stated values contingent on a specified event. The specific event is death in life insurance contracts, surviving in annuity contracts, loss of health in medical expense contracts and accident or illness in disability contracts. The life insurance company is referred to as the *insurer*, and the individual whose death causes the company to pay a claim is the *insured*. Three separate legal interests are created by a life insurance contract: the insured, the policy owner and the beneficiary. In a life insurance contract the policy owner and the insured may be the same person, and the third-party beneficiary may be the insured's estate, essentially placing the same party in all three positions. On the other hand, if a wife purchases insurance on her husband and makes a child the beneficiary, all three capacities are held by different people. The husband is the insured, the wife is the policy owner, and the child is the beneficiary.

Requirements of a Valid Contract

As for any other contract, four elements must exist for a life insurance contract to be valid:

1. The contract must be for a lawful purpose.
2. The parties to the contract must have capacity to enter the agreement.
3. There must be an offer and acceptance of the terms of the agreement.
4. Consideration must be exchanged.

Legality

To be a valid life insurance contract—to be legal—an agreement must not violate public policy (in the sense that it should not encourage antisocial behavior) or protect illegal or speculative ventures. Some people view life insurance as a gambling contract: the beneficiary is betting that the insured will die within the contract period. To prevent individuals from buying contracts on any life, the courts require the applicant to have an *insurable interest* in the life of the person insured before a valid life insurance contract can exist. If there is no insurable interest, the contract is viewed as a wager and thus as against public policy. The insurable interest requirement therefore differentiates insurance from gambling.

Insurable interest exists when one can show a "pecuniary interest in the continued life of the person whose death is the event insured against."[2] Some relationships producing insurable interest must be demonstrated, while in others there is a presumption of insurable interest. It is generally assumed that a person has an unquestioned insurable interest in his or her own life. The New York Insurance Code (Section 3205) states that "any person of lawful age may on his own initiative procure or effect a contract of insurance upon his own person."(Many large life insurance companies are licensed in New York State; as such, these companies must meet New York law wherever they operate.)

Also it is generally supported and recognized by courts that one has an insurable interest in the lives of others in the following circumstances:

- A husband in a wife and vice versa
- A parent in a minor child
- A minor child in a parent

The New York Insurance Code (Section 3205) states that insurable interest

shall mean: (a) In the case of persons related by blood or by law, a substantial interest engendered by love and affection; and (b) in the case of other persons, a lawful and substantial economic interest in the continued life . . . of the person insured.

In the latter instance (economic interest) the courts are more concerned with the financial interest of the applicant as opposed to insurable interest based on blood ties or affection. For example, a property settlement after a divorce may produce an insurable interest arising out of child support. A business partner may have an interest in the life of another partner to preserve the going-concern value of the firm. An employer may have an insurable interest in the life of a key employee. And a creditor may have an insurable interest in a debtor. Applicants for life insurance contracts who are not the insured, or where the interest is not presumed, must demonstrate an insurable interest. State statutes and insurance company guidelines dictate that in these cases the insured must consent to the life insurance contract.

When a creditor purchases life insurance on a debtor, the amount of insurance must bear a reasonable relation to the amount of the debt plus any insurance costs incurred. Many courts hold that all proceeds may be retained by the creditor. Some courts, on the other hand, hold that, if the contract is written for an amount many times the debt, the contract is generally set aside as a gambling contract and against public policy. If the policy is purchased by the debtor and the debtor assigns benefits to the creditor (or the creditor is placed in the position of a beneficiary), amounts above the debt are paid to a contingent beneficiary or the insured's estate. For example, Mr. Twiggs borrows $100,000 from the Union Loan Company and assigns the benefits on an existing $200,000 life insurance contract to Union. If Mr. Twiggs owes $75,000 at death, Union Loan may retain only $75,000 of any proceeds. The remainder is paid to either a beneficiary or the insured's estate.

The time when the insurable interest must exist is different in life insurance from that in property insurance. In life insurance insurable interest need exist only at the policy's inception and is sufficient to produce a valid legal contract. If the opposite were true—the insurable interest being required to exist when the loss occurs—undue hardship could result in many cases. Consider the case of a divorce. Mr. and Mrs. Twiggs have two children. Mrs. Twiggs purchases a whole life insurance contract on her husband to provide income to the family if death occurs and to provide savings for retirement. If the Twiggses divorce after the purchase of the contract, it would be unconscionable to deny child support or income to the remaining family upon the death of the insured. In this case a financial dependency exists. However, there are cases where there is no financial dependency, but the contract was originally purchased by the beneficiary to provide for a combination of retirement savings, estate tax problems and dependency income (support for the children). Undue hardship may result if death proceeds are denied based on the lack of insurable interest at the time of death.

Illegal Activities. Because of the nature of the life insurance contract, several events could legally prevent the insurer from paying proceeds, such as when the insured is murdered by the beneficiary, is executed by a public authority or commits suicide. This last topic will be explored in Chapter 10.

Murder. Depending on the situation, a beneficiary may collect policy proceeds even if involved in the insured's death. If an automobile accident occurs due to the beneficiary's negligence and the insured dies, payment will be made because the cause of death was clearly accidental and unintentional. Any policy purchased by the beneficiary with the intent to murder the insured can, however, be set aside because it is against public policy to protect illegal ventures or encourage the destruction of life. Nevertheless, if the policy was purchased in good faith without the intent to murder and the beneficiary later murdered the insured, the policy proceeds would be paid. To whom the proceeds would be paid is addressed by individual state law.

It is clear that, if the beneficiary wrongfully kills the insured, the proceeds of the contract will not be paid to the beneficiary, regardless of ownership. Proceeds are paid to the contingent beneficiary or the insured's estate. The beneficiary who commits murder can also be an heir to the estate, and state laws differ as to the partitioning of the estate's assets. Some states do not interfere with estate distributions; others do. In the latter the benefits are distributed among all innocent heirs.

Consider the case of *Lamb et al. v. Northwestern National Life Insurance Company*.[3] The Lamb case specifically addressed the issue of the definition of accidental death but also demonstrated that death proceeds are generally paid to the contingent beneficiaries if the primary beneficiary murders the insured:

> Edna and Charles Lamb returned to their home. . . . The couple had been drinking, and there apparently was an argument en route to the home. . . . The argu-

ment continued while the couple prepared for bed. Then, according to Edna Lamb, she, "started to lay down and . . . [Charles] swung at . . . [her] . . . [she] got up and set the clock. Turned off the lights, picked up two shells from somewhere. . . . [Charles] kept running his mouth . . . [Edna] went back over and put the shells in the gun that was underneath the bed. Closed the gun up, cocked it and picked it up and pulled the trigger. . . . [Charles] got quiet and . . . [Edna] walked out of the room and went down and called the police.

The children of the Lambs (contingent beneficiaries) claimed the basic death benefit of $20,000 and also sued for the double-indemnity accidental death benefit. The conclusion of the final case was that death of the insured was accidental and the contingent beneficiaries could recover the basic benefit and the additional $20,000. The rationale was that from the point of view of the insured (Charles), the result was "external, violent, unintentional, involuntary and, hence, accidental within the meaning of death by accidental means."

Even if the beneficiary is tried for murdering the insured, the conviction may be for a lesser offense. State statutory definitions of offenses (involuntary manslaughter, voluntary manslaughter, reckless homicide and first- and second-degree murder) vary, and there are no clear rules for determining when a beneficiary is to be denied collecting proceeds. The beneficiary does not always receive the policy proceeds if acquitted. Suits to force payment are on civil grounds; the rules of evidence for civil and criminal actions differ. Thus, even if the beneficiary is acquitted of murder, the life insurance company may be able to defend a suit for nonpayment of proceeds based on civil grounds (based on a preponderance of evidence as opposed to beyond a reasonable doubt).

Jones v. All American Life Insurance Company[4] illustrates the civil law defense for nonpayment even if the beneficiary is not convicted of a crime. Jones was named beneficiary of Felbert Hilliard's life insurance policy. Felbert died of a gunshot wound to his head. All American refused to pay the policy proceeds, based on the grounds that Jones murdered Hilliard, and an action was brought against All American to force payment. The plaintiff argued that she was entitled to the proceeds because she had never been convicted of any crime relating to the death of the insured.

During the jury trial the following evidence was presented. Death was caused by a small-caliber bullet, and the plaintiff owned such a gun at the time. The plaintiff and the insured had lived together. Several months before his death, he moved out and informed her that he would change the beneficiary on the life insurance policy. The day after his death, the carpet and bed linens had been washed, but some blood remained. Blood was found on the car. The trunk of the car had been cleaned, floor mats had been removed, and Hilliard's body exhibited abrasions suggesting that the body had been dragged.

The abundance of circumstantial evidence provided the jury with the means to conclude, with a preponderance of evidence, that Jones had killed Hilliard. Even though the plaintiff was never convicted of a crime, "it is a basic principle of law and equity that no [one] shall be permitted to take advantage of his [or her] own wrong, or [to] acquire property as a result of his [or her] crime."

Execution. Execution of an insured by public authorities for a crime does not destroy a beneficiary's right to receive proceeds. However, if the insured purchased a life insurance contract and failed to divulge all necessary information, the rules of concealment or misrepresentation would be used to deny payment of any death claim.

Capacity

Parties to the contract must also have the legal ability, or **capacity**, to contract. A life insurance company's legal capacity is derived from two sources. First, the power to act as an individual is granted by the corporate charter issued by the state. As long as the corporation acts within the bounds of its charter, it is said to have capacity. In addition, the state must grant a specific license to sell insurance. While most individuals have capacity to enter into insurance contracts, some groups lack legal capacity. Minors, the insane and the intoxicated are considered not to have legal capacity.

Minors. The law protects minors from being exploited by others under a number of circumstances. Generally, if a contract is not considered to be for a necessity, the minor may disaffirm the contract during minority and within a reasonable time after majority has been reached (typically age 18). Necessary contracts are ones supplying food, shelter, clothing, education or medical services.

When a competent party realizes a contract has been made with a minor, the contract cannot be avoided unless other contractual conditions have not been met. The mere fact that a minor is a party to the contract does not allow the insurer to avoid any obligations, because it would place the minor at a disadvantage. When the contract is disaffirmed by the minor, all parties to the contract are to return all value exchanged. However, if the minor no longer has the original value, the contract still can be disaffirmed, and the minor may recover all exchanged values without restoring the other party to its original position.

Life insurance contracts are not considered necessary. Therefore, when a life insurance contract is disaffirmed by the minor, premiums must be returned; and in some states the premiums are returned without a deduction for mortality costs and expenses. Minors need life insurance in some cases; and because of the problems of contracting with a minor, insurers require a parent or guardian to enter the contract for the minor's benefit.

Several states recognize the need for the minor (under age 18 or 21) to be a bona fide party to a contract. For example, in the state of New York, "A minor above the age of 14 years and 6 months shall be deemed competent to enter into a contract for, be an owner of, and exercise all rights relating to, a policy of life insurance."[5] Statutes such as these are referred to as *reduced-age statutes* and exist in a majority of the states.

The Insane and the Intoxicated. Insane and intoxicated people also lack the capacity to contract. It is assumed that the intoxicated or insane cannot comprehend the contractual duties expected. In both of these cases, when sanity is regained or the person is no longer intoxicated, the contract may be affirmed or disaffirmed. In the case of insane or mentally infirm people, usually a guardian is appointed to handle all legal affairs. The guardian may disaffirm a contract if made after the person was adjudged legally incompetent but before the appointment.

Offer and Acceptance

A contract is valid only when there is an *offer* and an **acceptance** of its terms and conditions. In a life insurance contract the written policy or application may control both who may accept and the conditions for acceptance. For example, some life insurance companies state in the application that there can be no acceptance unless there has been actual delivery of the policy. It is generally recognized that the insured makes the offer and the life insurance company may or may not accept it. The rules in this area are fairly complex. Offer and acceptance commonly involve a **conditional receipt.** Not all transactions involve one. A conditional receipt usually provides life insurance coverage before the contract is formally accepted, if underwriting rules are met.

In the normal sequence of events the life insurance agent presents the contract, its premium and its provisions to the applicant. An application with money is then submitted to the life insurance company. In this sequence the agent is said to be soliciting an offer, the applicant is offering to contract and the life insurance company can accept the offer, reject it or make a counteroffer. A counteroffer is actually a rejection with another offer, which the applicant can now accept or reject. Offering a rated policy, one with rates increased above standard, before acceptance, is considered a counteroffer.

As noted earlier, a life insurance contract cannot be started without some exchange of value, so money is normally tendered (consideration). Without the exchange, the life insurance company cannot accept the contract. There are, however, instances when it is desirable to submit the application without an exchange of value. A medically impaired individual who desires to find out how much the policy will cost and on what terms without actually starting the life insurance contract submits a *trial application.* Some life insurance companies require trial applications for all submissions. With this procedure, when the policy is sent to the agent and delivered to the applicant, it is considered an offer; the company has given the agent the power to offer the contract. The contract then starts when money changes hands.

Problems occur when the insured dies between the actual offer with tender and the acceptance. It can be difficult to explain to the estate or stated beneficiary that no contract existed when all underwriting rules were met and the premium was paid to the company. To avoid litigation in this circumstance the life insurance industry uses conditional receipts. Three types are most common. Two involve *conditions precedent* (a condition that must exist before coverage begins), and one requires a *condition subsequent* (coverage exists unless a condition is not met after the application is taken). Several forms of conditional receipts provide for temporary life insurance. These are the three types of conditional receipts:

1. A conditional receipt that requires home office approval before coverage exists. This type of premium receipt (condition that the insurer must act before coverage exists) provides the least amount of protection for the policyholder.

2. A conditional receipt that places insurance in force on the date of application or medical exam, whichever is later, and only if the insured meets the underwriting qualifications and rules when the policy is delivered. This requirement is also a condition precedent to coverage and provides protection to the applicant if the underwriting rules are met.
3. A conditional receipt that provides a certain amount of insurance for a maximum period of time or until the insurance company acts on the application, regardless of insurability. This type of conditional receipt provides the most protection for the insured and is called a **binding receipt.** At least some amount of coverage is available, and a condition subsequent exists for continuing coverage. If the applicant is found uninsurable, coverage terminates.

Consider two cases. In *Olsen v. Federal Kemper Life Assurance Company*[6] the conditional receipt issued at the time of the application was interpreted to deny death benefits to the beneficiary because a condition precedent was not met. The defendant completed a life insurance application under a conditional receipt on December 2, 1980. The receipt stated "that the company will incur no liability under this application until it has been received and approved, a policy issued and delivered . . . all while the health, habits and other conditions. . . . are as described in this application."

On January 2, 1981, Olsen learned he had cancer and failed to tell the agent or the insurance company. On January 16, 1981, the policy was delivered dated January 1, 1981, and the first premium was paid. Death occurred on February 14, 1981. As a consequence of the conditional receipt, the insurer denied coverage based on the condition precedent of good health upon delivery of the policy. The court found that the continuance of good health until actual delivery of the policy was a condition precedent to the effectiveness of the contract regardless of the policy issue date.

In *American Agency Life Insurance Company v. Russell*[7] a binding conditional receipt was issued providing $50,000 of coverage regardless of the insured's health condition. Russell applied for a $100,000 life insurance policy and paid the first premium. The conditional receipt provided $50,000 of insurance until the policy was formally approved, "provided the health of the proposed insured is as described in the application. . . . If you do not hear from the company within 60 days, notify the company and upon request and return of this receipt, the advance payment will be refunded." On August 17, 1979, the application was received at the home office, and on August 23 it was determined that Russell met underwriting standards. Russell died on August 25, 1979. At that point the policy had been typed, and there was no notification of approval by the company or the agent. American Agency was sued for the excess $50,000 of coverage. The court decided that notice of approval was a condition precedent to any recovery for the full $100,000.

Courts generally adhere to the literal terms of the life insurance contract's conditional receipt. However, sometimes courts adhere to the provisions of the conditional receipt in favor of the insured's interests.

Using Vending Machines to Market Insurance. Of limited importance are travel life insurance contracts marketed by vending machines. These life insurance contracts are designed to pay death benefits if death occurs by accident in the course of specific types of transportation. Typically, one purchases insurance from a machine, fills out all pertinent information, deposits part of the application and mails the remaining part to the insured's address. Insurance coverage is effective for only a short period of time.

It is clear that an application (an offer to contract) cannot be inspected by the life insurance company before the insured departs on the trip. Thus the offer is made by the vending machine to anyone meeting the stated requirements. The acceptance of the contract is made by filling out and depositing the application. As long as legal capacity exists and the contract does not violate the requirement of lawful purpose, a contract is made.

Processing Delay. Offers may specify a time period in which the offer is valid. Although one may place a time limit on an offer, in life insurance it is rarely done. If the life insurance company fails to respond, the applicant cannot construe the silence to be acceptance. Life insurance companies do have a duty to be prompt in their application-processing procedure. If injury occurs due to unreasonable delay in processing, civil penalties can be applied. The use of binding receipts (the third type of conditional receipt discussed earlier, providing some amount of coverage regardless of insurability) reduces the pressure on the life insurance company to speed processing, because some coverage is provided in the period between the actual offer and the acceptance. Binding receipts, however, increase the risk of the life insurance company in that coverage exists until the insured is advised that there is no coverage.

Delivery and Effective Date. Occasionally there may be a question as to whether a delivered policy is actually a contract and whether a contract exists when there has been no delivery. It is important, then, to determine when the contract goes into effect. The effective date is needed to determine whether death occurs within the policy period and to decide when the policy's contestability and restrictions against suicide terminate.

Where no conditional receipt exists, insurance contracts become effective when all conditions precedent are met. Typical conditions precedent include (1) that the application be made, (2) that the policy be issued by the life insurance company, (3) that the insured be in good health when the policy is actually delivered and (4) that the initial premium is paid. The date when all of the stated conditions are fulfilled is when the contract begins.

Regarding the third condition, what constitutes delivery is sometimes in question. Delivery can be *actual* or *constructive*. If there is actual delivery, the policy is physically received by the applicant. In constructive delivery, either an agent for the applicant receives the policy or the life insurance company relinquishes control with the intent of delivery. In the first case the life insurance agent might leave the policy with the spouse or secretary. In the second the life insurance company can place the policy in the mail to the insurance agent with only one act intended—delivery.

Sometimes life insurance policies are delivered to the applicant for inspection. In this case there is no actual contract as no money has changed hands. If the applicant dies while making a decision, it may be difficult for the life insurance company to prove that life insurance did not exist. Because of this problem it is common for applicants to sign a *policy inspection receipt.* These receipts indicate that the policy is in the hands of the applicant only for inspection purposes and that the policy does not provide coverage or constitute a contract.

On the other hand, a contract exists when all of the conditions precedent have been fulfilled even though there are statutory examination periods. Various states have passed laws requiring a ten-day examination period after the policy is delivered. If the owner desires to cancel the contract within the ten-day period, all premiums paid must be returned.

The practice of **backdating** policies also complicates determining when the contract starts. Backdating policies can legally lower the age of issue and in turn lower the premium. Backdating does not shorten any time limitations in the contract. However, some states limit the number of days backdating may take place.

Consideration

Consideration must be exchanged to produce a valid insurance contract. The promises outlined in the contract are exchanged for the insured's doing two things: making the first premium payment and making application statements that are representations about such things as health and employment. When premiums are financed, as is often the case with life insurance sold to college students, agents have the power to create promissory notes constituting an exchange of value. Default on the promissory note is treated separately from policy lapse. The life insurance premium has been paid, and any remedy for the creditor is controlled by the terms of the loan.

Life Insurance Contract Characteristics

Life insurance contracts are characteristically different from other business contracts. These legal characteristics provide insight into how life insurance contracts are treated when legal contests occur between parties to the contract or between beneficiaries and the life insurance company. The life insurance contract is said to be one of adhesion. It is also aleatory, conditional, unilateral, valued and of utmost good faith.

Adhesion

A contract of **adhesion** is interpreted against the writer. In life insurance the applicant has little control over the wording of the contract (though certain clauses and riders such as settlement or beneficiary clauses, are controlled partially by the policy owner). On the other hand, life insurance companies are subject to regulatory requirements. The company must word the contract to comply with any required statutory language. It is also their responsibility to make the contract clear. Thus any ambiguities are construed against the writer (the insurer).

Chapter 9 The Legal Framework of Life Insurance

Aleatory

As defined in Chapter 1, the life insurance contract is *aleatory* as opposed to *commutative*. In an aleatory contract, the exchange between the parties is known to be of unequal value. Life insurance death payments can be significantly greater than the premiums paid for the contract. Aleatory contracts may involve speculation and gambling. Insurance, gambling and speculative contracts are all based on an unequal exchange stemming from the occurrence of a chance event. However, the distinction between insurance and gambling should be made. Gambling is said to create risk where none existed, while insurance eliminates or reduces risk and makes the outcome more certain.

Conditional

The life insurance contract is also said to be a *conditional* contract. Performance by one party to the contract is conditional upon an act or promise of the other party. The life insurance company does not have to act unless the premium is paid, the insured contingency occurs and a claim is presented.

Unilateral

Only one party to the life insurance contract makes an enforceable promise; thus the contract is said to be a **unilateral contract** as opposed to bilateral. In a bilateral contract both parties must perform; and if one party does not, the remedy for the injured party is enforcement of performance or monetary damages. If the contract cannot be performed, it may be set aside. The life insurance contract is unilateral in that the performance of the life insurance company is enforced. The life insurance company must unquestionably accept premiums and abide by the terms of the original contract. The insured need not pay the premium unless there is a continued desire to maintain the contract. In addition, the insurance company cannot void the contract for lack of consideration (paying premiums) when the policy has a cash surrender value.

Valued

Insurance contracts are either **valued contracts** or **indemnity contracts**. An indemnity contract is one that attempts to return the insured to his or her original financial position. Examples of indemnity contracts are fire, inland marine and health insurance contracts.

Life insurance contracts are not indemnity contracts. There is no attempt to place an actual dollar amount on the loss of one's life, so the contract is considered to be valued. A valued contract pays the agreed amount when the contingency occurs. Although there are methods for determining human life values, these methods are used predominantly in civil wrongful death cases (legal liability). Other methods, such as the needs-based approach, attempt to answer the question of how much life insurance one should purchase to meet certain financial goals.

Because the principle of indemnity does not exist in life insurance, the principle of subrogation—that one who indemnifies another for a loss is entitled to recovery from any negligent third parties—also does not exist. Thus, if an insured is wrongfully killed in an automobile accident, the beneficiaries not only can collect the proceeds of the contract but also can sue the negligent party for damages. The life insurance company has no claim or interest in any recovery sought from the negligent third party and thus cannot recover any face amounts paid.

Utmost Good Faith

The life insurance contract is one of **utmost good faith**. Each party to the contract relies on the other's statements before the contract is begun. Either can be injured if important facts are misrepresented or concealed. The life insurance company relies on statements of the insured concerning health, age and employment activities. On the other hand, the applicant relies on statements of the agent concerning the cost and benefits of the policy. Because of the imposition of a higher degree of honesty on the life insurance transaction than on other business transactions, the law allows certain remedies if it can be shown that there was a concealment, a misrepresentation or a breach of warranty. A breach of warranty has little importance in the life insurance transaction, as will be shown.

A **concealment** is silence when there is an obligation to divulge information. The doctrine of utmost good faith imposes the responsibility on the applicant to divulge all material information. When a fact is concealed and it is considered **material**, the contract could be rescinded. A fact is considered material if the life insurance company would have denied the coverage, written the contract on a different form or charged a different premium based on the undisclosed information.

The strict application of this doctrine could produce hardship. If an insurance company fails to ask the appropriate questions and the applicant, ignorant of the appropriate questions, fails to reveal the information, rescission of the contract may occur. This point has been addressed in many cases.[8] The general rule with regard to a concealment is that failure to disclose a fact not asked by the agent or company will not provide the grounds for rescinding the contract unless the applicant intended to conceal fact(s) believed to be material. In other words, unless there was fraudulent intent to conceal (the element of deception), the failure to disclose information not requested does not ordinarily provide grounds to void the contract.

Representations are oral or written statements made before the contract is accepted. If the statements are incorrect and considered relevant to underwriting, the life insurance company can be injured. The New York Insurance Code (Section 3105) states that "no **misrepresentation** shall avoid any contract of insurance or defeat recovery thereunder unless such misrepresentation was material." Like concealment, a fact is considered material if the insurance company would have issued the contract (or not issued it) on different terms or at a different rate (premium). "In determining the question of materiality, evidence of the practice of the insurer which made such contract with respect to the acceptance or rejection of similar risks shall be admissible." (New York Insurance Code Section 3105)

In *Friedman v. Prudential Life Insurance Company*[9] the insurance company was allowed to rescind a contract based on a material misrepresentation. On February 3, 1982, a $37,000 life insurance policy was issued on Melvin Friedman, naming Mrs. Friedman the beneficiary. Melvin Friedman died on August 17, 1982. Because presentation of a death certificate is required before collecting proceeds, the certificate was requested and delivered. "The Certificate of Death stated that the immediate cause of . . . death was cardiac arrest, which was due to, or a consequence of, cardiogenic shock and chronic congestive cardiomyopathy, the onset of which had occurred years ago." The insurance company denied payment and returned the premium with interest. During the trial it was determined that the insured was treated for the undisclosed ailment and that the insurance company would not have issued the policy if the true facts had been known. As a result Prudential was allowed to rescind the contract and deny any liability.

Many statements made in applications are considered to be **statements of opinion** rather than representations. Statements of opinion arise when the insured is not in a position to know about an existing condition and believes something else to be true. Statements of opinion, even though false, could be considered material and will not allow the insurer to avoid the policy. Generally the element of deceit must be present, meaning that a statement known to be false at the time it was made must be proved to avoid payment.

In *Fuchs v. Old Line Life Insurance Co.*[10] the applicant made the statement that he was "free of any sickness or physical impairment." The applicant died of a heart attack, and it was revealed that the insured had suffered from a similar ailment two years before the application. From the point of view of the insured, there was no sickness, disability or impairment, because he was healed. Therefore the statement that the insurer relied on was considered a statement of opinion, and payment was made.

A *warranty* is considered a condition of the contract, and any breach of that condition will allow the insurer to avoid performance. With respect to life insurance, statements made in the application could in many cases be construed as a warranty instead of a representation. If the statement is considered a warranty, the company need only show a breach, and the contract can be rescinded. This could produce harsh results for a beneficiary expecting proceeds or for an insured who subsequently becomes uninsurable. Proceeds could be lost because of an innocent breach. And once the contract has been rescinded, the insured may no longer be able to purchase insurance due to advanced age or health problems.

Because the doctrine of warranty would impose hardship for even a trivial breach, most states consider all statements in the life insurance application to be representations. The New York Insurance Code Section 3204 states that "all statements . . . for the issuance, reinstatement, or renewal of any such policy or contract shall be deemed representations and not warranties."

Law of Agency

The concept of agency is extremely important to the life insurance transaction. Life insurance companies are typically corporations, and their existence is created in accordance with state law. Therefore insurance companies cannot operate without the use of agents to perform required functions. These functions include soliciting and underwriting contracts, performing medical inspections, adjusting claims and investing assets. Individuals fulfilling these duties are agents in the broad legal sense of the word. An agent is an individual who acts on behalf of another. For example, the life insurance agent solicits applications from the public on behalf of the insurance company.

In general, an agent can perform almost any task a principal can perform. There are, however, some exceptions. An agent cannot perform any personal service the principal is required to perform. The agent cannot vote for the principal; nor can an agent accept punishment for the principal. In addition, the principal must perform when special judgment is required.

There are several recognized duties the agent owes the principal:

- The agent has the duty to be loyal to the principal. In other words, the agent must place the principal's interest foremost in all activities connected to the agency.
- The agent must obey the principal's instructions so long as they are reasonable and legal.
- The agent must not be negligent (must use reasonable care in carrying out the principal's instructions).

In return, the principal owes the agent several duties. The principal must keep accurate records, compensate the agent for work or services performed and abide by other statutory requirements relating to employment such as withholding taxes, meeting Occupational Safety and Health Administration (OSHA) standards and meeting workers' compensation laws.

Types of Agents

The law of agency recognizes two types of agents. *General agents* are given the authority to perform acts over a period of time or to perform a series of acts. The emphasis in this relationship is on repeated activities of the agent for the benefit of the principal. Included in the general agent's activity are all acts performed in the normal course of the business in question. A *special agent* is one given the authority to perform only a specific task over a limited period of time. For example, if principal P wants agent G to enter negotiations and complete the purchase of a business, the agent is a general agent, because all activities for the specific purpose of the purchase are authorized. After the negotiations, if agent S is given the task of delivering the money for the purchase, S will be considered a special agent. Note, though, that these descriptions of general and special agents are not precise and that the use of these terms in both law and insurance is not consistent. The definitions of the general and special agents for normal business law can be confusing when applied to the law of agency in life insurance. In life insurance the terms *special* and *general* are used to denote different scopes of agent authorization, and the titles used to describe the agent vary from state to state. In the life insurance industry *general agent* usually refers to an individual who is given the power and authority, through an agency agreement, to solicit business in a certain geographic area. General agents are authorized to hire, educate and license special agents, or soliciting agents. The general agent does not have the power to accept offers to purchase life insurance, because that power is retained by the life insurance company and contracts must be completed by home office personnel. Special agents contact prospects, determine their needs and solicit applications for the purchase of life insurance.

Much confusion arises out of the imprecise definitions of the terms *special* and *general agent*, both in insurance and noninsurance transactions. State laws determine who is a special or general agent. However, regardless of the legal title, the task of the courts is to determine whether the person or entity had the authority to perform a certain task when the event or injury occurred.

Also adding to the confusion in the life insurance industry is the use of the term **broker**. Brokers conform to agency laws, but the legal principal-agent relationship of the broker exists between the applicant (principal) and the broker (agent). Note that a broker is a legal representative of the applicant and not of the life insurance company. Brokers seek insurance coverage, negotiate premiums and fill out applications on behalf of the insurance applicant. Many insurance marketing concerns represent themselves to the public as brokers. In several states, such as Ohio, the insurance code does not recognize brokers. All persons and entities engaged in the sale of insurance, even though they state they are brokers, are considered agents. Thus these "brokers" are usually agents who represent insurance companies.

It is important to determine whether the applicant in an insurance transaction is dealing with a broker or an agent. If the person is considered a broker, the principal-agent relationship lies between the applicant and the broker. Any knowledge divulged to the broker is not concurrent knowledge of the life insurance company. Thus, if the applicant provides material information to the broker that would impair the ability to secure coverage, and that information is also not communicated to the life insurance company, future problems may occur. Prior to any time limit on defenses, a concealment or misrepresentation may be claimed to contest any benefits.

If the same facts occur as above but the salesperson is considered an agent for the life insurance company, any knowledge of the agent is considered concurrent knowledge of the life insurance company. Concealment cannot be claimed, even though the information was not passed on to the home office, because the true facts are treated as if conveyed to the company by the agent.

Consider the case of *Northern National Life Insurance Company v. Lacy J. Miller Machine Company, Inc.*[11] Several minority stockholders of Miller Machine wanted to purchase life insurance to cover Lacy Miller, the president. In March 1979 insurance agent Brooks obtained an application for $100,000 of life insurance. Equitable Insurance declined the application based on medical reasons (heart trouble). In December 1979 a new group insurance plan being marketed was based on the "insured not to be known as terminally ill and that the insured is actively engaged in full-time employment." Lacy Miller signed a blank application, and agent Brooks filled it out based on prior meetings, interviews and past knowledge. During the proceedings it was shown that the information contained in the application concerning Miller's occupation and full-time status had been incorrect and that Brooks knew or should have known the true facts. The insurer tried to deny liability on the $100,000 policy.

The insurer was estopped from asserting fraud of its agent, and the life insurance company was required to pay the proceeds. The result was based on the following facts. The court found Brooks not to be Miller's agent; statements in the application were false; Brooks was found to be an agent for Northern National; Brooks had reason to know of the true facts; and false facts were inserted in the application.

Authority of the Life Insurance Agent

The life insurance agent receives authority to solicit applications and perform necessary and incidental sales activities in a contract called the *agency agreement*. The agency agreement spells out the agent's duties and obligations to the life insurance company, as well as the life insurance company's obligations to the agent. Typical considerations in the agreement include:

- the limits of the agent's authority and activities, such as what types of contracts may be solicited;
- the commission schedule to be paid on new and old business, and/or salary arrangements;
- survivorship rights in commissions;
- how the agreement may be terminated; and
- the type and amount of service and training to be provided by the company.

An agent's total authority to perform acts for the principal is delineated by the sum of the authority given in the agreement, what the agent actually believes his or her authority is and other reasonable acts to accomplish domiciled activities. When the agent and the life insurance company enter into the agency agreement, it is said that the agent's authority is *express*. Express authority includes all authority actually given (written) the agent to perform certain acts. Agents may also receive authority in other ways. When an agent is told to perform a certain act, it may be *implied* that the authority exists to take all reasonable and necessary steps to perform that act. For example, if an agent's job is to sell life insurance, implied is the authority to prospect, set up medical exams, take applications and accept premium payments. In addition to these rules, authority can be generated by an agent's actions. If the principal gives the public reason to believe that an agency relationship exists, there is said to be **apparent authority**. If an agent obtains applications and solicits life insurance without authority from the company, the appearance of agency exists from the point of view of the buyer of this insurance, and the company will be bound by this person's activities. Life insurance contracts cannot be started by the agent, but premiums might be collected or information exchanged, creating the agency.

Agency can also be created by *ratification*. If an agent or person repeatedly performs an unauthorized act, the principal ratifies that activity by not objecting in a timely fashion. For example, Mr. Whitfield, who is not an agent, continually solicits business and sends applications to the company. The company then issues the policies. The life insurance company, because it has previously accepted the applications and has not protested, cannot subsequently deny that an agency relationship exists and refuse performance on the contracts on this ground.

Sometimes agents in their sales presentation overstep their authority. Four areas commonly disputed are twisting, product misrepresentation, practicing law and rebating.

Twisting refers to the activity of persuading a client to drop an existing contract and replace it with another. The purpose of the product replacement may be to improve a client's coverage, but it also enriches the agent who earns a commission on the sale. In some instances replacement may harm the policy owner. The practice of twisting includes product misrepresentation, incomplete comparisons and misleading or defamatory statements made about the competitor's policies or financial condition.

Rebating is the practice of returning value as an inducement to buy the product. In most states all forms of rebating are forbidden. In a recent Florida case, "the District Court of Appeals . . . found that the Florida antirebating statutes constitute an unjustified exercise of the police power . . . and are therefore violative of the due process clause. . . ."[12] The court found no legitimate reason to maintain antirebate laws because there was no legitimate state interest in the protection of the public. Several arguments for antirebating statutes were presented that showed the existence of a legitimate state interest in protecting the public. These arguments included protecting the general public from unfair discrimination and from additional insolvencies. As of this writing, antirebating laws are still in effect except in the states of Florida and California.

In addition to twisting, misrepresenting and rebating, the agent must be careful not to engage in the unauthorized practice of law. Because it is illegal for life insurance agents to practice law, the agent must be careful not to provide services that must be performed by an attorney.

Creditors' Rights in Life Insurance Contracts

The phrase *creditors' rights in life insurance* refers to the ability of a creditor of either the insured or a beneficiary to attach life insurance values (cash value or policy proceeds) to pay for delinquent obligations. Federal and state governments recognize the value of life insurance in supplying protection to beneficiaries and generally exempt cash value and policy proceeds from creditors' claims. If creditors were freely able to attach the values at death or during the insured's lifetime, any benefit in owning life insurance would depend on the solvency of the insured while alive or the estate at death. Both federal and state laws pertain to creditors' rights, with the state laws segmented into rights of the insured's creditors and rights of the beneficiary's creditors.

Federal Law

The U.S. Congress allows state laws to control creditors' rights in life insurance policies. This includes federal bankruptcy proceedings. Therefore insurance policies are exempt from bankruptcy proceedings to the extent that state laws allow the exemption.

If the state law is silent concerning an exemption of cash value, then the cash value of the bankrupt policy owner is included in the proceeding, governed by the bankruptcy act, and the cash value is subject to creditor's claims. Some states allow only a limited exemption, so any excess over the exempt amount is included for distribution.

If, at the time of bankruptcy, a state exemption does not exist (or is limited), title to the property vests in the trustee on the date of the bankruptcy petition. At this point the policy owner can pay the amount of the vested interest (cash value) to the trustee to retain the ownership of the life insurance. Alternatively, the trustee will use the property for the satisfaction of any debts. If the bankrupt insured dies during the proceedings, the trustee is entitled only to the cash surrender value of the policy, not the total death benefit. Any excess amounts are paid to the beneficiary.

An exception to the priority of state laws occurs when the federal government is a creditor. Section 6334 of the Internal Revenue Code lists categories of property that are exempt from a government's tax lien. Life insurance products are not listed. Thus the federal government may seize cash surrender values up to the amount of the tax, interest and costs. The federal government may collect on the tax lien in one of two ways. A civil action is possible (IRC Section 7403), or the IRS may recover the cash surrender value directly from the insurer (IRC Section 6332). A civil action is considered the less efficient because it requires great expense and time, so the second method predominates use. After receipt of the direct attachment notice the life insurance company must pay the required amount within 90 days. Even when the policy is owned jointly, all cash values can be used to satisfy the tax lien (IRC Section 6013[d][3]).

It should be noted that the federal government gives insurance companies a "superpriority" status when a policy loan is granted after legal notice of the bankruptcy but before actual notice for payment of the lien (IRC Section 6623[b][9]). Thus in the case of **automatic premium loans (APLs)** the life insurance company is forced to comply with the APL selection because the contractual obligation is made prior to the lien. For example, Mr. Turner, who has been convicted of tax evasion, owns a life insurance policy with a considerable amount of cash value. If the insurer receives legal notice of the bankruptcy, it must honor the APL selection (the contractual obligation) if there are no premium payments before the actual notice for payment of the tax lien.

State Laws

All states have passed laws exempting, in some form, claims against life insurance contracts. States recognize the importance of providing protection for dependents whether or not the policy owner is solvent. State exemptions reduce the possibility of dependents becoming a burden on the public by making the needs of dependents (beneficiaries) superior to the claims of creditors. State exemption laws, however, will not go so far as to protect policyholders when there is an intent to defraud creditors by purchasing life insurance products. The amount a creditor can recover in these cases depends on the wording of the state's exemption statute and its interpretation. Individual state statutes and court decisions need to be consulted to determine the likely treatment of such fraud against creditors in the various states.

Rights of the Insured's Creditors

In general state exemption statutes protect the insured's cash value and proceeds from the claims of creditors. In a few states, however, the statutes are not broad enough to include protection for cash values. These amounts are then subject to federal bankruptcy rules and also to the statutes addressing fraud. In addition, state exemption laws address beneficiary designations. If death proceeds are payable to the policy owner or the insured (estate), state exemptions are generally not applicable, because all assets in the insured's estate are available to pay estate debts. Some states modify this general rule to allocate some estate assets for the benefit of certain dependents. In most states, however, there is generally no limit to the exemption amount as long as beneficiary requirements are met and there is no fraud against creditors.

The exemptions with regard to disability payments, annuities and endowments also vary by state. Disability benefits are generally not exempt, although some state's exemption statutes provide limited exemptions.[13] The exemptions for payments from annuities and endowment policies also depend on state law.

Creditors' Rights Against the Beneficiary

Ordinarily a creditor of a beneficiary does not have access to the insured's cash value, simply because the beneficiary has no vested property right in the life insurance contract. When the state statute exempts claims of the beneficiaries' creditors against cash value, it usually applies only to spousal relationships. For example, if a wife in New York[14] purchases a policy on her husband and makes herself beneficiary, she will be protected against the claims of both her and her husband's creditors even though both may have property interests in the contract.

When the beneficiary has a property right (for example, the owner of the contract) and no state exemption exists, creditors may be able to attach the cash values in the contract. In the case of an irrevocable beneficiary with no state exemption and *no* property right in the life insurance contract, creditors cannot attach the proceeds, because the beneficiary has only a contingent interest in the proceeds upon death and no right to the cash value.

As for the proceeds of the contract, several state exemption laws specifically prohibit the claims of the beneficiary's creditors against policy proceeds. When the law does not address this type of exemption, the law usually allows the policy owner to include a **spendthrift trust provision** in the life insurance contract. A spendthrift trust clause exempts proceeds of a life insurance contract from the beneficiary's creditor's claims. Most spendthrift trust provisions apply only when the proceeds are paid to the beneficiary other than the insured's estate. Also, most statutes provide protection under the spendthrift provisions only if the proceeds are paid under certain settlement methods (annuity form–fixed payment, fixed amount or annuity). After the proceeds are received by the beneficiary, creditors may be able to reach those amounts. The following is a typical spendthrift trust provision that can be included in the life insurance policy:

> The benefits payable to any beneficiary hereunder after the death of the Insured shall not be assignable nor transferable nor subject to commutation or encumbrance, nor to any legal process, execution, garnishment, or attachment proceedings.

An alternative to using the spendthrift trust clause in life insurance contracts is the *discretionary trust*. It is useful in states where the spendthrift trust clause is not allowed. In a discretionary trust an individual is entitled to assets of the trust at the discretion of the trustee. The beneficiary cannot force the trustee to liquidate trust property, because no present property interest exists. Thus creditors of the beneficiary cannot claim against any property held in trust.

Review Questions

1. How many legal interests are created when a life insurance contract is started? What are these legal interests? Can one entity hold more than one of these interests at a time?
2. What prerequisites exist to starting a valid life insurance contract?
3. How can one demonstrate insurable interest in the life of an insured? When must the insurable interest exist?
4. Explain why minors under certain ages, the insane and the intoxicated are not considered to have capacity to contract.
5. Why are conditional receipts used in the life insurance transaction?
6. Compare the legal characteristics of a life insurance contract to the legal characteristics of a contract to purchase clothes.
7. How can a life insurance contract be aleatory when both parties to the contract have exchanged negotiated values?
8. Why are warranties treated as representations in life insurance transactions?
9. What are the differences among a special agent, a general agent and a broker?
10. Discuss how an agent receives authority. How is authority limited by the life insurance company? How can the extent of authority be expanded by courts when viewed by the public?
11. Does state or federal law control creditors' rights in life insurance? Explain.
12. During the insured's lifetime, are life insurance values (cash value) attachable by creditors? Explain.
13. At death, if policy proceeds are paid into the estate, can creditors recover amounts owed?
14. What interest does a beneficiary have in a life insurance policy with respect to reaching cash values?
15. Explain why a spendthrift trust clause is useful in protecting policy proceeds from beneficiaries' creditors. How will a discretionary trust change the answer?

Endnotes

[1] Henry Campbell Black, *Black's Law Dictionary*, 5th ed. (St. Paul, Minn.: West Publishing, 1968), p. 394.

[2] Robert E. Keeton, *Insurance Law Basic Text* (St. Paul, Minn.: West Publishing, 1971), p. 120.

[3] *Lamb et al. v. Northwestern National Life Insurance Company*, 56 Md. App. 125; 467 A.2d 182 (1983).

[4] *Jones v. All American Life Insurance Company*, 68 N.C. App. 582; 316 S.E.2d 122 (1984).

[5] New York Insurance Code, Section 3207.

[6] *Olsen v. Federal Kemper Life Assurance Company*, 68 Ore. App. 90; 681 P.2d 144 (1984).

[7] *American Agency Life Insurance Company v. Russell*, 37 Wash. App. 110; 678 P.2d 1303 (1984).

[8] *Penn Mutual Life Insurance v. Mechanics' Savings Bank and Trust Company*, 72 F. 413 (1896); *Blair v. National Security Insurance Company*, 126 F.2d 955 (1942).

[9] *Friedman v. The Prudential Life Insurance Company of America*, 589 F.Supp. 1017 (1984).

[10] *Fuchs v. Old Line Insurance Co.*, 46 Wis.2d 67, 174 N.W.2d 273 (1970).

[11] *Northern National Life Insurance Company v. Lacy J. Miller Machine Company, Inc.*, 63 N.C. App. 424; 305 S.E.2d 568 (1983).

[12] William B. Scher, "Agents Fight Fla. Rebate Ruling," *National Underwriter (Life & Health Edition)*, November 3, 1984, pp. 11, 12.

[13] Alabama Code, Title 28A, Section 344, provides a $250-per-month limited exemption.

[14] New York Insurance Code Section 3212.

[15] *Advanced Underwriting Service* (Chicago: Dearborn Financial Publishing, Inc.), Section 18–8.

Bibliography

Advanced Underwriting Service. Chicago: Dearborn Financial Publishing, Inc.

Black, Kenneth Jr., and Harold Skipper, Jr. *Life Insurance,* 11th ed. Englewood Cliffs, N.J.: Prentice-Hall, 1987.

Greider, Janice, E., et al. *Law and the Life Insurance Contract*. Homewood, Ill.: Richard D. Irwin, 1984.

Keeton, Robert, E., and Alan I. Widiss. *Insurance Law Basic Text*. St. Paul, Minn.: West Publishing, 1988.

Mehr, Robert I., and Sandra G. Gustavson. *Life Insurance Theory and Practice*. Plano, Tex.: Business Publications, Inc. 1987.

Widiss, Alan, I., and Robert E. Keeton. *Insurance Law* (1988 Course Supplement). St. Paul, Minn.: West Publishing, 1988.

Chapter 10 | Life Insurance Policy Provisions

Chapter Objectives

- Discuss the mandatory and optional provisions of the life insurance contract
- Explore the ways nonforfeiture values can be used
- Discuss the common life insurance settlement methods
- Investigate the uses of participating dividends

Introduction

The performance of the life insurance contract is controlled by policy provisions, laws, court decisions and court interpretation. This chapter discusses life insurance policy provisions in light of this environment. Because the body of law controlling life insurance emerges from the states, contract provisions considered mandatory, optional or prohibited vary. Even if the wording of these provisions were consistent, states would interpret them differently. Thus no standard set of life insurance policies and provisions currently exist. Standard life insurance policies were mandated in several states after the Armstrong investigation of 1905 but were abandoned before 1910.[1] Subsequently New York mandated minimum language for various contractual requirements. The minimum language, coupled with the **Appleton Rule** (which broadens territorial enforcement by forcing life insurance companies selling insurance in New York to conform to New York laws wherever they sell insurance), provides the impetus for other states to adopt similar language requirements. Throughout this chapter, therefore, the New York Insurance Code will be quoted as having broad application.

Mandatory Policy Provisions

The New York Insurance Code, Section 3203, enforces mandatory provisions by use of the following paragraph:

> All life insurance policies, except as otherwise stated herein, delivered or issued for delivery in this state, shall contain in substance the following provi-

sions or provisions which the superintendent deems to be more favorable to policyholders:

This wording is typical of state law and allows contract wording more favorable than the mandated minimum. Any life insurance policy not conforming to the New York Insurance Code is interpreted automatically to include the minimum intent of the law. Provisions that are generally considered mandatory include:

- an entire-contract clause;
- an incontestable clause;
- a misstatement-of-age provision;
- a grace period;
- provisions dealing with nonforfeiture and surrender;
- a reinstatement provision;
- a provision describing settlement options; and
- a provision concerning apportionment of divisible surplus.

The Entire-Contract Provision

The **entire-contract clause** makes the policy issued with the application attached the total agreement between the parties to the contract. The application contains all of the pertinent underwriting and medical information. Most states do not allow the life insurance company to contest the contract based on statements in an application not attached to the policy. This is typical text of the entire-contract provision:

This policy and the application, a copy of which is attached when the policy is issued, constitute the entire contract.[2]

The purpose of the entire-contract provision is to discourage and eliminate the practice of *incorporation by reference*. Incorporation by reference can be used to simplify contract construction by including other documents by referring to them. Historically a few life insurance companies used incorporation by reference to include their corporate bylaws or charter as well as unattached applications. When provisions are included in the contract by reference, undisclosed limitations could alter a policy owner's benefits and rights. States prohibit incorporating the application by reference, because the practice can injure the insured by removing any opportunity to review and correct any errors in the application. In sum, entire-contract statutes protect the policy owner because all rights and duties are spelled out in the contract; the insurance company is protected because the insured cannot argue ignorance of provisions and statements made in the application.

Even though the entire-contract provision forces the intent of the parties to be contained in the policy, state laws and their interpretations modify and become a part of the contract. For example, if a mandatory provision is omitted, the policy is interpreted as if it exists. When provisions lack conformity to the minimum statutory requirements, the policy is interpreted as if it includes the required language. Moreover, entire-contract statutes apply only to the original intent of the parties at the inception of the contract; any subsequent, mutually agreed-on changes are treated as modifications.

Because laws and interpretations vary among states, determining court jurisdiction may be a problem in interstate disputes. Some states apply the *place-of-making* rule to determine which state law applies. This rule says that the contract is subject to the state law where performance of the last act to complete the contract occurred. The other states, not adhering to the place-of-making rule, decide which state law applies.

Incontestable Clause   Life insurance companies are barred by the *incontestable clause* from challenging the contract's validity after two years from the issue date. A typical incontestable clause reads:

> This policy shall be incontestable after it has been in force during the lifetime of the Insured for two years from the Date of Issue.

A two-year incontestable period is considered normal, but some insurance companies impose a one-year time limit. Even if there were material misrepresentations, concealments and (in many cases) fraud, the life insurance company could not contest the contract's validity after the prescribed period. The majority of life insurance companies include the words *during the lifetime of the insured* in the provision. When the clause states that the policy is contestable only within two years from the date of issue, a beneficiary knowing of a questionable fact would wait to submit the claim until the time limit expired.

The incontestable clause holds a special place in any insurance law discussion. Within the framework of normal contract law, the injured party may challenge a contract after any fraud is discovered but before any statute of limitations bars action. Further, the time limit starts when the fraud is discovered, not when the contract begins as in life insurance. The intent of the incontestable clause is for the insurer to agree to disregard fraud and lesser abuses of contract law after a specific length of time.

Before 1900 many life insurance companies voluntarily inserted a version of the incontestable clause to overcome some insurers' reputation for disputing the contract's validity on any fact not literally true. The incontestable clause protects the insured and any beneficiaries from the life insurance company contesting the validity of the contract long after underwriting facts should have been discovered. Two years is considered sufficient time to determine the suitability of the insured.

Even though the effect of the incontestable clause seems absolute, the life insurance company may still contest or terminate the contract in certain circumstances. Nonpayment of premium will terminate the contract if no nonforfeiture values exist. Moreover, benefit amounts may be adjusted or contested when the insured misstates his or her age or sex on the application or when the cause of death is questioned relative to accidental death benefit riders. Also, interpretation of the contracts may cause problems, and the validity of the entire contract may be in dispute. When gross fraud is involved, jurisdictions tend to set the contract aside, even if contested beyond the applicable period.

The incontestable clause is not applicable in these instances because the contests barred are generally those questioning the validity of the entire contract, not those attempting to interpret or enforce provisions. Other contestable points also not barred by the incontestable clause are contestable points such as:

- when the contract owner is determined to have no insurable interest at the time of issue;
- when the policy is purchased with the intent to murder; or
- when a person impersonates an insured for the application or medical exam.

In these cases the contract tends to be set aside and is said to be void from the beginning (void *ab initio*).

In *Welch v. Provident Life and Accident Insurance Company* a life insurance policy was found to be void and against public policy because it lacked insurable interest. Richard Morris and John Whitehead, owners of the corporation, applied for $100,000 of life insurance on Welch. Provident Life and Accident Insurance Company declined to issue the life insurance contract because there was no insurable interest. The beneficiary was then changed to Welch's son with the intent to change the beneficiary back to Morris and Whitehead once the policy was issued. The policy was then issued with the new beneficiary. Several issues were addressed (including the insured's health upon delivery), but it was found that even though the insured had a right to change the beneficiary to whomever he wanted, "Morris and Whitehead were the original procurers of the insurance, that it was never intended that there be any other beneficiary, and the contract of insurance was invalid ab initio because the procurers had no beneficiary interest in the life of the insured."[3]

Misstatement of Age

Issue age is the prime underwriting criterion for pricing life insurance; when it is misstated, the wrong premium will be charged for the exposure. An insured misrepresenting material facts, including important rating criteria, would ordinarily cause the insurance contract to be contested when reliance on the facts caused injury. Because insurance companies use either the age on the next, nearest or last birthday as an underwriting convention, statement of age must be in variance with the company's method for determining age to be considered a misstatement.

Not being able to document the insured's correct age causes problems for the life insurance industry. If the life insurance company is allowed to contest the entire contract after the death of the insured, based on age discrepancies, the beneficiary will be monetarily injured. If the misstatement of age is discovered while the insured is alive and is uninsurable, future life insurance replacement will be impossible. Most states follow the New York method of resolving the problem associated with any misstatement of age. New York Insurance Code Section 3203 requires that the following policy provision be included:

> If the age of the Insured has been misstated, any amount payable or benefit accruing under the policy shall be such as the premium would have purchased at the correct age.

The **misstatement-of-age provision** guarantees the beneficiary's right to receive policy proceeds if the insured's age was misrepresented. When the correct age is discovered before the insured's death, either the face amount is adjusted or the premiums are corrected to maintain the policy's face amount. Moreover, if the true age is discovered before the incontestable clause time limit is exceeded, the life insurance company may rescind the policy if applicable underwriting rules would have barred issuing the contract if the correct age had been known.

Misstatement of sex may also be a problem, though it is generally not a great one. Some insurance companies have elected to treat misstatement of sex in a way similar to misstatement of age. Widespread use of unisex mortality tables may eliminate the problem altogether.

Grace Period

The **grace period** is a length of time after the premium due date during which the contract remains in force even though premium payments have not been received. The following is the text of a typical grace period clause found in life insurance contracts.

> A grace period of 31 days shall be allowed for payment of a premium not paid on its due date. The policy shall continue in full force during the period. If the Insured dies during the grace period, the overdue premium shall be paid from the proceeds of the policy.

Statutorily the grace period is set at 31 days, but insurers may increase the period. If the insured dies during the grace period, premiums due are subtracted from any policy proceeds. Most state grace period provisions allow interest to be charged on any premium owed during the period. However, because the interest amount is usually insignificant, insurance companies tend not to impose the charge. Nonpayment of premiums may occur for many personal reasons. Whether the contract continues depends on the existence of cash value beyond the grace period. When there are no cash values, the grace period extends the contract for the applicable period when a lapse occurs, but the contract terminates if premiums are not paid after the grace period. When cash values exist, the contract continues beyond the grace period without additional premium payments. The most common methods by which the contract continues in this case are to elect the paid-up insurance option, elect the extended term option or make an automatic premium loan. These methods are discussed in the following section.

Nonforfeiture Options

New York Insurance Code Section 3203 requires that a **nonforfeiture option** be included in cash value life insurance products. Specifically the provision must show:

> the (guaranteed) cash surrender values and other options available in the event of default in a premium payment after premiums have been paid for a specified period, together with a table showing, in figures, all options available during each of the policy's first 20 years.

The origin of the cash or **nonforfeiture value** can be traced to the process of leveling the premium. Instead of paying an increasing premium each year, insureds pay a periodic level premium. In the early years of the policy the insured overpays the mortality expense, and in the later years the mortality expense is underpaid. The overpayments plus interest and a survivor benefit generate cash values. The leveling process producing the cash value is simply a funding technique to enhance the affordability and continuance of life insurance contracts. (The mathematics of the process is presented in Chapter 22.)

Historically, when the insured lapsed the policy (failed to pay the premium), the accumulated asset amount often was forfeited. As early as 1861, Massachusetts passed the first nonforfeiture legislation guaranteeing that four-fifths of the life insurance contract's cash value was to be used to purchase extended term insurance. Several other states then enacted similar legislation. By 1948 every state had appropriate nonforfeiture provisions mandating life insurance companies to guarantee certain values in the form of the cash surrender option, the extended term option and the reduced paid-up insurance option. (Alfred N. Guertin was appointed in 1937 to head a committee to study forfeitures and suggest legislation. The report led to the writing of two model bills by the NAIC. The standard nonforfeiture and the standard valuation laws are generally referred to as *Guertin legislation.*)

Figure 10.1A shows the relationship between a contract's cash value supplied by the nonforfeiture option and the amount of pure protection. As the insured persists and pays the premium, the cash value amount increases and the amount of protection decreases.

Cash Surrender Option

Cash surrender amounts are found in the policy's table of guaranteed values. The table lists the cash value according to the age of issue and the number of years the policy has been in force. Standard nonforfeiture legislation prescribes how to calculate the minimum cash value accruing to the benefit of the insured. Table 10.1 is an excerpt from the table of guaranteed values of a typical whole life insurance contract.

Cash values are not required until the end of the third year under the NAIC standard nonforfeiture legislation. However, some states require cash value amounts to be available at the end of the second year. The table values are guaranteed minimums, and many life insurance companies pay excess interest above the guaranteed rate, which leads to higher values.

If the insured wishes to terminate the contract, all of the guaranteed amount may be withdrawn:

> The Owner may surrender this policy for its cash value less any indebtedness. The policy shall terminate upon receipt at the Home Office of this policy and a written surrender of all claims. Receipt of the policy may be waived by the Company.
>
> The Company may defer paying the cash value for a period not exceeding six months from the date of surrender. If payment is deferred 30 days or more, interest shall be paid on the cash value less any indebtedness at the rate of 4% compounded annually from the date of surrender to the date of payment.

Generally the policy owner is required to deliver the contract to the life insurance company and request the surrender in writing. If the policy is lost, the life

**Figure 10.1
Conversion to Nonforfeiture Options**

A. **Normal whole life:**
   premium payments continue for all of one's life

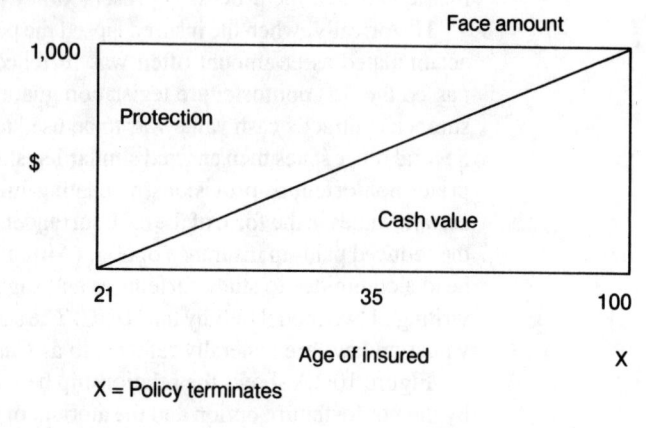

   X = Policy terminates

B. **Extended term option:**
   premium payments stop at conversion

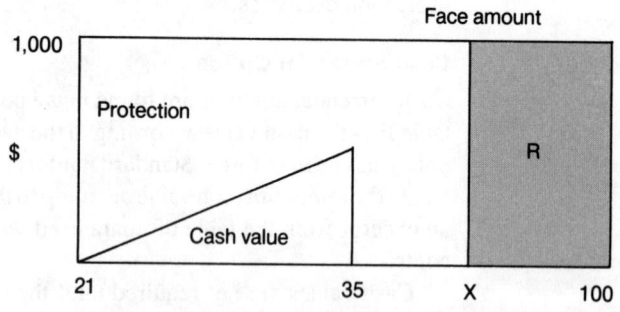

   X = Policy terminates
   R = Reduction in time

C. **Paid-up insurance option:**
   premium payments stop at conversion

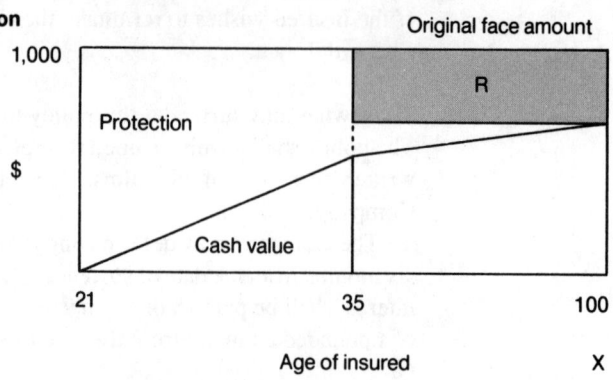

   X = Policy terminates
   R = Reduction in face amount

Table 10.1
Table of Guaranteed Values
(Male, age 20, per $1,000 face amount)

End of Policy Year	Cash or Loan Value	Paid-Up Insurance	Extended Term Years	Extended Term Days
1	$ 0.00	$ 0.00	0	0
2	0.00	0.00	0	0
3	4.09	13.00	1	214
4	15.12	46.00	6	38
5	26.46	78.00	10	253
6	38.09	110.00	14	248
7	50.01	142.00	17	205
Age 35	156.11	372.00	25	153
Age 62	567.46	811.00	17	85
Age 65	612.11	838.00	19	320

insurance company will have the policy owner sign a *lost policy receipt* as evidence of the surrender and to prove that a contract no longer exists. Problems arise if the insured dies during the process of surrendering the contract. The life insurance company would argue that only cash value should be paid even though the surrender process is incomplete. The beneficiary may insist that the face amount should be paid. In such cases the courts have generally decided in favor of the beneficiary, but there have been exceptions.

Extended Term Option

Instead of terminating the contract and receiving the cash value amount, the insured may continue death benefits in the form of term insurance without paying any additional premiums. In essence the insured purchases a single-premium term insurance contract for the original face amount for a predetermined period of years and days. If the insured outlives the time period, the contract terminates with no further benefits available. Individuals in poor health tend to select this option. As shown in Table 10.1, if the whole life insurance contract has been in force for seven years, the policy owner may convert to the **extended term option** by exchanging $50.01 for each $1,000 of face amount and in return receive extended term insurance for 17 years and 205 days. If the original policy was for $50,000, $50,000 of extended term insurance would be available as a death benefit for the designated period. As shown in Figure 10.1B, if the policy owner converts to the extended term option at age 35, the face amount of coverage is provided for a specified length of time in exchange for the cash value. The shaded area on the right represents the length of time lost due to the extended term conversion.

Reduced Paid-Up Insurance Option

If the insured no longer desires to pay insurance premiums, a reduced amount of whole life insurance is available. For example, Table 10.1 shows that, if the policy has been in force for seven years and the paid-up insurance option is chosen, $142 of whole life insurance will be available for each $1,000 of original face amount.

If the original face amount is $50,000, $7,100 ($142 × 50) is available as a death benefit under this option. In return for $50.01 per $1,000 of face amount the policy owner converts to a lower death benefit. The conversion is similar to purchasing the life insurance policy with a reduced death benefit at an older age, on a single-premium basis. Unlike the extended term option, cash values are still available with the paid-up insurance option after conversion.

This alternative is illustrated in Figure 10.1C. If the life insurance policy is converted to the paid-up insurance option at age 35, the policy owner receives a reduced face amount for the rest of the insured's life. The shaded area indicates the reduced face amount caused by discontinuing premiums and converting the policy to this option.

Policy Loans and Premium Default

Alternatively, the policy owner may take a portion of the cash value in the form of a loan and continue the policy in force.

> The Owner may obtain a policy loan by assignment of this policy to the Company. The amount of the loan, plus any existing indebtedness, shall not exceed the loan value. No loan shall be granted if the policy is in force as extended term insurance. The Company may defer making a loan for six months unless the loan is to be used to pay premiums on policies issued by the Company.

If all of the cash value is removed and the premium payments cease, the policy will terminate as if a surrender occurred. On the other hand, the insured may borrow the entire cash value amount in a traditional cash value policy and continue to pay the premium. A policy loan cannot occur once the policy has been converted to the extended term option, because no cash values exist.

As on any other loan, interest is charged on the indebtedness at the policy's loan rate. Older life insurance policies may charge 3 to 4 percent. Newer policies charge higher interest amounts, such as 7 to 8 percent. In addition, several states allow variable interest on loan amounts. An insured may wonder why interest is charged for borrowing his or her own funds. While the pooled funds are "owned" by the policy owners, any money removed reduces total assets; thus insufficient investment income will be earned to pay all death claims.

Because of the opportunity, cost of money and the low loan rate charged, policy owners tend to borrow the cash value of life insurance and invest the money at a higher rate of interest. This process, called *disintermediation,* is one factor encouraging life insurance companies to design new products such as universal life, paying market rates of interest.

When the policy owner wants to restore the original death benefit, the loan amount and any accrued interest must be repaid. However, the actual amount of indebtedness does not have to be paid in cash during the life of the insured. If the insured dies with a loan outstanding, any death benefit is reduced by the loan amount and any accrued interest. If interest is not paid periodically, it is possible for the outstanding indebtedness to reach or exceed the remaining loan or cash value. When this happens, the contract terminates after a required notification period.

The policy owner's right to borrow funds may be restricted if a beneficiary has been named irrevocably. In almost all cases consent of an irrevocable beneficiary is required to borrow funds. In addition, funds from life insurance contracts written on juveniles by the parent or guardian may be borrowed until the child reaches legal majority if the parent is the owner of the policy. If the minor owns the policy, parents generally cannot borrow any funds. If a legal guardian is appointed by the courts for the benefit of a child or an incompetent party, court approval of the use of the money usually is required to make sure funds are used for the benefit of the minor.

Premium Default. If the premium is overdue, the life insurance contract remains in force for the grace period (as explained earlier in this chapter). If the premium remains unpaid at the end of the grace period, the policy may still provide a death benefit, depending on the availability of cash value for an automatic premium loan or for an extended term conversion.

Upon application for life insurance, companies allow the policy owner to select the automatic premium loan (APL) option:

> A premium loan shall be granted to pay an overdue premium if the premium loan option is in effect. If the loan value, less any indebtedness, is insufficient to pay the overdue premium, a premium will be paid for any other frequency permitted by this policy for which the loan value less any indebtedness is sufficient. The premium loan option may be elected or revoked by written notice filed at the Home Office.

In some cases the APL is automatically included in the contract. The automatic premium loan option authorizes the life insurance company, upon default of a premium payment, to borrow the premium from any available cash value. The transaction and the effect on death benefits (if payable) are treated exactly the same as if the policy owner borrowed the premium amount under the loan provision and paid it to the life insurance company. Subsequent missed premium payments continue to increase the loan outstanding; if the cash value is exhausted, the contract terminates after the required notification period.

If an APL is not taken at the expiration of the grace period, the policy usually converts to the extended term nonforfeiture option. The extended term option normally is chosen over the paid-up insurance option because it provides a greater face amount. After the extended term policy expires, the contract terminates. When the policy is **rated**—(nonstandard, extra-hazard, increased-premium insurance)—life insurance companies generally use the paid-up insurance option to provide some amount of coverage whenever death occurs in cases when a health problem exists and it is assumed the insured is uninsurable.

There are advantages and disadvantages to selecting the extended term option or the APL alternative. If the extended term option is in force, the face amount is continued for a length of time determined by the insured's age, sex and cash value amount in the contract when default occurs. During illness, for example, this option provides a maximum amount of coverage for the extended time period. However, to place the contract back in its original condition, reinstatement (*see* next section) is necessary. If the APL is chosen, the face amount is reduced by the missed premiums and any accrued interest. Eventually, if premiums continue to be missed, the contract will terminate due to lack of any cash value for the loan. Under the APL, reinstatement is not necessary to restore the policy face. The owner merely repays the loan and any accrued interest. Because the amount of life insurance provided and its length of time depends on age, sex, premium payment plan, policy loan rate and the amount of available cash value, the choice of how coverage is to continue (extended term or APL) upon premium default warrants careful attention.

Reinstatement

After the policy is converted to one of the nonforfeiture options, the policy owner may wish to return to the contract's original terms at a later date. The objective of the *reinstatement provision* is to allow the owner to restore the face amount after a paid-up conversion or to restore coverage for life after an extended term conversion.

If the policy has not been surrendered for its cash value, it may be reinstated within five years after the due date of the unpaid premium provided the following conditions are satisfied:
  (a) Within 31 days following expiration of the grace period, reinstatement may be made without evidence of insurability during the lifetime of the Insured by payment of the overdue premium.
  (b) After 31 days following expiration of the grace period, reinstatment is subject to:
    (i) receipt of evidence of insurability of the Insured satisfactory to the Company;
    (ii) payment of all overdue premiums with interest from the due date of each at the rate of 6% compounded annually; or any lower rate established by the Company.
Any policy indebtedness existing on the due date of the unpaid premium, together with interest from that date, must be repaid or reinstated.

Regardless of whether the reinstatement provision is required by law, most life insurance contracts include a provision to reinstate lapsed insurance contracts. Even when no provision exists, life insurance companies may allow reinstatement for competitive reasons. In some cases, although not contractually bound to respond, insurance companies authorize a reinstatement even after the nonforfeiture option terminates.

An *original-age reinstatement* provision, which is the most common, allows insurance contracts to be reinstated if the insured is still insurable, pays any outstanding loans and interest, pays any unpaid premiums and accrued interest and requests reinstatement within the reinstatement period specified by the contract, which is usually three to five years after the lapse. The life insurance company must be returned to the identical financial condition it would have been in if the lapse had not occurred. Upon reinstatement the cash value and reserve amounts are restored.

Some insurance companies allow an *attained-age reinstatement*. In this case cash values do not have to be restored, and any subsequent premiums are based on the insured's attained age when reinstated. In both types of reinstatement the insurability requirement goes beyond evidence of good health. Life insurance companies may apply the same standards imposed when the original application was made. Life-style, hobbies, occupation and health will all be considered. If the insured is uninsurable at the time of the request, adverse selection will surely occur. Those requiring life insurance (feeling they are in poor health) will tend to seek reinstatement, and the life insurance underwriters try to prevent this abuse.

Even though evidence of insurability is still required, and the out-of-pocket payment may be larger, original-age reinstatements have advantages over purchases of new policies:

- When an old insurance contract is reinstated, the level periodic premium remains at its initial amount. If a new insurance contract were purchased, the premium would advance due to an increase in age.
- Upon reinstatement, cash values are immediately available for exercising any of the nonforfeiture options.
- The settlement provisions of the old contract may be more favorable. For example, if the life income option is calculated from a mortality table predicting higher mortality than the predictions used in a new contract, a higher annuity will be paid to the beneficiary under the old contract.
- The rate of interest on policy owner loans may be lower than in the new insurance contract.
- Costs of issuing a new insurance contract, including commissions and administrative fees, do not have to be paid when a contract is reinstated.

These benefits can be substantial. A disadvantage of reinstating an old insurance contract is the cash outflow associated with paying the back premiums and any loans and interest. However, the reinstatement of the cash value may offset this disadvantage.

Questions have arisen concerning the effects of renewing an old contract on the incontestable and suicide clauses. Majority opinion holds that the incontestable clause starts again, but only for any statements made for the purposes of reinstatement.[4] With few exceptions, the suicide provision does not start again, because the old contract is merely continued after reinstatement.

Settlement Options

Regardless of how thorough one is when planning the amount and timing of required death payments, a link must exist between the funding device and the methods for matching the actual payment with the required financial need. Some people use **settlement options** rather than taking the death benefits in a lump sum. Life insurance companies' services are available for investing any proceeds and distributing them in an orderly fashion. These options typically include the interest option, income for a fixed period, income set at a fixed amount, a life annuity with or without a guaranteed period and any other method agreed to by the life insurance company.

Payment of policy benefits upon surrender or maturity will be made in cash or under one of the payment plans described . . . if elected.

If policy benefits become payable by reason of the Insured's death, payment will be made under any payment plan then in effect. If no election of a payment plan is in effect, the proceeds will be held under the Interest Income Plan . . . with interest accumulating from the date of death until an election or cash withdrawal is made.

Even though the advantages of using the life insurance company's services are many, three major problems arise when a policy owner selects any mode of settlement. Anticipated needs, patterns of income and expenditures and life-style changes affect required amounts and patterns of funding. Frequent review and updating of the insured's financial plan and reevaluation of the settlement methods are required. A second serious problem involves inflation, the decline of purchasing power. Settlement options paying proceeds over a period of time may be insufficient for the needs of the beneficiary if inflation was not projected with fair accuracy. Third, the inability to predict accurately accumulated dividend amounts on participating policies introduces risk. Because future dividends are illustrated but not guaranteed, the financial planner will not know the exact amount of cash value available before death and the amount of proceeds to be paid when death occurs. The main disadvantage of using the settlement options to distribute proceeds is the relative inflexibility of distribution and investment options as compared to a trust arrangement.

Due to lack of investment flexibility for the beneficiary, incomplete financial planning by the policy owner (not designating the method of distribution or not directing settlement in an appropriate manner) or the beneficiary's desire for immediate cash wealth, most life insurance contracts are settled using the lump-sum method (*see* Table 10.2). Settlement mode may be selected any time during the policy period. If the owner of the life insurance contract has not irrevocably selected the settlement method before death, the beneficiary may select from the available options within a reasonable length of time. Typically, if no selection is made by either the owner or the beneficiary, a lump-sum payment is made. Once the lump sum is paid, all obligations of the contracting parties terminate. If the lump sum is not paid, the benefits can be placed in one of the other available settlement options.

Interest Option

When the **interest option** is chosen, the proceeds of the life insurance contract are left on deposit for the beneficiary. The policy owner may have directed how interest and principal are to be treated. For example, the policy owner may specify that only interest is to be paid to the beneficiary and the principal paid to another payee or the estate on a certain date or on the payee's death, whichever occurs first. The policy owner may specify a limited or full right of withdrawal for the initial beneficiary. Under the limited right to withdraw, part of the money may be removed by the beneficiary upon request; a contingent payee will be identified for the distribution of remaining funds. A typical formula might allow for 10 percent of the origi-

Table 10.2
Use of Settlement Options: Payments to Beneficiaries, September 1985

Payment Method	Percent of Policies Type of Policy		
	Ordinary*	Group	Industrial
Lump sum	98.0%	98.7%	100.0%
Life income	0.1	0.1	†
Annuity certain	0.5	0.9	†
Held at interest	0.6	0.2	†
All other	0.8	0.1	†
Total	100.0	100.0	100.0

*Credit life insurance on loans 10 years or less excluded
†Less than 0.05 percent
Source: *1990 Life Insurance Fact Book* (Washington, D.C.: American Council of Life Insurance, 1990), p. 47.

nal death benefit to be withdrawn by the beneficiary each year until proceeds are exhausted. Any amount may be removed upon demand when the payee has the full right of withdrawal.

When amounts are left on deposit with the life insurance company, interest is added at a guaranteed rate (currently 3.5 to 5.5 percent) and payable on an annual, semiannual, quarterly or monthly basis. Participating policies usually pay higher rates of return based on company earnings. Most insurance companies specify that interest earned must be distributed periodically to the payee. However, some insurance companies allow retention and compounding consistent with prevailing law preventing perpetuities.

The interest option may be useful in a variety of circumstances—for example, to produce an emergency fund for a beneficiary. If the beneficiary has the right to remove principal amounts, cash is readily available if required. Second, because an estate plan can call for deferred payments of principal, money may be left to earn interest until needed. And third, if proceeds are provided to supplement other sources of income (such as Social Security or a pension plan), the flexibility inherent in the interest option with full right of withdrawal allows latitude in withdrawing needed funds. Finally, depending on the contract, the interest option can keep principal amounts from being included in the first beneficiary's estate.

Fixed-Period Option

Under the **fixed-period option** proceeds are paid over a stated period of time, typically ranging from 1 to 30 years. The annual, semiannual, quarterly or monthly payment is estimated, using a conservative interest rate to liquidate the principal (death proceeds) over the chosen period. Any excess interest declared on the remaining principal is added to the payment(s). Because the time period is fixed, excess interest does not increase the period's length; this would be contrary to the policy owner's wishes.

Table 10.3 presents the payment amount on a fixed-period option for various payment lengths and frequencies for one company. For each $1,000 of policy proceeds the beneficiary receives the table amount periodically for a set number of

Table 10.3
Fixed-Period Amounts for Various Lengths of Time per $1,000 at 6 Percent

Payment Years	Annual	Semiannual	Quarterly	Monthly
1	$1,000.00	$507.39	$255.61	$85.64
5	223.96	113.82	57.38	19.24
10	128.18	65.26	32.93	11.05
15	97.13	49.53	25.02	8.40
20	82.25	42.00	21.23	7.13
25	73.80	37.73	19.08	6.41
30	68.54	35.08	17.75	5.97

Note: The principal amount ($1,000) is equal to the present value of an annuity due at 6 percent.

years. For example, if a monthly payment over ten years is desired and the policy proceeds equaled $75,000, $828.75 (75 × $11.05) would be the minimum payment amount. Uses of the fixed-period option include payments for readjustment income and payment for a four-year college education. The fixed-period option can provide readjustment income when it is necessary to allow sufficient time to reduce the beneficiary's standard of living.

Fixed-Amount Option

The **fixed-amount option** is similar to the fixed-period option in many respects. The most important difference is that the payment amount is fixed and the amount chosen determines the period over which the annuity is to be paid. Funds remaining to be paid are credited with interest, and when the principal is exhausted, the annuity terminates. With this option, if the life insurance company declares excess interest, the excess goes toward lengthening the time in which payments are made. Because the payment amount is fixed, the only factor allowed to change is the number of payments.

The fixed-amount option is considered more flexible than the fixed-period option. If the payee is given or retains partial or full right of withdrawal, equal withdrawals may be made without violating the requirement that the periodic payment amount remain the same. Only the number of payments will decline, because principal amounts have been withdrawn.

Life Annuity Option

Under the **life annuity option** a periodic payment is made as long as the payee survives. The various forms of life income options are equivalent to life annuity contracts. (*See* Chapter 5 for a more extensive treatment of life annuities.) Installments may be made monthly, quarterly, semiannually or annually. If a minimum number of payments is guaranteed, remaining payments are made to a surviving contingent payee. Otherwise the commuted value is paid to the last surviving payee's estate. When no minimum guarantees exist or the payee has at least received the guaranteed minimum, payments cease at death.

One of the advantages of a life annuity settlement is the guarantee of payments continuing as long as the recipient survives. Thus the beneficiary cannot outlive the proceeds. This guarantee is made possible by the pooling technique used in the insurance transaction. Individuals dying at an early age give up their right to receive further payments, while individuals living a long life continue to receive annuity payments. If one wished to produce the same effect by purchasing, for instance, a mutual fund, the investor would have to make choices relative to the expected length of life, the future investment rate of return and the amount to be withdrawn on a periodic basis. If any of the factors are estimated incorrectly, either the investor will survive beyond the exhaustion of principal or, when death occurs, principal will remain. (This argument, including a numerical analysis, was presented in Chapter 5.)

Life annuity payments depend on the sex and age of the individual receiving benefits and whether or not the contract is participating. An older individual selecting the life annuity option will receive higher annuity payments because life expectancy is shorter. Women tend to live longer than men, so women's rent payments are lower when sex-distinct mortality tables are used. With regard to taxation, all rent payments are split into principal and interest amounts. Principal amounts are not taxable. Interest amounts are included in taxable income. (Chapter 11 describes in more detail how annuities are taxed.)

Several variations of life annuity options exist. The *life income option* has no minimum number of payments guaranteed. When the payee dies, payments terminate regardless of the number of payments made. Because no minimum number of payments is guaranteed, the life income option provides the highest periodic payment among the various life annuity types discussed. The life income option would not be a good selection if the insured has a spouse, dependent parents or children who require financial assistance from the insured.

A second type of life annuity option is the *period certain life income option*. This option guarantees a minimum number of payments. If the payee dies before the minimum number is received, a contingent payee receives the benefits, or a commuted value is paid to the payee's estate. On the other hand, if the payee survives the guaranteed time, payments continue until death. Because of the guarantees associated with this form of life annuity, the payment amount is less than the payment under the pure life annuity option. Payment guarantees for any practical length of time are available. However, 10-, 15- and 20-year guarantees are most common.

A third type of life income option, providing even more of a guarantee, is the *installment or cash refund life income option*. If the sum of the payments received is not equal to the original death proceeds, payments continue to a contingent payee until the total amount of proceeds is distributed. When payments continue in the form of an annuity, the option is called an *installment refund annuity*. When the unpaid guaranteed amount is commuted and paid in one lump sum, the option is called a *cash refund option*.

Divisible Surplus Provision

One of the practices investigated by the Armstrong Committee in 1905 was the accumulation of excess surplus by mutual life insurance companies. Today such accumulations are paid to policy owners as participating dividends. Historically some mutual life insurance companies retained surpluses for several years. Thus, when the dividends were finally paid, only survivors participated. Surplus not currently distributed was forfeited to survivors in a later period.

The practice of forfeiting amounts to a group whose income depends on the forfeitures is similar to a scheme called a **tontine,** credited to Lorenzo Tonti in the 1600s.[5] A tontine was a scheme devised to raise money for the king and provide a pension for the people. Individuals participating would purchase shares in return for a guaranteed life income (percent of the shares purchased). When individuals in the pool died, interest payments terminated and were divided among the survivors. The last survivor therefore was in the position to make a great deal of money. As a by-product of the scheme the state would not have to repay the principal, because there were no survivors.

The New York Insurance Code, Section 3203, strictly forbids participating companies from retaining funds by requiring "that the insurer shall annually ascertain and apportion any divisible surplus accruing on the policy." Following is a typical divisible surplus policy provision.

> This policy shall share in the divisible surplus, if any, of the Company. This policy's share shall be determined annually and credited as a dividend. Payment of the first dividend is contingent upon payment of the premium or premiums for the second policy year and shall be credited proportionately as each premium is paid. Thereafter, each dividend shall be payable on the policy anniversary date.

Several options are available to the policy owner for using participating dividends. The policy owner may elect to take the dividends in cash, retain the dividends to accumulate with interest, buy paid-up additions of life insurance, use them to reduce current premiums, pay up the life insurance contract sooner than contractually stipulated or purchase one-year term insurance.

Dividend Options

Owners of participating life insurance contracts acquire the right to receive dividends. Dividends are considered a reimbursement of an overpayment, because the objective of the organization is to provide insurance at minimum cost. (*See* Chapter 24 for a discussion of mutual insurance companies.) The IRS does not consider participating dividends to be income; they therefore are not included in taxable income. The actual dividend amount depends on expenses, mortality, investment income and reserve requirements. If expenses or mortality is greater than anticipated or investment income lower, the dividend amount will tend to be lower than predicted, and vice versa. Initial premiums, overstating the expected costs of providing insurance, coupled with divisible surplus statutes, produce the annual dividend payments.

Cash Dividend Option. The policy owner may receive dividends in cash. Policy owners intending to take their dividends in this manner may be better off financially purchasing a comparable nonparticipating contract. However, the insured doing this loses the opportunity to participate in the long-term trends in mortality and expense charges, which tend to decline over time.

Interest Option. The life insurance company may be directed to retain the participating dividend distributions to accumulate interest. Life insurance contracts specify a guaranteed minimum rate of interest but generally credit higher rates. Accumulated interest amounts are distributed by the normal settlement and nonforfeiture procedures. Some insurance contracts specify that accumulated dividends and interest shall be used upon lapse to pay any past-due premium. When there is no applicable provision, dividend amounts may not be used to satisfy defaulted premium payments unless the policy owner consents to their use. When the policy owner leaves any dividends with the life insurer, any interest earned on the dividend amount is includable in taxable income because the IRS considers it constructively received.

Reduction of Premium Payments. Dividends may also be used to reduce current premium payments. Participating contracts allow the premium payer to reduce the remittance by the amount of the dividend stated on the premium notice. This may be advantageous for individuals desiring not to pay level premium payments over long periods of time. By continuing to reduce premium payments with dividend distributions, the policy owner will typically experience an increasing dividend and a reduction of the required net premium payment. At some point the dividend amount may equal or exceed the gross premium. Any dividend above the premium may be distributed, using the other dividend options. Dividends increase over time because the policy owner participates in an increasing asset pool that generates larger earnings as reserve amounts increase.

Paid-Up Additions. Paid-up additional amounts of participating life insurance may also be purchased with the dividends. This transaction is similar to purchasing life insurance at "net rates" with a single premium. That is, there is minimal loading for expenses, and the amount of insurance purchased is determined primarily by the age and sex of the insured and the amount of the dividend. For many people purchasing additional amounts of paid-up insurance is very efficient. There are no medical exams, nor are there commissions or other direct expenses to pay. Further, the additional amounts of life insurance may offset the eroding effect of inflation on the purchasing power of the initial face amount.

Paid-Up Insurance. Dividend payments also may be used to pay for the policy sooner than specified by the contract. Under this option dividends are allowed to accumulate at interest. When the sum of the cash value, the dividends and credited interest equals the net single premium for a policy at the attained age, the insured no longer need pay premiums. This amount is called the *present value of future benefits (PVFB)* (*see* Chapter 21). When the PVFB is accumulated, the insurer is placed in the position of being able to pay all future obligations under the contract without collecting any more premiums. If death occurs before the policy is paid up, any dividends and interest are added to the death benefit. In a similar fashion the policy owner may continue to pay premiums, effectively increasing the policy's death benefit.

One-Year Term. In addition to the common uses of dividends already described, many life insurance companies allow the policy owner to purchase varying amounts of one-year term insurance with the dividend distribution. Annually renewable term policies are sometimes associated with minimum premium deposit plans. In a minimum premium deposit plan the insured purchases a participating permanent contract, borrows any cash value increases and uses the dividend amounts to purchase sufficient term insurance to equal the cash value borrowed. Many life insurance companies do not allow the term insurance amount to exceed the guaranteed cash value stated in the policy. Aside from any such restrictions, the amount of term insurance purchased with the dividend is a function of age, gender and the dividend amount.

Optional Policy Provisions

Besides the mandatory policy provisions, life insurance companies are allowed to include other provisions not prohibited by statute. These optional clauses include provisions relating to the suicide of the insured, assignment of the contract and beneficiary designations.

Suicide of the Insured

Virtually all life insurance policies contain a clause restricting death payments when the insured commits suicide, while sane or insane, within two years after the policy date. Some companies reduce the time limit to one year.

> If within two years from the Date of Issue the Insured dies by suicide, the amount payable by the Company shall be limited to the premiums paid.

The purpose of the *suicide clause* is to protect the life insurance company from fraudulent death claims when the policy was bought with the intent to commit suicide. If the suicide clause were not allowed, insurance premiums would increase because of the inclusion of self-inflicted intentional deaths. On the other hand, if suicide deaths were totally eliminated, innocent beneficiaries would bear the cost of the insured's act. A suicide clause with a time limitation makes sense, because insurance rates can be loaded for suicide after a certain number of years while sufficiently insulating the insurance company from fraud.

If suicide occurs within the limited time period, the life insurance company need only return all premiums without any interest. If suicide is suspected within the limited time period and a death claim is denied, the burden of proof rests with the life insurance company. Because courts acknowledge the instinct for self-preservation, in the absence of substantial proof it is assumed death was unintentional.

In *Schelberger v. Eastern Savings Bank*[6] the insured died of an overdose of barbiturates. Because the insurance company failed to present sufficient evidence to overcome the strong presumption against suicide, proceeds of the life insurance contract were paid. During the presentation of the case it was shown that:

> The autopsy revealed a heavy concentration of barbiturates in the brain; so heavy was the concentration that it could only have been achieved by taking a

large number of pills. . . . Autopsy revealed a quantity of barbiturates in his stomach which had not yet been absorbed at the time of death. If taken one at a time, . . . he would have been asleep long before he could have taken any such quantity. . . . The medical examiner gave as his opinion that such a high number of pills could not have been taken inadvertently; it had to be purposeful and intentional.

The strength of the presumption against suicide is further illustrated by *Begley v. Prudential Insurance Company of America*.[7] Evidence showed that Begley was mentally depressed and suffered from various ailments. His body was found on the ground below his hospital room's window. No one witnessed the insured's fall, and the medical examiner had concluded that the insured "jumped or fell" from the room; ". . . the court of appeals in *Begley* held that, even with respect to accident coverage, where the evidence is evenly balanced, the jury must find accident as opposed to suicide."

Assignment of the Policy

Assignment has been defined as "a transfer or making over to another of the whole of any property, real or personal, in possession or in action, or of any estate or right therein."[8] The *assignment clause* in the life insurance contract allows the owner to assign the policy to another for the purpose of providing collateral or security and to transfer ownership interests. Unlike property insurance contracts, which may be assigned only with written consent of the insurance company, life insurance contracts may be assigned freely.

The Owner may transfer ownership of this policy by filing written evidence of transfer satisfactory to the Company at its Home Office and, unless waived by the Company, submitting the policy for endorsement to show the transfer.

To effect a collateral or secured interest in the life insurance contract, ownership rights of one party have to be transferred to another. For example, if the policy owner desires to use the cash value of the life insurance contract for security, a method is required to transfer the interest so the creditor may attach the values upon death or default. A collateral assignment is used in this case. A *collateral assignment* limits creditors' interest to any unpaid balances on the secured loan owed by the insured, any unpaid interest and any premiums paid by the creditor on the life insurance policy. An *absolute* assignment occurs when all unrestricted interests are transferred from one to another. In this case ownership is intended to be transferred unconditionally to another party.

For an assignment to be binding, most life insurance policies demand that the request be received in writing and filed at the home office. Validity of any assignment is not the responsibility of the life insurance company. The assignee's interest is subordinate to that of the life insurance company, and any beneficiary's or owner's interest is subordinate to that of the assignee. These requirements are considered necessary to handle assignments in an orderly fashion. If the assignment is not received in writing, the life insurance company cannot act on the request and therefore should have no liability if an unrecorded assignment is presented after proceeds have already been paid. In the case of duplicate or questionable assignments the process of **interpleader** is available to the insurer to settle any disputes. When the interpleader process is used, proceeds are paid into the court for a settlement decision, and the insurer is relieved of the responsibility for disputed claims.

The American Bankers Association (ABA) assignment form is commonly used for collateral assignments. This form provides a compromise agreement between the creditor's desire for an absolute assignment and the policy owner's desire to maintain control over the contract. Specifically, the following five rights pass from the policy owner to the assignee:

1. The assignee receives the right to collect the net proceeds by reason of death or maturity.
2. The right to surrender the policy is granted.
3. The assignee can borrow from the cash value of the policy.
4. The control of dividends and the dividend options is assigned.
5. The right to exercise nonforfeiture options passes to the assignee. The rights to receive disability benefits, to designate or change the beneficiary and to elect the settlement mode are specifically excluded from the assignment.

In return for receiving these rights, the assignee pledges to:

- return any balances remaining after applying proceeds to the debt (excesses are paid as though no assignment existed);
- not surrender or take a policy loan unless there has been a default; and
- not impair the policy owner's ability to change the beneficiary or mode of settlement.

Beneficiary Designations

Life insurance may be viewed as a method of providing a beneficiary's future income when an insured dies prematurely. Upon death the insured's present estate must be distributed by will or probate, and the document (the will) or state law (probate) determines who receives the distribution. The insured's future estate, capitalized by the life insurance contract, is created upon death by the life insurance contract, and the proceeds need to be distributed in an orderly fashion. The life insurance contract determines, through the use of the *beneficiary clause,* who receives the distribution. Even though much of the flexibility of designing payment patterns is lost after the policy matures as a death claim, the beneficiary may be given some flexibility in picking a settlement method if the owner allows an amount of discretion.

Generally policy owners having an insurable interest may designate any beneficiary, even if the beneficiary has no insurable interest. When community property rights are involved, when there are minor policy owners or when there are court restrictions, the right to choose a beneficiary may be restricted. In the case of a state with community property rights, each spouse has an interest in the life insurance contract if the policy is purchased with joint funds, so a beneficiary designation by only one spouse will be effective for only one-half of the proceeds.

Minors generally do not have the capacity to contract, and many life insurance companies therefore will not contract with them unless there is a statute specifically making the life insurance contract binding upon the minor. When minor owners are involved, some states restrict who can be named as a beneficiary and restrict any change of beneficiary on the policy. In the case of court restrictions a divorce decree may specify that certain beneficiaries be maintained and the premiums paid on life insurance policies for the purposes of guaranteeing child support or alimony.

Third-party ownership may also cause complications. Insurable interest must exist for the third party to receive any proceeds. For example, if a creditor takes out life insurance on the debtor, proceeds are payable only to the extent of the indebtedness, interest and policy premiums paid by the creditor. In the case of life insurance provided as an employee benefit, the beneficiary cannot be the employer.

With respect to estate taxation, the *insured,* the *beneficiary* and the *owner* have three distinct property interests in life insurance contracts. The way these three interests are set up determines whether the death proceeds are included in the insured's gross estate for estate tax purposes. Death proceeds generally will be included in the gross estate if the insured holds an incidence of ownership at the date of death (or held within three years of the date of death) *or* the insured's estate is the beneficiary of the policy proceeds.

Death proceeds will not be included in the gross estate if no incidence of ownership exists within three years of the date of death as long as policy proceeds are not paid to the estate. However, there will be a gift tax problem when the insured, the beneficiary and the owner are all named differently. For example, if the husband is the insured, the wife the owner and the child the beneficiary, the owner makes a gift equal to the death proceeds to the child when the insured dies. Depending on the amount of the gift, the owner may have to pay a gift tax on the transfer or use up some or all of his or her unified estate tax credit. (Chapter 12 explores estate and gift taxation.)

Revocable and Irrevocable Beneficiaries

Beneficiary clauses, unless otherwise indicated, are considered *revocable.* The policy owner may change the beneficiary as frequently as desired; thus revocable beneficiaries are considered to have only a contingent right in the life insurance contract. The beneficiary has the right to receive proceeds if and only if the policy owner does not change the designation and the contract, provided a death benefit is still in force. In general a policy owner should maintain the right to change the beneficiary unless an *irrevocable* status is required for creditors, for business relationships or where tax and estate planning considerations are involved.

Much of the flexibility of the policy is lost when an irrevocable beneficiary is named. First, the policy owner loses the right to change beneficiary arrangements and thus cannot make alterations when family relationships change. Second, during the insured's lifetime, control and disposition of the life insurance contract as property are contingent on the irrevocable beneficiary's agreement. Third, if the insured becomes uninsurable, the alternative of purchasing additional life insurance for the benefit of others no longer exists.

When an irrevocable beneficiary designation is used, the insured surrenders the right to change the beneficiary, and the contract for all practical purposes becomes jointly owned and the insured cannot exercise any right impairing the vested rights of the beneficiary without prior written consent. These vested rights include the insured's ability to assign, borrow from or surrender the policy.

[Margin note: These options are lost]

Much care should be used when an irrevocable beneficiary designation is made. First, it may be difficult to acquire the consent of the beneficiary even if the modification seems reasonable. Second, if minor beneficiaries are named, consent must be given by a legal guardian. The guardian cannot give away property of the minor, so getting consent in these cases may be impossible. This problem also extends to secondary or contingent beneficiaries named irrevocably. For example, John Webster names his daughter beneficiary in an irrevocable beneficiary clause, with proceeds going to any of the daughter's children if his daughter is not alive. Even if the primary beneficiary (the daughter) consents to the change of beneficiary, it may be impossible to overcome the vested rights of the minor children even if they agree to the change.

In addition, if a minor receives proceeds from a life insurance contract, receipts for payment may not be valid because the minor does not have the ability to contract. In such cases the life insurance company may use interpleader to distribute proceeds. Some state statutes allow for small payments to be made to a parent or guardian for the minor's benefit, while other states allow a limited direct payment to the minor. A trust arrangement may be used in certain circumstances to overcome some of these legal barriers to distribution.

Irrevocable beneficiary clauses can be *absolute* or *reversionary*. If the clause is absolute, the beneficiary has an absolute vested interest in the life insurance contract even when the beneficiary predeceases the insured. When a reversionary clause is included in the wording of the beneficiary designation, the right to modify the beneficiary clause reverts to the insured if the beneficiary predeceases the insured. At the beneficiary's death the owner regains control over all rights in the life insurance contract. The insured may then rewrite the beneficiary designation.

Levels of Beneficiaries

One or more primary beneficiaries may be named to receive policy proceeds. It is not uncommon for policy owners to declare a class of individuals instead of naming individuals. For example, if the primary beneficiary is intended to be all children of the insured, unborn children will not receive any proceeds if born children are named individually. Similar problems arise with adoptions and guardianships. In addition to primary beneficiaries, insureds may name a secondary layer to receive benefits if the primary beneficiaries predecease the insured. If all beneficiaries predecease the insured or if no beneficiary is named, proceeds are paid to the insured's estate if the insured is the owner; if the insured is not the owner, proceeds are paid to the owner or the owner's estate. In any case, if proceeds are paid to an estate, the property is distributed by will or, if no will exists, by state law. (Beneficiary designators may also distribute policy proceeds *per capita* or *per stirpes*. Per capita is based on a portion for each individual. Per stirpes is based on a branch of a family or line of descent.)

Common Disasters

Many individuals discount the possibility of the insured and the primary beneficiary dying in the same accident—a **common disaster.** Because, however, a problem arises from not knowing who dies first and how the proceeds are to be paid, this possibility deserves consideration.

Consider a man who names his wife as primary beneficiary and his ex-wife as contingent beneficiary. If both husband and wife are killed in an accident, it may be impossible to determine who died first. If the insured died first, the proceeds would go to his current wife and then to her estate to be distributed. But if the wife died first, the ex-wife receives the proceeds, skipping the children of the current marriage.

Common law fails to provide clear guidelines to alleviate the problem. Under common law, when there is no evidence indicating who died first, proceeds are paid to the insured's estate. The burden of providing evidence to show that the insured predeceased the beneficiary rests on the beneficiary's estate. This rule provides little comfort for the dependents of the beneficiary who were relying on policy proceeds. To alleviate the situation and provide uniform guidelines for the distribution of proceeds when there is a common disaster, all states and the District of Columbia, except Louisiana and Ohio, have either adopted in whole or modified and passed the **Uniform Simultaneous Death Act.**

Under this act, when there is no evidence to the contrary, it is assumed that the primary beneficiary predeceased the insured. This rule creates the desirable result of any proceeds going to the contingent beneficiary or, if no contingent beneficiary is named, to the estate of the insured. The act, however, falls short in dictating procedures for paying proceeds when the beneficiary survives by a short length of time.

There are several ways to deal with this latter problem. The first is to pay policy proceeds in installments, with a contingent beneficiary receiving any remaining payments. As a second solution, proceeds may be settled under the interest option with a right to withdraw. A contingent beneficiary can be named to receive any remaining proceeds if the primary beneficiary dies. In this case the beneficiary has access to required funds, but remaining funds are directed to a contingent beneficiary if the primary beneficiary dies from the disaster. Third, a common disaster clause may be written, including a condition stating that the primary beneficiary must survive the insured by a specific length of time to receive benefits. Otherwise proceeds would be paid to the contingent beneficiary.

Unearned Premiums at Death

Many life insurance companies include a clause refunding any **unearned premium** as part of the death benefit if the insured dies. Prepaid premiums are held by the insurer in anticipation of earning the dollars on the life insurance contract. Here is an example of this clause:

> The portion of any premium paid which applies to a period beyond the policy month in which the insured died shall be refunded as part of the proceeds of this policy.

Some insurers base the refund on the end of the month in which the insured dies. Others base the refund on the date of death. In applying the clause above, if an owner pays $767.00 for one-fourth of a year's coverage (pays four times a year) and dies in the first month, $511.33 ($767.00 × 2/3) would be added to the death benefit. If a year's premium of $3,068.00 ($767.00 × 4) was paid, and death occurred in the first month, $2,812.33 ($3,068 × 11/12) would be added to the death benefit. (Some policies do not address a refund of unearned premium as part of the death benefit. In these cases state laws apply.)

Change of Plan

After a policy is issued, the owner may want to change the plan of insurance. Many insurers allow the owner to change the type of permanent coverage. If the clause exists, the insurer either imposes conditions for the change or must consent to the change. This is an example of a change-of-plan provision:

> The Owner may change this policy to any permanent life or endowment plan offered by the Company on the Date of Issue of this policy. The change may be made upon payment of any cost and subject to the conditions determined by the Company. For a change made after the first year to a plan having a higher reserve, the cost shall not exceed the difference in cash values or the difference in reserves, whichever is greater plus 3 1/2 % of such difference.

War Exclusions

The question of death by terrorism may become a problem due to acts of terrorism arising out of a war declaration.[9] Very few life insurance policies contain an exclusion eliminating payment for death caused by war or death while in war or military service. Military service personnel can purchase life insurance from a limited number of companies without a war exclusion.

Common Policy Riders

In addition to the base plan of coverage, life insurers offer a variety of riders that add benefits to the insurance contract. These benefits raise the policy's premium. (Additional premiums for these riders exist only during benefit availability.) The accidental death benefit rider, the waiver-of-premium rider, the guaranteed insurability rider and the disability income rider are common.

Accidental Death Benefit Rider

The accidental death benefit pays additional face amounts if death occurs solely of accidental bodily injury. These riders are commonly referred to as **double-indemnity** or **multiple-indemnity riders** and are available typically to age 70. Some insurers impose a minimum age on the rider's availability. If the base policy is converted to the paid-up or extended term nonforfeiture option, the rider terminates, because no additional premiums are paid during these periods.

Typical exclusions found in the rider include death caused by declared or undeclared war or warlike action and death caused by riding in or piloting private aircraft, aircraft operated by the armed forces or descending from aircraft (skydiving).

Waiver-of-Premium Rider

The waiver-of-premium rider waives the premium if the insured is totally disabled until the death of the insured or a stated age. Typically if the insured is totally disabled before the policy's anniversary nearest the 60th birthday, the premium will be waived for life if the insured continues to be totally disabled. If disabled after the anniversary nearest age 60 but before the anniversary nearest age 65, the premium will be waived but only until age 65. (Variations of this rider also exist.)

Many definitions of total disability exist, but usually the following criteria must be met:

1. The total disability must be a result of bodily injury or disease and not be preexisting at the date of issue.
2. The disability must have existed continually for six months.
3. The disability must either
   - stop the insured from engaging in *an occupation* (the first 24 months of the total disability must stop the insured from engaging in his or her own occupation; after 24 months, it must prevent the insured from engaging in an occupation for which the insured is reasonably fit by "education, training, or experience") *or*
   - constitute loss of sight in both eyes, or hearing, or speech or the use of both hands or feet or a combination of one hand or foot (commonly referred to as a *presumptive total disability*).

Typically if the disability lasts longer than the six-month waiting period and premiums were paid within that period, a refund occurs. Proof of disability and proof of continuance of disability are also addressed in the rider. The insured must prove total disability exists according to the definition found in the contract, and proof of continued disability may be required by the insurer annually.

Guaranteed Insurability Rider

The guaranteed insurability option rider provides a series of optional purchase dates while waiving insurability requirements. Many insurers provide the option every three years starting at age 25 and ending at age 40. However, variations are found. In addition to the normal exercise date, options may be provided for births, marriages and adoptions. Some insurers reduce or offset the regular number of options by any additional options elected.

The type of coverage is usually restricted to whole life contracts. However, term coverage is sporadically offered within the option. The amount of coverage purchase is usually restricted by a minimum amount (e.g., $10,000) and a maximum set forth in the contract; the maximum amount may equal the face amount of the base policy. With respect to the waiver-of-premium option, many insurers include the option if it is included in the base policy.

Disability Income Rider

Many life insurance companies make available a disability income rider that provides the insured with spendable cash when disabled. The disability income rider typically provides $10 per month for each $1,000 of life insurance purchased. The insured must meet the definition of disability, and a waiting period that is typically six months must elapse for the insured to receive benefits. A maximum benefit based on a dollar amount (e.g., $1,000) or a percentage of predisability wage (e.g., 60 percent) may also apply. The definition of *disability* varies and is similar to the definition found in the individual disability income contracts discussed in Chapter 7. Age limitations for receiving benefits may apply. After the insured meets the requirements, any amount charged for this rider and premium payments are typically waived during the disability period.

Review Questions

1. Explain why entire-contract provisions are needed in life insurance contracts.
2. Why do states mandate to ignore fraud, misrepresentation and concealment by the use of the incontestable clause in a life insurance transaction?
3. Why doesn't the incontestable clause bar the life insurance company from changing policy proceeds when there has been a misstatement of age?
4. Describe the various nonforfeiture options. Is the automatic premium loan (APL) a nonforfeiture option?
5. Under what circumstances will a policy terminate when lapse occurs? When does a policy terminate under the various nonforfeiture options?
6. Discuss the advantages and disadvantages of implementing the automatic premium loan option.
7. Describe the process of reinstatement. Does the policy owner have the right to reinstate after a contract terminates?
8. Why do life insurance companies check insurability when reinstatement is requested? What is meant by insurability for reinstatement purposes?
9. Why would an individual want to reinstate an old life insurance contract?
10. How are the suicide and incontestable clauses affected by a reinstatement?
11. Why do you think that the lump-sum option is used predominantly in settling life insurance proceeds?
12. Explain how the amount of a life annuity settlement is determined at the death of the insured.
13. What is a participating dividend? Briefly describe the common dividend options. What factors influence the amount of the actual dividend paid?
14. How can life insurance law justify payment for self-inflicted intentional injury when suicide occurs?
15. Explain the difference between an absolute and a collateral assignment.
16. In what situations is the process of interpleader used?
17. What is the difference between a revocable and an irrevocable beneficiary? How can a policy owner regain the right to change beneficiaries if they have been designated irrevocably?

18. What methods are used to solve the problems created by the insured and primary beneficiary being injured in a common disaster?
19. Describe the purpose of the accidental death benefit rider, the waiver-of-premium rider, the guaranteed insurability rider and the disability income rider.

Endnotes

[1] H. Kruger and L. Waggoner, eds., *The Life Insurance Policy Contract* (Boston: Little, Brown, 1953).

[2] Special thanks to the American Council of Life Insurance (ACLI) for providing the sample policies quoted and referenced; all extracts in this chapter not otherwise attributed are excerpted from these policies.

[3] *Welch v. Provident Life & Accident Insurance Company,* No. 83-236-11 (Court of Appeals of Tennessee, Middle Section at Nashville), LEXIS, TENN Library, APP file.

[4] *Shellwood v. Equitable Life Insurance Co. of Iowa,* 230 Minn. 529, 42 N.W.2d 346 (1950), supports this view. A minority view holds that when a reinstatement occurs, it is a separate agreement, and therefore it may be contested.

[5] For an in-depth discussion of the tontine system, *see* Robert M. Jennings and Andrew P. Trout, *The Tontine: From the Reign of Louis XIV to the French Revolutionary Era* (Philadelphia: S. S. Huebner Foundation for Insurance Education, University of Pennsylvania, 1982; distributed by Richard D. Irwin, Homewood, Ill.).

[6] *Schelberger v. Eastern Savings Bank,* 461 N.Y.S.2d 785; 93 A.D.2d 188 (1983).

[7] *Begley v. Prudential Mutual Life Insurance Co.,* 1 N.Y.2d 530; 136 N.E.2d 839 (1956).

[8] Henry Campbell Black, *Black's Law Dictionary,* 5th ed. (St. Paul, Minn.: West Publishing, 1968), p. 153.

[9] Steven Sullivan, "War Exclusions: When Is Terrorism an Act of War?" *Life Association News,* March 1991, p. 5.

Bibliography

Black, Kenneth Jr., and Harold Skipper, Jr. *Life Insurance,* 11th ed. Englewood Cliffs, N.J.: Prentice-Hall, 1987.

Greider, Janice, E., et al. *Law and the Life Insurance Contract.* Homewood, Ill.: Richard D. Irwin, 1984.

Keeton, Robert, E., and Alan I. Widiss. *Insurance Law.* St. Paul, Minn.: West Publishing, 1988.

Mehr, Robert I., and Sandra G. Gustavson. *Life Insurance Theory and Practice.* Plano, Tex.: Business Publications, Inc. 1987.

Thornton, John H., and Kennes C. Huntley. "A Survey of Life Insurance Policy Provisions." *Journal of the American Society of CLU & ChFC,* May 1990, p. 72.

Chapter 11 | The Federal Income Tax

Chapter Objectives

- Explain the taxation of the life insurance transaction
- Distinguish taxpaying from tax-reporting entities
- Describe the taxation of some securities transactions
- Discuss some advanced topics in life insurance taxation

Introduction

Life insurance products are often sold, at least in part, based on their tax advantages. While it would overstate the case to describe the life insurance purchase as a "tax-driven" transaction, it would not be an exaggeration to note that many decisions to purchase life insurance involve tax considerations. For example, to compute the amount of life insurance needed in given cases, a planner should realize that holding a lump sum of life insurance proceeds in a mutual fund or in a trust produces different tax consequences from taking the proceeds as a lifetime income (annuity) from the insurer. Indeed, life insurance, financial planning and the federal income tax are inextricably intertwined. For example, determining the appropriate amount of life insurance for many people requires calculating their after-tax income. Also, the particular tax implications of the life insurance transaction can be understood only in the broader context of the whole federal income tax procedure. And, because people often purchase life insurance as an investment alternative, it is important to understand how investments are taxed. For these three reasons an entire chapter is devoted to the federal income tax.

Most readers will have had some background in federal income taxation, so this chapter does not attempt to provide a full tax primer. However, to understand the taxation of life insurance products readers may be aided by a review of taxable entities as defined by the Internal Revenue Service and by a discussion of the fundamental tax treatment of investment vehicles that investors may be comparing to life insurance products in their financial planning. Following this general material are specific sections on taxation of life insurance.

Taxable Entities

The Internal Revenue Code (IRC) identifies several distinct types of taxable entities. The IRC makes an important distinction between *taxpaying* entities and *tax-reporting* entities. Both taxpaying entities and tax-reporting entities file returns. However, the returns of tax-reporting entities are informational, and the tax liabilities reported appear on the return of taxpaying entities. For example, tax returns of partnerships are informational; the implied tax liabilities on partnership income ultimately appear on individual returns.

Taxable entities are classified as follows:

- Individuals
- Corporations, including corporations (regular) and corporations (small-business tax conduits)
- Trusts and estates
- Partnerships (tax-reporting conduits)

Individuals

American citizens and resident and nonresident aliens with gross income greater than a specified minimum amount, including people with self-employment income, file *Form 1040, the U.S. Individual Income Tax Return*. (Forms 1040A and 1040EZ are designed for taxpayers with uncomplicated reporting needs.) Dozens of forms and schedules may accompany Form 1040. Frequently used are these:

- Schedule A—Itemized deductions
- Schedule B—Interest and dividend income
- Schedule C—Profit or loss from business or profession
- Schedule D—Capital gains and losses
- Schedule E—Supplemental income schedule
- Form 6251—Alternative minimum tax individuals
- Form 2106—Employee business expenses

Married people have the option of filing a joint return or separate returns, a decision that should be made by calculating taxes on both single and joint returns. (Total taxes may be lower if separate returns are filed when one spouse has a large income and large deductible expenses.) Children under age 14 can report taxable income on their parents' return or can file separate returns. Single parents and other taxpayers meeting specified criteria may file "head of household" returns. (*See* Table 11.1 for 1991 tax rates.)

Corporations

The IRC recognizes two major types of **corporations**: regular corporations, called *C corporations*, and corporations electing to have their income taxed to their shareholders, called *S corporations*. (Special rules apply to banks, insurance companies, regulated investment companies and real estate investment trusts.) C corporations report their entire taxable income from domestic and foreign sources and pay taxes based on this income. Income distributed to shareholders, called

Table 11.1
1991 Federal Income Tax Rates

Unmarried Individuals

Taxable Income Over	But Not Over	Tax	+ % on Excess	Of the Amount Over
$ 0	$20,350	$ 0	15	$ 0
20,350	49,300	3,053	28	20,350
49,300	—	11,159	31	49,300

Joint Returns & Surviving Spouses

Taxable Income Over	But Not Over	Tax	+ % on Excess	Of the Amount Over
$ 0	$34,000	$ 0	15	$ 0
34,000	82,150	5,100	28	34,000
82,150	—	18,582	31	82,150

Heads of Households

Taxable Income Over	But Not Over	Tax	+ % on Excess	Of the Amount Over
$ 0	$27,300	$ 0	15	$ 0
27,300	70,450	4,095	28	27,300
70,450	—	16,177	31	70,450

Married Individuals Filing Separate Returns

Taxable Income Over	But Not Over	Tax	+ % on Excess	Of the Amount Over
$ 0	$17,000	$ 0	15	$ 0
17,000	41,075	2,550	28	17,000
41,075	—	9,291	31	41,075

Estates and Trusts

Taxable Income Over	But Not Over	Tax	+ % on Excess	Of the Amount Over
$ 0	$ 3,450	$ 0	15	$ 0
3,450	10,350	518	28	3,450
10,350	—	2,450	31	10,350

dividends, is taxed a second time when reported by recipients on Schedule B of Form 1040. If C corporations unreasonably retain their income rather than paying dividends, a special tax is applied.

S corporations avoid paying the corporate income tax because the shareholders agreed to be taxed as individuals. For tax purposes an S corporation is a tax-reporting entity rather than a taxpaying entity. Despite their tax treatment, S corporations retain limited liability and other corporate advantages, such as indefinite life.

To qualify for S corporation status a corporation must meet three criteria:

Chapter 11 The Federal Income Tax

1. There must be no more than 35 shareholders. They all must agree to S corporation status.
2. Shareholders must be U.S. citizens, residents or domestic estates or trusts.
3. There can be only one class of stock.

Because the current tax laws have lowered the highest individual tax rate below the highest corporate tax rate, more eligible corporations probably will elect to qualify as S corporations. However, election of S corporation status is a complex issue, and the question should be given careful attention by a tax professional.

Trusts and Estates

Trusts and estates may be either taxpaying or tax-reporting entities. Rules governing income taxation of these entities are complex, and the following summary statement conveys only one basic idea. In general, if a trust or an estate retains ordinary income, such income is subject to taxation in the trust or estate. If trusts and estates distribute income, such income is taxed when reported on the recipient's Form 1040.

Partnerships

Partnerships are tax-reporting entities. They are formed when two or more people join together to carry on a trade or business. The partners agree to share profits or losses and each partner agrees to contribute cash, property, labor or skill. Each year the partnership files an informational return with the IRS. Partners include their share of income or loss on their Form 1040. (Actual tax law applying to partnerships is extensive and complex; this chapter provides only a summary statement.)

Taxing Securities Transactions

The variety and complexity of security transactions is difficult to appreciate. Reading the *Wall Street Journal* or other financial papers conveys an idea of the scope of the transactions made in our capitalistic economy. Most of these transactions have specific and often peculiar tax implications. This chapter could not possibly cover all of these tax concerns; what follows is a simplified review of a few common transactions frequently made by investors.

People often purchase life insurance and annuities at least in part for their savings values, so it is logical to compare the after-tax consequences of life insurance transactions to the after-tax results of alternative investment opportunities.

U.S. Savings Bonds

Banks and savings and loan associations sell U.S. savings bonds, called *Series EE bonds*. These bonds sell at a discount. That is, the purchaser pays one-half the face value of the bonds and earns income when redeeming the bonds at face value. The government guarantees a minimum interest rate if the bonds are held for at least five years. If prevailing interest rates are greater than the minimum guaranteed rate, the bonds earn higher interest rates equal to 85 percent of the market rate for five-year **Treasury securities.**

Interest earned on EE bonds usually is taxed in the year the bonds are redeemed. Thus EE bonds provide a period of tax deferral on interest income. Interest equals the difference between the amount paid for the bonds and the redemption value. The after-tax return on an EE bond is found by multiplying the before-tax rate by one minus the individual's marginal tax rate.

☐ **Example**

John Benton is in the 28-percent marginal tax bracket. He earns $500 interest when he redeems his EE bonds in 1989. John must pay $140 (.28 × $500) in taxes on his EE bond earnings. In computing his after-tax rate of return, John must calculate his yield using $360 ($500 interest − $140 taxes) as his after-tax return.

Assuming John held the bonds for eight years, his approximate after-tax yield could be found by dividing $360 (after-tax return) by $500 (initial deposit) by the eight-year holding period.

$$\frac{(360/500)}{8} = .09$$

This is only an approximate return. Financiers use a more complicated formula recognizing that investors earn interest annually and not in a lump sum when bonds are redeemed.

EE bonds can be converted to HH bonds instead of being redeemed. If they are converted, no tax is due on the conversion date, but interest earned on the HH bonds is taxable when received. The government pays semiannual interest on HH bonds.

Beginning in 1990, interest on EE bonds purchased after December 31, 1989, and redeemed to finance college expenses is free of income tax if certain conditions are met. These conditions involve ownership of the bonds, age of the purchaser and income of the purchaser. For joint returns the interest exclusion for these bonds phases out for incomes above $60,000. For incomes above $90,000, interest earned on the bonds is fully taxable.

Corporate Bonds

Many corporations raise money by selling **corporate bonds**, which represent debt to the company. Bonds may be secured (mortgage bonds) or unsecured (debentures). Some bonds have coupons attached. The owner redeems the coupons when they are due. Owners of registered bonds receive interest checks by mail.

☐ **Example**

Glen Greenlee receives bond interest of $600 from AT&T on January 1 and July 1. At year's end Glen reports $1,200 in bond interest on Form 1040, Schedule B.

Assume Glen paid $10,000 for the bond three years ago. Assume he sells the bond for $11,000 on January 1, before any interest has accrued. Glen has a long-term gain in the $1,000 difference between his purchase price and the selling price.

If Glen sells the bond at a point when interest has accrued, any gain on the sale must be divided between accrued interest (ordinary income) and capital gains (losses). Assuming he sells the bond for $11,000 on October 1, he would have earned three months' interest, or $300. Therefore, when filing his taxes he divides the $1,000 gain into $300 in bond interest and $700 in capital gain.

Zero-Coupon Bonds

Some corporate and municipal bonds are sold at a discount, like EE bonds. They pay no annual interest but are redeemable at face amount at maturity. Each year the difference between the market value and the face value of these bonds decreases. At maturity, of course, the market and face value are equal.

For zero-coupon corporate bonds issued after March 1, 1984, the government requires owners to report the annual increase in value of these securities. Owners of tax-exempt (municipal and state) **zero-coupon bonds** do not report interest income from these securities.

Dividend Income

Owners of corporate stock or mutual funds may receive cash dividends. These dividends are fully taxable in the year received. Owners of mutual funds also may receive dividends that include some portion of capital gains. These capital gains are reported separately from the dividends but are taxed at the same rate.

Stock dividends or stock splits do not result in taxable income. These transactions do not change the worth of the owner's investment.

Taxing Life Insurance Transactions: Fundamentals[1]

Coverage of the taxation of the life insurance transaction has been divided into two sections, fundamentals and advanced topics, based primarily on the frequency of the transaction. The first section covers the taxation of proceeds from life insurance policies and annuities received at death or during the insured's lifetime. Advanced topics include the taxation of policy loan interest costs, the tax consequences of exchanging one policy for another and rules governing the deductibility of life insurance premiums by business firms.

Life Insurance Defined

To be taxed as life insurance contracts, policies issued after December 31, 1984, must be classified as life insurance contracts under state law and meet a mathematical IRS test.

Internal Revenue Code Section 1035

Section 1035 (b) of the IRC contains the following definitions:

Endowment contract: A contract of endowment insurance is a contract with a life insurance company which depends, in part, on the life expectancy of the insured, but which must be payable in full in a single payment during his life.

Annuity contract: An annuity contract is a contract to which [the preceding paragraph] applies but which may be payable during the life of the annuitant only in installments.

Life insurance contract: A contract of life insurance is a contract to which [the paragraph on endowment contract] applies but which is not ordinarily payable in full during the life of the insured.

Statutory Definition

"Life insurance" [means] every insurance upon the lives of human beings and every insurance appertaining thereto. The business of life insurance shall be deemed to include the granting of endowment benefits; additional benefits in the event of death by accident or accidental means; additional benefits operating to safeguard the contract from lapse or to provide a special surrender value, in the event of total and permanent disability of the insured; and optional modes of settlement of proceeds.[2]

IRS Classification

The Technical and Miscellaneous Revenue Act of 1988 (TAMRA) became law on November 10, 1988. In the period before its enactment life insurance agents sold substantial amounts of single-premium whole life insurance as a tax shelter. And it was a great tax shelter. There was no tax on the annual investment earnings, and insurance companies were allowing policyholders to borrow the annual investment earnings at no cost. Moreover, insurers were allowing policyholders to invest their cash values in many different investment media. One purpose of TAMRA was to end what most observers felt was an abusive application of the tax advantages afforded the life insurance transaction.

The method used to end the abusive tax shelter sales, without affecting the tax advantages traditionally accorded life insurance transactions, was to define a class of contracts known as *modified endowment contracts (MECs)*, introduced in Chapter 3.[3] The technical definition of a MEC is complicated. A simple version is: any contract entered after June 20, 1988, that fails a "seven-pay test." (Policies issued before this date were grandfathered. However, substantial changes to these contracts forfeit the protected status.) The seven-pay limit is the amount equal to the level annual premium needed to fully pay up the original face amount by the end of the seventh year. If the insured pays more than the seven-pay limit, the contract is categorized as a MEC and loses many tax advantages afforded other life insurance contracts. Thus single-payment life insurance or any policy paid up with fewer than seven payments is a MEC.

Premiums

Premiums for individual life insurance are not a tax-deductible item. Health insurance premiums are deductible if (1) the taxpayer itemizes deductions and (2) total allowable medical care costs, including health insurance premiums, exceed 7.5 percent of adjusted gross income. The deduction equals the amount of allowable medical care costs exceeding 7.5 percent of adjusted gross income. Benefits received from health insurance policies reduce the amount of medical expenses allowable as an itemized deduction.

☐ **Example**

Jennifer McKinnley has an adjusted gross income of $40,000. She has medical expenses of $8,000 and pays individual health insurance premiums of $2,000. Her insurer pays $4,000 of the $8,000 in medical expenses. Her itemized medical deduction is calculated as follows:

Medical expenses	$8,000
Health insurance	2,000
Insurance recovery	(4,000)
Net expense	6,000
7.5% AGI	(3,000)
Amount deductible	$3,000

Proceeds Payable at Death

Life insurance proceeds payable at death generally are excluded from the beneficiary's gross income.[4] For example, if a daughter receives $100,000 as beneficiary of her mother's life insurance, the daughter reports no taxable income upon receipt of the lump sum of cash.

Two exceptions apply to this general rule. First, gross income includes death proceeds where there has been a **transfer for value**, which occurs when the current owner sells an existing policy to another person. The new owner may exclude the amount paid for the policy and any subsequent premiums paid from income tax.[5]

For example, suppose Smith, the insured, sold a $20,000 life insurance policy he owned to Jones for $8,000. Or, assume Jones agreed to cancel an $8,000 debt if Smith transfers ownership of the policy to him. When Jones subsequently receives the face amount at Smith's death, Jones must report $12,000 ($20,000 face value −$8,000 amount paid) of the proceeds as income. If Jones had paid premiums of $1,000, only $11,000 would be taxed.

Second, gross income includes some portion of the death proceeds if they are received in installments instead of as a lump sum. Only an amount equal to the original lump sum may be excluded from income. Interest earned on the lump-sum proceeds left on deposit with the insurer must be included in gross income.

For example, assume the widow Green has a choice of receiving the death proceeds as $100,000 cash or as a series of ten payments of $12,000. If she chooses the latter payment, she must include $2,000 in her gross income each year for the ten-year period. If she chooses a life income option instead, she will be taxed as if she were receiving an annuity for which she paid $100,000. (Annuity taxation is discussed later in the chapter.)

Surrender for Cash

If the life insurance policy is surrendered and the surrender value exceeds the policy's adjusted basis, the sum of premiums paid less dividends received, the difference is taxed as ordinary income. (The taxation of partial withdrawals not resulting in surrender is complex. Taxation depends on the timing of the withdrawal. Different rules apply to withdrawals made in the first five years, between the 6th and 15th years, or after 15 years.) Losses on surrender are not deductible.

For example, Caine paid premiums equal to $20,000 during the ten years the policy was in force. During this time he received $6,000 in dividends. His adjusted basis in the policy is $14,000 ($20,000 − $6,000). If he surrenders the policy for $16,000, he must report $2,000 ($16,000 − $14,000) as ordinary income.

When endowment life insurance contracts mature as a survival claim, they are treated similarly to the surrender of the policy for its cash value. That is, the owner may deduct the net premiums from the surrender value, treating the balance as ordinary income in the year of the policy claim. The effect of this calculation is to subject interest earned on the endowment to the income tax.

Dividends

Dividends received from a contract issued on a participating basis are excluded from income tax until they exceed the net premiums paid. These dividends historically have been viewed as a return of premium payment and not as income. Any tax-free dividends the policy owner receives on a traditional life insurance contract reduce the owner's adjusted basis in the contract.

In the foregoing example, Caine reported no taxable income on the $6,000 in dividends received. If he were to receive more dividends than he paid in premiums, he would have no basis in the policy and would have to report all future dividends in excess of his premium payments as taxable income.

Annuities[6]

Individual Purchases

The portion of annuity liquidation payments representing the return of premium is excluded from gross income. The portion of each payment received representing interest earned is taxable. To determine the percentage of payments included in gross income, an *exclusion ratio* must be calculated. This ratio is found by dividing the premium paid for the annuity by the expected return:

$$\text{Exclusion ratio} = \frac{\text{Investment in contract}}{\text{Expected return}}$$

IRS annuity tables determine the expected return. Table 11.2 reproduces a portion of one of these tables.

☐ Example

Ben Hill pays $40,000 for an annuity. The insurer promises Ben $5,000 a year for life. Ben is age 65. The IRS *Ordinary Life Annuities—One Life—Expected Return Multiples* table shows Ben to have an expected life of 20 years. The total expected return from the contract is 20 times $5,000, or $100,000. The exclusion ratio is $40,000/$100,000, or .40. Consequently 40 percent ($2,000) of each year's $5,000 annuity income is considered the return of Ben's premium and is excluded from income. The remaining $3,000 must be reported as income each year. The exclusion ratio remains constant for the next 20 years if Ben lives that long.

Table 11.2
Ordinary Life Annuities—One Life—Expected Return Multiples

Age	Multiple	Age	Multiple
50	33.1	65	20.0
51	32.2	66	19.2
52	31.3	67	18.4
53	30.4	68	17.6
54	29.5	69	16.8
55	28.6	70	16.0
56	27.7	71	15.3
57	26.8	72	14.6
58	25.9	73	13.9
59	25.0	74	13.2
60	24.2	75	12.5
61	23.3	76	11.9
62	22.5	77	11.2
63	21.6	78	10.6
64	20.8	79	10.0

Pension Plan

Many private pension plans provide annuity benefits to retired workers. If the employee/retiree contributed nothing to the pension during the working years, the total amount received each year will be included in gross income. On the other hand, if the employee paid for some portion of the pension with after-tax contributions, the employee will be entitled to an exclusion when receiving pension benefits. The employee's total exclusion is limited to the amount contributed. If pension recipients die before their basis is recovered, the unrecovered amount can be deducted on the final tax return. Once the employee's basis is recovered, no additional annuity income can be excluded.

☐ **Example**

Frances DeKalb contributed $50,000 to a pension plan during a 40-year working career. In retirement Frances is promised a pension of $10,000 a year for life. Frances's life expectancy according to the IRS is 15 years; thus the expected value of her pension is $150,000. Frances must calculate an exclusion ratio. It is found by dividing her contribution by the expected value of the pension, $50,000/$150,000, or 33 percent. Frances may exclude $3,333 (.33 × $10,000) of each pension payment and must include $6,667 in her gross income. After she recovers her $50,000 basis in 15 years ($50,000/$3,333), her gross income includes all additional receipts.

Premature Distributions

Cash withdrawals from deferred annuities before age 59 1/2 may result in taxation and a tax penalty. If the cash value exceeds the annuitant's adjusted basis, the amount withdrawn is included in income. (Loans are considered withdrawals.) The taxable amount equals the difference between the cash value and the owner's basis. In addition, a penalty of 10 percent of the amount includible in income also applies unless the annuitant dies or is disabled. The penalty can be avoided if the amount withdrawn is taken in payments spread over the annuitant's lifetime.

☐ **Example**

Richard Bell, age 38, makes ten installments of $1,200 for a deferred annuity. At the end of the tenth year the policy has a cash value of $18,000. Richard withdraws the cash value and ends the contract. The tax consequences are:

Ordinary income ($18,000 − $12,000) = $6,000
Penalty (.10 × $6,000) = 600

If Richard is in the 28-percent marginal tax bracket, his withdrawal results in income taxes of $2,280 (.28 × $6,000 = $1,680 + $600).

Taxing Life Insurance Transactions: Advanced Topics

Policy Loans and Interest Costs

Policies having a cash surrender value allow the owner to borrow an amount up to the cash value. Insurers charge interest on these policyholder loans. For individuals in nonbusiness circumstances no deduction is allowed for interest incurred on these loans. (This rule did not, however, always apply. Previously, if four of the first seven annual premiums were paid without borrowing, interest costs on individual life insurance loans was deductible. The four-out-of-the-first-seven rule led to a class of life insurance purchases called *minimum deposit life insurance*. The purpose of this plan was to provide the purchaser with an income tax deduction on money borrowed to finance the purchase of life insurance. This was a tax-driven scheme.)

Exchange of Life Insurance Policies

Under IRC Section 1035, if one life insurance policy is exchanged for another, no gain or loss is recognized unless the value of the new contract, plus any cash received, exceeds the cash basis of the old policy. An exchange is tax-free if no cash or other property is received in the exchange. If a gain is recognized, it is treated as ordinary income.

These rules apply when:

- one life insurance policy is exchanged for another;
- a life insurance policy is exchanged for an annuity; or
- one annuity contract is exchanged for another.

Insurance Premiums

As noted, individual life insurance premium payments are not deductible. Insurance premiums paid by a business usually are deductible as business expenses. Premiums paid by a business on behalf of an employee are reported as income by the employee. An important exception to this last rule is the premium paid by an employer for the first

$50,000 of group term life insurance. These group life insurance premiums are deductible by the employer but create no taxable income for the employee.

The rules with respect to **split-dollar life insurance** are complex. Under this plan an employer pays part of the premium and the employee pays part. The employer's cost equals the increase in the policy's cash value. The employee pays the difference. At the employee's death the employer receives an amount equal to the cash value. In other words, it receives an amount equal to the premiums it paid, and its only cost is forgone interest. The employee's beneficiary receives an amount equal to the difference between the face and the cash value. Under the split-dollar arrangement the employee is taxed on the total value of all benefits received, less any premiums paid.

Financial Planning Issues

Life insurance generally is a tax-favored transaction, but care must be taken to achieve tax-favored results. Many tax rules apply to the life insurance transaction. Some rules have tax-favorable results; other rules have unfavorable consequences. For example, one favorable rule allows tax deferral on the "inside buildup," or investment returns, on most life insurance and annuity contracts. Another allows receipt of death benefits free of income tax. Other rules have unfavorable consequences, including tax penalties for early withdrawal from specified insurance transactions and inclusion of policy proceeds in gross income in some cases of transfer for value. Favorable tax considerations may be an important reason to arrange a life insurance transaction.

One justification for the favorable tax treatment accorded the life insurance transaction is that society is better off if people purchase life insurance. If the government did not encourage the purchase of life insurance, the argument goes, the government's (taxpayers') burden for welfare and other subsidies would be greater.

During planning, savings and investment alternatives should be judged on an after-tax basis. Tax considerations enter most investment decisions, as do considerations of risk and other characteristics of a specific alternative. To reach logical conclusions only after-tax results should be compared. Sometimes computing an after-tax return is easy; the before-tax return is multiplied by one minus the person's marginal tax rate. Sometimes computing an after-tax return is complex and only estimated outcomes are possible. Calculating future returns on participating life insurance requires estimating several factors, including the year of surrender, dividends paid and appropriate tax and insurance company penalties.

In general, investors and financial planners should keep in mind three overall strategies to reduce individual income taxes:

1. Reducing reported income
2. Delaying recognition of reportable income
3. Shifting income to lower tax brackets

A fourth strategy, converting ordinary income into capital gains, historically has achieved favorable tax results. This strategy succeeds when capital gains are taxed at lower rates than ordinary income, but since 1987 capital gains have been taxed at the same rate as other income, so this strategy presently is not effective.[7] However, in his 1991 State of the Union address, President Bush proposed reintroducing the differential between capital gains and ordinary income. If this proposal should become law, this fourth strategy will again be an effective means of lowering tax liability.

Review Questions

1. As the beneficiary of his uncle's life insurance policy, Dean receives $100,000 in cash when his uncle dies. How much taxable income does he report if his uncle paid only $15,000 in premiums before death? How much income would Dean report if his uncle's adjusted basis in the policy were $10,000?

2. As beneficiary of her father's life insurance, Marian takes the $500,000 death benefit in six annual installments of $100,000. What are the tax consequences?

3. Lou paid annual premiums of $4,000 for his life insurance. He received dividends on the policy of $1,000 each year. If he surrenders the policy for its cash value of $6,000 at the end of the fourth year (after paying four premiums and receiving four dividends, with premiums paid at the beginning of the year and dividends received at the end of the year), what is the tax consequence? If he surrenders the policy for $35,000 at the beginning of the tenth year, what are the tax consequences?

4. Gary paid $200,000 for an annuity. He made this payment on his 50th birthday. He is now 65 and begins to receive $3,000 a month in income from his annuity. Calculate Gary's taxable income. (Hint: you must use the IRS life expectancy table.)

5. Shelly, age 65, made no contributions to her pension plan during her working years. Her employer paid the entire cost. She retired this year and received $12,000 in pension payments. How much of this amount is taxable income?
    a. Assume Shelly had $100,000 deducted from her salary for her pension over her 40-year working career. How much of her annual $12,000 pension is taxable?

Endnotes

[1] For extensive technical explanations of this material *see* Jeffrey W. Tegeler and Dan W. Smith, "Life Insurance Tax and Planning Considerations," *Journal of the American Society of CLU and ChFC*, November 1989, pp. 48–56; and J. Timothy Lynch, "A Guide to the Life Insurance Provisions of the 1988 Tax Law," *Journal of the American Society of CLU and ChFC*, November 1989, pp. 58–72. Both articles footnote the IRC extensively.

[2] New York Insurance Code Section 1113(1).

[3]IRC Section 7702(A).

[4]IRC Section 101(a)(1).

[5]IRC Section 101(a)(2). *See* Thomas F. Commito, "Transfer for Value Rulings Offer Planning Opportunities," *Journal of the American Society of CLU & ChFC,* November 1991, pp. 38–43.

[6]This material applies to nonqualified annuities. Qualified annuities, also known as *tax-deferred annuities*, are associated with 403(b), Keogh and other tax-advantaged retirement plans, described in Chapter 16. One major difference between qualified and nonqualified annuities is that qualified annuities are purchased with before-tax dollars; as a result, when the annuity is liquidated, the entire withdrawal is included in taxable income in the year received. For comprehensive coverage of annuity taxation, *see* J. Mark Poerio, "Everything You Wanted to Know about the Taxation of Annuities," *Life Association News*, April 1991, pp. 50–62.

[7]IRC Section 1201(a).

Bibliography

Adney, John T., and Mark E. Griffin. "The Great Single Premium Life Insurance Controversy: Past and Prologue—Part I." *Journal of the American Society of CLU & ChFC* 43, May 1989, pp. 64–74.

Auster, Rolf. "Traps to Avoid to Deduct Interest on Life Insurance Related Loans." *Journal of the American Society of CLU & ChFC* 41, May 1987, pp. 80–83.

Dorfman, Mark S., and Saul W. Adelman. "TDA and Non-TDA Investments after the 1986 Tax Reform Act." *Journal of the American Society of CLU & ChFC* 42, January 1988, pp. 54–57.

Friedman, Douglas I. "Section 1035 Exchanges and Modified Endowments." *Journal of the American Society of CLU & ChFC* 43, July 1989, pp. 62–67.

Hira, Labh S. "Tax Reform Act Changes to Section 403(b) Plans." *Journal of the American Society of CLU & ChFC* 41, September 1987, pp. 56–59.

Hira, Labh S. "Taxation of Distributions from Section 403(b) Plans." *Journal of the American Society of CLU & ChFC* 43, January 1989, pp. 52–55.

Jenkins, Gary E. "The Impact of Choice of Entity Selection upon Compensation and Fringe Benefit Planning after Tax Reform." *Journal of the American Society of CLU & ChFC* 42, March 1988, pp. 30–39.

The Life Insurance Counselor: Federal Income Taxation of Life Insurance. Chicago: American Bar Association, 1989.

Lurie, Alvin D. "TAMROLI: Reflections on Life after TAMRA." *Journal of the American Society of CLU & ChFC* 45, March 1991, pp. 44–53.

Lynch, J. Timothy. "A Guide to the Life Insurance Provisions of the 1988 Tax Law." *Journal of the American Society of CLU & ChFC* 43, November 1989, pp. 58–72.

Magner, James C., and Steve Kotler. "The Alternative Minimum Tax and Corporate-Owned Life Insurance." *Journal of the American Society of CLU & ChFC* 42, January 1988, pp. 24–30.

McFadden, John J. "Planning Qualified Plan and TDA Distributions." *Journal of the American Society of CLU & ChFC* 40, September 1986, pp. 48–55.

Mittelman, Alan J. "S Corporation Buy-Sell Agreements after the Tax Reform Act of 1986." *Journal of the American Society of CLU & ChFC* 42, 1988, pp. 36–43.

Morgan, Charles C. "The Internal Revenue Code of 1986: The Interest Deduction, Policy Loans and Universal Life Insurance." *Journal of the American Society of CLU & ChFC* 41, January 1987, pp. 30–43.

Samson, William D., and Robert W. McLeod. "Choosing Between C versus S Corporate Status in the Closely Held Corporation." *Journal of the American Society of CLU & ChFC* 44, September 1990, pp. 62–75.

Shechtman, Richard G. "The Corporate Alternative Minimum Tax—Hidden Traps for Corporate Owned Life Insurance." *Journal of the American Society of CLU & ChFC* 42, November 1988, pp. 32–36.

Stoeber, Edward A. "Taxation of Withdrawals from Life Insurance Policies." *Journal of the American Society of CLU & ChFC* 42, November 1988, pp. 42–49.

Tegeler, Jeffrey W., and Dan W. Smith. "Life Insurance Tax and Planning Considerations." *Journal of the American Society of CLU & ChFC* 43, November 1989, pp. 48–56.

Tucker, Michael J., and Ross Quarles. "The Excise Tax on Excess Retirement Benefit Distributions and Accumulations." *Journal of the American Society of CLU & ChFC* 44, May 1990, pp. 48–51.

Waldron, Gary L. "Another Look at Section 2035 Transfers of Life Insurance." *Journal of the American Society of CLU & ChFC* 42, March 1988, pp. 48–54.

Chapter 12: The Federal Gift and Estate Tax

Chapter Objectives

- Explain the federal estate tax calculation
- Explain the federal gift tax calculation
- Explain methods of reducing the transfer tax liability
- Present estate and gift tax terminology
- Explain the estate consequences of the life insurance transaction

Introduction

This chapter presents material needed to understand one use for life insurance proceeds, providing liquidity to estates after property owners die. Obviously people of wealth need cash to pay taxes, repay debts and current bills and pay estate administration costs when they die. Unfortunately, such oversimplified statements lead to misunderstanding and mistakes. Just how rich must a property owner be before life insurance is needed to provide estate liquidity? Should people who are wealthy sell some property to pay their taxes? These questions require careful answers. Providing the answers requires knowledge of the federal gift and estate tax.

At the outset readers should understand that the federal estate tax affects relatively few Americans. The tax applies only to decedents having taxable estates greater than $600,000. On the other hand, many owners of small businesses, farmers, investors, physicians and others do have taxable estates, and they purchase millions of dollars of life insurance to facilitate the transfer of their estates to their families. Moreover, the need for estate liquidity to facilitate property transfer at death is not limited to people with a federal estate tax liability. People of moderate means also require life insurance for estate transfer purposes.

As was true for the preceding chapter's explanation of the federal income tax, this chapter omits considerable technical detail on gift and estate taxation that can be found in accounting and law texts.

Table 12.1
Federal Estate Tax Model

	Gross Estate
less	Deductions
plus	Taxable gifts
equals	Tax base
compute	Tentative tax liability
subtract	Post-1976 gift tax paid
subtract	Unified credit
subtract	Other credits
equals	**Federal estate tax liability**

Overview of the Federal Estate Tax

Purposes

Like the federal income tax, the federal **estate tax** raises money for the government. Because the tax affects so few Americans, however, the federal estate tax is not a significant source of federal revenue. In one recent year the estate tax raised .83 percent of total government revenue compared to 43.3 percent raised by the individual income tax and 1.8 percent raised by customs duties.[1]

A second justification for this tax is its effect on wealth concentration. Without the estate tax, people argue, large estates would stay in families for generations; the rich would get richer, and wealth would concentrate. Economists identify wealth concentration as a main contributor to the Depression and other economic swings. Politicians also realize that society is less stable when, for example, 3 percent of the population is wealthy and 97 percent poor.

A third purpose of the tax is the encouragement it provides for gift giving, the transfer of wealth from older to younger generations. Presumably society is more vital and progressive after such intergenerational wealth transfers.

Unified Transfer Tax

The federal estate tax applies to property transferred at death. The federal gift tax applies to lifetime property transfers. The federal estate tax and the federal gift tax are unified. The two taxes have identical rates and one unified credit. The federal estate tax calculation requires adding taxable gifts back to wealth on hand at death. By creating a **unified transfer tax**, the government is attempting to create a tax environment in which tax consequences are approximately the same whether the property owner dies owning property or gives it away while living. A later section in the chapter points out, however, that the unification is not perfect and that lifetime gifting can be an advantageous tax strategy.

The Federal Estate Tax

Gross Estate

A calculation of federal estate tax liability begins with the gross estate, which includes all of the decedent's property. Some property interests in real estate (land and things permanently attached to land), personal property (tangible property other than real property) and intangible property (e.g., investment securities and patents) are easy to identify but hard to value. Other property interests are more difficult to identify. Along with all real, personal, tangible and intangible property, the decedent's gross estate includes each of the following property interests.

Joint Interests

The total amount of jointly owned property is included, with two exceptions. First, only one-half of property owned jointly with a spouse is included. Second, any amount of property jointly owned with people other than the decedent's spouse is excluded to the extent that co-owners have paid for their share.

☐ **Example**

Tom owned $100,000 of real estate jointly with his wife. At death Tom's estate includes only $50,000.

If Tom owned the property jointly with his brother, Dick, $100,000 would be included in Tom's estate unless Dick could prove he paid for a portion of the property. The portion of property attributed to Dick's contributions is excluded from Tom's estate.

Assume the property was originally purchased for $60,000. Tom paid $40,000 or two-thirds of the cost. Dick paid $20,000, one-third of the cost. At Tom's death $66,667 ($2/3 \times \$100,000$) is included in his gross estate.

Community Property

Eight states, with Texas and California being the two largest, have community property laws. These laws give spouses equal interest in property acquired during their marriage. All of the decedent's interest in community property, as established by state law, is included in the gross estate.

Powers of Appointment

If the decedent has a general power to distribute property held in trust, the property under the decedent's control is included in the gross estate. If the decedent holds only a limited power, the property is not included in the gross estate. Those who hold a general **power of appointment** can distribute the property to themselves, their estate, their creditors or other eligible parties. Those who hold limited power of appointment cannot appoint the property for their own benefit.

☐ Example

Edith is trustee of a $1 million trust created by her father. Each year she can appoint the income from the trust to herself or her children. Edith's gross estate includes the $1 million even if she never appointed any income to herself.

Assume Edith could appoint the income from the trust only to her brothers and sisters. She could not appoint herself, her creditors or her estate. In that case, the $1 million would not be included in her estate.

Some Property Transferred within Three Years of Death

Most property transferred within three years of death is not included in the gross estate, though in the past such property was added back under "contemplation of death" provisions. However, property not included in the gross estate is still included in the estate tax base when post-1976 gifts are added to the total taxable property. The point at which the property is included in the estate tax base is important: property added back to the gross estate is valued at the date-of-death value; property included in the post-1976 gifts category is valued at the date-of-gift value. In the case of life insurance the date-of-death value is the face amount; the date-of-gift value is essentially the cash value.

Property transferred within three years of death that is added back to the gross estate includes:

- gifts of life insurance;
- property transferred with retained life estate or other interest; and
- revocable transfers.

A gift of life insurance occurs if the policy is absolutely assigned by one party to another. The second party may be a person or a trust. In either case, if the policy owner fails to live three years from the date of the gift, the face amount of life insurance is included in the estate.

Gifts with retained life interest occur if a person transfers property to another but retains the right to use or receive income from the property during his or her lifetime. A transfer with retained life interest would occur, for example, if a father transferred ownership of a business to a child but retained the right to some percentage of the future income.

Revocable gifts allow the giver to reacquire the property. Special rules apply if a reversionary interest is greater than 5 percent of the value of the property gifted. For example, if a father (age 45) gave a grandfather (age 80) some property with the provision that the property reverts to the father if the grandfather predeceases him, the value of the reversionary interest would exceed 5 percent of the property value. If the father failed to live for three years after making such a gift, the date-of-death value of the property would be included in the father's estate along with any gift taxes paid on the transfer.

Note that, if any of these three items are added back to the decedent's gross estate, they are added back at their date-of-death value, not the date-of-gift value.

Moreover, any gift tax paid on the transfer is also added to the decedent's gross estate. Adding back the gift tax is called *grossing up* the estate.

Life Insurance

The gross estate includes life insurance proceeds if they are payable to the estate or used for the benefit of the estate. Proceeds are also included if the decedent had any incident of ownership—the right to name the beneficiary, to make a policyholder loan or to choose the dividend option—in the policy at death.

☐ **Example**

Assume Nathan died with $100,000 of life insurance. This amount will be included in his estate if:

- he names his estate or his executor as beneficiary;
- he names his son (or a trust) as beneficiary, but the beneficiary uses the life insurance proceeds to pay Nathan's estate taxes;
- Nathan gave the policy away within three years of death; or
- Nathan had any incident of ownership in the policy at his death.

Annuity, Pension or Profit-Sharing Plans or Trusts

This area of the estate tax law is difficult to summarize. In general the decedent's gross estate includes the present value of amounts receivable by other annuitants (e.g., coannuitant's share of joint-and-last-survivor annuities) or because of refund features (e.g., contingent beneficiary's shares of cash refund annuities). For people dying after 1984 the amount included in the decedent's gross estate arising from qualified pension plans is affected by any contributions made by the decedent.[2]

Property Valuation

Property included in the gross estate is included at its fair market value at the date of death. An alternative valuation date of six months after the decedent's death may be selected by the executor as the date for calculating the fair market value. If the alternative date is chosen, it applies to all property in the estate. The alternative date would be an efficient choice in cases where the property comprising the majority of the estate has diminished significantly in value during the six months following death. Such a loss might arise from business reversals caused by the owner's death or by a stock market decline. The diminished estate would be less able to pay the estate tax, which explains why the government allows the alternative valuation date.

As an example of when the executor would choose the alternative valuation date, consider an estate worth $3.5 million at the date of death. Federal estate and other death transfer costs might amount to $750,000. Assume the value of the closely held business assets comprising the bulk of the estate declines markedly in the six months following the owner's death, so the value of the estate is only

$900,000 when the taxes are payable. In this case, without the alternative valuation date provision there would be severe hardship in paying the tax liability on the $3.5 million estate.

Farms and closely held businesses may be valued on a special basis that is less than the fair market value.[3] The rules covering special valuation of this type of property are complex and are not presented here. Note that, if the heirs divert property from its special use within ten years following the decedent's death, the law provides for a recapture of any forgone tax with interest.

Deductions

The next step in the federal estate tax calculation is to take deductions from the gross estate. Deductions are allowed for:

- funeral expenses;
- administrative expenses of settling the estate;
- repayment of debts;
- uninsured losses; and
- charitable transfers (in general, to achieve tax-deductible status the charity must be for exclusively religious, scientific, charitable, literary or educational purposes).

One allowable deduction requires additional explanation and special attention in the estate plans of married people: the *marital deduction*. (Several planning issues related to the marital deduction are covered in Chapter 17.) Since 1982, all property passing from a deceased spouse to a surviving spouse has reduced the deceased spouse's gross estate. That is, if the first spouse to die leaves his or her entire estate to the surviving spouse, there is no federal estate tax at that spouse's death. The government's purpose is to tax the transfer at the subsequent death of the surviving spouse. Estate taxation can be eliminated or postponed if the surviving spouse consumes all the property or remarries.

To qualify for the marital deduction, property given to a spouse must not be a **terminable interest**. That is, the right to use, give away or enjoy the property must not end at the surviving spouse's death, remarriage or any other predetermined event. However, the tax law allows for an important exception to the terminable interest rule.

Despite being an interest in property that terminates at death, **qualified terminable interest property (QTIP)** can be eligible for the marital deduction. QTIP trusts allow property to be enjoyed by a surviving spouse during his or her lifetime, but at the death of the second spouse the property is distributed by designation of the first spouse to die.

☐ **Example**

Richard and Peggy are married. It is a second marriage for both of them. Both have children by this marriage and by their first marriage. At Richard's death he wants to pass his property to Peggy for her lifetime, then to the children of this marriage. The QTIP arrangement allows achievement of his objective.

To be eligible for the marital deduction, QTIP property must meet the following conditions:

- All income from the property must go to the surviving spouse.
- The income must be payable at least annually.
- There must not exist any provision for the appointment of property to anybody but the surviving spouse during the survivor's lifetime.

The executor of the estate of the first spouse to die makes the election to classify property as QTIP. This election is irrevocable. With a QTIP election the decision is made after the probate process has begun and the gross estate has been valued. The QTIP election is a postdeath planning technique.

Adjusted Taxable Gifts

The following rules do not apply to the gifts already included in the gross estate because they were made within three years of death. This section applies to all other post-1976 gifts. After deductions are made from the gross estate, adjusted taxable gifts are added to the remainder, producing the tax base. The logic for adding back gifts is to create indifference, from a tax standpoint, between gifting property and passing property at death. Because the unified transfer tax rates are progressive, if gifts were not added back, for example, a person transferring a $1 million estate by four gifts of $250,000 would pay lower taxes than a person dying with a gross estate of $1 million.

☐ **Example**

As a textbook example, assume a very simple tax structure. The tax rate on gifts or estates of amounts up to $1 million is 10 percent. The tax on amounts of $1 million or more is 50 percent.

If A gave four gifts of $250,000, A pays $100,000 ($250,000 × .1 = $25,000; $25,000 × 4) in gift taxes. A dies owning no wealth. If B dies with an estate of $1 million, B pays $500,000 in taxes ($1,000,000 × .5).

What is C's tax liability if C gives one $250,000 gift and dies with an estate of $750,000? C would pay $100,000 (.1 × $250,000 plus .1 × $750,000).

Now, however, assume the tax law causes A and C to add their prior gifts back to their taxable estates. Even though A died without wealth, he would be subject to tax on an estate of $1 million at the 50 percent rate. He would get a credit for the $100,000 in prior gift taxes paid but would owe $400,000 ($500,000 in tax liability less $100,000 in gift tax credit). (In practice, when estates have insufficient assets to pay tax liabilities, the IRS can use tax liens and other methods to extract taxes due from the gift beneficiaries.) Likewise, C would have the $250,000 gift added to the gross estate of $750,000 and would have a tax liability of $500,000 and a credit for the $25,000 in gift taxes paid.

Despite having to add adjusted taxable gifts back to the decedent's estate, gifting retains desirable characteristics for the following reasons.

When adding gifts to the estate, the amount added to the estate is the value at date of gift. If property appreciates after gifting, the appreciation is not subjected to the estate tax.

☐ **Example**

Sam gives his daughter, Diane, 1,000 shares of common stock. The date-of-gift value is $100,000. At Sam's death the stock is worth $1 million. Only $100,000 is considered when calculating adjusted taxable gifts to add back to the estate.

Note that it is not necessary to add $100,000 back to Sam's estate because each person has an *annual gift tax exclusion* of $10,000. The government allows each person to give $10,000 each year to any number of recipients free of the federal gift tax. Thus Sam's *adjusted* gift to Diane is $90,000 ($100,000 gift less $10,000 annual exclusion). If Sam's wife, Sue, joins him in making the gift, the annual exclusion is increased to $20,000, leaving $80,000 as the adjusted taxable gift. The annual gift tax exclusion is $20,000 even if Sue did not directly give property to Diane, as long as she legally joins in the gift.

If gift taxes are paid on adjusted taxable gifts, the amount of gift taxes is removed from the gross estate and a credit is available for the gift taxes paid.

Sometimes gifting property is not advantageous. First, payment of gift taxes, after exhausting the unified credit, implies an opportunity cost of the tax payment. Second, if property declines in value instead of appreciating, the decedent's gross estate would be smaller if the property had not been gifted. Remember, the date-of-gift value is added back to the estate.

Estimated Estate Tax Liability

Table 12.2 reproduces the unified tax rate schedule for people giving gifts or dying after 1988.

☐ **Example**

James Polk had a gross estate of $5,000,000. He had deductions of $2,500,000. He gave gifts of $1,000,000 in 1988. His tentative tax liability is:

Gross estate	$5,000,000
Deductions	2,500,000
Adjusted Gifts	990,000
Tax base	$3,490,000

Tentative tax liability
$1,290,800 + .55 ($3,490,000 − $3,000,000) = $1,560,300

Tax Credits

The government allows several credits against the tentative tax liability. Allowable credits include these:

- State death taxes
- Gift taxes on gifts included in the gross estate

Chapter 12 The Federal Gift and Estate Tax   253

Table 12.2
Federal Transfer Taxes: Unified Rate Schedule

A More Than	B But Not More Than	C Tax On A	D Rate On Excess
$ 0	$ 10,000	$ 0	18%
10,000	20,000	1,800	20
20,000	40,000	3,800	22
40,000	60,000	8,200	24
60,000	80,000	13,000	26
80,000	100,000	18,200	28
100,000	150,000	23,800	30
150,000	250,000	38,800	32
250,000	500,000	70,800	34
500,000	750,000	155,800	37
750,000	1,000,000	248,300	39
1,000,000	1,250,000	345,800	41
1,250,000	1,500,000	448,300	43
1,500,000	2,000,000	555,800	45
2,000,000	2,500,000	780,800	49
2,500,000	3,000,000	1,205,800	53
3,000,000		1,290,800	55

- Federal estate taxes previously paid on property included in the gross estate: A regularly diminishing percentage of credit is allowed. After ten years this credit is exhausted. (This credit is available, for example, if a person inherited taxed property and died within six years of the inheritance. The decedent's gross estate includes the inherited property, but a credit is allowed for a percentage of the taxes paid on the inherited property.)
- Foreign death taxes
- The **unified credit**: Each person is allowed one lifetime credit of $192,800 against his or her combined gift or estate tax liability. If taxable gifts are given, presumably the credit will be used at that point to offset the gift tax liability. Any credit used to offset the gift tax liability is subtracted from the amount of credit available to reduce the estate tax liability.

☐ **Example**

Sally gives $610,000 to her son Arnold. Her taxable gift is $600,000. The gift tax on this amount is $192,800. Sally uses her unified credit to offset this tax and pays no federal gift tax on this gift. If she gives Arnie $610,000 next year, she will pay $235,000. (The difference between the tax of $192,800 on the first gift and the $235,000 tax on the second gift illustrates the effect of a progressive marginal tax schedule with prior taxable gifts added to the current gift. The procedure for calculating the gift tax on a series of gifts is explained and illustrated shortly. After studying that material readers should return to this example and calculate the tax on the second gift. The tax base is $1,200,000, and a credit of $192,800 is allowed for the first gift.)

If she dies with $1 million in property, she will add back both adjusted gifts of $600,000, producing an estate tax base of $2,200,000 ($1,000,000 + $600,000 + $600,000). She calculates a tentative tax liability of $878,800 [$780,800 + (.49 × $200,000)], from which she subtracts her unified credit of $192,800 and the $235,000 she previously paid in gift taxes, leaving a net tax liability of $451,000 ($878,800 tentative tax liability − $192,800 unified credit − $235,000 gift tax previously paid).

Arranging Life Insurance Ownership

As discussed in Chapter 1, a life insurance policy creates three legal interests: the insured, the beneficiary and the owner. Only natural people can be insureds, while charities, corporations, trusts and other legal entities can be beneficiaries and owners.

When coordinating life insurance into an estate plan, the ownership of the life insurance is of critical importance. If the decedent's estate receives the proceeds, if the proceeds are used to pay the estate's obligations or if the decedent retained any of the incidents of ownership in the policy, the gross estate includes the proceeds. Also, if the decedent either gave away or absolutely assigned the rights in the policy within three years of death, the gross estate includes the proceeds.

The objective of minimizing taxes requires that the proceeds not be included in the estate. In smaller estates, where the life insurance proceeds combined with all other assets are less than $600,000, the estate can be named beneficiary. In other cases, where the property owner desires to keep the proceeds out of the gross estate but still make the cash available, the owner may name a spouse, a child or a life insurance trust as owner and beneficiary of the policy. Ownership of the policy by a trust also should be considered where minors are the intended beneficiary, because life insurance companies will not release proceeds directly to minors. The spouse, child or trust, once receiving the proceeds, may use the cash to purchase assets from the decedent's estate or make loans of cash to the estate. Either of these two transactions will put cash into the estate without subjecting the proceeds to the estate tax.

Two additional rules apply if the proceeds are to be kept from the decedent's estate. First, any transfer of an existing policy must precede the insured's death by more than three years. Second, there must not be more than a 5 percent chance, determined actuarially, that the policy will revert to the original owner. For example, if a 55-year-old daughter were to give a policy to her 77-year-old mother, there clearly would be a substantial chance that the ownership of the policy would revert to the daughter, and the policy proceeds would therefore be included in the daughter's estate.

However, the transfer of an existing policy can have the effect of causing taxes to be paid earlier than if the transfer were not made. In this instance, if the new owner of the existing policy should predecease the insured, the new owner's estate includes the cash surrender value, and this value is subject to the estate tax, although the insured is living.

☐ **Example**

Father assigns ownership of a life insurance policy having a $15,000 cash value to Mother. Son is the beneficiary. If Mother predeceases Father, Mother's estate will include the $15,000 cash value. (IRS regulations term this amount *replacement cost*, which is usually about equal to the cash value.) The face value is not included, because Father is alive.

If the owner and beneficiary are different people, when the insured dies the owner makes a taxable gift of the death proceeds to the beneficiary. A person makes a taxable gift if he or she buys a life insurance policy naming another party as owner and a third party as beneficiary. Future premiums paid on such a policy are also gifts.

☐ **Example**

If Father (from the previous example) dies causing $150,000 in proceeds to be paid to Son, Mother has made a taxable gift of $150,000.

The Federal Gift Tax

For the purpose of the federal gift tax, a **gift** is any transfer of property for less than its fair market value.

☐ **Example**

Ray Conway gives his daughter some stock worth $50,000. Ray sells his son some land having a fair market value of $55,000 for $5,000. Ray makes an "interest-free" loan to his daughter. If he had loaned the money on a fair market value basis, it would have produced $50,000 in interest income for Ray.
In each case Ray made a $50,000 gift.

From a legal standpoint a valid gift has three requirements:

1. The donor must give up all rights in the property. Incomplete gifts or gifts with strings attached can produce unintended and adverse tax consequences.
2. There must be actual or constructive delivery of the gift property.
3. A donee (or a qualified representative of a minor or incapacitated donee) must accept the gift.

Gift Tax Exclusion

A gift must be a *present interest* to qualify for the $10,000 annual gift tax exclusion. A present interest means the donee can use and enjoy the property immediately. A *future interest*, such as that held by the beneficiary of a life insurance policy, implies a period when the holder cannot use or enjoy the property.

The Crummey Trust

The Crummey Trust arrangement deals with the gifting problems presented if one person pays life insurance premiums for another. Payment of a life insurance premium involves a gift of a future interest, because the beneficiary cannot use the gift when it is made. In the Crummey Trust arrangement an unfunded trust owns a life insurance policy. Regular (annual) cash deposits are made to the trust. After the deposit is made, the beneficiary has limited time to withdraw the cash from the trust. If the cash is not withdrawn, the trustee uses it to pay the life insurance premium. In this instance the donor made a gift of present value because the beneficiary has a chance to withdraw the cash.

Two basic requirements must be met to make the arrangement valid: there must be an adequate period for the cash withdrawal to be made, and adequate notice must be given to the person authorized to make the cash withdrawal. In the case of minors a guardian, who may not simultaneously be the donor, must be notified of the availability of cash in the trust.

The Crummey Trust arrangement allows payments of up to $10,000 in premiums ($20,000 if two donors make the gift) each year using the annual gift exclusion. Without using the Crummey Trust arrangement, anyone who paid, for example, $10,000 in premiums for a life insurance policy on someone else's life would be making a taxable gift.

Tax Advantages of Gifts

Lifetime gifts can be used in several ways to serve tax purposes.

Interspousal Gifts

Interspousal gifts can be made to ensure that both spouses have sufficient property to take advantage of the unified federal estate and gift tax credit. This advantage arises in cases where one spouse's assets exceed the minimum assets subject to the estate tax and the other's do not. Interspousal gifts in this instance can reduce or eliminate the federal estate tax and increase the amount of property passing to children.

☐ **Example**

Peter and Amanda Johnson are married. This year Amanda inherited $5 million from her father. Peter has less than $10,000 in assets. Amanda gives Peter $1 million, allowing Peter to pass $600,000 to their children free of the federal estate tax. If Amanda had not made the gift and Peter died before Amanda, his $600,000 exemption would be lost.

Gifts of Income-Producing Property to Children

Such gifts may result in the income received by the child being taxed at lower rates than if the income were received by the donor. The "kiddie tax" rules implemented in 1986 and the reduction in marginal tax bracket spread, however, have reduced this advantage.

Multiple Donees

Gifts up to a maximum of $10,000 per donee may be excluded each year from taxable gift giving. With enough donees and enough time, much wealth can be passed to others in this way, free of the federal transfer tax.

Gifts to Charities

In addition to giving gifts to family members, many people enjoy making gifts to charitable organizations. The tax rules governing charitable giving are fairly complex. For example, there is an important distinction between public charities and private foundations, with different limits on gifts applicable to each category. In general, charitable gifts are limited for federal *income* tax purposes to 50 percent of taxable income but are not subject to any percentage limitation for federal *estate* tax purposes. Like gifts to individuals, charitable gifts may be made outright or may involve the use of a trust.

Probate versus Gifting

In some circumstances gifting may not be the most tax-advantageous strategy for passing property between generations. For example, property that has appreciated greatly may be more advantageously passed through the probate process after the owner's death. Property received at death receives a **stepped-up basis**. That is, the basis for the new owner is the value of the property at the original owner's death, not the original owner's cost basis.

☐ **Example**

Jim Lawrence owns property with a fair market value of $100,000. He acquired the property ten years ago for $40,000. If he gives this property to his daughter, $90,000 ($100,000 current value less the $10,000 annual gift exclusion) would be added back to Jim's estate at death. Also, the daughter's basis in the property, if she sells it, is $40,000. Here, where the donee sells appreciated property, her position would be better if she received the property at her father's death and had the $100,000 basis.

Federal Gift Tax Calculation

Table 12.3 presents a summary of the federal gift tax calculation.

☐ **Example**

Kay Garland gives her sister $510,000 on January 1, 1986, 1987 and 1988. She had given no gifts before 1986. Her gift tax calculations are as follows.

Table 12.3
Federal Gift Tax Calculation

	Current year's gross gifts
less	
	Annual exclusion(s) and deductions
equals	
	Current taxable gifts
plus	
	Total prior taxable gifts
equals	
	Gift tax base
compute	
	Tentative tax liability
less	
	Tentative tax on total prior taxable gifts
leaves	
	Tentative tax on current gifts
less	
	Unused unified credit
equals	
	Net current gift tax

Gift 1, 1986
Gross gift	$ 510,000
Annual exclusion	−10,000
Taxable gift	$ 500,000
Gift tax	155,800
Unused unified credit 192,800	
Gift tax paid (remaining credit $192,800 − $155,800 = $37,000)	—0—

Gift 2, 1987
Gross gift	$ 510,000
Annual exclusion	−10,000
Taxable gift	$ 500,000
Prior taxable gifts	+500,000
Tax base	$1,000,000
Tentative gift tax	$ 345,800
Tentative tax on prior gifts	−155,800
Tentative tax on current gifts	$ 190,000
Unused unified credit	−37,000
Gift tax paid	$ 153,000

Gift 3, 1988
Gross gift	$ 510,000
Annual exclusion	−10,000
Taxable gift	$ 500,000

Prior taxable gifts	$1,000,000
Tax base	$1,500,000
Tentative gift tax	$ 555,800
Tentative tax on prior gifts	−345,800
Tentative tax on current gifts	$ 210,000
Unused unified credit	—0—
Gift tax paid	$ 210,000

Valuation and Deductions

As was the case with estate property, some gifts are more obvious than others. It is beyond the scope of this book to describe all the different types of property that can be gifted and how such property is valued. (For example, release of a general power of appointment constitutes a taxable gift.) In general, gifted property is valued at its fair market value at the time of the gift.

If a donor transfers an annuity, the value of the gift is determined by the donee's life expectancy. If a life insurance policy is gifted, the replacement cost of the policy, considering outstanding loans, determines the value of the gift.

Gifts to specified charities, such as religious, scientific or educational institutions, are fully deductible. An unlimited marital deduction also is available for gifts between spouses.

Generation-Skipping Transfer Tax

One additional federal tax requires mention. Again, the subject is quite technical and so loosely connected to the subject of life insurance that full treatment is not provided here. In a few financial planning situations involving millions of dollars of property this tax can have very serious implications, because the tax rate applied is the maximum federal estate tax rate.

Since 1986 direct transfers to persons more than one generation below the grantor are taxed as "direct-skip" transfers. That is, gifts from grandfather to grandchild or great grandchild are taxed.

Each transferor has a $1 million lifetime exemption and a $2 million exemption for direct skips to grandchildren. These exemptions can be doubled if spouses join in gifts.

Financial Planning Issues

This chapter explored estate and gift taxation and how life insurance fits into a financial plan with respect to these taxes.

Many business owners and farmers want to keep the business or farm in the family. The government places a tax on the transfer of assets at death. The tax, with rates as high as 55 percent, can create a substantial need for cash. If an adequate amount of life insurance proceeds is available, the death of the property owner, which creates the need for cash, also can be the event that provides the cash, the life insurance proceeds. For the plan to be effective, the amount of cash available must equal the amount needed. The federal estate tax must be calculated to reveal the amount needed. (Chapter 17 presents a comprehensive estate planning problem. The material in this chapter provides the background needed to understand that example.)

Policy ownership and beneficiary designation are significant factors in determining the estate tax consequences of any life insurance transaction. Often several combinations of ownership and beneficiary designations are possible in family or business situations, including the possibility of ownership by a trust. This chapter discussed the tax consequences of various ownership and beneficiary combinations.

Life insurance policies present many gifting possibilities. Policies with substantial cash values can be given away to family members or to charity. Sums of money can be given to pay premiums on life insurance policies. Care always must be taken to arrange these transactions to achieve the desired tax effect.

Review Questions

1. Carlos Santa Cruz died owning the following assets. Calculate the amount of his gross estate.
   a. Apartment building with a book value of $123,000 and a fair market value of $345,000. The purchase price was $200,000.
   b. Three vehicles purchased for $45,000, now worth $23,300.
   c. A home with a fair market value of $500,000, a replacement cost of $400,000 and a purchase price of $250,000. The home has an outstanding mortgage loan of $100,000.
   d. Common stock purchased for $400,000 that could now be sold for $250,000.

2. Bob Newton has a general power of appointment over a $5 million trust. His grandmother set up the trust 15 years ago. He can appoint the annual income of about $400,000 to himself, his three children or his three sisters. He has never appointed any of the income to himself but has split the income in equal shares between his children and his sisters. When Bob dies, how much property from this trust is included in his estate?

3. Melanie Hempstead dies. She owned $50,000 in life insurance provided by her employer and $200,000 of individually purchased life insurance. What amount of this life insurance is included in her gross estate? If, last year, she

gave the individually purchased life insurance to her daughter, who is also the beneficiary, would your answer change?

4. Steve White died with $1,000,000 in cash. His funeral expenses were $8,000, and the cost of settling his estate was $10,000. Calculate Steve's federal estate tax liability.
   a. Assume Steve gave $300,000 to the Red Cross. Recalculate his estate tax liability.
   b. Assume Steve gave $300,000 to his wife instead of the Red Cross. Recalculate his estate tax liability.

5. Sebastian Sevier gave $1 million in taxable gifts of common stock to his children in 1990. He dies in 1992 owning $2 million in assets. Calculate his tentative tax liability. Calculate the amount of taxes payable at his death.

6. Bea Wilson gave a gift of $1,010,000 to her sister in 1988 and 1989. These were the only gifts she ever gave. Show the calculations needed to calculate her gift tax liability.

Endnotes

[1] *U.S. Statistical Abstract, 1989* (Washington, D.C., U.S. Government Printing Office).

[2] Readers interested in technical areas such as this one should consult the IRS or the *Advanced Underwriting Service* (Chicago: Dearborn Financial Publishing, Inc.).

[3] IRC Section 2032A.

Bibliography

Chandler, Darlene K. "The Irrevocable Life Insurance Trust and Section 2035: New Guideposts to Effective Estate Planning?" *Journal of the American Society of CLU & ChFC* 41, July 1987, pp. 52–56.

Duncan, Douglas W. "Life Insurance Planning to Minimize Generation Skipping Transfer Taxes." *Journal of the American Society of CLU & ChFC* 42, May 1988, pp. 46–56.

Jurinski, James J. "Pre-death Transfers of Life Insurance in Community Property States." *Journal of the American Society of CLU & ChFC* 44, March 1990, pp. 34–39.

Mittelman, Alan J. "Irrevocable Life Insurance Trusts and the Generation-Skipping Transfer Tax." *Journal of the American Society of CLU & ChFC* 42, November 1989, pp. 88–95.

1991 Federal Tax Course. Englewood Cliffs, N.J.: Prentice-Hall, 1991.

Prestopino, C. J. *Introduction to Estate Planning*, 2d ed. Homewood, Ill.: Richard D. Irwin, 1989.

Stone, Edward H. "Crummey Rules Have Changed." *Journal of the American Society of CLU & ChFC* 43, September 1989, pp. 34–38.

Whitney, Victor P. "Unique Funding for Charitable Remainder Trusts." *Journal of the American Society of CLU & ChFC* 44, July 1990, pp. 36–40.

Chapter 13 | Financial Mathematics and Investments

Chapter Objectives

- Review the mathematics underlying time-value-of-money problems
- Discuss criteria for selecting investments for reallocating consumption
- Discuss common performance measurements used to compare investments

Introduction

During adult life people make consumption and investment decisions to balance their need for immediate consumption with the desire to accumulate wealth. Investing, purchasing appropriate amounts of life, health and annuity coverage and engaging in financial planning provide certainty to a family's future consumption pattern.

This chapter focuses on three issues underlying this lifelong process. First is the importance of the time value of money. How does the time value of money influence financial planning decisions? The amount of interest paid on investments influences the amount that needs to be deposited on a periodic basis to meet certain financial goals. Inflation and deflation can also modify the purchasing power of the dollar, especially over long periods of time. This chapter presents the mathematical techniques used to solve a variety of time-value-of-money problems.

Second is the unique position of cash value life insurance among the different types of investments available. What investments can be substituted for cash value life insurance, allowing consumers to allocate lifetime consumption? Cash value life insurance has a unique function and a shared function. No other contract can promise a death benefit *whenever* death occurs (the unique function). Other investments, however, compete with its shared function, accumulating savings. Alternative investments include stocks, bonds, U.S. Treasury securities and collectibles. Each investment has specific characteristics with respect to liquidity, risk and return. Various investments will be examined with regard to those characteristics. The goal is to provide a background in investment topics and to describe alternatives to cash value life insurance for saving.

Third is the difficulty of making intelligent long-term projections of income, expenses and investment returns. Long-term financial planning is difficult because the future is unknown. Individuals, however, must make intelligent decisions based on incomplete information, and they must make projections based on reasonable assumptions of future conditions. Personal computers and spreadsheet software simplify the process, allowing for changes in income and expense patterns and providing instantaneous recalculation of results based on the changes made in the assumptions or formulas. The chapter presents examples solved algebraically and by a computer spreadsheet program. (Lotus 1-2-3 spreadsheet formulas, a product of Lotus Development Corp., are used, but other spreadsheet programs have similar formulas and work just as well.)

Financial Mathematics

The impact of compound interest on financial decisions is significant especially when long periods are involved. The reader is assumed to be somewhat familiar with present value and future value concepts; only a brief review of these concepts is included here.[1]

Future Value of $1

When money is invested at a positive interest rate, the sum grows to a larger amount, the future value, by a specific factor $(1 + i)^n$. This relationship is expressed algebraically as:

$$FV = PV \times (1 + i)^n \quad \text{(Formula 13.1)}$$

where:

FV = future value amount
PV = present value amount
i = interest rate
n = the number of periods the money is to be invested at rate i.

For example, if $1,000 is deposited at an interest rate of 7 percent for one period (in this example, one year), the future value will be $1,070. If the $1,070 is now invested for one year at 7 percent, the original $1,000 will grow to $1,144.90. This can be calculated by using Formula 13.1:

$FV = \$1,000 \times 1.07 \times 1.07$ or
$FV = \$1,000 \times 1.07^2$
$FV = \$1,000 \times 1.1449$
$FV = \$1,144.90$

Many financial problems can be solved with Formula 13.1.

☐ **Example**

How much will a depositor accumulate at the end of four years if $1,500 is deposited now at 8 percent interest compounded annually?

$$FV = PV \times (1+i)^n$$
$$FV = \$1{,}500 \times (1.08)^4$$
$$FV = \$1{,}500 \times 1.3604$$
$$FV = \$2{,}040.60$$

What yearly rate of return is generated if $1,500 grows to $2,000 in five years when interest is compounded annually? (To solve for i, one may simply use future value time-value-of-money tables.)

$$FV = PV \times (1+i)^n$$
$$\$2{,}000 = \$1{,}500\,(1+i)^5$$

$$\frac{\$2{,}000}{\$1{,}500} = (1+i)^5$$
$$1.333 = (1+i)^5$$
$$1.333^{1/5} = (1+i)$$
$$i = 1 - 1.333^{1/5}$$
$$i = 0.059$$

Use the following spreadsheet formula to calculate future value factors. For 8 percent for four periods (*see* the first example) use:

$$+(1+.08)\char`\^4 = 1.3604$$

The 5th root of 1.333 or the periodic growth rate for the second example is:

$$1.333\char`\^(1/5) = 1.059$$

Present Value of $1

The process of calculating the future value of an amount growing at some stated rate can be reversed. This concept is called **present value**. One question answered with present value is how much must be deposited so the investment will grow to a stated amount at some future point. Calculating the present value (Formula 13.2) of an amount is just the inverse of calculating the future value amount:

$$PV = FV \times \left(\frac{1}{1+i}\right)^n \qquad \textbf{(Formula 13.2)}$$

☐ **Example**

How much money must be deposited today so that in ten years $20,000 will be accumulated if the interest rate is 12 percent?

$$PV = FV \times \left(\frac{1}{1+i}\right)^n$$
$$PV = \$20{,}000 \times \left(\frac{1}{1+.12}\right)^{10}$$
$$PV = \$20{,}000 \times 0.322$$
$$PV = \$6{,}440.00$$

Present values and present value factors are used extensively in calculating life insurance premiums, and the reader should be familiar with and be able to solve problems using formulas 13.1 and 13.2. (These and other formulas are reproduced in Appendix A to this text.)

Use the following spreadsheet formula to calculate present value factors. For 6 percent for five periods, use:

$$+1/((1+.06)^5) = 0.7472$$

Annuities

Not all cash flows occur as one lump sum. Many investments involve a series of equal payments. Streams of equal payments are called *annuities*. (This is a financial definition which should be distinguished from its life insurance use to describe a specific type of contract, as defined in Chapter 5.) One must be careful when analyzing annuities. Single payments or streams of payments can occur at the end of a period or at the beginning of a period, thus affecting the compounding process. When a payment is made at the *end* of a period, as in the present value and future value calculations discussed so far, the annuity is called an *ordinary annuity*. When the payment occurs at the *beginning* of the period, the annuity is called an **annuity due**. Formulas 13.3 and 13.4 provide the formulas for calculating the present value of an annuity and an annuity due.

$$PV_a = A x \sum_{t=1}^{n} [1/(1+i)]^t \quad \text{(Ordinary Annuity, Formula 13.3)}$$

$$PV_d = A x \sum_{t=1}^{n-1} [1/(1+i)]^t + 1 \quad \text{(Annuity Due, Formula 13.4)}$$

An example will help distinguish between the two. If people receive an annuity (A = $100) consisting of two payments, and the discount rate is 10 percent, the respective present values of the ordinary annuity and the annuity due are computed as follows:

Ordinary annuity:
$PV_a = (\$100 \times .909) + (\$100 \times .826)$
$PV_a = \$173.50$

Annuity due:
$PV_d = (\$100 \times 1.00) + (\$100 \times .909)$
$PV_d = \$190.90$

In the ordinary annuity calculation the first payment is discounted one year and the second payment is discounted two years. In the annuity due calculation payment is received at the beginning of the period, and the present value of the first payment is equal to $100. The second payment is discounted for only one year.

Tables are constructed to provide present value and future value annuity factors consisting of sums of the present value and future value factors. Looking at the example, the sum of the present value factors in the ordinary annuity case is 1.735 (.909 + .826), and the sum of the annuity due factors is 1.909 (1.00 + .909). The factors 1.735 and 1.909 appear in their respective tables for a two-year

Table 13.1
Illustration of an Annuity and an Annuity Due

	A	B	C	D	E	F
1	Present value of education fund					
2						
3	Inv. rate			0.05		
4						
5				1992	1993	1994
6	Education expense			0	$7,000	$7,000
7	PV of education fund					
8	Annuity			12,396	13,016	6,667
9						
10	Annuity due			13,016	13,667	7,000
11						

annuity under the discount rate of 10 percent. The formulas to calculate the time-value-of-money factors are found in Appendix A to this book.

Table 13.1 demonstrates how the present value of an *annuity* and how the present value of an *annuity due* may be calculated using a spreadsheet program. The method demonstrated assumes that computer software calculates the present value of a stream of equally spaced, regular or irregular dollar amounts. The @NPV function performs the task in Lotus 1-2-3 and other programs. Table 13.1 shows the calculation of the present value of a hypothetical education fund. Assume that $7,000 is needed for expenses in the years 1993 and 1994. Then calculate the present value of the stream of payments at the beginning of each year.

The formula used for the ordinary annuity for 1992 (cell D8) in Table 13.1 is equal to @NPV(D3,D6...F6) and equals the sum of the present value of the numbers found in D6, E6 and F6. The discount rate is found in cell D3. (The "$" sign is used in formulas to fix the cell as an absolute reference if the formula is copied.) The formula for the annuity due (cell D10) is equal to +D6+@NPV −(D3,E6...F6). This adds the number found in cell D6 to the present value of education amounts found in cells E6 and F6. (The formula in F10 is **+F6** because the present value of one payment received immediately is equal to that number.)

☐ **Examples**

If Mr. Wilkinson wants to retire in ten years with $100,000 dollars in savings, how much must be deposited at the end of each year (*PMT*) so that the $10,000 will be available? Assume a 7 percent annual interest rate.

$$FV_a = PMT \times FVAF \text{ at } 7\% \text{ for 10 periods}$$
$$\$100,000 = PMT \times 13.816$$
$$PMT = \$100,000 / 13.816$$
$$PMT = \$7,237.98$$

where:

$FVAF$ = future value annuity factor

Mr. Wilkinson will have $100,000 available at the end of ten years if $7,237.98 is deposited at the end of each period and if funds deposited earn 7 percent.

How much will the annual payment be if $50,000 is borrowed to purchase a house over 30 years at a 10 percent annual rate? Each loan payment is made at the end of the year.

$$PV_a = PMT \times PVAF \text{ at } 10\% \text{ for } 30 \text{ periods}$$
$$\$50{,}000 = PMT \times 9.4269$$
$$PMT = \$50{,}000 / 9.4269$$
$$PMT = \$5{,}303.97$$

where:

$PVAF$ = present value annuity factor

Thus, at 10 percent the bank is indifferent between receiving $50,000 now and receiving $5,303.97 at the end of each year for the next 30 years.

If Mrs. Webster can afford a payment of $200 at the end of each year for 12 years, what is the maximum that can be borrowed if the interest rate is 12 percent?

$$PV_a = PMT \times PVAF \text{ at } 12\% \text{ for } 12 \text{ periods}$$
$$PV_a = \$200 \times 6.194$$
$$PV_a = \$1{,}238.80$$

At a 12% loan rate, Mrs. Webster makes 12 $200 annual payments to repay the $1,238 loan.

The following spreadsheet formulas calculate the present value and future value of an annuity:

@FV(payments, interest, term): Future value of an annuity (payments made at the end of the period).

@PV(payments, interest, term): Present value of an annuity (payments made at the end of the period).

@NPV(interest, range): Net present value of a range of amounts (payments made at the end of period).

@TERM(payments, interest, future value): Calculates the number of payments made at the end of period necessary to accumulate the future value at the interest rate.

To adjust for an annuity due, use:

@FV(payments, interest, term) * (1 + interest)
@PV(payments, interest, term) * (1 + interest)
@TERM(payment, interest, future value/(1 + interest))

Table 13.2
Mortgage Calculator

	A	B	C	D	E	F	G
1	Mortgage Calculator						
2							
3							
4	Assumptions:						Balance End
5	Principal			$80,000		Per.	of Period
6	Interest rate			0.100		0	$80,000
7	Years			10		1	74,980
8	Payments per yr.			1		2	69,459
9						3	63,385
10	Output:					4	56,704
11	Total # payments			10		5	49,355
12	Rate per period			0.1		6	41,270
13	PV factor			6.145		7	32,378
14	Periodic payment			$13,020		8	22,596
15						9	11,836
16						10	0
17							

☐ **Example: Mortgage Balance Calculator**

While constructing your financial plan, you may need to calculate the remaining balance of a loan. The following is a generalized mortgage calculator. Some money management programs have this function built in, but escrow amounts, private mortgage insurance and other loan peculiarities often result in only a close approximation of your actual results. Table 13.2 shows the results of calculating the remaining balance at the end of each year for an $80,000, ten-year (payable at the end of each year), 10 percent mortgage loan.

The mortgage payment is equal to the principal amount divided by the present value of an annuity factor:

@PV(1, interest, term) calculates the present value of a $1 annuity.
$80,000/@PV(1,0.1,10) = $13,020

The following formula alternatively can be used to calculate the mortgage payment:

@PMT(principal, interest, term)

The outstanding principal balance at the end of the year is calculated by subtracting the principal payment from the beginning principal amount:

beginning principal − [payment − (beginning principal × interest rate)]

Investing: Reallocating Consumption

As discussed early in this book, any savings program represents a reallocation of consumption. From the standpoint of financial efficiency, determining the goal for saving also determines the investment strategy and the savings medium used. An investor whose savings goal is short-term, for example, would not choose to put funds into investments that are difficult to liquidate or whose liquidation would cause adverse tax consequences. When people save or reallocate consumption to the future, funds are invested to take advantage of growth opportunities. A variety of investments with different risk, return and liquidity characteristics compete with cash value life and annuity contracts for personal savings. Some of these investments, including cash value life insurance, enjoy a favorable tax status.

Investment decisions must be based on the simultaneous consideration of liquidity, safety, current yield and growth potential and taxability.

Liquidity

Liquidity means an investment can be turned into cash quickly, without suffering a decline in value attributed solely to changing the investment into cash. This concept is distinguished from a change in the value due solely to market conditions.

☐ **Example**

A $1,000, 8 percent coupon, 30-year bond is purchased at 100 percent of its maturity value, or $1,000. If market interest rates decline to 6 percent, the market price of the bond will increase. The bond is considered liquid because an active secondary financial market exists, allowing easy cash sales. (A small transaction charge reduces the proceeds.) The bond's value has increased due to market conditions.

The most liquid investments, such as bank deposits, may be turned into cash quickly without penalty. Investments in publicly traded securities are easily marketable. When securities are bought or sold, transaction costs usually apply, and there is a slight delay in obtaining the cash after the sale. Certificates of deposit (CDs) can be converted to cash quickly, but substantial penalties may apply if the CDs are cashed in before maturity. Investments in real estate or business ventures are less liquid than publicly traded securities. Cash sales of real estate or business assets often require a long time, a considerable concession in price and the payment of substantial transaction costs.

Investments with maximum liquidity typically have lower rates of return than less liquid investments. Maximum current liquidity is not required for investments made to finance retirement income, especially when the investments are made during middle age. As an investor approaches the retirement years, a portion of his or her investments should be systematically switched from illiquid to liquid investments.

Safety

Safety—or its opposite, riskiness—relates to the variability of realized and expected returns. The return on a safe investment held to maturity can be predicted accurately in advance, and the possibility of monetary loss is low. Short-term U.S. government obligations, Treasury notes, are often spoken of as being risk-free

**Figure 13.1
Relative Risk of Common Investments**

```
                              Risk
  Low ─────────────────────────┼───────────────────────── High

  U.S.      Commercial  Long-term        Long-term    Preferred   Common
  Treasury  paper       government       corporate    stock       stock
  bills                 bonds            bonds
```

because the return is predictable and the chance of loss is assumed to be nonexistent. Long-term U.S. government bonds and notes are subject to loss of value when interest rates rise but are assumed to have no risk of default.

The greater the riskiness of an investment, the greater the variation in possible gains or losses. As a general rule, the greater the investment's safety, the lower its expected return. While safety is important in saving for retirement, maximum safety is not required. The investor may be willing to sacrifice some safety to achieve greater yield.

U.S. investments considered low-risk include Treasury bills, considered to be virtually risk free, while common stocks (especially of small, newer companies) are the highest-risk investments. Refer to Figure 13.1.

Risk, or the uncertainty associated with an investment's results, can be categorized in a variety of ways and arises from several sources. The most important sources of risk are:

- purchasing power risk;
- market risk;
- interest rate risk; and
- issue-specific risk.

Purchasing Power Risk

The loss of purchasing power caused by the general rise in prices is one risk investors must be concerned about, especially over long time periods. If prices increase, the purchasing power of a fixed amount of principal declines. Typically, investors seek investments producing rates of return that, at least, compensate for lost purchasing power. These investments are considered *hedges against inflation*. Investors must realize that these investments do not guarantee a stable purchasing power level but provide the opportunity to achieve the results.

Fixed types of securities such as bonds, CDs, savings accounts and life insurance cash values (in traditional products) are not good hedges against inflation. Equity investments or stock securities are better inflation hedges than fixed investments. However, no sure hedge exists against inflation. In times of low or moderate inflation rates a portfolio of equity investments may increase in value and offset the effects of the reduction in purchasing power. However, in times of rapid inflation the value of stock tends to fall dramatically if the government uses monetary policy to fight general price increases.

Market Risk

Market risk refers to the general trend of changes in the value of the securities market. Market risk may be the result of inflationary expectations, political announcements, the risk of war, unexpected insolvencies or default, changes in international monetary exchange rates or comparative advantage shifts in the expanding global economy. Investors summarize these trends by labeling the market a *bull* or a *bear* market. If the market, as measured by one of the many indexes, is falling, it is labeled a bear market; if rising, a bull market. Thus an investor is subject to market risk due to timing of the purchases or sales.

☐ **Example**

Harry Smith needs to liquidate a sufficient amount of shares in a high-quality mutual fund to replace the roof on his house. Because a bull market has existed for two years, Harry needs to liquidate only 100 shares to pay for his roof. If a bear market existed for two years, Harry would have to liquidate 200 shares to produce the required amount of cash.

Interest Rate Risk

Changes in the level of interest rates can increase or decrease investment value. An inverse relationship exists between investment values and changes in interest rates. When interest rates decline, investment values tend to increase. When interest rates increase, investment values tend to decline.

☐ **Example**

Sara Butler purchased a high-quality $1,000 bond. The bond pays $80.00 interest per year (8 percent coupon). If interest rates increase such that a comparable bond yields 12 percent, the value of Sara's bond falls. Because the bond pays only $80.00 annually, the value (what someone would pay for it) declines to produce a yield of 12 percent.

$$\begin{aligned}
\text{Current yield before} &= 8\% \ (\$80.00/\$1{,}000) \\
\text{Current yield after} &= 12\% \ (\$80.00/\$666.66) \\
\text{Price} \times 0.12 &= \$80.00 \\
\text{Price} &= \$80.00/0.12 \\
\text{Price} &= \$666.66
\end{aligned}$$

The longer the maturity, the more sensitive is this relationship. The price of a 30-year bond changes more dramatically than that of a 10-year bond because both market values equal the present value of all future cash flows.

☐ **Example**

Compare the difference in market value of a $1,000, 8 percent bond purchased at par (maturity value). If prevailing rates of return change to 12 percent from 8 percent, the following theoretical market value results.

The present value of $80 for ten years plus a maturity value for $1,000 at 12 percent equals $774.

The present value of $80 for 30 years plus a maturity value for $1,000 at 12 percent equals $678.

Year	Payment	PV	Pmt × PV
1	$80	0.893	$ 71.43
2	80	0.797	63.78
3	80	0.712	56.94
4	80	0.636	50.84
5	80	0.567	45.39
6	80	0.507	40.53
7	80	0.452	36.19
8	80	0.404	32.31
9	80	0.361	28.85
10	1,080	0.322	347.73
		Sum of PV amounts	$773.99
1	$80	0.893	$ 71.43
2	80	0.797	63.78
3	80	0.712	56.94
4	80	0.636	50.84
5	80	0.567	45.39
6	80	0.507	40.53
7	80	0.452	36.19
8	80	0.404	32.31
9	80	0.361	28.85
10	80	0.322	25.76
11	80	0.287	23.00
12	80	0.257	20.53
13	80	0.229	18.33
14	80	0.205	16.37
15	80	0.183	14.62
16	80	0.163	13.05
17	80	0.146	11.65
18	80	0.130	10.40
19	80	0.116	9.29
20	80	0.104	8.29
21	80	0.093	7.40
22	80	0.083	6.61
23	80	0.074	5.90
24	80	0.066	5.27
25	80	0.059	4.71
26	80	0.053	4.20
27	80	0.047	3.75
28	80	0.042	3.35
29	80	0.037	2.99
30	1,080	0.033	36.05
		Sum of PV amounts	$677.79

This table shows the calculation on a year-by-year basis. Alternatively, present value of annuity factors may be used to discount the annual payment. Present value of $1 factor may be used to discount the $1,000 maturity amount.

Issue-Specific Risk

Issue-specific risk, default or financial risk arises from changes in the issuer's financial condition. These changes may lead to decreased security for bondholders, a reduction in the dividend amount to stockholders, failure to pay or default on bond interest payments and inability to retire or refinance outstanding debt. Issue-specific risk may reduce if the profitability of the firm improves. Therefore issue-specific risk focuses on the timing and magnitude of expected cash flows and the cash flow's certainty.

☐ **Example**

Purchasers of Rydex bonds have increased their required rate of return to 15 percent. This increase is the result of Rydex's rise in the proportion of debt to equity financing. Bondholders view the issue as riskier because the amount of debt has increased in the capital structure and it is more difficult to make the required interest payments.

Current Yield and Growth Potential

Current yield and growth potential may be combined and spoken of as the total return on an investment. Total return is always of concern because, if one investment is chosen, another must be forgone. Holding other factors constant, rational investors choose investments with the highest total return. However, other factors cannot be held constant in the real world, nor can investors ever have all the information needed to make the optimal choice. The theory that rationality is bounded by the costs of acquiring information applies to investment decision making. In general, the higher an investment's potential total return, the lower its safety. If an investor wants more return, it will be accompanied by more risk.

Taxability

The possibility of deferring or eliminating federal, state and/or local taxes is a consideration in many savings decisions and is especially germane to a discussion of saving for retirement. Investments may have no tax advantages and be fully taxable, produce **tax-free** income or produce **tax-deferred** income.[3]

Taxable Investments

Investments with no tax advantage require owners to pay tax on current income and pay tax on any capital gains when sold. Taxable investments are not limited to common or preferred stock but include investments such as rare coins, artwork and antiques.

☐ **Example**

Jake purchases 100 shares of Rydex stock for $32. During the year he receives a $1.50 per share dividend. Jake must report $150 as dividend income. Next year, Jake sells the stock for $36 per share. Assuming no transaction costs, the capital gain of $400 ([$36 − $32] × 100 shares) is taxable in the year sold.

Tax-Deferred vs. Tax-Free Investments

An important distinction exists between tax-deferred and tax-free investments. *Tax-free* investments such as state and local bonds generally are free of federal income taxes. However, any capital gains and losses are treated as taxable events. *Tax-deferred* income arises when income that otherwise would be currently taxed is given special treatment, delaying imposition of the tax. Ultimately, however, the tax must be paid. Important sources of tax-deferred income include the cash value of life insurance contracts, annuities and U.S. savings bonds. The cash value increases of life insurance contracts are tax-deferred. If the contract matures as a death claim, the policy face including the cash value is usually paid tax-free to the beneficiary. The face amount, however, can be included in the insured's estate and subject to federal estate taxes. Depending on the type of plan, the amount contributed to the tax-advantaged account can be deductible for income tax purposes. In such cases, when a taxable event occurs, all funds received are taxable, because no tax was ever paid on the principal or investment earnings. Examples of tax-deductible and tax-deferred investments include the individual retirement account (IRA) under certain circumstances, the Section 401(k) plan and the Section 403(b) plan. (The IRA and the 403(b) plans are described in Chapter 16.) The IRA and 403(b) plans have tax penalties if withdrawals are made before age 59$\frac{1}{2}$.

A Numerical Comparison

Assume an individual earns $4,000 and has three options for investing the money: (1) a fully taxable investment, (2) an investment with investment earnings tax-deferred and (3) an investment with the tax on current income *and* investment earnings deferred. Table 13.3 shows the results of using $4,000 of before-tax income to make the various investments.

In the first option, the fully taxable investment, only $2,800 is invested because taxes must be paid on the $4,000 of income. Taxes at the rate of 30 percent are also paid on investment income earned each year. With the second option, where only investment earnings are tax-deferred, $2,800 is invested because tax must be paid on the $4,000 of earnings. In this case investment earnings are tax-deferred—tax is paid on earnings only when withdrawn. The original $2,800 is not taxable at withdrawal because it has already been taxed. The third option defers tax on current income and investment earnings. Taxes are paid on current income (the $4,000) and investment earnings when withdrawn. Table 13.3 shows that wealth after taxes is maximized if current taxable income is reduced by the contribution and earnings are deferred until withdrawn. A fourth option is also illustrated by Table 13.3. If a tax-free investment is made with after-tax dollars ($2,800), the resulting wealth after 20 years equals $13,051. (Tax-free investments usually pay lower rates of return. For the purpose of this comparison, however, the tax-free investment also earns 8 percent.)

Chapter 13 Financial Mathematics and Investments

Table 13.3
Comparison of Investment Results
Based on Tax Method

	Fully Taxable*	Tax-Deferred on Earnings†	Current Income Reduced and Tax-Deferred‡
Amount Before Tax	$4,000	$4,000	$4,000
Tax Rate	0.30	0.30	0.30
Invested Funds	2,800	2,800	4,000
Rate of Return	0.08	0.08	0.08
Year	Account Balance	Account Balance	Account Balance
1	$2,957	$3,024	$4,320
2	3,122	3,266	4,666
3	3,297	3,527	5,039
4	3,482	3,809	5,442
5	3,677	4,114	5,877
6	3,883	4,443	6,347
7	4,100	4,799	6,855
8	4,330	5,183	7,404
9	4,572	5,597	7,996
10	4,828	6,045	8,636
11	5,099	6,529	9,327
12	5,384	7,051	10,073
13	5,686	7,615	10,878
14	6,004	8,224	11,749
15	6,340	8,882	12,689
16	6,695	9,593	13,704
17	7,070	10,360	14,800
18	7,466	11,189	15,984
19	7,884	12,084	17,263
20	8,326	13,051	18,644
Taxation method	Taxes paid	Taxes payable on earnings = 0.30 × ($13,051 − $2,800)	Taxes payable on total amount = 0.30 × $18,644
		Penalties may apply when withdrawn early.	
Wealth after Taxes	$8,326	$9,976	$13,051

This example assumes all funds are withdrawn at the end of 20 years.
*Investments such as CDs and mutual funds
†Investments such as cash value life insurance and series EE bonds
‡Investments such as tax-deferred IRA, 401(k) and 403(b) plans

Table 13.4 shows how frequently suggested alternatives compare to life insurance in the investment characteristics just discussed.

Performance Measurements

People need to monitor and measure accurately the performance of their investments. Because one goal of the investor is to maximize the rate of return and capi-

Table 13.4
Characteristics of Selected Investments

Type	Liquidity	Safety	Current Yield	Growth Potential	Tax
Whole Life Insurance	Cash value is highly liquid.	Cash value amount scheduled.	Cash value amount scheduled.	Cash value amount scheduled.	No tax as cash value increases. Possible tax on surrender.
Universal Life Insurance	Highly liquid. Fees may apply to withdrawals.	Cash value based on investment results.	Based on investment results. Added to cash value.	Based on investment results.	No tax as cash value increases. Possible tax on surrender.
Corporate Bonds	Active secondary market. Commission paid on transaction.	Ranges from high grade to "junk."	Based on coupon rate.	Value inversely related to interest rates.	Current income and capital gains taxable.
U.S. Treasuries	Active secondary market. Commission paid on transaction or direct purchases.	No default risk.	Based on coupon rate.	Value inversely related to interest rates.	No state and local tax on interest. Capital gains taxable.
Common Stock	Active secondary market. Commission paid on transaction.	Low to high risk depending on issue.	Based on dividend payment.	High growth possible. Depends on issue.	Tax on dividends and capital gains.
Preferred Stock	Active secondary market. Commission paid on transaction.	Low to high risk depending on issue.	Based on coupon rate.	Limited due to fixed distribution.	Tax on dividends and capital gains.

tal gains of the investment, it is important to calculate and know the rate of return. The following section provides a description of various performance measures with examples. These measures include the price-to-earnings ratio (P/E), the current yield, the holding period return and yield and the yield to maturity. In addition, the difference between after-tax and before-tax yields and returns is discussed.

Price-to-Earnings Ratio (P/E)

The **price-to-earnings (P/E)** ratio is calculated by dividing the current market price of a share of common stock by its earnings per share. The P/E ratio measures the willingness of investors (in market price) to pay for the right to the future earnings of the corporation.

$$\text{P/E ratio} = \frac{\text{current market price}}{\text{earnings available for common shareholders}} \quad \textbf{(Formula 13.5)}$$

☐ **Example**

Ardmore stock is selling for $26.00. Over the latest 12 months Ardmore earned $2.20 per share. The P/E ratio is equal to 11.81 ($26.00/$2.20).

A high P/E ratio usually signals that investors expect the earnings of the corporation to grow and they are willing to increase the price so as to participate in the expected profitability of the firm. Lower P/E ratios may be found where the company pays out most of its earnings in current dividends, when the company is quite stable in earnings or when investors feel it has little future growth prospects. Investors should compare P/E ratios of a particular stock to those of similar companies and to past information to become more familiar with the market's assessment of the stock's performance and to spot any trends based on this calculation.

The reciprocal of the P/E ratio is the earnings-to-price ratio (E/P). The earnings-to-price ratio provides the stockholder with the earnings rate of return relative to the market price of the stock.

☐ **Example**

The earnings-to-price ratio for Ardmore is 8.46 percent ($2.20/$26.00). Based on the stock price, $2.20 of earnings is generated on a $26.00 investment. The investor does not receive the $2.20. The dividend actually paid may be greater or less than the earnings per share.

Current Yield

The current yield measures the annual benefit an investor receives from investment income. The current yield is equal to the actual dividend or interest received divided by the current market price. The current yield does not include any rate of return for expected capital gains, although the market price reflects investors' expectations of future payments as well as market value adjustments.

$$\text{Current yield} = \frac{\text{investment income (annual)}}{\text{current market price}} \quad \textbf{(Formula 13.6)}$$

☐ **Example**

The current distribution of Ardmore's 7 percent preferred stock (par value equals $100) is $7.00. The current market price is $82.00. The current yield is 8.53 percent ($7.00/$82.00).

Holding Period Yields and Return

Investments are typically held over long periods of time, and investors not only benefit from the annual distribution of dividends and interest, but their wealth increases or decreases based on the security's underlying market value. The holding period yield (HPY) and the holding period return (HPR) are useful in calculating the *geometric* rate of return or the growth rate of the investment.

$$\text{Holding period return (HPR)} = \frac{\text{Total current value of the investment}}{\text{Original amount of investment}} \quad \text{(Formula 13.7)}$$

$$\text{Holding period yield (HPY)} = \text{HPR} - 1 \quad \text{(Formula 13.8)}$$

☐ **Example**

Six years ago Randal Smith purchased 100 shares of Ardmore stock at $18.00. He has reinvested all dividends through Ardmore's reinvestment plan. He now owns 187 shares at the $26.00 current market price. His original investment was $1,800 (100 × $18.00). The current value is $4,862 (187 × $26.00). With a holding period of six years, the HPR is 2.70 ($4,862/$1,800). The HPY is 1.70 (2.70 − 1). Randal's stock is worth 2.7 times the amount paid, and he will receive 1.7 times his investment in new wealth.

Randal's geometric rate of return is the annual rate of return making an investment of $1,800 grow to $4,862 in six years. The annual geometric rate of return is 18.01 percent, calculated as follows.

$$\$4{,}862 = \$1{,}800\,(1+X)^6$$
$$\frac{\$4{,}862}{\$1{,}800} = (1+X)^6$$
$$2.70 = (1+X)^6$$
$$2.70^{1/6} = (1+X)$$
$$1+X = 1.1801$$
$$X = 18.01\%$$

The annual geometric rate of return is calculated by using the following formula:
$+ ((4862/1800) \wedge (1/6)) - 1 = 0.1801$

Yield to Maturity

The yield to maturity is used with investments paying an amount annually with the principal paid to the investor upon maturity. Bonds and other debt securities fall into this category. Bonds pay a fixed coupon rate annually based on the par or face amount of the bond. (Most bonds pay half the coupon rate on a semiannual basis.) The bond matures at a stated date, at which time the par amount is returned to the investor. The yield to maturity measures the rate of return of the bond based on its purchase price if the bond is held to maturity. If the bond is sold before maturity, the market price is paid based on prevailing economic conditions.

The yield to maturity is equal to the internal rate of return (IRR) on the investment. The IRR may be calculated directly, or an estimating formula may be used.

Yield to maturity (estimate) = (Formula 13.9)

$$\frac{\text{annual coupon interest} + \binom{\text{discount}}{\text{or}}/\text{number of years to maturity}}{(\text{current market price} + \text{par value})/2}$$

☐ **Example**

Assume an 8.5 percent bond (par $1,000) is currently selling for $802 and has 12 years to maturity. The discount is $198 ($1,000 − $802). The yield to maturity is 11.27 percent, and the current yield is 10.60 percent.

$$\frac{85 + (198/12)}{(802 + 1,000)/2} = \frac{85 + 16.5}{901} = 11.27\%$$

The current yield is 10.60 percent (85/$802).

If the current market price is $1,037, the premium is $37. The yield to maturity is 8.042 percent, and the current yield is 8.196 percent.

$$\frac{85 - (37/12)}{(1,037 + 1,000)/2} = \frac{85 - 3.083}{1,018.5} = 8.042\%$$

The current yield is 8.196 percent (85/$1,037).

If the market price of the bond is selling at a price equal to par, the coupon rate equals the yield to maturity. If the market price increases, the yield to maturity decreases—an inverse relationship. If market interest rates increase, the bond's market price decreases. The amount of change is a function of time to maturity and the magnitude of the interest rate change.

Alternatively, the internal rate of return may be calculated by using the following spreadsheet formula:

@IRR(guess, range)
where guess is a starting interest rate for the estimating procedure and range is the range of cells containing the periodic cash flows.

After-Tax Yields and Rates of Return

As noted earlier, investors need to be sensitive to after-tax investment results. It is difficult to compare investments if the tax obligations vary. Therefore, to compare investments with different tax obligations an after-tax rate should be used. However, the applicable tax rate and the timing of the adjustment depend on the investment's taxability. Again, investments are either taxable currently, tax-free or tax-deferred. Capital gains are usually taxable, but in some cases taxes may be deferred. Some investments made with before-tax dollars are taxable when constructively received.

☐ Examples

Arnold buys 100 shares of stock with after-tax income. Any dividends are taxable in the year received. When Arnold sells the stock, taxable gains or losses will be realized.

Arnold also makes contributions to a 403(b) plan. Payroll amounts are invested on a before-tax basis. Any earnings or capital gains in the plan are deferred until distributions are made.

Both investments may be generating the same before-tax rate of return. However, the after-tax consequences are different.

The after-tax yield on a fully taxable investment equals its before-tax yield multiplied by one minus the tax rate.

Arnold invests in a tax-free municipal bond. If the bond pays 7.35 percent of its market price, the after-tax yield is 7.35 percent.

An alternative common stock investment is yielding 5.23 percent. Arnold is in the 28 percent marginal tax bracket. His after-tax dividend yield is calculated by the following.

$$\text{Yield} \times (1 - \text{tax rate}) =$$
$$5.23\% \times (1 - 0.28) = 3.76\%$$

Review Questions

1. Why are time-value-of-money calculations important in financial planning?
2. Life insurance products can be broken into a unique and a shared function. What are the unique function and the shared function of the life insurance product? Explain.
3. Distinguish between the process of calculating the present value of $1 and calculating the future value of $1.
4. What is the difference between an annuity and an annuity due? Identify a cash flow following an annuity pattern and one following the annuity due pattern.
5. What four factors should be investigated before any investment is made? Explain each. Provide examples of situations where an investment need *does not* match the investment's characteristics. What problems result from this mismatch?
6. What is meant by purchasing power risk, market risk, interest rate risk and issue-specific risk? Explain each.
7. What is the difference between tax-deferred and tax-free investments? What financial factors go into the decision to invest in one versus the other?
8. What is the difference between a fixed-income and an equity investment? What can an investor expect to receive from each?

Endnotes

[1] For a detailed source, *see* Elbert B. Greynolds, Jr., Julius S. Aronofsky and Robert J. Frame, *Financial Analysis Using Calculators: Time Value of Money* (New York: McGraw-Hill, 1980).

[2] Some of this material is adapted with permission from Mark S. Dorfman and Saul W. Adelman, *The Dow Jones–Irwin Guide to Life Insurance*, (Chicago: Dow Jones–Irwin, 1988).

[3] *See also* M. S. Dorfman and S. W. Adelman, "Comparing the TDA to a Non-TDA Investment Program for Accumulating and Liquidating Wealth," *CLU Journal*, January 1983, p. 40.

Bibliography

Branch, Ben. *Investments: Principles and Practices*, 2nd ed., Chicago: Dearborn Financial Publishing, Inc., 1989.

Greynolds, Elbert B., Jr., et al. *Financial Analysis Using Calculators: Time Value of Money*. New York: McGraw-Hill, 1980.

Widicus, Wilbur W., and Thomas E. Stitzel. *Personal Investing*, 5th ed. Homewood, Ill.: Richard D. Irwin, 1989.

Chapter 14 Social Security

Chapter Objectives

- Explain Social Security benefit eligibility
- Explain Social Security benefit types
- Explain Social Security benefit calculations
- Explain limits on Social Security benefits
- Present a case study of Social Security benefit planning

Introduction

In the United States, Social Security is the foundation on which an individual's financial plans should be built. In fact, because participation is compulsory, Social Security can be seen as the common denominator of financial planning. However, by design Social Security is only one leg of a tripod of financial protection. The other two legs are employer-provided benefits and individual financial assets, including individually purchased life insurance. For some people, unfortunately, Social Security is not the foundation of their financial plans; it is the entire structure.

This chapter has a somewhat narrow focus; it covers aspects of Social Security that apply to most Americans but does not address the history, philosophy or financing of the system. These topics are important and interesting but are not needed to understand the role Social Security plays in individual life insurance plans.[1] There is also no coverage of the controversies surrounding the program, including the accumulation and investment of large surpluses during the next 20 years and the doubt of critics about the likelihood that individuals will receive retirement benefits promised in the future. The bibliography at the end of this chapter contains references to some Social Security literature. The chapter also does not allow calculation of current individual benefits (the Social Security system now provides a statement of estimated benefits for individuals who request this information in writing). Rather, the chapter shows how the calculations are made. Many numbers used in Social Security calculations are indexed annually for inflation. The formulas presented are subject to less frequent change.

Chapter 14 Social Security

As used throughout this chapter, **Social Security** refers to a federal social insurance program enacted by Congress in 1935 and subsequently amended. The program is more formally known as the Old Age, Survivors, Disability and Hospital Insurance Program (OASDHI).[2]

Eligibility for Social Security Benefits

Payment of Social Security Taxes

People receiving Social Security benefits either have a history of employment or are related to somebody with an employment history. Eligibility to receive a Social Security benefit depends on several factors. The two most important are:

1. having a minimum amount of earnings that have been subject to the Social Security tax and
2. experiencing a specified life event such as living to a particular age, dying or becoming disabled.

The Social Security tax is based only on the amount of earnings up to a stated maximum. Amounts earned beyond this maximum are not subjected to the Social Security tax, nor do they earn benefits for the worker. Table 14.1 provides recent rates for the tax and maximum earnings subject to the Social Security tax.

For employees, Social Security taxes are a percentage of wages. These taxes are the familiar FICA (Federal Insurance Contributions Act) deduction on paycheck stubs. Employers also pay a Social Security tax equal to the employee's share. Self-employed workers pay the combined employer-employee rate but may deduct one-half the tax as a business expense on their income tax return.

☐ **Example**

In 1991 Tess Garland earns $30,000 working for Large Industries as an accountant. Large deducts $2,295 (.0765 × $30,000) from her salary and pays a matching amount of Social Security tax.

Helen Russell earns $70,000. Her employer deducts $4,325.80 from Helen's pay and pays a matching amount of tax. Helen's tax calculation is: (.0765 × $53,400) + (.0145 × ($70,000 − $53,400)) = $4,085.10 + $240.70 = $4,325.80.

Louise Fayette, a self-employed computer consultant, earned $40,000. Her Social Security tax is $6,120 (.153 × $40,000), but she can deduct half, $3,060, from her income tax, saving her $3,060 times her marginal tax rate.

Social Security covers about 95 percent of the country's workers. Two groups of employees not covered are permanent federal civil service employees hired before 1983 and the employees of some state and local government units that never joined the Social Security program or opted out of the program after joining. (The 1983 Amendments to the Social Security Act ended the option of leaving Social Security for state and local governments that had previously elected coverage.

Table 14.1
Social Security Taxes

Year	Employee Tax Rate	Maximum Wages Subject to Tax
1984	6.70	$37,800
1985	7.05	39,600
1986	7.15	42,000
1987	7.15	43,800
1988	7.51	45,000
1989	7.51	48,000
1990	7.65	51,300
1991	7.65*	53,400†

*6.2% of this total is for old age and survivors insurance, and 1.45% is for hospital insurance.
†After 1990 this number is automatically adjusted based on the increase in the average national wage. Effective January 1, 1991, the 1.45 percent hospital insurance tax applies to salaries up to $125,000.

About 30 percent of state and local government employees are now not covered under Social Security.)

Quarters of Coverage

Workers earn one *quarter of coverage (QC)* each year their covered earnings exceed a stated minimum. After earning 40 quarters of coverage (QC) a worker has *fully insured status*. In 1991, $540 in wage or self-employment income was required for each QC earned. Workers earning $2,160 or more during 1991 earned four QCs. No more than four QCs can be earned in one year. (Workers do not need to earn covered income in four separate quarters to receive four QCs; some baseball stars, for example, could earn four QCs in one day.) The amount required to earn one QCs is subject to annual change.

Fully Insured Status

Fully insured status normally takes ten years (40 QCs) of covered employment. Fully insured status qualifies a worker for retirement and survivor benefits. Fully insured status combined with disability-insured status is needed for disability benefits.

To be fully insured younger workers must have at least one quarter for each year after their 21st birthday and before the year of death or disability. In any case, a minimum of six quarters of coverage must be earned.

☐ **Example**

Adam Appling was 21 in 1980 and died in 1990. He needed nine QCs (the number of years in 1981 to 1989) to be fully insured. If Adam earned the required QCs before his death, including QCs earned before his 21st birthday, he would be fully insured. Therefore, his survivor(s) would be eligible for Social Security benefits.

Currently Insured Status

Workers who earn six QCs in the 14 quarters before death or disability but have insufficient QCs for fully insured status are still eligible for currently insured status. Currently insured status does not qualify a worker for many benefits, the main one being a survivor benefit for a deceased worker's dependent children and widowed spouse taking care of these children.

☐ **Example**

Anne Atkinson was 21 in 1970. She died in 1985. She had worked from 1983 until her death, acquiring eight QCs. Fully insured status requires 14 QCs (1984 − 1970 = 14 years).

Anne's eight QCs are inadequate for fully insured status. However, earning eight QCs immediately before death qualifies her for currently insured status. With currently insured status, if Anne had any eligible children, they would be entitled to Social Security survivor benefits, as would her surviving husband.

Disability-Insured Status

Disability-insured status requires 20 QCs in the 40 calendar quarters preceding and including the quarter in which disability occurs. More liberal rules apply to individuals disabled before age 31. The Social Security definition of **disability** is "the inability to engage in any substantial gainful activity by reason of any medically determinable physical or mental impairment which can be expected to result in death or which has lasted or can be expected to last for a continuous period of not less than 12 months."[3] This definition is generally more difficult to meet than many group disability insurance definitions that refer to "meeting all the requirements of the insured's own occupation."

Again, workers must pass the test for both *fully* insured and *disability*-insured status to receive benefits. Both tests must be passed to preclude a fully insured worker who has not been in covered employment for a long period before disability from claiming the benefit. Disability income is supposed to replace lost wage income. A disabling illness or injury presumably should not cause unemployed people to lose wage income. If a fully insured active worker is disabled, both tests ordinarily will be passed.

☐ **Example**

Emily Bacon earned fully insured status, 40 QCs, before interrupting her employment to raise three children. When the youngest child was ten years old, she returned to covered employment. At age 55, after seven years' work during the second period of covered employment, she was disabled. Emily could meet both the fully insured and the disability-insured eligibility tests, because she earned 28 QCs (7 years × 4 quarters) immediately before disability.

The quarters of coverage earned in the second employment period were not sufficient to earn fully insured status by themselves, nor was it necessary for them to be. Fully insured status cannot be lost once earned.

If the disability had occurred during the second period of work but before she earned 20 QCs, the disability-insured status test would not have been passed. Therefore disability benefits would not be paid despite Emily's fully insured status.

Table 14.2
Quarters of Coverage Required for Benefit Eligibility

Quarters of Coverage	Status	Benefits Earned
40	Fully insured	1. Retirement 2. Survivors 3. Disability*
6 of 14, prior to death or disability	Currently insured	Survivors
20 of 40 prior to disability— in conjunction with fully insured status	Disability insured	Disability

*If also disability insured

Table 14.2 reviews the quarters-of-coverage requirements for the three different categories of insured status.

Categories of Benefits and Beneficiaries

The Social Security Act of 1935 provided only a retirement benefit, for workers 65 or older. Amendments in 1939 added benefits for dependents of retired workers and created a survivor benefit category. In 1956 amendments added benefits for totally and permanently disabled workers. Today's Social Security program provides three categories of benefits: retirement, survivor and disability benefits. The hospital benefits under the Medicare program are available only to people receiving or eligible to receive a retirement benefit, a disability benefit or benefits due to kidney disease. Chapter 8 describes Medicare benefits.

Retirement Benefits

A fully insured worker at age 65 is entitled to receive a monthly check from the Social Security Administration. This accurate, but deceptively simple, statement requires further explanation.

Primary Insurance Amount (PIA)

All Social Security benefits, including the retirement benefit, are a function of the worker's PIA. The calculation of the PIA is explained in the chapter appendix. For now the PIA may be thought of as a single sum of money. Calculating this amount requires consideration of (1) a worker's covered earnings over the years, (2) an indexing procedure allowing for price changes over a working career and (3) the year the worker reaches age 62.

Normal Retirement

Fully insured workers are entitled to 100 percent of their PIA upon retirement at the normal retirement age. Historically the **normal retirement age** has been 65, and that is the age assumed in all calculations and illustrations here. The Social Security reforms passed in 1983, however, will gradually increase the normal retirement age until it reaches age 67 in 2027; it will apply to people born after 1959.

Early Retirement

Workers can retire at age 62 and receive a reduced monthly benefit. The early retirement benefit reduction is expressed as a percentage reduction of the PIA. The reduction equals five-ninths of 1 percent for each of the first 36 months of retirement before the 65th birthday. Retirement at age 62 produces a 20 percent reduction in the monthly benefit (3 years × 12 months × 5/9). When the normal retirement age is 67, workers retiring at age 62 will face a 33 percent reduction in benefits (60 months × 5/9 percent per month).

☐ **Example**

Ed Montgomery retires at age 64. His PIA is $1,000. His Social Security retirement benefit is reduced by 12 (months) × 5/9 percent, or 6.67 percent. He receives (1 − .0667) × $1,000 or $933.30 each month in retirement.

An approximate actuarial equivalence exists between people taking the early retirement benefit and those retiring at age 65. That is, the worker retiring at age 62 receives 80 percent of the PIA, calculated in the year of retirement. The 20 percent reduction applies until the benefit ends at death. The worker retiring at age 65 receives 100 percent of the PIA until death. Thus early retirement has two potential penalties and one potential advantage.

Retired workers dying between ages 62 and 65 receive no retirement benefit unless they take the early retirement benefit. For workers living long lives after age 65 or having significant earnings increases in the years between ages 62 and 65, the 20 percent reduction is one penalty. Calculating the PIA on a smaller base is a second penalty. For workers in poor health or for those with poor job prospects the early retirement benefit obviously can be valuable. Healthy workers should plan carefully before making the retirement decision.[4]

If a worker elects early retirement but subsequently returns to work, the reduction of benefits applies only to the months during which the retirement benefit was received. This limited reduction is irreversible.

☐ **Example**

Ronnie Baldwin retires at age 62 but returns to work one year later. A 6.67 percent reduction (12 × 5/9) will be made in his monthly retirement benefit when his PIA is redetermined at his later retirement.

Delayed Retirement

Some workers choose delayed retirement after their normal retirement age. If a worker delays retirement, the PIA is increased one-fourth of 1 percent for each month (3 percent per year) of delay. The 1983 amendments to the Social Security Act schedule a gradual increase in this credit. From 3.5 percent for workers reaching age 65 in 1990, the credit rises to 8 percent for each year of delayed retirement for workers reaching age 66 in 2008. With a federal law (the **Age Discrimination**

in Employment Act, as amended in 1978) prevents mandatory retirement at any age. With increased life expectancies, delayed retirement may prove useful to many workers.

Spousal Retirement Benefit

If a fully insured and retired worker is married, the spouse, aged 65 or older, may receive a benefit equal to 50 percent of the worker's PIA. The combined benefit for a retired worker and spouse, each aged 65 at the initial claim, is 150 percent of the worker's PIA.

At age 62 the spouse of a *retired* worker may elect to take a reduced retirement benefit. The reduction is based on the full 50 percent benefit available at age 65. The reduction is calculated by multiplying 25/36 by 1 percent by the number of months the spouse is under age 65 when the early benefit is taken. Election of the spousal retirement benefit at age 63 calls for a benefit of $1 - (2 \times 12 \times 25/36) = (1 - .1667)$ or 83.33 percent of 50 percent of the retired spouse's PIA. A reduced spousal benefit taken at age 62 produces a reduction factor of 75 percent now. The reduction factor rises to 65 percent when the normal retirement age reaches 67.

☐ **Example**

Bud Woodruff retired this year at age 65. His PIA is $1,000. His wife, Kay, will receive a retirement benefit of $500 if she waits until age 65 to claim benefits. She is now 62. If she chooses to receive a benefit this year, it will be calculated as follows:

$$3 \times 12 = 36 \text{ months reduction factor}$$
$$36 \times 25/36 = 25 \text{ percent reduction}$$
$$1 - .25 = 75 \text{ percent of benefit}$$
$$.75 \times \$500 = \$375 \text{ monthly benefit}$$

The spouse of a *retired* worker may receive a retirement benefit of 50 percent of the PIA if caring for a child under age 16 or a disabled child. The spouse may be any age. The disabled child may be any age if the disability occurred before age 22. The issue of disability and dependency may be questions of fact requiring adjudication by the Social Security Administration. Questions can be raised in some cases involving stepchildren, adopted children and custody of minors.

Dependent Benefits

Each eligible child of a retired worker is entitled to a Social Security benefit equal to 50 percent of the retired worker's PIA. *Eligible child* means one who is (1) unmarried and (2) under age 18 or 19 if still in high school. A child disabled before age 22 remains an eligible child. While the parent's benefits end when the eligible child reaches age 16, the nondisabled child's benefits continue until age 18 (or age 19 if the child is still in high school).

If one or more eligible children and a spouse, all linked to a retired worker's PIA, are receiving benefits, the total amount of these benefits is subject to a limit

Chapter 14 Social Security

Table 14.3
Summary of Retirement Benefits*

Category	Benefit†
Worker at normal retirement age	100 percent PIA
Worker 62–64	100 percent PIA (calculated at retirement age) *minus* 5/9 of 1 percent for each month under age 65
Spouse at 65	50 percent of worker's PIA
Spouse 62–64	50 percent of worker's PIA *minus* 25/36 of 1 percent for each month under age 65
Spouse (any age) caring for eligible child	50 percent of worker's PIA
Eligible child	50 percent of worker's PIA

*Assuming a normal retirement age of 65
†All benefits subject to reduction by earnings test and maximum family benefit limit.

called the *maximum family benefit (MFB)*. If this limit is exceeded by the initial calculation of benefits, a proportional reduction is made to keep the total of the benefits within the prescribed limits. (A mathematical example of the MFB appears later in this chapter.)

In cases of divorce after a minimum of ten years of marriage, the divorced spouse of a *retired* worker may apply for the spouse's benefits. The maximum family benefit calculation does not include the divorced spouse's benefits. If the divorced worker has remarried, two or more spouses may each receive a retirement benefit based on the worker's PIA.

If a spouse of a retired worker has an earnings record producing a retirement benefit greater than the spousal retirement benefit, the larger of the two amounts will be chosen. The sum of both benefits is not paid.

Table 14.3 provides a review of the Social Security retirement benefits just described.

Survivor Benefits

If a fully insured worker dies, a Social Security survivor benefit is available for a spouse, a divorced spouse, an eligible child and dependent parents. (The survivor benefit is a monthly benefit and should not be confused with the one-time lump-sum death benefit of $255.) Benefits are a percentage of the deceased worker's PIA.

The spouse of a fully-insured deceased worker is entitled at the normal retirement age to a retirement benefit of 100 percent of the decedent's PIA. An early retirement benefit for spouses of deceased workers is available at age 60, but the benefit will be reduced, using the same approach used to reduce benefits for early retirement when there is a living spouse. (The reduction factor at age 60 for spouses of deceased workers is 71.5 percent. For those claiming benefits at ages after 60 but before the normal retirement age, the reduction factor is determined proportionately between 71.5 percent and 100 percent. Benefits are available at a rate of 71.5 percent of the PIA when a disabled surviving spouse of a fully insured deceased worker claims benefits at ages 50–59.)

Table 14.4
Review of Survivor Benefits*

Category	Benefit†
Fully insured worker (deceased)	Spouse
At age 65	100 percent of worker's PIA
60–64	PIA reduced by 19/40 of 1 percent for each month under age 65
Age 50–59 if disabled	71.5 percent of PIA
If caring for eligible child	75 percent of PIA
Eligible children	75 percent of PIA
Dependent parents	82.5 percent of PIA (75% each if 2 parents)
Currently insured worker (deceased)	
Spouse caring for eligible child	75 percent of PIA
Eligible child	75 percent of PIA

*Assuming a normal retirement age of 65
†All benefits subject to reduction by earnings test and maximum family benefit limit.

The spouse of a fully insured or currently insured deceased worker is eligible for benefits while caring for an eligible child. Eligible children can receive benefits in their own right. The benefits equal 75 percent of the deceased worker's PIA, subject to the maximum family benefit limitation. Survivor benefits are the only significant benefits available for workers having currently insured status.

The period of a nondisabled child's dependency ends at age 18 (unless attending high school and then at age 19). The surviving spouse's survivor benefits end when the child reaches age 16. If the surviving spouse is younger than age 60 when the youngest child in a family reaches age 16 (and there is no eligible disabled child), there will be a period when no Social Security benefits are available. Often called the "widow's blackout" period, this period must be given careful consideration in family financial planning.

☐ **Example**

Reba Redding was 34 when her husband, Don, died. Her youngest child was 10. Reba's survivor benefits end in 6 years when she is 40 and the child is 16. Reba will be eligible for an early retirement benefit 20 years after her survivor benefits end (40 + 20 = 60). It will be 25 years after the survivor benefits end before she is eligible for a full spousal retirement benefit.

If a deceased fully insured worker was supporting his or her parents, the parents may receive, when they are 62 or older, a survivor benefit based on the deceased worker's PIA. One such parent receives 82.5 percent of the PIA; two receive 75 percent each.

Table 14.4 provides a review of Social Security survivor benefits.

Disability Benefits

As already stated, to receive disability benefits the worker must be both fully insured and disability-insured and must satisfy the Social Security definition of dis-

Table 14.5
Summary of Disability Benefits*

Category	Benefit†
Worker—both fully insured and disability-insured	100 percent PIA
Spouse	
Caring for eligible child	50 percent PIA
At age 65	50 percent PIA
Age 62–64	50 percent PIA reduced by 25/36 of 1 percent for each month under age 65
Eligible child	50 percent PIA

*Assuming a normal retirement age of 65
†All benefits subject to reduction by earnings test or maximum family benefit limit.

ability, quoted earlier. The disability must be present for at least five months before a worker can receive benefits. A fully insured and disability-insured worker satisfying these conditions is eligible for a monthly benefit equal to the PIA.

Besides the disabled worker, disability benefits (a percentage of the worker's PIA) are available to a spouse or eligible children. The spouse of a *disabled* worker may receive full benefits at age 65 or while caring for an eligible child. Reduced benefits are available to the spouse at age 62.

Establishing disability can be a problem. Cases of blindness and many terminal diseases are obviously disabling. Other physical or mental problems may require judgmental decisions. Because Social Security benefits generally are not taxable and some people prefer disability income to employment income, abuse of the system must be guarded against. Judgments regarding a worker's claim for benefits are made by state agencies, such as vocational rehabilitation agencies.

People receiving workers' compensation benefits because of a work-related injury cannot simultaneously claim a full Social Security disability benefit. Workers' compensation and Social Security disability benefits are coordinated so that total benefits do not exceed 80 percent of average current earnings. It is not in society's interest to create a disincentive for disabled workers to return to employment. Likewise, many employer-provided group long-term disability plans are integrated with both Social Security and workers' compensation benefits. Injured workers with integrated group disability insurance who receive government disability benefits find their employer-provided coverage reduced so that the total benefit does not exceed a target level.[5]

Table 14.5 reviews the essentials of Social Security disability benefits.

Limitations on Benefits

The Maximum Family Benefit

Two very important limitations can reduce Social Security benefits: the maximum family benefit and the earnings test. The *maximum family benefit* places a limit on the total dollars paid to a family, based on one worker's earnings and resulting PIA. A formula approach is used to calculate the maximum family benefit. (For a particular PIA, the MFB is the same for retirement benefits and survivor benefits but is generally lower for disability benefits.) The reader interested in current maximum family benefit limits should review current Social Security literature, because the limits change each year.

If a family had, for example, five eligible children and an eligible spouse, each entitled to receive *survivor* benefits, the maximum family benefit limit would be exceeded. When this limit is exceeded, the benefit for each recipient is reduced in the same proportion. (If beneficiaries receive different percentage benefits based on the same PIA [e.g., 81.5 percent and 75 percent], benefits are reduced based on a proportional share.) If a *retirement* benefit is paid to a living worker and to the worker's dependents, the worker's benefit is subtracted from the MFB limit and paid to the worker in its entirety. The remainder is then split proportionally by the remaining beneficiaries. In general the percentage reduction is determined by the ratio of the maximum family benefit limit divided by the total benefits originally calculated.

☐ **Examples**

Assume the Social Security benefit structure called for *survivor* benefits equal to 75 percent of the PIA for each beneficiary. Assume a PIA of $1,000 and five eligible beneficiaries, each of whose primary benefit is $750. At first $3,750 in benefits (5 × $750) is calculated. Assume the maximum family benefit is $1,750. Then each benefit would be reduced proportionately. That is, each $750 benefit would be multiplied by 1,750/3,750 or .4667. The benefit paid is .47 × $750, or $350 to each beneficiary.

Assume the benefit above is a *retirement* benefit instead of a survivor benefit. Assume Dad retired with a PIA of $1,000. Assume Mom and three eligible children are entitled to benefits equal to 50 percent of Dad's PIA, or $500. Assume a MFB of $1,750.

First, Dad's $1,000 benefit would be subtracted from the MFB ($1,750 − $1,000) leaving $750 to be divided by the other beneficiaries. Next, the four $500 benefits would be reduced by the fraction (remaining MFB/original benefit calculation). Mathematically, $750/$2,000 = .375. The remaining benefits equal .375 × $500, or $187.50.

The $1,750 in MFB would be distributed $1,000 to Dad and $187.50 each to Mom and the three children.

Earnings Test

The retirement, dependent and survivor benefits paid to workers, their spouses and their dependent parents or children may be reduced if the beneficiary earns income from employment beyond a specified limit in a particular year. The limit is called the *earnings test* or, sometimes, the *retirement test*. Limits for 1991 are (1) over age 70, no limit; (2) ages 65–69, $9,720; (3) younger than 65, $7,080. These limits change annually. After 1990 people between ages 65 and 69 lose $1 in Social Security benefits for every $3 earned beyond the limit. People under age 65 lose $1 for every $2 earned.

☐ Examples

Kay, age 48, a surviving spouse with an eligible child, is scheduled to receive a $650 monthly benefit, or $7,800 annually. She works part-time, earning $10,000. Her Social Security benefits are reduced. She has excess earnings of $10,000 − $7,080 (the earning limit for people under 65 in 1991), or $2,920. Her benefits are reduced by $2,920/2, or $1,460, from $7,800 to $6,340. If her child has no earned income, the child's benefits are not reduced.

Jim, age 68, is scheduled to receive a retirement benefit of $7,800 annually. He earns $15,000 in a part-time job. In 1991 his excess earnings equal $5,280 ($15,000 − $9,720). His benefits are reduced by $5,280/3, or $1,760, from $7,800 to $6,040.

The purpose of these tests is to restrict Social Security benefits to people actually retired or, with survivor benefits, to those who actually were dependent on the worker. This Social Security provision is designed to preclude paying benefits to workers or relatives who are independently self-supporting as a result of earnings. (Special provisions apply to disabled beneficiaries, because sizable earnings may indicate they are no longer disabled within the definition of the law.)

Despite the reasonable goal of restricting Social Security benefits to those in need or to those actually retired, in practice the earnings test (especially when applied to retired workers) has produced questionable results. Among current retirees, low Social Security benefits are often the only source of income rather than being the intended floor of protection. Social Security benefits often allow only subsistence living. If people in this economic condition supplement their Social Security income by working full-time or part-time, and their employment income exceeds the earnings test limit, then their Social Security benefit is reduced. The reduction of $1 for every $3 is, in essence, a 33 percent tax.

Contrast the condition of an impoverished person with that of a second person receiving the maximum Social Security retirement benefit. The second person saved regularly and in retirement receives $1 million in dividend and interest income each year. Nonwage income does not reduce Social Security retirement benefits, though it is subject to federal income taxation. The wealthier person receives a full Social Security retirement benefit.

The logic for this apparent anomaly is that Social Security retirement benefits are supposed to go only to actually retired workers. Second, taxing nonwage income by reducing Social Security benefits taxes and discourages the very savings Social Security is designed to supplement in retirement. These arguments have not persuaded many critics, and the retirement test remains controversial.

The earnings test applies to most people receiving Social Security benefits. However, if one beneficiary (a surviving spouse, for example) has benefits reduced or eliminated, it does not affect the benefits received by other beneficiaries, such as eligible children. The maximum family benefit provision applies after the effect of the earnings test has been considered.

Taxation of Benefits

Part of the 1983 Social Security amendments subjected Social Security benefits to the federal income tax for the first time. Taxing Social Security benefits improves the financial status of the system because the U.S. Treasury returns the tax proceeds to the Social Security Administration. Taxation applies only to upper income levels. When one-half the recipient's Social Security benefits together with other income exceeds a specified base amount, the federal income tax is applied to half the excess. For this calculation "other income" includes tax-free interest income earned on state and municipal bonds. In 1991 the base amounts are $25,000 for single taxpayers and $32,000 for married taxpayers filing joint tax returns. The amount included in taxable income is limited to one-half the Social Security benefits.

☐ **Example**

Andy and Joyce Stone receive $60,000 in pension, interest and dividend income. Of this amount $20,000 is interest on state of California bonds. Andy and Joyce receive $9,000 in Social Security retirement benefits.

Adding $4,500 (one-half of their Social Security income) to their total retirement income of $60,000 produces a figure of $64,500. This is $32,500 more than the applicable threshold of $32,000. Thus one-half of $32,500, or $16,250, of their Social Security benefits would be taxable, except for the rule that no more than half the benefits are taxable.

When calculating their federal income tax, they add $4,500 (.5 × $9,000) to their taxable income of $40,000. (The $40,000 equals $60,000 total income less $20,000 in state bond interest.)

Those favoring this taxation note the measure increases revenue, adding financial strength to the Social Security program. Second, taxing benefits makes the treatment of Social Security benefits more nearly comparable to the taxation of private pension plans. The application of the tax to only one-half the benefits avoids taxing the employee's contributions, which were taxed initially. This is similar to the treatment given to private pensions. Third, the tax compensates for the fact that the benefits received are disproportionately large relative to contributions for people currently receiving benefits.

Benefit Increases

Before 1975 Congress would occasionally increase the dollar amounts received by Social Security beneficiaries. Such increases were sometimes motivated by political considerations, rising price levels or available "surpluses" in Social Security trust funds. Beginning in 1975, benefit increases called a **cost-of-living adjustment (COLA)** became automatic. Whenever the consumer price index (CPI) rises, Social Security benefits are increased by the same percentage as the increase in the CPI. Such annual increases allow Social Security recipients to maintain their purchasing power. Few other groups in our economy have such a guarantee.

Financial Planning Issues

Social Security benefits should be included in financial plans. Social Security retirement benefits are comparable to the employer-provided pension and to income received from individually purchased annuities. When estimating retirement income, individuals should consider the amounts from each of these sources. Social Security survivor benefits supplement income from employer-provided group life insurance and individually purchased life insurance. Social Security disability benefits must be integrated with workers' compensation benefits and other disability benefits. Financial planners must know what benefits Social Security provides, who is eligible for benefits and how benefit amounts are calculated, despite the view of some critics who challenge the future availability or value of these benefits.

In the process of planning, individuals should take into account the fact that eligible workers can take early, normal or delayed retirement. Early retirement benefits may be reduced by 20 percent depending on how soon the worker retires, and the benefit reduction is irreversible. Normal retirement age is the first time a worker can retire with unreduced benefits. Normal retirement ages will increase slowly after the year 2003. Beginning in 1990, delayed retirement can increase benefits by between 3 and 8 percent for each year of delay after the normal retirement age. (The 8 percent increase applies to people reaching normal retirement age in 2008 and thereafter.) The increase is permanent. Spouses of retired workers also can choose early or normal retirement. Financial planners must understand the issues raised when advising people on the choice of retirement age. Planners and their clients should also account for the limits, reduction and taxation to which Social Security benefits are subject. Earnings above stated limits can reduce Social Security benefits from 33 to 50 percent. Social Security benefits also may be subject to federal income tax for some middle- and upper-income people. Despite the potential for change, financial planners must know the prevailing rules on earning limits and taxation before integrating Social Security benefits into a financial plan.

Case Study: The Banks Family

Facts and Data

Robert and Sally Banks are both 40 years old in 1991. They were married at age 23 and now have two children, Randy (15 years old) and Lisa (10). Robert is a chemical engineer working for one of the country's largest agricultural chemical firms. Sally worked at a large department store as an interior designer and home fashion consultant for two years before Randy's birth. Since then, she has not been employed outside the home. Robert is both fully insured and disability-insured. Sally has only 12 quarters of coverage from her work as a teenager and her later employment after graduating from college. Based on an estimated average indexed monthly earnings (AIME) of $1,780, Robert estimates his PIA will be $776. (See chapter appendix.) This figure is used in making the family's financial plans.

If he were to die now, Robert estimates the survivor benefits shown in Exhibit 14.1 will be available from Social Security.

Exhibit 14.1 is divided into two parts to illustrate the effect of an MFB of $1,390. The first part of the table shows the original calculation of benefits, while the second part illustrates the benefits the family will receive because the MFB was exceeded. The reduction factor used is $1,390/$1,746 for the first three years. Thereafter no reduction in benefits is called for, because the limit is not exceeded once Randy is 18.

Before reduction for the MFB, Sally receives a survivor benefit equal to 75 percent of Robert's PIA (.75 × $776 = $582) until Lisa, the younger child, reaches age 16, at which time Sally will be age 46. Both Lisa and Randy receive benefits equal to 75 percent of Robert's PIA until their 18th birthdays.

Exhibit 14.1
Survivor Benefits, Banks Family

Part 1: Original Calculation Based on PIA of $776

Sally
Age	40	41	42	43	44	45		
Benefit	582	582	582	582	582	582		

Randy
Age	15	16	17					
Benefit	582	582	582					

Lisa
Age	10	11	12	13	14	15	16	17
Benefit	582	582	582	582	582	582	582	582

Total
Family	1,746	1,746	1,746	1,164	1,164	1,164	582	582

Part 2: Recalculation for Maximum Family Benefit of $1,390

Sally
Age	40	41	42	43	44	45		
Benefit	463	463	463	582	582	582		

Randy
Age	15	16	17					
Benefit	463	463	463					

Lisa
Age	10	11	12	13	14	15	16	17
Benefit	463	463	463	582	582	582	582	582

Total
Family	1,389	1,389	1,389	1,164	1,164	1,164	582	582

Though it is not shown in Exhibit 14.1, Sally is eligible for a widow's benefit equal to 100 percent of Robert's PIA at age 66, her normal retirement age because she was born in 1950. Should Sally become disabled within seven years of Lisa reaching age 16, a benefit is available after she reaches age 50. A reduced widow's benefit is available at her 60th birthday. In any case, Exhibit 14.1 clearly illustrates the widow's blackout period for Sally, as there is a period between Sally's last survivor benefit when she is age 46 and the beginning of her next possible Social Security benefit.

The children's benefits end at their 18th birthday. When Randy's benefits end, the benefits of the remaining beneficiaries are increased because the MFB is no longer exceeded. Note in Part 2 of the exhibit that Sally and Lisa's benefits increase from $463 to $582 after Randy reaches age 18.

The illustrated benefits in Exhibit 14.1 do not allow for expected increases in benefits due to the Social Security COLA. The projection assumes neither Sally nor her children have employment income above the limit imposed by the earnings test.

In the event of his immediate disability, Robert estimates the disability benefits shown in Exhibit 14.2 would be available from Social Security. It is assumed the disability is not work-related, eliminating the problem of integrating the Social Security benefits with workers' compensation insurance benefits.

Robert's disability benefit equals 100 percent of his PIA and begins in the sixth month after the onset of his disability. The benefit lasts until Robert dies or recovers. Sally's benefit, which equals 50 percent of Robert's PIA, lasts only until Lisa reaches age 16. The benefit resumes at 100 percent of Robert's PIA when Sally reaches age 66. Reduced benefits would be available to Sally at age 62. The children's benefits each equal 50 percent of Robert's PIA, and they last until each child reaches age 18.

As was the case with the survivor benefits, the

Exhibit 14.2
Disability Benefits, Banks Family

Part 1: Original Calculation

Robert									
Age	40	41	42	43	44	45	46	47	48
Benefit	776	776	776	776	776	776	776	776	776
Sally									
Age	40	41	42	43	44	45			
Benefit	388	388	388	388	388	388			
Randy									
Age	15	16	17						
Benefit	388	388	388						
Lisa									
Age	10	11	12	13	14	15	16	17	
Benefit	388	388	388	388	388	388	388	388	
Total Family	1,940	1,940	1,940	1,552	1,552	1,552	1,164	1,164	776

Part 2: Recalculation for Maximum Family Benefit of $1,164

Robert									
Age	40	41	42	43	44	45	46	47	48
Benefit	776	776	776	776	776	776	776	776	776
Sally									
Age	40	41	42	43	44	45			
Benefit	129	129	129	194	194	194			
Randy									
Age	15	16	17						
Benefit	129	129	129						
Lisa									
Age	10	11	12	13	14	15	16	17	
Benefit	129	129	129	194	194	194	388	388	
Total Family	1,164	1,164	1,164	1,164	1,164	1,164	1,164	1,164	776

MFB limit is exceeded. An MFB limit of $1,164 is associated with a PIA of $776. (Note that the MFB for disability beneficiaries is usually lower than for old-age retirement and survivor beneficiaries. It is never more than one-and-a-half times the PIA.) The reduction takes effect by providing Robert with 100 percent of his benefit, then reducing the remaining benefits proportionately as illustrated.

Other Points

Since Sally does not have the required quarters of coverage for fully or currently insured status, her premature death or disability will cause financial problems that will have to be resolved with other resources. Presumably the main source of income in the event of Sally's premature death or disability would be Robert's earnings. Because Robert is fully insured, he can anticipate receiving a retirement benefit and the survivor and disability benefits presented in the preceding tables.

After making an estimate of available Social Security benefits, the next step in integrating Social Security benefits into financial plans is estimating the need for income in the event of premature death or disability. The next two chapters show this calculation and the integration of Social Security benefits with employer-provided (death, disability and retirement) benefits and individually purchased life and health insurance.

Appendix:
Calculating the Primary Insurance Amount (PIA)

All Social Security benefits are a function of the PIA. This appendix presents the calculation of the PIA in detail, including the indexing approach underlying the procedure. This procedure is used for people reaching age 62 after 1978.

Average Indexed Monthly Earnings (AIME)

Each worker's PIA calculation is unique and involves a two-phase mathematical procedure. The first phase is the calculation of the average indexed monthly earnings (AIME). The focus of the AIME calculation is to develop a number that fairly represents a worker's average monthly income over a working career, allowing for the effects of inflation on wages.

The AIME calculation begins by adding the number of years after the worker's 21st birthday and before the year when age 62 is reached (40 years for people born after 1929). Next, 5 years are subtracted, leaving a 35-year total for consideration. In the case of death or disability before age 62, where the PIA is needed to calculate benefits for survivors or the disabled worker, the measuring period is the number of years after age 21 and before the year of death or disability, minus 5 years, subject to a minimum number of years in some cases.

Given the actual earnings for the years of employment considered in the AIME calculation, the next step is to index the earnings so they are all on a comparable price basis over this rather long period. The indexing is done by multiplying the worker's actual earnings by a factor. The indexing factor is found by dividing the average national wage in the year that is two years before the insured's 62nd birthday (or death or disability if earlier) by the average national wage in the year of the earnings.

Table 14.6 shows a hypothetical and abbreviated example of a 10-year indexing procedure, using the AIME approach. Please note the example is abbreviated to cover only 10 years. The typical calculation at retirement covers 35 years.

Given the total of a worker's averaged indexed *annual* earnings for the 35 highest years, the next step is to divide this total by the number of months in the working career being considered. In the case of a 35-year calculation the total earnings are divided by 420 months (35 × 12) to produce the sought-after AIME. Calculation of the AIME ends Phase 1 of the PIA calculation.

Calculating the PIA from the AIME

Phase 2 involves the metamorphosis of the AIME into a PIA and requires a second procedure that appears complex but is actually fairly straightforward. The formula calls for the use of indexed "bend points" combined with constant percentage factors, as the following formula shows:

90 percent of bend point 1   **(Formula 14.1)**
+ 32 percent of bend point 2
+ 15 percent of excess beyond bend point 3
= the PIA

Table 14.6
Hypothetical AIME Calculation

Column	2	3	4	5	6
Year	Actual Wage	Average National Wage in This Year	Average National Wage in Year Used for Indexing	Indexing Ratio Column (4)/(3)	Indexed Wage Column (2)/(5)
1	10,000	12,000	40,000	3.33	33,333
2	10,800	14,440	40,000	2.98	32,142
3	11,664	15,052	40,000	2.66	30,994
4	12,597	16,859	40,000	2.37	29,887
5	14,604	18,882	40,000	2.12	28,820
6	14,693	21,148	40,000	1.89	27,791
7	15,868	23,685	40,000	1.69	26,798
8	17,138	26,528	40,000	1.51	25,841
9	18,509	29,711	40,000	1.35	24,912
10	19,990	33,276	40,000	1.20	24,028

Total to 10 years or 120 months 284,558
AIME equals (284,558/120) = 2,371

The bend points for the cohorts becoming age 62 change each year to allow for inflation. The base year for the calculation is 1979. The bend points for any year are found by multiplying the 1979 bend points by a ratio of the national average wage for the second year preceding the given year to the national average wage for 1977. The bend points for 1979 were $180, $905 and $1,085, respectively, and the average national wage was $9,779. Assume for example the conversion of a $1,200 AIME into a $468 PIA. The AIME was calculated in the manner presented in Table 14.6; but the calculation covered 35 years, and the national average wage was $9,779 instead of the $40,000 used in the example. Using formula 14.1:

$$\begin{aligned}
.90 \times \$180 &= \$162 \\
+ .32 \times \$905 &= \$289 \\
+ .15 \times \$115 &= \$17 \quad (115 = 1,200 - 1,085) \\
\$1,200 & \$468 \\
\text{AIME} & \text{PIA}
\end{aligned}$$

As a second example, assume the percentage change in national wages between 1977 and a given year was 30 percent. That is, the average national wage went from $9,779 to $12,712. Then the PIA formula would be:

$$\begin{aligned}
1.3 \times \$180 &= \$234 = \text{bend point 1} \\
1.3 \times \$905 &= \$1,176 = \text{bend point 2} \\
1.3 \times \$1,085 &= \$1,410 = \text{bend point 3}
\end{aligned}$$

Using the new bend points, with formula 14.1, the result is calculated as follows:

.9 × $234 + .32 of next $1,176 + .15 of excess over $1,410 = PIA.

Table 14.7
Sample Transformations of AIME into PIA

If AIME is $1,000
  .9 ×   356 = 320.40
  .32 × 644 = <u>206.08</u> (644 = 1,000 − 356)
       PIA = 526.48

Replacement ratio is (PIA/AIME) 526/1,000 = 52.6%

If AIME is $2,000
  .9 ×   356 = 320.40
  .32 × 1,644 = <u>526.08</u> (1,644 = 2,000 − 356)
       PIA = 846.48

Replacement ratio is (PIA/AIME) 846/2,000 = 42.3%

If AIME is $3,000
  .9 ×   356 = 320.40
  .32 × 1,789 = 572.48 (1,789 = 2,145 − 356)
  .15 ×   855 = <u>128.25</u> (855 = 3,000 − 2,145)
       PIA = 1,021.13

Replacement ratio is (PIA/AIME) 1,021/3,000 = 34%

For 1990 cases, the formula called for 90 percent of the first $356, plus 32 percent of the amount between $356 and $2,145, plus 15 percent of the amount in excess of $2,145.

Table 14.7 presents three examples of PIA calculations using 1989 bend points.

Combining Phase 1 (AIME calculation) with Phase 2 (PIA calculation) produces the basis of all individual benefits as explained throughout this chapter. Two summary points may be made. First, the indexing of the wages used to produce the AIME is offset by the indexing of the bend points in the PIA calculation. Offsetting indexing is done to produce "vertical equity," or a comparability of benefits among cohorts retiring in different years.

Second, as the AIME increases, so does the PIA; but the rate of increase in the PIA is less, leading to a lower **replacement ratio** (PIA/AIME) of earnings for workers with higher incomes. That is, higher incomes produce higher PIAs, but a lower percentage of preretirement income is replaced for people earning the higher incomes. The inverse replacement ratio relationship between income and Social Security benefits reflects the philosophy of social adequacy, relating some part of the Social Security benefit to workers' needs.

Review Questions

1. How does a person earn fully insured status?
2. What benefits are available to those having fully insured status? Currently insured status?

3. Why are there two tests for eligibility for disability benefits?
4. What is the effect of early retirement on Social Security benefits? In what circumstances should early retirement be recommended? When should delayed retirement be recommended?
5. Who is eligible to receive survivor benefits from Social Security?
6. Do you think the Social Security survivor benefits illustrated for the Banks family reflect a Social Security program whose benefits are too generous, adequate or inadequate? Explain your answer.
7. Mary worked in covered employment from January 1, 1985, until December 31, 1990. She died on January 1, 1991.
   a. If she was born in 1950, what is her insured status?
   b. If she was born in 1965, what is her insured status?
   c. If she was born in 1950 and previously worked from 1970 to 1978 before returning to work in 1985, what is her insured status?
8. Bill worked in covered employment from January 1, 1985, until December 31, 1990. He was disabled on January 1, 1991.
   a. If he was born in 1950, is he eligible for benefits?
   b. If he had worked from 1975 until 1990, is he eligible for benefits?
9. Henry earned $30,000 in covered employment in 1990. How much Social Security tax was deducted from his salary? If Henry was self-employed, how much tax would he pay?
10. Grace retires at age 65. Her PIA is $1,500. If she had taken early retirement at age 62, what would her retirement benefit have been then (use the same PIA).
    a. Assume Grace's husband took a retirement benefit at age 65 based on his wife's earnings and calculate this benefit.
    b. Assume Grace's husband took an early retirement benefit at age 63 based on his wife's earnings and calculate this benefit.
11. Doreen earns $62,000 in 1990. How many QCs did she earn? How much Social Security tax did she pay?

Endnotes

[1] The information in this chapter comes from *The Social Security Handbook—1988*, 10th edition, SSA Publication No. 05-10135, (Washington, D.C.: U.S. Department of Health and Human Services, October 1988). The entire Social Security program includes welfare and other benefits not covered in this text.

[2] See the *Social Security Bulletin*, July 1989, for the official comprehensive coverage of these points.

[3] *Social Security Handbook—1988*, p. 81.

[4] R. J. Doyle, Jr., "When to Take Early Social Security Retirement Benefits," *Journal of the American Society of CLU and ChFC*, January 1990, pp. 30-37. Paul S. Marshall and Robert J. Myers, "Retirement Planning: An Evaluation of the Delayed Social Security Benefit Option," *Journal of the American Society of CLU and ChFC*, July 1990, pp. 30-37.

[5]Burton T. Beam, Jr., and John J. McFadden, *Employee Benefits*, 3rd ed. (Chicago, Dearborn Financial Publishing, Inc., 1992). pp. 155–156.

Bibliography

Aaron, Henry J., et al. *Can America Afford to Grow Old? Paying for Social Security*. Washington, D.C.: Brookings Institution, 1989.

Bernstein, Merton C., and Joan B. *Social Security: The System That Works*. New York: Basic Books, 1988.

Doyle, Jr., Robert J. "When to Take Early Social Security Retirement Benefits." *Journal of the American Society of CLU & ChFC* 44, January 1990, pp. 30–37.

Marshall, Paul S., and Robert J. Myers. "Retirement Planning: An Evaluation of the Delayed Social Security Benefit Option." *Journal of the American Society of CLU & ChFC* 44, July 1990, pp. 54–65.

Myers, Robert J. *Social Security*, 3rd ed. Homewood, Ill.: Richard D. Irwin, 1985.

Myers, Robert J. "Social Security and the Federal Budget: Some Mirages, Myths and Solutions." *Journal of the American Society of CLU & ChFC* 43, March 1989, pp. 58–63.

Rejda, George E. *Social Insurance and Economic Security*, 4th ed. Englewood Cliffs, N.J.: Prentice-Hall, 1991.

Social Security Bulletin. Washington, D.C.: U.S. GPO, periodical.

Social Security Handbook, 10th ed. Washington, D.C.: U.S. GPO, 1988.

Chapter 15 | Financial Planning: The Early Adult Years

Chapter Objectives

- Explain the concept and process of financial planning during the early adult years
- Explain and illustrate the needs-based purchase of life insurance in the financial planning context
- Discuss the process of choosing the appropriate life insurance policy from a desirable insurer
- Describe inflation's impact on financial plans
- Illustrate the integration of life insurance into the financial planning process by means of an annotated case study

Introduction

The prevailing financial environment contains many capable and clever consumers of financial services. Other people, however, pay little attention to their financial affairs. These people are content to leave their savings in bank passbook accounts and to determine the amount of life insurance they need by their ability to pay premiums. Unfortunately, the price for financial ignorance has increased significantly in the past decades.

The financial environment of the 1990s is complex. Making distinctions among the hundreds of financial alternatives offered by banks, stock brokerages, credit unions and life insurance companies can be tricky. Purchasing life insurance in the right amount from the right carrier is challenging. Integrating all financial transactions into an efficient, clearly directed, likely-to-succeed strategy requires a large amount of knowledge, a considerable amount of time and continuing attention. We call the development of such a strategy **financial planning.** This chapter explains how to integrate life insurance into the financial plans of young adults.

The Default Financial Plan

In the United States, personal financial plans always exist. People who fail to construct a financial plan can always rely on the Procrustean plan provided by the state and federal governments. This "one size fits all" plan is made up of government's *bankruptcy* laws (useful to those who fail to allocate lifetime income properly or those who experience uninsured losses), *welfare* provisions (useful to essentially the same group, as well as others unwilling or unable to compete in our economic society), **intestacy** provisions (for those who die without valid wills) and *social insurance* programs (which by design provide minimum amounts of coverage on which people are supposed to build their financial plans).

Fortunately many Americans prefer to develop their own custom-designed plans. Employing home computers or financial service firms to allow them to use the same principles of cash budgeting and forecasting used by business firms gives many individuals confidence. While the expense of financial planning can be significant, the cost of financial ignorance can be substantially greater.

Life Insurance and Financial Planning

Life and health insurance products play a key role in the financial planning process throughout adult life. Insurance is especially important to young adults. Life insurance policies add certainty to a lifetime consumption plan. If a wage earner dies prematurely, insurance proceeds can replace the purchasing power the deceased would have provided survivors. Life insurance allows families to maintain their standard of living and achieve cherished goals, including educating children. Life insurance policies also function as long-term savings vehicles. Health insurance provides disability income protection and protection from the financial devastation of serious illness. Financial planners agree that a logically developed life insurance program should be the foundation of most young adults' financial plans.

The Early Adult Years

The early adult years last roughly from ages 20 to 45. Typically, first marriages take place, educations are completed, careers begun, children reared and debts incurred for housing and consumer durables. Of course, not all people follow this traditional pattern. The American demographic data presented in Chapter 2 reveal an increasing number of never-married people, of couples postponing or having fewer children and of divorced people. The financial plans of never-married people are different from those of married people with two dependent children. Regardless of family status during the early adult years, however, all young adults face the potential of premature death or disability. Most young adults need financial plans to solve the personal or business problems caused by these catastrophes. Purchasing life and health insurance in adequate amounts is an indispensable part of such plans.

Foundations of Financial Planning

Sound financial plans are built on the following foundation:

- Accurate and comprehensive personal financial information
- Professional expertise in legal, accounting, insurance and related areas
- Knowledge of personal values and risk tolerance
- An understanding of inflation's impact on financial plans

Individual financial plans may involve elaborate computer-generated, regularly updated written documents. Some people employ accountants, lawyers, investment advisers, life insurance agents or financial planners to help develop their plans. Other people prefer homemade plans, employing experts only when needed. Successful financial plans, whether developed by professionals or by laypeople, must be built on the same foundation.

Accurate and Comprehensive Financial Information

All successful financial planning must be based on accurate and comprehensive financial information. How to gather essential information is discussed later in the chapter.

Expertise Needed

In the 1990s preparing a complete financial plan requires expertise in the following five areas:

1. The law
2. Accountancy and tax planning
3. Life insurance planning
4. Property and liability insurance planning
5. Investment planning

Only attorneys can draft wills, trusts and contracts for other people. Laypeople who draft legal documents or provide legal advice, are committing a crime called the **unauthorized practice of law.** Completing most financial plans requires legal expertise and advice. Often this service must be purchased. Today people attempting to complete their financial plans without paying for outside expertise can tap the computer software available to help them construct valid wills and other legal documents.

Today many people at all income levels use accountants or professional tax preparers to complete tax returns. Accountants also can be used to estimate the value of business property such as partnership interests or the fair market value of small businesses and farms. Wealthy people are likely to need an accountant's services to study alternative tax strategies. Again, computer software packages are available to help people complete their regular bookkeeping and prepare tax forms. Some people presumably derive some satisfaction from completing both assignments with a pencil and calculator.

Life insurance agents usually are essential when developing financial plans. Except for mail order policies and savings bank life insurance, people cannot put life insurance policies in force without dealing with a life insurance agent or broker. Three states—New York, Connecticut and Massachusetts—allow the operation of savings bank life insurance. Professional life insurance agents provide extensive product knowledge, and many have computer facilities for calculating life insurance needs.

Property insurance agents provide needed product knowledge and risk management checklists. Again, people cannot implement their financial plans without the services of a property insurance agent, nor would most people want to do so. Wealthy people often need to purchase coverage for jewelry, furs or other property requiring special (inland marine) insurance forms. Liability exposures, especially any hobby or business exposures that standard homeowners' forms exclude from coverage, need careful attention when completing this aspect of financial plans.

The wide array of investment alternatives makes investment expertise and advice essential for many people. People purchasing stocks, bonds, municipal securities, mutual funds or even certificates of deposit often need to consult with experts to identify the most efficient choices. To stay current on the alternatives in the financial markets requires considerable time and research. Managing investments, however, is a part of financial planning that many laypeople apparently enjoy.

Complicated financial plans require coordination of the different professionals employed. These plans require somebody to make sure the required wills, insurance policies, investments and other essential elements are implemented, complete and current. People calling themselves *financial planners* have assumed this responsibility. Because most states do not restrict the term *financial planner,* people with varying degrees of knowledge and ability have used it. Clients relying on professional expertise must be assured of their planner's integrity. Neither reputable planners nor astute clients would allow the professional to operate without some amount of client oversight and input. After integrity, the most desirable qualities of a financial planner include expertise, an ability to communicate clearly, stability in the profession and a commitment to service.

Because so much expertise is required to complete a comprehensive financial plan, it can be expensive to rely exclusively on professional help. Often it would be difficult to calculate the cost of a professionally prepared financial plan because some experts, such as accountants and lawyers, charge hourly fees, while others (life insurance agents and investment advisers) embed their fees (commissions) within transaction costs. It is likely that only upper-income people with accumulated wealth rely exclusively on fee-for-service professional help to develop their financial plans. This is also the group that is likely to benefit the most from complex planning.

Many Americans prefer to do things themselves. Thus many middle-income families do not have comprehensive, well-coordinated financial plans but have taken a patchwork approach, completing some tasks themselves, perhaps investment management, and purchasing some expert help, such as legal document drafting. Because most Americans fall within this group, society has a considerable stake in the success of these financial plans. Often the responsibility for providing needed assistance falls to the life insurance agent. Sometimes the life insurance agent provides indispensable services. Providing financial planning services can justify the relatively high transaction costs often associated with buying life insurance.

Knowledge of Personal Values and Risk Tolerance

People should understand their personal values so as to rank their financial priorities effectively. In the young adult years planning requires a trade-off between current and future consumption. Individuals also need to evaluate their risk tolerance because financial planning requires a trade-off between risk and return alternatives.

Because scarcity of financial resources is the rule, financial plans require rank-ordering of preferences. People must choose between living in a single-family home and renting an apartment, between driving a new car and taking expensive vacations. Parents choose between public and private education for their children; people choose between dining out regularly and eating at home.

After consumption alternatives are ranked, overall consumption must be balanced against the need to save. Savings goals—typically including building up funds for emergencies, retirement needs, children's education, vacations and the purchase of large items—also must be rank-ordered.

A sound financial plan must be constructed in light of a person's attitude toward accepting risk. Unfortunately for planners, people's reaction to risk is difficult to measure, probably changes over time and depends on the situation faced. Individuals using self-searching or intuition or professional planners using questionnaires and interviews should come to some conclusion about a person's risk tolerance. Only then should financial plans be constructed. High-risk plans for low-tolerance people or low-risk plans for aggressive investors are not likely to be carried out or followed for long.

Before developing financial strategies, clients should be placed in one of three groups. The following three categories are roughly drawn, but any attempt at greater precision might lead to unwarranted conclusions:

- *Risk-tolerant* people are aware of the chance of loss and willingly bear significantly increased chances of loss in expectation of slight gains. These people are aggressive investors but not gamblers. Gamblers create risk for thrills.
- *Risk-averse* people are made uncomfortable by appreciable chances of loss and forgo significantly increased chances of gains for slightly diminished chances of loss
- *Risk-neutral* people engage in mathematically fair trade-offs between the potential for loss and the chance of gain.

All financial transactions involve some chance of loss or the possibility of unfavorable outcomes. Some people can tolerate such possibilities and still "sleep comfortably." Other people spend much effort trying to avoid all possibility of loss. *Realistically, the possibility of loss cannot be avoided; it can only be managed.* All financial plans involve risk, and the best any individual can do is find an acceptable combination of risk and return based on his or her personality. People with low risk tolerance must accept lower returns. Higher returns are associated with higher risk. The opposite conclusion does not hold. Very risky investments do not guarantee higher returns.

Figure 15.1 shows an accepted risk-return investment relationship. Even the lowest return possibility, short-term U.S. government securities, is accompanied by some risk because there are three different types of risk:

- Default risk
- Interest rate risk
- Purchasing power risk

This material is a brief review of material presented more extensively in Chapter 13. Some authorities would include reinvestment risk as an additional category. Reinvestment risk describes the potential for gain or loss caused by the

Figure 15.1
Risk-Return Characteristics of Investment Alternatives

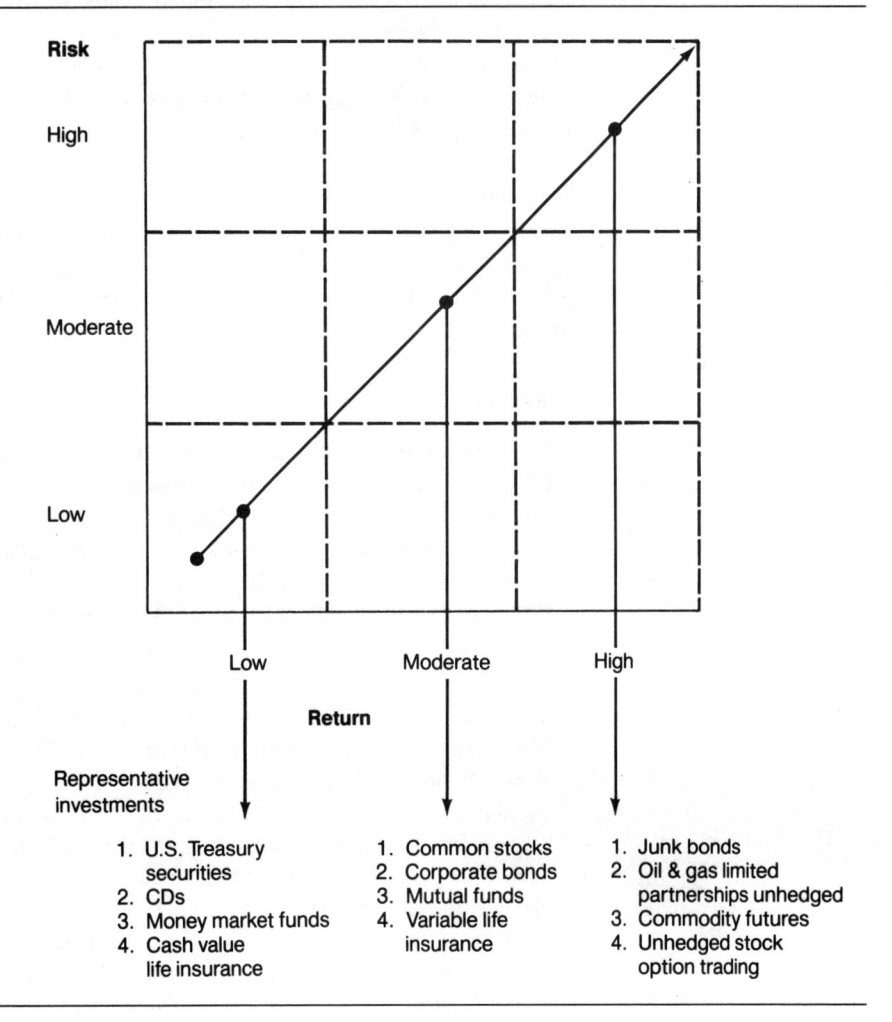

[Graph showing Risk (vertical axis: Low, Moderate, High) vs Return (horizontal axis: Low, Moderate, High) with a diagonal line from low-low to high-high.]

Representative investments

Low Return	Moderate Return	High Return
1. U.S. Treasury securities	1. Common stocks	1. Junk bonds
2. CDs	2. Corporate bonds	2. Oil & gas limited partnerships unhedged
3. Money market funds	3. Mutual funds	3. Commodity futures
4. Cash value life insurance	4. Variable life insurance	4. Unhedged stock option trading

timing and opportunity costs of differential cash flows produced by alternative investment choices. An investment with high cash flows in its early years presents more reinvestment risk than a similar investment with level cash flows or with high cash flows in its later years.

Default risk

Default risk is the possibility that the invested principal will not be returned, that creditors or businesses will fail and the investment will be lost. People assume no default risk with federally insured bank deposits or U.S. Treasury securities.

Interest Rate Risk

Changes in interest rates affect the market value of fixed-rate securities. People holding fixed-rate securities, including U.S. Treasury issues, experience losses in market value when interest rates rise. The longer the term of the security, the greater the loss. The opposite result occurs when interest rates decline: people experience gains.

Purchasing Power Risk

Purchasing power risk describes the possible loss of purchasing power caused by inflation and taxes. People who postpone consumption and save are financially worse off when inflation and taxation more than offset the investment return on their savings.

☐ **Example**

Becky deposits $20,000 in the bank for five years at 5 percent interest. She could have purchased a Plymouth Voyager with her money but decided to save instead. After five years Becky has earned 3.5 percent on her investment after taxes, assuming a 30 percent marginal tax rate. She can withdraw $23,754. Unfortunately, because inflation averaged 6 percent each year, Becky's Plymouth Voyager now costs $26,765, and she cannot afford it.

Inflation

Like risk, inflation considerations pervade all financial plans. Inflation is measured by changes in the **consumer price index (CPI).** The Department of Labor releases data on the CPI monthly, with changes widely reported in the media and followed closely in the nation's financial markets. While the annual rate of inflation has moderated since the mid-1980s, the potential for periods of rapid inflation remains. Few politicians or economists maintain that inflation has been eliminated or that a permanent method of control has been found.

Forecasting future inflation rates for use in financial plans is difficult. In the 1980s inflation as measured by changes in the CPI ranged from about 13 percent (1980) to about 4 percent (1983–1988). Table 15.1 reproduces the CPI for the past ten years.

Inflation may be defined as an overexpansion of the economy in which the production of goods and services cannot balance the claims being made on this production. One observable result is price increases. Inflation, however defined and understood, produces much economic instability.

An extensive discussion of the causes and cures for inflation is beyond the scope of this text. The following description is meant to be only a primer on the subject.

The initial and subsequently aggravating causes of inflation include the following:

- A wage-price spiral in which a ratchetlike action of wage increases leads to price increases, which in turn lead to additional wage increases and so forth.

Table 15.1
Consumer Price Index: 1980–1989

Year	CPI	Percent Change
1980	82.4	
1981	90.9	10.32
1982	96.5	6.16
1983	99.6	3.21
1984	103.9	4.32
1985	107.6	3.56
1986	109.6	1.86
1987	113.6	3.65
1988	118.3	4.14
1989	124.0	4.82

Source: *Statistical Abstract of the United States* (U.S. GPO, annual).

Among the necessary conditions for this ratchet action are strong unions able to enforce wage and nonproductivity demands and producers relying on nonprice competition (e.g., advertising) to promote the sale of their products.

- Exogenous commodity price shocks and international economic interdependence, causing one country's inflation to be imported by other nations.
- Governmental monetary and fiscal policy allowing either spending to exceed taxation (deficit spending) or the money supply to grow at a faster rate than productive output.
- Political considerations encouraging legislative stalemates in developing effective economic policies and establishing spending and taxing policies that contribute to the inflationary pattern. Because the only inflation control known to be effective involves politically unpopular moves such as raising interest rates and instituting austerity programs accompanied by unemployment, control of inflation in a democracy is not easily accomplished through the political process.
- Inadequate knowledge of the political or the economic processes and their interaction.
- Anticipation of additional inflation by producers and consumers, causing distortions in purchasing patterns. Advance purchases lead to even greater distortions than otherwise would be the case. Included in this category are automatic wage increases (cost-of-living adjustments) formulated into wage contracts and into government transfer payments such as Social Security.

These six causes are not mutually exclusive, nor is the list exhaustive. But the review should clarify how deeply rooted in both the political and economic processes the inflationary problem is and why practical solutions to the problem of economic stability seem so difficult to achieve.

Examples of the effects of inflation are not hard to find or to describe. A typical "market basket" of goods costing $100 in 1969 cost $334 in 1989. The worker purchasing the same market basket of goods in both years probably had many pay increases in the period, but even a doubled salary provided significantly less purchasing power than 20 years earlier. Homeowners paying $28,000 for a home in the 1960s might find their property worth $128,000 30 years later, but often purchasing a newer home or a residence in a retirement community may be more than can be afforded after the sale of their current house.

One problem caused by inflation is called **disintermediation**. Disintermediation describes a process in which people withdraw their money from a financial intermediary (such as a life insurance company or bank) to invest at a higher yield. With respect to life insurance companies, the process involves policy owners borrowing some or all of the cash values accumulated in a permanent form of life insurance and investing these funds at higher rates than the insurer charges as interest on the loan. With older life insurance policies having annual interest charges of 5 or 6 percent and with many newer policies charging only 8 percent interest, it is attractive for insureds to borrow from their cash value during inflationary periods, when available investments provide returns greater than the interest charged.

From the consumer's standpoint inflation makes the traditional life insurance transaction appear less valuable than it would be under stable economic conditions. All financial planning is difficult in an inflationary period. Financial planning in fixed dollars, including determining an adequate amount of life insurance, becomes risky, and plans rapidly become obsolete.

For example, a young family with a financial plan based on a $50,000 face amount of insurance would find the postdeath funds grossly inadequate if inflation caused prices to double after the plan went into effect. If they needed $50,000 of purchasing power before prices doubled, they now need $100,000 to accomplish the same objectives. (Repaying a fixed-dollar mortgage is an exception.) The possibility of life insurance plans becoming immediately obsolete does not enhance the apparent value of the purchase.

Second, from the life insurance consumer's standpoint, inflation makes the investment/savings aspect of traditional cash value life insurance look like a poor alternative. People abandon cash value products during inflationary periods if they believe alternative investment returns are greater than those being earned on cash values. During inflationary periods it becomes progressively easier to implement successfully a buy-term-and-invest-the-difference strategy. If nothing else, inflation has modified the investing behavior of a significant segment of consumers by making them more sophisticated financially, and much more yield-conscious. This behavior holds true for banking, life insurance and all other financial transactions.

The Financial Planning Process

Constructing comprehensive financial plans requires a six-step process. A regular annual review is an ongoing part of the process. The six steps are as follows:

1. Collect facts and data.
2. Analyze information.
3. Establish goals.

4. Develop strategies.
5. Implement strategy.
6. Prepare financial reports.

Step 1: Collect Facts and Data

Sound financial planning begins by collecting accurate and comprehensive financial information and data. The financial data typically are presented in a cash flow statement and a statement of net worth. Required financial records should accompany the data. A record of assets typically includes the following information:

- Name of asset
- Date acquired
- Cost basis
- Community property or joint tenancy (if applicable); owner(s) names
- Property to be disposed by will or trust
- Property available to be liquidated for estate settlement needs

Special attention should be given to business interests, including identifying any prearranged plans for sale at the owner's death, disability or retirement. A detailed record of all outstanding debts and liabilities is also required.

Data needed for financial statements come from income tax returns, bank statements, stock brokerage statements, life and property insurance policies and other records. The current market value of some assets, including bank deposits and marketable securities, is readily determined. The market value of other assets must be estimated, including the value of a house that has been occupied for 20 years. The difference between total asset value and total indebtedness equals the person's or family's net worth.

Personal statements do not need to account for the last penny, as do business firms. People can rely on close estimates. However, statements used in divorce proceedings or loan applications must be accurate.

A statement of **net worth** appears in Table 15.2. Table 15.3 presents a typical format for a cash flow statement. These textbook illustrations present broad categories, not detailed accounts. In practice housing expense might be broken down into mortgage repayment, utilities, maintenance and new furniture and appliance accounts if such detail is needed. The greater the detail provided, the more tedious the budget is to maintain. Also, detailed budgets can cause users to lose the forest in all the trees and are less likely to be kept current. Some home computer programs tie checkbook and cash budgets together, minimizing the bookkeeping problem. These programs do not, however, solve the data overkill problem.

Financial plans must be based on current personal information. Planners use fact finders or checklists to collect relevant data. Like financial statements, fact finders can be brief or extensively detailed. Figure 15.2 presents a brief fact finder.

Step 2: Analyze Information

After collecting financial and personal information the planner should analyze it for problems and weaknesses. Typical financial problems include the following items:

Table 15.2
Statement of Net Worth

Assets		
	Checking account	$ 1,000
	Certificate of deposit	5,000
	Mutual fund	8,000
	100 shares of IBM common stock	12,000
	Home, 123 Main Street	130,000
Total Assets		156,000
Debts		
	Home mortgage loan	80,000
	Credit card balance	2,500
	Car loan	11,000
Total Debt		93,500
Net Worth		**$ 62,500**

- Incomplete financial information
- Regular spending in excess of income ("too much month left at the end of the money")
- Too much debt
- Inadequate accumulated wealth
- No will, no funeral plans, no directions for survivors
- No savings plan to achieve desired goals
- Inattention to tax planning possibilities
- Inefficient investment decisions
- Inadequate life insurance, health insurance, property and liability insurance

Table 15.3
Cash Flow Statement

Income		
	H salary	$35,000
	W salary	35,000
	Investment income	3,000
Total Income		73,000
Taxes		
	Federal income	15,000
	Social Security	4,000
	State and local income	5,000
	Real estate	2,000
Total Taxes		26,000
Disposable Income		47,000
Expenses		
	Housing	12,000
	Food	7,000
	Transportation	5,000
	Health	1,500
	Vacations, large purchases	4,500
	All other	10,000
Total Expenses		40,000
Amount Saved (Borrowed)		**$ 7,000**

Chapter 15 Financial Planning: The Early Adult Years   315

Figure 15.2
Personal Information

1. General Information
    H Name, Social Security number, birth date
    W Name, Social Security number, birth date
    H employer, W employer
    Date married, previous marriages
    Names of dependents: Children, parents, others
2. Personal Documents Available
    Income tax returns
    Gift tax returns
    Wills, trusts
    Business agreements
    Insurance contracts
    Employee benefit documents
3. Professional Advisers
    Attorney
    Accountant
    Banker
    Life insurance agent
    Property insurance agent
    Stockbroker
4. Savings Objectives
    Support for family members
    Emergency fund
    College education
    Retirement fund
    Other
5. Personal Attitudes
    Planned retirement age
    Attitude toward risk
    Ability to manage money, H, W
    Ability of dependents to manage money

These or other deficiencies uncovered during the analysis of financial data and personal information should be noted in a financial report prepared for clients. It would be unusual to find people without financial problems in these complex times.

Step 3: Establish Goals

Personal financial planning is a means to an end. The end is achieving specified financial goals. The third step in the process is establishing reasonable, attainable and desirable financial goals. On a trip without a destination any road will do. Once a destination is chosen, however, some routes prove more efficient than others. Thus the choice of goals determines in some measure the route to be taken.

Typical financial goals include the following:

- Control spending and increase saving, accumulate wealth
- Protect family from financial consequences of premature death, disability, uninsured property losses or liability claims
- Repay debts

Figure 15.3
Statement of Financial Goals

Postdeath needs:	
Annual income for *spouse* until youngest child reaches age _____	$_____
Annual income for *child* until youngest child reaches age _____	$_____
Annual income for spouse after period of child dependency ends	$_____
Death expenses	$_____
Emergency fund	$_____
Mortgage repayment	$_____
Other debt repayment	$_____
Education fund	$_____
Estate settlement fund	$_____
Disability income needs	$_____
Retirement income needs	$_____

- Fund college educations
- Fund retirement
- Fund business purchase or house down payment
- Fund anticipated bequests

Financial goals *must* be expressed in dollars. A desire to "save" is not an acceptable goal. Saving 10 percent of disposable income or $200 each month is what people need to specify. The planner's role is to quantify goals; the client makes the choices.

Figure 15.3 presents a summary checklist for quantifying financial goals. The detail provided for postdeath needs is greater than that shown for disability or retirement needs. Some planners might prefer detail in these categories similar to that shown for postdeath needs.

Step 4: Develop Strategies

The number of "successful" financial strategies appearing in the popular press and the shelves full of how-to books in chain bookstores are a direct function of the number of financial experts. One type of financial "expert" has made money in real estate, common stock, uncommon stocks, oil well partnerships, junk bonds, gold, mutual funds or another activity. Other purveyors of financial advice use their books to expose the flaws of real estate, common stock, uncommon stocks, oil well partnerships, junk bonds or whole life insurance. A third type of expert provides financial advice for just one group, perhaps women, older people, single people, poor people, former bankrupts or future bankrupts. Financial strategy literature is prodigious, contradictory and often self-serving. Adding to this mixture of propaganda and literature are the following personal finance strategies, suggestions that are neither comprehensive nor innovative but form the philosophical basis of a sound personal financial plan. These rules always apply to all people.

1. *Never risk more than you can afford to lose.* Every financial plan requires adequate amounts of life, health, property and liability insurance.¹ This rule never varies.
2. *Always save.* As some people put it, "Pay yourself first." Insurance adds certainty to financial plans; saving adds flexibility. People save for many reasons ranging from protecting against emergencies to making future purchases. Without savings, financial plans have little flexibility. People accumulate wealth when their investments grow. As one adviser put it, "You don't get rich working for your money; you get rich when your money works for you."
3. *Hold wealth based on a safety-first financial pyramid (See Figure 15.1.)* Percentage rules vary on this point, but holding 30 percent of all assets in low-risk assets provides a solid foundation for middle-income people. This layer includes bank deposits, U.S. Treasury securities, cash value life insurance and money market mutual funds.

    About half of all assets can be held in moderately risky/moderate-return assets. The percentage of assets of this type held depends on a person's risk tolerance. However, even the least risk-tolerant people should hold some of these assets because they offer protection against purchasing power loss. This layer includes common stocks, mutual funds and direct business investments. Only the remaining percentage should be ventured in high-risk/high-return possibilities and then only if the person can tolerate losses financially and psychologically.
4. *If financial expertise is needed, pay for it.* Ignorance is the most expensive education. There are no free lunches. Financial counselors should be chosen more for their integrity and willingness to educate than for their one-season track record or low fees. Advisers should show a continuing interest in their own education and should be able to prove their financial and educational accomplishments.
5. *Wealth should be managed.* People should not rely entirely on experts but should read reports and remain involved in the financial planning process. Decisions require regular review. People change, circumstances change and the economy changes. Money management is never static.
6. *Conservation rules.* Financial estimates should be based on realistic or conservative assumptions. Worst-case possibilities, including the immediate death of wage earners, should be considered. Unrealistic investment returns, especially if projected over long periods, produce false security where great danger may lurk.

Step 5: Implement Strategy

The obvious step is not the easiest step. Procrastination in carrying out financial plans is common. Subtle psychological explanations also may account for lack of action. Most financial strategies require action. Lawyers must draft wills, trusts, guardianships, powers of attorney and contracts. Insurance contracts must be purchased, investments made, savings accumulated. All this activity is obvious to financial planners. Motivating people to act is often their most difficult assignment.

Figure 15.4
Seven Questions to Ask When Preparing a Written Report

1. Is the opening paragraph specific, accurate, appealing?
2. Is all the writing honest and to the point?
3. Do the conclusions logically follow from the material presented?
4. Are financial data presented carefully and as simply as is appropriate? Would a graphic presentation help?
5. Is the report written in the active voice rather than the passive voice? ("We recommend establishing a guardianship for Sue" rather than "It is recommended a guardianship be established for your minor child.")
6. Will readers understand all the terminology used, or do some terms require definition?
7. Has the document been checked for correct grammar, style and spelling?

Step 6: Prepare Financial Report

A financial report is the culmination of the financial planning process. The report should document all data and information collected. Problems should be identified in writing and quantified goals made clear. Strategies should be documented, with reasons provided for advice given. (Review of college entrance examination scores reveals that mathematical scores are higher than verbal scores. Clearly communicating in English is at least as difficult as communicating in mathematics. Figure 15.4 provides a very brief review of some essentials for preparing written reports.)

A typical financial report has the following contents, mirroring the financial planning process.

- Cover letter
- Facts and data
- Analysis of problems and weaknesses
- Quantified goals presented
- Steps required to meet goals
- Timetable for implementing plans

Special Planning Problems

College Funding

Many arguments favor a college education. The "be all that you can be" argument tops the list. A college education should promote clear and logical thinking, an appreciation of the arts and sciences and the ability to read, write and do mathematics at advanced levels. College-educated people provide democracies with educated citizens needed for the functioning of this complex political system. College education increases students' employment potential. A college education facilitates communication and interaction with other college-educated people. For these reasons most American high school graduates enter college.

College Costs

The cost of college education varies greatly in the United States. In 1990 city colleges and state-supported schools were estimated to cost about $25,000, with private institutions costing about $60,000 for a bachelor's degree. Our nation's most prestigious private universities cost about $100,000 for an undergraduate education. Unfortunately, college costs have been increasing faster than the general inflation rate. Using a 7 percent annual inflation factor public educations will cost about $37,000 in 5 years, $51,000 in 10 years and $88,000 in 18 years. The comparable figures for private universities are $78,000 (5 years), $110,000 (10 years) and $190,000 (18 years). Families faced with the need to provide a child's college education are well advised to plan early and carefully.

Several strategies lead to successful college funding, including the following:

- Direct funding
- Cash value life insurance
- Property transfer to minors

Direct Funding

The simplest funding plan is to have the parents own the assets accumulating in the college fund. Retaining asset ownership means the savings are available for emergencies or other purposes. Retention also means the owners continue to pay applicable federal, state or local income tax. Appropriate investments for college funding include growth stock mutual funds, zero-coupon bonds and U.S. savings bonds, which offer special advantages for middle-income families when used to fund college educations.[2]

Direct ownership of the college fund assets should always be accompanied by an adequate amount of term life insurance. The life insurance need ends after the education is complete. Life insurance is necessary to cover the possibility of the wage earner(s) dying before accumulating adequate assets. Disability coverage to replace lost income and savings also should be purchased.

Cash Value Life Insurance

Cash value life insurance can be used to fund a child's education. Traditional whole life, universal life and variable life insurance policies can all be used. The insured is the parent(s), the wage earner whose income is providing the accumulating savings. If the parent dies before accumulating adequate assets, the death benefit provides the cash needed to pay for the college education. If the parent lives, the cash value can fund the education. The cash value may be taken as a policy loan or in total if the owner surrenders the policy.

☐ **Example**

Edward Byron began a $150,000 whole life insurance policy at age 23, when his daughter Karen was born. If he had died prematurely, part of the proceeds would have provided funds for Karen's education. Edward survived well past the years of Karen's college education, but when Karen was 18, he borrowed the $39,000 needed to pay tuition and other expenses from the insurance company. The $39,000 loan and accumulated interest reduced the available proceeds at Edward's death. Because the need for a college education was already satisfied, the reduction did not upset the Byrons' financial plans.

Cash value life insurance has two significant advantages in funding college educations. First, savings increase with each premium payment. Second, the needed funds are available if a wage earner dies. Thus, whether the insured lives or dies, the education is funded. The life insurance company guarantees the results. Finally, the cash value life insurance policy can be accompanied by disability income and waiver-of-premium riders to protect against the impact of this potential catastrophe.

The rate of return on cash value life insurance may not be as great as some alternatives. However, the financial guarantee of a financially sound life insurance company may provide a better combination of risk and return than other alternatives.

Asset Transfer to Minors

The Tax Reform Act of 1986 requires the nonearned (investment) income of children under age 14 to be taxed at their parents' marginal rates. This "**kiddie tax**" removed much of the prior motivation for transferring property to minors. (*See* Chapter 12 for a complete explanation of the kiddie tax.) Despite the kiddie tax, gifts to minors still allow donors to use the annual $10,000 ($20,000 for joint gifts) federal gift tax exclusion, transfer assets with future appreciation potential, reduce probate estate size and accomplish other logical objectives. Therefore this section will examine two approaches to transferring property to minors: the Uniform Gifts to Minors Act and the trust.

UGMA. The **Uniform Gifts to Minors Act (UGMA)** is model legislation in effect in many states. Other states have adopted a more recent model called the *Uniform Transfers to Minors Act (UTMA)*. The UTMA allows a broader class of assets to be transferred. (Some states have slight deviations from the model laws. For simplicity, the single acronym, UGMA, is used to represent both model laws in this section.) The UGMA is needed because minors lack legal capacity to enter contracts. Thus property transferred directly to a minor cannot be managed easily.

The UGMA overcomes the difficulties of a direct property transfer to minors without the expenses and complications of the trust. The UGMA requires appointment of a custodian for the transferred property until the child reaches age 18. An attorney is not required for these transfers.

State law determines the type of property that may be transferred under the UGMA. The following types of property typically may be transferred (as noted, the UTMA allows more types of property to be transferred than the UGMA):

- Bank accounts and certificates of deposit
- Securities: common stock, corporate and tax-exempt bonds and mutual funds
- Transfer of life insurance and annuities (in some states)

Property transferred to a child using the UGMA becomes the child's property when the child reaches age 18. Except in cases of the child's death, property generally is not recoverable by the donor. Income from transferred property cannot be used to provide the normal child support parents legally must provide.

The UGMA may provide psychological rewards because of the love and trust involved. One potential disadvantage lies in the possibility that the donee will not use the funds for the purpose envisioned by the donor. The gift is irrevocable, and some donors may regret this outcome.

Trusts. The trust is an alternative to the direct or UGMA transfer of property to a minor. A trust is a legal arrangement allowing one party, the trustee, to manage property for another party, the beneficiary. Trusts are not a practical alternative for the transfer of small amounts of property.

The Internal Revenue Code identifies two types of trusts that can be used to hold property for minors, while still allowing the donor to claim the annual $10,000 gift tax exclusion. (The annual gift tax exclusion is for present interests transferred from donor to donee. A gift to a trust ordinarily would not be a present interest. The gift tax and the annual exclusion are described in Chapter 12. The Crummey Trust, also described in Chapter 12, allows donors to use the annual gift tax exclusion to fund a life insurance purchase.) **The Section 2503(c) trust** requires both income and principal to be expended before the minor's 21st birthday. Distributed income is taxable to the minor; accumulated income is taxable to the trust.

☐ **Example**

Grandfather gives Granddaughter $10,000 each year from ages one through eight. He places the money in a 2503(c) trust. The terms of the trust make the annual income available to Granddaughter after her 16th birthday. Any residual value in the trust must be paid to Granddaughter at her 21st birthday.

Grandfather should not be named trustee of this trust, because that causes the trust assets to be included in his estate if he dies before Granddaughter reaches age 21. If Granddaughter dies before age 21, the trust assets pass to her estate.

The **Section 2503(b) trust** is similar to the 2503(c) trust, except that the trust principal need not be paid to the minor donee before age 21 or ever. On the other hand, the 2503(b) must distribute the income to the minor at least annually.

☐ **Example**

Grandfather and Grandmother jointly give $20,000 each year for five years to a trust set up under the terms of IRC Section 2503(b). The gifts begin at their grandson's 14th birthday. The gifts qualify for the annual $20,000 gift tax exclusion available for joint gifts. Each year the grandson must receive the income from the trust. At the grandson's 23rd birthday the trust is dissolved and the principal is transferred to Aunt Mary.

Evaluating Life Insurance Alternatives

Implementing a life insurance program requires purchase of a specific policy, from a specific life insurance company. This step is taken after determining the needed amount of coverage. Implementation requires the following steps:

1. Gather information.
2. Analyze proposals.
3. Choose policy type and company.

Information

Life insurance is sold by more than 2,000 insurers and more than 100,000 agents and brokers. Some companies operate nationally, some locally. Some offer a complete portfolio of policies, some only a few different contracts. Some insurers have operated for more than 100 years; some companies have operated for less than 100 months. The largest 50 life insurers control most of the market. Most of the largest 20 companies operate on the mutual basis. Some newer companies, offering either term life insurance or innovative cash value products, have grown rapidly in the past decade. A consumer making a purchase decision has many choices.

The year 1991 saw several insolvencies of large life insurance companies, including one of the twenty largest. In addition, some financial ratings firms lowered their ratings of many prominent insurers. In this environment, many insurance consumers (and insurance agents) were more cautious in choosing life insurance companies. In 1991, at least five financial ratings companies provided evaluations of life insurance company financial strength or "claims paying ability." This group included: A. M. Best Company, Standard & Poors, Moody's Investors Services, Duff & Phelps Credit Rating Company and Weiss Research. The ratings companies themselves caused some controversy, either because of the fees they charged life insurers to receive a rating (up to $28,000) or because of the fees one company charged consumers requesting a rating (about $45 for an indepth review of an insurer). In using the financial ratings firms' reviews, the consumer must realize that:

- the ratings firms may not agree on a specific life insurance company's merits;
- not all life insurance "experts" agree on the quality of a given ratings firm's ratings;
- one letter grade cannot tell the "whole" story of a life insurance company;
- slight differences in letter grades probably do not make a sound basis for choosing one insurer over another; and
- life insurance companies with high ratings can sell policies that are not the most efficient choices for many consumers

While financial strength ratings are important, a consumer must consider the source of the rating. However, if two or more ratings services agree on a "poor" rating, consumers should probably look for an alternative carrier.[3]

Analysis

It is unlikely that any two companies' proposals will follow the same mathematical format, making comparisons of purchase alternatives difficult. Despite the mathematical approach used, the following items should be reviewed for comparable policy types:

- Annual premiums
- Year-end cash values
- Projected dividends
- Year-end death benefits
- Surrender charges
- Policyholder loan charges

Meaningful comparisons can be made only if insurers use reasonable interest and dividend assumptions. Unrealistically high interest assumptions, especially if presented for a long period, lead to disappointment. Such proposals should be weeded out quickly. If life insurance companies use different methods to calculate investment credits—for example, one company uses the portfolio method while others use new money methods—care must be taken to assess the impact of these approaches on the policy comparisons. It is wise to ask insurers for a comparison of their predicted and the historical (actual) results. Usually applicants need not make the comparisons themselves; often competing agents are more than willing to compare their proposals, pointing out problems and deficiencies in other companies' proposals.

The appropriate policy type depends on several factors. The following are most important:

- *Ability to pay premiums relative to the coverage needed.* If a large amount of coverage is required, and disposable income is limited, term life insurance is the appropriate purchase.
- *Ability to accept risk.* Aggressive investors probably will follow the buy-term-and-invest-the-difference plan. Risk-averse investors may be most comfortable with traditional whole life insurance and the accompanying guarantees. Risk-neutral investors may prefer investment-oriented contracts such as universal life insurance or variable life insurance.
- *Need to save.* Savings discipline. Many people need to save and benefit from the compulsory savings program of cash value life insurance. These people should purchase cash value life insurance if they have adequate disposable income and can purchase adequate coverage. A combination of term and cash value life insurance is often appropriate.

Decision

After choosing a policy type and company, an application must be completed, and usually a medical examination taken. The rates used in sales presentations are standard rates. Review of medical evidence and information contained in applications may cause the insurer to propose substandard rates. Two different insurers may reach different underwriting decisions. If one insurer proposes substandard rates, an application can be made with a different insurer. If the applicant is satisfied with the underwriting decision, all required steps to put the policy in force should be completed in short order.

An Annotated Case Study:
The Cook Family: Calculating the Life Insurance Need

Facts and Data

Joe and Joyce Cook are 34 years old. They live in Columbus, Ohio. Their one child, Jill, is 12. Joe works as an engineer for the local electric utility. Joyce is a research chemist with a large food processing company. Joyce's parents are deceased. Joe's parents are alive, and his father works for the U.S. Postal Service. Joe's parents live in Detroit.

Two years ago, using money Joyce inherited from her parents' estate, the Cooks made a down payment on a new house. What current assets they now have also can be traced to this inheritance. Joe and Joyce each have two sisters. Only Joyce's older sister lives near the Cooks.

The Cooks' statement of net worth and most recent cash flow statement appear as Exhibit 15.1 and Exhibit 15.2 respectively. The information in Exhibit 15.2 is slightly incorrect. In 1991 the Cooks know from year-end balances that they used about $1,000 of their savings, despite the cash flow statement showing a $369 cash surplus.

Comment: The Cooks' average tax rate and marginal federal tax rate are each 28 percent in Exhibit 15.2. In progressive tax structures average tax rates are less than marginal tax rates. However, combining the Cooks' state and local income taxes with their federal income taxes produces the result described.

The Social Security tax is calculated as 7.65 percent of each salary because neither salary exceeds the covered maximum. The covered maximum earnings base and the tax percentage have changed annually in recent years. Readers needing current information should contact the Social Security Administration.

The Cooks have no individually purchased life or disability insurance. Each has $15,000 of group life insurance. Each employer provides a health insurance plan covering all family members. The Cooks have employer-provided group disability insurance coverage that replaces 66 percent of lost income in the event of total disability. Each of the Cooks has earned fully insured and disability-insured status under Social Security. The Cooks maintain adequate insurance on their house and automobile.

Both Cooks are optimistic about their financial future. Both have made progress in their careers and feel future advancement should follow. They want a second child and have been trying to increase their family for several years. If they have a second child, they assume Joyce will stay home until this child is about six years old. After the younger child is six, Joyce wants to return to work. Joyce expressed concern about having to dip into their savings last year. Joe was less concerned because he felt the money "went into the house."

When confronted with the question "What are your plans if either or both spouses were to die prematurely or become disabled?" the Cooks admitted having given the matter little thought. They lacked formal plans but assumed one of their sisters would raise Jill if they both died prematurely. They also felt that if one parent died prematurely the surviving spouse would raise Jill while continuing to work. They thought the surviving parent's earnings would provide adequate income for the family. The Cooks have no will and no written financial plans.

The Cooks stated that if a reduction in current consumption were made to increase savings, it would have to come from their vacation and entertainment budgets. Of the $4,000 they spent on recreation last year, about $500 was spent on their hobby of collecting old glass bottles. The Cooks felt they could easily postpone adding to their collection and reduce their vacation and entertainment expenditures by $750 without unacceptable changes in their life-style. On the other hand, while desiring to increase their savings, the Cooks want to buy a second car. Their main savings goal is to fund Jill's college education. They feel this goal is more important than getting a new car, so they are shopping for a used one.

Exhibit 15.1
Cook Family Statement of Net Worth
December 31, 1991

Assets	
Cash and checking	$ 1,500
Money market fund	3,000
100 shares common stock (market value)	5,500
Car (market value)	6,500
House (market value)	100,000
Total assets	116,500
Liabilities	
Credit card	1,200
Car loan	3,500
Home mortgage loan	78,292
Total liabilities	82,992
Net worth	33,508
Total liabilities and net worth	$116,500

Analysis

Review of the data and information provided by the Cooks reveals the following financial problems:

- No will, no estate plans, no funeral plans, no plans covering the possibility of simultaneous deaths
- Inadequate life insurance
- Inadequate disability insurance
- Inadequate savings
- Inadequate accumulated wealth
- No plans to achieve financial goals

Exhibit 15.3 uses the Cooks' cash flow statement for 1991 as the basis of a nine-year projection. The projection ends when Jill reaches age 21. The spending and savings percentages are projected to remain

Exhibit 15.2
Cook Family Cash Flow Statement
January 1 to December 31, 1991

Income		
Joe's salary	$28,000	
Joyce's salary	28,000	
Investment income	680	
Gross income	56,680	
Income taxes (fed., state, local)	15,870	
Real estate tax	1,200	
Social Security (FICA)	4,284	
Total taxes	21,354	
Disposable income	35,326	
		(percent of disposable income)
Expenses		
Housing (mortgage pmt. = $8,813)	12,484	35.3%
Transportation	5,899	16.7%
Food	5,334	15.1%
Vacation/entertainment	4,239	12.0%
All other	7,000	19.8%
Total expenses	34,957	99.0%
Net cash flow	$ 369	1.0%

Exhibit 15.3
Cook Family Cash Flow Statement
Seven-Year Projection, 1992–1999

Assumptions
Salary growth rate 2%
Inflation rate 5%
Rate of return on investments 8%
Improve standard of living 4%

Jill's age	12	13	14	15	16	17	18	19	20
Year	1991 (actual)	1992	1993	1994	1995	1996	1997	1998	1999
Income									
Joe's salary	$28,000	$29,960	$32,057	$34,301	$36,702	$39,271	$42,020	$44,962	$48,109
Joyce's salary	28,000	29,960	32,057	34,301	36,702	39,271	42,020	44,962	48,109
Investment income	680	710	766	850	961	981	1,012	1,050	1,094
Gross income	56,680	60,630	64,880	69,452	74,366	79,524	85,052	90,974	97,312
Income taxes (fed., state, local)	15,870	16,976	18,167	19,447	22,310	23,857	25,516	27,292	29,194
Real estate tax	1,200	1,200	1,200	1,200	1,200	1,200	1,200	1,200	1,200
Social Security (FICA)	4,284	4,584	4,905	5,248	5,615	6,009	6,429	6,879	7,361
Total taxes	21,354	22,760	24,271	25,895	29,125	31,066	33,145	35,371	37,754
Disposable income	35,326	37,869	40,609	43,558	45,241	48,458	51,908	55,603	59,558
Expenses									
Housing (mortgage pmt. = $8,813)	12,484	12,668	12,860	13,063	13,275	13,498	13,732	13,978	14,237
Transportation	5,899	6,430	7,009	7,640	8,327	9,077	9,894	10,784	11,755
Food	5,334	5,814	6,338	6,908	7,530	8,207	8,946	9,751	10,629
Vacation/entertainment	4,239	4,621	5,036	5,490	5,984	6,522	7,109	7,749	8,447
All other	7,000	7,630	8,317	9,065	9,881	10,770	11,740	12,796	13,948
Total expenses	34,957	37,163	39,560	42,165	44,997	48,075	51,421	55,059	59,015
Net cash flow	369	707	1,049	1,392	244	383	486	543	543
Accumulated net cash flow		1,076	2,125	3,517	3,761	4,144	4,630	5,174	5,717
Total savings	8,869	9,576	10,625	12,017	12,261	12,644	13,130	13,674	14,217

constant. A 5 percent inflation factor is used. Moreover, as their incomes increase, the Cooks are assumed to increase their standard of living by 4 percent each year, as this has been their historical pattern. That is, like many members of a "consuming" generation, the Cooks have purchased a better car, taken better vacations and purchased other, more expensive items as their incomes grew. Their savings rate remains constant. A 2 percent compound annual increase in both salaries is assumed because this pattern is representative. From a financial planning standpoint, this assumption is not conservative.

Exhibit 15.3 illustrates the problems highlighted in the analysis section. Specifically, despite beginning the period with $8,500 in investments and having a total disposable income of almost $400,000, they end the period saving less than $6,000. Their final total savings amounts to only $14,217.

Establish Goals

After reviewing Exhibit 15.3, the Cooks quickly decide they need financial counseling. They understand the need to execute a will, purchase life insurance and establish financial goals. This chapter covers the development of financial plans for only their two most important financial goals:

1. To save $20,000 in a college fund before Jill's 18th birthday. The amount to be saved assumes Jill will go to a state university whose tuition and other costs are about $8,000 in 1991 and are estimated to be $12,500 annually when Jill begins college. The college fund will be supplemented by annual cash flow to provide the needed withdrawals.
2. To purchase adequate life and disability insurance.

Saving for College

Exhibit 15.4 reflects an increase in savings and an inflation factor of 5 percent in addition to the 2 percent merit raises. To increase the Cooks' savings, a 2 percent increase in their standard of living is assumed as their incomes increase. (Exhibit 15.3 assumed a 4 percent increase in this amount.) In addition, a $750 reduction is shown in their vacation/entertainment expenditures. Taxes and expenses are increased proportionately by the 5 percent inflation factor. The net result is an increase in savings from $707 to $2,116 in 1992. Saving from cash flow increases from a projected $5,717 (Exhibit 15.3) to $43,460 (Exhibit 15.4) over the nine-year period. Most important, the Cooks still have a savings balance after financing Jill's college education. The Cooks feel this balance could be used to educate a second child or as the beginning of their retirement fund.

Comment: The "investment income" line in Figure 15.4 is calculated by multiplying the rate of return on investments (.08) by the accumulated savings at the end of the preceding year.

The Cooks' savings program illustrates the reallocation of lifetime consumption. Current consumption must be postponed to allow for increased future consumption. People must take a long-run view of their consumption to achieve their financial goals.

Life Insurance Planning

The Cooks' family and financial circumstances require a well-developed plan covering the possibility of Joe's or Joyce's premature death. These plans appear as two financial models. (The problem of disability is not covered in these two models. The Cooks have employer-provided group disability insurance coverage that replaces 66 percent of lost income in the event of total disability. Each of the Cooks has earned fully insured and disability-insured status under Social Security.)

Model 1: Joe dies and Joyce continues work as a chemist (Exhibit 15.5). Because Joe and Joyce have similar salaries, Model 1 also can illustrate the financial consequences of Joyce dying while Joe continues to work. In this case the financial consequences will be the same despite the order of death. If there are significant disparities in salaries, separate models should be used to illustrate the financial consequences of the husband predeceasing the wife and vice versa.

Model 2: Joe dies and Joyce stops working outside the home (Exhibit 15.6).

Model 1

Exhibit 15.5 is derived from the data presented in Exhibit 15.4. Exhibit 15.5 assumes Joe's immediate death with Joyce continuing to work at the food com-

Exhibit 15.4
Cook Family Cash Flow Statement

Increased Savings

Seven-Year Projection, 1992–1999

Assumptions
Salary growth rate	2%	
Inflation rate	5%	
Rate of return on investments		8%
Improve standard of living		2%

Jill's age	12	13	14	15	16	17	18	19	20
Year	1991 (actual)	1992	1993	1994	1995	1996	1997	1998	1999
Income									
Joe's salary	$28,000	$29,960	$32,057	$34,301	$36,702	$39,271	$42,020	$44,962	$48,109
Joyce's salary	28,000	29,960	32,057	34,301	36,702	39,271	42,020	44,962	48,109
Investment income	680	710	879	1,142	1,510	1,877	1,360	1,918	2,618
Gross income	56,680	60,630	64,993	69,744	74,915	80,420	85,401	91,842	98,836
Income taxes (fed., state, local)	15,870	16,976	18,198	19,528	22,474	24,126	25,620	27,552	29,651
Real estate tax	1,200	1,200	1,200	1,200	1,200	1,200	1,200	1,200	1,200
Social Security (FICA)	4,284	4,584	4,905	5,248	5,615	6,009	6,429	6,879	7,361
Total taxes	21,354	22,760	24,303	25,976	29,290	31,334	33,249	35,632	38,212
Disposable income	35,326	37,869	40,690	43,768	45,625	49,085	52,151	56,210	60,625
Expenses									
Housing	12,484	12,580	12,682	12,788	12,900	13,017	13,140	13,269	13,405
Transportation	5,899	6,312	6,754	7,227	7,733	8,274	8,853	9,473	10,136
Food	5,334	5,708	6,107	6,535	6,992	7,481	8,005	8,566	9,165
Vacation/entertainment	4,239	3,664	3,847	4,039	4,241	4,453	4,676	4,909	5,155
All other	7,000	7,490	8,014	8,575	9,176	9,818	10,505	11,240	12,027
Total expenses	34,957	35,754	37,404	39,164	41,041	43,043	45,179	47,458	49,889
Net cash flow	369	2,116	3,286	4,604	4,584	6,042	6,972	8,752	10,736
Accumulated net cash flow		2,484	5,771	10,374	14,958	21,000	27,972	36,724	47,460
College costs						(12,500)	(12,500)	(12,500)	(12,500)
Total savings	8,869	10,984	14,271	18,874	23,458	17,000	11,472	7,724	5,960
Education calculation									
Tuition payments						12,500	12,500	12,500	12,500
PV of tuition		32,866	35,495	38,335	41,402	44,714	34,791	24,074	12,500

Chapter 15 Financial Planning: The Early Adult Years 329

Exhibit 15.5
Cook Family Life Insurance Plan: Model 1

Joe Dies, Joyce Continues to Work

Seven-Year Projection, 1992–1999

Assumptions
Salary growth rate 2%
Inflation rate 5%
Rate of return on investments 8%
Improve standard of living 2%

Jill's age	12	13	14	15	16	17	18	19	20
Year	1991 (actual)	1992	1993	1994	1995	1996	1997	1998	1999
Income									
Joe's salary	$28,000								
Joyce's salary	28,000	29,960	32,057	34,301	36,702	39,271	42,020	44,962	48,109
Jill's survivor benefit		3,000	3,150	3,308	3,473	3,647	3,829	4,021	4,222
Investment income	680	0	2,881	3,555	4,317	5,177	6,145	5,906	5,614
Gross income	56,680	32,960	38,089	41,164	44,492	48,095	48,165	50,868	53,724
Income taxes (fed., state, local)	15,870	6,592	7,618	8,233	8,898	9,619	9,633	10,174	10,745
Real estate tax	1,200	1,200	1,200	1,200	1,200	1,200	1,200	1,200	1,200
Social Security (FICA)	4,284	2,292	2,452	2,624	2,808	3,004	3,215	3,440	3,680
Total taxes	21,354	10,084	11,270	12,057	12,906	13,823	14,048	14,813	15,625
Disposable income	35,326	22,876	26,818	29,107	31,586	34,272	34,118	36,055	38,099
Expenses									
Housing (mortgage pmt. = $8,813)	12,484	3,855	4,047	4,250	4,462	4,685	4,919	5,165	5,424
Transportation (²⁄₃ orig.)	5,899	4,166	4,458	4,770	5,104	5,461	5,843	6,252	6,690
Food (²⁄₃ orig.)	5,334	3,767	4,031	4,313	4,615	4,938	5,283	5,653	6,049
Vacation/entertainment (²⁄₃ orig.)	4,239	2,994	3,203	3,427	3,667	3,924	4,199	4,493	4,807
All other (²⁄₃ orig.)	7,000	4,943	5,289	5,660	6,056	6,480	6,933	7,419	7,938
Total expenses	34,957	19,725	21,028	22,419	23,904	25,488	27,178	28,982	30,908

Exhibit 15.5 (continued)

Jill's age Year		12 1991 (actual)	13 1992	14 1993	15 1994	16 1995	17 1996	18 1997	19 1998	20 1999
Net cash flow		369	3,151	5,790	6,687	7,682	8,784	6,939	7,072	7,191
Accumulated net cash flow			3,151	8,941	15,629	23,311	32,095	39,035	46,107	53,298
Total savings		8,869								
Postdeath funds needed										
Repayment of mortgage			77,307	76,225	75,034	73,724	72,283	70,698	68,954	67,036
Education fund			32,866	35,495	38,335	41,402	44,714	34,791	24,074	12,500
Emergency fund			15,000	15,000	15,000	15,000	15,000	15,000	15,000	15,000
Total			125,173	126,720	128,369	130,125	131,996	120,488	108,028	94,536
Assets available										
Group life insurance			15,000	15,000	15,000	15,000	15,000	15,000	15,000	15,000
Current assets			8,869							
Total			23,869	15,000	15,000	15,000	15,000	15,000	15,000	15,000
Life insurance needed			101,304	111,720	113,369	115,125	116,996	105,488	93,028	79,536
Mortgage calculation										
Principal	80,000									
Interest	0.10									
Years	25									
PV factor	9.08									
Annual mortgage payment	8,813									
Bal. beg. yr.	80,000	79,187	78,292	77,307	76,225	75,034	73,724	72,283	70,698	68,954	67,036
Education calculation										
Tuition payments							12,500	12,500	12,500	12,500
PV of tuition			32,866	35,495	38,335	41,402	44,714	34,791	24,074	12,500

Exhibit 15.6
Cook Family Life Insurance Plan: Model 2

Joe Dies, Joyce Remains Home

Seven-Year Projection, 1992–1999

Assumptions
Salary growth rate	2%
Inflation rate	5%
Rate of return on investments	5.6%
Improve standard of living	2%

Jill's age Year	12 1991 (actual)	13 1992	14 1993	15 1994	16 1995	17 1996	18 1997	19 1998	20 1999
Jill's age	12	13	14	15	16	17	18	19	20
Joyce's age	34	35	36	37	38	39	40	41	42
Income									
Joe's salary	$28,000								
Joyce's salary	28,000								
Joyce's survivor benefit		3,000	3,150	3,308					
Jill's survivor benefit		3,000	3,150	3,308	3,473	3,647			
Investment income	476								
Gross income	56,476	6,000	6,300	6,615	3,473	3,647	0	0	0
Income taxes (fed., state, local)	15,813								
Real estate tax	1,200	1,200	1,200	1,200	1,200	1,200	1,200	1,200	1,200
Social Security (FICA)	4,284								
Total taxes	21,297	1,200	1,200	1,200	1,200	1,200	1,200	1,200	1,200
Disposable income	35,179	4,800	5,100	5,415	2,273	2,447	(1,200)	(1,200)	(1,200)
Expenses									
Housing	12,484	3,855	4,047	4,250	4,462	4,685	4,919	5,165	5,424
Transportation	5,875	6,286	6,726	7,197	7,701	8,240	8,817	9,434	10,094
Food (²/₃ orig.)	5,312	3,751	4,014	4,295	4,596	4,917	5,261	5,630	6,024
Vacation/entertainment (²/₃ orig.)	4,221	2,981	3,190	3,413	3,652	3,908	4,181	4,474	4,787
All other (²/₃ orig.)	7,000	4,943	5,289	5,660	6,056	6,480	6,933	7,419	7,938
Living expenses	34,892	21,817	23,267	24,814	26,466	28,230	30,112	32,122	34,267

Exhibit 15.6 (continued)

Jill's age	12	13	14	15	16	17	18	19	20
Year	1991 (actual)	1992	1993	1994	1995	1996	1997	1998	1999
Net cash flow	286	(17,017)	(18,167)	(19,399)	(24,193)	(25,783)	(31,312)	(33,322)	(35,467)
Total savings	8,786								
Postdeath funds needed									
Maintain standard living (annuity due)		164,989	156,259	145,826	133,506	115,434	94,672	66,908	35,467
Repayment of mortgage		77,307	76,225	75,034	73,724	72,283	70,698	68,954	67,036
Education fund		32,866	35,495	38,335	41,402	44,714	34,791	24,074	12,500
Emergency fund		15,000	15,000	15,000	15,000	15,000	15,000	15,000	15,000
Total funds needed		290,163	282,979	274,195	263,632	247,431	215,160	174,935	163,589
Assets available									
Group life insurance		15,000	15,000	15,000	15,000	15,000	15,000	15,000	15,000
Current assets		8,786							
Total assets available		23,786	15,000	15,000	15,000	15,000	15,000	15,000	15,000
Life Insurance Needed		266,376	267,979	259,195	248,632	232,431	200,160	159,935	115,003

pany. Joe's death directly affects the following elements of Exhibit 15.4:

- Joe's salary ends.
- Social Security survivor benefits are available.
- Investment income drops in 1992 as all current assets are used to meet postdeath needs. In 1993 and thereafter investment income is earned on the education fund provided by life insurance proceeds and on accumulated net cash flow.
- The marginal and average income tax rates drop. Jill's survivor benefit is not taxable. Real estate taxes remain constant. Social Security tax applies only to Joyce's salary.
- With the mortgage repaid, housing expenses are reduced by the mortgage payment. In this case the mortgage interest cost is 10 percent, while available investment earnings are 8 percent. As long as this relationship prevails, the Cooks plan to repay the mortgage with life insurance proceeds. If investment returns on low-risk investments exceed the mortgage interest rates, the life insurance proceeds will be invested and the mortgage not repaid.
- With one less family member, other expenses are reduced by one-third.

The Cooks' current income and expense factors reflect annual 5 percent increases caused by inflation. In addition, Joyce receives an annual 2 percent merit wage increase. (Using constant inflation or merit wage factors over long periods greatly distorts results. Spreadsheets should be recast regularly to be meaningful.)

Cash Inflow

Since both Joe and Joyce have fully insured status, Jill is entitled to a survivor benefit if either her mother or father dies before she is age 18. Joyce also is entitled to a survivor benefit. Because her salary is greater than the minimum specified by the earnings test, she receives no benefit. If Joyce dies, Jill and Joe are entitled to a survivor benefit, but Joe would fail the earnings test if he continued working. Jill's benefit ends at her 18th birthday. The family's disposable income in this model is the sum of Joyce's after-tax income plus Jill's Social Security benefit.

Expenses

Housing expenses consist of maintenance, utilities, insurance and the replacement of Joe's services. These expenses continue even after the mortgage loan is repaid with life insurance proceeds. Thus when comparing the data shown for 1991 and 1992, housing expenses drop from $12,484 to $3,855. The difference equals the mortgage payment of $8,813, with the balance adjusted for inflation at 5 percent.

Comment: $12,484 - 8,813 = 3,671 \times 1.05 = 3,855$.

The declining balance of the mortgage loan is calculated at the bottom of Exhibit 15.5. The results are slightly inaccurate since calculations are shown on an annual basis, while monthly payments actually are required. (See Chapter 13, Financial Mathematics, for a description and an example of calculating a mortgage loan balance.) The mortgage payment can be calculated by dividing the principal by the present value (PV) factor combining 25 years and 10 percent interest.

Comment: Using the spreadsheet's @PMT function with the following argument—@PMT (principal, rate, time)—produces the required payment. Other spreadsheet financial functions can break down the mortgage payment into its interest and principal repayment components, if necessary. (The author of this chapter used the QUATTRO PRO spreadsheet program by Borland International, Inc., to develop the exhibits used in this chapter. Other popular spreadsheet programs probably have similar financial functions, but users should review the order of their arguments.)

Repayment of the mortgage is not a legal necessity at Joe's death. If prevailing interest rates exceed the interest rate on a fixed mortgage, repayment of the mortgage would not be desirable, since investment income on the life insurance proceeds would exceed the mortgage loan interest costs.

The food category shows significant change. With one less person, the family's cost of food eaten at home decreases. However, more meals are eaten away from home.

Postdeath Funds Required

The Cooks' life insurance plan illustrates fulfillment of the following three goals:

1. The repayment of the mortgage
2. The provision of an education fund for Jill
3. The provision of a sufficient amount of cash to allow the family to maintain its standard of living

The plan assumes the cost of Jill's education is $12,500 a year for four years. The $12,500 annual cost represents the estimated annual cost for the type of college education the Cooks want to provide for Jill based on a 1991 cost of $8,000. These payments are made between Jill's 17th and 20th birthdays. The calculation of the educational expense is shown at the bottom of this exhibit, with the result shown in the Education Fund row. The Education Fund is the lump sum needed to pay the projected educational expense, if the fund grows at the investment return rate of 8 percent. The fund balance increases each year because there is less time to earn interest on the lump sum.

If the Cooks survive and successfully achieve their savings goal shown in Exhibit 15.4, the amount saved for Jill's education reduces this need for life insurance proceeds. The education fund projection is for an *annuity due,* because the tuition is paid at the beginning and not the end of the year. (*See* Chapter 13, Table 13.1 for a description and an example of an annuity due.)

Comment: Calculating the present value of an annuity due with a spreadsheet requires lagging the series one year. For example, to make the calculation in cell H15 the formula would call for "+G15 +@NPV(.8, G16 . . . N16)." Some spreadsheet programs have a toggle in their advanced financial functions for calculating an annuity due.

Death and emergency fund expenses are assumed to be $15,000 and to remain constant. The $15,000 allowance is considered adequate. Because net cash flow is positive during this period, the family does not require life insurance proceeds to assist the family in maintaining its standard of living. However, most of the investment income arises as a return on the life insurance proceeds in the education fund. This investment income cannot be used for living expenses without depleting the education fund. Many families and financial counselors would be more comfortable with a cash cushion available after the mortgage is repaid and the education funded. A $25,000 cushion against outrageous fortune would add a margin of safety to this plan.

Postdeath Assets

If Joe dies, his group life insurance policy provides a $15,000 benefit. The Cooks have about $8,900 of current assets available in 1991. Subtracting postdeath assets from postdeath needs yields the amount of life insurance required to fund the three goals set in this model. This amount initially equals $101,304 in 1992. Each year Joe lives and the family saves money, the family's net worth increases. Accumulating assets and investment income should be incorporated into regular revisions of the financial plan once the savings are in hand.

Total life insurance needed diminishes each year Joe lives, because another year's payments reduce the mortgage loan, more savings accumulate and another year of support is provided for Jill. Exhibit 15.5 shows the amount of life insurance as an increasing amount for the first several years. The reason for an increasing need when logic suggests a decreasing need is that the projected accumulated current assets shown in this exhibit have not been added to the postdeath assets available. This approach makes the life insurance needed projection conservative. Exhibit 15.5 assumes death is immediate, in which case the projected savings will not be made. When the savings are actually in hand, they can be added to the current assets available to meet postdeath needs. Then the amount of life insurance required does indeed diminish.

If the lump sum is withdrawn in the sequence projected, with the remaining balance earning exactly 8 percent, no funds remain after the final withdrawal.

Model 2

Exhibit 15.6 is the second postdeath model prepared for the Cooks. It presents an alternative to the model presented in Exhibit 15.5. These plans are mutually exclusive. The difference between them is found in the assumption made regarding Joyce's employment if Joe dies. Model 1 assumes Joyce continues to work as a chemist if Joe dies. In this model, Joyce ends her employment if Joe dies. If there were two children at the time of Joe's death, the family felt this alternative would be their first choice. They also recognized that Joyce might be able to work part-time, but this was unlikely.

Cash Inflow

Joyce and Jill are each entitled to a Social Security survivor benefit. Since she has no wage income, Joyce receives a cash benefit. The family benefit is estimated to be $6,300 for 1993 and is automatically indexed by the consumer price index. In this model a 5 percent compound annual rate applies. Joyce's benefit ends when Jill reaches age 16. Jill's benefit ends at her 18th birthday.

After 1991 no investment income is shown. The current assets that had been earning income can be used for final expenses. If these funds are used for that purpose, they will no longer earn investment income, and the principle of using conservative estimates requires assuming no further investment returns on this amount. On the other hand, if a lump sum of life insurance proceeds is received, taxable investment income will be earned whether these assets are held directly or placed in a trust. This investment income is not shown directly in the exhibit. Rather the use of an after-tax discount rate of return on investments in the net present value calculations used in the standard of living maintenance fund and the education fund imply that investment income is earned and taxed and that the fund balances are liquidated in precisely the pattern projected.

Expenses

The expense pattern in Model 2 is identical to that in Model 1. It requires no further explanation. While the cash flow is positive when Joyce continues to work after Joe's death, the cash flow is negative, by a substantial amount, when Joyce does not continue outside employment after Joe's death.

Postdeath Funds Required

The amount shown in Exhibit 15.6 as needed to maintain the family's standard of living is the present value of the cash flow deficits. That is, the amount shown in this row is the lump sum of cash needed to cover all the deficit cash flows calculated in the preceding step. The discount rate assumes an 8 percent before-tax investment rate of return. An after-tax rate of return is used in the calculation because any investment income earned on the insurance proceeds is taxed in the year received. The after-tax rate of return is 5.6 percent assuming a 30 percent tax rate (.08 × (1 − .3) = .056). In other words, if the indicated lump sum were on hand at death, if the fund were depleted exactly as shown in the projection of net cash flow and if the fund balance grew at 5.6 percent each year, then the fund would have a zero balance in the year 2000.

Comment: Because the net cash flows are negative after Joe's death, the spreadsheet calculation requires the absolute value function. If calculation is made in cell N5, the formula would be "@ABS(+M5+@NPV(.056,M6 . . . M15)). Also, an annuity due calculation is used because funds are needed at the beginning of the period rather than after the first year's investment return has been earned.

Calculating the postdeath funds required follows the same pattern presented in Exhibit 15.5. In Exhibit 15.6 the required amount of life insurance equals $266,376 in 1992.

Implement Strategy

The Cook case shows how life insurance planning fits within the framework of a comprehensive financial plan. Beginning with a cash flow statement and a statement of net worth and then moving to two likely postdeath alternatives (models), the Cooks can make informed decisions about their life insurance needs. Model 1, assuming the surviving spouse continues employment at the death of the other spouse, calls for $101,304 of life insurance on both lives in 1992. Model 2 assumes Joyce stays home if Joe dies. This model calls for $266,376 of life insurance on Joe's life. Joyce's life would still be insured for $101,304 in this case.

In practice, after estimating the amount of insurance, the next step is determining the appropriate type of policy considering the amount of premium expense the Cooks can afford. The Cooks need a large amount of life insurance relative to their disposable income. Therefore term life insurance should be used for most or all of their needs at this time. The policies should be both renewable and convertible to provide needed financial flexibility. The Cooks could use a whole life policy to save for Jill's college education while simultaneously providing life insurance protection for the family.

If funds are available, a planner might recommend consideration of the purchase of a disability income insurance policy as well. Individual disability policies may have more liberal definitions of disability than that found in group coverage or in the Social Security definition. An individual policy might define permanent disability as being "unable to engage in the insured's *own* occupation," as opposed to the Social Security definition of "unable to engage in *any* occupation. . . ." Desirable individual disability policies also have shorter waiting periods for benefits, typically 90 days, while Social Security requires a six-month wait. An individual disability income insurance policy providing $1,500 a month income for a man of Joe's age would cost about $750 annually.

Financial Planning Report

This presentation illustrates life insurance planning. The exhibits in the Cook case allow the computation of an adequate amount of life insurance. An accompanying financial report would have the following elements:

- Cover letter
- Review of personal information
- Specification of the Cooks' goals and objectives
- Identification of current problems
- Statement of net worth and cash flow
- Statement of assumptions and projections to estimate funds required for postdeath resources

This case study did not cover many important considerations. The following topics would surely receive attention in a comprehensive financial report:

- The need for two wills and a guardianship for Jill
- A disability loss projection
- A simultaneous death projection
- An investment plan including an estimate of retirement income needs (development of a retirement funding plan is the subject of the following chapter) and postdeath investment advice
- An analysis of property and liability insurance needs

A comprehensive financial report would include an estate plan covering the transfer of the Cooks' estates at death. A will for each of the Cooks is necessary, despite the small amount of their current assets, which is the reason the Cooks gave for not having a will. An attorney should be retained to prepare all needed legal documents, including the formal establishment of a guardianship for Jill in the event both parents die while she is still a minor.

Much attention would be devoted to developing plans for the most likely possibility in this situation: that both parents remain alive and healthy for the entire period of Jill's minority, that assets will be accumulated and invested and that a college education will be provided for Jill.

A comprehensive financial report would discuss the impact of long-term disability of any of the family members. Thorough financial plans call for a forecast of an income statement showing the effects of disability.

Families also should consider the possibility of simultaneous deaths. Directions to a surviving spouse or guardian for managing the lump sum of life insurance proceeds are needed. Investment directions are especially useful if survivors are neither skilled in investing nor desirous of managing money. In these cases a settlement option other than the lump sum option may be appropriate. The trust is another useful alternative for managing and distributing insurance proceeds.

A comprehensive financial report also should cover property and liability loss exposures. The Cooks own a house and two vehicles requiring adequate insurance. Most planners suggest personal liability umbrella policies to add protection against large legal liability losses.

☐ **Practice Cases**

The Brantley Family

Ben Brantley is 29. His wife, Elizabeth, is 26. Ben and Elizabeth were married 8 years ago. They have two children, Donald, age 3, and Robert, age 5. Ben is manager and one-fourth owner of a franchised fast-food restaurant. The business operates as a subchapter S corporation. Ben averages about 60 hours of work each week. Last year he earned $70,000 before taxes. The $70,000 included his share, $20,000, of the restaurant's profits.

The remaining three-fourths of the franchise is owned by Elizabeth's father, who hopes to sell his interest to Ben sometime in the next 15 years. Ben feels he should save at least $100,000 to purchase his father-in-law's interest in the restaurant. Additional financing to make the purchase will come from loans. If Ben dies prematurely, his father-in-law has agreed to purchase Ben's interest in the restaurant, but his agreement is not in writing.

Ben acquired his interest in the business eight years ago using a wedding gift of $5,000 from his father-in-law and borrowing $100,000 from the bank. When the gift was given, the restaurant had a fair market value of $400,000. The current value is $1 million. The restaurant has increased in value at an average annual rate of 3 percent more than the increase in the CPI.

Neither Ben nor Elizabeth completed college, but they plan to be able to send both of their sons to college if this is the boys' choice. Ben has a $40,000 group life insurance policy from the restaurant and a $25,000 ordinary whole life policy purchased five years ago when

Exhibit 15.7
Brantley Family
Statement of Net Worth
(End of Last Year)

Assets	
Cash, checking and CDs	$15,000
Home	85,000
Interest in restaurant (at mkt.)	250,000
Total assets	350,000
Liabilities and Net Worth	
Home mortgage loan	63,809
Bank loan	28,245
Total liabilities	92,054
Net worth	257,946
Total liabilities and net worth	350,000

Robert was born. The restaurant also has a group health insurance plan covering Ben and his family. The restaurant has no pension plan. Ben is fully insured and disability-insured for Social Security calculations. Elizabeth is a homemaker and qualifies for no Social Security benefits based on her own earnings.

The Brantleys' statement of net worth and cash flow statement are shown in Exhibits 15.7 and 15.8.

Ben and Elizabeth are comfortable with their lifestyle. They both accept the risks inherent in the restaurant business. They realize most of their savings are invested in the business. They plan to continue living modestly after their current bank loan is repaid in two years to save enough money to purchase the remaining interest in the restaurant.

Assignment

You are to develop a financial plan for the Brantleys, including a life insurance plan allowing Mrs. Brantley

Exhibit 15.8
Brantley Family
Statement of Cash Flow
(Last year)

Income	
Ben's salary	$50,000
Restaurant profits	20,000
Less taxes:	(21,500)
Federal marginal rate = 28%	
State marginal rate = 5%	
FICA = 15.1%	
Disposable Income (DPI)	48,500
Expenses	
Food (14% DPI)	6,790
Housing (20% DPI)	9,700
Transportation (12% DPI)	5,820
Health (6% DPI)	2,910
Vacation/entertainment (4% DPI)	1,940
Repay bank loan	16,275
All other (10% DPI)	4,850
Total expenses	48,285
Savings	215
Total expenses and savings	48,500

**Exhibit 15.9
Representative Life Insurance Rates
Nonparticipating Rates
Cash Value Projected, Not Guaranteed
(All Data per $1,000)**

Ben Brantley, age 29

Age	Term	Whole Life	Cash Value
29	2.08	9.25	0
30	2.10		0
31	2.12		5
32	2.14		8
33	2.16		13
34	2.20		19
35	2.27		26
36	2.38		34
37	2.52		43
38	2.68		52
39	2.87		62
40	3.08		72
41	3.31		83
42	3.57		93
43	3.86		107
44	4.18		118
45	4.53		130
46	4.92		142
47	5.34		155
48	5.81		165
49	6.33		180
50	6.90		196
51	7.53		212
52	8.21		225
53	8.96		245
54	9.79		267
55	10.70		290

to remain at home during the entire period of the children's minority (to age 18). Ben's PIA is $650. Both Ben and Elizabeth are in good health.

1. Prepare a written financial report following the steps outlined in the chapter. The report should not exceed five pages.
2. Prepare a set of financial projections to accompany the written report. Be sure the written report and the financial projections are carefully integrated.
3. Assume inflation equals the most recent published annual rate.
4. Construct a line graph showing the Brantleys' need for life insurance and a pie chart showing their current consumption pattern.
5. Extra Credit: Develop an insurance solution for the business continuation problem presented if Ben Brantley's father-in-law dies before Ben purchases his three-quarter interest in the restaurant. (This assignment should be attempted only after reading Chapter 20 on business continuation life insurance.)

Mortgage and Loan Terms

The Brantleys purchased their home four years ago for $85,000. They made a 20 percent down payment. The terms of the mortgage loan are for 25 years. The $100,000 loan to finance Ben's interest in the restaurant was made eight years ago. The bank loan's terms are 10 percent annual interest for 10

Exhibit 15.10
Dean Upson
Statement of Cash Flow
(Most Recent Year)

Income	
Teaching salary	$26,000
Summer work (for brother)	9,000
Taxes	(8,750)
(state = 3%, FICA = 7.51%)	
Child support	(6,000)
Disposable personal income	20,250
Expenses	
Food (Dean only)	5,200
Apartment rent	6,000
Car (sports car)	5,200
All other	3,850
Total expenses	20,250

years. The balance shown in the statement of net worth, $28,245, is for the beginning of the loan's 9th year. Two more annual payments remain.

The Upson Family

Dean Upson is 26. He married Kate when they were 21. They were divorced three years later. While married, they had a child, Kathy. Kathy is now 4. As a result of the divorce, Dean must pay Kate $500 a month child support until Kathy is age 18. He has also agreed to insure his life for $50,000, naming Kate and Kathy as beneficiaries. He has a $50,000, 5-year term life insurance policy currently in force. By court order this policy must remain in force until Kathy is 18. If Dean dies before Kathy is 18, the insurance proceeds relieve his estate from any additional liability to Kate or Kathy. He still is fond of both of them and sees Kathy one weekend a month. Besides providing child support until Kathy is 18, he has agreed to provide one-half the cost of sending Kathy to college.

Dean remarried three months ago. His second wife, Joan, is also age 26. She is a high school teacher and has two children, Dan and Rick, by a former marriage. Dean is also a high school teacher, as was his first wife. Dean's employer provides $25,000 of group life insurance, complete health insurance and deposits an amount equal to 10 percent of Dean's salary each year in a pension plan. Dean has earned 24 quarters of Social Security coverage. His current estimated PIA is $500. Dean works in the

Exhibit 15.11
Dean Upson
Statement of Net Worth
(End of Last Year)

Cash in bank	$3,000
Car (mkt. value)	5,500
Pension	15,000
Total assets	23,500
Car loan	3,500
Net worth	20,000

Exhibit 15.12
Representative Life Insurance Rates
Nonparticipating Rates
Cash Value Projected, Not Guaranteed
(All Data per $1,000)

Dean Upson, Joan Upson, both age 26

Age	Term	Whole Life	Cash Value
26	1.89	8.10	0
27	1.89		1
28	1.90		3
29	2.08		4
30	2.10		5
31	2.12		7
32	2.14		8
33	2.16		13
34	2.20		19
35	2.27		26
36	2.38		34
37	2.52		43
38	2.68		52
39	2.87		62
40	3.08		72
41	3.31		83
42	3.57		93
43	3.86		107
44	4.18		118
45	4.53		130
46	4.92		142
47	5.34		155
48	5.81		165
49	6.33		180
50	6.90		196
51	7.53		212
52	8.21		225
53	8.96		245
54	9.79		267
55	10.70		290

summer for his brother, who owns and operates a construction company. This work will be available for the foreseeable future.

Dean's cash flow statement and statement of net worth for last year are shown in Exhibits 15.10 and 15.11.

Assignment

You are to develop a comprehensive financial plan for Dean and Joan Upson. Their goals include the following:
- Saving more money for a down payment on a house.
- Buying more life insurance if he needs it. Joan's former husband is not in a financial position to provide a college education for his and Joan's children. Dean and Joan assume they will have to educate these children and any born of their marriage. They have no plans for more children. Joan will continue working if Dean dies prematurely. Both Dean and Joan are insurable.

Dean's wife, Joan, earned $30,000 last year and received $7,200 in child support payments. Her children are ages three and five. At the time of her marriage to Dean she had neither financial assets nor liabilities.

1. Prepare a written financial report following the steps outlined in the chapter. The report should not exceed five pages.
2. Prepare a set of financial projections to accompany the written report. Be sure the written report and the financial projections are carefully integrated. Represented life insurance rates are found in Exhibit 15.12.
3. Assume inflation equals the most recent published annual rate.
4. Construct a line graph showing the Upsons' need for life insurance and a pie chart showing their current consumption pattern.

Review Questions

1. Why does the government provide a default financial plan for everybody?
2. Do most people you know engage in financial planning? Do you think home computers will have an effect on the amount of financial planning done?
3. Why is a knowledge of personal values needed in completing a financial plan?
4. What was the rate of inflation last year? Why is it important to factor inflation into personal financial plans?
5. Describe the alternative methods of financing a college education. What are the advantages of each method?

Endnotes

[1] For an extended discussion of personal property risk management, *see* M. S. Dorfman, *Introduction to Risk Management and Insurance,* 4th ed. (Englewood Cliffs, N.J.: Prentice-Hall, 1991).

[2] *See* Francis D. Burke, Jr., "Financial Planning," *Journal of the American Society of CLU & ChFC,* July 1990, p. 19, for technical details on holding U.S. savings bonds.

[3] *See* "The Rating Game," *Life Association News,* September 1991, for a thorough discussion of life insurance company financial ratings services.

Bibliography

Brenner, George D. "Coping with the Finances of Educating Children," *Journal of the American Society of CLU & ChFC* 44, March 1990, pp. 58–60.

Burke, Jr., Francis D. "Financial Planning." *Journal of the American Society of CLU & ChFC* 44, July, 1990, pp. 19–20.

Crowe, Robert M., ed. *Fundamentals of Financial Planning.* Bryn Mawr, Pa.: American College, 1990.

Lee, Keun Chang, and Stephen P. D'Arcy. "The Optimal Investment Strategy Through Variable Universal Life Insurance." *Journal of Risk and Insurance* 56, June 1989, pp. 201–217.

Leimberg, Stephan R., et al. *The Tools and Techniques of Financial Planning,* 3rd ed. Cincinnati: National Underwriter, 1988.

Lynch, J. Timothy. "How to Find the Right Insurer." *Journal of the American Society of CLU & ChFC* 41, July 1987, pp. 58–68.

Nordstrom, Kenneth V. "Financial Planning for Singles." *Journal of the American Society of CLU & ChFC* 44, July 1990, pp. 30–34.

Chapter 16 — Financial Planning: The Middle Years

Chapter Objectives

- Explain the difficulties of establishing retirement goals during middle age
- Describe the interplay of physical, psychological and family factors when making retirement plans
- Explain the calculations used to estimate the need for retirement funding
- Present information on the IRA and 403(b) plans used for retirement funding
- Illustrate preretirement financial planning with an annotated case study

Introduction

This chapter is about people in the middle of the financial life cycle. Their young adult years have passed, and their retirement period lies ahead. In general they are characterized by one or more of the following:

- The legal and financial independence of children
- The accumulation of significant amounts of financial assets or the lack of significant debt (depending on prevailing tax provisions and the relationship between the debt's cost and available investment returns), including a home mortgage
- Maximum career advancement and income

In the financial life cycle such a position is identified as the *preretirement planning period*. It generally occurs between the ages of 45 and 60.

Some aspects of retirement funding occur long before middle age. Participation in Social Security and employer-provided pension plans begins in the early stages of employment. However, sometimes during middle age the focus of financial planning changes from the concerns of early adult life to the concerns of middle life, with an emphasis on saving for retirement.

The evolution is a gradual one. Through a series of modifications to existing financial plans, emphasis shifts gradually as children get older and complete their education and as debts are repaid or financial assets accumulated. In modifying financial behavior to address this problem, the availability of savings and the proximity of retirement are key factors. Though individual financial circumstances are unique—not every person marries, remains married or rears children, for example—each person surviving to mid-life faces the problem of planning to finance a retirement period.

Several life insurance products are useful in funding retirement. The deferred annuity, for example, is designed for this purpose, and any cash value life insurance contract can be converted to an annuity if the protection is no longer needed. However, unlike funding premature death needs, where no good alternatives to life insurance exist, many other investments are effective in funding retirement. The annotated case study presented in this chapter illustrates the different cash flow patterns when a mutual fund and a deferred annuity are used as alternative approaches to funding retirement.

This chapter analyzes the preretirement financial planning process, including the roles of psychological, physical and family factors in setting financial goals. The chapter gives primary attention to calculating the amount of resources needed to finance the retirement period. The calculation involves integrating all sources of postretirement income with the estimated need for funds and then examining any estimated differences between funds available and funds required. The mid-life financial plan is designed to fill any projected gaps between available and required resources.

Solving the Problems of an Aging Society: Mid-life Concerns

While this chapter focuses on individual financial plans for retirement, attention also must be drawn to the societal problems that could affect people currently in the middle years of the financial life cycle. For example, the fact that the average age of Americans is increasing affects such things as the ratio of retired to active workers, demands made on the health care delivery system (especially long-term care) and the types of public services desired (parks versus schools for example). Each of these serious concerns deserves attention.

A second national problem is inadequate capital formation. If society as a whole saves less than necessary to maintain or improve its productive assets such as factories, roads and schools, the collective well-being of its members must decrease. The sector holding and investing society's savings (Social Security, private pension plans or individuals) determines how the savings are invested. A question of immediate concern is spending Social Security surpluses on current government operations. Current spending usually does not enhance the nation's asset base and leaves the economy less able to support an enlarged population of retired people. In contrast, individual or private pension investment in corporate securities could have a beneficial effect if corporations used the proceeds for new plants and equipment.

Third is the related problem of poor savings habits among Americans. Explanations for the recent trend of individuals failing to save significantly may be found in the tax code, the preference for immediate consumption or the substitution of anticipated private pensions and Social Security benefits for personal savings.

> The evidence is clear: The overwhelming bulk of the population does not save sufficiently for old age. Home equity accounts for the bulk of most people's wealth, but these assets are not readily or willingly converted to spendable funds as people grow older.[1]

Each of these problems is serious. Within the next decade or so, individuals and society must make choices with broad impact. How will society's scarce resources be distributed among the generations? How will savings be held? What role will government play in the provision of retirement income and health services? These questions will become increasingly crucial as the "baby boom" generation leaves the preretirement period it is now entering and begins to retire sometime after 2010.

Preretirement Financial Planning

Although the emphasis is shifting somewhat from funding premature death to funding retirement, the same general sequence of steps is followed for middle-years planning as for early-years planning. (To avoid duplication, however, this list and the description of the financial planning process are abbreviated versions of the material presented in Chapter 15.)

1. Collect and analyze data and other relevant information.
2. Specify financial goals.
3. Implement strategy.
4. Monitor and modify plan to meet changing circumstances and goals.

Step 1: Collect and Analyze Data and Other Relevant Information

Much of the financial information needed to develop a retirement plan is the same as that used to develop plans for premature death. A sound retirement funding plan requires:

- a statement of net worth and projections of cash flows;
- estimates of the amount and sources of retirement income, including Social Security, private pension or other employer-provided retirement benefits; and
- a review of existing legal documents, including wills, insurance contracts and business continuation arrangements.

Step 2: Specify Financial Goals

In many respects, specifying financial goals for retirement while a person is still in middle age is more difficult than developing financial goals during the early adult years. It is relatively easy to calculate the amount needed to repay a mortgage or fund a college education and to estimate the amount needed to maintain a family during the children's dependency. However, accurately estimating the amount needed to fund a retirement period is much more complex, in part because the length of the period remains indeterminate until close to life's end. Estimates of retirement needs made by a 50-year-old may involve expenditures planned for 40 years in the future.

The indeterminate length of the retirement period is not the only problem faced when a middle-aged person develops a retirement funding plan. Society has had little experience with the long periods of retirement estimated for the people retiring in the next several decades. (In recent years frequent and extensive congressional hearings have been held with much public comment as American society develops a national aging policy. The resulting printed proceedings provide a wealth of information about societal aspects of the aging problem.) The future may present new forms of retirement communities with new financial requirements for residency. Also, new opportunities may arise for the aged to work part-time or engage in expanded educational opportunities. Because future trends are difficult to anticipate, initial retirement plans should be flexible. Financial plans requiring early and regular savings for retirement—even if they later prove somewhat inaccurate—are better than no plans at all. An inadequately funded retirement can be an enduring disaster.

In summary, a person planning for retirement must solve the following problems:

- Estimating the length of life and future health status (and the same for a spouse where applicable)
- Forecasting the amount and sources of preretirement and postretirement income
- Predicting the amount and type of retirement expenses
- Estimating the age of retirement
- Gauging the impact of inflation on preretirement and postretirement finances
- Anticipating the possibility of dependent children or parents or both

Solving these problems is an imposing task, but these complex problems are not insurmountable. The following section suggests several useful considerations when developing solutions.

Step 3: Implement Strategy

After collecting and analyzing data and developing plans, the next step is to implement the plans. Plans (budgets) calling for saving must be followed. Investments must be made. Once set aside, money must be left to accumulate and not used for current consumption. Legal documents needed for business continuation agreements, life insurance or trusts must be in place. In small business firms employee benefit plans often must be installed or modified. An unimplemented financial plan is ineffective at least and self-deceptive at best.

Step 4: Monitor and Modify the Plan

The key word in preretirement financial planning is *flexibility*. Preretirement financial plans must be flexible to accommodate changes in financial status, health, marital status and goals. As significant changes occur, the plans must be adapted to fit the new circumstances.

Important Considerations in Specifying Financial Goals

The following four categories of factors play a role in setting goals for this period regardless of the many variations among individual preretirement financial plans.

- Physical factors
- Psychological factors
- Family considerations
- Financial considerations

Physical Factors

Many retired people retain much vigor in their later years. They are as capable of working, playing and thinking after age 65 as they were in middle life. Such vigor may be retained for long periods in retirement, thus creating the need for a long planning horizon. The false stereotype of aged invalids sitting around a TV set all day should not be the basis of financial plans for retirement.

Some people retire early because of physical impairments. Consequently their capabilities in retirement may be limited, their planning horizons relatively short and their needs for health-related expenditures above average. Because both current and estimated health status plays such a critical role in the amount and timing of the expenses expected in retirement, a planner should develop an estimate of the impact of these factors on each financial plan. It may be neither necessary nor possible to predict the exact number of years a person will live. Usually a prediction of the number of decades will suffice.

The types of goods and services consumed and the point in the retirement period at which the consumption takes place are often a function of physical capabilities, and such an estimate should be made where it is reasonable to do so.

In middle age it may be difficult to predict health during retirement, but the planner can get some clues by asking questions about the following subjects:

- Current health status (future health or health problems are usually contingent on current health)
- The longevity of parents (one generation's longevity is related to the previous generation's longevity)
- Marital status (married people tend to live longer)
- Economic status (higher income, better nutrition, better health care and longevity are positively correlated)
- Relationship of height to weight (significantly overweight people tend to live shorter lives and experience more health problems)
- Exercise pattern (people who have followed a regular exercise program tend toward increased longevity)
- Alcohol and tobacco consumption (both tend to reduce longevity and increase morbidity)
- Gender (females tend to live longer than males)

Because early predictions of life expectancy after retirement may prove inaccurate, the conservative approach dictates planning for a longer rather than a shorter period.

Figure 16.1 presents some U.S. Census Bureau estimates of retirement periods for living cohorts. Though these are group estimates that cannot be directly transferred to individuals, the data do provide some insight into expected retirement periods.

Psychological Factors: Motivation to Save for Retirement

Psychological factors are often as important as economic factors in understanding why some financial transactions, such as the purchase of life insurance, occur. As discussed in Chapter 2, some people find the contemplation of death distressing. Those who react similarly to contemplating retirement and old age will have difficulty with preretirement financial planning. Other people eagerly anticipate end-

Figure 16.1
Expected Retirement Periods: Life Expectancy at Age 65, 1900–2050

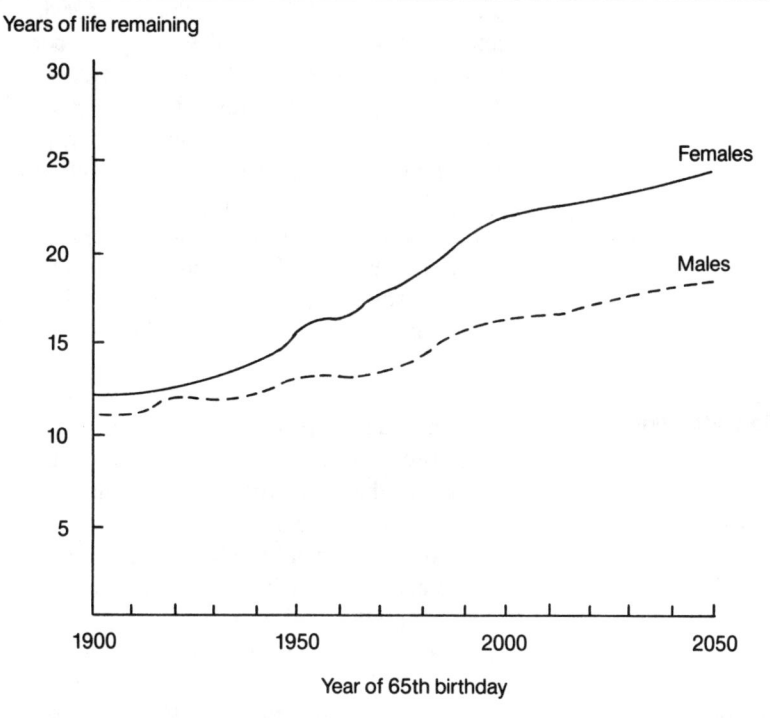

Source: Cynthia M. Taeuber, *America in Transition: An Aging Society,* Series of Current Population Reports, Series P-23, no. 128 (Washington, D.C.: U.S. Department of Commerce, Bureau of Census, September 1983), p. 5.

ing full-time employment and find pleasure in participating in preretirement financial planning. To ease anxiety and provide planning assistance, some employers regularly conduct preretirement seminars for their employees nearing retirement.

Some people are hard to motivate to plan for their retirement because they misunderstand what retirement will be like. They believe the period will be characterized by physical deterioration, loneliness and boredom. Other workers are hard to motivate because they fear loss of social status once active employment ends.

Getting young people to focus on financing their retirement, especially when the event is 30 or more years away, is a motivational chore. Young people often recognize the possibility of dying, and many can be convinced to plan for premature death. Funding a retirement period, however, may appear to be a remote problem for people age 45 or younger. Financial planners must always stress these two facts: (1) Reallocating consumption from the last 10, or even 20, years of a working career to a 20- to 40-year retirement period is a difficult financial problem. Retirement funding begun within 10 years of retirement is often bound to fail to provide adequate resources to maintain a standard of living comparable to that enjoyed before retirement. (2) The longer the planning period, the greater the ability of compound interest to increase assets. Stressing these facts is especially important in light of the overestimate by many individuals of the amount of benefits provided by Social Security or private pension plans. Even when combined, the retirement benefits of Social Security and company pensions often fall short.

In all cases a planner should be sensitive to the psychological implications of discussing aging and retirement. One or more courses in gerontology and familiarity with the literature of gerontology may prove invaluable in helping both planners and their clients make reasonable retirement plans. As society continues to age, public awareness of the possibility of long and successful retirement periods will assist the planner in motivating people to plan for retirement. Education and observing more people enjoying retirement should lower existing psychological barriers to making preretirement plans. However, in many current cases the financial planner must provide the needed education and motivation.

Family Considerations

Family considerations undoubtedly play a major role in the development of preretirement financial plans. Marital status is a particularly important consideration. Single people have greater freedom to move and a greater need to live in a retirement community than do married people because of the greater need for both companionship and health support in old age. People caring for dependent children or being cared for by their children may face geographic or financial constraints in preretirement planning. Sometimes people planning retirement may be caring for or planning care for their retired parents. The phenomenon of 60-year-olds caring for very old parents will become more prevalent as each successive cohort lives longer.

Financial Considerations

As is true in planning for the early adult years, a person's present financial circumstances in large part determine the starting point and the direction of retirement plans. However, planning during the preretirement period is more complex. Often more possibilities or alternatives exist when estimating future cash inflows and outflows. One or both spouses may plan to work full-time or part-time during the early retirement years. Retirement may be a difficult point to identify for some people if the term is defined as the "cessation of employment." Partial retirement may be especially appealing to the self-employed, who usually have more control over their choice to work than does the employee of a large corporation with a rigid retirement policy. (The *Age Discrimination in Employment Act* forbids mandatory retirement or other discrimination against older workers. However, corporate pension plans and corporate cultures are often keyed to the Social Security normal retirement age.) Farmers provide an example of an occupation where the exact point of retirement may be hard to identify because disengagement from work and from work-related income often is gradual.

Because a middle-aged person may be unsure of the amount and source(s) of retirement income, the planner may want to evaluate more than one set of assumptions. Using electronic spreadsheets, it is a simple task to construct several projections. But the problem of data overkill—losing the forest in the trees—serves as a constraint on the process.

Pension plan income may be expressed as a percentage of the salary earned in the years just before retirement. Social Security benefits are calculated using indexed career earnings. The amount of individual investments and the return earned on these investments are hard to estimate, as are the amount and timing of any inheritances or the amount and direction of intrafamily transfers. The impact of inflation on both income and expenses is difficult to estimate. Assuming constant inflation rates over long periods can greatly distort results.

Many different financial circumstances might affect a person in middle age or later. The emphatic point is that successful solutions to the retirement funding problem must begin early, must focus clearly on one or a few likely outcomes and must be flexible. Beginning early is more important than having the initial plans prove accurate.

Statement of Goals

Simultaneous consideration of the four categories of factors just presented (physical, psychological, family and financial) should lead to a set of reasonable and attainable financial goals for retirement. The goals must be quantified. They may be expressed as a dollar amount of assets to be available at the beginning of a retirement period or a dollar amount of income per month during retirement.

Replacement Ratios

Considerable discussion exists in the academic and professional employee benefits literature about the appropriate ratio of retirement to preretirement income. In the early 1980s the President's Commission on Pension Policy set forth a replacement ratio of 50 percent as a standard for pension plans. In recent years some actuarial studies have suggested using a 70 percent **replacement ratio** target.

While a replacement ratio may be a useful concept in pension plan design, it misses the mark as a basis for individual retirement funding. Retirement funding should be based on the preretirement standard of living, not on preretirement income. For many people it is preretirement expenses, not preretirement income, that determine postretirement expenses. For example, a person earning $60,000 a year but saving $10,000 for retirement while still enjoying a comfortable standard of living requires a different replacement ratio to maintain that standard of living from the person saving a greater or lesser percentage of preretirement income. Granted, one's preretirement standard of living depends on preretirement disposable income, and budgets are often expressed as a percentage of disposable income. However, neither of these facts should obscure the conclusion that maintaining the retiree's standard of living is the important goal, not replacing a given level of income.

The Role of Life Insurance in the Middle Years

Life insurance products can be used effectively to fund both premature death and retirement.

Premature Death Protection

While planning retirement finances should receive priority attention during middle age, plans for premature death or disability remain important. Even if children are educated and financially independent, mortgages and all other significant personal debts are repaid, some savings have been accumulated and income exceeds expenses by a good margin, financial problems associated with death or disability may remain.

In nearly all cases people need a final expense fund or death fund to cover the expenses of a last illness and all other death costs. Most people require emergency funds and adequate cash resources at death. Sometimes a debt retirement fund may be required to repay outstanding business debts. In other cases the financial future of dependent children, parents or a spouse with physical or mental problems is a concern. Such needs should be met by a dependent support fund backed by adequate life insurance.

Most of the needs just described are categorized as permanent needs. They do not diminish over time as did the majority of needs calculated for young adults. Solving these problems requires permanent life insurance.

Individual savings are likely to be greater in middle age than during the young adult period. Available savings reduce the need for life insurance. Social Security survivor benefits also meet a portion of the need for postdeath resources.

The most logical way to determine the amount of life or disability insurance needed during middle age is to construct a financial model similar to the models presented in the preceding chapter. As always, immediate death or disability is the foundational premise. Spreadsheet models of postdeath financial requirements can accommodate changes both in financial circumstances and in inflation estimates. Because the recommended approach to building a model for predeath or disability financing is the same for people in middle age as it is for young adults, no exhibits of the process are presented in this chapter.

Retirement Funding Insurance authorities recommend two categories of life insurance contracts to fund retirement income: cash value life insurance and annuities. Both types of contracts have the advantage of tax deferral on the "inside buildup." That is, the income earned on the investment portion of these contracts is not taxed until received. Moreover, if a life insurance policy is exchanged for an annuity at retirement, the deferred tax on the investment earnings is spread over the duration of the annuity receipts. The longer the tax deferral period, the greater is the tax advantage.

Explanations of cash value life insurance and annuities are given in Chapters 3, 4 and 5. Relevant tax considerations and examples are presented in Chapter 11. Logical comparisons to other investments are covered in Chapter 13. None of this material is repeated here. The focus of this chapter is defining and analyzing the retirement problem, not the tools used to solve the problem. Suffice it to note that life insurance products offer the advantage of safety and liquidity and often offer a competitive return commensurate with the high level of safety provided.

The IRA, Keogh Plan and Section 403(b) Plan

Individual Retirement Account (IRA)[2] Individual retirement accounts (IRAs) are designed to encourage people to save for retirement. Tax laws allow qualified people to make limited tax-deductible contributions and allow IRA accounts to earn tax-deferred investment income. Congress passed the original IRA provisions as part of the **Employment Retirement Income Security Act of 1974 (ERISA)**. Eligibility rules were broadened in 1982 and then restricted by the *Tax Reform Act of 1986* for tax years after December 31, 1986.

Tax rules current in 1991 distinguish between deductible and nondeductible IRA contributions. Deductible contributions can be made only by people in certain categories to be presented shortly. Other people can make nondeductible contributions. The advantage of making nondeductible contributions lies in the tax deferral accorded investment income.

The maximum limits on contributions are the same for deductible and nondeductible contributions. In general the maximum limits are $2,000 of *earned* income for each person, $4,000 of *earned* income for a two-earner married couple. (Complex rules apply to married couples filing separate returns.)

Eligibility for Deductible Contributions

In 1991 people in the following categories could make deductible IRA contributions for the tax year of 1990:

- Single people not covered by an employer-provided pension
- Married couples where neither spouse is covered by an employer-provided pension. (Special rules apply to married couples filing separate returns. One-earner married couples may contribute $2,250 on a deductible basis.)
- Single people having an adjusted gross income of $25,000 or less and married couples having adjusted gross incomes of $40,000 or less, who are covered by an employer-provided pension. (A phase-out of the deductible IRA contributions applies to single people with adjusted gross income between $25,000 and $35,000 and married couples with adjusted gross income between $40,000 and $50,000.)

☐ **Example**

Ralph Newton earned $25,000 in 1989. He wants to save $2,000 for his retirement. He is considering opening an IRA and uses the following mathematical model to evaluate the results.

	IRA	No IRA
Gross income	$25,000	$25,000
IRA contribution	2,000	0
Adjusted gross income	23,000	25,000
Personal exemption	(2,000)	(2,000)
Standard deduction	(3,100)	(3,100)
Taxable income	17,900	19,900
Income tax	(2,681)	(3,154)
Disposable income	15,219	16,746

If Ralph makes the IRA contribution, his disposable income is $15,219, but he has $2,000 in an IRA for a total of $17,219. This amount is greater than his disposable income if the IRA contribution is not made. However, if Ralph makes the IRA contribution, the taxes are deferred and not eliminated, so absolute dollar comparisons can be misleading. Also, if he makes the IRA contribution, Ralph cannot withdraw the money without penalty before age $59 1/2$. Because he is 55 now, the early withdrawal penalty is not troublesome. Younger people may feel differently. (It is possible to determine mathematically the break-even point between contributing to an IRA, withdrawing funds early and paying the penalty tax and opting for a non-tax-deferred alternative.)

Investment Alternatives

IRA funds must be held by qualified trustees or by a life insurance company. If a life insurance company holds the funds, the IRA contracts must be annuities, and no death benefit may be provided. Qualified trustees include banks, other savings institutions including federal credit unions, mutual funds and stock brokerages providing self-directed IRA accounts. Most of the investment alternatives provided by these institutions are available for IRA use. However, no collectible items (e.g., paintings, jewelry and baseball cards) can be used to fund IRAs.

Rollovers

Money may be placed in an IRA by a rollover. A **rollover** occurs when money from an IRA or another retirement plan is placed with a new trustee. For example, a rollover occurs if an investor takes IRA funds from one mutual fund and places them with another fund. Rollovers may occur when an employee switches jobs and takes vested retirement benefits from a pension plan or when an employer terminates a pension plan and makes payments of vested benefits to individual employees. If the employee takes the vested benefits and places them in an IRA, this transaction is considered a rollover. A rollover also would occur if a person switched from one investment medium to another, such as from a mutual fund to a bank. In general a person has 60 days to move funds from one IRA trustee to another without recognizing taxable income on the exchange.

Taxation

IRA withdrawals are taxed as ordinary income in the year received. Any portion of a payment attributed to a nondeductible contribution is not taxed a second time. In other words, only withdrawals of deductible contributions and tax-deferred interest are taxed.

In general age $59 1/2$ is the earliest time that withdrawals can be made without penalty. Early withdrawal from an IRA incurs a 10 percent tax penalty in addition to the ordinary income tax arising when the withdrawal is added to the person's taxable income. Exceptions to the premature withdrawal penalty exist in cases of death or disability before age $59 1/2$. Withdrawal of funds must begin by age $70 1/2$.

Simplified Employee Pensions (SEPs)

Some employers operate an employer IRA, also known as **simplified employee pension** plans. Employees participating in these plans receive immediate vesting of all sums contributed and may have some flexibility in directing the underlying investments. Vesting means the employee is irrevocably entitled to all the employer's contributions made to fund the employee's pension. In other pension plans an employee leaving employment before vesting is not entitled to the employer's contribution.

Keogh Plans

Keogh plans allow self-employed people to take a deduction from their adjusted gross income for money contributed to a retirement fund. These plans are also called *H.R.-10 Plans*.

Keogh plans are available to sole proprietors or active partners in a partnership. They are also available to full-time employees in other businesses who have their own business as a sideline. If the self-employed person has employees, they must be included in the plan.

Basically Keogh plans allow participants to contribute 25 percent of their earned income up to a $30,000 limit. However, self-employment earnings must be reduced by the amount of the Keogh contribution and the self-employment Social Security tax. These two reductions reduce the effective percentage limit to less than 20 percent of self-employment income before making the Keogh contribution. (The IRS provides a four-step format to calculate the maximum deductible Keogh contribution; the format is not reproduced here. Keogh plan administrators typically will calculate maximum contributions when plans are begun.[3]) Once a participant selects a contribution level, it must be continued each year if a money purchase plan is installed.

A profit-sharing Keogh plan allows contributions to vary. Profit-sharing plans limit contributions to 15 percent of earned income rather than the 25 percent limit applied to money purchase plans.

The assets accumulating in a Keogh plan must be held by a bank or any other independent custodian. The custodian typically provides all the forms needed to set up the account and either charges a flat annual fee or bases the fee on the amount of assets administered. Plans must be set up in writing before the end of the taxable year for which the deduction is claimed.

Distributions from Keogh plans must begin by age 70$\frac{1}{2}$. Minimum distributions must be based on life expectancies of the owner or over the joint life expectancy of the owner and spouse. Withdrawals from Keogh plans before age 59$\frac{1}{2}$ result in a tax penalty, except in cases of death or permanent disability.

Section 403(b) Plans[4]

Section 403(b) of the Internal Revenue Code establishes a plan for employees of specified nonprofit institutions to save for their retirement on a tax-advantaged basis. The plan was developed because nonprofit employers do not pay taxes and therefore do not benefit from tax deductions. Consequently Congress felt these employers did not have sufficient motivation to provide adequate pension programs.

Section 403(b) provides tax advantages and penalties similar to those associated with IRAs. Briefly, qualified contributions are made with before-tax dollars, investment income is tax-deferred until received and early withdrawal results in a 10 percent tax penalty in addition to any applicable ordinary income tax.

Covered Employees

Section 501 (c) (3) and Section 171 (b) (1) of the IRC specify employers eligible to operate 403(b) plans. The following categories of nonprofit, tax-exempt employers are among those eligible:

- Universities (public and private)
- State-operated educational institutions
- Hospitals
- Museums
- Parochial schools
- Religious organizations
- Zoos

The following categories of nonprofit employers are not eligible to establish 403(b) plans for their employees:

- Chambers of commerce
- Fraternal orders and associations
- Credit unions

Allowable Investments

When Congress passed the original enabling legislation in the 1950s only annuity contracts provided by life insurance companies were permitted as funding vehicles for 403(b) plans. Thus the plans became known as *tax-sheltered annuity plans (TSAs)* or *tax-deferred annuity plans (TDAs)*. Eligible annuity contracts include both fixed-benefit and variable annuities. ERISA broadened the allowable investments to include shares of mutual funds held in custodial accounts.

Contributions

Employees of eligible institutions are allowed to enter voluntary salary reduction agreements with their employer. When the agreement is effective, the employer contributes the money determined by the employee to the qualified carrier on the employee's behalf. The employer determines which carriers can operate a 403(b) program for their employees.

The funds are immediately vested in the employee. The employee, however, cannot pledge or assign the contract or otherwise realize funds from the arrangement except at retirement. In case of death or disability funds may be withdrawn without penalty.

The maximum amount an employee can contribute to a 403(b) plan is established in Section 415 of the IRC. This area is very complex, and generalizations are hazardous. Nevertheless, the basic limitation is a maximum of 20 percent of current salary times the number of years of prior service, less amounts previously contributed to retirement plans. Amounts less than the maximum may be contributed.

Taxation

All withdrawals, whenever made, must be added to taxable income in the year made. In the unlikely event that withdrawals include a portion of income from an after-tax contribution, no additional tax is due. Early withdrawals result in a 10 percent penalty imposed by the IRS. Insurance carriers and mutual funds also may impose their own penalties for early withdrawal. Withdrawals from a TDA in retirement are taxed as ordinary income. They are not afforded capital gains treatment.

Planning to Fund Retirement

Before the advent of the personal computer, building a financial model of the retirement period presented insurmountable problems. Making the required financial projections without an electronic spreadsheet is out of the question because the calculations involve long-range compounding and discounting of dissimilar cash flows. Because an initial projection made during middle age covers a long period, it is unlikely to prove accurate. The most important thing is for the initial model to be constructed carefully. If it is, subsequent changes can be incorporated easily. Thus it is the completeness and not the numerical accuracy of the initial model that is of greatest concern.

Constructing a preretirement financial plan requires projecting income, expenses and the gaps between them. Possible advances in health care or improvement in a person's health maintenance activities dictate that conservative estimates—long life spans—should be used in initial projections.

Income

Individuals enjoying high income in middle age are likely to have a greater variety and a greater amount of income in retirement than those less well off. Possible retirement income sources include the following categories:

- Continuing employment of the person or spouse
- Social Security benefits
- Employer-provided pension(s)
- Payments from IRAs or tax-deferred annuities
- Deferred-compensation arrangements
- Individual investment income
- Inheritances, trusts and royalties

Estimating income from these sources requires evaluating their likelihood of being received and of the impact of inflation on the estimate. Sophisticated approaches may be applied to discount these income flows, especially those that seem risky. As an alternative, the planner can prepare three budgets: "optimistic," "pessimistic" and "most likely." However, the problem of data overkill places a restraint on such practices.

Table 16.1
Percentage Analysis of Typical Retirement Budget

Part 1: Expenditures Categorized by Age

	65–74	Percent	75+	Percent
Avg. expenditure	$18,888	100%	$12,230	100%
Food	2,971	16%	2,104	17%
Housing	5,965	32%	4,521	37%
Clothes	1,035	5%	545	4%
Transportation	3,274	17%	1,394	11%
Health	1,688	9%	1,596	14%
Entertainment	873	5%	308	3%
All other	3,082	16%	1,762	14%
		100%		100%

Part 2: Expenditures Categorized by Income Level

	$10–15,000	Percent	$40,000+	Percent
Avg. expenditure	$15,076		$40,858	
Food	2,660	18%	5,478	13%
Housing	5,018	33%	10,363	25%
Clothes	768	5%	1,874	5%
Transportation	3,091	21%	7,565	19%
Health	1,718	11%	2,509	6%
Entertainment	466	3%	1,836	4%
All other	1,355	9%	11,233	28%
		100%		100%

Source: *Consumer Expenditure Survey, 1987,* Department of Labor, June 1990, Bulletin 2354. U.S. Doc L2.3: 2354.

Expenses

In the process of preparing an initial model during middle age, the amount and type of expenses a person will experience in retirement are difficult to estimate accurately. Guidance in preparing estimates is available from analysis of the expenditure pattern of the current cohort of retirees. Table 16.1 presents some relevant data.

The first part of Table 16.1 shows that the pattern of expenditures is not constant over the retirement period. People in their 60s, 70s and early 80s may find that travel and other leisure activities consume more of their income than people in their late 80s, 90s and older. Older people may find that health care costs and housing take an increasing percentage of their budget. People with impaired health have a different pattern of expenditures, regardless of age, than people in good health.

Part 2 of the table relates expenditures to the amount of retirement income available. In cases of either extreme poverty or extreme wealth this percentage analysis is not meaningful, but the breakdown can provide useful guidance in developing plans for average cases.

People living in nursing homes or retirement communities may find their pattern of expenditures determined in large part by their environment. During middle age it may be difficult to predict whether one will choose—or be forced by the impaired health of one or both spouses—to seek admission to a long-term care facility or another type of adult community. Thus there should be sufficient flexibility in plans prepared during middle age to allow for unforeseen contingencies.

Differences Between Income and Expenses

For many people projecting a retirement budget, the decline in income will be greater than the decline in expenditures. Filling any gaps requires reallocating consumption from the preretirement to the postretirement period. *Developing a reallocation strategy is the main function of preretirement financial planning.*

Predicting a decline in projected retirement income is based on historical analysis of general retirement income sources. For many people now retired, Social Security is the main (and often the only) source of income. Exclusive reliance on Social Security may not continue to be the case for future cohorts of retirees. Yet it appears that for many retirees Social Security will provide a substantial proportion of retirement income. Social Security is designed to provide less than half of a person's preretirement income for those at the lower income levels. The replacement ratio of retirement to preretirement income goes down as income increases. Future retirees can anticipate even lower replacement ratios as scheduled changes in the Social Security program take effect.

Many current workers will receive employer-provided pensions. (Chapters 18 and 19 cover employee benefit plans, including pensions.) The two basic types of private pension plans are called *defined benefit plans* and *defined contribution plans*. In a **defined benefit plan**, the output, which is the worker's benefit, is predetermined by formula, and the input, the employer's contribution, fluctuates. With defined benefit plans the worker's benefit can be projected fairly accurately before retirement takes place, because the benefit is based on a formula. A typical defined benefit formula might be 2 percent of the average wage in the highest five years of earnings multiplied by the number of years of covered service.

In **defined contribution plans** the inputs, the employer's contributions, are predetermined, and the output, which is the employee's pension, fluctuates. Projecting future benefits is more difficult with the defined contribution plan. An example of a defined contribution plan might involve the employer specifying it will contribute 6 percent of the employee's salary annually during the worker's employment period. Benefits are not guaranteed but are determined at retirement. During the accumulation period salaries vary, and so do investment results. Projecting a retirement benefit for a middle-aged employee may be educated guesswork until just before retirement.

What generalizations about gaps between income and outgo can be made? One is that a person's retirement expenditure pattern is related to the preretirement pattern. That is, in general, maintaining a standard of living costs a middle-income person more than a lower-income person and less than a higher-income person.

An Annotated Case Study: The Candlers

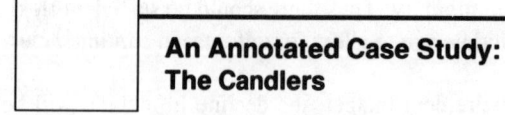

Facts and Data

George and Frances Candler of Milwaukee, Wisconsin, have been married for 32 years. Both are 55 years old. Both are active and healthy, and they enjoy golfing and sailing. They have three adult children, the youngest of whom is age 22. The two older children are married, and each couple has one child. The youngest Candler child is single. The Candler children all have had college educations and are pursuing promising careers.

George and Frances live in the house they have occupied for the past 30 years. They repaid their mortgage loan four years ago. The Candlers have no intention of selling the house, despite three unused bedrooms.

George is a manufacturer's representative for a medium-sized machine tools manufacturer. He makes extended sales trips one week of every month. In recent years roughly half his compensation has been salary and half commission income. George's commission income is cyclical, unlike his salary income, which has risen at a regular annual rate of 3 percent.

George is good at his job, and he enjoys it very much. However, he plans to retire at age 65. Frances currently is not employed, although she previously worked part-time as a real estate agent. In recent years her main area of interest outside her home has been volunteer work at the local public library, including service on the board of directors.

George's employer, Grinder Brothers Machine Tools, Inc., provides a pension with a formula benefit calling for 1.50 percent of an employee's average salary earned in the five years preceding retirement, for each year of covered employment. This formula requires calculating an average salary for the five years before retirement and multiplying it by the number of years worked for Grinder Brothers. If George retires on his 65th birthday, as planned, he will have 30 years of covered employment. Because about half his compensation has been commission and because commissions do not count in the pension benefit computation, George wants to develop a financial plan providing for an adequate income during retirement.

George currently has $50,000 in group life insurance that will remain in force only as long as he is employed. In addition, he has $50,000 of individually purchased whole life insurance. George feels he has adequate life insurance protection in light of his current family situation and needs.

Statement of Net Worth

The Candlers' statement of net worth, Exhibit 16.1, shows an accumulation of assets, no significant debt and a $227,000 net worth, more than half of which represents equity in their home. George has invested $1,000 a month in a balanced-growth mutual fund for the past three years and plans to contribute at this rate until retirement. He has accumulated a total of $45,000, and this makes him feel confident about his future retirement.

Projected Cash Flow Statements to Retirement

The projected cash flow statements, Exhibit 16.2, cover the years until George's planned retirement. The 1992 results reflect the actual cash flows through the Candlers' checking accounts and their income tax records. The projections in the years after 1992 are based on the following assumptions:

- The Candlers' consumption pattern remains similar to 1992.
- Inflation equals 6 percent annually.
- George's wages will increase at 3 percent annually.
- George's commissions are based on random events.

Exhibit 16.1
Candler Family
Statement of Net Worth
December 31, 1992

Personal property	$ 56,000
Home (market value)	120,000
Cash/checking	4,000
Mutual fund	45,000
Life insurance (cash value)	14,000
Total assets	239,000
Car loan/credit card balance	12,000
Net worth	227,000
Liabilities and net worth	$239,000

- George's mutual fund produces a 6 percent annual cash dividend and a 3 percent annual growth rate, for a total annual return of 9 percent. The total return rate ignores transaction costs but reflects an average return for growth common stock mutual funds. All savings are added to the mutual fund.

Comment: The 6 percent cash dividend appears in the "Investments" line of the income section. It is calculated by multiplying the ending balance in the mutual fund in the preceding year by .06.

The 3 percent growth factor is incorporated by multiplying the ending balance in the preceding year by .03 and adding this amount to the savings in a given year to calculate the ending balance for that year.

For example, the $88,263 ending balance in the mutual fund in 1995 is calculated by adding 3 percent of 1994's balance to the cash savings in 1995, then adding this total to the ending balance in 1994 ($2,183 + $13,316 + $72,764 = $88,263).

The investment income for 1995 is 6 percent of 1994's balance (.06 × $72,764 = $4,336).

The Candlers like to entertain and are members of a country club. They also drive over 15,000 miles each year to visit their children and grandchildren and for other pleasure purposes. Their housing costs are reduced as their mortgage loan was repaid four years ago.

Comment: "Disposable income" results from subtracting "total taxes" from "gross income." Taxes are a set percentage of taxable income. In practice taxes are likely to be a changing percentage as income grows or as tax laws change. This technicality is incorporated in a later exhibit.

The Candlers saved about $11,000 in 1992. With the children educated and the mortgage repaid, this is the most savings the Candlers have ever made. All savings went into the mutual fund. The Candlers plan to continue putting all their savings into this mutual fund as George is not interested in investment management and feels comfortable with the risks inherent in growth stocks.

When George and Frances reviewed Exhibit 16.2, they were excited and pleased as the results seemed realistic and showed them accumulating about $176,000 in savings before retirement. Exhibit 16.2 shows their spending increasing in years when George's commission income increases. In the "good" years the Candlers always purchase a new Chrysler New Yorker and take longer vacations, often going to the Caribbean in the winter.

Because the accumulated savings did not include their home equity, the Candlers were confident of their financial security in retirement. They knew they would be eligible for Social Security and Medicare besides receiving George's pension and the investment income from the mutual fund. They assumed they could continue their present life-style with little or no change. That is the assumption on which Exhibit 16.3, projected retirement budget, is built.

Projected Retirement Budget

The Candlers' projected retirement budget rests on the following assumptions:

Exhibit 16.2
Candler Family
Projected Income Statements Until Retirement

Assumptions	Inflation factor	6%
	Average wage increase	3%
	Investment return	6%

Year	1992 (actual)	1993	1994	1995	1996	1997	1998	1999	2000
George's age	56	57	58	59	60	61	62	63	64
Salary	30,000	30,900	31,827	32,782	33,765	34,778	35,822	36,896	38,003
Commissions	30,000	31,177	36,724	36,755	35,160	43,976	31,598	46,140	46,561
Investments	2,100	2,700	3,480	4,366	5,296	6,253	7,284	8,230	9,379
Gross income	62,100	64,777	72,031	73,903	74,221	85,007	74,704	91,267	93,943
Exemptions and deductions	(8,000)	(8,480)	(8,989)	(9,528)	(10,100)	(10,706)	(11,348)	(12,029)	(12,751)
Taxable income	54,100	56,297	63,043	64,375	64,121	74,301	63,355	79,238	81,193
Federal income tax	11,902	12,385	13,869	14,162	14,107	20,804	17,739	22,187	22,734
FICA	4,000	4,240	4,494	4,764	5,050	5,353	5,674	6,015	6,375
State/local	5,410	5,630	6,304	6,437	6,412	7,430	6,336	7,924	8,119
Property	2,200	2,332	2,472	2,620	2,777	2,944	3,121	3,308	3,506
Total taxes	23,512	24,587	27,140	27,984	28,346	36,531	32,870	39,433	40,735
Disposable income	38,588	40,190	44,891	45,918	45,875	48,476	41,834	51,834	53,208
Food	5,788	6,028	6,734	6,888	6,881	7,271	6,275	7,775	7,981
Transportation	6,174	6,430	7,183	7,347	7,340	7,756	6,693	8,293	8,513
Housing	1,929	2,009	2,245	2,296	2,294	2,424	2,092	2,592	2,660
Clothing	2,315	2,411	2,693	2,755	2,752	2,909	2,510	3,110	3,192
Entertainment	3,859	4,019	4,489	4,592	4,587	4,848	4,183	5,183	5,321
Charity	1,544	1,608	1,796	1,837	1,835	1,939	1,673	2,073	2,128
All other	5,788	6,028	6,734	6,888	6,881	7,271	6,275	7,775	7,981
Total	27,397	28,535	31,873	32,602	32,571	34,418	29,702	36,802	37,778
Savings	11,191	11,655	13,019	13,316	13,304	14,058	12,132	15,032	15,430
End. bal. mutual fund	45,000	58,005	72,764	88,263	104,215	121,399	137,173	156,320	176,440

Exhibit 16.3
Candler Family
Projected Retirement Budget

Assumptions		Inflation factor			6%								
		Pension adjustment			3%								
		Investment yield			6%								

Year	2001	2002	2003	2004	2005	2006	2007	2008	2009	2010	2011	2012	2013
George's age	65	66	67	68	69	70	71	72	73	74	75	76	77
Pension	16,134	16,618	17,116	17,630	18,159	18,703	19,265	19,843	20,438	21,051	21,682	22,333	23,003
Social Security													
George	4,800	5,088	5,393	5,717	6,060	6,423	6,809	7,217	7,650	8,109	8,596	9,112	9,659
Frances	2,400	2,544	2,697	2,858	3,030	3,212	3,404	3,609	3,825	4,055	4,298	4,556	4,829
Mutual fund	10,586	11,222	11,895	12,609	13,365	14,167	15,017	15,918	16,873	17,885	18,959	20,096	21,302
Cash inflow	33,921	35,471	37,101	38,814	40,614	42,506	44,495	46,587	48,787	51,101	53,535	56,097	58,793
Taxable gross	26,720	27,839	29,011	30,238	31,524	32,870	34,282	35,761	37,311	38,936	40,641	42,429	44,305
Ded. and exempt	(6,000)	(6,360)	(6,742)	(7,146)	(7,575)	(8,029)	(8,511)	(9,022)	(9,563)	(10,137)	(10,745)	(11,390)	(12,073)
Taxable income	20,720	21,479	22,270	23,092	23,949	24,841	25,770	26,739	27,748	28,800	29,896	31,039	32,232
Federal income tax	3,108	3,222	3,340	3,464	3,592	3,726	3,866	4,011	4,162	4,320	4,484	4,656	4,835
State/local	1,450	1,504	1,559	1,616	1,676	1,739	1,804	1,872	1,942	2,016	2,093	2,173	2,256
Property	3,506	3,717	3,940	4,176	4,427	4,692	4,974	5,272	5,589	5,924	6,280	6,656	7,056
Total	8,065	8,442	8,839	9,257	9,696	10,157	10,643	11,155	11,693	12,260	12,857	13,485	14,147
Disposable cash inflow	25,856	27,029	28,262	29,557	30,918	32,348	33,851	35,432	37,093	38,841	40,679	42,612	44,646
Food	8,460	8,968	9,506	10,076	10,681	11,108	11,552	12,014	12,495	12,995	12,995	12,995	12,995
Transportation	9,024	9,566	10,140	10,748	11,393	11,848	12,085	12,327	12,574	12,825	12,825	12,825	12,825
Housing	2,820	2,989	3,169	3,359	3,560	3,703	3,925	4,160	4,410	4,675	4,675	4,955	5,252
Clothing	3,384	3,587	3,802	4,030	4,272	4,443	4,710	4,992	5,292	5,609	5,609	5,946	6,303
Entertainment	5,640	5,978	6,337	6,717	7,120	7,405	7,850	8,321	8,820	9,349	9,349	9,910	10,505
Charity	2,256	2,391	2,535	2,687	2,848	2,962	3,140	3,328	3,528	3,740	3,740	3,964	4,202
All other	8,460	8,968	9,506	10,076	10,681	11,108	11,997	12,956	13,993	15,112	15,112	16,321	17,627
Health	2,500	2,650	2,809	2,978	3,156	3,282	3,479	3,688	3,909	4,144	4,393	4,656	4,936
Cash outflow	42,545	45,097	47,803	50,671	53,712	55,860	58,738	61,787	65,020	68,449	68,697	71,572	74,644
Shortfall	(16,688)	(18,068)	(19,541)	(21,114)	(22,793)	(23,512)	(24,886)	(26,356)	(27,927)	(29,608)	(28,019)	(28,960)	(29,998)
P.V. SHORTFALL	272,035												

Exhibit 16.3 (continued)

Year	2014	2015	2016	2017	2018	2019	2020	2021	2022	2023	2024	2025
George's age	78	79	80	81	82	83	84	85	86	87	88	89
Pension	23,693	24,404	25,136	25,890	26,667	27,467	28,291	29,139	30,014	30,914	31,841	32,797
Social Security												
George	10,238	10,852	11,503	12,194	12,925	13,701	14,523	15,394	16,318	17,297	18,335	19,435
Frances	5,119	5,426	5,752	6,097	6,463	6,850	7,261	7,697	8,159	8,648	9,167	9,717
Mutual fund	22,580	23,935	25,371	26,893	28,507	30,217	32,030	33,952	35,989	38,148	40,437	42,864
Cash inflow	61,630	64,617	67,762	71,074	74,561	78,235	82,105	86,183	90,480	95,008	99,781	104,813
Taxable gross	46,273	48,339	50,507	52,783	55,173	57,684	60,321	63,091	66,003	69,062	72,279	75,660
Ded. and exempt	(12,798)	(13,565)	(14,379)	(15,242)	(16,157)	(17,126)	(18,154)	(19,243)	(20,397)	(21,621)	(22,918)	(24,294)
Taxable income	33,475	34,773	36,127	37,541	39,017	40,558	42,167	43,849	45,605	47,441	49,360	51,367
Federal income tax	5,021	5,216	5,419	5,631	5,853	6,084	6,325	6,577	6,841	7,116	7,404	7,705
State/local	2,343	2,434	2,529	2,628	2,731	2,839	2,952	3,069	3,192	3,321	3,455	3,596
Property	7,479	7,928	8,403	8,908	9,442	10,009	10,609	11,246	11,920	12,636	13,394	14,197
Total	14,844	15,578	16,351	17,167	18,026	18,931	19,886	20,892	21,954	23,073	24,253	25,498
Disposable cash inflow	46,786	49,039	51,411	53,907	56,536	59,304	62,219	65,290	68,526	71,935	75,528	79,314
Food	12,995	12,995	12,215	11,482	10,793	10,146	9,537	8,965	8,427	7,921	7,446	6,999
Transportation	12,825	12,825	12,056	11,332	10,652	10,013	9,412	8,848	8,317	7,485	6,737	6,063
Housing	5,567	5,901	6,256	6,631	7,029	7,450	7,897	8,371	8,874	9,406	9,970	10,569
Clothing	5,672	5,105	4,595	4,135	3,722	3,350	2,345	1,641	1,149	804	563	394
Entertainment	11,135	11,803	12,511	13,262	14,057	14,901	15,795	11,846	8,885	6,663	4,998	3,748
Charity	4,454	4,721	5,004	5,305	5,623	5,960	6,318	6,697	7,099	7,525	7,976	8,455
All other	19,037	20,560	20,560	20,560	20,560	20,560	20,560	20,560	20,560	20,560	20,560	20,560
Health	5,232	5,546	5,878	6,231	6,605	7,001	7,421	7,867	8,339	8,839	9,369	9,931
Cash outflow	76,917	79,456	79,075	78,938	79,041	79,381	79,286	74,795	71,648	69,204	67,619	66,719
Shortfall	(30,131)	(30,417)	(27,664)	(25,031)	(22,506)	(20,078)	(17,066)	(9,504)	(3,122)	2,731	7,909	12,595

George's pension results from the Grinder Brothers' formula. Payments grow at an annual 6 percent rate. The pension payment growth is not guaranteed, but the Grinder Brothers have a well-earned reputation for treating their retired employees fairly. They have increased pension payments for their current retirees irregularly for the past several years, based on the availability of "excess" investment income in the pension trust.

Comment: Using an electronic spreadsheet, the pension benefit is calculated as follows: ".45 * (@avg(L11...L16))". In practice a linked spreadsheet addressing the last five years of wage income was used on Exhibit 16.2. The alternative is to build Exhibit 16.3 to the right of 16.2. The .45 is the result of the pension formula calling for 1.5 percent of wage income for each year worked, in this case 30 years.

George's Social Security retirement income is based on an estimate received from the Social Security Administration. Frances's own retirement benefit is less than 50 percent of George's benefit because she worked part-time only after their youngest child was in eighth grade. Therefore she receives a Social Security benefit based on George's earnings.

Comment: Both Social Security benefits are indexed for inflation. The formula in cell D6 is "+C6 * (1 + F3), where F3 is the absolute address of the inflation factor. Writing the formula in this fashion allows changing all projections, including an inflation factor in F3, with one entry.

The income from investments is calculated by assuming a 6 percent return on the preceding year's ending balance in the mutual fund. In retirement the Candlers planned to spend the income from the fund but not reduce the principal.

Taxable gross income does not include Social Security benefits. Current law calls for taxing half a recipient's Social Security benefit once income exceeds a specified threshold. This complication was not built into Exhibit 16.3. Federal income tax exemptions are increased for people over age 65. In the Candlers' case the increased exemptions are more than offset by reduced itemized deductions. Specifically the federal deduction for state and local income taxes will be significantly less when the Candlers' income drops in retirement.

Expenses in retirement at first follow the pattern existing just before retirement, including an adjustment for inflation. However, after a while, food, transportation, clothing and entertainment expenses decline, while health expenses increase. Because of the Candlers' current good health the pattern of decline in expenses is gradual until they reach age 85.

The result of these calculations is projected expenses in excess of income for all the retirement years. These excess expenses have a present value of $272,035. This figure represents the lump sum needed to fund the deficits if the remaining balance earns exactly 6 percent.

The Candlers are surprised and concerned when they review the projected retirement budget with a shortfall more than double their projected savings. They realize some changes in their preretirement and postretirement plans are necessary if they are to maintain a postretirement standard of living comparable to that enjoyed during George's working years.

Retirement Funding with Deferred Annuity

A review of the retirement budget's projected outcome made clear to the Candlers that their preretirement plans needed changes. Their financial planner recommended two significant changes. First, the planner recommended purchasing a **deferred annuity** with their preretirement savings accumulation. Second, the planner recommended modifying their preretirement consumption plans to increase savings.

Annuity Purchase

Purchasing a series of single-premium deferred annuities increases accumulated savings from $176,440, shown in Exhibit 16.2 to $250,222, shown in Exhibit 16.4.

Comment: The $250,222 referred to in Exhibit 16.4 is the total of the balance in the annuity account, which is assumed to grow at 6 percent per year, and the balance in the mutual fund, assumed to be growing at 3 percent a year, plus paying a 6 percent annual dividend shown as investment income. Because the mutual fund begins at $45,000 after 3 percent growth for eight years, it has an ending balance of $57,004.

The formula used for computing the annuity balance in cell E47 is (D47 * (1 + E8)) + E46, where E8 is the absolute address of the investment rate of return and E46 is the annual net cash flow. The 6 percent growth in the annuity is the "guaranteed" rate, which is likely to be exceeded in actual results, making these estimates conservative.

Exhibit 16.4
Candler Family
Projected Income Statements Until Retirement: Revised

Assumptions	Inflation factor	6%
	Average salary increase	3%

Year	1992	1993	1994	1995	1996	1997	1998	1999	2000
	(actual)								
George's age	56	57	58	59	60	61	62	63	64
Salary	30,000	30,900	31,827	32,782	33,765	34,778	35,822	36,896	38,003
Commissions	30,000	31,177	36,724	36,755	35,160	43,976	31,598	46,140	46,561
Investments	2,100	2,226	2,360	2,501	2,651	2,810	2,979	3,158	3,347
Gross income	62,100	64,303	70,911	72,038	71,576	81,564	70,398	86,194	87,911
Exemptions and deductions	(8,000)	(8,480)	(8,989)	(9,528)	(10,100)	(10,706)	(11,348)	(12,029)	(12,751)
Taxable Income	54,100	55,823	61,922	62,510	61,477	70,859	59,050	74,165	75,160
Federal income tax	11,902	12,281	13,623	13,752	13,525	17,715	12,991	18,541	18,790
FICA	4,000	4,240	4,494	4,764	5,050	5,353	5,674	6,015	6,375
State/local	5,410	5,582	6,192	6,251	6,148	7,086	5,905	7,416	7,516
Property	2,200	2,332	2,472	2,620	2,777	2,944	3,121	3,308	3,506
Total taxes	23,512	24,435	26,781	27,387	27,500	33,098	27,691	35,280	36,188
Disposable income	38,588	39,868	44,129	44,651	44,077	48,467	42,708	50,914	51,723
Food	5,788	5,183	5,737	5,805	5,730	6,301	5,552	6,619	6,724
Transportation	6,174	4,784	5,296	5,358	5,289	5,816	5,125	6,110	6,207
Housing	1,929	1,993	2,206	2,233	2,204	2,423	2,135	2,546	2,586
Clothing	2,315	1,993	2,206	2,233	2,204	2,423	2,135	2,546	2,586
Entertainment	3,859	3,189	3,530	3,572	3,526	3,877	3,417	4,073	4,138
Charity	1,544	1,595	1,765	1,786	1,763	1,939	1,708	2,037	2,069
All other	5,788	3,987	4,413	4,465	4,408	4,847	4,271	5,091	5,172
Total	27,397	22,725	25,154	25,451	25,124	27,626	24,343	29,021	29,482
Net cash flow	11,191	17,143	18,976	19,200	18,953	20,841	18,364	21,893	22,241
Annuity		17,143	37,147	58,576	81,043	106,747	131,516	161,300	193,218
Mutual fund	45,000								57,004
Total financial assets									250,222

Exhibit 16.5
Candler Family
Projected Retirement Budget: Revised

Assumptions				
Inflation factor			6%	
Pension adjustment			3%	
Investment yield			6%	

Year	2001	2002	2003	2004	2005	2006	2007	2008	2009	2010	2011	2012
George's age	65	66	67	68	69	70	71	72	73	74	75	76
Pension	16,134	16,618	17,116	17,630	18,159	18,703	19,265	19,843	20,438	21,051	21,682	22,333
Social Security												
George	4,800	5,088	5,393	5,717	6,060	6,423	6,809	7,217	7,650	8,109	8,596	9,112
Frances	2,400	2,544	2,697	2,858	3,030	3,212	3,404	3,609	3,825	4,055	4,298	4,556
Mutual fund	3,420	3,625	3,843	4,073	4,318	4,577	4,851	5,142	5,451	5,778	6,125	6,492
Annuity	13,500	13,500	13,500	13,500	13,500	13,500	13,500	13,500	13,500	13,500	13,500	13,500
Cash inflow	40,254	41,375	42,549	43,778	45,066	46,415	47,829	49,311	50,864	52,493	54,201	55,993
Taxable gross	33,054	33,743	34,459	35,203	35,976	36,780	37,616	38,485	39,389	40,329	41,307	42,325
Ded. and exempt	(10,000)	(10,600)	(11,236)	(11,910)	(12,625)	(13,382)	(14,185)	(15,036)	(15,938)	(16,895)	(17,908)	(18,983)
Taxable income	23,054	23,143	23,223	23,293	23,352	23,398	23,431	23,449	23,450	23,434	23,399	23,342
Federal income tax	4,611	4,629	4,645	4,659	4,670	4,680	4,686	4,690	4,690	4,687	5,148	5,135
Fed. tax rate	20%	20%	20%	20%	20%	20%	20%	20%	20%	20%	22%	22%
State/local	1,614	1,620	1,626	1,631	1,635	1,638	1,640	1,641	1,642	1,640	1,638	1,634
Property	3,506	3,717	3,940	4,176	4,427	4,692	4,974	5,272	5,589	5,924	6,280	6,656
Total taxes	9,731	9,966	10,210	10,466	10,732	11,010	11,300	11,604	11,921	12,252	13,065	13,426
Disposable cash inflow	30,523	31,409	32,339	33,313	34,334	35,405	36,529	37,707	38,944	40,242	41,136	42,567
Food	7,127	7,555	8,008	8,489	8,998	9,538	9,920	10,316	10,729	11,158	11,158	11,158
Transportation	6,579	6,974	7,392	7,836	8,306	8,804	8,981	9,160	9,343	9,530	9,530	9,530
Housing	2,741	2,906	3,080	3,265	3,461	3,669	3,889	4,122	4,369	4,631	4,631	4,909
Clothing	2,741	2,906	3,080	3,265	3,461	3,669	3,889	4,122	4,369	4,631	4,631	4,909
Entertainment	4,386	4,649	4,928	5,224	5,537	5,870	6,222	6,595	6,991	7,410	7,410	7,855
Charity	2,193	2,325	2,464	2,612	2,769	2,935	3,111	3,298	3,495	3,705	3,705	3,927
All other	5,483	5,812	6,160	6,530	6,922	7,337	7,924	8,558	9,243	9,982	9,982	10,781
Health	2,500	2,650	2,809	2,978	3,156	3,346	3,546	3,759	3,985	4,224	4,477	4,746
Cash outflow	33,751	35,776	37,923	40,198	42,610	45,167	47,480	49,930	52,524	55,272	55,526	57,816
Shortfall	(3,299)	(4,367)	(5,584)	(6,885)	(8,276)	(9,761)	(10,952)	(12,223)	(13,580)	(15,031)	(14,390)	(15,249)

P.V. SHORTFALL 132,279

Exhibit 16.5 (continued)

Year	2013	2014	2015	2016	2017	2018	2019	2020	2021	2022	2023	2024	2025
George's age	77	78	79	80	81	82	83	84	85	86	87	88	89
Pension	23,003	23,693	24,404	25,136	25,890	26,667	27,467	28,291	29,139	30,014	30,914	31,841	32,797
Social Security													
George	9,659	10,238	10,852	11,503	12,194	12,925	13,701	14,523	15,394	16,318	17,297	18,335	19,435
Frances	4,829	5,119	5,426	5,752	6,097	6,463	6,850	7,261	7,697	8,159	8,648	9,167	9,717
Mutual fund	6,882	7,295	7,732	8,196	8,688	9,209	9,762	10,348	10,968	11,627	12,324	13,064	13,847
Annuity	13,500	13,500	13,500	13,500	13,500	13,500	13,500	13,500	13,500	13,500	13,500	13,500	13,500
Cash inflow	57,872	59,845	61,915	64,087	66,369	68,764	71,280	73,923	76,699	79,617	82,684	85,907	89,296
Taxable gross	43,385	44,488	45,636	46,832	48,078	49,376	50,729	52,138	53,608	55,140	56,738	58,405	60,144
Ded. and exempt	(20,122)	(21,329)	(22,609)	(23,966)	(25,404)	(26,928)	(28,543)	(30,256)	(32,071)	(33,996)	(36,035)	(38,197)	(40,489)
Taxable Income	23,263	23,158	23,027	22,867	22,674	22,448	22,185	21,882	21,536	21,144	20,703	20,207	19,655
Federal income tax	5,118	5,095	8,998	9,333	9,682	10,045	10,424	10,819	11,230	11,659	12,107	12,573	13,060
Fed. tax rate	22%	22%	28%	28%	28%	28%	28%	28%	28%	28%	28%	28%	28%
State/local	1,628	1,621	1,612	1,601	1,587	1,571	1,553	1,532	1,508	1,480	1,449	1,415	1,376
Property	7,056	7,479	7,928	8,403	8,908	9,442	10,009	10,609	11,246	11,920	12,636	13,394	14,197
Total Taxes	13,802	14,195	18,538	19,337	20,177	21,059	21,986	22,960	23,984	25,060	26,192	27,382	28,634
Disposable cash inflow	44,070	45,650	43,377	44,750	46,192	47,705	49,294	50,963	52,715	54,557	56,492	58,525	60,662
Food	11,158	11,158	11,158	10,489	9,859	9,268	8,712	8,189	7,698	7,236	6,802	6,394	6,010
Transportation	9,530	9,530	9,530	8,958	8,421	7,916	7,441	6,994	6,575	6,180	5,562	5,006	4,505
Housing	5,204	5,516	5,847	6,198	6,570	6,964	7,382	7,825	8,294	8,792	9,319	9,878	10,471
Clothing	5,204	4,683	4,215	3,794	3,414	3,073	2,766	1,936	1,355	949	664	465	325
Entertainment	8,326	8,826	9,355	9,917	10,512	11,142	11,811	12,519	9,390	7,042	5,282	3,961	2,971
Charity	4,163	4,413	4,678	4,958	5,256	5,571	5,905	6,260	6,635	7,033	7,455	7,903	8,377
All other	11,643	12,574	13,580	13,580	13,580	13,580	13,580	13,580	13,580	13,580	13,580	13,580	13,580
Health	5,030	5,332	5,652	5,991	6,351	6,732	7,136	7,564	8,018	8,499	9,009	9,549	10,122
Cash outflow	60,259	62,033	64,016	63,885	63,963	64,246	64,732	64,867	61,545	59,311	57,673	56,737	56,362
Shortfall	(16,189)	(16,384)	(20,640)	(19,135)	(17,771)	(16,541)	(15,438)	(13,905)	(8,829)	(4,754)	(1,182)	1,789	4,300

One reason the Exhibit 16.4 savings are greater than the amount shown in Exhibit 16.2 is that the annuity accumulation includes the deferred taxes and the income earned on the deferred taxes. Because the planner recommends that the Candlers annuitize the savings in retirement, using a joint-and-one-half survivor annuity, the cash flow in retirement also will be significantly greater than the investment income shown in Exhibit 16.3. In fact the increase in cash flow, when combined with the second recommended change, reduces by about half the deficit predicted in the original retirement budget.

The Candlers realize purchasing the annuity means the funds they would have passed to their children will be smaller than if they retained the undepleted mutual fund investment as originally planned. They also realize that their equity in their home, the face value of the life insurance, the mutual fund investment and other assets will be available for bequests. They feel the security provided by the annuity is more important than leaving a large estate, because their children are grown and financially independent.

Modifying Consumption

The planner also recommended that current consumption during the preretirement years should be reduced about 15 percent. The Candlers felt this reduction could be achieved by eating out less frequently, taking fewer trips each year and adding one year to the average time they traded automobiles. None of these changes greatly altered their life-style or interfered with their current activities.

Two advantages arise when the Candlers modify their consumption. First, annual savings increase substantially. Second, by reducing their preretirement consumption they have a lower level of consumption to support during retirement. The Candlers agree that a moderate change in preretirement consumption is more desirable than an abrupt change at or after retirement.

They are satisfied with the revised retirement budget presented in Exhibit 16.5.

Conclusion

Exhibit 16.5 shows a projected retirement budget for the Candlers revised to include the annuity income and the modified consumption pattern introduced in Exhibit 16.4.

The most conspicuous comparison between Exhibit 16.3 and Exhibit 16.5 is that the present value of the deficit is reduced from $247,494 to about $132,000. This estimate pleases the Candlers. Though a deficit remains, it is mostly offset by the Candlers' home equity. Also, this exhibit relies on a conservative estimate of annuity income, as will be explained shortly.

The income amounts shown in Exhibit 16.3 and Exhibit 16.5 differ substantially. In Exhibit 16.3 the mutual fund yields 6 percent, and capital gains increases the fund balance annually by an additional 3 percent, for a 9 percent annual compounded rate of return. In Exhibit 16.5 the dividend yield on the mutual fund is much less because no additional contributions are made after 1991. Instead, all the Candlers' savings are used to purchase an annuity.

Comment: The mutual fund income shown in the year 2001 is 6 percent of the ending balance in the mutual fund in the year 2000 (.06 × $57,004 = $3,420). Technically we should show the mutual fund balance increasing annually at a 3 percent rate, which would increase the annual income slightly more than the 6 percent shown. This complexity has not been added to the model.

The annuity income illustrated is for a joint-and-one-half survivor fixed-benefit annuity. Not all the annuity's cash flow is subject to income tax. Only the accumulated investment earnings, not the return of principal, are taxable. (Chapter 11 describes the mechanics of annuity taxation.) The excluded cash flow increases the Candlers' "ded. and exempt" amount in the tax calculation. Also note that an irregularly increasing average federal tax rate is incorporated, as shown in the table. As taxable income increases in a progressive tax scheme, the average tax rate also increases. The federal income tax rules current in 1991 involve disappearing itemized deductions for certain high-income people. We have not overly complicated the tax estimates to allow for this technicality.

In the projection the annuity benefit is constant. In practice it is likely that the benefit will grow, because the insurer will pay increased benefits if it earns "excess interest" beyond the guaranteed amount illustrated. Using a fixed-benefit illustration makes the projection more conservative. It is likely that the cash outflow deficits shown lasting through age 81 will be offset by increased annuity income.

☐ Practice Cases

The Walker Case

William and Susan Walker are 47 and 44 respectively. William is a pilot for a large commercial airline. Susan has not been employed outside their home since their first child, Matthew, was born 17 years ago. They have two younger children, Michael, age 15, and Debbie, age 10.

Because William has a considerable amount of free time when he isn't flying, he has a second job with a real estate firm as a part-time broker. He also owns and manages a six-unit apartment building, purchased last year. William's real estate income is quite cyclical and should be represented by relatively random increases and decreases.

The Walker cash flow statement and statement of net worth appear in Exhibits 16.6 and 16.7. You are to develop a comprehensive financial plan for the Walkers, with special emphasis on the retirement period.

Both William's and Susan's parents are still alive and in good health. William's parents, both of whom are age 71, will need $500 each month in financial support from William, who is an only child. William plans to provide this support for his parents once his children complete their college education. Thus far a small pension and Social Security benefits have allowed William's parents a modestly comfortable retirement, but their entire savings are in their house, estimated to be worth about $50,000.

William and Susan are in good health. They belong to a country club and exercise regularly. Their children are all healthy. All plan to go to college. William is both fully insured and disability-insured for Social Security, and his salary has been above the maxi-

Exhibit 16.6
The Walkers' Cash Flow Statement (Last Year)

Income	
Pilot's salary	$ 95,000
Investment income	5,000
Real estate commissions	15,000
Apartment net income	25,000
Taxable Gross Income	140,000
Taxes (federal, state, local income, FICA, personal property and real estate produce an average tax rate of 32% of taxable gross income)	(44,800)
Disposable Income	95,200
Expenses	
Food	14,000
Entertainment	9,000
House	14,000
Clothes	7,000
Transportation	14,000
Health	4,500
Vacation	5,000
Contributions	4,000
All other	9,000
Total Expenses	80,500
Savings	$ 14,700

Exhibit 16.7
The Walkers' Statement of Net Worth (End of Last Year)

Assets	
House (market value)	$200,000
Cars (three)	27,000
Apartment bldg.	350,000
Common stocks	65,000
Cash in bank and money market fund	15,000
Total assets	657,000
Liabilities	
Home mortgage loan	82,394
Apartment bldg. loan	293,999
Total liabilities	376,393
Net worth	280,607
Total liabilities and net worth	$657,000

Notes:
1. The home was purchased 10 years ago for $135,000. Mortgage terms were a 20-year loan, 10 percent interest and a 20% down payment.
2. The apartment building was purchased for $350,000 last year. It is fully rented to college students and is located six blocks from a large branch campus of the state university. The apartment loan calls for a 15 percent down payment, 12 percent fixed rate of interest and a 25-year loan.
3. William's pension is calculated by a formula calling for 2 percent of final salary for each year of service. William will have 25 years of covered service when he plans to retire at age 60. The pension is *not* indexed for inflation. William's pay raises have kept pace with inflation.
4. William currently has $100,000 of individual whole life insurance. He also has $100,000 of group term life insurance, which remains in force until retirement.
5. William has a 15-year-old will giving all his property to Susan. Susan has no will.

---

mum covered wage for the past 15 years. William's Social Security PIA is estimated to be $700 and will keep pace with inflation.

When asked to specify some important financial goals, the Walkers developed the following list:

- Provide college education for three children, graduate school if needed.
- Purchase a summer home or condominium.
- Retire at age 60.
- Be prepared to support William's parents if needed.

Assignment

You are to develop a financial plan for the Walkers. (A table with monthly annuity installments is included at the end of the practice cases.)

1. You are to write a cover letter analyzing and explaining their current financial situation.
2. You are to develop a retirement plan based on their current consumption pattern.
3. You are to analyze their current insurance program (assignment optional with instructor).
4. You are to recommend any changes you feel will improve the Walkers' financial plans.

The Smith Case

Ellen Smith is a vice president of a large hotel chain with its headquarters in New York. She earned an MBA from a well-respected school. She is a very effective administrator, is well liked and feels she has very good possibilities for advancement. Ellen is 54 and has always been single. She is an avid scuba diver and travels around the world collecting large seashells and other underwater specimens. She has made several donations of live specimens to the city aquarium and serves on its board of directors. (She receives no compensation as a board member.) Her only living relative is her younger brother, Donald, who is married and has two teenage children. In most years she spends the Christmas holiday with

Exhibit 16.8
Ellen Smith: Cash Flow Statement (Last Year)

Income	
Salary	$75,000
Dividends and interest	12,000
Gross income	87,000
Deductions and exemptions	(10,000)
Adjusted gross income	77,000
Taxes (all, marginal rate = 35%)	27,000
Disposable Income	60,000 (87,000 − 27,000)
Expenses	
Food	6,000
Rent	9,000
Transportation	4,000
Travel	10,000
All other	14,000
Total expenses	43,000
Savings	17,000 (60,000 − 43,000)
Total expenses and savings	$60,000

her brother. She gets along well with Donald and loaned him $10,000 as part of a down payment on a house. Donald lives on the West Coast, while Ellen lives in New York.

Ellen has an average earnings record for Social Security, but her income has increased rapidly in the past ten years. Fifteen percent of her income in recent years came from an annual bonus. The bonus is based on her employer's profitability, which is quite variable. Ellen's Social Security PIA currently is estimated to be $600 and will keep pace with inflation.

She has no current plans for retirement but began

Exhibit 16.9
Ellen Smith: Statement of Net Worth (End of Last Year)

Assets	
Mutual fund—growth	$ 50,000
Common stock portfolio	65,000
Cash, CDs, money market fund	40,000
Loan to brother	10,000
Total assets	165,000
Liabilities	0
Net worth	$165,000

Notes:
1. Donald has made no repayments on the loan, and it is understood that he will not do so until he can afford it or Ellen needs the money. It is most unlikely that Donald will be able to repay the loan as he has been unemployed or partially employed several times in the past few years. His employment prospects are not good, but he is presently working full-time.
2. Ellen expects a pension of about one-half her salary at retirement, which she believes will be at 65. She expects average Social Security benefits.
3. Ellen has no individual life insurance, but she is insurable at standard rates. She has $100,000 of group term life insurance. Donald is her beneficiary.
4. Ellen has a will naming her brother and his family as sole and contingent beneficiaries.

Exhibit 16.10
Monthly Annuity Installments per $1,000 of Deposit*

Male

Age	Life Income	10 Yrs Certain	20 Yrs Certain	Cash Refund
60	5.91	5.68	5.10	5.30
61	6.06	5.80	5.16	5.40
62	6.22	5.93	5.21	5.51
63	6.39	6.07	5.27	5.63
64	6.58	6.21	5.33	5.75
65	6.77	6.35	5.38	5.88
66	6.99	6.50	5.43	6.02
67	7.21	6.66	5.48	6.16
68	7.46	6.83	5.52	6.32
69	7.72	7.00	5.56	6.48
70	8.00	7.17	5.60	6.65
75	9.79	8.07	5.72	7.68
80	12.44	8.93	5.75	9.10

Female

Age	Life Income	10 Yrs Certain	20 Yrs Certain	Cash Refund
60	5.27	5.17	4.87	4.94
61	5.40	5.28	4.94	5.03
62	5.53	5.40	5.01	5.14
63	5.67	5.52	5.08	5.24
64	5.82	5.66	5.15	5.36
65	5.98	5.80	5.22	5.48
66	6.16	5.95	5.28	5.61
67	6.36	6.10	5.35	5.75
68	6.57	6.27	5.40	5.89
69	6.80	6.45	5.46	6.05
70	7.04	6.63	5.51	6.21
75	8.66	7.64	5.68	7.21
80	11.16	8.64	5.74	8.55

*Joint-and-survivor annuity tables present hundreds of combinations of male and female ages and installments, which cannot be presented here.

to invest in the stock market several years ago. She owns only safe utility and other blue chip stocks. She does not feel comfortable with risky investments.

Ellen's goals include helping her brother provide college educations for her nieces, of whom she is very fond. She also wants to continue her current consumption pattern in retirement, including the possibility of doing more travel than she had been able to do during her working years.

Assignment

Based on her cash flow statement, shown in Exhibit 16.8, and her statement of net worth, shown in Exhibit 16.9, you are to develop a financial plan for Ellen Smith.

1. You are to write a cover letter analyzing and explaining Ellen Smith's current financial situation.
2. You are to develop a retirement plan based on her current consumption pattern. This plan should include providing $10,000 a year for her nieces' college education. The oldest niece is now 15 and the youngest is 13.
3. You are to analyze her current insurance program (assignment optional with instructor).
4. You are to recommend any changes you feel will improve her financial plans.

Review Questions

1. What financial characteristics distinguish the middle years of adult life?
2. What are the problems that arise when a 50-year-old begins to develop a set of preretirement financial goals? How does the financial planner deal with these problems?
3. Describe the role of physical factors, psychological factors, family considerations and financial considerations in developing financial plans.
4. Describe the most likely needs for life insurance in the middle years.
5. Do you believe the expenditure pattern in retirement will differ from the preretirement pattern? Do you think there will be differences in the consumption pattern throughout the retirement period? Describe some of these differences.
6. What are the characteristics of the investments that are most appropriately used to fund retirement? What trade-offs must be made when choosing a retirement investment?
7. Why is tax deferral an important consideration when funding retirement income?
8. What are the important characteristics of an IRA? TDA?
9. Explain why you think the Candlers have or do not have sufficient life insurance.
10. What role did an IRA play in the Candlers' financial plan?

Endnotes

[1] Schulz, J. H., *The Economics of Aging*, 4th ed. Dover, Mass.: Auburn House Publishing Co., 1988, p. 253.

[2] For a comprehensive discussion and explanation of this complex subject, *see* N. H. Tarver and A. L. Mortensen, *IRA Manual*. Chicago: Dearborn Financial Publishing, Inc., 1987. For updated tax rules on IRAs, consult a tax service such as those provided by Prentice-Hall or the Commerce Clearing House.

[3] *See* the *Advanced Underwriting Service*, Current Comment 1991. Chicago: Dearborn Financial Publishing, Inc., annual, pp. 34-35.

[4] For a comprehensive explanation of the many complex provisions pertaining to Section 403 (b) plans, *see* N. H. Tarver and A. L. Mortensen, *Section 403(b) Manual*, 8th ed. (Chicago: Dearborn Financial Publishing, Inc., 1991).

Bibliography

Boroson, Warren. *Keys to Retirement Planning*. Hauppauge, N.Y.: Barron's Educational Series, 1990.

Doyle, Robert J., and Don Wright, eds. *Retirement Planning Handbook*, Vols. 1 & 2. Bryn Mawr, Pa.: American College, 1989.

Graves, Edward E., et al. *Retirement Planning for Individuals*, 2nd ed. Bryn Mawr, Pa.: American College, 1990.

Leimberg, S., and J. McFadden. *Employee Benefit and Retirement Planning*. Cincinnati: National Underwriter Co., 1989.

Palmer, Bruce A. "Tax Reform and Retirement Income Replacement Ratios." *Journal of Risk and Insurance* 56, December 1989, pp. 702–725.

Schmahl, W., ed. *Redefining the Process of Retirement*. New York: Springer-Verlag New York, 1989.

Schulz, J. H. *The Economics of Aging*, 4th ed. Dover, Mass.: Auburn House Publishing Co., 1988.

Streng, William P. *Tax Planning for Retirement*. New York: Warren Gorham & Lamont, 1989.

Webb, Thomas L. "Retirement Planning Alternatives." *Journal of the American Society of CLU & ChFC* 43, July 1989, pp. 54–60.

Chapter 17 | Financial Planning: The Later Adult Years

Chapter Objectives

- Define and explain the need for estate planning
- Explain the variety of professional expertise needed to complete a complex estate plan
- Explain the steps involved in developing an estate plan
- Describe the legal process of transferring property at death
- Explain the role life insurance plays in the estate planning process
- Illustrate the estate planning process with a comprehensive case study

Introduction

Adult life cannot be divided precisely into trimesters. It is obvious, however, that the pattern of predominant financial concerns changes slowly but clearly during adult life. Financial problems associated with premature death and disability are the predominant concerns of young adults. In the middle adult years the need to fund the retirement period dominates the financial plan. The focus of the financial plan in the third trimester is the consumption and ultimate distribution of accumulated wealth.

The third trimester of adult life generally is distinguished by retirement from full-time employment, by the financial independence of children and by the peak of accumulated wealth. Other characteristics that appear include the receipt of Social Security and private pension income, a change in emphasis in the expenditure pattern toward greater consumption of leisure and health maintenance activities and, for many people, a change in residence.

The term *old age* adds little to this description, as experts distinguish between the "young old" and the "old old" person. Indeed much of the stereotyping about old age is either wrong or inapplicable in individual cases. A specific chronological age does not universally distinguish the onset of this period, though the normal retirement age for receipt of Social Security benefits provides a convenient benchmark. It is the shift in emphasis from wealth accumulation to wealth liquidation that marks the period analyzed in this chapter. This shift in emphasis has created a special term for the financial planning done during this period of life. It is called *estate planning.*

Estate Planning Defined

Estate planning means developing financial plans covering the liquidation and distribution of accumulated wealth. Comprehensive estate plans encompass the wealth owner's consumption expenditures until death and gift giving during the person's life. An estate plan may include rearrangement of the form in which wealth is held, gift giving, the sale or transfer of business assets and often the purchase of life insurance.

Professional Skills Required

Legal expertise is needed to complete an estate plan, regardless of the size of the estate. Only lawyers can provide legal advice or draft legal documents such as wills, trust agreements, powers of appointment and contracts to buy or sell assets. (Some documents may not need to be drafted by an attorney to be legally enforceable if they are used personally.) As mentioned in earlier chapters, a layperson who creates these documents for a third party is violating an unauthorized practice of law statute, which is a part of each state's criminal code. Because tax laws governing estate planning issues tend to be complex and because courts frequently make decisions covering estate planning matters, sound estate plans require professional legal advice.

Life insurance expertise also is usually required in estate planning, especially in larger estates where problems of providing liquidity, funding bequests or making charitable gifts often involve the purchase of life insurance. Life insurance salespeople may be needed to advise in arranging policy ownership or choosing settlement options. Frequently the life insurance salesperson is the professional initially uncovering the need for an estate plan.

Because many estates, large and small, use trusts to reach estate planning goals, bank trust officers with experience in estate planning can prove useful. In situations involving minors, spendthrifts or heirs without money management skills, trusts can play an indispensable role in achieving desired objectives.

Developing estate plans often requires accounting expertise to establish the fair market value of property or to capitalize complex business income streams. These problems require the accountant to capitalize historic or estimated earnings or unscramble intermingled earning streams. The more complex the property owned, the more likely an accountant's services will be needed. If an accountant has been preparing a person's income tax return, the accountant is a ready source of much information required to develop the estate plan. The accountant, while preparing tax returns, may be the professional uncovering the need for an estate plan.

Estate planning, especially in the larger and more complex cases, requires more professional expertise than does the financial planning associated with the earlier periods of life. Moreover, some aspects of an estate plan should be in place regardless of age or the amount of wealth involved. For example, a will is necessary at age 28 and at age 68. Trusts, guardianships and buy-and-sell agreements should be in place long before a person enters the last trimester of adult life.

The Estate Planning Process

The sequence of steps for later-years planning is again similar to that for the first two trimesters of the financial life cycle:

1. Collect and analyze information.
2. Set objectives.
3. Implement estate plan.
4. Review and update plan.

Step 1: Collect and Analyze Information

The first step in the estate planning process is evaluating the wealth owner's existing estate plan. This is accomplished with a hypothetical probate analysis. A hypothetical probate answers the question "If the wealth owner died today, where would his or her property go and what expenses would arise in the transfer?"

Often no estate plan exists, in which case local intestacy laws govern the distribution of estate assets. Many people, because of procrastination, fear of death or busy lives, give no thought to the disposition of their property at death. More unfortunately, in cases involving dependent children, no thought is given to dependents' care and custody if both parents die simultaneously.

The following questions should be answered in the process of developing comprehensive estate plans.

- What is the size of a person's gross estate? How much property is owned? When was it acquired? What is its current value? What is the owner's basis in the property?
- What legal documents exist? Are wills, powers of appointment, guardianships, trusts, buy-and-sell agreements already in place? Do these documents reflect current conditions?
- How is property titled? Does the person really own outright all the property believed to be owned?
- What previous gifts were given? To whom? When? What property values were involved?
- Who are all the relatives, charities and others a person might want to consider when transferring property during life and at death? Can all potential beneficiaries manage their financial affairs, or will professional financial management be needed?
- How much life insurance is currently owned? Are the proceeds adequate to accomplish estate planning goals? Is policy ownership arranged in the most efficient way? Are there outstanding policy loans?
- What employee benefits will be included in the estate? What benefits are available to survivors? Should current arrangements be modified?
- What gifts or inheritances might be received?

Step 2: Set Objectives

After determining and analyzing the current facts, the next step is developing clear statements covering:

- *lifetime goals*—the use and disposition of funds during the owner's life;
- *death transfer objectives*—determining the precise beneficiaries of wealth at the owner's death; and
- *transfer and tax minimization strategies*—conveying the maximum amount of property to heirs at minimum transfer cost.

These objective are listed in order of their importance.

Lifetime Objectives

The first objective in developing an estate plan is to provide for the wealth owner's enjoyment of life. This objective may involve continuing participation in business or farming, moving to an adult community or participating in an adult educational program. There should be a projected budget coordinating available assets with the activities the individual or family desires.

In most cases attending to lifetime needs dominates all other objectives. For example, in some situations it may be argued that early gifting of a business interest makes sense from a tax or a death transfer standpoint. However, the loss of purpose or of self-esteem felt by the donor may more than offset any potential financial gain.

After the objectives for future living and well-being have been planned, a program for gift giving can be considered. For some people there is great joy in sharing property with relatives or a favorite charity. A second purpose can be served when a gift-giving program is begun between older and younger generations involved in a family business; the business may be made more successful. There is a time when a business needs youthful enthusiasm and commitment and an ownership interest is an appropriate reward for years of service.

Gift giving during one's lifetime can fulfill psychological goals. Ernest Becker identified the feeling of being a hero, of having one's wealth do good before and after death, as important motivators of human behavior.[1] Thus lifetime gifting may serve important psychological purposes. For example, gifting may increase self-esteem, allow one to express love or allow one to atone for past mistakes.

Chapter 12 presented the tax advantages and disadvantages arising from gifting. Some of these are reviewed briefly in the following lists.

Advantages of gifting include these:

- Interspousal gifts can be made to assure that both spouses have sufficient property to take advantage of the unified federal estate and gift tax credit. This advantage arises in cases where one spouse's assets exceed the minimum assets subject to the estate tax and the other's do not. Interspousal gifts in this instance can reduce or eliminate the federal estate tax.
- Gifts up to a maximum of $10,000 per donee ($20,000 if joint gifts) may be excluded each year from taxable gift giving. With enough donees and enough time, much wealth can be passed to others in this way, free of the federal transfer tax.

- Future appreciation of gifted property is kept from the donor's estate, resulting in lower estate taxes and probate costs.

Disadvantages of gifting include these:

- Gifted property may be needed by the donor for unforeseen reasons.
- Gifted property may depreciate rather than appreciate, in which case the donor might be better able to use the tax loss than the donee.
- Large gifts can cause the (premature) payment of the federal transfer tax and associated lost investment income on any tax paid.
- Gifted property retains the donor's basis. Property passed at death receives a stepped-up basis. If property is later sold for a profit, the capital gains tax will be less if the stepped-up basis is greater than the donor's basis. In an inflationary environment and for rapidly appreciating property, forgoing the stepped-up basis can be costly.

Death Transfer Objectives

As discussed in Chapter 2 and reviewed in Chapter 15, contemplation of death presents a difficult psychological problem for some people. Nonetheless it is unavoidable in the estate planning process. The satisfaction of knowing that their assets can achieve objectives even after their death can provide psychological rewards to help offset the discomfort felt by such people.

Developing death transfer objectives means identifying precisely those people or organizations the individual wishes to enjoy his or her property after death. In cases of two or more marriages with children by each marriage, when some children have proved either more worthy or more needy or where a spouse is wealthy in his or her own right, the development of death transfer objectives may prove difficult.

The need is for clear designation of the intended recipients of the assets, including the designation of beneficiaries of life insurance policies. Most death transfer objectives are established in a valid will. Transfers of life insurance proceeds and employee benefit plan proceeds (group life insurance) are established by contract. For families it is important that husband and wife each have valid and consistent wills, because either spouse, regardless of age, may predecease the other.

In cases where there are minors, a guardian should be nominated in the parent's will. A court must make the appointment official. The guardian also may be the trustee for the minor's assets, though these duties are separable. The requirements for a guardian do not involve money management skills. In cases where assets are sufficiently large, a trust arrangement involving a bank may prove desirable to both the guardian and the minor.

Simultaneous Deaths. The potential for the simultaneous death of both parents should be considered in developing death transfer objectives. Most states have passed the Uniform Simultaneous Death Act as part of their probate code. In general these rules provide that if one spouse does not survive the other by at least 120

Figure 17.1
Calculation of the Federal Estate Tax

1. Calculate the decedent's gross estate
2. *Subtract* allowable deductions
3. *Add* taxable gifts
4. The result is the tax base.
5. Compute the tentative tax liability
6. *Subtract* gift tax on post-1976 gifts
7. *Subtract* other allowable credits
8. The result is the federal estate tax liability.

hours it is assumed that the property owner survived the other spouse. That is, when spouses die simultaneously, the deceased husband's property is distributed as if he survived his wife. Similarly, the wife's property is distributed as if she survived her husband.

Many estate planners go further than the state provisions and deal explicitly with the possibility of simultaneous deaths or deaths that are not simultaneous but less than six months apart. If both spouses die simultaneously, many problems must be faced, including the loss of the spousal transfer tax advantages. Thorough estate plans present at least two hypothetical probate exhibits, one based on the assumption that the husband dies first and one assuming the wife dies first. Additional calculations might involve estimating the results of simultaneous deaths.

Tax Objectives

After identifying living objectives and death transfer objectives, the third category of objectives to be integrated into the estate plan is tax-minimizing strategies. The overriding concern at this point is to minimize the decedent's or the family's total tax burden, including state and federal death and income taxes and other transfer costs. Another way of stating this goal is that the estate plan should maximize the net wealth passing to heirs after all tax and administration expenses have been subtracted.

To achieve this objective the planner must have a comprehensive and current knowledge of the relevant tax laws and court decisions. Chapter 12 explains the federal transfer tax provisions. Figure 17.1 provides a brief summary of the federal estate tax calculation.

Step 3: Implement the Plan

Once an estate is inventoried and analyzed, an estate plan can be developed. After developing the estate plan, the next step is implementing the plan. Many cases require new legal documents, and sometimes existing documents need updating. If executors, guardians or trustees are needed, they must be identified. Planned gifts should be given, especially if the annual gift tax exclusion is to be used. Trusts must be set up and ownership of property transferred to the trustee. If needed, life insurance policies must be put into effect. Small businesses often require buy-and-sell arrangements. Neglecting these steps causes even the most efficient estate plan to fail.

Step 4: Review and Update

An estate plan requires regular review. Tax laws change. Births, deaths, health-related problems (including disability) and divorces change plans. Sales or acquisitions of assets may require changes in wills and other legal documents. The more complicated a person's wealth holdings and financial transactions, the more important it is to keep an estate plan current.

Property Transfers at Death

Probate

The third period of adult life ends in death. At death the decedent's assets pass to the living through a legal process known as *probate*. Probate is a court proceeding used to pass the title of the decedent's property to parties named in a will or, in cases where no valid will exists, to distribute the property under the state laws of intestacy.

The probate process can be avoided if people die owning no wealth. Some people plan to avoid probate by putting all their property into a living trust or by arranging the joint ownership of property with a desired heir. (Living trusts are described later in this chapter.)

Joint ownership means two or more people hold title to the same property. *Joint tenancy* means only two people share the interest. *Tenancy in common* means more than two people share the property. With joint ownership the surviving owner(s) receives the deceased owner's shares automatically. (There are several valid arguments to be made on both sides of the decision to avoid probate. This discussion is beyond the scope of this book but is covered in detail in the Prestopino text cited in the bibliography at the end of the chapter.) Thus property owned at death may pass to heirs in a prearranged fashion by the way title is held, or title may be assigned by probate at the direction of a valid will or intestacy laws.

Intestacy

Every state has a law covering the transfer of property from the dead to the living when the wealth owner leaves no legally enforceable will. These laws differ in the various states, but many states follow the *Uniform Probate Code*. In general these laws outline the shares taken by living relatives or deceased wealth owners. The shares are determined by the closeness of the blood relationship between the deceased and the living, with special treatment given to a surviving spouse.

☐ **Example**

In states basing their laws of inheritance on English common law a surviving spouse receives the first $50,000 plus one-half the balance of the intestate estate if there is no surviving issue but the decedent is survived by a parent.

For example, when Rick Dumas dies leaving no children, his wife, Cindy, receives $50,000 plus one-half of the balance of his $1 million estate [$50,000

+ .5 × ($1,000,000 − $50,000) = $525,000]. Rick's parents share the balance ($1,000,000 − $525,000 = $475,000) equally.

Assume Rick is not survived by his parents, but by children of his marriage to Cindy. In this case the mathematical results are the same; Cindy receives $525,000, and the children share $475,000 equally.

Wills

A **will** is a legally enforceable declaration allowing people to distribute their property at death according to their preferences. A will also can be used to nominate a guardian for minors or set up trusts.

A valid will has three mandatory features established in state law:

1. The will must be made while the person is capable of understanding the document—"of sound and disposing mind," as the phrase for legal capacity is often put.
2. The document must be witnessed properly.
3. A will must be in a written form acceptable in the probate court having jurisdiction over the decedent's estate.

At death the terms of the will are carried out by an executor named in the document. The courts will appoint an administrator to distribute estates of people dying intestate.

Distributions are either per stirpes or per capita. *Per stirpes* means by the root. In effect this distribution means that if a party entitled to receive a share of an estate in turn dies before receiving this share, decedents of this party get a proportional share of the bequest.

☐ **Example**

Grandfather dies leaving an estate divided equally by three daughters. One daughter preceded her father in death. This daughter had two sons. Under a per-stirpes distribution of the grandfather's will, these two sons each receive half their mother's one-third share of the estate. Each receives one-sixth of the grandfather's estate.

A *per-capita* distribution means an estate is divided on an equal-share basis by surviving heirs. In the preceding example four heirs survived—two daughters and two sons of a deceased daughter. Each surviving heir would receive one-quarter of the estate.

Trusts

A trust is a legal device in which one party (the grantor or donor) transfers property to a second party (the trustee) to manage for a third party (the beneficiary). If the trust is established during the grantor's lifetime, it is called a **living** or **inter vivos** trust. If a trust is established in a will, it is called a **testamentary** trust. If the grantor can change the terms of the trust or terminate the agreement, the trust is called a **revocable** trust. If the terms of the trust cannot be altered by the grantor, the trust is an *irrevocable* trust. A trust with property in it is a **funded** trust, while a trust with no present property but with the right to receive property—such as life insurance proceeds—in the future is an *unfunded* trust.

Trusts can be used to achieve many estate planning objectives, including:

- managing property for minors or financially inexperienced adults;
- taking advantage of some beneficial provisions in the tax code;
- removing property from an estate, thus lowering the cost of probate; and
- expediting and adding certainty to buy-and-sell agreements used in the estate plan.

Living Trusts

A living trust can be used as a will substitute. If property is put in this type of trust, it will be distributed according to the trust's terms. Property put in trust is owned by the trust and is not part of the decedent's estate. Living trusts are initially more expensive than wills, but because the property avoids the probate process, they could ultimately prove to be more cost-efficient. (Resolving this issue mathematically involves estimating life spans and making present value calculations, which will not be demonstrated here.)

If the income from the living trust is available to the wealth owner during his or her lifetime, the trust is called a **grantor trust**. No tax advantages accrue to the grantor trust as all income is taxed to the donor. Often the grantor of the living trust also will be the trustee or cotrustee. The advantages claimed for the living trust over the will include increased privacy, increased speed of disposition and lower potential for challenge by dissatisfied family members. Wills can be contested according to well-established legal rules. Trusts are much less susceptible to contest.

The Marital Deduction

The unlimited marital deduction provided for in the federal estate tax requires careful planning in many family situations. Because the deduction is unlimited, it allows the estate of the first spouse to die to pass to the surviving spouse free of the federal estate tax. The IRC allows this deduction when a present nonterminable interest in property is transferred from decedent to spouse. A nonterminable interest is one that does not end at the spouse's death, at remarriage or when a specific age is attained.

Because the marital deduction is unlimited, the estate tax can be eliminated by transferring all the decedent's assets to a surviving spouse. However, for estates greater than $600,000, this often is not the most efficient strategy if the aim is to minimize total taxes paid after both husband and wife die.

First, giving the entire estate to a spouse means the loss of one unified tax credit. (However, if the combined estates will not exceed the minimum amount subject to the tax, $600,000, it makes no difference from an estate tax standpoint whether the first spouse to die uses the available credit.) Second, in cases where the surviving spouse has sufficient assets to allow a comfortable standard of living, adding more assets to the estate serves to increase the amount of income tax during the surviving spouse's lifetime and death taxes and probate costs at death. The progressive marginal tax rates of the federal income and estate taxes magnify this penalty.

Credit Shelter Bypass Trust

In large estates the **credit shelter bypass trust** (also known as the *A–B trust*) arrangement traditionally has proved useful. The credit shelter bypass trust involves the creation of separate but coordinated trusts: one qualifying for the estate tax marital deduction, the other not qualifying. One trust receives the property qualifying for the marital deduction, and the other receives the nonqualified property. The property not qualifying for the marital deduction can provide the surviving spouse with lifetime income and be subject to a limited power of appointment by the surviving spouse. The limited power means the property is not included in the surviving spouse's estate at death. The purpose of the credit shelter bypass trust is to allow each spouse to use his or her $192,800 unified transfer credit, which is lost if the entire estate passes to a surviving spouse. The effect is to allow $1,200,000 to pass tax-free to children or other nonspousal heirs, rather than the $600,000 that passes free of tax at the second death if the credit shelter bypass trust is not used.

A formula approach can be used to decide the proportion of assets placed in each trust to minimize total taxes paid after both deaths. One target amount to be placed in the nonqualified trust would be $600,000. This amount uses all of the unified estate tax credit. (The $600,000 amount assumes the full $192,800 credit is available, with none of it previously used to cover gift tax liability. If some amount has been used for gift tax liability, the amount put in the nonmaritally qualified trust is reduced to use all the remaining credit.) If assets exceed the exempt amount, then the formula calls for the remaining property to be put into the qualified trust. The credit shelter bypass trust results in no federal estate taxes at the first death and a lower estate tax liability (compared to giving the entire estate outright to the surviving spouse) after both deaths.

☐ **Example**

Dave and Donna Loneoak have similar wills, and each has $1 million in assets. Each will provides that $600,000 be put in a trust with life income provided for the spouse and the principal passing to their children at the surviving spouse's death. Because both spouses have equal assets, the result is not affected by the order of death.

Because this arrangement involves a terminable interest, the property in the trust does not qualify for the marital deduction. Because the surviving spouse never has title to the trust property and has no general power of appointment over the trust, the $600,000 is not included in the spouse's estate. The remaining $400,000 in the estate of the first spouse to die passes to the second spouse. There is no federal estate tax at the first death under this arrangement because $400,000 passes to a surviving spouse and $600,000 is the exempt equivalent of the unified credit of $192,800.

Assuming no gifts, growth in property values or other changes, there will be tax at the surviving spouse's death, as that person will have an estate of $1,400,000 ($1 million of his or her own property and $400,000 inherited from the first spouse to die). This spouse also has an exempt amount of $600,000. The federal estate tax at this death equals $320,000. The remainder of this estate, $1,080,000, ($1,400,000 assets − $320,000 FET) passes to the children. After both deaths the children receive $1,680,000 ($600,000 from the first death plus $1,080,000 from the second).

Contrast this result to the amount passing to the children if all property passes from one spouse to the survivor at the first death and from the surviving spouse to the children at the second. In this case the children receive a total of $1,412,000, about 19 percent less than if the credit shelter bypass trust were used.

Table 17.1 presents these results.

QTIP Trust

To qualify for the marital deduction the property given to a spouse must not be a terminable interest. That is, the right to use, give away or enjoy the property must not end at the surviving spouse's death, remarriage or any other predetermined event. However, the tax law does allow for an important exception to the terminable interest rule. Despite being an interest in property that terminates at death, qualified terminable interest property (QTIP) can be eligible for the marital deduction. To be eligible for the marital deduction QTIP property must meet the following conditions:

- All income from the property must go to the surviving spouse.
- The income must be payable at least annually.
- There must not be any provision for the appointment of property to anybody but the surviving spouse during the survivor's lifetime.

The QTIP election, for example, allows property to be directed to a couple's children at the first parent's death, while still allowing the property to qualify for the marital deduction. Despite being directed to the children, the income from the property must go to the surviving spouse until the second death. Then the property is included in the estate of the second spouse to die and is subject to the estate tax. Thus the effect of the QTIP provision is to delay, from the first to the second death, the estate tax on property in which the survivor has a terminable interest.

The executor of the estate of the first spouse to die makes the election to classify property as QTIP. This election is irrevocable. It is the election by the executor that sets the QTIP trust apart from the credit shelter bypass trust approach. Under the credit shelter bypass trust the decision on what amount of property to include in the trust is made before the first spouse's death. With a QTIP trust this decision can be made after the probate process has begun and the gross estate has been valued. The QTIP arrangement is a postmortem planning technique.

Life Insurance in Estate Planning

One purpose of the extensive discussion of estate planning is to provide sufficient background for readers to appreciate the role life insurance plays in the estate plan. Life insurance is often essential in a comprehensive estate plan. It allows

Table 17.1
Advantages of Credit Shelter Bypass Trust, Dave and Donna Loneoak

Part I: No Trust Used

At first death:
Estate		$1,000,000
Marital deduction		1,000,000
Taxable estate		0

At second death:
Estate		1,000,000
From spouse		1,000,000
Taxable estate		2,000,000
Tentative tax	780,800	
Unified credit	192,800	
Estate tax		588,000

Property Passing to Children | | 1,412,000

Part 2: Credit Shelter Bypass

At first death:
Estate		1,000,000	
Marital deduction	400,000		
Bypass trust	600,000		
Taxable estate			600,000
Tentative tax			192,800
Unified credit			192,800
Estate tax			0

At second death:
Estate		1,000,000
From spouse		400,000
Taxable estate		1,400,000
Tentative tax	512,800	
Unified credit	192,800	
Estate tax		320,000

Property Passing to Children | 1,080,000
Property from Trust | 600,000
Total Property to Children | $1,680,000

---

people to achieve their living, death transfer and tax objectives. To comprise a useful part of a well-developed estate plan, ownership of the life insurance must be arranged with care, the amount of insurance purchased must be appropriately related to the projected needs and the premiums must be affordable. Because term insurance usually is unavailable after age 65, the estate planning need for life insurance involves cash value life insurance such as whole life or universal life insurance.

In smaller estates life insurance proceeds may comprise most of the estate's assets and may be a prime source for funding the decedent's bequests. In other cases, when particular assets are destined for specific heirs, life insurance proceeds can be used to fund equalizing bequests.

☐ **Example**

Farmer Brown wants to leave his entire farm to the child engaged in the actual farming. He also wants to give a bequest of equal value to the child that has gone to live in the city. An amount of life insurance equal to the value of the farm can be used to fund the gift to the city dweller.

Life insurance is frequently used to add liquidity (cash) to larger estates. Larger estates need liquidity because the assets usually are held in real property, business investments or other assets that cannot quickly be turned into cash. The federal estate tax must be paid in cash within nine months of the estate owner's death, though extensions can be arranged. Probate costs also require cash, as does the need to repay debts, costs of final illness and state death taxes. Life insurance, if carefully arranged, can add the liquidity to meet these needs.

Buy-and-sell agreements allow the transfer of business interests from the decedent's estate to predetermined buyers at a predetermined price. Life insurance owned by the purchaser on the life of the decedent can be used to fund the purchase. Life insurance also can be used to fund other employment-related benefits promising payments to an employee's estate or survivors.

Ownership of Life Insurance

In coordinating life insurance into an estate plan, the ownership of the life insurance is of critical importance. If the decedent's estate receives the proceeds or if the decedent retained any of the incidents of ownership in the policy, the proceeds are included in the gross estate. Also, if the decedent either gave away or absolutely assigned the rights in the policy within three years of death, the gross estate includes the proceeds.

In general, payment of premiums by the decedent will not cause the proceeds to be included in the gross estate. The objective of minimizing taxes requires that the proceeds *not* be included in the estate, yet the living and death transfer objectives just outlined require that the proceeds be available to the estate. Resolving these antagonistic objectives has been a key difficulty in the estate planner's assignment.

In smaller estates, where the life insurance proceeds combined with all other assets are less than $600,000, the minimum amount subject to tax, the estate can be named beneficiary. In other cases, where it is desired to keep the proceeds out of the gross estate but still make the cash available, the insured may name a spouse or a life insurance trust as the owner-beneficiary of the policy. (Ownership of the policy by a trust also should be considered where minors are the intended beneficiary, since life insurance companies will not release proceeds directly to minors.) The trust, once it receives the proceeds, may be authorized to purchase assets from the decedent's estate for cash or may be authorized to make loans of cash to the estate. Either of these two transactions puts cash into the estate without subjecting the proceeds to the estate tax.

Two additional rules apply if the proceeds are to be kept from the decedent's estate. First, any transfer of an existing policy must precede the insured's death by more than three years. Second, there must not be more than a 5 percent chance, determined actuarially, that the policy will revert to the original owner. For example, if a 55-year-old daughter were to give to her 77-year-old mother a policy in which the daughter was the insured and owner, there clearly would be a substantial chance that the ownership of the policy would revert to the daughter. If the daughter should predecease the mother, the policy proceeds would be included in the daughter's estate.

Sometimes the transfer of an existing policy can cause taxes to be paid earlier than if the transfer were not made. For example, if the new owner of the existing policy should predecease the insured, the cash surrender value is included in the new owner's estate even though the insured remains alive.

Life Insurance Trusts In large estates the irrevocable life insurance trust has proved useful in achieving estate planning objectives. The trust is named the owner-beneficiary of the policy. The insured may neither be a trustee nor in a position to influence the trust's government in any other capacity, such as being director of a corporation that is named a trustee. If the trust, after the insured's death, has cash assets from life insurance proceeds, it can purchase business interests, farmland or other items from the estate, or it can make loans to the estate. All transactions should be at fair market value. The result is to put the cash in the estate while keeping the life insurance proceeds from being subject to the federal estate tax. (To accomplish this result the decedent must live for three years after the life insurance policy funding the trust is purchased, and the decedent must be in a position to receive no economic benefit from the policy. Moreover, careful drafting of the trust is necessary to avoid the appearance of directing the trust to pay the decedent's estate tax obligation.) The services of an attorney are required in establishing a life insurance or any other trust and in developing the appropriate wording to achieve the estate owner's objectives.

A Comparison Between Individuals and the Life Insurance Trust as a Beneficiary

Either an individual or a trust can be chosen as policy beneficiary. In small estates not subject to the federal estate tax it is usual to choose an individual beneficiary or the decedent's estate. Individuals are chosen because it is simple and inexpensive and because insurers provide several settlement options providing money management in cases where individuals do not want money management responsibilities. However, these settlement options often are not sufficiently flexible to meet peculiar needs (for example, beneficiaries may be under legal disability or incompetent), do not allow consolidation of policies from different carriers or other sources of income and may offer uncompetitive rates of return. Therefore, the trust, which overcomes these problems, is often chosen to receive policy proceeds.

The trust can be quite flexible in terms of payments made to beneficiaries and investment possibilities. A trust reduces probate costs if the alternative is the estate receiving the life insurance proceeds. And a trust can integrate the life insurance proceeds with all other estate assets. Perhaps most important, in taxable estates the life insurance trust can make the proceeds available to the decedent's estate without increasing the estate's tax liability.

The disadvantages of the trust include the initial cost to draft the document and any maintenance expense if a professional trustee is employed. Moreover, the trust document is relatively complex and thus difficult for laypeople to understand. Sometimes a surviving spouse may feel the trust was employed because of the decedent's lack of confidence, and this psychological cost must be counted in the equation.

Survivor or Second-Death Policies

In some cases estate planners recommend purchase of life insurance policies that pay only after the second of two deaths. The theory behind this arrangement is to pass the entire estate from the first spouse to die to the surviving spouse. This transfer exempts the entire estate from the estate tax at the first death because of the unlimited marital deduction. At the second death, assuming an estate tax liability exists, there also will be life insurance proceeds to provide needed cash.

Survivor life insurance premiums can be significantly lower than two individual policies. Premiums are a function of the clients' ages and the carrier's actuarial assumptions. However, in cases where the wife is younger than the husband, significant premium savings are possible. Some actuaries feel that premiums should rise after the first death, because the policy becomes an individual life insurance policy at that point. Other companies apparently reflect this possibility in their initial premiums. As this material is being written, competition among carriers has produced diverse products and diverse approaches to pricing.

Recent data provided by the Life Insurance Marketing and Research Association (LIMRA) indicate growing acceptance of second-death policies. Comparing the first six months of 1990 to the first six months of 1989 shows the following changes: annualized premiums increased 153 percent; the face amount of coverage increased 162 percent to a total of about $10 billion; and the number of policies in force increased 171 percent to about 8,000. During this period the average policy size remained about constant at $1.3 million, with an average annual premium of $20,000.[2]

The goal of making the proceeds available to the estate without causing them to increase the size of the taxable estate is the same for a second-death policy as it is for a single-life policy. Reaching this goal often requires using a life insurance trust.

An Annotated Case Study: The Petersons

Facts and Data

"J.T." and Mildred Peterson are 72 and 70 years old, respectively. Both are in fairly good health. Four years ago J.T. retired from active participation in the construction company he founded. His annual after-tax disposable income from ownership of the company and his other investments is $1 million. The company is incorporated with 1,000 shares of stock. J.T. owns 800 shares; his oldest child, Jim, owns 200 shares. Jim purchased the shares from his father more than ten years ago at fair market value.

Jim now operates the company. The other two children are a daughter, Molly, and the youngest child, John. All three of the Peterson children are married; they each have two children and, except for Jim, do not live near Minneapolis, their hometown. Exhibit 17.1 shows the Petersons' current estates.

The Petersons both have wills, which they made many years ago. The wills are identical, leaving all property to the surviving spouse with their three children sharing the estate equally at the death of the second parent. The Petersons' living objectives are to continue living independently for as long as possible and then to enter an adult community that is about five miles from their home. They have already been placed on a waiting list for this community. Their death transfer objectives are to allow the surviving spouse to move to the adult community as planned and to pass control of the business to Jim, with the income shared about equally with their children or their grandchildren (per stirpes) if any child predeceases them.

After collecting needed information and analyzing the Petersons' current estates and wills, an estate planner prepared Exhibit 17.2 based on the assumption that J.T. dies now and Mildred dies several years later. For simplicity's sake, no growth is assumed in the value of the assets in this initial exhibit.

Based on the data presented in Exhibit 17.2, the Petersons desire an estate plan that is as "simple as possible" and is designed to (1) provide adequate support for the surviving spouse and (2) transfer control of the business to Jim (51 percent or more of the shares of stock) and the remainder of the assets to the other two children or grandchildren. The Petersons' third objective is to minimize their estate tax liability.

If Jim dies, no family member will be available to operate the firm, and J.T. realizes that the firm would

Exhibit 17.1
The Petersons' Current Estates as of January 1, 1991

J.T.'s estate:	
Personal property, cash and investments	$400,000
80% ownership in JTP Construction	12,000,000*
Commercial real estate (current appraisal)	1,000,000
Life insurance policy (face value)	85,000
Total	13,485,000
Mildred's estate:	
Personal property, cash and investments	$400,000
The Peterson residence	180,000
Florida condominium	125,000
Total	705,000

*JTP fair market value; son Jim owns the remaining 20 percent.

Exhibit 17.2
Hypothetical Estate Tax Calculation: Current Wills
J.T. Dies First

J.T.'s gross estate:	$13,485,000
Less: expenses	200,000
Adjusted gross estate	13,285,000
Marital deduction	13,285,000
Taxable estate	0
Mildred's gross estate	
Own assets	705,000
J.T.'s bequest	13,285,000
Less: expenses	300,000
Adjusted gross estate	13,690,000
Tentative tax	7,170,300[1]
Less: unified credit	192,800
Federal estate tax	6,977,500
Passed to children	6,712,500[2]

Notes:
[1] $1,290,800 + (.55 × [13,690,000 − 3,000,000])
[2] $13,690,000 − $6,977,500

have to be sold. At this point no buyer has been identified, but both Jim and J.T. will begin to work on this business continuation problem, giving it the highest priority.

The estate planning team includes the Petersons' lawyer, their accountant (who prepares their individual and business tax returns) and a life insurance salesperson recommended by Jim.

Solution[3]

The alternatives developed by the team include the following suggestions:

1. Institute a gift-giving program, giving gifts of $20,000 to each child and grandchild. These gifts qualify for the annual joint gift-giving exclusion, so no tax is payable, nor do they have to be re-added to the Petersons' gross estates. With three children and six grandchildren, these tax-free gifts remove $180,000 of property each year from J.T.'s estate. Jim's gift should be shares of JTC, Inc. stock. (The longer J.T. lives, the greater the percentage of JTP Construction that can be transferred to Jim. The effect of such a transfer in terms of "freezing" asset values and creating a minority interest, especially if some shares are transferred to a trust or outright to other family members, is governed by IRC 2036[c.] In 1990 revised provisions of this section, retroactive to 1987, were enacted.) All gifts to minors should be in trust.

2. Revise and update both wills. Use the unlimited marital deduction to pass all but $600,000 of the estate of the first spouse to die to the surviving spouse. This strategy defers any federal estate tax until the surviving spouse's death. The $600,000 not going to the surviving spouse fully uses the unified transfer credit.

This plan requires the purchase of a survivor life insurance policy for $6 million. Because both Petersons are insurable, the annual premium would be about $136,000. While this premium is large, the face amount of coverage is large, and the premiums could be considerably less than the estate tax liability if the policy matures as a death claim in the early years. (One large life insurance company writes survivor life insurance policies in amounts up to $30 million.) Because J.T. has a current income of $1 million, the premiums are affordable. In fact the premiums reduce the size of his gross estate, thereby lowering probate costs and estate taxes.

The policy is to be owned by a life insurance trust that also will be the beneficiary. At the second death—and the order is not important in this instance—the shares of stock in JTP Construction in the surviving spouse's estate can be purchased with the insurance proceeds. The shares can be held in trust until the youngest Peterson grandchild reaches age 35. Jim and the local bank are to be named cotrustees of the trust, leaving Jim in control of the business.

At the second death the trust's purchase of shares leaves $6 million in cash in the decedent's estate. This cash is the source of funds to pay the federal estate tax obligation.

3. The Petersons' estates are grossly disproportionate. While Mildred's estate currently exceeds $600,000, it is comprised partially of illiquid assets providing no income. J.T. should use the unlimited marital deduction to gift his $1 million in commercial real estate to Mildred at this time. (While a $1 million gift is illustrated, larger gifts, including some shares of JTP Construction, would also be appropriate.) Their marriage is stable, and there is no concern about divorce. This gift will add more certainty to the possibility that Mildred could use all her unified credit should she predecease J.T.
4. The ownership of the existing life insurance policy is to be transferred to the life insurance trust. If J.T. dies within three years of the gift, the entire proceeds will be included in his estate. If he outlives the three-year period, the cash value of the policy (approximately $22,000) is included in J.T.'s gross estate as a taxable gift.

Conclusion

As shown in Exhibit 17.3, the new estate plan allows $7,042,500 ($600,000 at the first death and $6,442,500 at the second death) to pass directly to the children rather than the $6,712,500 passing under the existing plan. The difference equals $330,000. However, the new plan also includes $6 million (plus the $85,000 policy) in life insurance proceeds not shown in Exhibit 17.3. Under the new arrangement the trust purchases JTP shares for cash at the second death. Assume the cash then is used to pay almost all the estate tax. Then, the proposed plan actually leaves the children with about $13 million ($7 million passed directly plus $6 million in life insurance proceeds) and with continued control of the family company.

☐ Practice Cases

The Calhoun Family

Ed and Emma Calhoun are each 62 years old, and both are in good health. Ed is a nationally known college professor of electrical engineering whose theories about electrical circuits have had many applications in computers. As a result of breakthroughs made by Ed and his students, Ed receives at least $200,000 a year in patent income and at least $100,000 in consultation and director fees. Ed's income has risen very rapidly. Just ten years ago, before his first successful patent, his only income was his teaching salary.

One of two daughters (twins) of the deceased founder of a nationally known candy company, Emma has inherited a considerable amount of income and assets (shown in Exhibits 17.4 and 17.5). Her inheritance may be doubled, as she is her never-married sister Edith's nearest living relative. The trust for the two sisters ends at the death of the last living sister, when the heirs of each sister receive the residual of the trust. Emma is the executor of Edith's will; she and her children are the primary and contingent beneficiaries.

Ed has been a professor all his working career except for a four-year period of duty in the U.S. Navy. Ed has a moderate hearing loss resulting from a war injury and is entitled to all veterans' benefits, including health care at a veterans' hospital.

The Calhouns have three children: Mark, a successful professor of mathematics at a large university; Susan, a homemaker; and Judy, who is 19, unemployed, supported by her parents and has yet to develop any clear goals. Mark and Susan each have two children, ages 3 and 8. Her parents consider Judy immature and irresponsible because she did not go to college, whereas her brother earned a PhD and her sister earned a master's degree in library science.

Ed and Emma feel they need financial counseling. They think they need an estate plan, as they currently have wills made more than 20 years ago, each spouse leaving his or her entire estate to the other at death. In both cases the contingent beneficiaries are the three children under a share-and-share-alike formula. At times they have expressed a desire to disinherit Judy, but now they want to give her access to minimal support but not necessarily an equal share of the assets unless she "shapes up."

**Exhibit 17.3
Hypothetical Estate Tax Calculation: New Estate Plan
J.T. Dies First**

At J.T.'s death:	
J.T.'s gross estate	$12,485,000[1]
Less: expenses	200,000
Adjusted gross estate	12,285,000
Marital deduction	11,685,000[2]
Taxable estate	600,000
Tentative tax	192,800
Less: unified credit	192,800
Federal estate tax	0
At Mildred's death:	
Mildred's assets	1,705,000[3]
From J.T.'s estate	11,685,000
Less: expenses	300,000
Adjusted gross estate	13,090,000[4]
Tentative tax	6,840,300[5]
Less: unified credit	192,800
Federal estate tax	6,647,500
Passed to children	6,442,500[6]

Notes:
[1] previous estate less $1 million gift to Mildred
[2] $12,485,000 − $600,000 (Unified Transfer Credit) = $11,685,000
[3] previous estate plus $1 million gift from J.T.
[4] For simplicity's sake, assume no growth in assets and annual exclusion gifts come from current income.
[5] $1,290,800 + [.55 × (13,090,000 − 3,000,000)]
[6] Mildred's adjusted gross estate less federal estate tax. The assets in the life insurance trust, $6 million and $85,000, also are passed to the children, producing a total transfer of $12,527,500.

Assignment

You are to develop a plan that addresses the retirement funding issue and the estate planning issues, including three hypothetical probates, illustrating:

1. the results before your estate planning suggestions, assuming Ed dies first;
2. the probate after your suggestions and assuming Ed is the first spouse to die; and
3. the probate after your suggestions and assuming Emma is the first spouse to die.

The Pulaski Family

Val and Jean Pulaski were married four years ago. Each had been married previously. Val's first wife, May, died nine years ago after a brief illness. Val and May had three children, John, June and Patricia. Val is now 58, John is 31, June 29 and Patricia 23. Patricia and June are single.

Patricia still lives at home and works as an accountant in her father's business. She has an undergraduate degree in accounting from a well-known school. She is a capable accountant, but she has few friends. Val wants her to own and operate his business after his death. She is capable and willing to do so. Val wants the profits of the business shared with her sister.

June is divorced and is raising two children, Amos and Erin, ages 3 and 6. Her former husband provides child support but not regularly as he is frequently unemployed. His alcohol and drug abuse problems led to the divorce, and there is no likelihood of the marriage being rejoined. June relies on her parents for regular financial support.

John is married. He lives and works in New York as a stockbroker with a large securities firm. John's

Exhibit 17.4
Ed and Emma Calhoun
Cash Flow Statement (Last Year)

Ed's Income:	
University salary	$ 65,000
Patent income	250,000
Consulting	112,000
Investment income	76,000
Total	503,000
Emma's Income:	
Trust income	168,000
Investment income	100,000
Total	268,000
Total Income	771,000
(Less taxes)	292,400
Disposable income	478,600
Expenses:	
Cost of living*	100,000
Gifts to children	30,000
Charitable gifts**	15,000
Total	145,000
Added to savings	$ 333,600

*Ed was too busy to be specific about the categories of expenses, but he added up all the charges from his monthly bank check statements. He did not double-count the gifts to his children, which were $10,000 to each child.
**Split evenly between Ed's university and the Calhouns' church.

Exhibit 17.5
Ed and Emma Calhoun
Statement of Net Worth (Last Year)

Ed's Assets:	
House	$ 175,000
Stocks and bonds	800,000
Checking account	35,000
Total	1,010,000
Emma's Assets:	
Half-interest in father's trust	2,000,000
Stocks and bonds	2,500,000
Total	$4,500,000

Notes:
1. The Calhouns have no liabilities.
2. Ed's portfolio is split evenly among three blue-chip stocks, GM, IBM, and GE, and several issues of long-term federal securities. He has no interest in managing his investments and a very low tolerance for risk. His basis in his stock portfolio is about half of its current market value of $200,000. At times he has found as much as $70,000 in his checking account. Ed has $12,000 in paid-up servicemen's life insurance, $50,000 in group life insurance from the university and $50,000 in individual whole life insurance, paid up at age 65.
3. Ed is entitled to a university pension of $1,000 a month beginning at age 65. He estimates his Social Security PIA then will be $750.

Exhibit 17.6
Financial Statements for Val Pulaski

Cash Flow Statement (Last Year)

Net income from dairy: $1,000,000	
Dividends & interest $25,000	
Total income	$ 1,025,000
Less:	
Federal income tax	300,000
Social Security tax	4,000
State & local income tax: $76,000	
Total taxes	380,000
Disposable income	645,000
Cost of living (food, clothes, transp.)	100,000
Support for June	48,000
Charity	25,000
Vacations, club dues, travel	60,000
Total costs	233,000
Net savings (90% put back in dairy)	412,000

Statement of Net Worth

Dairy (fair market value)	$20,000,000
(cost basis $14,000,000)	
(dairy is incorporated, 100% of stock owned by Val)	
Cash, stock & bonds	500,000
Home (no mortgage)	300,000
Vehicles (1 Mercedes, 1 Jeep, 1 Lincoln, all new)	100,000
Personal property	150,000
Total assets	21,050,000
Loan on dairy—remaining balance	6,000,000
Net worth	$15,050,000

---

wife, Allison, is an executive in an advertising firm. John and Allison had combined incomes of more than $200,000 for the past three years. Their marriage is not stable, and they were separated for a period. They plan no children. Allison does not get along very well with Val Pulaski.

Jean Pulaski's first marriage also ended in divorce. She is now 63 and has an insignificant amount of financial assets. There were no children of Jean's first marriage. Jean has known Val since childhood, and they were married about a year after her divorce became final. Their marriage is a happy one. Val and Jean live with Patricia in a large unmortgaged home.

Val Pulaski owns and operates a medium-sized regional dairy. The company has been successful, earning about $2 million each year before interest and taxes. Val purchased the dairy ten years ago for $10 million. He has added about $4 million in improvements since the original purchase. When the purchase was made, he borrowed $8 million on a floating-rate loan to finance the purchase. The loan now has a $6 million balance. Last year's interest charge was $600,000. The terms of the loan call for interest at the prime rate and repayment in 15 more years. Val recently had an offer to purchase the dairy made by a large national dairy and food processor. The offer was for $20 million, which Val feels represents the fair market value of the business. Val enjoys work and has resisted selling.

Val indicates that he would like to leave much of the income from his dairy to Jean during her lifetime but then wants the property to be passed to his children, with most of the property going to Patricia, who will run the dairy, and June and her children. He wants Patricia to have legal control of the dairy at his death and thereafter for her lifetime. Val plans to sell the dairy if Patricia predeceases him. If Patricia were to predecease June, he hopes the dairy could be sold quickly and profitably. He feels John can take care of himself, and he does not like John's wife, Allison, very much.

None of the people described in this case has a will. The elder Pulaskis own no life insurance. Both are insurable. June is the beneficiary of a $25,000 policy on her former husband's life, but he frequently neglects or is unable to pay the premiums.

Exhibit 17.6 shows the Pulaskis' financial data.

Assignment

You are to develop an estate plan that includes three hypothetical probates:

1. the results before your estate planning suggestions, assuming Val dies first;
2. the probate after your suggestions and assuming Val is the first spouse to die; and
3. the probate after your suggestions and assuming Jean is the first spouse to die.

Review Questions

1. What is required for a person to have a valid will? What is the purpose of the will in the estate plan?
2. Why are so many experts needed to complete a thorough estate plan? What role can a financial planner play on an estate planning team?
3. List several uses for trusts in an estate plan.
4. When are gifts an appropriate estate planning technique? What are some drawbacks to gifting?
5. Describe some problems that might be caused if the parents of two young children were to die simultaneously. What provisions should be made in a will concerning simultaneous deaths? What are the consequences if one spouse survives the other by only a few days?
6. What categories of property are included in the gross estate? How is property generally valued for estate tax purposes? What are the important exceptions to the rule?
7. How can life insurance be made available to an estate without increasing the size of the gross estate?
8. Describe the credit shelter bypass trust arrangement and its purpose in the estate plan.
9. Explain how the estate planner was able to reduce the Petersons' estate tax liability about 30 percent.

Endnotes

[1] Ernest Becker, *Escape From Evil* (New York: Free Press, 1975), p. 81.

[2] *Life Association News*, March 1991, p. 38.

[3] We wish to acknowledge several valuable comments and suggestions made by James R. Newell, CLU. Any shortcomings remain those of the authors.

Bibliography

Belin, David W. *Creative Estate Planning for the Nineteen Nineties: A Guide for Middle & Upper Income Americans*. New York: Macmillan, 1991.

Comstock, Paul. "Planned Giving Issues and Techniques under Tax Reform." *Journal of the American Society of CLU & ChFC* 42, January 1988, pp. 60–65.

Cooper, Robert W. "Retirement Planning: Client Needs and Professional Services." *Journal of the American Society of CLU & ChFC* 42, November 1988, pp. 68–79.

Jurinski, James John. "Pre-death Transfer of Life Insurance in Community Property States." *Journal of the American Society of CLU & ChFC* 44, March 1990, pp. 34–39.

Leimberg, Stephan R. and Jeff A. Schnepper. "SPLIT Interest Purchase of Property (SPLIT)." *Journal of the American Society of CLU & ChFC* 41, November 1987, pp. 44–55.

Mittelman, Alan J. "Irrevocable Life Insurance Trusts and the Generation-Skipping Transfer Tax." *Journal of the American Society of CLU & ChFC* 42, November 1988, pp. 88–95.

Nordstrom, Kenneth V. "Estate Planning for Unmarried Individuals." *Journal of the American Society of CLU & ChFC* 41, September 1987, pp. 39–46.

Oshins, Richard A. "GRITS and Splits: Turning the Tables on the IRS and Insuring the Victory." *Journal of the American Society of CLU & ChFC* 41, November 1987, pp. 84–93.

Stone, Edward H. "Crummey Rules Have Changed." *Journal of the American Society of CLU & ChFC* 43, September 1989, pp. 34–48.

Stone, Edward H. "Estate Tax-Free Life Insurance." *Journal of the American Society of CLU & ChFC* 44, May 1990, pp. 52–61.

Whitney, Victor P. "Unique Funding for Charitable Remainder Trusts." *Journal of the American Society of CLU & ChFC* 44, July 1990, pp. 36–40.

Chapter 18 — Employee Benefits: Group Insurance

Chapter Objectives

- Explain the role benefits play in our society
- Describe the advantages the government, employers and employees gain from the mixed private and public employee benefit system
- Identify the factors underwriters consider when rating group insurance
- Describe group term life insurance, group disability insurance and group health insurance

Introduction

One definition of *employee benefits* is "any reward moving from an employer to an employee other than wages." The definition includes the following types of benefits:

- Government-mandated benefits: Social Security, workers' compensation and unemployment insurance
- Group life insurance
- Group disability income insurance
- Group health insurance
- Pension plans
- All other benefits, including vacations, day care, employee discounts and reimbursement for educational expenses

Importance of Employee Benefits

In 1989 the cost of employee benefit plans reached an average of $11,527 per employee. Benefit costs of the employers surveyed by the U.S. Chamber of Commerce reached 38 percent of payroll in 1989. The chamber estimated total benefit payments made by all U.S. employers was about $965 billion in 1989. The fastest-rising component of the employee benefits bill was health care costs, which rose to $2,853 per employee in 1989 from $2,538 in 1988, a 12.4 percent increase. In

1987 health care costs per employee were $2,189, which was about 30 percent less than the 1989 figure.[1]

These data show that employee benefits have wide societal and individual effects and thus deserve careful study. The largest group affected by employee benefits is, of course, employees. Employees of the largest U.S. corporations and many working for smaller employers receive these benefits. In recent years state and federal legislation that would make one benefit, group health insurance, mandatory for all employees has been proposed.

Many others are affected by employee benefits as well. For example, personnel administrators need to understand the insurance aspects of employee benefits because these benefits can account for more than 40 percent of payroll expense in some companies. People working in the insurance industry as underwriters, actuaries or salespeople obviously need to understand the technical features of employee benefits. Financial planners need to understand the topic to integrate employer-provided benefits into clients' financial plans. Accountants must understand the topic as several auditing issues involve the liabilities created by promises to deliver benefits many years in the future.

No other society relies as much as the United States on the private market to deliver the basic framework of economic security to its citizens. If our democracy is to function well, Americans should be well informed about the provision of their economic security. In recent years, several employee benefits have merited national attention. Demographic forecasts, especially data indicating the aging of our society, suggest this attention will continue and likely increase.

This chapter provides the basic vocabulary and information needed to understand many employee benefit issues. As is true elsewhere in this text, readers should consult more narrowly focused books for more comprehensive information (*see* the bibliography at the end of this chapter).

The Advantages for the Government, Employer and Employee

The Government

When the United States was born, it was an agricultural society, and as such its people were assumed to be self-sufficient. When a disaster such as premature death or disability occurred, family members provided the support needed. Extended families lived close enough to help one another. In addition, few people lived long enough or were sufficiently wealthy to retire from work.

Industrialization destroyed the agrarian pattern. People left the land and lost the self-sufficiency of growing their own food. Society became interdependent, relying on a monetary exchange system for transactions. Families were more likely to be separated geographically. Improved sanitation and health care increased life expectancy. One result was a potentially long retirement period, often involving economic and physical dependency. The use of machinery and fossil fuel shortened workweeks, providing leisure time.

Society was revolutionized, and so was the method of providing economic security to its members. Instead of the family, the government assumed responsibility for providing economic security. This change did not take place suddenly; rather it was a gradual evolution from the view of individual responsibility for one's welfare to collective or social responsibility. As a result of this process, the governments of all industrialized societies provide some level of economic security for their citizens.

The American approach relies primarily on free enterprise. The government provides a foundation of benefits, but employers and private insurers provide the key portion of the economic security program for most American workers. This approach has many advantages. First, the competition of free enterprise promotes efficiency. When insurers, preferred provider organizations and health maintenance organizations each can provide group health coverage and compete for business in terms of price and quality, society benefits from the invisible hand of competition. Second, the large amount of capital required to fund pension plans remains in the private economy, which is desirable for a free-enterprise, capitalistic system.

The free enterprise approach also has disadvantages. Coverage is neither uniform nor universal. The unemployed, part-time employees and employees of companies with no benefits or minimal benefit programs may be cut off from needed services. Inadequate health care access is an especially troublesome social issue involving about 35 million Americans. Also, the tax revenues forgone when the government induces employers to provide employee benefits by granting tax breaks mean taxes must go up to replace that revenue. Critics maintain that such a tax policy often helps upper- and middle-income citizens at the expense of lower-income people. The tax advantages given employee benefits also distort the economic welfare distribution. For example, some critics maintain that the tax advantage given group health insurance may account for overconsumption of this good and be a prime reason for the uncontrollable rise in health care costs.[2] These critics argue that tax policy encourages employers to provide health insurance and that the insurance benefits encourage people to use more health care services than they would if they paid for their health care costs directly.

The government receives the following advantages from our mixed government and private employee benefits system:

- Fewer people depend on the government for support (welfare).
- Private pensions and life insurance reduce pressure to expand the Social Security program.
- The government avoids control of the economy if the funds held to finance the benefits system remain in private hands.

The Employer

An employer receives the following advantages when providing employee benefits to workers:

- Tax advantages
- The capability to attract, retain, motivate and reward employees beyond providing straight wages
- The ability to protect the firm's investment in its employees' human capital
- The ability to provide room for the promotion of young workers

Tax Advantages

If an employer were given the option of paying employees either $14 an hour in wages or $10 an hour in wages and $4 in benefits, why might the second alternative be chosen? Some tax advantages favor the second approach. Both wages and benefits are deductible from gross income, so no direct tax advantages arise from the deductibility of employee benefits. However, assume the employer's goal is to provide a given amount of dollars of pension benefit to each employee, $500 a month for example. Then, because no tax is payable on the investment income during the employee's working years, the employer does not have to put as much into the fund to accumulate the desired amount.

Attract, Retain and Motivate

Employee benefits allow the employer to *attract, retain* and *motivate* the employee more effectively than straight wages. In a competitive job market, if one employer's total compensation package is viewed as less desirable than all others, presumably that employer will have difficulty finding and keeping good workers. Likewise, if one employer has a better compensation program than other employers, it will have an advantage in hiring the best workers. If employees view the combination of wages and employee benefits as more desirable than wages alone, competitive employers must provide them to employ the best people. Given the tax advantages (described later in the chapter) afforded employee benefits from the employee's standpoint, competitive employers must offer them.

Reward and Commitment

Creative employers and benefit planners can use employee benefit packages to provide a solution to the universal problem of motivating and rewarding valuable employees. "Golden handcuffs," profit-sharing plans and deferred compensation programs can boost morale, increase commitment to the firm's goals and reward superior performance. Often the reward can be provided on a tax-advantaged basis.

Protect Human Capital

A firm's accounting balance sheet never lists all of its most important assets. It always omits human capital—its employees. Intelligent risk managers use life insurance and disability insurance to replace income losses arising when key people die or are disabled. In a similar vein, health insurance, wellness programs and substance abuse programs may allow a firm to recover the services of valuable employees before they are irretrievably lost.

Mobility

When younger employees replace retiring employees, many positive results often occur. Sometimes, however, a firm loses irreplaceable skills, while in other cases a firm can acquire new skills, new enthusiasm, new endurance, all at a salary considerably less than that of the retiring worker. A pension plan eases the transition to retirement and thereby opens positions for younger workers.

The Employee

Employees usually prefer employee benefits to straight salary because of tax advantages. They receive some benefits income tax-free, while other benefits allow the advantage of tax deferral on investment income.

Employees need not report the premiums for the first $50,000 of group term life insurance or premiums spent on group health insurance on their federal tax return. Depending on the worker's marginal tax bracket, this benefit can be worth a considerable amount.

Tax deferral allows the employer to take an immediate income tax deduction when making contributions to a pension plan, but the employee reports no income until the pension is received. Forty years, for example, may elapse between the employer's payment and the employee's receipt of taxable income. Tax deferral provides two advantages. First, postponing tax payment allows interest to be earned on dollars "owed" to the government. Second, deferral allows the compound interest to accumulate on a tax deferred basis.

☐ Example

Gene Green receives straight wages and must pay taxes on his marginal $1,000 of income at a 30 percent rate. He can invest $700 after taxes. Each year he also must pay 30 percent of his investment earnings in taxes. Sue Blue postpones the taxes on the marginal $1,000 contributed to her pension plan. The full $1,000 is invested. Furthermore, she also postpones the taxes on all the income the $1,000 produces. In the long term, though she owes taxes when she makes withdrawals, Sue's position will be superior to Gene's. Table 18.1 illustrates this distinction.

When the employer and employee are the same person, these tax advantages are even more valuable. For the employer the life, health and disability insurance premiums and pension plan deposits are tax-deductible business expenses; for the employee these benefits are received tax-free or on a tax-deferred basis. Professional corporations, such as those formed by doctors and lawyers and small businesses, allow owners significant tax planning possibilities using employee benefits.

Employees receive other advantages from employee benefit programs, including the following:

- Compulsory saving for retirement accompanied by professional money management
- Group insurance's lower cost than for comparable individual coverage

Table 18.1
Illustration of the Advantages of Tax Deferral
(Interest rate = 8%)

	Gene Green					Sue Blue			
Year	Deposit	Taxes	Interest	Taxes	Fund Balance	Deposit	Interest	Fund Balance	Taxes	Balance After Tax
1	1,000.00	300.00	56.00	16.80	739.20	1,000.00	80.00	1,080.00		
2			59.14	17.74	780.60		86.40	1,166.40		
3			62.45	18.73	824.31		93.31	1,259.71		
4			65.94	19.78	870.47		100.78	1,360.49		
5			69.64	20.89	919.22		108.84	1,469.33		
6			73.54	22.06	970.69		117.55	1,586.87		
7			77.66	23.30	1,025.05		126.95	1,713.82		
8			82.00	24.60	1,082.45		137.11	1,850.93		
9			86.60	25.98	1,143.07		148.07	1,999.00		
10			91.45	27.43	1,207.08		159.92	2,158.92		
11			96.57	28.97	1,274.68		172.71	2,331.64		
12			101.97	30.59	1,346.06		186.53	2,518.17		
13			107.68	32.31	1,421.44		201.45	2,719.62		
14			113.72	34.11	1,501.04		217.57	2,937.19		
15			120.08	36.03	1,585.10		234.98	3,172.17		
16			126.81	38.04	1,673.87		253.77	3,425.94		
17			133.91	40.17	1,767.60		274.08	3,700.02		
18			141.41	42.42	1,866.59		296.00	3,996.02		
19			149.33	44.80	1,971.12		319.68	4,315.70		
20			157.69	47.31	2,081.50		345.26	4,660.96		
21			166.52	49.96	2,198.06		372.88	5,033.83		
22			175.85	52.75	2,321.16		402.71	5,436.54		
23			185.69	55.71	2,451.14		434.92	5,871.46		
24			196.09	58.83	2,588.40		469.72	6,341.18		
25			207.07	62.12	2,733.35		507.29	6,848.48		
26			218.67	65.60	2,886.42		547.88	7,396.35		
27			230.91	69.27	3,048.06		591.71	7,988.06		
28			243.84	73.15	3,218.75		639.04	8,627.11		
29			257.50	77.25	3,399.00		690.17	9,317.27		
30			271.92	81.58	3,589.35		745.38	10,062.66	3,018.80	7,043.86

- Availability of group insurance coverage for some employees to whom individual coverage is unavailable

Characteristics of Insured Employee Benefits

Before this chapter discusses the three types of insurance commonly provided by employers, readers should understand how group insurance is characterized, particularly how it is underwritten.

General Features

Group insurance provides coverage for many people under one master contract. Typical groups covered include all the employees of one employer or all the members of a labor union. Group insurance can be written on all the debtors (credit card holders with outstanding balances) of one creditor (bank, credit union or department store). Insurers have offered group coverage to all members of social fraternities and sororities or all the alumni of a particular university. The most important characteristic of the covered group is that it not be formed solely to purchase group insurance. About half the states require a minimum number of covered workers—usually ten—before group insurance can be written.

Another eligible group is the multiemployer trust (MET). Multiemployer trusts represent groups of employers and employees in one industry; for example, construction. The MET allows this group to combine their numbers and purchase group insurance more advantageously than any member could individually. Unfortunately, several METs have experienced fraud and mismanagement in recent years, leaving some workers without coverage.

Group life, disability and health insurance require a contract between an employer and an insurer. Many large employers self-insure their health benefits but allow third-party administrators to operate the plans. Each employee receives a *certificate of participation* and an explanation of the benefits provided, but the "insured" technically is the employer.

As mentioned elsewhere in this book, group insurance costs less per person than comparable individual insurance because medical examinations usually are not required, the employer often provides administrative services and the insurer's acquisition costs are lower.

Group Underwriting

Minimizing the effects of adverse selection, introduced earlier in this text, is one purpose of insurance underwriting for both group and individual coverage. Careful underwriting classifies applicants based on loss expectancy. The insurer then charges an appropriate price or declines the application.

A second purpose of group insurance underwriting is to control the administrative expense of providing the insurance. Careful underwriting allows the insurer to charge an appropriate premium for groups predicted to incur greater than average expenses or to decline coverage if it appears the group will not allow full expense recovery.

The following factors influence the group insurance underwriting decision:
- Claims history
- Demographics
- Stability
- Size and credibility
- Past carrier changes
- Benefit calculation

Claims History

The biggest factor entering into the group underwriter's decision about a particular group applicant is the group's historic claims pattern. No simple statement can summarize this mathematically complex decision area. Groups with relatively high but statistically expected "smooth" and credible claims histories are generally considered more desirable applicants than groups with wide cyclical swings in their claims histories or a history of unpredictably large claims. Underwriters and actuaries use sophisticated mathematical tools in appraising a group's claims history, but in the final analysis human judgment, including an appraisal of the agent submitting the application and the managers of the group, always plays a role in the underwriting decision.

Demographics

Because the group is underwritten as a whole, insurers adjust the premium based on group demographics. Factors influencing the premium include the balance between men and women and between older and younger employees.

Stability

Stability is determined by employee turnover. Groups with either no departures or abnormally high employee turnover are not looked on favorably. If turnover is low, the group will age, and insurance costs will increase. If turnover is high, administrative expense will increase.

Size and Credibility

As explained in Chapter 7, the insurer might offer a large group experience-rated premiums. Credible groups having fewer deaths, disabilities or hospitalizations receive lower premiums. Small groups must wait several years before insurers give their experience sufficient credibility to lower premiums.

Carrier Changes

Underwriters are not favorably impressed with applications from insureds that frequently switch insurers, because insurers do not recover acquisition expenses in the first year or two. Groups with a history of frequent carrier changes are not likely to be profitable to the insurer.

Benefit Calculation

Group underwriters prefer covered people to have little or no choice in benefit type or amount. This is one safeguard against adverse selection. In large groups of employees, limited benefit choice is the rule. In the case of a small business, when the business owner purchases the group coverage and is also a plan beneficiary, the underwriter pays special attention to the reasonableness of the benefit levels.

Group Life Insurance

When a covered employee dies, *group term life insurance* provides a death benefit to the employee's beneficiary. Policies typically last for one year. When the term expires, the policy can be renewed. These policies have no savings values.

The average age of the covered employees determines the premiums for group term life insurance. Unlike an individual, a group's average age does not necessarily increase every calendar year. In fact when several older employees retire and are replaced by younger employees, the group's average age goes down. Thus the average age of a group is affected by the age and number of employees flowing in and out of the group.

Most employers will cover full-time workers, but some may offer the coverage to part-time employees too. Some employers also offer coverage, often in reduced amounts, to retired employees.

Benefit Amounts

A *flat amount benefit* provides the same amount of coverage for each employee or category of employees. For example, a $25,000 flat amount benefit provides $25,000 if a covered worker dies. An alternative benefit formula bases the insurance amount on a *position schedule*. For example, a position schedule may provide a benefit of $40,000 for salaried workers and $20,000 for hourly workers. A third approach establishes the insurance benefit as a *percentage of earnings*. For example, the death benefit may equal one year's salary or, alternatively, 150 percent of salary. Finally, combinations of these approaches are possible. For example, a *percentage of earnings position schedule* may provide 200 percent of salary for upper-level managers, 150 percent for middle managers, 100 percent for all other employees. To retain their tax-advantaged status, employee benefits must not violate the discrimination provisions of the Internal Revenue Code (IRC). If plans discriminate in favor of the highly compensated, tax advantages are lost. (As this material is being written, the rules governing nondiscrimination in employee benefits are not final, because IRC Section 89 rules have been repealed and have not yet been replaced with final provisions, though temporary safe harbors are known. The "90-50" rule is a good example of a nondiscrimination requirement. This Section 89 rule required that at least 90 percent of the non–highly compensated employees must be eligible to receive a benefit equal to at least 50 percent of the largest benefit available to highly compensated employees.)

Beneficiary Designation, Assignment and Settlement Options

The employee is allowed free choice when designating a beneficiary, though some states prohibit the employer from being named an employee's beneficiary. Unless they name their beneficiary irrevocably, employees can change beneficiaries freely by properly notifying the insurer.

Employees may assign contract rights if they give the insurer proper notification. A valid assignment transfers all ownership rights the employee has in the contract. Estate planning considerations may motivate assignment of group life insurance.

The employee during life or the beneficiary after the employee's death may choose a settlement option. Available options are comparable to the settlement options available with individual insurance, including lump-sum payment, lifetime income or payments for a limited period. The default option is a lump sum of cash. If the beneficiary designation is unclear, the insurer uses the facility of payment clause or the interpleader process to transfer the death proceeds. (*See* Chapter 10 for a discussion of these legal issues.)

Conversion

Group term life insurance contracts allow covered employees to convert group insurance coverage to individual insurance if they leave the group. Insurers do not require evidence of insurability for conversion, but other conditions may apply, such as a time limit for making the change.

The conversion right is rarely exercised except by people who are otherwise uninsurable. The insurance must be converted to a cash value type of coverage with premiums calculated at the insured's age at the time of conversion. People who are changing jobs usually opt for the group life insurance offered by the new employer rather than an expensive conversion. Those who remain unemployed often cannot afford an expensive conversion.

Taxation

The federal income taxation of group term life insurance allows the employer a deduction for premiums paid, as long as an employee's total compensation is reasonable.[3] The employee does not report the premium as income, as long as the insurance benefit is less than $50,000.[4] To receive this favorable tax treatment, group life insurance plans must not discriminate in favor of highly compensated employees. (The IRC has a set of mathematical tests to determine if highly compensated employees receive unacceptably high benefits relative to non–highly compensated employees. One example of this type of test is that the largest benefit received by the highly compensated cannot be more than 50 percent greater than the lowest benefit available to the non–highly compensated. The nondiscrimination rules covering welfare [nonpension] plans were presented in Section 89 of the IRC. This highly complex set of requirements was repealed in 1990. These rules are being revised as of this writing.)

If the benefit is greater than $50,000, the premiums for the insurance in excess of $50,000 are included in the employee's taxable income based on a government table (*see* Table 18.2) showing increasing cost for each $1,000 of coverage based on the employee's age.

☐ **Example**

Lona Boyd is 45 years old and receives a $200,000 group life insurance benefit from her employer. She includes the premium for ($200,000 − $50,000) $150,000 of group life insurance in her taxable income. This is calculated as

Table 18.2
Premiums for $1,000 of Group Term Life Insurance

Age	Monthly Cost
Under 30	.08
30–34	.09
35–39	.11
40–44	.17
45–49	.29
50–54	.48
55–59	.75
60–64	1.17
65–69	2.10
70 and above	3.76

$0.29 (cost per thousand each month) × 12 (months) × 150 (thousands of coverage), or $522.

When group life insurance proceeds are received in a lump sum, the beneficiary recognizes no taxable income. When the settlement option pays the proceeds over time, combining interest income with the lump-sum proceeds, only the interest earnings are taxable. (*See* Chapter 11 for details of taxation of life insurance proceeds.)

Group Life Insurance in Individual Financial Plans

Most financial advisers recommend that people not rely entirely on group term life insurance or even a combination group term life insurance and Social Security survivor benefits for their life insurance program. Most people will see group life insurance as one leg of a financial security tripod, with Social Security and individual life insurance being the other two legs, for the following reasons:

- The benefits may be inadequate to meet all financial needs and goals. This outcome is likely, because group benefit amounts are set without considering employee needs.
- The benefits may be unavailable if employment ends or the employer cancels the plan due to bankruptcy or merger. As noted earlier, conversion to individual insurance is unlikely.
- Group term life insurance involves no savings, and the savings feature of individual cash value life insurance may be important to some people. Some employers make cash value life insurance or group universal life insurance available as an optional part of their employee benefit program.

Other Benefits

Supplemental life insurance plans allow the employee to purchase additional amounts of coverage. Because of the possibility of adverse selection, the employee is given a limited choice of amounts for purchase, with a maximum total amount of coverage predetermined. For example, the supplemental plan may allow a covered employee to purchase supplemental insurance equal to the amount provided in the basic plan. If the basic plan provides $25,000 in coverage, the supplemental plan allows a second $25,000 to be purchased. If a maximum total coverage limit of $40,000 is provided, the employee can purchase only $15,000 of supplemental coverage. The employee might pay the full cost of the supplemental coverage, or the employer might subsidize some of the purchase. Because the supplemental coverage involves the potential for adverse selection, the cost can be higher than the basic coverage, and the employee should compare the cost to other purchase alternatives. Some insurers require evidence of insurability if supplemental insurance is purchased, and this can limit the effects of adverse selection and lower the cost.

Accidental death and dismemberment coverage pays an additional amount when covered workers die or are severely injured by accident. Benefits are stated as a percentage of a *principal sum*. For example, death caused by a common carrier (such as a scheduled airline) may result in payment of three times the principal sum. For other accidental causes of death the policy may pay twice the principal sum. Accidental loss of body parts (an eye, a hand, a foot) is scheduled for payment at 50 percent of the principal sum.

Accident policies can be employer-provided as part of the basic coverage or made elective with the cost covered by employee contributions. While the nominal cost of this insurance appears low, the insurance still can be expensive relative to the potential for claims payment. Financial plans should never be based on the possibility of accidental death.

Postretirement Life Insurance

The group life insurance plans described so far provide coverage for active workers. Retired workers generally do not need life insurance as much as young workers. By the time of retirement, home loans are repaid, children are financially independent and wage income, by definition, does not need replacement. Nevertheless, in some cases, especially involving professional corporations and small businesses, employers provide life insurance coverage to retired employees.

Employers fund postretirement coverage in the form of current funding, retired lives reserves and cash value policies.

Current Funding

Larger employers providing a life insurance benefit to retired employees can include the retired workers with active employees when reporting the insured group census to the insurer. If the number of retired workers is not large relative to the active group, the impact on the group insurance cost is slight. If group demographics change and the retired employees become a significant percentage of the insured pool, costs must rise. Often the death benefit provided each retired worker is less than that provided active employees. The smaller death benefit provided retired workers reduces the increasing cost of their coverage.

Retired Lives Reserves[5]

Before the Tax Reform Act of 1984 employers could prefund the cost of providing life insurance to retired workers on a tax-advantaged basis. Simply put, retired lives reserves are deposits made to a trust. At retirement the trust funds pay the cost of group term coverage on retired workers. These plans still may be established, but current tax rules provide no encouragement to do so.

Cash Value Policies

Several postretirement group life insurance plans involve a combination of term and cash value life insurance. Insurers have designed several policy types for the employee benefits market. The usual arrangement is for the employer to pay the term portion of the cost, with the employee paying for the cash value life insurance. Splitting the premium this way preserves the tax advantages accorded term insurance by Internal Revenue Code Section 79. The employer's paying for the cost of cash value life insurance creates taxable income for the employee in the year the premium is paid.

At retirement the employee can continue to pay for the cash value life insurance, take a reduced amount of paid-up coverage or surrender the policy for cash. Because the employee's payments funded the coverage, the employee has an adjusted cost basis in the policy, thus limiting any federal income tax liability.

Group universal life insurance policies fall into the category of cash value life insurance. During the late 1980s group universal life insurance enjoyed some popularity because it allowed employees to purchase this attractive form of permanent life insurance at group rates and relieved employers of any perceived need to provide life insurance for retired employees.

Group Disability Income Insurance

The loss potential—in both frequency and severity—of total and permanent disability caused by accident or illness is greater than the loss potential of premature death. Disability occurs about four times more frequently than premature death at ages younger than 55, and while premature death ends wages, permanent disability ends wages *and* is likely to be accompanied by substantial medical and rehabilitative expenses.

When an employee is disabled by a work-related accident or illness, workers' compensation benefits pay medical expenses, replace income and provide for rehabilitation. Workers' compensation benefits rarely replace all lost income. Moreover, not all permanent disabilities are work-related. Legal liability may provide compensation for some non-work-related disability, but the legal recovery process can be slow, unsure and expensive. Employers wanting to provide adequate work-related and non-work-related disability coverage for workers and their families furnish disability income insurance as one part of their employee benefit program.

Short-Term Disability   Short-term programs continue the employee's salary for six months or less. Often these plans, usually called *sick leave plans*, are not insured, although some union-negotiated plans are insured. Employers offering this benefit credit employees with a number of "sick days" for a given period of time worked. For example, an employee may earn one "sick day" for each month of employment. If the employee takes more sick days than are earned, the employee's pay is reduced.

Long-Term Disability

Long-term disability benefit plans typically cover full-time employees only. Long-term benefits begin after a waiting period (for example, six months) and last for a period of years (for example, five or ten) or until a specified age (for example, 65) is reached.

For two reasons employers usually purchase commercial insurance when providing long-term disability coverage: (1) because purchased coverage causes the insurer, not the employer, to make the disability determination, absorbing any ill will generated by a negative decision; (2) because the disability exposure can produce catastrophic losses for large, but especially for small, employers.

Several problems must be solved when offering long-term disability insurance. *Permanent disability* must be defined. Definitions may be liberal (unable to perform the tasks of the occupation for which the person is trained) or strict (unable to perform the tasks of any occupation for which the person might be trained). Some policies combine both definitions, applying the liberal definition for the first few years of disability, then shifting to the strict definition if the disability persists.

☐ **Example**

Mr. Bore, a teacher, suffers a permanent voice loss in 1990. He meets the liberal disability definition because he cannot fulfill his classroom responsibilities. After three years his policy shifts to the strict definition. At this point he no longer meets the definition of permanent disability, because he can fulfill the requirements of an administrative position.

Underwriting Problems

Home office underwriters, the insurance company employees pricing the group insurance application, have learned painful lessons about adverse selection when providing long-term disability insurance. Especially in times of economic recession, people tend to increase claim frequency. Because some losses are open to question and some are within the insured's control, both preloss underwriting and postloss claims adjusting take on added importance.

Benefit Amounts

Disability compensation must not encourage malingering. To achieve this goal compensation is limited to some percentage of the predisability income, such as $66^{2}/_{3}$ percent. All sources of disability income should be considered when calculating the disability insurance benefit, including Social Security and workers' compensation benefits. Plans that consider Social Security benefits when determining disability insurance benefits are called **integrated plans**.

Exclusions

Long-term disability insurance typically excludes payment for losses arising out of:

- self-inflicted injuries, including suicide attempts;
- the commission of a felony;

- preexisting conditions; and
- war.

Most policies limit benefits when disability is caused by mental illness or substance abuse.

Taxation

The IRC allows the employer to deduct the cost of purchasing disability insurance coverage. The employee does not have to report the cost of the employer's contribution as taxable income. However, if the employee receives payments because of disability, these payments are included in the employee's taxable income in the year received. If, however, the employee paid the premium for the disability income protection, there is no federal income tax on the benefits. If the employer and the employee each paid part of the premiums, the amount of disability income attributed to the employee's contribution is not subject to income tax.

Group Health Insurance

Employers provide group health insurance to active full-time employees. Many employers also provide coverage for employees' dependents, and some employers continue health insurance coverage for their retired employees. (In 1991 the Federal Accounting Standards Board [FASB] set 1993 as a target date for companies to begin showing the liability for postretirement health benefits on their financial statements. For large corporations the liability can be billions of dollars. For example, IBM Corporation recognized a onetime charge of more than $2 billion in the first quarter of 1991.)

Health Insurance Providers

Private group health insurance comes from the same sources as individually purchased coverage. About 90 percent of Americans with private health insurance acquired their benefits as part of an employee benefit program. Blue Cross and Blue Shield Plans, insurance companies, preferred provider organizations (PPOs) and health maintenance organizations (HMOs) are the usual sources of group health insurance. Additionally, large employers may self-insure some or all of their health insurance costs. (Chapter 7 presents features and provisions of individual health insurance contracts and describes health care providers more thoroughly. To avoid repetition, this chapter presents only a brief review of overlapping material.)

HMOs provide extensive health care, including physical examinations, in exchange for monthly payments called *capitation payments*. Once the capitation payment is determined for a period (such as six months or a year), it does not change because of utilization. PPOs, such as hospitals, provide services on a contract basis to employers. They do not provide prepaid benefits like HMOs, but they bill the user (employer) at prearranged prices when service is rendered. Incentives, such as reduced coverage if a non-PPO is used, are used to encourage employees to get their health care needs met by the PPO.

Health Insurance Contracts

Group health insurance typically covers the employee and eligible dependents. Eligible dependents include a spouse, if the employee and spouse are not separated, and children under a specified age, such as 19.

Group health insurance benefits are provided under a *basic medical* insurance policy or a *major medical* insurance policy.

Basic Medical Insurance

Basic medical insurance provides a limited amount of insurance (for example, $5,000 or $10,000) for expenses incurred if the insured is hospitalized. Contracts define the term *hospital* to exclude nursing homes, substance abuse treatment centers and other locations providing custodial care.

Covered hospital expenses include room charges, X-rays and supplies and charges for use of special facilities such as operating rooms or intensive care units. Basic medical policies cover many outpatient expenses, including emergency room costs.

These contracts cover physicians' charges for services delivered in the hospital. Insurers either determine payments for doctors' charges on the *reasonable and customary* (R & C) charge or use a scheduled approach. Insurers determine R & C payments for given geographic areas. Usually physicians accept this amount as full payment. The *scheduled approach* lists the payments available for every service a doctor may perform. Sometimes when the scheduled amount is less than the doctor charged, the patient must pay the difference.

Basic medical policies provide *first-dollar coverage* usually without any participation by the insured. That is, there is no deductible or coinsurance provision. Thus, if the insured incurs a $970 fee for using the emergency room, the insurance pays the full amount.

Typical exclusions are payments for regular physical examinations and for elective cosmetic surgery. Some new policies broaden coverage by providing payment for hospice care, outpatient surgical centers and a limited amount of home health care.

Major Medical Insurance

Group major medical insurance generally has high policy limits or sometimes no-maximum limits. It also has a deductible provision and a coinsurance, or participation, provision. The insured pays an initial deductible amount and a percentage of all claims in excess of the deductible. Caps are usually placed on the total amount an insured must pay in a calendar year. If the sum of the deductible and the participation payments exceeds the cap (for example, $1,000), the major medical insurance pays 100 percent of the claim up to the policy limits.

☐ **Example**

Betty Worker has $50,000 in covered expenses in one calendar year. Her employer's policy has a $250 deductible, an 80-20 coinsurance provision and a $1,000 cap on the insured's annual payments. Her insurance benefit is calculated in Table 18.3.

Table 18.3
Calculation of Betty Worker's Major Medical Insurance Claim

Covered expenses	$50,000
(less deductible)	250
	49,750
For the next $3,750 of the claim the insured pays 20% ($750) and the insurer pays 80% ($3,000)*	
80% coinsurance until cap	3,000
100% insured after cap	46,000
Total paid by insurer	$49,000
Total paid by insured	$1,000

*The algebraic solution is .2(X) + $250 = $1,000, where X is the maximum amount of the claim the insured must participate in. In this example it is $3,750. Eighty percent of this amount is the $3,000 paid by the insurer shown in the table. When the claim exceeds $3,750, the insurer pays 100% of the remainder ($50,000 − 250 − 3,750 = $46,000).

Insurers write major medical insurance on either a *supplementary* or a *comprehensive* basis. Supplementary policies coordinate with an underlying basic medical insurance policy. The basic medical policy pays the initial claim, then the major medical insurance policy begins to pay.

Comprehensive major medical policies have no underlying basic medical insurance. The major medical insurance policy pays the entire claim, less any applicable deductible and participation provision.

General Provisions of Group Health Insurance Contracts

The Consolidated Omnibus Budget Reconciliation Act of 1985 (COBRA) requires employers to allow workers leaving the group, spouses of deceased employees and divorced spouses to continue group health insurance coverage for up to 36 months after a "qualifying event," such as separation from work, death or divorce. The person continuing the coverage must pay the group premium to the employer, but this cost is less than individually purchased coverage.

Benefits

The contract between insurer and employer determines the coverage and the cost. Major medical insurance typically covers the following expense categories:

- Hospital charges
- Physician charges
- Prescription drugs
- X-rays and anesthetics
- Ambulance charges

Exclusions

Several exclusions generally apply to group health insurance policies. The following exclusions are typical:

- *Coverage for custodial care*. This exclusion eliminates coverage when the insured is in a facility that is not trying to improve the status of the patient's health.

- *Coverage of physical examinations.* Unlike HMOs, insured plans, including those offered by Blue Cross/Blue Shield, do not pay for regular examinations.
- *Coverage for elective cosmetic surgery.*
- *Coverage for preexisting conditions.* The definition of preexisting conditions varies, but it generally means a condition for which the employee was being treated when the coverage began.
- *Most group health insurance policies place limits on the amounts they will pay for mental health problems and often place limits on payments for health problems arising from substance abuse.*

Coordination of Benefits

Coordination of benefit clauses in health insurance contracts enforces the principle of indemnity. Indemnity requires the insured to be reimbursed for covered losses, but not enriched. Because many families have two working spouses, because many children are reared in families where parents are divorced and remarried and because many families have medical expense coverage provided by personal automobile policies for losses arising from automobile accidents, duplicate health insurance is a common possibility. Coordination of benefit clauses determines which policy pays first (provides *primary* coverage) and which policy pays second (provides *excess* coverage). If the policy wording does not clearly handle duplicate coverage questions, state law resolves the issue.

Cost Containment

The rapid rise in health care costs has led employers to make considerable efforts to contain health care costs or shift some of these costs to employees. Many employers have instituted measures such as wellness programs (including emphasis on physical fitness and elimination of smoking and drinking), precertification before surgery (when a medical technician reviews and approves the anticipated length of stay), second opinions before surgery, case management for AIDs victims and victims of other catastrophic illnesses and postclaims audits of medical bills. Despite all these measures, employers' health insurance premiums rose at double-digit rates throughout the 1980s and into the early 1990s.

Review Questions

1. Describe the employer's goals in offering employee benefits.
2. Why do employees prefer employee benefits to straight wage income?
3. List three different approaches for determining a group life insurance benefit.
4. Give two different definitions of *permanent disability*.
5. What are some of the differences between basic and major medical insurance policies?
6. Describe the different business management functional areas having an interest in employee benefits.

7. What are the federal government's benefits and costs in encouraging private employers and benefit providers to maintain the current American employee benefit system?

8. Describe and explain the importance of the various factors considered by the home office group insurance underwriter.

9. Explain the taxation of group life and group health insurance benefits from the employee's standpoint.

10. Describe accidental death and dismemberment coverage and explain why some critics downplay its value.

11. What is postretirement life insurance? Describe the alternative ways in which it can be financed.

Endnotes

[1]*Business Insurance*, December 10, 1990, p. 1.

[2]*See* C. Havighurst, "The Questionable Cost-Containment Record of Commercial Health Insurers," *Health Care in America*, H. E. Frech III, ed. (San Francisco: Pacific Research Institute for Public Policy, 1988), pp. 232-234.

[3]Internal Revenue Code Section 162.

[4]Internal Revenue Code Section 79.

[5]For more comprehensive coverage of this topic, see B.T. Beam, Jr., and J. J. McFadden, *Employee Benefits*, 3rd ed. (Chicago: Dearborn Financial Publishing, Inc., 1992), pp. 124-131.

Bibliography

Regularly updated reporting services by Prentice-Hall (*Pension and Profit Sharing Service*) and Dearborn Financial Publishing, Inc., (*Advanced Underwriting Service*) provide technical analysis of recent tax rulings and other material involving employee benefit plans.

Beam, Burton T., Jr. "Cafeteria Plans: What's on the Menu Now?" *Journal of the American Society of CLU & ChFC* 41, November 1987, pp. 58-65.

Beam, Burton T., Jr., and Edward E. Graves. "Group Universal Life Insurance." *Journal of the American Society of CLU & ChFC* 41, January 1987, pp. 46-52.

Beam, Burton T., Jr., and John J. McFadden. *Employee Benefits*, 3rd ed. Chicago: Dearborn Financial Publishing, Inc., 1992.

Curtis, James A. "The Future of Employee Benefits after Tax Reform." *Employee Benefits Journal* 14, December 1989, pp. 21-24.

Frech, H.E., III, ed. *Health Care in America*. San Francisco: Pacific Research Institute for Public Policy, 1988.

Glazer, David A. "Wage Continuation Plans as an Executive Fringe Benefit." *Journal of the American Society of CLU & ChFC* 44, November 1990, pp. 68-73.

Hansman, Robert J. "Group 'Carve Outs' Revisited." *Journal of the American Society of CLU & ChFC* 42, July 1988, pp. 72-77.

Nordberg, Jean and Gary Bohline. "Cafeteria Plans: On the Brink of a Breakthrough?" *Journal of the American Society of CLU & ChFC* 42, July 1988, pp. 54-58.

Rhine, Sherrie L. W. "The Determinants of Fringe Benefits: Additional Evidence." *Journal of Risk and Insurance* 54, December 1987, pp. 790-799.

Rosenbloom, Jerry S., and G. Victor Hallman. *Employee Benefit Planning*, 3rd ed. Englewood Cliffs, N.J.: Prentice-Hall, 1991.

Stacy, Donald R. "Effect of the Age Act on Employee Benefit Plan Design." *Journal of the American Society of CLU & ChFC* 44, May 1990, pp. 62–72.

Sutton-Bell, Nancy. "Financing the Long-Term Care Risk." *Journal of the American Society of CLU & ChFC* 42, September 1988, pp. 72–78.

Sutton-Bell, Nancy, and Jerry D. Todd. "Auditing the Employee Benefits Program." *Benefits Quarterly* 5, Fourth Quarter 1989, pp. 51–67.

Chapter 19 | Employee Benefits: Pension Plans

Chapter Objectives

- Describe the role of private pensions in a free-enterprise economy
- Explain the difference between qualified and nonqualified pension plans
- Describe the main federal laws governing pension plans
- Discuss alternatives for eligibility, employee contributions and retirement age provisions
- Describe defined benefit and defined contribution plans and the advantages and disadvantages of each
- Explain the role of life insurance products used for funding pensions
- Describe profit-sharing, 401(k), 403(b), Keogh and cafeteria plans

Introduction

The post–Industrial Revolution forces that created the need for employer-provided group life, health and disability insurance also made private pensions a necessity:[1]

- Longer life spans, resulting from improved health care knowledge and less grinding physical labor
- The breakup of the large, closely knit nuclear family, with the accompanying loss of family ability to support retired members
- A money-based economy, facilitating storing wealth for long periods
- The social insurance program implemented in the United States, with its "floor of protection" philosophy, which assumes supplementary employer-provided pension programs
- Greatly increased worker productivity as fossil fuels were substituted for human labor and animal power, allowing fewer active workers to support more retired workers

In 1875 the American Express Company became the first American corporation to provide pension plans for its employees. By the turn of the 20th century, however, only a few corporations had formal pension plans in place. Only after World War II did private pensions become the generally accepted norm for the largest American corporations.

The Social Security program, which provided workers with a "foundation" pension, began paying its first benefits just before World War II. From its inception in 1935 until the present, Social Security was designed to be only one leg of a tripod of economic security for American workers.

The employer-sponsored pension plans that are another leg of the tripod (individual savings being the third) provide retirement income to eligible employees. The employer's and the employee's purposes are best served when pension income, as measured by the replacement ratio, is "adequate."

The replacement ratio is calculated as retirement income divided by preretirement income. Typically, when designing pension plans, employers consider pension income combined with Social Security retirement benefits and other sources of employee retirement income in calculating the replacement ratio. Replacement ratios less than 100 percent do provide adequate retirement income, because the retired employee presumably has no work-related expenses, such as commuting expense, pays no Social Security tax on pension income and is not saving to fund retirement income. Pension experts believe a replacement ratio between 50 and 70 percent allows retired workers to maintain a standard of living comparable to that enjoyed during the working years. This chapter describes how private pension plans help individuals attain that goal.

Private Pensions and Free Enterprise

The government, employers and employees all experience benefits and costs from the uniquely American approach to providing employee benefits. (Chapter 18 presents more extensive coverage of these issues.)

Government

The government loses tax revenues, estimated to be more than $70 billion annually, because of the tax incentives provided to private employers to establish and maintain private pension plans. In exchange for this revenue loss the government transfers the liability for providing pensions to private employers. More important, the private pension system allows the free-enterprise sector of the economy to retain control of the hundreds of billions of dollars used to fund pension promises. It would be hard to conceive of our economy operating its capital markets on its current scale if pension funds were held by the government or if private citizens, with their propensity to consume, were responsible for funding their own retirements. Thus the government benefits from the current system by reducing pressure on the Social Security and welfare systems and by maintaining the private enterprise capital markets.

The Employer

Private pensions allow employers to reward employees for their contributions to the firm's success. Good pension programs allow employers to attract, retain and

Chapter 19 Employee Benefits: Pension Plans 419

motivate productive employees. Pensions also facilitate labor mobility within companies, allowing older workers to retire with adequate income, thus creating promotion possibilities for younger workers. The tax incentives provided to employers by the government allow these objectives to be achieved at a lower cost than otherwise would be the case.

The Employee

Employees benefit greatly from our private pension system. Covered employees participate in a compulsory savings program managed by professional investment advisers. Most significantly, private pension plans enjoy significant tax advantages, described shortly.

Qualified and Nonqualified Pension Plans

One of the most important distinctions made in pension plan terminology is between qualified and nonqualified plans. **Qualified pension plans** meet the requirements of Internal Revenue Code Sections 401(a) and 403(a). These plans receive significant tax advantages. **Nonqualified pension plans** neither meet the IRC requirements nor receive special tax advantages but still can be useful to employers who want to provide supplemental benefits to selected employees.

Qualified Plans

Qualified pension plans receive the following beneficial tax treatment:

1. The employer's contributions to a qualified plan are deductible in the year made.[2]
2. Interest earned on pension plan assets is not taxed until received by the employee. That is, investment income on pension plan assets accumulates on a tax-deferred basis.[3]
3. Despite the employer's receiving a current tax deduction for pension payments, employees do not report taxable income until they receive pension benefits.[4]

The taxation of pension benefits is complex and does not lend itself to simplification or easy summary.[5] Generally, when a retired worker receives pension income, any portion of the income attributed to the *employee's* after-tax contributions is excluded from further taxation; the remainder, the employer's contributions and investment earnings, is subject to taxation. If employees make no contribution to their pensions, the entire amount received during retirement is reported as taxable income. (In practice applying this general principle to individual circumstance can be quite complex and often requires professional tax advice. When lump-sum distributions are taken instead of lifetime income, special tax rules apply.)

In practice, employers preparing to install a qualified pension plan seek an advance ruling from the IRS to determine whether the proposed plan provisions meet IRC requirements. If the plan is acceptable, the IRS issues a favorable determination letter. If the plan is unacceptable to the IRS, it makes its objections clear so the proposed plan can be modified to conform to IRS requirements. If the employer chooses not to modify the proposal, the IRS objections can be negotiated or the initial findings appealed. After the plan is in operation, the IRS may audit the plan and "disqualify" it if the approved plan was modified or is not adhered to in practice.

The actual legal requirements for plan qualification (described later in this chapter) are complex, but they can be understood in terms of two overriding government goals. First, *plans should not discriminate in favor of highly compensated employees*. Second, *plans should be operated in a financially sound manner*.

Nonqualified Pension Plans[6]

Many corporations promise their upper-level management employees extra retirement benefits, unavailable to most employees. Offering these benefits helps the employer attract, retain and motivate the firm's key personnel. Deferred compensation plans allow employees to shift taxable income from the years of their highest income to their retirement years, when tax treatment may be more favorable.

Nonqualified plans do not receive the tax advantages available to qualified plans. The general rule is that contributions to a nonqualified pension plan are deductible by the employer and taxable to the employee in the year the employer makes the transfer, and the assets transferred are not subject to a substantial risk of forfeiture.[7] Many companies use nonqualified plans to supplement qualified pensions because they may discriminate in favor of the highly compensated and because neither IRS approval nor cumbersome regulation or administrative procedures are required.

Typical plans require a participating employee to take a reduction in current pay or forgo future raises. The employer promises the employee future benefits equaling the current income forgone. If the employee dies before receiving the promised benefits, the employer makes payment to the employee's beneficiaries.

Supplemental Executive Retirement Program

A popular nonqualified plan is the **supplemental executive retirement program (SERP)**. Employers often fund SERPs with life insurance contracts. These programs typically have the following provisions:

- The corporation is the owner and beneficiary of life insurance on the favored executive's life.
- The benefit is based on an unsecured promise, and the employee is an unsecured creditor in the event of bankruptcy. Because the promise is unsecured, the employee reports no current taxable income, nor does the employer receive a current tax deduction. (If the promised benefit were secured, the employee would have to report current income. Many employers use "rabbi" trusts—so-called because the first such arrangement was designed to benefit a rabbi—to provide some protection to nonqualified benefit recipients. To achieve its aim, the rabbi trust must comply with strict IRS regulations.)
- The promised benefit is taxable when received in retirement, at which time the corporation is allowed a tax deduction.

- At retirement the corporation funds the employee's benefits with policyholder loans against the cash value.

Federal Regulation of Pension Plans

Pension regulation involves some very long and complex legislation, court decisions and administrative interpretations of these laws. (It is very likely changes will be made in some particulars of these rules while this book is in print. Readers needing current information will find it in the *Advanced Underwriting Service* cited at the end of this chapter.)

The Internal Revenue Code contains extensive regulations covering pension plans. Several of these provisions are described in this chapter. Other important federal laws affecting private pension plans include the following:

- Employment Retirement Income Security Act of 1974 (ERISA)
- Age Discrimination in Employment Act (ADEA)
- Civil Rights Act of 1964
- Retirement Equity Act of 1984 (REA)

Employment Retirement Income Security Act of 1974 (ERISA)[8]

This is the most far-reaching federal law covering pension plans. Its overall purpose is to protect the rights of pension plan participants. All qualified pension plans must comply with ERISA requirements.

ERISA requirements may be categorized and summarized as follows:

Reporting and Disclosure Requirements

ERISA requires employers to provide employees with easily understood plan descriptions and annual benefit statements. Annual reports also must be submitted to the government. Plans with more than 100 employees must submit more extensive reports than smaller plans.

Fiduciary Requirements

Those responsible for holding and investing pension assets must be careful to protect the assets and minimize risk of loss. Pension plan assets must be segregated from the employer's assets and must not be diverted to any use except providing plan benefits.

Minimum Plan Requirements

These requirements fall into four areas:

1. *Eligibility*: Plans should cover all employees over age 21 with one full year of service.
2. *Nondiscrimination*: Plans should not provide unfairly large benefits to highly compensated employees. Employer contributions to the plan also must be fair.

The Internal Revenue Service determines the meaning of *fair* using formulas and "safe harbor" provisions.

3. *Funding*: Defined benefit plans must be funded in advance according to the requirements of ERISA. Regular payments must be made to defined contribution plans. (Defined benefit and defined contribution plans are described shortly.) The employer must give up control of funds used to finance qualified pension plans.

4. *Vesting*: After a specified period, the employee is given a right to the employer's contribution to the pension plan. That is, if the employee leaves employment after the period when pension benefits are 100 percent vested, any contributions made by the employer belong to the employee. For example, a plan may provide for no vested benefits before five years of service are completed, with 100 percent vesting after that. This is called *five-year cliff vesting*. One purpose of the vesting requirement is to discourage employers from firing employees just before retirement.

Vesting does not mean benefits may be taken in cash at the point of termination, though in the case of a small amount of benefits this may be allowed. Generally, if benefits are vested, the employee will be eligible for whatever pension benefit is called for at the normal retirement age.

Plan Termination Insurance

This part of ERISA created the *Pension Benefit Guarantee Corporation (PBGC)*. The PBGC is a government agency that collects an insurance premium from all plan sponsors and in return stands ready to assume the liabilities of insolvent plans. Only defined benefit plans create liabilities of the type the PBGC assumes. (The U.S. Supreme Court issued a landmark decision on June 18, 1990, covering the PBGC's scope of authority. In *Pension Benefit Guaranty Corp. v. LTV Corp.* [58 U.S.L.W. 4831] the Court upheld the PBGC decision to restore a terminated plan to the employer. Simply put, LTV transferred $2.3 billion of liabilities from an underfunded pension plan to the PBGC and then started a new plan. The Court found LTV used the government insurance program to subsidize its subsequent benefit plan, and this was unacceptable. It was feared that, if the Court had ruled differently, a great raid on the U.S. Treasury and the solvent pension plans of other employers, by way of increased PBGC premiums, could have occurred.)

Age Discrimination in Employment Act (ADEA)

The ADEA prohibits discrimination against employees in the protected age group (ages 40 to 70). ADEA prevents employers from forcing employees to retire before age 70. It also prevents plan provisions, such as those relating to contributions or benefits, from discriminating against individuals in the protected group.

The Civil Rights Act of 1964

This act prevents employers from discriminating in pension plan benefits based on gender or race. This was the law the U.S. Supreme Court relied on in reaching decisions in the *Manhart* and *Norris* cases.[9] As a result of these two Court rulings, pension plans may not collect unequal contributions or pay unequal benefits based on gender.

The Retirement Equity Act of 1984 (REA)[10]

REA amended several aspects of ERISA. Its rules affect requirements for qualified pension plans in the following areas.[11]

- *Participation and vesting provisions.*
- *Maternity and paternity leave.* REA rules specify conditions under which employees can take unpaid leave without sacrificing their job.
- *Breaks in service.* A break in service occurs when an employee leaves active employment—to raise a child, for example—and subsequently returns. REA rules determine how the length of the break affects other pension rules such as vesting provisions.
- *Survivor benefits.*
- *Qualified domestic relations orders.* ERISA prohibits the assignment or alienation of pension benefits. Federal law also preempts state law. Thus, before REA, some conflict existed about a local court's ability to consider pension assets in divorce settlements. REA amends ERISA, allowing state courts to consider pension assets when providing alimony for divorced spouses and child support payments.

Most significant is that REA requires married workers to take their pension benefit as a joint-and-survivor (or one-half survivor) annuity, unless the nonemployee spouse consents to another type of distribution. This law prevents, for example, the retired employee from taking a lump-sum payment unless the spouse agrees, in writing, to this alternative.

Tax Reform Act of 1986[12]

The Tax Reform Act of 1986 was the most comprehensive revision of the IRC since 1954. Its provisions affected a wide range of transactions made by individuals, estates, corporations and pension plans. The provisions affecting pension plans were supposed to do the following:

- Severely limit previous practices allowing large tax deductions for highly compensated people
- Restrict plan loans
- Broaden plan participation
- Limit favorable tax treatment of plan distributions
- Increase the types and amounts of tax penalties

Omnibus Budget Reconciliation Act of 1987[13]

This act was intended to "tidy up" some loose ends legislators felt were left by the Tax Reform Act of 1986. Two areas of provisions affected pension plans:

- Funding requirements for underfunded plans were strengthened.
- Defined benefit plans perceived to be overfunded tax shelters faced new contribution limits, and other restrictions regulating actuarial assumptions were enacted.

Eligibility, Contributions and Retirement Age

Eligibility

The pension plan document determines rules for eligibility. To comply with ERISA nondiscrimination requirements, plans must cover almost all full-time employees. Exceptions may be made for part-time and seasonal workers. If the plan excludes part-time workers, a definition of *part-time* that is acceptable to the IRS must be used.

If age and service requirements determine eligibility, the minimum age cannot be greater than 21. The service requirement—the amount of time before a new employee can participate in the plan—cannot exceed one year.

Contributions

Qualified pension plans may be funded entirely by employers or by a combination of employer and employee contributions. Employer-pay-all plans are called *noncontributory pension plans*. Plans funded in part with employee dollars are called *contributory plans*.

Historically many pension plans were contributory plans. Currently noncontributory plans are more popular. One argument favoring contributory plans is that they allow the plan to provide larger pension benefits than if employer contributions are the sole funding source. Sometimes it is argued that contributory plans increase employee awareness and appreciation for the program. Each of these points is arguable, especially the larger-benefit assertion. Because employee pension contributions come from after-tax income, it could be argued logically that employees would be better off financially to have the employer reduce their salaries to make pension contributions.

Noncontributory plans are easier to administer. No efforts are necessary to convince reluctant employees to participate. As we just stated, tax rules also favor the noncontributory plan. An employee's contribution to a contributory plan is not tax-deductible when made, while the employer's contribution to a noncontributory plan is a deductible business expense. (Employees making after-tax contributions to their pension can deduct their contributions from taxable income when the pension is received in retirement.) Thus the noncontributory plan allows more of the pension benefit to be funded by favorable federal tax policy.

Retirement Age

To estimate pension benefits and calculate funding liabilities, pension plans establish a normal retirement age. The normal retirement age is the earliest age at which a full pension benefit can be taken. Not all employees retire at the normal retirement age; some retire sooner and some later. Thus pension plans must have provisions for a range of retirement ages. The normal retirement age is required for pension calculations; it is not a mandatory retirement age.

Many pension plans link the retirement age to a minimum number of years of service.

Example

The Loud Noise Company pension plan allows employees to retire with full benefits at age 65 if the employee has at least five years of covered employment. Retirement with full benefits is allowed at age 60 with 20 years of covered employment, and retirement is allowed at age 55 with 30 years of covered employment.

Many plans allow early retirement with reduced benefits. In cases where employees have impaired health or reduced earnings prospects, these early retirement provisions help employees. In cases where employers can benefit from hiring new workers with better skills at reduced salaries, early retirement provisions can help the employer. At times some employers provide special inducements to encourage early retirement. These employers typically offer employees near retirement age an increased number of years of pension plan credit in return for their taking early retirement.

Example

The Loud Noise Company allows workers to retire with actuarially reduced benefits between ages 55 and 64. In 1988 the company agreed to add two more years of credit to the actual years of covered employment for all employees taking early retirement with more than 25 years of service. Under this option, for example, an employee retiring with 25 years of actual service would be given credit for 27 years. If the pension plan called for a benefit of 1 percent for each year of covered service, the employee's benefit would be based on 27 percent, not 25 percent. Because employers do not agree to make these offers each year, these inducements may affect employees needing an extra incentive to retire early.

Actuarially reduced benefits means both mortality and interest assumptions are used to calculate the reduced benefits. These assumptions are necessary because early retirees deprive the pension plan of investment earnings and mortality gains. Mortality gains arise from people dying before taking pension benefits.

The Age Discrimination in Employment Act prevents employers from enforcing a mandatory retirement age. Therefore, pension plans must have provisions for employees delaying retirement beyond the normal retirement age. Plan provisions differ but generally provide for actuarially determined increments to pension benefits for each year (month) of delayed retirement.[14]

Benefits

Defined Benefit Plans   Defined benefit pension plans use a formula to determine the employee's pension benefit. (Maximum benefit levels are established by IRC Section 415.) Determining the projected pension benefit simultaneously establishes the employer's funding obligations. Because defined benefit pension plans predetermine benefits, they create legal liabilities for employers.

Defined benefit pension plans use the following types of formulas:

Flat Percentage Formula

This benefit formula provides retired employees with a percentage of preretirement income; for example, 25 or 50 percent. A *flat amount formula* provides retired employees with a fixed-dollar benefit, such as $400 a month. These benefit formulas are not popular because they ignore the employee's length of service.

Unit Benefit Formula

This formula calculates the pension benefit by multiplying the years of covered employment by a predetermined percentage of salary, typically between 1 and 2 percent. The product of this calculation is then multiplied by some measure of salary, such as an average of the last five years of salary or the average of the highest three years of salary. (*See* the annotated case study in Chapter 16.)

□ **Example**

Michael Bloomington worked for the Big Company for 25 years. The Big Company pension plan provides each worker with 2 percent of salary for each year of covered employment. Michael's pension is based on 50 percent of his preretirement income.

Service-Only Formula

Some union-negotiated pension plans calculate pension benefits based exclusively on years of service. For example, each year of service may earn the covered worker $25 of monthly income. Under such a plan a worker with 30 years of service receives a pension of $750 (30 × $25) a month.

Defined Contribution Plans

Defined contribution plans fix the employer's input; the employee's pension benefit remains undetermined until retirement. While the pension benefit remains undetermined until the employee retires, the input to defined contribution plans is designed to be sufficiently large to fund adequate retirement benefits. (Maximum contribution limits to pension plans are established by IRC Section 415.) This type of pension plan creates no legal liabilities for the employer with respect to plan funding if the employer makes the required contributions. The employee bears the investment risk with defined contribution pension plans.

Money Purchase Plans

Employers make contributions to money purchase plans based on a predetermined formula. One arrangement requires the employer to contribute a constant percentage of the employee's salary, usually between 5 and 10 percent, to the pension plan. A second formula determines the employer's pension contribution as a percentage of total payroll, with individual employees receiving their allocation based on the proportion of their compensation to total compensation paid out by the employer. Another type of money purchase plan calls for a flat-dollar annual contribution for each employee, such as $3,000.

Target Benefit Plans

Target benefit plans are hybrids between defined benefit and defined contribution plans. Legally they are defined contribution plans and thus do not create legal liabilities with respect to underfunding. In practice the employer makes a target contribution that, if actuarial estimates are realized, results in a predetermined pension benefit. The pension benefit can be based on a formula comparable to any defined benefit plan. For example, the employer can project target benefits based on a flat percentage formula or a unit benefit formula.

Target benefit plans became increasingly popular in the late 1980s. Not only do these plans eliminate the legal liabilities associated with defined benefit plan funding, but they shift the investment risk to the employees, allowing them to receive superior investment results if realized. Moreover, in small business cases where the owner is older than other employees, the target benefit plan may allow greater tax-deductible pension contributions for the owner than other defined contribution plans. Also adding to their attractiveness, target benefit plans, because they are defined contribution plans, are easier to administer and involve less regulation than defined benefit plans.

Cash Balance Plans[15]

The *cash balance plan* is another recently developed hybrid pension plan. It requires an account balance for each employee. As in a defined contribution plan, the employer contributes a percentage of the employee's salary each year. Unlike in a defined contribution plan, the employer guarantees a growth rate on the balance. Typically the guaranteed growth rate equals the interest rate on one-year Treasury bills. Similar to the defined benefit plan, the guaranteed growth rate shifts the investment risk to the employer.

The cash balance plan is popular for two reasons. First, the plan is easier to understand than defined benefit plans and thus is thought to provide better motivation for employees. Experts believe few employees understand the actuarial assumptions of the final average pay plans, and the fact that benefits can be obtained only at retirement makes these benefits appear remote to younger employees. Plan designers believe employees will respond more favorably to a plan in which the employee receives quarterly or annual statements showing regular employer contributions and compound interest gains.

Second, cash balance plans provide relatively greater benefits for employees with shorter service spans. Defined benefit plans providing benefits based on a 30-year career often do not provide much reward to employees with relatively shorter service periods. For example, a plan providing 2 percent of final average salary for each year of employment gives an employee with 10 years of service only 20 percent of final average salary. Given work service patterns in recent decades, many employees might consider a 10-year service period a long rather than a short service period. Thus the cash balance plan's ability to reward short service spans more adequately can be an important attraction to younger employees.

Advantages and Disadvantages of Defined Benefit and Defined Contribution Plans

During the 1980s most discontinued pension plans were defined benefit plans, while most new plans were defined contribution plans. Here is a summary of the advantages and disadvantages of each plan type:

- Defined contribution plans are less complex to begin and administer.
- Defined contribution plans allow younger employees to accrue benefits more rapidly than defined benefit plans. This advantage might help a company that has a young work force or that is trying to attract young workers.
- Defined contribution plans do not create legal liabilities for underfunding if required annual contributions are made. Therefore defined contribution plans do not have to pay PBGC premiums, which may represent a significant cost advantage.
- Defined contribution plans are more easily portable for employees changing jobs than are defined benefit plans.
- Defined contribution plans shift investment risk from the employer to the employee. In periods of good investment results this is an advantage to employees. During periods of poor investment performance this is an advantage to employers.
- Defined benefit plans offer greater tax sheltering potential for older owner-employees.
- Defined benefit plans allow funding for past service. *Past service benefits* apply to years counted in the pension formula but "earned" in years before the pension plan was installed. For example, if the pension plan was installed in 1975, but an employee began employment in 1965, the initial ten years of employment could count toward a pension benefit in a defined benefit plan, but they would not increase benefits in a defined contribution plan.
- Defined benefit plans produce more predictable results for employees needing an estimate of retirement benefits.
- Defined benefit plans are more likely to provide adequate benefits for lower-paid workers than defined contribution plans. This latter assertion is more likely to hold if plans have a voluntary contribution component, because lower-paid workers are less able to make contributions, even if they are matched by employers' contributions.

Inflation Considerations

Inflation distorts the plans of employers and employees, of active workers and retired people. It may be retired employees who suffer the most from inflation, because their pensions often provide only fixed benefits. The monthly income they receive at retirement may be fixed for the next two decades or longer. Rapid inflation during the period of active employment also can significantly impact retirement income. Retirement benefits based on career average earnings unadjusted for inflation may require inclusion of many years of low nominal wages.

Because both employer and employee are served best when pensions provide adequate retirement income, pension plans must allow for inflation. Ideally, pension benefits should be inflated by the same percentage as the annual increase in the consumer price index (CPI). Social Security follows this approach with its annual cost-of-living adjustment (COLA). Social Security operates on a pay-as-you-go basis, and its inflow is based on the inflated earnings of the currently employed, allowing it to increase benefits to retired workers.

Private employers cannot afford to make the generous promise of an annual COLA for two reasons. First, such a promise would create an open-ended liability on their balance sheet, with the possibility of potential bankruptcy in periods of rapid inflation. Second, because private pensions are funded in advance, retroactive contributions cannot be required to fund unanticipated liabilities caused by inflation. Therefore private employers try to compensate for the effect of inflation on pension benefits through plan design or ad hoc increases in pension benefits when funds are available.

Basing defined benefits on the average of the highest years of wages (e.g., the three highest years) is one way to eliminate years of low nominal earnings. This approach allows initial replacement ratios to reflect the worker's standard of living before retirement. Unfortunately, if inflation persists during the worker's retirement, purchasing power will be eroded without benefit increases.

Defined contribution plans adjust for inflation differently. Money purchase plans and other defined contribution plans transfer investment gains and losses directly to the employee. During inflationary periods common stock prices are subject to the same price inflation as consumer goods. Thus, if inflation exists during a working career, investment gains should help offset relatively low contributions based on low nominal wages. Again, this adjustment does not help the retired worker offset purchasing power loss during retirement. Only the continuation of inflated investment results and ad hoc benefit increases can ameliorate the loss of purchasing power in retirement.

Vesting

Rather than remain with their current employer until retirement, most employees change jobs several times during their working years. Some workers die or are disabled, and some are fired or voluntarily leave the work force. Pension plans must provide for employees' leaving their jobs before retirement. (ERISA provides the legal rules covering this area.)

In the event of a preretirement withdrawal from a pension plan, employees are always entitled to all contributions they made to the pension plan and the net investment income attributable to their contributions. At withdrawal the employer need not provide the employee a lump sum of cash but must provide the appropriate pension benefit at retirement.

Employees' rights to their own contributions are straightforward, but their rights to the employer's pension contributions can be complicated. The benefit the employee earns each year is called the *accrued benefit*. For example, if the plan uses a benefit formula calling for 1 percent of final salary for each year of covered employment, the employer must deposit a sum, the *present value* of the promise, that will fund the benefit. The term *vested benefit* means the withdrawing employee has a legal right to receive the employer's contributions funding accrued pension benefits.

ERISA sets minimum vesting standards. Two approaches are acceptable. Five-year cliff vesting, mentioned earlier, provides that the employee's benefits are fully vested after the fifth year of covered employment. The second acceptable vesting technique allows the gradual vesting of benefits between the third and seventh year of covered employment. This approach calls for 20 percent of the accrued benefits to be vested in the third year, with an additional 20 percent of the benefits vesting each year thereafter, until 100 percent of the benefits are vested after the seventh year.

The Role of Insurance in Qualified Pension Plans

Insurance is one of two ways qualified pension plans may be funded. The other arrangement uses trusts. Plans funded exclusively by insurance contracts are exempt from IRC minimum funding requirements. Noninsured plans must meet minimum funding requirements, including rules governing interest and actuarial assumptions.

Whether trusts or life insurance contracts are used, the pension cycle is the same. During the period of active employment, money is contributed to the pension plan. After retirement, payments are received from the pension plan. The services of an insurance company can be used in one or both of the phases of the cycle. That is, the insurer can provide services during the accumulation phase, the liquidation phase or both.

If an employee's pension benefit is funded individually while the benefit is accumulating, the pension benefit is called an *allocated* benefit. An employer's purchase of an annuity or a life insurance policy for each employee is called **allocated funding** of a pension plan. Small employers often use allocated funding. Large employers typically do not allocate their pension funds; rather they contribute an actuarially determined amount to a pool of assets from which payments are made to retired employees. When pension plan assets are not segregated for individual employees, the pension funding method is called *unallocated funding*. Trusts are used to hold the unallocated funds because of their benefit and investment flexibility. That is, while ERISA provisions hold investment advisers and trust fund fiduciaries to the highest levels of responsibility for the funds they oversee, the trust still is more flexible than individually purchased insurance contracts.

To compete with trusts, insurance companies offer unallocated funding alternatives called *group deposit administration contracts* and *immediate participation guarantee contracts*. The group deposit administration contract is just a pool of money until the worker retires, at which time an individual annuity is purchased. The immediate participation guarantee contract remains unallocated even after the employee retires. Even in retirement, pension payments come directly from the pool of pension assets without the guarantees associated with the purchase of an annuity. If the assets are inadequate to make the promised payments in any unallocated funding approach, the employer legally is responsible for any deficit. When insurance contracts are used in an allocated approach, the insurance company guarantees mortality, expense and investment risks.

Insurance Contracts Allocated pension plan funding uses either individual retirement annuities or individual life insurance contracts.

Individual Retirement Annuity

Small pension plans logically can use individual deferred annuities to provide retirement income. The annuity's purpose is to provide retirement income whether purchased by individuals or by pension plans. Plans using individual annuities typically involve a trustee who legally owns the policies and pays the premiums. Insurers price the annuities in terms of $10 per month of retirement income. When plans are initiated, the employer estimates the employee's pension and purchases the appropriate annuity. If an employee's estimated pension increases, additional contracts must be purchased.

☐ **Example**

The Sonic Boom Record Company estimates one of its workers, Tom White, will be entitled to receive a pension of $1,500 a month at age 65. Sonic's pension insurer pays $8 per month for each $1,000 of annuity premium on deposit. Sonic will need $187,500 ($1,500/$8 × $1,000) of annuity premium on deposit to provide Tom's pension.

The Sonic Boom Company can fund this amount over the 30 years of Tom's career, paying a level annual annuity deposit of about $1,700. If Tom's estimated pension increases, additional deposits and additional contracts will be needed.

Whether life insurance contracts or annuities fund pensions, the insurer guarantees payments and the employer is relieved of funding liability if the premiums are paid. If employees live unexpectedly long lives or investment returns are lower than expected, the insurer, not the employer, bears the extra costs. Typically insurers use conservative projections when making such guarantees. These conservative projections cause the insurance alternative to compare less favorably to the unallocated funding approach during periods when high investment returns are available.

Other disadvantages to funding pensions with individual insurance contracts include the following:

- *No contribution flexibility.* Insured plans rely on regularly scheduled premium payments. When trusts are used, increased investment returns can result in lower pension contributions for employers.
- *No advanced discount in anticipation of labor turnover.* Trusteed plans can anticipate such turnover resulting in lower annual contributions for employers. With insured plans nonvested benefits can be reacquired by employers when nonvested employees actually leave the plan.

Group Deferred Annuity

Employers with between 10 and 25 employees often use **group deferred annuities** to fund pension benefits. Employers with fewer employees use individual annuities, and employers with more than 25 employees often use group deposit administration accounts (GDA). The GDA funding plan involves one master contract. The employer usually owns the contract and pays the premiums. Annual premiums allow the employer to purchase units of deferred paid-up annuities that match the accrued pension obligations created during the year. This plan works especially well with unit benefit formulas. For each year of active employment the employer purchases a paid-up annuity providing the estimated amount of benefit.

☐ Example

The Bigger Boom Record Company deposits $1,700 each year to fund Helen Black's pension. Helen's pension plan benefit formula calls for multiplying 1 percent by the number of years of covered employment by the average of Helen's salary in her last three years of employment. If Helen works for 30 years, and her average annual salary in her last three years is $60,000, her annual pension is found by multiplying .3 by $60,000, or $18,000. Based on the insurer's payment of $8 per month for each $1,000 of annuity deposit, Bigger Boom's annual deposits will fund Helen's pension.

Life Insurance Contracts Funding Pension Plans

If a pension plan is funded with life insurance rather than deferred annuities, IRS rules limit the type of life insurance contracts used. Death benefits must be "incidental" to the pension benefit. *Incidental* means the death benefit must not be more than 100 times greater than the monthly pension benefit. For example, if the monthly pension benefit is $400, no more than $40,000 in cash value life insurance can be used to fund the benefit. Most traditional whole life contracts cannot meet the incidental death benefit test and still provide the required pension benefit. Thus, if whole life insurance is used to fund a pension, the employer also must contribute to a side fund used to supplement the cash values funding the pension. When an employer uses a side fund to supplement a whole life insurance policy, the plan is called a *combination plan*.

Retirement income policies build cash values more rapidly than whole life policies. Retirement income policies are designed to meet the need for an individual life insurance contract that funds a pension benefit with only incidental death benefits. Retirement income policies lost popularity in the 1980s because they had noncompetitive rates of return and were less flexible than available alternatives. When using retirement income or whole life insurance policies, insurers require medical examinations.

Profit Sharing, 401(k), 403(b), ESOP, Keogh Plans and Cafeteria Plans

Profit-Sharing Plans

Profit-sharing plans are one type of defined contribution plan. Unlike in qualified pension plans, the employer is not committed to regular annual contributions, but contributions must be "recurring and substantial."[16] In years when the firm's profits permit, the employer credits each employee with a share of the firm's profit. The payments may be in cash or may be deferred. Cash payments result in current income tax liabilities for employees.

Deferred profit-sharing plans may be qualified like pension plans. If they are qualified, they get the same tax deferral advantages and must meet qualification requirements similar to those for pension plans. One important requirement for qualification is that the formula dividing the employer's contributions among participants not discriminate in favor of the highly compensated. Typically the employer's contribution is allocated to individual participants based on the fraction (participant's compensation/total compensation of all plan participants). For example, if A's compensation is $80,000, and the total compensation of all plan participants is $800,000, A would be entitled to 10 percent of the employer's contribution in this year. A second important rule limits deductible employer contributions to 15 percent of total compensation of the plan's participants.[17]

Because profit-sharing plans do not produce predictable benefits on which to base retirement income, they usually supplement other pension plans. The primary goal of profit-sharing plans is often employee motivation, so these plans have more liberal rules than qualified retirement plans regarding early withdrawals and participant loans. (The 10 percent federal income tax early withdrawal penalty applies.) When profit-sharing plans are combined with other qualified plans, the total employer contribution for all plans cannot exceed 25 percent of total compensation of plan participants.

401(k) Cash or Deferred Arrangements

A **Section 401(k) plan** (the plan gets its name from the relevant section of the IRC, as does the 403[b] plan) is a profit-sharing plan allowing an employee a choice between taking income in cash or putting the income into a qualified plan. If the employee chooses to defer the income, all the advantages of tax deferral are available. The ability to choose between current or tax-deferred income explains much of this plan's popularity. A second explanation is the limit of contributions an employee can make, which currently is significantly higher than the limit applying to IRA contributions.

The Tax Reform Act of 1986 limits contributions to 401(k) plans to $7,000 indexed annually for inflation. (The 1991 limit, for example, is $8,475.) Once funds are deposited in 401(k) plans, withdrawals before age $59^{1}/_{2}$ are subject to a 10 percent tax penalty in addition to any ordinary income tax liability, unless the early withdrawal is attributed to the employee's death or disability. Moreover, employees can make withdrawals only of their own contributions; they cannot withdraw investment earnings or matching employer contributions. The employee's benefit vests immediately.

403(b) Plans, Tax-Deferred Annuities (TDAs)

The employees of nonprofit organizations such as schools, hospitals and museums have a special section of the IRC devoted to them. Congress justifies this special tax advantage because nonprofit employers do not have the same incentive as tax-paying employers to provide for their employees' welfare.

Originally the law allowed the employees of the specified nonprofit institutions voluntarily to reduce their salary (and their income tax liability) to purchase deferred annuities. Subsequently the law was amended to allow contributions to mutual funds. Limits apply to the amounts an employee can contribute to a TDA, and early withdrawal results in a 10 percent tax penalty. (Chapter 16 presents a more comprehensive explanation of these plans.)

Employee Stock Ownership Plans (ESOPs)

An ESOP can be viewed as a defined contribution profit-sharing plan with a very distinct feature: the employer contributions are made in company stock. Thus the employees' accounts are reported as a number of shares of stock. The ESOP allows the employer to raise capital on a tax-advantaged basis, and it allows employees to participate in a firm's success. The ESOP provisions can be especially useful for small corporations requiring a buyer at the death or retirement of the owner(s).

Provisions of the IRC allow companies to borrow money from lending institutions, such as banks, to acquire stock for an ESOP. The stock is pledged as collateral for the loan. When the loan is repaid, the entire repayment, not just the interest charge, is treated as a tax-deductible expense. However, recent tax law changes curtail the tax-exempt interest provisions.

ESOPs provide employers some important tax advantages, including the following:

- Stockholders can sell shares to the ESOP and defer capital gains taxation.
- Company contributions to acquire shares or retire debt are tax-deductible.
- Employees are not currently taxed on employers' contributions.

Keogh Plans

Before 1983 Keogh plans were used to provide retirement benefits for the self-employed. Prior to 1983 qualified plans had restrictions applying to pensions for partners and sole proprietors. These restrictions no longer apply, and many partnership and proprietorships now use qualified plans for all employees, including the owners. (Chapter 16 presents a more comprehensive explanation of these plans.)

Cafeteria Plans

In the past few years some employers have given employees a choice of benefits. In some cases employees are given an amount of money to spend, with minimum participation required in each benefit type. This type of plan allows an employee, for example, to trade a higher deductible on the major medical plan in exchange for a dependent care allowance. Each person or family will have a different priority of needs, and the flexibility of having a larger or smaller major medical deductible in exchange for a day-care allowance can be valuable. Flexibility can benefit families with two working spouses and overlapping health insurance benefits. Likewise families with no children or with grown children can benefit from tailoring their employee benefits to their peculiar circumstances.

Because of administrative difficulties and some issues involving taxation, cafeteria plans have not yet been widely adopted. **Cafeteria plans** are also known as *flexible-benefit plans* or **Section 125 plans**.

Review Questions

1. Describe the main reason for qualifying pension plans.
2. What is the main difference between defined benefit and defined contribution pension plans?
3. List four requirements for qualifying a pension plan.
4. Describe four of the federal laws that apply to pension plans.
5. Describe an important difference between pension plans funded with insurance contracts and those funded using trusts.
6. What is the general rule regarding the taxation of pension benefits?
7. Describe a few characteristics of profit-sharing plans, 401(k) plans and ESOPs.
8. Explain some of the employer's motivations in installing and maintaining a pension plan.
9. What is a nonqualified pension plan?

Endnotes

[1] For a comprehensive description of these factors, *see* R. C. Atchley, *Social Forces and Aging*, 6th ed. (Belmont, Calif.: Wadsworth Publishing Co., 1990), Chapters 9 and 16. *See also* D. M. McGill and D. S. Grubbs, Jr., *Fundamentals of Private Pensions*, 6th ed. (Homewood, Ill.: Richard D. Irwin, 1989), Chapter 1.

[2] Internal Revenue Code Sections 162, 212 and 404(a).

[3] IRC Sections 401(a) and 501(a).

[4] IRC Sections 72, 402 and 403.

[5] *See* the *Advanced Underwriting Service*. Chicago: Dearborn Financial Publishing, Inc. (annual), Section 17(d) for a comprehensive treatment of the taxation of pension plans.

[6] *See* Stephan R. Leimberg and Linda I. Feldman, *The Deferred Compensation Handbook: A Guide to Nonqualified Plans*, for comprehensive coverage of this material.

[7] IRC Section 402.

[8] Public Law 93-406. *See* McGill and Grubbs, Jr., *Fundamentals of Private Pensions*, pp. 51-58, for the history of ERISA.

[9] *City of Los Angeles, Department of Water and Power v. Marie Manhart*, U.S. Supreme Court, 1978 (434 U.S. 815). *Arizona Governing Committee for Tax Deferred Annuity and Deferred Compensation Plans, etc., et al. Petitioners Nathalie Norris etc.*, U.S. Supreme Court, 1982 (No. 82-52).

[10]Public Law 98-397.

[11]For current details on these provisions *see* the *Advanced Underwriting Service*. Chicago: Dearborn Financial Publishing, Inc. (annual), Section 17(c).

[12]Public Law 99-514.

[13]Public Law 100-203.

[14]ADEA Section 4, ERISA Section 204 and IRC Section 411.

[15]*Business Insurance,* November 19, 1990, pp. 3, 8.

[16]IRC Section 401-1(b) (ii).

[17]IRC, Section 404(a) (3).

[18]Dickson C. Buxton, "ESOP and Business Perpetuation Plans," *Journal of the American Society of CLU & ChFC* 44, November 1990, pp. 34–44.

Bibliography

Advanced Underwriting Service (Volume 4). Chicago: Dearborn Financial Publishing, Inc. (A monthly updated reporting service especially useful in determining current pension information.)

Barefoot, Jeffrey C. "Supplemental Executive Retirement Programs after TRA '86." *Journal of the American Society of CLU & ChFC* 42, September 1988, pp. 48–54.

Beam, Burton T., Jr., and John J. McFadden. *Employee Benefits*, 3rd ed. Chicago: Dearborn Financial Publishing, Inc., 1992.

Buxton, Dickson C. "ESOP and Business Perpetuation Plans." *Journal of the American Society of CLU & ChFC* 44, November 1990, pp. 34–44.

Canan, Michael. *Qualified Retirement & Other Employee Benefit Plans*. St. Paul, Minn.: West Publishing Co., 1989.

Canan, Michael J., and William B. Mitchell. *Employee Fringe & Welfare Benefit Plans*. St. Paul, Minn.: West Publishing Co., 1990.

Easton, Albert E. "Replacing the Qualified Joint and Survivor Option with Life Insurance." *Journal of the American Society of CLU & ChFC* 44, September 1990, pp. 78–82.

Hira, Labh S. "Taxation of Distributions from Section 403(b) Plans." *Journal of the American Society of CLU & ChFC* 43, January 1989, pp. 52–55.

Holland, Roger G., and Nancy A. Sutton. "The Liability Nature of Unfunded Pension Obligations Since ERISA." *Journal of Risk and Insurance* 55, March 1988, pp. 32–58.

J. K. Lasser Tax Institute Staff. *J. K. Lasser's Retirement Plan Handbook, 1989-90: IRAs, 401(k)s, Keoghs & Other Retirement Plans*. Englewood Cliffs, N.J.: Prentice-Hall, 1988.

Leimberg, Stephan R. and Linda I. Feldman. *The Deferred Compensation Handbook: A Guide to Nonqualified Plans*. Chicago: Dearborn Financial Publishing, Inc., 1989.

Leimberg, Stephan R., and John J. McFadden. "Nonqualified Deferred Compensation: A Critical Look." *Journal of the American Society of CLU & ChFC* 44, May 1990, pp. 32–45.

Miller, Ralph G. "Should I Pull My Money Out of My Retirement Plan—A Tougher Question Under Section 4980A." *Journal of the American Society of CLU & ChFC* 45, May 1991, pp. 52–65.

Myers, Daniel A., Richard V. Burkhauser, and Karen C. Holden. "The Transition from Wife to Widow: The Importance of Survivor Benefits to Widows." *Journal of Risk and Insurance* 54, December 1987, pp. 752–759.

Myers, Robert J. *Social Security*, 3rd ed. Homewood, Ill.: Richard D. Irwin, 1985.

Nielson, Norma. "Testing Life Insurance as a Substitute for Survivor's Pension Benefits." *Journal of the American Society of CLU & ChFC* 42, March 1988, pp. 56–62.

Palmer, Bruce A. "Tax Reform and Retirement Income Replacement Ratios." *Journal of Risk and Insurance* 56, December 1989, pp. 702–725.

Rosenbloom, Jerry S., and G. Victor Hallman. *Employee Benefit Planning*, 3rd ed. Englewood Cliffs, N.J.: Prentice-Hall, 1990.

Spalding, Albert D. "Nonqualified Retirement Plans Enter a New Era after Tax Reform." *Journal of the American Society of CLU & ChFC* 42, May 1988, pp. 58–63.

Tucker, Michael J., and Ross Quarles. "The Excise Tax on Excess Retirement Benefit Distributions and Accumulations." *Journal of the American Society of CLU & ChFC* 44, May 1990, pp. 48–51.

Chapter 20 | Business Uses of Life and Disability Insurance

Chapter Objectives

- Explain the problems associated with the loss of life or health of a key employee
- Identify business continuation problems based on the type of organizational structure
- Show how the proper use of insurance products solves many of the problems caused by the loss of life or health in the business environment
- Describe the use of nonqualified plans in providing special benefits to employees.

Introduction

The value of a business as a "going concern" is often closely tied to the continued productivity of human capital. Human capital is subject to the unfavorable contingencies of death or loss of health before normal retirement. How can a firm protect its future earnings from the death or disability of a key person? What problems are encountered when an owner dies and the business organization is a sole proprietorship? A partnership? A closely held corporation? How can a business provide extraordinary benefits to key personnel and not to the entire workforce?

The financial problems caused by the life contingencies of death and disability can be overcome with the proper use of life and health insurance. Due to the nature of the triggering mechanism in these insurance contracts, the contingency causing the financial loss simultaneously produces the contractual solution.

When a firm is financially dependent upon certain key employees, death or disability may substantially reduce income or increase expenses of the organization. Key employee life and disabilty insurance provides funds to pay for the financial problems associated with the loss of a valuable employee and simultaneously provides other benefits, including a measure of credit protection.

When a business owner dies, the organization may or may not continue, depending on the organizational structure. If no prior arrangements identify a buyer and a seller and establish a price, the going concern value may be lost.

Nonqualified plans, which are discriminatory and therefore do not enjoy the same tax advantages of qualified plans, may be used to enhance the benefit packages of key employees.

This chapter explores the financial problems caused by the death or disabilty of business owners or employees, and then examines how life insurance products, coupled with other contractual arrangements, provide solutions to these problems.

Professionals Involved in Business Insurance

The problems encountered in the so-called *business insurance* area can be quite complex and have profound effects on a variety of areas such as business organizational form, wills, estate administration and probate, liquidations, property distribution, income tax, estate tax and creditors' rights. (Because of the technical nature of this material and continual revisions of tax code, readers should consult an up-to-date tax and law service for the most recent information.) Because of the variety of problems encountered in the key employee, business continuation and nonqualified plan areas, professional service is required to ensure the anticipated outcome of these plans. Minimally, an attorney, an accountant and a life insurance agent are required. In some cases, depending on the structure of the plan, trust officers are included.

Legal Counsel For a variety of reasons attorneys are needed to handle business insurance problems. The legal nature of the business organization, wills, estates and trusts must be understood so potential problems based on life contingencies can be assessed properly and legal solutions suggested. The attorney provides the technical insight as well as the legal ability to structure the necessary documents and perform other functions such as title transfer.

Accountant Accountants are included in structuring business continuation plans, key employee plans and deferred compensation plans because of the resource, tax, valuation and accounting implications. Accounting issues must be understood so that the transactions are represented properly on financial statements. Concerned parties need to understand the potential impact on the balance sheet, income statement, cash flows and taxes.

Life Insurance Agent The life insurance agent's primary duty is to identify potential problems based on life contingencies and motivate all concerned to take steps leading to a workable solution. After the client understands the problems and is properly motivated, the life insurance agent may become the coordinator of the other professionals involved. The focus of the life underwriter's job is to provide the products to fund the solutions identified by the team.

Trust Officer In many instances the professional services of a bank trust officer are required. Many solutions to business problems need a third-party administrator for the proper separation of assets, management, administration, preservation and distribution. Common examples include handling life insurance trusts, administering assets for minors and other incompetent individuals and taking advantage of favorable portions of the tax code.

Key Employee Insurance

Identifying key employees is the first step in resolving key employee life and disability insurance problems. Key employees may perform a wide variety of tasks and be responsible for any number of activities. A **key employee** is defined as any person whose death or disability would cause severe financial harm to the organization, whether it is a sole proprietorship, a partnership or a corporation. Key employees include salespersons who have valuable contacts and knowledge, individuals involved in unique and ongoing research and development and owners or managers whose skill is integral to motivating and rewarding employees.

Depending on the characteristics of the organization, an employee's or owner's death or disability may cause varying degrees of financial harm. Organizations that have extreme key employee dependency problems exhibit the following characteristics:

- Managers are few, authority is concentrated and no method exists for the continuous hiring and training of managers or employees resulting in a defined career path.
- The firm is illiquid. There is little room for mistakes in cash flow management, and any abnormal cash requirement poses a liquidity problem.
- Capital cannot be borrowed by the firm without the owners providing their personal guarantee for repayment.
- A small number of people occupy sensitive roles or positions.

The opposite characteristics are found in organizations tending not to have significant key employee life and disability problems:

- Management and authority is not concentrated, there is a defined career path and there is a hiring and training program to support the continuing needs of the organization.
- Liquidity is sufficient to meet a variety of unexpected contingencies.
- Capital can be borrowed in the organization's name and without the personal guarantee or signature of its owners.
- No one individual monopolizes sensitive or key positions. Most positions have trained replacements available in the business, or they can be easily attracted in the labor marketplace.

Typically, smaller organizations have key employee problems and exhibit at least one of the characteristics that may result in severe financial problems from the death or disability of one individual. Larger organizations tend to have fewer key employee problems due to the higher incidence of preparation for the flow of employees. In addition, larger firms tend to have better access to capital without the personal guarantees of their owners. However, many organizations, large and small, are highly dependent on the abilities of a few capable people.

Administratively, setting up a key employee life or disability plan is usually simple. Professional help and advice, however, are always recommended. Corporate key employee plans require a resolution from the board of directors indicating that an economic problem exists and the financial extent or value of the problem. In addition, a company officer needs to be empowered to act in setting up the plan. With respect to a partnership, no resolution is required, but usually a partner who is not the insured signs the life or disability insurance application on behalf of the partnership. In a sole proprietorship the sole proprietor executes the entire agreement. In all cases the key employee must consent to the life insurance product and usually does so by signing the insurance application.

Problems Caused by Death

The financial losses caused by a key employee's death depend on the position held within the organization. A reduction in sales or an increase in expenses may result in smaller profit margins and lost profits. Death of individuals involved in important research and development efforts or people who influence the effectiveness of the organization by their motivating influence can dramatically reduce future profits.

Cost of Replacement and Training

The cost of finding and training another employee adds to the firm's loss. Payroll cost is only one component. Assuming an acceptable candidate is available, a variety of search costs will be incurred. To attract a candidate an increased sum of money or benefits may have to be offered. Training the new employee may take considerable time before the same level of productivity is reached. A new person will need some time to establish relationships with customers, suppliers and fellow workers.

Beyond the impact on current and future financial performance, a series of credit issues surrounding the death or disability of a key employee exists. If financial performance depends greatly on the continuing lives of a few people, the ability to secure credit will be impaired after a key employee dies. If the creditworthiness of the firm cannot be based on its own strength, financial institutions require other security, usually personal notes, collateral or other performance guarantees of owners. If an owner dies, funds may become unavailable; if available, the interest rate will be higher than before. Personal notes, payable immediately at death, can cause cash demands on the estate and premature liquidation of business assets to meet these financial obligations. Many times, for owners, creditors and heirs, the result is the destruction or substantial financial impairment of the business. (Business continuation problems are discussed later in this chapter.)

Disability Problems

All the problems just discussed also arise if a person becomes disabled before normal retirement. The financial impact of disability may range from minor to amounts exceeding the damage done by an employee's death. Total disability impacts income and expense patterns in a fashion similar to death. However, the business may feel an obligation to support the key employee by continuing income or paying medical or other expenses. A formal salary continuation plan implemented prior to disability would communicate the organization's policy with regard to the amount of continued salary and the length of time paid, placing a limit on the moral obligation of the firm.

Benefits of Using Life Insurance

Most of these problems can be solved with the proper use of insurance products. The benefits of using life and disability insurance products include:

- credit enhancement,
- key person indemnification,
- retention of the firm's going concern value and
- liquidity enhancement.

Credit Enhancement. Key employee life insurance is a sign of the attentive nature of management. Life insurance improves the borrower's credit standing and provides a degree of creditor protection in the event of the insured's death. Lending institutions tend to act more favorably when life insurance exists and may grant loans containing better credit terms for longer periods, allowing the borrower to take advantage of stable financing and possibly lower interest rates.

Key Person Indemnification. The use of life insurance provides for key person indemnification. The business receives funds for the loss it suffers due to the untimely death of the key employee. The various financial losses the firm suffers include loss of sales, increase in expenses and the cost of hiring and training a new employee.

Retention of Going Concern Value. When a key employee dies or is disabled, the *going concern* value may be reduced. The going concern value is generally the market value set by a willing buyer and a willing seller under normal circumstances. *Normal circumstances* implies no duress or any unusual circumstances such as the death or disability of one of the key employees. Proper use of life and disability contracts can compensate the firm for a reduction in the going concern value. If arranged properly, the value of the firm is stabilized by a hedging process. The event reducing the value of the firm is counterbalanced by a contract providing replacement of those values.

Liquidity Enhancement. Cash value life insurance is a source of funds and an asset that may be used for collateral. Borrowing cash value may be prudent for a number of reasons:

1. There is no credit analysis or reporting, and policy loans cannot be denied. (Many life insurance contracts include a six-month waiting clause to postpone distribution of borrowed amounts. However, the provision is rarely imposed.)
2. Even though premium payments are thought of as an expense, the cash value increase due to the premium, as well as earnings on past accumulations, boosts the organization's assets. The boost in assets increases the firm's surplus because assets must equal liabilities plus owner's equity.

3. Any increase in cash value is not currently taxable.
4. The contract's loan rate may be below currently available commercial rates.

Term insurance policies may be used for key employee problems if the only need is indemnification for death. If other benefits are desired, such as accumulation of cash for a retirement plan or a source of funds for collateral, cash value plans are useful because the accumulated values may be used for funding retirement benefits or be a source of collateral. (The reader should be aware of the accumulated earnings tax. The IRS imposes additional tax when retention of capital generally exceeds $250,000 and is not necessary for ordinary business needs. A $150,000 limit applies to selected professional service corporations. Also, an increasing cash value could subject the firm to the alternative minimum tax [AMT].) The premium waiver benefit associated with insurance contracts may be desirable. Once the premium is waived, the released funds may be used toward a salary continuation plan.

Determination of Insurable Value—Life Insurance

Insurable value must be established once a business recognizes that a key employee exposure exists. Valuation should not be arbitrary. An analysis of the exposure should accurately estimate the firm's potential financial loss. A variety of techniques provides guidance in indirectly measuring insurable value or the theoretical loss to the firm. These techniques include a variation on the human life value approach, an approach that capitalizes excess salary and a technique that estimates the person's contributions to the firm's earnings.

The human life value approach discounts the employee's annual expected earnings less maintenance expenses over the person's expected work life. (This technique is a variation of the human life value approach suggested by S. S. Huebner.) Maintenance expenses include federal, state and local taxes as well as the cost of the person's self-maintenance. The employee's work life is either life expectancy or retirement, whichever occurs first. Theoretically the human life value provides an estimate of an owner's loss to his or her family, and an owner/key employee may want to estimate the insurable value based on this point of view.

☐ **Example**

Harry Butler, age 52, is a sole proprietor. He earns $62,000 annually. Assume self-maintenance expense (taxes, food and clothing) consumes 55 percent of his salary. Harry's life expectancy is to age 72; however, normal retirement age is 65. At 8 percent Harry's human life value is estimated as follows:

$$\$62,000 \times (1.0 - 0.55) = \$27,900$$
13 years to work until retirement

Present value of an annuity of $27,900 for 13 years at 8 percent equals $220,515.

The human life value approach is more appropriate in determining loss to the family when the business is a sole proprietorship. Maintaining the going concern value is not considered in this example.

Capitalizing excess salary theoretically calculates a value for the person's talents not readily replaceable by the firm. This method discounts the difference between the employee's salary and the salary required to hire a replacement to perform essentially the job's *routine* duties. The discounting period is the time necessary to train someone to *fully* replace the key employee.

☐ **Example**

Arnold Hamilton is a valuable long-term employee with a current salary of $120,000. The cost of a replacement employee to perform Arnold's routine duties is estimated to be $50,000. It will take the replacement six years to fully develop the skills necessary to replace Arnold. Arnold's value to the firm equals $323,601:

Current Earnings	$120,000
Routine replacement	50,000
Difference	70,000

The present value of a $70,000 annuity at 8 percent for six years equals $323,601.

This technique assumes the firm benefits at least $70,000 by paying the difference above the mere replacement value of the routine duties. The $323,601 represents the present value of the firm's loss if benefits of hiring the key employee are assumed to equal $120,000.

Calculating the contribution of the employee to the firm is the most complex of the three methods described. In this method the average book value or stockholder's equity is calculated over a representative number of years. This value is then multiplied by an easily obtainable and representative rate of return for the same period. The resulting amount is equal to earnings the owners alternatively would make without the talent of management. The firm's average income is subtracted. The resulting figure is theoretically the annual contribution of management. The value sought is the annual value contributed by management multiplied by the number of years required to replace management. This calculation ignores the time value of money and a phase-in of the new management's contribution. These factors can be taken into account. Variations of this method result in the annual contribution by management, the annual contribution of a particular manager (assuming a certain percent contributed by the individual), the gross loss of management until replacement and the gross loss of an individual until replacement.

☐ **Example**

If the book value of a firm equals $1,000,000 and a fair rate of return equals 10 percent:

Fair return in dollars = 0.10 × $1,000,000 = $100,000.

If average income equals $300,000, the return attributed to management is $200,000 (300,000 − 100,000). If it takes four years to replace management, the value of management equals $800,000 (4 × $200,000). If the manager-employee is assumed to contribute one-third of the talent, the value of the manager-employee is $266,666 ($1/3$ × $800,000).

Determination of Insurable Value—Disability Insurance

Many of the considerations discussed for life insurance are included in determining the amount of disability income or overhead replacement coverage and the length of the benefit period. For example, business overhead insurance is generally arranged for service organizations such as a dentist. When the dentist is disabled for a period of time, income is needed to cover the operating expenses such as office payroll (overhead coverage) and provide income for the dentist during the disability period (disability income).

Tax Consequences—Life Insurance

Because key employee life insurance is purchased by the firm for its benefit the business pays the premium, owns the policy and is the beneficiary. Premiums are not deductible for income tax purposes when the expense is not considered ordinary and necessary or when the business directly or indirectly benefits from a life insurance policy. When individuals (stockholders or partners) sit in the three positions of owner, premium payer and beneficiary, the deduction is not allowed because the expense either is considered a personal expense or is made in anticipation of receiving tax-free income as a beneficiary. Because premiums generally are not tax-deductible, the benefits paid to the beneficiary generally are not taxable. However, in some cases taxes are paid if benefits are distributed as dividends.

Consider the case of a C corporation receiving death benefits from a key employee life insurance contract. Premium payments are not tax-deductible for income tax purposes. When the benefits are paid, they are not included in taxable income. Once received, however, the proceeds lose their identity as tax-free income; when paid as a dividend, they become taxable to the recipient as dividend income. (Even though key employee arrangements are designed to indemnify the firm, the receipt of cash may allow normal dividend distributions.) If the same situation occurs in a Subchapter S corporation, the same result occurs. With respect to a partnership, any benefits received are similarly not taxable. However, unlike for the corporate entity, proceeds do not lose their identity once paid and can be distributed to the partners without incurring any tax. The main difference between a C corporation and an S corporation rests in the manner of reporting taxes. In a C corporation corporate taxes are paid and reported by the organization. In an S corporation the individual stockholders report taxable income on their personal returns and are responsible for the tax payment. Taxable earning information is supplied by the corporation on IRS form K-1.

Transfer for Value

Transfer-for-value rules modify the treatment of key employee life insurance for income tax purposes. A transfer for value occurs if a life insurance policy is exchanged for consideration. Generally new life insurance policies are purchased for key employee insurance. However, in some cases existing policies may be used for a variety of reasons, including insurability problems. If a life insurance contract is transferred for value, the death proceeds are included in income tax to the extent that it exceeds the cost basis (the sum of premiums and consideration paid less any dividends received). A series of exceptions to this rule applies. One of the exceptions arises if an in-force policy is transferred for key employee life insurance to a corporation or partnership. If the insured is a partner, a shareholder or an officer of the firm, the transfer-for-value rule does not apply, and proceeds are not included in taxable income. (Note that if the insured is only an employee of the organization, the transfer-for-value rule applies.)

☐ **Example**

Randall Jones, a key employee-nonowner, sells a $200,000 life insurance contract to Sampson Co. for its replacement value ($30,000). Sampson names itself beneficiary and owner. No additional premiums have been paid when Randall dies. Because of the transfer-for-value rule, $170,000 is included in Sampson's taxable income.

If Randall Jones is a shareholder-employee, the transfer-for-value rule does not apply, and the $200,000 is received tax-free.

In neither case is the $30,000 tax-deductible when the exchange occurs.

Termination of Employment

If the insured leaves the firm or the policy is no longer needed, the business has the legal right to continue paying the life insurance premiums and will receive the death proceeds even though there is no continuing insurable interest. (Insurable interest need exist only when the contract is started in life insurance. No continuing interest is required to maintain or collect on a valid life insurance policy.) As an alternative, the firm may elect to sell the policy for its replacement value (the cash surrender value) to the insured or may surrender it for cash. If no longer insurable, the insured may want to purchase the contract for its replacement value.

Estate Tax Consequences

Death proceeds are included in the gross estate if (1) the insured, at the time of death, possessed any of the incidences of ownership, (2) proceeds are paid to the estate of the insured or (3) proceeds are payable for the benefit of the insured's estate. Therefore, when the insured is a key employee-nonowner and the firm owns the contract, the policy is not included in the insured's gross estate. Several complicating situations can arise. For example, if a partner is a key employee and the proceeds are paid to the partnership, the value of the deceased partner's interest increases for federal estate tax purposes. This points out an advantage of fixing the value of a business in a buy-and-sell agreement, which is discussed later. All individuals know the value and can plan for the estate tax consequences. If the value is set by formula, it will be more difficult to plan for estate taxes.

When a stockholder is a key employee, the proportionate share of the policy proceeds will be included in the gross estate of the key employee when the individual has a controlling interest. Controlling interest in the organization is usually defined as actual or equitable interest of more than 50 percent of the controlling voting power. The rules regarding inclusion of policy proceeds are complex due to the fact that the corporation's value increases when the proceeds are paid and the value of the stock is included in the stockholder's estate. An argument can be made that the value of the firm was reduced by the employee's death and the life insurance policy has made restitution for the value and no increase of the value of the stock has taken place.

Tax Consequences—Disability Insurance

Disability insurance purchased on a key employee with the firm identified as the beneficiary or owner is taxed similarly to life insurance. That is, premiums are generally not deductible, and benefits are not taxable. There is an exception to this rule. Premiums paid for disability insurance designed to reimburse the firm's overhead expense are deductible for income tax purposes. The proceeds are taxable to the firm but can be deducted immediately as an ordinary and necessary business expense.

Business Continuation Problems

Maintaining and transferring the going concern value of the firm upon the disability or death of an owner is the focus of the business continuation problem. The *going concern* value is usually much greater than the firm's *liquidation value*. The going concern value is the firm's market value determined at arm's length between willing and knowledgeable buyers and sellers. The firm's liquidation value is the amount paid when the seller's price is influenced by the necessity to sell in a short period of time. Much value can be lost if a business is sold under duress to meet family, tax or other cash needs. These untimely sales are sometimes referred to as *forced sales* or *liquidations*. Depending on the form of the organizational structure, the ease or difficulty of maintaining the going concern value of a firm and the ease of transferring ownership varies. Sole proprietorships, partnerships and closely held corporations all have similar problems with regard to maintaining value and transferring wealth.

The Sole Proprietorship

Assets held by a sole proprietor are indistinguishable from the assets of the business. So-called "business assets" may be used to pay for personal obligations, and personally held assets may be used to satisfy business indebtedness. The sole proprietor may identify assets as "personal" or "business"; however, the law does not make the distinction.

Disability of the Sole Proprietor

Short- or long-term disability of the sole proprietor threatens the existence of the firm and certainly reduces its value. Typically the income and value of the business depends on the personality and the expertise of the owner. With these qualities lost, clients may purchase products or services from other sources. Loyalty will go only so far in retaining a good working relationship, regardless of whether the disability is partial or total, temporary or permanent. Options for continuing business during the disability include substitution of a spouse and hiring an employee.

The substitution of a spouse may not be a viable solution if the talents and expertise of the sole proprietor are not replaced. Business income and the going concern value will decline in these circumstances. Hiring an employee may prove far short of an optimum solution. In this case the employee increases payroll (in addition to the amounts paid to the owner). If employees prove valuable, they will demand higher wages. A third solution is to sell the "business" assets. In this case the going concern value will decline due to the forced sale.

Because these solutions may not be satisfactory, the purchase of sufficient amounts of disability income coverage is prudent. The amount purchased need not be 100 percent of the predisability net income. Because of the tax treatment of disability benefits, 60 to 70 percent may be all that is necessary to replace after-tax spendable funds. Disability income coverage is used to supply income during the length of the disability. Proceeds can also be used to purchase the talents of an employee without necessarily eroding the owner's income. The insurance coverage could be used to compensate for the loss of the going concern value in the event of a forced sale.

In the planning stages both permanent and short-term disability should be analyzed, and consideration should be given to purchase sufficient disability coverage to:

- make a reasonable sale to an outsider without the immediate need for liquidation;
- provide sufficient funds for the phase-in of an interested and responsible family member; or
- provide sufficient funds until a child can take over the business.

Problems Caused by Death

A proprietor's death causes a variety of problems due to the nature of the business entity. The assets of the owner are inseparable from business assets, so all assets in the decedent's estate are available for final estate settlement. Business assets may have to be used to settle the estate. Personal assets likewise may have to be used to pay business debts. All assets therefore transfer to an executor if a valid will exists. (For the purpose of this discussion the terms *administrator* and *executor* are used to describe the individual responsible for the orderly resolution of the estate.) An administrator handles the assets of intestate decedents. The administrator assembles and accounts for all assets and liabilities of the decedent and settles the estate in an expeditious manner. In cases where a spouse or relative does not administer the estate, the executor's responsibility may run counter to the desires of the spouse or heirs. Within the constraints of the administrator's duties the business may be liquidated, or an attempt may be made to continue the business. Neither of these options produces wholly satisfactory results for the heirs.

Liquidation. The administrator's responsibility is to wrap up the decedent's affairs, repay any debts and dispose of remaining assets consistent with law. An exception occurs when the will contains express instructions to continue the business or all heirs agree to continue and assume responsibility for the results, good or bad. If an heir is a minor, it may be impossible to get consent to continue the business and accept responsibility. In this case continuing the operation of the business may not be possible. Otherwise the responsibility of the administrator is to dispose of the business quickly. Operation of the business after death and before liquidation will be allowed by the court if it is deemed prudent. In any event the administrator will be held liable for any losses or additional indebtedness incurred from operating the business any longer than needed to wind up the decedent's affairs.

Upon liquidation the proceeds may be less than the business liabilities, and personal assets may have to be liquidated to settle remaining claims. Sufficient amounts of life insurance (cash) payable to the estate, trust or spouse to cover debts, administrative costs and estate taxes may prevent the liquidation of personal assets to meet these cash demands. (A trust or spouse can loan dollars or purchase estate assets for cash.)

Continued Operation by Administrator. The administrator, at the direction of the will or in variance of the will, may attempt to operate the business. All personal and business debts must be paid before an attempt is made to operate on a long-term basis, and funds may be insufficient to operate the business after all business and personal obligations are paid. If sufficient assets remain, the decision to operate the business is a voluntary one, even though the will expressly authorizes the act. Because of this, any debts or losses incurred will be the responsibility of the administrator. The administrator may seek restitution from the remaining assets of the estate if the authorized continued operation produces increased debt or net losses. However, by that time there may be insufficient assets in the estate, and the administrator will be held personally responsible. Cautious administrators will therefore tend not to operate the business due to the potential for personal liability.

The Need for Cash

The need for cash in the estate should be self-evident. Cash in the estate reduces the need for quick liquidation of the assets at an inopportune time. Costs of administration, the repayment of debt and taxes can be paid for if a sufficient amount of life insurance proceeds is available. Cash in the estate is useful if business creditors demand immediate repayment and tighten credit standards due to the uncertainty of payment. Tightened credit standards may hamper the "business as usual" appearance and make it difficult to operate due to cash flow problems.

Additional cash in the estate may also provide surplus funds for the administrator if the business is continued. There will be more flexibility in deciding the course of action so as to maximize the wealth of the heirs.

Operation by Heirs. Once all obligations of the estate have been settled, the heirs may decide to operate the business. For a wide variety of reasons, it is likely that the income to the heirs will be lower than normal for a number of years. Life insurance on the owner could make up the difference between predeath and postdeath income, enhance the creditworthiness of the business and possibly minimize the necessity of infusions of capital by the heirs. Heirs may find continuing the business drains their own funds. In retrospect some firms should have sold the business or otherwise terminated it upon the death of the owner because the heirs lacked needed expertise. (It is impossible to know the correct course of action without the advantage of knowing the future. Therefore many professionals recommend disposal of the business as the best course of action.)

The Sale of the Business. The sale of the business may be arranged by the administrator, or it may be prearranged before death occurs. Life insurance is usually needed to fund the purchase. When the owner dies, cash is needed to settle the estate, compensate for the reduction in going concern and goodwill value, maintain the business and service for new and existing customers, provide support for credit transactions, replace the lost human capital and provide income to the family. Cash is needed to support these needs for an indefinite period of time until a purchase can be arranged or the business once again becomes self-sustaining.

Predisability and Predeath Arrangements

Many of the problems caused by the death or disability of the owner are resolved by prearranging a sale. Employees, competitors and family members including children are logical people to purchase the business. Incorporation may prove useful if minors are involved. (The stock should be held in trust until the child is able to handle affairs. Typically key employees also purchase a minor interest in the stock and run the business until the child is able to contribute.)

Buy-and-sell agreements specify the particulars of the transfer and are agreed to before the death or disability occurs. The buy-and-sell agreement obligates one party to buy and directs the estate (the owner in the case of disability) to sell at a prearranged price or formula. The advantages of this arrangement include:

- identification of a buyer before death,
- setting the price in a "normal" supply-and-demand environment,
- maintaining values for the heirs and
- arranging for a smooth transition.

Funding the transaction then becomes the problem. Assuming the owner is insurable, the buyer purchases life insurance on the sole proprietor. The buyer makes himself or herself the owner and beneficiary of the life insurance policy. The life insurance amount may fund the entire purchase or handle the down payment, with the remaining amount paid by a note with funds generated from the business. When death occurs, the buyer-beneficiary receives sufficient funds to make the exchange with the estate. The estate receives the cash, the buyer receives the business and, if a fair value is used, the transaction value is used to value that part of the decedent's gross estate for IRS purposes. (Just as long as it was an arm's-length agreement, the IRS will concur with the value.) The use of a trust in monitoring and enforcing the transaction is often useful. In this case policy proceeds are paid to the trust. The trustee holds the business interest and must comply with the wording of the trust document directing the sale. Thus the trust adds certainty to the transaction.

Business buy-and-sell agreements may also be funded by disability income coverage in the event of a defined disability. The agreement should define disability exactly the same way as the disability insurance contract. A separate disability income contract could be purchased, or a disability income rider attached to the life insurance contract may suffice. The premium waiver rider should also be considered. If disability occurs, the life insurance values will be maintained until death, or the cash value of the life insurance policy may be used (borrowed) to pay a part of the purchase price. Then, upon the owner's death, the difference between the face amount and the borrowed funds and accrued interest is paid as a death benefit.

Partnerships

Partnerships allow two or more people to combine their skills and share profits as well as losses according to a partnership agreement. Legally it is not necessary to have a partnership agreement. However, it is advisable to have one and to agree on such things as the proportion of ownership, the work load, the sharing of profits and losses, the procedures for terminating the partnership and the entry of new partners. In a *general partnership,* all partners are personally responsible for all partnership debts. *Limited partnerships* have at least one general partner. Limited partners cannot actively engage in the management of the business. The most limited partners can lose is their investment, and they share in the profits as agreed.

Disability of a Partner

Disability of a contributing partner presents essentially the same problems as the disability of a key employee. Depending on the terms in the partnership agreement, income to the disabled partner could continue based on either the percent of active participation or the ownership interest. In any event, a moral obligation to continue income may prevail, and in many disability cases the income to the business and the partners falls. In the long run the partner is often replaced or bought out. Disability income coverage purchased by each partner provides a solution. The income produced by the disability contract can replace the disabled partner's income, or the partner can receive payment directly and agree to terminate the partnership draw if disabled. (The definition of disability needs to be consistent between the disability contract and the partnership agreement.)

Disability of a limited partner tends not to be a problem. The limited partner is not active in the business by definition, and the disability does not affect operations or the organization's financial results. Liquidation of the limited partner's share may become a problem depending on the limited partner's need for cash during the disability.

Problems Caused by Death of a Partner

The law allows only voluntary associations, so a partner's death leads to the partnership dissolution unless there is a provision to the contrary in the partnership agreement. No new partner may be permitted without the consent of all surviving partners, and therefore no partner may prearrange a new partner (heir) for the business relationship in the case of his or her own death. All partners are allowed to associate freely and form a new organization after the death of a partner and dissolution of the partnership.

Two courses of action exist after a partner's death. The business is either liquidated or reorganized. The law generally requires liquidation unless the adult heirs consent to leaving assets within the partnership and the surviving partners agree. (Minor heirs cannot give consent, so liquidation is the only course unless a prearranged buy-and-sell agreement exists.) In this case the heirs become partners. If the heirs do not consent to leaving the assets in the partnership and/or the partners do not accept the heirs, liquidation of the partnership is necessary.

Role of the Deceased Partner's Estate. The role of the deceased partner's estate is to settle all obligations and distribute property consistent with law. Partnership assets may be required to settle the estate, and the estate may be held responsible for the partnership's debts. Sufficient life insurance may provide funds to avoid forced liquidation and minimize depletion of partnership assets (possibly avoiding a reduction of the surviving partner's assets).

Obligations of Surviving Partners. In the absence of a buy-and-sell agreement the surviving partners become liquidating trustees. Liquidating trustees are responsible for the prompt and orderly liquidation of the partnership, and it is their responsibility to provide an accounting to the estate administrator. Practically, they are responsible for liquidating and destroying their own jobs when their desire may be to continue the business. Options to continue the business include purchasing the heir's interest, taking a purchaser of the heir's interest as a partner and taking the deceased's heirs as partners. Problems encountered include setting the price, funding the purchase and agreeing on the acceptability of the new partners.

In some cases partners arrange to will their portion of the partnership to existing partners. This plan may make sense where it is intended to pass assets between actively involved spouses or siblings.

Buy-and-Sell Agreements. Arranging for a sale of a partner's interest before a death or disability is the preferred method of resolving the conflict between the surviving partners' desire to continue the business and maximize wealth and the heir's desire for cash. Properly funded buy-and-sell agreements prearrange asset transfer in the case of death or disability. (It is desirable but not necessary to address both death and disability in the buy-and-sell agreement.)

Life insurance can be used for full or partial funding of the purchase price, and coverage can be arranged using a cross-purchase plan or an entity purchase plan. Each partner in the **cross-purchase** plan buys and owns life insurance on the life of the other partners. If a partner dies, the survivors receive the cash and the estate receives the partnership interest. A swap is made at the prearranged price or formula, and the share value (basis) is set for future transfers. The cross-purchase agreement is equitable because, even with great disparities in age or proportion of ownership, the partner pays for and receives benefits fairly. The plan is also quite flexible, because a partner can elect to purchase a smaller proportion, leaving the remainder for the other partners.

☐ Examples

John, Sally and Jane are all one-third partners in a partnership currently valued at $750,000. Using a cross-purchase agreement funded by life insurance, each partner applies for, owns and is the beneficiary of $125,000 of life insurance on the other two partners. There are six contracts involved.

If John dies, Sally and Jane both will receive $125,000 in cash as beneficiaries. John's interest will be purchased for the $250,000 ($125,000 × 2). The estate receives the cash, and the surviving partners each purchase half of John's interest. Sally and Jane become half owners of the partnership after John's death. They may then institute a revised buy-and-sell agreement and purchase additional life insurance to prearrange a transfer if Sally or Jane dies.

John and Sally are both age 55. Jane is 40. Jane pays a relatively higher premium on John and Sally than John and Sally pay on Jane. Even though the premium amounts are different, they are proportional to the expectation of collection.

If John and Sally each own 40 percent of the firm and Jane 20 percent, Jane's premium payment will be greater than John's and Sally's because of the ownership disparity. This result is mathematically fair because the premium payment is proportional to the probability of benefiting and the size of the potential gain.

The cross-purchase plan becomes cumbersome once more than a few partners exist. For two partners only two contracts are needed. For n partners, $n \times (n-1)$ contracts are required.

☐ Example

Four partners decide to enter into a buy-and-sell agreement. To fund the plan, each of the 4 (n) partners purchases 3 ($n-1$) contracts for a total of 12 ($n \times [n-1]$) contracts.

The **entity purchase** plan makes more sense when the number of contracts required becomes unmanageable. In this case the partnership pays for the contracts and is both the owner and the beneficiary. This plan coupled with a proper buy-and-sell agreement provides funds to the entity (the partnership) to purchase the deceased partner's interest from the estate at the prearranged price or formula. Premiums are not deductible by the partnership, because the expense is not considered necessary. Death benefits are not taxable. If cash value life insurance is used, the cash value is included as an asset of the partnership and is subject to creditors' claims.

As mentioned earlier, the cross-purchase plan is equitable with regard to costs and benefits. The entity purchase plan, however, is not wholly fair in that the burden of premium payment falls more heavily on the partners owning larger interests. In addition, because partners pay proportionately the same amount, younger partners, having a longer life expectancy, benefit more than older partners.

When setting the purchase price, consideration should be made for the cash values held by the firm on the survivors' lives and the proceeds paid to the firm on the death of the partner. That is, the deceased partner had an interest in the cash value contained in the life insurance contract(s) of the surviving partners, and when death occurs, the proceeds are paid to the partnership and essentially split among the surviving partners in proportion to their ownership. The inability to modify this proportion is a disadvantage under the entity purchase plan.

The Close Corporation

The closely held corporation and the partnership have similar business problems. A closely held corporation—or *close corporation,* as it is commonly called—is owned by a few stockholders. Publicly held corporate organizations do not have the same problems as the closely held form because an actively traded market exists in the securities and an ownership interest may be sold easily without loss in value. Key employee life insurance addresses the problem of maintaining the organization's value when a key person dies or is disabled. Typically most of the stockholders in a close corporation are active in the daily operation of the organization. The corporation usually pays owners a salary instead of distributing dividends because dividends are subject to both corporate and personal income. The major difference between the partnership and the closely held corporation is that the ownership interest is represented by shares of stock as opposed to being inseparable from the partner's assets. If a stockholder dies, however, the organization continues, and the ownership interest represented by shares of stock must be distributed in some manner.

Disability of a Stockholder

The disabled stockholder often continues to receive salary through a formal or informal salary continuation plan. Because the stockholder is being supported without contributing at predisability levels, the firm's income often declines. For short-term disabilities, a salary continuation plan supported by sufficient disability income coverage is advisable. For longer or permanent disabilities, a stock redemption agreement passing the ownership interest of the disabled stockholder to the organization at a prearranged price or formula should exist. Financing arrangements for redeeming the ownership interest include continued support funded by business income and a disability income contract. (The definition of disability must be consistent in the stock redemption agreement and the disability contract.) The disabled stockholder might prefer the security of the disability income contract as opposed to relying on the continued profitability of the organization.

Death of a Stockholder

Even though ownership passes to an heir, problems similar to those that affect partnerships arise when a stockholder of a closely held corporation dies. Surviving stockholders have no control over unwanted co-owners; anyone legally owning the stock is an owner.

From the business point of view, several options exist:

- Bring the new owner into the firm to participate in operations and management.
- Pay a dividend stream to the heir equivalent to the salary before death. (The total dividend amount paid is based on number of shares and dividend amount per share. Paying a dividend causes all owners to receive dividend income.)
- Purchase the stock from the estate, heir or purchaser of the heir's interest.
- Pay only salary, and no dividends, to participating owners.

If the firm employs the new owner, there is no guarantee of a positive contribution to the business. The amount or quality of the contribution may cause problems among the owners. If the new owner is not employed by the firm, the survivors may resent his or her lack of contribution and the distribution of earnings based on ownership and not effort. On the other hand, if the new owner is not an employee, he or she may not receive any income because the organization may pay salaries instead of dividends.

There are other problems associated with minority and majority stockholders. A minority stockholder can be at the mercy of the majority ones. A minority stockholder-heir may desire to sell the stock at a high price while the others want to buy it at a low price. A minority heir may be "squeezed out" by the inability to participate truly in management and by the lack of income or dividends.

A majority heir may also be at a disadvantage. Majority owners may not receive the cooperation of the working minority stockholders, meaning the value of the firm will decline. It is also possible for the active minority to pressure the inactive majority owner for additional salary or other concessions.

Properly Funded Buy-and-Sell Arrangements. When an owner dies, the uncertainty, the possible decline in business value and the potential uneasy relationship among the remaining owners are serious problems. A properly funded buy-and-sell agreement solves these problems by arranging before the stockholder's death (or disability) how and to whom the stock is to be transferred and how the purchase is to be funded.

Buy-and-sell agreements as they apply to closely held corporations are similar in form and intent to those used by partnerships or sole proprietors. Typically these agreements are arranged as a cross-purchase plan or a **stock redemption plan.** These plans are similar to the partnership cross-purchase and entity plans already discussed. In the cross-purchase plan each stockholder purchases life insurance on the other stockholders in an amount sufficient to purchase the percentage of the stock. The purchaser is the owner and beneficiary of the insurance contract. If a death occurs, the life insurance contract provides proceeds sufficient to purchase the interest, and the estate sells the stock to the survivors in the proportion dictated by the buy-and-sell agreement. The estate/heirs receive cash, and the surviving stockholders receive the stock.

In the stock repurchase plan, the corporation buys, owns and is the beneficiary of the life insurance on each stockholder. If a stockholder dies, the corporation receives the cash and is obligated to buy the stock held by the estate. (In most states stock repurchases may be made only out of surplus capital. In selecting the amount of life insurance to buy, consideration must be given to paying any negative surplus and providing sufficient funds to repurchase the stock.) A trust is often useful in adding certainty to the transaction. Premium waiver riders and disability income riders attached to the life insurance contract may also help maintain and fund the life insurance during a period of disability and somewhat compensate for a reduction in profitability and the maintenance of income for the disabled stockholder.

The buy-and-sell agreement should also address the problem of an employee-stockholder who voluntarily leaves the organization. Arrangements should be made for the transfer of stock ownership and disposition of the life insurance contracts. The life insurance contracts may be purchased at their replacement value by the departing stockholder, or the continuing stockholders may use the cash value in the contract to help fund the purchase of the stock.

Tax Aspects of Funding Buy-and-Sell Agreements with Life Insurance. Premiums paid by the corporation (entity or stock redemption plan) or by the individual (cross-purchase plan) are not deductible for income tax purposes. When death proceeds are paid to the corporation or the individual, the proceeds are received free from any income tax. When the corporation receives the proceeds under the stock redemption plan, the value of the firm may increase unless the valuation method takes this into consideration.

The stockholders may also run afoul of the transfer-for-value rule, making a portion of the policy proceeds a taxable gain. This may happen when the corporation buys a life insurance contract from the stockholder to fund the stock redemption plan or a stock redemption plan is converted to a cross-purchase plan. (Transfer-for-value rules are complex and allow for exceptions when a transfer occurs between partners. However, transfers between stockholders and corporations generally fall under transfer-for-value rules.)

Section 302 and 303 Stock Redemptions. Under a cross-purchase plan, there is no tax to the decedent's estate when payment is received from the purchaser due to the stepped-up basis at death. When the owner dies, the value of the business is included in the estate at its date-of-death value. When the purchase is made, no new value is added to the estate due to the swap of the business interest for cash. Any proceeds paid to the purchaser from the life insurance contract similarly are not taxed. Under the stock refunding plans additional problems arise from the fact that a distribution to purchase stock may be viewed either as a sale, an exchange or as a dividend. If it is classified as a dividend, a taxable event occurs, and the cost basis is increased by the dividend amount. If the transaction is classified as a sale or an exchange, the cost basis does not change. As a general rule, any distribution to a stockholder will be treated as a dividend unless it meets specific rules established in IRC Sections 302 and 303.

Section 302. Under Section 302 of the Internal Revenue Code, if the corporation redeems *all* of the shareholder's shares and all interests in the organization are terminated, a capital transaction occurs (sale or exchange), and the purchase is not considered a dividend. The problem arises in that "all shares" include shares owned or constructively owned by the estate. (Attribution rules are found in IRC Section 318 and include the tests for waiving family attribution rules.) Shares owned by a beneficiary of the estate are deemed to be owned by the estate under the complex rules.

Section 303. Under Section 303, stock may be refunded under certain conditions without being treated as a dividend. Section 303 is helpful when the stock value is a major portion of the stockholder's estate and it is desirable to avoid a forced sale of stock, estate assets or business assets to pay estate debts and taxes.

The requirements for a 303 stock redemption include the following:

- The value of the redeemed stock must be includable in the estate of the stockholder.
- The value of the stock redeemed must be more than 35 percent of the value of the adjusted gross estate.
- The dollar amount limit is equal to the sum of all federal and state estate and inheritance taxes and funeral and administrative expenses.
- The redemption must occur within three years and 90 days after the estate tax is filed (which is due nine months after death).
- The person whose shares are redeemed must be legally obligated to pay the expenses listed in the third requirement.

☐ **Example**

Arthur Sharp owns 50 percent of the outstanding shares of Apex. Apex is valued at $5 million. Arthur's estate is valued at $3.5 million as follows:

Business 50%	2.5 million
Other Assets	1.0 million
Adjusted Gross Estate	3.5 million

Estate shrinkage costs are $1.5 million. Because Arthur meets Section 303 rules, stock worth $1.5 million may be purchased by the corporation and be treated as a sale or an exchange (35 percent requirement = $3.5 million × 0.35 = $1.225 million). Sums beyond the $1.5 million (estate shrinkage costs) are treated as a dividend unless Section 302 rules are met if all shares are redeemed by the corporation.

Notice that a Section 303 stock redemption allows favorable tax treatment for an amount equal to the funeral, administrative and tax payments. A partial redemption in excess of this amount is treated as a dividend. One additional benefit of using a 303 redemption is that the attribution rules discussed under the Section 302 stock redemption do not apply.

It is clear that a Section 302 and a Section 303 redemption require the corporation to have sufficient unencumbered cash to make the exchange. Life insurance is a logical solution. The corporation applies for, owns and is the beneficiary of sufficient life insurance to refund part or all of the deceased partner's stock. If the stockholder is not insurable or decides not to use life insurance, a sinking fund may be used. A sinking fund, however, which is included in corporate assets and subject to claims of creditors, may cause a greater problem. Pressure to use the funds for other business purposes may exist. Funds retained for a 303 redemption are considered for reasonable business needs and not subject to the accumulated earnings tax.

Nonqualified Employee Compensation Plans

As life and disability insurance contracts are used to solve key employee and business continuation problems, life and annuity contracts are used to provide special or supplementary benefits to select employees. These plans are generally set up to:

- attract and retain key employees,
- provide supplemental benefits beyond the existing qualified plan,
- provide a plan-in-lieu of a qualified plan for selected employees and
- take advantage of provisions in the tax code to the advantage of certain employees.

Qualified versus Nonqualified Plans

Qualified plans meet IRS nondiscrimination tests and allow the employer to deduct expenses of the plan while taxable income is not imputed to the employee until it is received. (*See* Chapters 18 and 19, where qualified employee benefits are discussed.) *Nonqualified* plans are designed to provide benefits to specific valuable employees. They do not meet the tests for qualified plans, nor do they benefit from preferential tax treatment. Generally, nonqualified plans are categorized as **deferred compensation plans** and **salary continuation plans**. Deferred compensation plans require the employee to reduce current income or forgo a bonus or raise. Presumably the money will be received at a later date, when the recipient possibly is in a lower tax bracket. These plans are often referred to as *in-lieu-of plans*. Salary continuation plans require no comparable reduction in current compensation but are agreements to continue salary after a specific event, such as retirement, and for a specific length of time (a fixed number of years, to a certain age or upon the occurrence of an event such as death).

For an employee to avoid constructive receipt of income for income tax purposes under nonqualified plans, there must be a substantial risk of forfeiture. "Substantial risk of forfeiture" occurs if the employee's benefit is contingent on future performance or services. The employer cannot reduce its taxable income until there is constructive receipt by the employee, and consequently the employee pays taxes on the income only when received. Because the tax consequences are similar in deferred compensation and salary continuation plans, this chapter refers to both as deferred compensation plans.

Funded versus Unfunded Plans

Nonqualified plans are classified as either *funded* or *unfunded*. A funded plan exists when an employer transfers assets to an account or a trust specifically to secure the promise for future compensation. Earmarking general assets of the business with no legal link to the specific promise does not create a funded plan. An unfunded plan exists when no formal allocation of assets occurs *and* the employee depends solely on the unsecured pledge of the employer. Unfunded plans provide no security to the employee and therefore are not protected from the claims of general creditors when the employer is in bankruptcy. A *secular trust* may be used to fund nonqualified deferred compensation benefits. In a secular trust, funds are not subject to the claims of general creditors, and the employee recognizes income and pays taxes on contributions and earnings at the current marginal tax rate. The employer is entitled to the deduction. In the *rabbi* trust contributions are made to an irrevocable trust and are not taxed to the employee as current taxable income, and the employer receives no tax deduction. The assets in the trust must remain subject to the employer's creditors. These plans are not considered "formally funded."

Estate Tax Treatment

If the employee dies while receiving distributions from a deferred compensation plan and benefits terminate, nothing is included in the gross estate for estate tax purposes. If, however, payments are to continue to a beneficiary, the commuted or present value is included for estate tax purposes.

Death during the deferral period causes different problems. If there is an enforceable right in a deferred compensation plan, the estate will include the present value of those rights. Payments to a named beneficiary and not the employee may be considered a *death-benefit-only* plan, and the commuted value generally will be included in the gross estate. This occurs whether the rights were forfeitable or not.

Use of Life and Annuity Insurance for Funding Plans

Life insurance is useful in funding deferred compensation plans. Funding, however, needs to be *informal.* That is, the funding mechanism must not provide any vested or nonforfeitable rights or interests in the deferred compensation plan. Because of this, the employer, in an informal funding plan, is the owner, the premium payer and the beneficiary. The employer may merely purchase life, annuity or disability insurance on the employee and name the corporation as the beneficiary. Premiums paid are not deductible, and benefits received are not taxable. Funds then may be used to pay the deferred compensation arrangement. Funding deferred compensation plans with life insurance on an informal basis provides the following benefits:

- If deferred compensation death benefits are triggered, the life insurance contract can provide funds to pay for the obligation. Any accumulated amounts in a sinking fund may fall short if the employee dies "early."
- Cash values may be used to meet partially or fully the deferred compensation obligations upon retirement. If other assets are available, the policy may be maintained until death occurs; then the employer collects the death proceeds.

☐ **Example**

Randy Harrow's deferred compensation plan is funded informally with cash value life insurance. If death occurs, funds will be sufficient to complete the plan for Randy's wife. If Randy retires, deferred compensation will be paid out of corporate earnings. The corporation will continue to pay premiums on the life insurance contract, and when death occurs, the corporation will receive the death benefits.

- The inside buildup in cash value life insurance contracts accumulates tax-free until the policy is surrendered (taxes are paid on the surrender value in excess of cost basis). (*See* Chapter 11.)

- The premium waiver and disability income riders are available either to waive the premium while the insured is disabled or to provide cash during disability. The waiver-of-premium rider can free up funds to use for compensation during a disability, and the disability income rider can provide some, if not all, of the remaining obligation.
- Life income settlement options may be used to shift the risk from the employer to the insurance company. In these plans it is necessary to make sure the benefits are not paid directly to the employee. If so, the entire benefit would become taxable to the employee or beneficiary in one year.

☐ **Examples**

Randy Harrow (*see* preceding example) dies. The corporation settles the contract using the life income option based on Randy's wife. The corporation will receive the annuity rent as long as Randy's wife survives. Just as long as the benefits are not payable directly to Randy's wife, the income will not all be taxable in one year.

Upon retirement Randy's employer uses the cash value in the life insurance contract to purchase a joint and survivor life income annuity on Randy and his wife, payable to the corporation. The corporation receives the benefits and simultaneously pays the amount due under the compensation plan.

Split-Dollar Life Insurance Plans

Split-dollar life insurance is a funding technique and not a type or form of life insurance. The term *split-dollar* refers to cooperation in splitting the death benefits and the living benefits of cash value life insurance contracts between two parties. Premium payments usually are also split. Typically the split-dollar plan is arranged between an insured (employee) and an employer, but it may be useful in a variety of relationships such as between a stockholder and corporation, parent and child, buyer and seller (partnerships and sole proprietorships), among others. The split-dollar plan may be used in a wide variety of situations, including funding a sole proprietor's or partnership's buy-sell agreement[s] as well as helping fund family life insurance plans. The objective of the split-dollar plan is to provide a permanent cash value life insurance contract on an insured while simultaneously sharing the burden of its cost.

The Basic Split-Dollar Plan. In the basic or "classical" split-dollar arrangement (used as an employee fringe benefit) the employer and employee agree to purchase a cash value life insurance contract and split the funding of the plan as well as the rights under the contract. Typically the employee pays the portion of the premium exceeding the annual increase in the cash value. The employer pays an amount equal to the annual cash value increase. Upon the death of the insured the employer is reimbursed for an amount equal to its cost (which equals the cash value amount), and an employee's beneficiary receives the remaining distribution. In the classical split-dollar plan the employee may pay all of the premium in the first few years because there is no increase in the cash value for the first year or two due to acquisition costs. In later years the employee's contribution to the premium declines while the employee's death benefit also declines (because the employer receives the cash value at death, which is subtracted from the face). Using dividends or purchasing additional coverage under a guaranteed insurability rider may allow the death benefits (face amount less cash value) to be maintained at a fairly stable level.

Most split-dollar plans are set up using a variation of either the *endorsement system* or the *collateral system.* In the endorsement system, life insurance is applied for and owned by the employer. The split-dollar arrangement requires the employee to reimburse the employer for the portion of the premium that exceeds the increase in cash value. The employer is named a beneficiary for an amount equal to the cash value, and the employee names a beneficiary for the excess. The split-dollar endorsement to the life insurance contract modifies the ownership rights of the employer so the insured controls the beneficiary designation. If the plan is terminated, the policy is surrendered by the employer, or the insured may purchase the policy for its replacement cost (cash or surrender value).

In the collateral system the employee applies for and owns the life insurance contract. The employee designates a beneficiary. The employer provides an interest-free loan for an amount equal to the increase in cash value. The employee then uses the life insurance policy for collateral on the loan and a formal collateral assignment of the policy is made. At death, the collateral assignment repays the loan (equal to the accumulated cash value) and the remaining policy proceeds are paid to the beneficiary.

Income Tax Treatment for the Employer. The employer is not able to reduce its taxable income by any amounts paid in premiums under a split-dollar plan because the employer is directly or indirectly a beneficiary under the life insurance policy. When death benefits are paid, the employer recaptures capital equal to the cost of the life insurance policy. The opportunity cost of the cash value (forgone interest) is an additional cost to the employer.

Income Tax Treatment for the Employee. The employee, on the other hand, receives a *taxable economic benefit* under split-dollar arrangements and must report the value as a taxable amount. The economic benefit calculated using the *P.S.-58 Rate Table* (Table 20.1), or the standard term rates available for a one-year original-issue term policy may be substituted. The P.S.-58 table provides the cost of pure life insurance protection taxable to the employee and is based on certain actuarial assumptions. The value should be computed using the lower of the two, resulting in a lower economic benefit and consequently a lower tax liability. Policy proceeds are received income tax-free unless the plan runs afoul of the transfer-for-value rules or fails to meet the definition of life insurance and is classified as an investment contract.

Table 20.2, on page 463, provides an example of calculating the economic benefit included in the insured's taxable income.

Each year the employee will pay a tax based on the marginal income tax rate on the amount found in the column labeled "Taxable Income." If death occurs after

Table 20.1
P.S.-58 Rates*

Age	Premiums	Age	Premiums
15	1.27	49	8.53
16	1.38	50	9.22
17	1.48	51	9.97
18	1.52	52	10.79
19	1.56	53	11.69
20	1.61	54	12.67
21	1.67	55	13.74
22	1.73	56	14.91
23	1.79	57	16.18
24	1.86	58	17.56
25	1.93	59	19.08
26	2.02	60	20.73
27	2.11	61	22.53
28	2.20	62	24.50
29	2.31	63	26.63
30	2.43	64	28.98
31	2.57	65	31.51
32	2.70	66	34.28
33	2.86	67	37.31
34	3.02	68	40.59
35	3.21	69	44.17
36	3.41	70	48.06
37	3.63	71	52.29
38	3.87	72	56.89
39	4.14	73	61.89
40	4.42	74	67.33
41	4.73	75	73.23
42	5.07	76	79.63
43	5.44	77	86.57
44	5.85	78	94.09
45	6.30	79	102.23
46	6.78	80	111.04
47	7.32	81	120.57
48	7.89		

*For premium rates for ages under 15 and over 81, see Appendix C, *Tax Facts (1991)*, (Cincinnati: National Underwriter Company), p. 710.

the end of year 4 but before the beginning of year 5, the beneficiary receives $47,989 and the employer $2,011 (the cash value).

Estate Tax Treatment at Insured's Death

Under both the collateral assignment system and the endorsement system, the life insurance proceeds may be included in the gross estate. If the insured dies possessing an incidence of ownership, if proceeds are paid to the estate or if proceeds are used for estate obligations, the proceeds are then subject to estate tax. Under the collateral system, because the insured typically owns the life insurance contract, the value of the gross estate is increased by the policy proceeds less any debt owed under

Table 20.2
Split-Dollar Life Insurance—Taxable Income

End of Policy Year	Cash Value	Change in Cash Value	P.S.-58 Rate	Employee's Contribution	Employee's Death Benefit	Employee's Taxable Income
1	0	0	3.63	927	50,000	181.50
2	515	515	3.87	412	49,485	191.51
3	1,253	738	4.14	189	48,747	201.81
4	2,011	758	4.42	169	47,989	212.11
5	2,786	775	4.73	152	47,214	223.32
6	3,579	793	5.07	134	46,421	235.35
7	4,390	811	5.44	116	45,610	248.12
8	5,220	830	5.85	97	44,780	261.96
9	6,068	848	6.30	79	43,932	276.77
10	6,932	864	6.78	63	43,068	292.00

Premium $927.00
Face $50,000
Age 37

the split-dollar arrangement. If the owner, however, is the beneficiary and the insured has no incidence of ownership, no values will be included. In this case, instead of the insured being a party to the split-dollar arrangement, the beneficiary is.

Under the endorsement system the employer owns the contract. However, the insured usually modifies the ownership rights. One of the ways the insured controls the contract is to require the employer to obtain consent of the insured to change the beneficiary designation. Because this is an ownership right, the face value is included in the gross estate. One possible way to avoid the inclusion is to require the beneficiary's permission to change the beneficiary, not the insured's permission. Thus, if the insured dies, no ownership rights are possessed, and therefore the value will not be included in the gross estate. (Even though no incidence of ownership exists, attribution rules applied to an employee–majority stockholder could cause amounts not paid for the corporation's benefit to be attributed and included in the gross estate.)

Review Questions

1. What is a key employee? What characteristics are generally found in businesses having key employee problems? What characteristics are generally found in businesses having no key employee problems?

2. What potential problems are encountered when a key employee dies? What potential problems are encountered when a key employee is disabled?

3. What cost factors influence the amount of financial loss when a key employee dies or is disabled?

4. What are the advantages of using life and disability insurance to indemnify the business?
5. Explain the tax consequences of a business applying for, owning and receiving benefits from life and disability insurance contracts.
6. What generally happens to a business when an owner dies or is disabled in a sole proprietorship, a partnership and a closely held corporation?
7. Why is it not advisable for the administrator of a sole proprietor to attempt to run the business?
8. What is the purpose of a buy-and-sell agreement? Describe the difference between a cross-purchase and an entity purchase agreement as it applies to the partnership or closely held corporation.
9. What is the difference between a Section 302 and Section 303 stock redemption? Why is it advisable for an exchange to be treated as a capital transaction and not a dividend?
10. What is the difference between a qualified and a nonqualified plan? What is the difference between a deferred compensation and a salary reduction plan?
11. Why are nonqualified plans used in the business environment? Describe the tax consequences for the nonqualified plan with respect to the business, the insured, the beneficiary and the estate.
12. Describe the operation of a typical split-dollar life insurance plan. What is the difference between the collateral system and the endorsement system in setting up the plan?

Bibliography

Advanced Underwriter Service, Chicago: Dearborn Financial Publishing, Inc.

Black, Kenneth, Jr., and Harold Skipper, Jr. *Life Insurance,* 11th ed. Englewood Cliffs, N.J.: Prentice-Hall, Inc., 1987.

Culhane, Floyd C. "Split Dollar: Is It All Smoke and Mirrors?" *Life Association News,* May 1990, pp. 57–60.

Mehr, Robert I., and Sandra G. Gustavson. *Life Insurance Theory and Practice, 4th ed.* Plano, Tex.: Business Publications, Inc., 1987.

Tax Facts 1 (1991), Cincinnati: National Underwriter Company.

Weinberg, Michael D. "Funding the 1990s Buy/Sell Agreement." *Life Association News,* May 1990, pp. 83–86.

White, Edwin H., and Herbert Chasman. *Business Insurance,* 5th ed. Englewood Cliffs, N.J.: Prentice-Hall, 1980.

Chapter 21: The Net Single Premium

Chapter Objectives

- Discuss the importance of life insurance mathematics
- Investigate the component parts of the life insurance premium
- Demonstrate how the net single premium is calculated for traditional life insurance contracts
- Demonstrate how the net single premium is calculated for annuity contracts

Introduction

No study of life insurance would be complete without an examination of the mathematics used in calculating the insurance premium. Mathematics allows the accurate calculation of life insurance premiums and provides the foundation for the life insurance transaction. The amount of the premium, the contractual obligations, the investment return, the mortality experience, expenses and taxes all shape and mold the balance sheet and income statements of life insurance companies.

The background material and the method for calculating the *net single premium* will be presented in this chapter. The net single premium is the onetime charge the insurance company requires the policyholder to pay to fulfill the promise specified in the contract. The premium is referred to as *net* because it assumes payment is only for mortality costs. No expenses of providing the insurance contract (such as taxes, overhead and additions to surplus) are included. *Single* denotes that the premium will be paid only once. The policy owner need not pay another premium, and the insurer will remain obligated to pay all benefits.

Knowing how to calculate the net single premium is the first step in understanding the mathematics of life insurance. In subsequent chapters additional mathematical topics will be explored:

- Calculating a level amount of premium to be paid each period (the level premium)
- Policy reserve values (a balance sheet liability)
- The gross premium (the premium that includes taxes, overhead and additions to surplus)

The Mathematics of Life Insurance

There are three reasons for studying the mathematics of life insurance. Perhaps the most important is that life insurance contracts call for monetary payments from the insurer, usually a long time after the policy begins. Thus the insurance company needs to calculate very accurately the amount of money needed to deliver its future promises to policyholders. Underpricing the contract will ultimately lead to losses. Overpricing the contract can lead to reduced sales due to competitive pressures. Fewer policies sold at a higher price is undesirable, other factors being the same, because the life insurance company's mortality predictions will be less accurate and will in turn increase the variability of operating results. (The law of large numbers states that, the larger the sample size, the closer will the actual approach the expected experience of the group.) Thus serious mistakes in pricing the life insurance product can harm the life insurance company's profit picture and threaten its existence.

The second reason for studying life insurance mathematics is that the premium charged is a function of the event insured. Mathematical models are used to predict the relative frequency of the insured event and to calculate the premium required to insure that event. It is important to know how these models (such as a mortality table) are developed so as to better understand the calculation of the life insurance premium. If the insured event is death, the price (premium) is a function of mortality, or death, rates. Health and disability premiums depend on morbidity rates, and life annuity contracts depend on survivor rates, which are the inverse of mortality rates. (Different tables are used, however, because the experience of groups of people seeking life insurance is different from that of groups seeking annuity contracts.)

The third reason for studying life insurance mathematics is that the contracts often last for many years (obligations of more than 100 years are possible when settlement options are considered), and the time value of money is very important. It is well established that the value of $1 received today is worth more than $1 received ten years from now. The time value of money comes into play in life insurance mathematics in many ways. Money received can be invested for long periods of time until funds are needed to pay claims. During this accumulation phase the insurance company relies on compound interest to provide sufficient funds to pay the benefits called for by the contract. If a lump-sum settlement is not chosen at death, the investment rate also influences the amount of proceeds paid to the beneficiary. For example, the amount or length of payments under the fixed-period, fixed-amount and life annuity options depends partially on the rate of return earned on the invested funds.

It is clear from this brief discussion that the basis for operating a successful life insurance company is the calculation of the proper insurance rate; that is, the company's success depends on accurate mathematics. Therefore it is evident that, once a life insurance contract is sold, the initial premium charged will continue to have a dynamic impact on the company's financial statements and well-being throughout the life of the contract.

Composition of the Premium

The life insurance premium is a function of four factors:

1. The time value of money
2. The probability of the insured event occurring
3. The amount to be paid if the insured event occurs
4. The amounts added to the premiums for expenses, additions to surplus and taxes

The gross premium needed to complete the contractual promise(s) can be calculated only when all of these factors are considered. The first part of this calculation focuses on the *net* single premium, which is derived from considering the amount paid when the event occurs, the time value of money and the probability of the event. Amounts added to the premium for expenses, additions to surplus and taxes are considered in subsequent chapters.

The Time Value of Money: The First Component

The impact of compound interest on the life insurance premium calculation is significant when long contractual periods are involved. The time value of money is one of the important building blocks of the premium. Readers who have difficulty making the calculations and to whom time-value-of-money concepts are unfamiliar should review Chapter 13.

Mortality: The Second Component

The probability of loss is the second component considered when the premium is calculated. The probability of loss is the expected frequency of the loss occurring and is stated as a fraction. For example, if 100 individuals are expected to die out of a group of 10,000, the expected probability is 0.01 (100/10,000).

In life insurance, mortality rates depend on many factors. The most important factor is age. A group of 20-year-olds will live longer than a group of 60-year-olds, though some 60-year-olds will outlive some 20-year-olds. Other significant factors are sex, health, life-style, hazardous occupations or hobbies and the length of time the person has been insured. In calculating the probability of loss, companies must consider, on the average, that females tend to live longer than males, that healthy people tend to live longer than the unhealthy and that people who do not drink, smoke or engage in hazardous occupations or hobbies also tend to live longer.

Newly insured groups experience a lower mortality rate than groups insured for several years and of the same age. Males aged 35 who have just successfully passed a life insurance medical exam will generally show a lower mortality rate than men aged 35 who have been insured for several years. The lower mortality rate for the new group is a result of the use of a medical examination for preselection purposes. This is known as the **medical selection effect**.

Life insurance companies use mathematical models for predicting death rates. There are many mathematical models describing a function that can predict the number of survivors of a cohort (group) of lives over time. One job of the life insurance actuary is to select a mathematical model (**mortality table**) that accurately reflects the mortality rates the life insurance company expects to experience. Thus a life insurance company must select or create a mortality table reflecting expected experience so that accurate predictions may be obtained. Continuous mathematical models, even though they produce smooth curves, do not reflect the mortality rates accurately at all ages; therefore the parameters of the mathematical model, coefficients that shape the function, must be refined so mortality or morbidity predictions are generally accurate when large numbers of insureds are considered in the pool.

Life insurance companies also can construct mortality or morbidity tables by selecting a large group of individuals and observing its mortality rate. A large cohort of lives is selected for observation at a certain age (usually age zero for life insurance), and the experience of the group is tabulated over many years until there are no survivors. If ten million male lives were selected for observation at age zero, accurate statistics could be developed by following the cohort and dividing the number of people who die during each year by the number of people who began that year, to derive the frequency or probability of death. If the radix (the number of individuals that start the group) is large, one would assume that the rate of deaths per year would change in a smooth fashion; but irregularities do occur. A process of graduation is used to smooth any apparent inconsistencies in the annual experience so that the tabular rates are closer to the theoretical rates. To illustrate how to construct and interpret a mortality table, the 1980 Commissioners Standard Ordinary (CSO) Table (Table 21.1) will be used in this chapter. (Table 21.14, the 1980 CSO Mortality Table and the 1983 Annuity Table for male and female lives, starts on page 485. The 1980 CSO Table is based on experience from 1970 to 1975. The 1983 Annuity Table is based on 1971 to 1976 experience. Table 21.1 follows a cohort of ten million and provides the numbers used throughout this chapter. Table 21.14 is based on rates per 1,000 and provides survival probabilities.) The 1980 CSO Table will also be used to illustrate the calculation of life insurance premiums in the material to follow.

Interpreting Mortality Tables

The 1980 CSO Table starts age age zero (x) with ten million male lives as its radix. (In 1898 the International Congress of Actuaries established a system of notation for actuarial literature. The following notation will be used where convenient in this and the following chapters: x = age; q_x = probability of dying during age x [d_x / l_x]; px = probability of surviving age x [l_{x+1}/l_x]; l_x = number living at age x [$l_{x-1} - d_{x-1}$]; dx = the number dying during age x [$l_x - l_{x-1}$].) Out of the ten million lives that start the year (l_x), it is expected that 41,800 will die (d_x) during the year, leaving 9,958,200 to start the next year. The probability of a person dying during the year ($q_{x=0}$) is equal to d_0/l_0 = 41,800 / 10,000,000 or 4.180 deaths per thousand. Similarly, the yearly probability of dying during age 40 (q_{40}) is equal to d_{40}/l_{40} = 28,319 / 9,377,225 or 3.020 deaths per thousand. And the yearly probability of dying between age 99 and 100 (q_{99}) is d_{99} / l_{99} = 10,757 / 10,757 = 1.00.

Thus the 1980 CSO mortality rate assumes no one survives to age 100. The yearly probability of surviving (p_x) is simply unity (1) minus the yearly probability of dying.

$$p_x = 1 - q_x$$

Chapter 21 The Net Single Premium

Table 21.1
1980 Commissioners Standard Ordinary (1970–1975) Male Lives

Age	Number Alive at the Start of the Year l_x	Number Dying during the Year d_x	Yearly Probability of Dying q_x	Yearly Probability of Surviving p_x
0	10,000,000	41,800	0.004180	0.995820
1	9,958,200	10,655	0.001070	0.998930
2	9,947,545	9,848	0.000990	0.999010
3	9,937,697	9,739	0.000980	0.999020
4	9,927,958	9,432	0.000950	0.999050
5	9,918,526	8,927	0.000900	0.999100
6	9,909,599	8,522	0.000860	0.999140
7	9,901,077	7,921	0.000800	0.999200
8	9,893,156	7,519	0.000760	0.999240
9	9,885,637	7,315	0.000740	0.999260
10	9,878,322	7,211	0.000730	0.999270
11	9,871,111	7,601	0.000770	0.999230
12	9,863,510	8,384	0.000850	0.999150
13	9,855,126	9,757	0.000990	0.999010
14	9,845,369	11,322	0.001150	0.998850
15	9,834,047	13,079	0.001330	0.998670
16	9,820,968	14,830	0.001510	0.998490
17	9,806,138	16,376	0.001670	0.998330
18	9,789,762	17,426	0.001780	0.998220
19	9,772,336	18,177	0.001860	0.998140
20	9,754,159	18,533	0.001900	0.998100
21	9,735,626	18,595	0.001910	0.998090
22	9,717,031	18,365	0.001890	0.998110
23	9,698,666	18,040	0.001860	0.998140
24	9,680,626	17,619	0.001820	0.998180
25	9,663,007	17,104	0.001770	0.998230
26	9,645,903	16,687	0.001730	0.998270
27	9,629,216	16,466	0.001710	0.998290
28	9,612,750	16,342	0.001700	0.998300
29	9,596,408	16,410	0.001710	0.998290
30	9,579,998	16,573	0.001730	0.998270
31	9,563,425	17,023	0.001780	0.998220
32	9,546,402	17,470	0.001830	0.998170
33	9,528,932	18,200	0.001910	0.998090
34	9,510,732	19,021	0.002000	0.998000
35	9,491,711	20,028	0.002110	0.997890
36	9,471,683	21,217	0.002240	0.997760
37	9,450,466	22,681	0.002400	0.997600
38	9,427,785	24,324	0.002580	0.997420
39	9,403,461	26,236	0.002790	0.997210
40	9,377,225	28,319	0.003020	0.996980
41	9,348,906	30,758	0.003290	0.996710
42	9,318,148	33,173	0.003560	0.996440
43	9,284,975	35,933	0.003870	0.996130
44	9,249,042	38,753	0.004190	0.995810
45	9,210,289	41,907	0.004550	0.995450
46	9,168,382	45,108	0.004920	0.995080
47	9,123,274	48,536	0.005320	0.994680
48	9,074,738	52,089	0.005740	0.994260
49	9,022,649	56,031	0.006210	0.993790
50	8,966,618	60,166	0.006710	0.993290
51	8,906,452	65,017	0.007300	0.992700
52	8,841,435	70,378	0.007960	0.992040

Table 21.1 (continued)
1980 Commissioners Standard Ordinary (1970–1975) Male Lives

Age	Number Alive at the Start of the Year l_x	Number Dying during the Year d_x	Yearly Probability of Dying q_x	Yearly Probability of Surviving p_x
53	8,771,057	76,396	0.008710	0.991290
54	8,694,661	83,121	0.009560	0.990440
55	8,611,540	90,163	0.010470	0.989530
56	8,521,377	97,655	0.011460	0.988540
57	8,423,722	105,212	0.012490	0.987510
58	8,318,510	113,049	0.013590	0.986410
59	8,205,461	121,195	0.014770	0.985230
60	8,084,266	129,995	0.016080	0.983920
61	7,954,271	139,518	0.017540	0.982460
62	7,814,753	149,965	0.019190	0.980810
63	7,664,788	161,420	0.021060	0.978940
64	7,503,368	173,628	0.023140	0.976860
65	7,329,740	186,322	0.025420	0.974580
66	7,143,418	198,944	0.027850	0.972150
67	6,944,474	211,390	0.030440	0.969560
68	6,733,084	223,471	0.033190	0.966810
69	6,509,613	235,453	0.036170	0.963830
70	6,274,160	247,892	0.039510	0.960490
71	6,026,268	260,937	0.043300	0.956700
72	5,765,331	274,718	0.047650	0.952350
73	5,490,613	289,026	0.052640	0.947360
74	5,201,587	302,680	0.058190	0.941810
75	4,898,907	314,461	0.064190	0.935810
76	4,584,446	323,341	0.070530	0.929470
77	4,261,105	328,616	0.077120	0.922880
78	3,932,489	329,936	0.083900	0.916100
79	3,602,553	328,012	0.091050	0.908950
80	3,274,541	323,656	0.098840	0.901160
81	2,950,885	317,161	0.107480	0.892520
82	2,633,724	308,804	0.117250	0.882750
83	2,324,920	298,194	0.128260	0.871740
84	2,026,726	284,248	0.140250	0.859750
85	1,742,478	266,512	0.152950	0.847050
86	1,475,966	245,143	0.166090	0.833910
87	1,230,823	220,994	0.179550	0.820450
88	1,009,829	195,170	0.193270	0.806730
89	814,659	168,871	0.207290	0.792710
90	645,788	143,216	0.221769	0.778231
91	502,572	119,100	0.236981	0.763019
92	383,472	97,191	0.253450	0.746550
93	286,281	77,900	0.272110	0.727890
94	208,381	61,660	0.295900	0.704100
95	146,721	48,412	0.329960	0.670040
96	98,309	37,805	0.384553	0.615447
97	60,504	29,054	0.480200	0.519800
98	31,450	20,693	0.657965	0.342035
99	10,757	10,757	1.000000	0.000000

Calculating the probability of dying or surviving for a period of years is a relatively easy task, using the mortality tables supplied. For example, for a male aged 35, what is the probability of dying within the next ten years and the probability of surviving the ten-year period? (Use Table 21.1.)

The probability of dying within the next ten-year period is equal to the number of people who die within the ten-year period ($l_{35} - l_{45}$) divided by the number of people starting the cohort at age 35 (l_{35}).

$$q = \frac{(l_{35} - l_{45})}{l_{35}} = \frac{9{,}491{,}711 - 9{,}210{,}289}{9{,}491{,}711} = 0.0296$$

Similarly, the probability of surviving the ten-year period is equal to the number of people who survive the ten-year period divided by the number of people who started the cohort.

$$p = \frac{l_{45}}{l_{35}} = \frac{9{,}210{,}289}{9{,}491{,}711} = 0.9704$$

or

$$p = 1 - 0.0296 = 0.9704$$

The number living is taken from age 45 because l_{45} is the number of people alive at the beginning of age 45, which is equal to the number of individuals alive at the end of age 44.

Care must be taken in interpreting such probabilities. Predictions of mortality are accurate only when applied to a large number of lives. It could be argued that it is erroneous to state that the probability of death of a particular male age 40 is 0.003020 because one male is an insufficient number on which to base any credible predictions. On the other hand, it is accurate to say that, out of 100,000 men age 40, 302 are expected to die during the year. It is impossible to make accurate predictions based on a group consisting of one individual.

The 1980 CSO Table is a conservative table in that the death rates of insured lives were overstated initially and based on 1970 to 1975 data. Because death rates have declined since the table was developed, the 1980 CSO Table is even more overstated. Life insurance companies are not required to use any particular mortality table for calculating their rates. However, life insurance companies are required to use the 1980 CSO Table for calculating the legal reserves on their balance sheet, thus imposing a form of indirect rate regulation. (As of this writing, all states have adopted the 1980 CSO Table for calculating reserves. The death rates predicted in the 1980 CSO Table are generally lower than the death rates predicted by the previously used 1958 CSO Table.)

Annuity Tables. Because people who purchase annuities exhibit better mortality rates (fewer deaths per thousand) than people who purchase life insurance contracts, different tables must be constructed for use with annuity contracts than for life insurance contracts. The 1983 **Annuity Table** with Projection (Table 21.2) is commonly used for predicting mortality among a group of individuals purchasing annuities. The table is similar to the 1980 CSO Table except that the annuity table

Table 21.2
Commissioners 1983 Individual Annuity Table
(1971–1976 Projected to 1980) Male Lives

Age	Number Alive at the Start of the Year l_x	Number Dying during the Year d_x	Yearly Probability of Dying q_x	Yearly Probability of Surviving p_x
5	10,000,000	3,770	0.000377	0.999623
6	9,996,230	3,499	0.000350	0.999650
7	9,992,731	3,328	0.000333	0.999667
8	9,989,403	3,516	0.000352	0.999648
9	9,985,887	3,675	0.000368	0.999632
10	9,982,212	3,813	0.000382	0.999618
11	9,978,399	3,931	0.000394	0.999606
12	9,974,468	4,040	0.000405	0.999595
13	9,970,428	4,138	0.000415	0.999585
14	9,966,290	4,236	0.000425	0.999575
15	9,962,054	4,333	0.000435	0.999565
16	9,957,721	4,441	0.000446	0.999554
17	9,953,280	4,559	0.000458	0.999542
18	9,948,721	4,696	0.000472	0.999528
19	9,944,025	4,853	0.000488	0.999512
20	9,939,172	5,019	0.000505	0.999495
21	9,934,153	5,215	0.000525	0.999475
22	9,928,938	5,421	0.000546	0.999454
23	9,923,517	5,656	0.000570	0.999430
24	9,917,861	5,911	0.000596	0.999404
25	9,911,950	6,165	0.000622	0.999378
26	9,905,785	6,439	0.000650	0.999350
27	9,899,346	6,702	0.000677	0.999323
28	9,892,644	6,964	0.000704	0.999296
29	9,885,680	7,226	0.000731	0.999269
30	9,878,454	7,498	0.000759	0.999241
31	9,870,956	7,759	0.000786	0.999214
32	9,863,197	8,029	0.000814	0.999186
33	9,855,168	8,308	0.000843	0.999157
34	9,846,860	8,626	0.000876	0.999124
35	9,838,234	9,022	0.000917	0.999083
36	9,829,212	9,515	0.000968	0.999032
37	9,819,697	10,134	0.001032	0.998968
38	9,809,563	10,928	0.001114	0.998886
39	9,798,635	11,915	0.001216	0.998784
40	9,786,720	13,124	0.001341	0.998659
41	9,773,596	14,582	0.001492	0.998508
42	9,759,014	16,327	0.001673	0.998327
43	9,742,687	18,375	0.001886	0.998114
44	9,724,312	20,703	0.002129	0.997871
45	9,703,609	23,279	0.002399	0.997601
46	9,680,330	26,069	0.002693	0.997307
47	9,654,261	29,050	0.003009	0.996991
48	9,625,211	32,177	0.003343	0.996657
49	9,593,034	35,437	0.003694	0.996306
50	9,557,597	38,775	0.004057	0.995943
51	9,518,822	42,178	0.004431	0.995569
52	9,476,644	45,602	0.004812	0.995188
53	9,431,042	49,023	0.005198	0.994802
54	9,382,019	52,455	0.005591	0.994409
55	9,329,564	55,921	0.005994	0.994006
56	9,273,643	59,435	0.006409	0.993591
57	9,214,208	63,016	0.006839	0.993161
58	9,151,192	66,712	0.007290	0.992710
59	9,084,480	70,695	0.007782	0.992218

Chapter 21 The Net Single Premium

Table 21.2 (continued)
Commissioners 1983 Individual Annuity Table
(1971–1976 Projected to 1980) Male Lives

Age	Number Alive at the Start of the Year l_x	Number Dying during the Year d_x	Yearly Probability of Dying q_x	Yearly Probability of Surviving p_x
60	9,013,785	75,157	0.008338	0.991662
61	8,938,628	80,296	0.008983	0.991017
62	8,858,332	86,280	0.009740	0.990260
63	8,772,052	93,247	0.010630	0.989370
64	8,678,805	101,230	0.011664	0.988336
65	8,577,575	110,230	0.012851	0.987149
66	8,467,345	120,228	0.014199	0.985801
67	8,347,117	131,192	0.015717	0.984283
68	8,215,925	143,072	0.017414	0.982586
69	8,072,853	155,774	0.019296	0.980704
70	7,917,079	169,196	0.021371	0.978629
71	7,747,883	183,214	0.023647	0.976353
72	7,564,669	197,672	0.026131	0.973869
73	7,366,997	212,427	0.028835	0.971165
74	7,154,570	227,472	0.031794	0.968206
75	6,927,098	242,767	0.035046	0.964954
76	6,684,331	258,222	0.038631	0.961369
77	6,426,109	273,669	0.042587	0.957413
78	6,152,440	288,863	0.046951	0.953049
79	5,863,577	303,469	0.051755	0.948245
80	5,560,108	317,071	0.057026	0.942974
81	5,243,037	329,216	0.062791	0.937209
82	4,913,821	339,452	0.069081	0.930919
83	4,574,369	347,231	0.075908	0.924092
84	4,227,138	351,825	0.083230	0.916770
85	3,875,313	352,603	0.090987	0.909013
86	3,522,710	349,178	0.099122	0.900878
87	3,173,532	341,399	0.107577	0.892423
88	2,832,133	329,422	0.116316	0.883684
89	2,502,711	313,825	0.125394	0.874606
90	2,188,886	295,252	0.134887	0.865113
91	1,893,634	274,336	0.144873	0.855127
92	1,619,298	251,686	0.155429	0.844571
93	1,367,612	227,884	0.166629	0.833371
94	1,139,728	203,484	0.178537	0.821463
95	936,244	179,023	0.191214	0.808786
96	757,221	155,019	0.204721	0.795279
97	602,202	131,955	0.219121	0.780879
98	470,247	110,383	0.234734	0.765266
99	359,864	90,646	0.251890	0.748110
100	269,218	72,933	0.270907	0.729093
101	196,285	57,337	0.292111	0.707889
102	138,948	43,883	0.315823	0.684177
103	95,065	32,548	0.342376	0.657624
104	62,517	23,262	0.372091	0.627909
105	39,255	15,909	0.405273	0.594727
106	23,346	10,325	0.442260	0.557740
107	13,021	6,294	0.483373	0.516627
108	6,727	3,559	0.529062	0.470938
109	3,168	1,835	0.579230	0.420770
110	1,333	846	0.634659	0.365341
111	487	339	0.696099	0.303901
112	148	113	0.763514	0.236486
113	35	29	0.828571	0.171429
114	6	5	0.833333	0.166667
115	1	1	1.000000	0.000000

Table 21.3
Selected Mortality Table Statistics
Deaths per Thousand

Age	1958 Mortality	1980 Mortality	1949 Annuity	1983 Annuity	U.S. Population
0	7.08	4.18			12.60
5	1.35	0.90			0.37
15	1.46	1.33	0.54	0.44	0.69
25	1.93	1.77	0.77	0.62	1.32
35	2.51	2.11	1.39	0.92	1.59
45	5.35	4.55	3.63	2.40	3.66
55	13.00	10.47	10.57	5.99	9.02
65	31.75	25.42	23.07	12.85	20.59
75	73.37	64.19	54.50	35.05	45.07
85	161.14	152.95	134.18	90.99	107.25
95	351.24	329.96	316.83	191.21	229.76
99	1000.00	1000.00	431.20	251.89	280.30
105			638.96	405.28	335.39
109			1000.00	579.35	359.88
115				1000.00	

All males lives except U.S. population.
1949 Annuity Table is not projected.
1983 Individual Annuity Table (based on 1971–1976 experience) projected to 1983.
1980 CSO Table (based on 1970–1975 experience) increased to produce conservative statistics.

starts at age 5, and every annuitant is assumed to die before age 116. The 1983 Annuity Table is based on 1971 to 1976 data and is interpreted similarly to the 1980 CSO Mortality Table. For a comparison of several mortality tables, refer to Table 21.3. The 1980 CSO Mortality and 1983 Annuity Tables are compared graphically in Figure 21.1 on the following page.

Many annuity tables are labeled *projected*. A projected table predicts a lower mortality rate (higher survivor rate) than similar tables that are not projected. Projected tables are derived by taking the mortality rates predicted by nonprojected tables and adjusting them for anticipated mortality trends. As mortality rates decline, annuity tables become less conservative. If mortality is less than predicted (longevity increases), more money than anticipated must be paid in rent, and the life insurance company could experience financial loss. Declining mortality rates in life insurance contracts are not a problem; if fewer people die than expected, the life insurance company will not be threatened financially.

Types of Mortality Tables. As stated, mortality rates differ between newly insured individuals and those insured for several years. The effect of this selection process eventually disappears, and the mortality rates of the two groups at the same age will not differ significantly. Mortality tables showing this ripple effect from the age of issue to a later date (three to four years) are called *select* mortality tables. The mortality rate depends first on the age of the group and second on the number of years since the group has gone through the insurance company's selection process. Thus a lower mortality rate is experienced for a select group aged 35 versus a

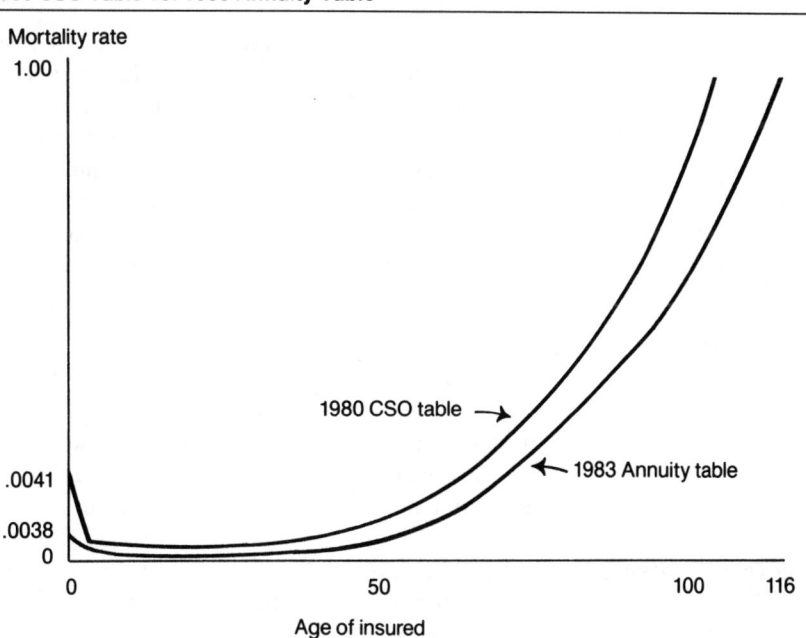

Figure 21.1
1980 CSO Table vs. 1983 Annuity Table

group aged 35 insured for a short period. When the effect of the selection finally erodes, the mortality rate for a male aged 35 who has been insured for 5 years is approximately equal to one insured for many years. As the number of years being insured increases, the select mortality rates converge into the mortality rates of groups insured for many years; thus the select mortality rates will evolve into *ultimate* mortality rates. The 1980 CSO Table and the 1983 Annuity Table are examples of ultimate mortality tables.

Calculating the Net Single Premium

The **net single premium (NSP)** equals the amount of money the life insurance company must have on hand at the beginning of the contract term to perform according to its contractual obligations. Because it does not include any amounts for taxes, operating expenses or additions to surplus, it is not representative of the premium a consumer will pay. It is, however, a very useful teaching device that has actuarial applications. Calculating the net single premium involves determining the present value of the benefits to be provided by the contract. This statement will become clearer as the calculation process is presented.

NSP Assumptions

The following presentation of the mathematics underlying the net single premium assumes several unrealistic assumptions so as to simplify the calculation process.

To make the net single premium equal the present value of the future benefits, these assumptions are made:

- The group insured is large enough to produce absolutely predictable results. In other words, the mortality rate of the group insured is equal to the mortality rate predicted by the table being used, in this case the 1980 CSO Table. (An implied extension to this assumption is that all insureds are the same age and sex and that all are in good health. If unisex mortality tables are used, males and females may be mixed in the same proportion used in constructing the table. The result, regardless, must be absolutely predictable.)
- All premiums are collected at exactly the same instant at the beginning of the contract year
- All death claims are paid at the end of the policy year.

In practice actuarial calculations start with these simplifying assumptions and use various techniques to handle problems generated by grouping individuals with unequal birth dates in a given year and collecting premiums and paying death claims throughout the policy year. The reader should evaluate the effect on the net single premium when there are violations of one or more of these assumptions.

The Term Insurance Contract

Term life insurance contracts promise to pay $1,000 to a beneficiary if the insured dies within the term specified. (It will be assumed that life insurance contracts are issued only for $1,000 for illustrative purposes. Life insurance policies are purchased for any practical amount. The premium calculation is similar except that the benefit changes or the resulting net single premium may be multiplied by the face amount desired in thousands.) Term insurance contracts may last for many years but are considered temporary contracts because an individual generally cannot renew the contract past age 65 to 75. (The ability to renew varies from company to company. Some insurance companies issue term to age 99 and charge the required premiums. Many people cannot renew because they cannot afford the price.)

The net single premium of a $1,000 one-year term insurance contract is equal to the probability of the insured dying multiplied by the benefit if death occurs ($1,000) and again multiplied by a present value factor (PVF). Using the 1980 CSO Table and a 4 percent interest factor, the net single premium for a male aged 30 would be calculated as follows:

$$\begin{aligned} \text{NSP} &= d_{30}/l_{30} \times \$1,000 \times 1/[(1 + .04)^1] \\ &= 16,573 / 9,579,998 \times \$1,000 \times 0.9615 \\ &= .00173 \times \$1,000 \times 0.9615 \\ &= \$1.6635 \end{aligned}$$

Thus, if the life insurance company collects $1.6635 from 10,000 insureds and the premium is invested at 4 percent, approximately $17,300 (10,000 × $1.6635 × 1.04) will be accumulated. If exactly 0.00173 times the number of insureds in the group die, there will be enough assets to pay the death benefits at the end of the year (.00173 × 10,000 × $1,000 = $17,300), and the insurance company will break even after all death claims have been paid.

Chapter 21 The Net Single Premium

Table 21.4
NSP Five-Year Term Policy

Year	Age	Yearly Probability of Death	×	Benefit	×	PVF	=	Yearly NSP
1	30	16,573 / 9,579,998		1,000		0.962		1.663
2	31	17,023 / 9,579,998		1,000		0.925		1.643
3	32	17,470 / 9,579,998		1,000		0.889		1.621
4	33	18,200 / 9,579,998		1,000		0.855		1.624
5	34	19,021 / 9,579,998		1,000		0.822		1.632
		Net single premium						8.183

This calculation assumes that the investment rate is 4 percent for illustrative purposes only. Though life insurance companies use varying rates, the rates used do tend to be on the conservative (low) side. Four percent undoubtedly seems low compared to current interest rates, but from the life insurance companies' point of view the interest rate elected *must* be conservative. Because of the possible length of the life insurance contract, the debtor/creditor position of the company toward its insureds and beneficiaries and investment laws and regulations, investment of funds must be low-risk/low-return. When the interest rate is chosen for the calculation of the insurance premium, a conservative posture must be reflected. Otherwise, if high-risk investments are made and capital is lost due to a flawed investment policy, sufficient funds may not be available to pay claims as they come due.

Multiple-Year Term Contracts

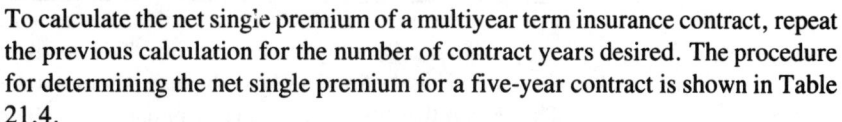

To calculate the net single premium of a multiyear term insurance contract, repeat the previous calculation for the number of contract years desired. The procedure for determining the net single premium for a five-year contract is shown in Table 21.4.

The net single premium calculation for the first year is exactly the same for the one-year term policy at age 30. In the second year, at age 31, the probability of death is calculated by taking the number of deaths predicted in the second year and dividing that number by the number of individuals starting the group at age 30. The probability required is the *conditional probability* of an individual dying in the second year given that the individual started at age 30. As stated earlier, the probability of an individual dying during his or her 31st year is not the same as the probability of death for the person who started the group in an earlier year.

The sum of the five probabilities shown in Table 21.4 equals the probability of dying during the five-year period (88,287 / 9,579,998 = 0.00921). Notice that the sum does not equal one because many individuals in the group will survive. Death is not a certainty in the term contract, whereas in the permanent forms of insurance a death claim will certainly be paid if the insured does not allow the policy to lapse. The probability of surviving the five-year period is 0.99079 (1 − 0.00921).

The present value factor (PVF) in Table 21.4 is the present value factor of $1, given the number of years the money will be invested. The amount of money needed to pay the mortality costs for the third year is $1.823 ($1,000 × 17,470 / 9,579,998). If the present value of $1.823 ($1.621) is invested at 4 percent, a sufficient amount of money will be available to pay death claims.

Again, present value tables may be used, or the factor (PVF) may be calculated using the following formula:

$$PVF = 1 / (1 + i)^n$$

where:

i = rate of interest per period
n = the number of periods discounted

A quick method for determining the number of discounting periods (n) in the formula is to take the age of the individual for that contract year, subtract from that number the age at issue and add one to the result. In the preceding example, for the year when the insured is 34 the number of discounting periods is 5 years (34 − 30 + 1).

Calculating the net single premium of a 10-year, 15-year or term to age 65 contract follows the same procedure, except more years of calculations are included in the final sum.

Whole Life Insurance

Determining the net single premium for a whole life insurance contract is similar to calculating the net single premium for the term insurance contract. Whole life insurance contracts are considered permanent insurance contracts because the insured can maintain the policy throughout life. Because of the permanent nature of the contract, a calculation must be made for each year that there is a possibility of a benefit payment. The 1980 CSO Table assumes each insured has died by his or her 100th birthday, so calculations need be made only through age 99. Even if this assumption is violated and the insured lives longer than age 99, the insurance company will not collect any more premiums. The life insurance company will assume the insured has died and will pay the face amount of the policy as a maturity value. The reason that the life insurance company pays the claim even if the insured is alive will become evident in Chapter 23, where policy reserves and cash values are studied.

Table 21.5 extends the example of calculating the net single premium for the one-year and five-year term policies for the whole life policy. The first line is exactly the same as for the one-year term policy, and the first five lines are exactly the same as for the five-year term policy. The calculations continue for 70 years. Only the first and last five years for the whole life calculation are shown.

The net single premium for a whole life insurance policy is equal to $209.18, using the 1980 CSO Table and a 4 percent interest rate.

Endowment Insurance

The endowment life insurance contract provides both a death and a survivor benefit. If the insured dies during the term of the contract, the face amount is paid to the beneficiary. But if the insured survives the term of the contract, the face value is paid to the policy owner insured. Thus the net single premium calculation must take into account not only the contingency of death but also the possibility of the insured's surviving the endowment period. The net single premium associated

Table 21.5
NSP Whole Life Insurance

Year	Age	Yearly Probability of Death	x	Benefit	x	PVF	=	Yearly NSP
1	30	16,573 / 9,579,998		1,000		0.962		1.663
2	31	17,023 / 9,579,998		1,000		0.925		1.643
3	32	17,470 / 9,579,998		1,000		0.889		1.621
4	33	18,200 / 9,579,998		1,000		0.855		1.624
5	34	19,021 / 9,579,998		1,000		0.822		1.632
.	.	.		.		.		.
.	.	.		.		.		.
.	.	.		.		.		.
66	95	48,412 / 9,579,998		1,000		0.075		0.380
67	96	37,805 / 9,579,998		1,000		0.072		0.285
68	97	29,054 / 9,579,998		1,000		0.069		0.211
69	98	20,693 / 9,579,998		1,000		0.067		0.144
70	99	10,757 / 9,579,998		1,000		0.064		0.072
		Net single premium						209.185

with the first benefit, to pay upon death, is calculated exactly as for a term insurance policy (Table 21.6). The second benefit (Table 21.7), payment if the insured survives, is added to the net single premium of the first benefit to equal the net single premium of the endowment insurance policy. (The mathematics exploring the endowment contract is provided for historical purposes only, because a very small proportion of life insurance sold is of this form. In 1985 less than .5 percent of the total life insurance in force was of the endowment type.)

At the beginning of year six (end of year five), 9,491,711 individuals have survived out of the original 9,579,998 (99.1 percent). The benefit ($1,000) and the present value factor remain unchanged from the last calculation of the first promise (to pay upon death).

Annuities

Instead of needing contracts that pay either upon death or at the end of a specified period if the insured survives, individuals may require a contract to make periodic payments over a length of time. Annuity contracts are defined as ones requiring insurance companies to make regular payments. Often annuity payments are made

Table 21.6
Endowment Contract: Death Benefit

Year	Age	Yearly Probability of Death	x	Benefit	x	PVF	=	Yearly NSP
1	30	16,573 / 9,579,998		1,000		0.962		1.663
2	31	17,023 / 9,579,998		1,000		0.925		1.643
3	32	17,470 / 9,579,998		1,000		0.889		1.621
4	33	18,200 / 9,579,998		1,000		0.855		1.624
5	34	19,021 / 9,579,998		1,000		0.822		1.632
		NSP to pay death benefit						8.183

Table 21.7
Endowment Contract: Survivor Benefit

Year	Age	Yearly Probability of Death	×	Benefit	×	PVF	=	Yearly NSP
5	35	9,491,711 / 9,579,998		1,000		0.822		814.352
		+ NSP death benefit						8.183
		NSP for 5-year endowment						822.536

to a beneficiary as one of the settlement options under the life insurance contract. Among the annuity type of settlement options provided by most life insurance companies are the fixed-payment option, the fixed-amount option and the life income option.

Other applications of annuity contracts include use in deferred compensation plans and individual retirement or group pension plans. Because the mathematical complexity increases substantially when joint-life annuities are considered, this discussion will be confined to single-life annuities. Joint-life and group annuities are written on two or more lives, and the probabilities of survival (payment) depend on compound probabilities.

Annuity Certain

Not all annuities are paid based on a life contingency. Some annuities pay rent for a period of time and terminate on a certain date regardless of whether the insured lives or dies. (The term *rent* means "payment" when used in conjunction with annuities.) Such a contract is called an *annuity certain*. The net single premium of an annuity paying a stated amount each period can be calculated by discounting the rent at an appropriate rate for the proper discounting period. Because no life contingencies are involved, the present value of an annuity factor can be used for the calculation. As an alternative method of calculating the factor, a present value factor can be applied to each payment separately to determine the present value of the stream of payments. The calculation is shown in Table 21.8 for the net single premium for a male aged 65 purchasing a ten-year annuity certain ($100 each year at a 4 percent discount rate). (Factors such as age and sex in this example are irrelevant because payment is not contingent upon surviving.)

The net single premium for the promise to pay $100 each year for ten years is $811.30. If the insurance company earns 4 percent on its investments and pays $100 per year for ten years, nothing will be left after the tenth payment. Notice the first payment is discounted for one year; amounts deposited at the beginning of the year have time to earn interest.

Immediate versus Deferred Annuity

Table 21.8 is an example of an immediate annuity. Suppose, however, the insured wished to deposit sufficient money in one lump sum to fund the premium five years before the annuity payments are begun by the insurer. In this case, for a deferred

Table 21.8
Immediate Annuity Certain

Year	Yearly Payment	×	PVF	=	NSP
1	100.00		0.962		$ 96.20
2	100.00		0.925		$ 92.50
3	100.00		0.889		$ 88.90
4	100.00		0.855		$ 85.50
5	100.00		0.822		$ 82.20
6	100.00		0.790		$ 79.00
7	100.00		0.760		$ 76.00
8	100.00		0.731		$ 73.10
9	100.00		0.703		$ 70.30
10	100.00		0.676		$ 67.60
	Total net single premium				$811.30

or Payment × PVAF 4%, 10 periods = Net single premium
$100.00 × 8.113 = $811.30

annuity two adjustments must be made to the calculation. First, a shift in the payment pattern occurs from the end of the year to the beginning of the year. From the insurance company's point of view, the first payment is made at the end of the fifth year or the beginning of the sixth year. Second, the premium for the annuity must be discounted for five years because the insurance company will have use of the money without having to make payments to the insured. (Instead of applying a deferral factor as illustrated, the present value factor for each year that appropriately reflects the payment pattern may be used. This note applies to all of the examples showing how to calculate the net single premiums for deferred annuities.) Table 21.9 shows the calculations for a ten-year annuity certain, deferred five years.

If $693.52 is deposited and left for five years at 4 percent, $100 may be withdrawn at the beginning of each of the next ten years, whereupon the principal will be exhausted. Again, no life contingencies are involved in the calculation.

Temporary Annuities

Temporary annuities pay the insured if and only if the insured is alive; however, payments also cease once a predetermined number of payments have been made. To calculate a ten-year temporary annuity starting at age 65, the annuity certain calculation must be adjusted for the life contingency (Table 21.10).

According to the 1983 Annuity Table, 8,577,575 individuals are in the initial group. Of that number, 8,467,345 will collect the first rent payment because they will survive the first year. Similarly, 8,347,117 members will collect the second rent payment because they will survive out of the original group. The probability of receiving a rent payment for the remaining eight years is calculated in a fashion similar to that for the first two years. Because there is no promise to pay beyond the tenth year regardless of whether the insured is alive, no more calculations need to be made.

If the temporary annuity is deferred instead of immediate, the premium is determined by first changing the time-value-of-money calculation from the simple

Table 21.9
Deferred Annuity Certain

Year	Yearly Payment	x	PVF	=	NSP
1	100.00		1.000		$100.00
2	100.00		0.962		$ 96.20
3	100.00		0.925		$ 92.50
4	100.00		0.889		$ 88.90
5	100.00		0.855		$ 85.50
6	100.00		0.822		$ 82.20
7	100.00		0.790		$ 79.00
8	100.00		0.760		$ 76.00
9	100.00		0.731		$ 73.10
10	100.00		0.703		$ 70.30
	Total net single premium				$843.70

Discount $843.70 for 5 years:
$843.70 × 0.822 = $693.52

annuity to an annuity due; second, that result is discounted for the number of years of deferral. Care must be taken, however, in making the adjustment. Adjustments such as those illustrated in Table 21.9 and Table 21.11 assume that if the insured dies within the accumulation period all monies will be returned to a beneficiary of the insured's estate with a nominal amount of interest added. If the opposite is true, the amounts are forfeited to the group, and the survivor rate must be calculated differently (see Table 21.12). The survivor rate is calculated by using the number of people who will receive the rent relative to the number of people starting the group at the beginning of the accumulation period, not at the time that the rent starts.

Assume Joe Wilcox has two children. Joe decides to start saving for retirement and purchases a temporary annuity deferred for 25 years. It would be in Joe's best interest to purchase the annuity contract with the refund feature. If Joe dies before

Table 21.10
Temporary Annuity

Age	Year	Yearly Probability of Survival	x	Payment	x	PVF	=	NSP
66	1	8,467,345 / 8,577,575		100.00		0.962		$ 94.92
67	2	8,347,117 / 8,577,575		100.00		0.925		$ 89.97
68	3	8,215,925 / 8,577,575		100.00		0.889		$ 85.15
69	4	8,072,853 / 8,577,575		100.00		0.855		$ 80.45
70	5	7,917,079 / 8,577,575		100.00		0.822		$ 75.86
71	6	7,747,883 / 8,577,575		100.00		0.790		$ 71.39
72	7	7,564,669 / 8,577,575		100.00		0.760		$ 67.02
73	8	7,366,997 / 8,577,575		100.00		0.731		$ 62.76
74	9	7,154,570 / 8,577,575		100.00		0.703		$ 58.60
75	10	6,927,098 / 8,577,575		100.00		0.676		$ 54.56
		Net single premium						$740.68

Table 21.11
10-Year Temporary Annuity, Age 65, Deferred 5 Years:
Refund during Accumulation

Age	Year	Yearly Probability of Survival	× Payment	× PVF	= NSP
65	1	8,577,575 / 8,577,575	100.00	1.000	$100.00
66	2	8,467,345 / 8,577,575	100.00	0.962	$ 94.96
67	3	8,347,117 / 8,577,575	100.00	0.925	$ 90.01
68	4	8,215,925 / 8,577,575	100.00	0.889	$ 85.15
69	5	8,072,853 / 8,577,575	100.00	0.855	$ 80.46
70	6	7,917,079 / 8,577,575	100.00	0.822	$ 75.87
71	7	7,747,883 / 8,577,575	100.00	0.790	$ 71.35
72	8	7,564,669 / 8,577,575	100.00	0.760	$ 67.02
73	9	7,366,997 / 8,577,575	100.00	0.731	$ 62.78
74	10	7,154,570 / 8,577,575	100.00	0.703	$ 58.64

	$786.24
Deferral factor	×0.822
Net single premium	$646.29

his children are on their own, the accumulated savings should go toward the children's support.

On the other hand, consider the case of Fred Wheeler, who is single and desires to save for retirement. Fred has no dependents and has no plans for marriage; he would tend to choose an annuity contract without a refund feature because the premium would be less expensive and the financial security of dependents is not a consideration.

Note the difference between Table 21.11 and Table 12.12. In Table 21.11 the number of individuals starting the group is equal to 8,577,575 at age 65. The 1983 Annuity Table predicts that 8,577,575 individuals will be alive at the beginning of age 65. On the other hand, in Table 21.12, because there is no refund of accumu-

Table 21.12
10-Year Temporary Annuity, Age 65, Deferred 5 Years:
No Refund during Accumulation

Age	Year	Yearly Probability of Survival	× Payment	× PVF	= NSP
65	1	8,577,575 / 9,013,785	100.00	1.000	$ 95.16
66	2	8,467,345 / 9,013,785	100.00	0.962	$ 90.37
67	3	8,347,117 / 9,013,785	100.00	0.925	$ 85.66
68	4	8,215,925 / 9,013,785	100.00	0.889	$ 81.03
69	5	8,072,853 / 9,013,785	100.00	0.855	$ 76.57
70	6	7,917,079 / 9,013,785	100.00	0.822	$ 72.20
71	7	7,747,883 / 9,013,785	100.00	0.790	$ 67.91
72	8	7,564,669 / 9,013,785	100.00	0.760	$ 63.78
73	9	7,366,997 / 9,013,785	100.00	0.731	$ 59.74
74	10	7,154,570 / 9,013,785	100.00	0.703	$ 55.80

	$748.22
Deferral factor	×0.822
Net single premium	$615.04

Table 21.13
Whole Life Immediate Annuity

Age	Year	Yearly Probability of Survival	× Payment	× PVF	= NSP
65	1	8,467,345 / 8,577,575	100.00	0.962	$ 94.92
66	2	8,347,117 / 8,577,575	100.00	0.925	$ 89.97
67	3	8,215,925 / 8,577,575	100.00	0.889	$ 85.15
.	.	.	.	.	.
.	.	.	.	.	.
.	.	.	.	.	.
113	49	6 / 8,577,575	100.00	0.146	$ 0.00
114	50	1 / 8,577,575	100.00	0.141	$ 0.00
115	51	0 / 8,577,575	100.00	0.135	$ 0.00
		Net single premium			$1,194.03

lated savings, the denominator is equal to the number of individuals starting the accumulation process at age 60.

Whole Life Annuities

The whole life annuity contract pays rent until the insured dies. To determine the net single premium for a whole life annuity, merely extend the number of calculations in the temporary annuity calculation by adding the remaining discounted survival benefits. For brevity, the first and the last three years of the whole life immediate annuity are shown in Table 21.13. The 1983 Annuity Table predicts that there will be no survivors in the 116th year; thus calculations cease in the 115th year.

The same methods used to modify the immediate temporary annuity to a deferred temporary annuity are used to convert the whole life annuity from immediate to deferred. First, recognize that the payments are made at the beginning of each period (annuity due) instead of the end of the period. Second, because of the shift in the timing of the payment the time-value-of-money factors must also change accordingly. Again, this modification assumes that during the accumulation period assets held by the insurance company are refunded upon the death of the insured with a nominal amount of interest added. If there is no refund during accumulation, as explained earlier, the survivor rate must be adjusted to reflect the number of individuals initially starting the accumulation process.

Guaranteed Payments

Many individuals will not buy an annuity contract where there is the distinct possibility of forfeiting large sums of money to the insurance company (benefit of survivorship) if death occurs early in the annuity distribution period. Because of this fact, life insurance companies offer annuity contracts with minimum guarantees included. For example, a whole life annuity contract could be written with the first ten payments guaranteed irrespective of life contingencies. In this case the net single premium is calculated by adjusting the probability of receiving the benefit ($100 in the preceding examples) to certainty (1). It should be clear by now that, if

Chapter 21 The Net Single Premium

Table 21.14
1980 Standard Ordinary Mortality Table and the 1983 Annuity Table

	Commissioners 1980 Standard Ordinary Mortality Table (1970–1975)				1983 Individual Annuity Table (1971–1976) Projected			
	Males		Females		Males		Females	
Age	Deaths per 1,000	Life Expect.	Deaths per 1,000	Life Expect.	Deaths per 1,000	Life Expect.	Deaths per 1,000	Life Expect.
0	4.18	70.83	2.89	75.83	—	—	—	—
1	1.07	70.13	0.87	75.04	—	—	—	—
2	0.99	69.20	0.81	74.11	—	—	—	—
3	0.98	68.27	0.79	73.17	—	—	—	—
4	0.95	67.34	0.77	72.23	—	—	—	—
5	0.90	66.40	0.76	71.28	0.38	74.10	0.19	79.36
6	0.86	65.46	0.73	70.34	0.35	73.12	0.16	78.37
7	0.80	64.52	0.72	69.39	0.33	72.15	0.13	77.39
8	0.76	63.57	0.70	68.44	0.35	71.17	0.13	76.40
9	0.74	62.62	0.69	67.48	0.37	70.20	0.14	75.41
10	0.73	61.66	0.68	66.53	0.38	69.22	0.14	74.42
11	0.77	60.71	0.69	65.58	0.39	68.25	0.15	73.43
12	0.85	59.75	0.72	64.62	0.41	67.28	0.16	72.44
13	0.99	58.80	0.75	63.67	0.42	66.30	0.17	71.45
14	1.15	57.86	0.80	62.71	0.43	65.33	0.18	70.46
15	1.33	56.93	0.85	61.76	0.44	64.36	0.19	69.47
16	1.51	56.00	0.90	60.82	0.45	63.39	0.20	68.49
17	1.67	55.09	0.95	59.87	0.46	62.42	0.21	67.50
18	1.78	54.18	0.98	58.93	0.47	61.44	0.23	66.51
19	1.86	53.27	1.02	57.98	0.49	60.47	0.24	65.53
20	1.90	52.37	1.05	57.04	0.51	59.50	0.26	64.55
21	1.91	51.47	1.07	56.10	0.53	58.53	0.28	63.56
22	1.89	50.57	1.09	55.16	0.55	57.56	0.29	62.58
23	1.86	49.66	1.11	54.22	0.57	56.59	0.31	61.60
24	1.82	48.75	1.14	53.28	0.60	55.63	0.33	60.62
25	1.77	47.84	1.16	52.34	0.62	54.66	0.35	59.64
26	1.73	46.93	1.19	51.40	0.65	53.69	0.37	58.66
27	1.71	46.01	1.22	50.46	0.68	52.73	0.39	57.68
28	1.70	45.09	1.26	49.52	0.70	51.76	0.41	56.70
29	1.71	44.16	1.30	48.59	0.73	50.80	0.42	55.72
30	1.73	43.24	1.35	47.65	0.76	49.83	0.44	54.75
31	1.78	42.31	1.40	46.71	0.79	48.87	0.46	53.77
32	1.83	41.38	1.45	45.78	0.81	47.91	0.48	52.80
33	1.91	40.46	1.50	44.84	0.84	46.95	0.50	51.82
34	2.00	39.54	1.58	43.91	0.88	45.99	0.52	50.85
35	2.11	38.61	1.65	42.98	0.92	45.03	0.55	49.87
36	2.24	37.69	1.76	42.05	0.97	44.07	0.57	48.90
37	2.40	36.78	1.89	41.12	1.03	43.11	0.61	47.93
38	2.58	35.87	2.04	40.20	1.11	42.15	0.65	46.96
39	2.79	34.96	2.22	39.28	1.22	41.20	0.69	45.99
40	3.02	34.05	2.42	38.36	1.34	40.25	0.74	45.02
41	3.29	33.16	2.64	37.46	1.49	39.30	0.80	44.05
42	3.56	32.26	2.87	36.55	1.67	38.36	0.87	43.09
43	3.87	31.38	3.09	35.66	1.89	37.43	0.94	42.12
44	4.19	30.50	3.32	34.77	2.13	36.50	1.03	41.16
45	4.55	29.62	3.56	33.88	2.40	35.57	1.12	40.20
46	4.92	28.76	3.80	33.00	2.69	34.66	1.23	39.25
47	5.32	27.90	4.05	32.12	3.01	33.75	1.36	38.30
48	5.74	27.04	4.33	31.25	3.34	32.85	1.50	37.35

Table 21.14 (continued)
1980 Standard Ordinary Mortality Table and the 1983 Annuity Table

| | Commissioners 1980 Standard Ordinary Mortality Table (1970–1975) |||| 1983 Individual Annuity Table (1971–1976) Projected ||||
| | Males || Females || Males || Females ||
Age	Deaths per 1,000	Life Expect.	Deaths per 1,000	Life Expect.	Deaths per 1,000	Life Expect.	Deaths per 1,000	Life Expect.
49	6.21	26.20	4.63	30.39	3.69	31.96	1.66	36.40
50	6.71	25.36	4.96	29.53	4.06	31.07	1.83	35.46
51	7.30	24.52	5.31	28.67	4.43	30.20	2.02	34.53
52	7.96	23.70	5.70	27.82	4.81	29.33	2.22	33.59
53	8.71	22.89	6.15	26.98	5.20	28.47	2.43	32.67
54	9.56	22.08	6.61	26.14	5.59	27.62	2.65	31.75
55	10.47	21.29	7.09	25.31	5.99	26.77	2.89	30.83
56	11.46	20.51	7.57	24.49	6.41	25.93	3.15	29.92
57	12.49	19.74	8.03	23.67	6.84	25.09	3.43	29.01
58	13.59	18.99	8.47	22.86	7.29	24.26	3.74	28.11
59	14.77	18.24	8.94	22.05	7.78	23.44	4.08	27.21
60	16.08	17.51	9.47	21.25	8.34	22.62	4.47	26.32
61	17.54	16.79	10.13	20.44	8.98	21.80	4.91	25.44
62	19.19	16.08	10.96	19.65	9.74	20.99	5.41	24.56
63	21.06	15.38	12.02	18.86	10.63	20.20	5.99	23.69
64	23.14	14.70	13.25	18.08	11.66	19.41	6.63	22.83
65	25.42	14.04	14.59	17.32	12.85	18.63	7.34	21.98
66	27.85	13.39	16.00	16.57	14.20	17.87	8.09	21.14
67	30.44	12.76	17.43	15.83	15.72	17.12	8.89	20.31
68	33.19	12.14	18.84	15.10	17.41	16.38	9.73	19.49
69	36.17	11.54	20.36	14.38	19.30	15.66	10.65	18.67
70	39.51	10.96	22.11	13.67	21.37	14.96	11.70	17.87
71	43.30	10.39	24.23	12.97	23.65	14.28	12.91	17.07
72	47.65	9.84	26.87	12.28	26.13	13.61	14.32	16.29
73	52.64	9.30	30.11	11.60	28.84	12.96	15.98	15.52
74	58.19	8.79	33.93	10.95	31.79	12.33	17.91	14.76
75	64.19	8.31	38.24	10.32	35.05	11.72	20.13	14.02
76	70.53	7.84	42.97	9.71	38.63	11.13	22.65	13.30
77	77.12	7.40	48.04	9.12	42.59	10.56	25.51	12.60
78	83.90	6.97	53.45	8.55	46.95	10.00	28.72	11.91
79	91.05	6.57	59.35	8.01	51.76	9.47	32.33	11.25
80	98.84	6.18	65.99	7.48	57.03	8.96	36.40	10.61
81	107.48	5.80	73.60	6.98	62.79	8.47	40.98	9.99
82	117.25	5.44	82.40	6.49	69.08	8.01	46.12	9.40
83	128.26	5.09	92.53	6.03	75.91	7.57	51.89	8.83
84	140.25	4.77	103.81	5.59	83.23	7.15	58.34	8.28
85	152.95	4.46	116.10	5.18	90.99	6.75	65.52	7.77
86	166.09	4.18	129.29	4.80	99.12	6.37	73.49	7.28
87	179.55	3.91	143.32	4.43	107.58	6.02	82.32	6.81
88	193.27	3.66	158.18	4.09	116.32	5.69	92.02	6.38
89	207.29	3.41	173.94	3.77	125.39	5.37	102.49	5.98
90	221.77	3.18	190.75	3.45	134.89	5.07	113.61	5.60
91	236.98	2.94	208.87	3.15	144.87	4.78	125.23	5.26
92	253.45	2.70	228.81	2.85	155.43	4.50	137.22	4.94
93	272.11	2.44	251.51	2.55	166.63	4.24	149.46	4.64
94	295.90	2.17	279.31	2.24	178.54	3.99	161.83	4.37
95	329.96	1.87	317.32	1.91	191.21	3.75	174.23	4.12
96	384.55	1.54	375.74	1.56	204.72	3.51	186.54	3.88
97	480.20	1.20	474.97	1.21	219.12	3.29	198.65	3.65

Table 21.14 (continued)
1980 Standard Ordinary Mortality Table and the 1983 Annuity Table

| | Commissioners 1980 Standard Ordinary Mortality Table (1970–1975) |||| 1983 Individual Annuity Table (1971–1976) Projected ||||
| | Males || Females || Males || Females ||
Age	Deaths per 1,000	Life Expect.	Deaths per 1,000	Life Expect.	Deaths per 1,000	Life Expect.	Deaths per 1,000	Life Expect.
98	657.98	0.84	655.85	0.84	234.74	3.07	211.10	3.44
99	1000.00	0.50	1000.00	0.50	251.89	2.86	224.45	3.22
100					270.91	2.66	239.22	3.01
101					292.11	2.46	255.95	2.80
102					315.83	2.26	275.20	2.59
103					342.38	2.08	297.50	2.38
104					372.09	1.90	323.39	2.18
105					405.28	1.73	353.41	1.98
106					442.28	1.57	388.11	1.79
107					483.41	1.41	428.02	1.60
108					528.99	1.27	473.69	1.43
109					579.35	1.13	525.66	1.26
110					634.81	1.01	584.46	1.11
111					695.70	0.89	650.65	0.97
112					762.34	0.78	724.75	0.83
113					835.06	0.70	807.32	0.71
114					914.17	0.67	898.89	0.60
115					1000.00	0.50	1000.00	0.50

the first ten payments are guaranteed, the net single premium must rise, all other factors being the same, because the rent must be paid whether or not the insured is alive.

Refund Features

The same rationale that applies to a refund feature applies to various forms of guaranteed payment features of annuity contracts. Some insureds avoid annuity contracts where the possibility exists of not receiving at least the premium amount in rent payments over the life of the contract. Therefore some annuity contracts contain a refund feature that returns the difference between the premium paid and the sum of the rents received either in a lump sum or on an installment basis. These contracts are called **installment** or **cash refund annuity contracts**. The refund feature added to the annuity contract generally increases the net single premium (When comparing an installment or cash refund annuity contract to an annuity contract with a long period of guaranteed payments, one may find the installment or cash refund annuity less expensive for the same amount of periodic rent payment.) The insured always receives at least the amount paid for the insurance contract, so the insurance company's source of revenue must be the excess interest generated by investing the funds.

Review Questions

1. What factors enter into the calculation of the life insurance premium?
2. Why is the time value of money so important in pricing the life insurance contract?
3. What is the difference between an annuity table and a mortality table? Why do annuity tables project probabilities to an older age than mortality tables?
4. List the assumptions used in the text for calculating the net single premium (NSP). Why are these assumptions needed?
5. Set up the formula and calculate the net single premium for a one-year term policy (age 40, $1,000 face amount, 5 percent interest, 1980 CSO Mortality Table).
6. Extend the formula and calculation in question 5 to a five-year term policy.
7. Set up the net single premium calculation of a whole life policy. Use the assumptions in question 5 and show only the first five and last five years of the required calculation.
8. Refer to question 6. Show the modifications to the formula required in order to calculate the net single premium for an endowment policy. Calculate the net single premium for a five-year endowment policy.
9. Calculate the net single premium for an annuity certain (no life contingencies considered; $100 per year for five years at 8 percent). Calculate the net single premium of an annuity certain, deferred five years.
10. Refer to question 9. Calculate the net single premium of a five-year temporary life annuity for a male age 70 (use the 1983 Annuity Table).
11. How does the calculation of the annuity NSP change when a refund during accumulation is considered as opposed to no refund during accumulation?
12. Set up the calculation of the NSP for a whole life immediate annuity. (Show the first five and last five years of the calculation for a male aged 60 at 8 percent interest.)

Bibliography

Batten, Robert W. *Mortality Table Construction*. Englewood Cliffs, N.J.: Prentice-Hall, 1978.

Benjamin, B., and H. W. Haycocks. *The Analysis of Mortality and Other Actuarial Statistics*. London: The Syndics of the Cambridge University Press, 1970.

Harper, Floyd S., and Lewis C. Workman. *Fundamental Mathematics of Life Insurance*. Homewood, Ill.: Richard D. Irwin, 1970.

Huebner, S. S., and Kenneth Black, Jr. *Life Insurance*, 11th ed. Englewood Cliffs, N.J.: Prentice-Hall, 1987.

Jordan, C. W. *Life Contingencies*, 2d ed. Chicago: Society of Actuaries, 1967.

Pedoe, Arthur, and Colin E. Jack. *Life Insurance, Annuities and Pensions*, 3d ed. Toronto: University of Toronto Press, 1978.

Chapter 22 | Leveling the Net Single Premium

Chapter Objectives

- Review the assumptions used in calculating the net single premium
- Describe what is meant by the present value of future benefits
- Explain the mathematics involved in leveling the net single premium for life insurance
- Explain the mathematics involved in leveling the net single premium for annuity contracts

Introduction

Most consumers purchase life insurance in installments rather than paying one premium at the inception of the contract. A male aged 30 would have to pay a lump sum of $20,918 to purchase $100,000 of whole life insurance. This amount is the net single premium, assuming the 1980 CSO Table and a 4 percent interest rate, as calculated according to procedures in Chapter 21. Gross premiums would include loading for expenses, taxes and additions to surplus, all actually paid to the life insurance company. Using the 1958 CSO and 4 percent, the amount would be approximately $26,500. This large premium would make the purchase of any practical amount of life insurance impossible for most people. Instead of paying one large amount or purchasing term insurance annually, of course, people may purchase life insurance by paying equal periodic installments—the level premium. This chapter describes the process for leveling the net single premium. Using this method, the policy owner "overpays" the mortality expense in the early years of the contract and "underpays" the mortality expense in the later years. This chapter describes the logic underlying the development of the level-payment plans and the mathematics to calculate that amount.

An Overview of the Level Premium

As stated, most people cannot afford the purchase of large amounts of life insurance on a single-premium basis. One alternative is to purchase a series of one-year renewable term insurance contracts. With this alternative, as premiums increase, the insured will begin to question the need for owning the life insurance contract, especially if he or she expects to continue in good health. And clearly the insured will feel a need to renew the contract if he or she perceives a possibility of premature death. This self-selection process produces adverse selection. Less healthy people will tend to remain in the insurance pool while the healthy will tend to select themselves out. As a result of self-selection, the mortality rate of the remaining insured group will be higher than originally expected, and the premiums will be inadequate to pay death claims as they become due. One solution to this problem is to adjust the mortality table to reflect this antiselection process. Simply adjusting the mortality table is not an adequate solution to the problem of adverse selection, however, because affordable insurance coverage will still not be available at older ages, and self-selection will continue.

The insurance industry, seeking a solution to the dual problems of affordability at older ages and adverse selection, devised a method to level the premiums to make the ownership of life insurance practical in the later years. (The process *is* actually self-selection. The difference between self-selection and adverse selection is that in adverse selection people are seeking coverage when losses are likely; self-selection occurs when people remove themselves from or stay in a group that is already insured.) The *level premium* may be thought of as an annuity paid to the life insurance company to purchase a life insurance contract that will pay a claim whenever death occurs. (The annuity is also contingent upon surviving and the desire to continue the life insurance contract.) Once the net single premium is calculated for the desired contract (see Chapter 21), a periodic payment can be calculated so the net level premium exceeds the mortality cost in the early years of the contract; in the later years the mortality cost will exceed the net level premium (see Figure 22.1). The overpayments (with respect to the mortality cost) in the early years, plus interest added, pay for the underpayments in the later years of the contract. (The survivor benefit also provides funds to pay the benefits promised by the contract. The survivor benefit will be discussed later.)

At the beginning of each policy year, level premium payments plus balances remaining from the prior year are invested at a positive rate of interest. And if the mortality rate and the investment rate have been calculated correctly, the insurance company will have sufficient funds available to pay all death claims at the end of the year. The insurance company will also have the overpayments plus accrued interest called *reserves*. The accrued overpayments plus future premiums collected plus interest will be sufficient to pay all claims. The leveling process produces *reserves*, and in the discussion to follow, the link between the premium leveling process and the reserves generated by life insurance contracts will be explained.

Net Single Premium Assumptions Revisited

In Chapter 21 several assumptions were made to develop the mathematics of the NSP calculation and reduce its difficulty. All of these assumptions are violated in

Figure 22.1
The Leveling Process

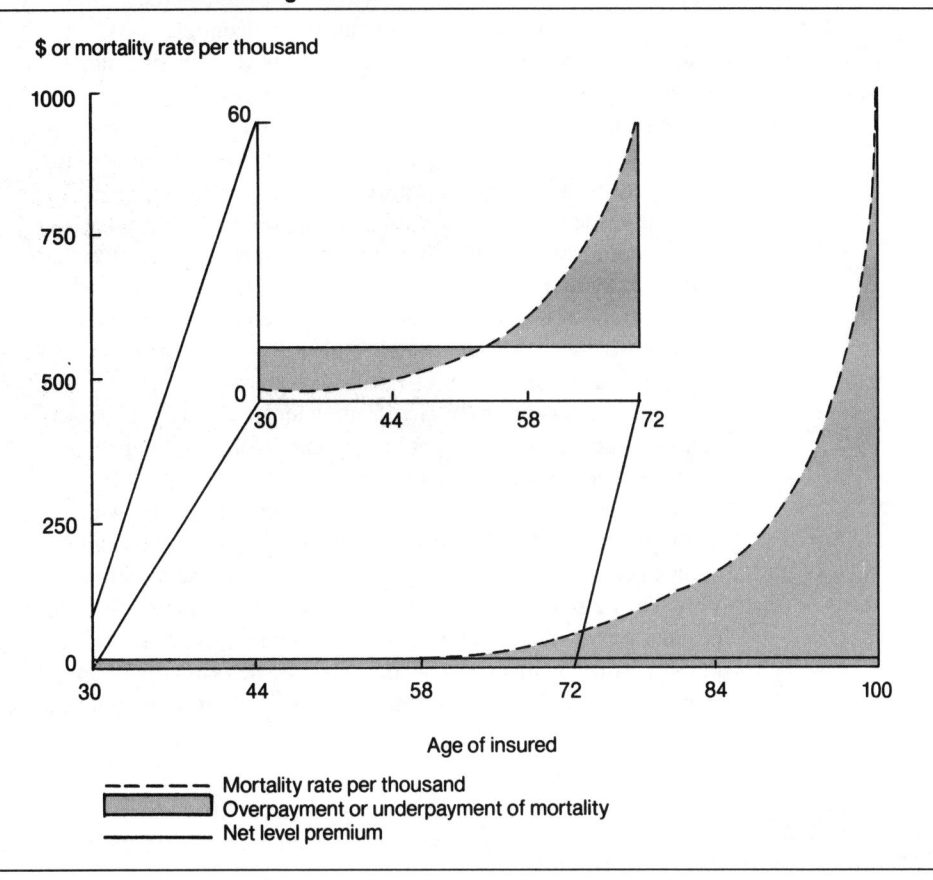

$ or mortality rate per thousand

- - - - - Mortality rate per thousand
▨ Overpayment or underpayment of mortality
─── Net level premium

Age of insured

practice. Several of the assumptions will be relaxed in this chapter, so this section reviews them to clarify their influence on the level premium.

The first assumption made for the NSP calculation is that the net single premium is paid in full at the beginning of the contract term. The net single premium is the present value of the future benefits to be provided by the contract or the actuarial present value. The financial promises made by the life insurance contract are discounted for the time value of money and the probability of a death claim occurring. When the premium payment equals the net single premium, the insured need never pay another premium, and the life insurance company will have sufficient funds to fulfill the actuarial obligations promised by the policy.

The second assumption used to simplify the NSP calculations is that all death proceeds are paid at the end of each policy year and all premiums are collected at the beginning. If the insured buys the contract at the beginning of the year and dies during the year, the life insurance company has time to earn investment income for the entire year until the claim is paid at the end of the year.

The third assumption used to simplify the NSP calculation is that the actual mortality rate experienced is equal to the rate predicted by the table selected. (The 1980 CSO Table is used for the life insurance examples in this chapter.) This third assumption is required so no risk exists in predicting the financial outcome due to mortality considerations.

The final assumption is that amounts paid to the life insurance company are used to pay only for mortality costs; no additional amounts are included for operating expenses, additions to surplus or taxes.

With respect to an interest rate assumption, readers must recognize that investments made by life insurance companies are conservative because all future claims under all insurance policies must be paid. Therefore relatively long-term, low-risk (and consequently relatively low-return) investments are sought. Financial disaster would occur if the life insurance company discounted the financial promise(s) at a high interest rate and subsequently could not earn the projected rate unless there happened to be an offsetting underwriting gain. In addition to the possibility of not achieving target investment income, a company may lose principal amounts when risky investments are made.

In practice, life insurance companies do not operate within these restrictive assumptions relating to their financial and operating environment. Life insurance companies pay claims and receive premium payments throughout the calendar year. They also do not adhere exclusively to the 1980 CSO Mortality Table. Various mortality tables are used in calculating rates, and there are wide fluctuations in rates of return on investments. However, these assumptions are still made to simplify matters so that reasonably accurate and conservative calculations can be made.

The Present Value of Future Benefits

The net single premium for a whole life insurance contract is calculated by summing the present value of future benefits to be provided by the contract (*see* Chapter 21). For a hypothetical male aged 30 to purchase a $1,000 whole life contract, the net single premium was calculated at $209.18, assuming a 4 percent interest rate. If a net single premium of $209.18 is paid at the beginning of the contract period, $8.37 (209.18 × .04) is added to the net single premium due to the investment income during the year; $1.73 ([16,573/9,579,998] × [$1,000]) is subtracted from that sum due to the insured's contribution to mortality costs. Figure 22.2 shows that, when this calculation is continued for a hypothetical insured who survives through age 99, the cash amount accumulated increases over time. Amounts under the curve are commonly referred to as the *cash value, nonforfeiture value,* or *reserve amount.*

Note that the line drawn from $209.18 at age 30 to $1,000 at age 100 is called the *present value of future benefits* line. An individual who wishes to purchase a life insurance policy will purchase the contract for an amount equal to the present value of the future benefits for the given age of the individual, otherwise known as

Figure 22.2
Present Value of Future Benefits

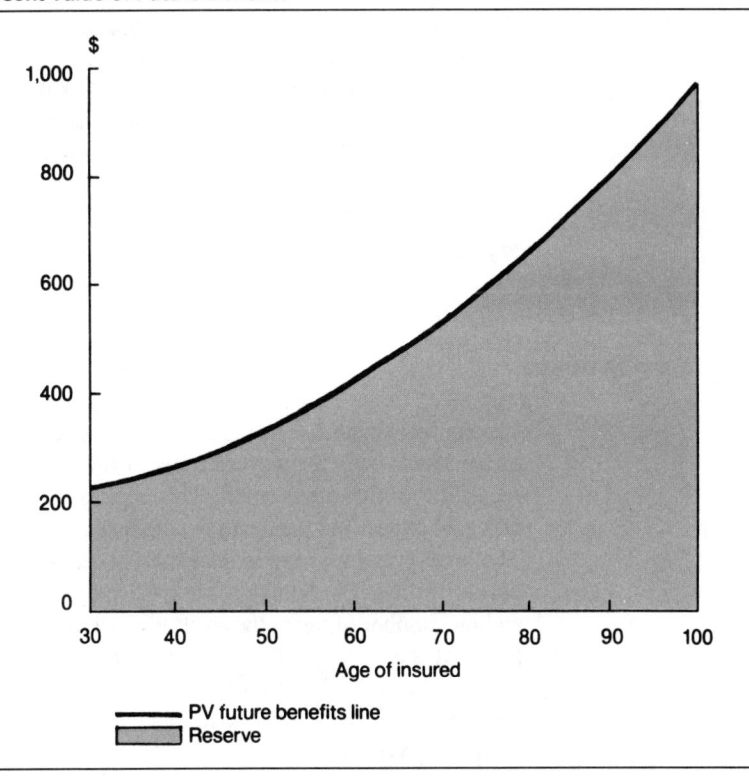

—— PV future benefits line
▨ Reserve

the net single premium. The net single premium amount ($209.18) was calculated for the male aged 30. For males aged 35 and 40 a net single premium of $246.82 and $290.81 respectively would have to be paid. At age 99 the present value of future benefits would simply be $1,000 discounted for the time value of money, because death is assumed to be a certainty during the year ($1,000 × [10,757/10,757] × $1/1.04^1$ = $961.54).

Note that, if the life insurance company accepts premium payments over the life of the insurance contract, several of the preceding assumptions are violated. The first violation is that the entire net single premium will not be received at the beginning of the contract term. In lieu of the NSP the life insurance company accepts a series of payments. Therefore the insurer will not generate interest earnings on the whole NSP from the inception of the contract. Second, because most insureds will not survive the premium-paying period, the life insurance company must forgo collecting any additional premiums from these individuals, reducing the funds flowing to the insurer. Thus the level-premium plan produces two sources of "loss" relative to the NSP: (1) loss resulting from the premature termination of premium installments and (2) loss arising from lower investment income. (A third loss of funds arises from lapses—policy owners not continuing the contract. When a lapse occurs, however, the contractual obligation is modified or terminated.)

Because of "missing" premiums and interest, the life insurance company cannot divide the net single premium by the number of premium payments desired. The problems associated with these "missing" amounts are solved by the leveling process. In addition, two other problems are solved. First, if insureds pay a relatively small periodic premium for each $1,000 of life insurance, they will be able to afford larger face amounts. Second, the problem of adverse selection at advanced ages is minimized because the premium stays constant over the life of the payment term, creating no inducement for the healthy individuals to leave the pool. (Actually the problem remains, but not to the extreme extent encouraged by paying ever-increasing premiums.)

The Leveling Process

The **net level premium** is the amount of money paid to the life insurance company on a periodic basis to purchase a life insurance contract that will pay a death claim regardless of the age at death. This applies to the whole life contract. Term policies are leveled, but the death benefit is available only during the contract's term. The level premium may be payable for the term of the contract or for a shorter period of time. The number of periodic payments depends on the contract chosen and the number of years the insured desires to pay premiums. (The frequency of payment is assumed to be once per year, although the premium for life insurance policies can be paid on a more frequent basis.) It is interesting to note that, everything being equal, the life insurance company should be indifferent toward the premium payment plan selected.

An Analogy

To develop the mathematics for leveling the net single premium, the mortgage calculation similar to the one in Chapter 13 will be used. Suppose Mr. Worth is contemplating the purchase of a $40,000 house. Mr. Worth wants to know the annual payment amount for a 4 percent, 20-year amortization schedule. To solve this problem, time-value-of-money techniques are used. The present value of the stream of payments to the bank is equal to $40,000 at 4 percent. Below is the formula used to calculate the annual payment.

$$PV = PMT \times PVAF \text{ at 4 percent for 20 years}$$

where:

$$PV = \text{present value}$$
$$PMT = \text{yearly payment amount}$$
$$PVAF = \text{present value annuity factor of \$1}$$
$$\$40,000 = PMT \times 13.590$$
$$PMT = \frac{\$40,000}{13.590} = \$2,943.34$$

The bank is indifferent as to whether it receives the principal now (not lending the money) or later through annual installments. (Most mortgages are, however, paid on a monthly basis. In this example the rate would be .04/12 and for 240 [12 × 20] periods.) This is the case because the borrower's installment payments compensate the bank for the interest that could have been earned on an alternative investment. In a similar fashion a life insurance contract can be purchased on an installment basis, except that two modifications must be made to the payment determination.

Modification 1

In the mortgage example, payments are assumed to be made at the end of each year, and a present-value-of-an-annuity factor was used. On the other hand, premiums paid to a life insurance company are made at the beginning of each year, requiring a different mathematical adjustment for the time value of money. Instead of using the present-value-of-an-annuity factor, an annuity due factor must be substituted.

$$PV = PMT \times PVAF_d \text{ at } 4\% \text{ for } 20 \text{ years}$$
$$PVAF_d = \text{present-value-annuity-due factor of } \$1$$

The $PVAF_d$ factor is calculated by summing 20 present value factors (Table 22.1). The first factor is equal to one because payments are made at the beginning of the year instead of at the end of the year, as in the ordinary annuity. Note that the individual factors in Table 22.1 may be calculated by using an appropriate formula in the appendix to this book or time-value-of-money tables may be used. If a present-value-of-an-ordinary-annuity table is used, the sum of the individual factors must be shifted one year. The present-value-of-an-annuity-due factor can also be calculated by adding one to the present value of an annuity factor for 19 years.

☐ Example

To get the present value of an annuity due for 25 years at 5%, add 1 to the present-value-of-an-annuity table factor for 24 years at 5% (13.799 + 1 = 14.799). The present value of an ordinary annuity may alternatively be multiplied by [1 + i]. The present-value-of-an-annuity factor for 25 years at 5% equals 14.094, and 14.094 × 1.05 = 14.799. The present-value-of-an-annuity-due factor for 25 years at 5% is 14.799.

To change the timing of the payments (in the preceding mortgage example) from the beginning of the year to the end of the year, determine the payment by substituting the annuity due factor for the annuity factor.

$$\$40,000 = PMT \times 14.137$$
$$PMT = \frac{\$40,000}{14.137} = \$2,829.45$$

The yearly payment is reduced to $2,829.45 from $2,943.34. The payment declined because (1) the borrower does not have use of all the money the first year

**Table 22.1
Present Value of an Annuity Due
Calculation at 4 Percent: 20 Years**

Year	Factor	Year	Factor
1	1.000	11	0.676
2	0.962	12	0.650
3	0.925	13	0.625
4	0.889	14	0.601
5	0.855	15	0.577
6	0.822	16	0.555
7	0.790	17	0.534
8	0.760	18	0.513
9	0.731	19	0.494
10	0.703	20	0.475
	Present value of an annuity due		14.137

because the first payment is made right away and (2) in subsequent years, payments are made at the beginning of each year instead of the end of each year. This calculation is similar to the leveling calculation of the life insurance contract, except there is one additional modification.

Modification 2

If the insured dies during the premium-paying period, subsequent payments will cease. When this happens, the assumption of collecting the NSP at the beginning of the contract period obviously is violated. Thus an additional adjustment must be made for missing premiums. The first and second adjustments are made by substituting a *life annuity due* factor for the annuity due factor. The nature of this second adjustment is explained in the following section.

Leveling the Term Insurance Contract

Switching to the life insurance transaction, Mr. Worth decides to purchase a five-year term insurance contract. The net single premium for the five-year term insurance contract is equal to $8.183 (*see* Chapter 21). Instead of paying $8.183 for the contract, Mr. Worth wants to pay in equal annual installments and only if he is alive. Dividing the net single premium by five does not provide the correct level premium. If the net single premium is divided by an ordinary annuity factor, the timing of the payments (beginning versus the end of the period) is not correct, and it does not account for missing premiums. An appropriate adjustment is made for the timing of the payments and the missing premiums and interest when a *temporary life annuity due factor* (Table 22.2) is substituted for the annuity due factor.

$$PV = PMT \times PVTLAD \text{ at } 4\% \text{ for 5 years, age 30}$$
$$NSP = NLP \times PVTLAD$$
$$NLP = NSP / PVTLAD$$

Table 22.2
Temporary Life Annuity Due Calculation
(Male, age 30, 5 payments, 1980 CSO, 4 percent)

Year	Interest Factor	×	Probability of Survival	=	PVTLAD Factor
1	1.000		9,579,998/9,579,998		1.000
2	0.962		9,563,425/9,579,998		0.960
3	0.925		9,546,402/9,579,998		0.922
4	0.889		9,528,932/9,579,998		0.884
5	0.855		9,510,732/9,579,998		0.849
			Temporary life annuity due		4.615

where:

PV = present value amount (*NSP*)
PMT = yearly payment or net level premium (*NLP*)
$PVTLAD$ = present value of a temporary life annuity due
$\$8.183 = PMT \times 4.615$
$PMT = \$8.183/4.615 = 1.774$

The net level premium for the five-year term policy is equal to 1.774 ($8.183/4.615), which Mr. Worth will pay for each $1,000 of life insurance at the beginning of each contract year if he is alive to do so.

The calculation in Table 22.2 is mathematically similar to the mortgage problem but is adjusted for the problems associated with violating several of the original restrictive assumptions.

Before it is shown that the calculation produces the correct net level premium, the nature of the temporary life annuity due (TLAD) calculated in Table 22.2 needs to be discussed. A life annuity due (LAD) factor is calculated by taking the sum of an interest discount factor for $1 times a survivor factor for the five years. In the example, the number 4.615 is called a *temporary life annuity due factor*. It is called *temporary* because the number is not calculated for the whole life of the individual, and the word *life* is used because the sum takes into account the probability that the individual will survive to pay the premium. Therefore this factor adjusts for the lack of premium payments and interest thereon when the insured dies.

A *whole* life annuity due factor must be calculated for leveling the net single premiums on whole life insurance contracts that are paid each and every year (through age 99). When life insurance premiums are not paid when due, the contract lapses. The process of leveling the premium must also account for these lapsed contracts people who survive but do not pay. Adjusting the life insurance premium for the lapse of insurance contracts is discussed in Chapter 23.

Following is proof that $1.774 is the correct leveled premium. If 1,000 insureds, all aged 30, each purchase a five-year term insurance contract, the following financial results occur:

Year 1:
 1,000 Insureds pay 1.774 (rounded)   1,773.50
 Interest at 4%   70.94
 Death claims
  16,573/9,579,998
  × 1,000 × $1,000   1,729.96
 Ending balance   114.48
  Reserve per surviving policy   0.11

Year 2:
 998.270 Insureds pay 1.774   1,770.43
  Beginning balance   114.48
  Interest at 4%   75.40
  Death claims
   17,023/9,579,998
   × 1,000 × $1,000   1,776.93
  Ending balance   183.38
   Reserve per surviving policy   0.18

Year 3:
 996.493 Insureds pay 1.774   1,767.28
  Beginning balance   183.38
  Interest at 4%   78.03
  Death claims
   17,470/9,579,998
   × 1,000 × $1,000   1,823.59
  Ending balance   205.09
   Reserve per surviving policy   0.21

Year 4:
 994.670 Insureds pay 1.774   1,764.05
  Beginning balance   205.09
  Interest at 4%   78.77
  Death claims
   18,200/9,579,998
   × 1,000 × $1,000   1,899.79
  Ending balance   148.11
   Reserve per surviving policy   0.15

Year 5:
 992.770 Insureds pay 1.774   1,760.68
  Beginning balance   148.11
  Interest at 4%   76.35
  Death claims
   19,021/9,579,998
   × 1,000 × $1,000   1,985.49
  Ending balance   (0.35)
   Reserve per surviving policy   (0.00)

At the beginning of each year the surviving insureds pay the required premium of $1.774 for $1,000 of life insurance. During each year the remaining balances plus the new premium payments earn 4 percent interest. At the end of each year the expected number of death claims are paid. Dividing the ending balance each year by the number of survivors results in the reserve per policy. If 1,000 insureds purchase the five-year term contract, $1,773.50 will be collected in net premiums in the first year. This amount is invested at 4 percent, and investment income of $70.94 will be added to the premium amount.

At the end of the year 1.729 (16,573/9,579,998) insureds are expected to die out of each 1,000 insureds. Because the pool starts with 1,000 insureds, 1.729 death claims are expected to be paid. The amount paid as death claims ($1,729.96) reduces the sum of the net premium plus investment income to $114.48. If the ending balance is divided by the number of insureds surviving (998.270), an amount equal to the reserve per surviving policy results. This reserve amount can be thought of as the overpayment plus interest added in the first year to compensate partially for the underpayment in the later years. The calculations for the five years demonstrate that the leveling process is at work. In the early policy years the insureds are overpaying the predicted mortality rate so that underpayments may be made in the later years. After the end of the fifth year all contractual promises have been met by the life insurance company, and all sums have been liquidated.

Leveling the Whole Life Insurance Contract

Determining the level premium for the whole life insurance contract is similar to leveling the premium for the term policy. In reviewing the procedure for calculating the level premium for the one-year and the five-year term contract, notice that the TLAD is calculated for the maximum length of time the premiums are to be paid. Notice that the one-year term net single premium is already leveled because the TLAD is always equal to 1.00. Also note that the possibility of purchasing the one-year term contract and not paying the premium does not exist. In the five-year term policy the TLAD was calculated for the full five years. Logic dictates that in leveling the whole life premium the LAD calculation must be performed for each year a premium payment potentially can be made. For the hypothetical male aged 30, 70 yearly payments are possible. The first payment is made at the beginning of the year the insured is age 30 and the last at the beginning of the year the insured is age 99. Age 99 is the last year for a premium payment because the 1980 CSO Table predicts that all insureds who reach age 99 will die before age 100. Thus the probability of surviving and paying a premium for the next year (age 100) is zero. The LAD calculation for the hypothetical 30-year-old male is calculated for 70 years. Table 22.3 shows the LAD calculation for the first five and the last five years. The first five lines in Table 22.3 are the same as the first five lines in Table 22.2.

The sum of the 70 calculations starting at age 30 and ending at age 99 provides the LAD figure needed for leveling the whole life contract for a 30-year-old male. The last line of the table may be thought of as the present value of the contingent

Table 22.3
Life Annuity Due Calculation
(Male, age 30, 70 payments, 1980 CSO, 4 percent)

Age	Year	Interest Factor	×	Probability of Survival	=	LAD Factor
30	1	1.000		9,579,998/9,579,998		1.000
31	2	0.962		9,563,425/9,579,998		0.960
32	3	0.925		9,546,402/9,579,998		0.922
33	4	0.889		9,528,932/9,579,998		0.884
34	5	0.855		9,510,732/9,579,998		0.849
.	.	.		.		.
.	.	.		.		.
.	.	.		.		.
95	66	0.078		146,721/9,579,998		0.001
96	67	0.075		98,309/9,579,998		0.001
97	68	0.072		60,504/9,579,998		0.000
98	69	0.069		31,450/9,579,998		0.000
99	70	0.067		10,757/9,579,998		0.000
				Life annuity due		20.563

promise to pay $1 in 70 years if the insured is still alive. Dividing the NSP ($209.185) by the life annuity due (LAD) factor results in the leveled premium.

$$NLP = NSP/LAD$$
$$NLP = \frac{\$209.185}{20.563} = \$10.172$$

Leveling the NSP for ages other than 30 requires calculating a new net single premium for the selected age and an LAD figure commensurate with the age of issue. When the net single premium was calculated in Chapter 21, the iterative calculations were made for the number of years a benefit could possibly be paid. In this chapter the LAD calculation is made for the number of payments (years) scheduled. Thus the number of years used for the iterative calculation is the duration of time that a benefit payment or a premium payment could possibly be made for the type of contract specified.

Leveling the Premium for an Endowment Policy

The logic presented in the preceding section is also used to determine the level premium for the endowment policy. The net single premium for the five-year endowment policy for a 30-year-old male is equal to $822.53. This net single premium is composed of $8.183 to pay for death benefits and $814.35 to pay a survivor benefit. (*See* Chapter 21, where the net single premium was calculated for the endowment contract.) The survivorship promise occurs at the end of the fifth year. If five installments are needed for this endowment contract, the number of years of potential benefits and the number of potential premium payments are equal.

The five-year TLAD (4.615) that is used to level the five-year term contract is the same TLAD required to level the five-year endowment contract. The net single premium for the endowment contract is divided by the temporary life annuity due (4.615), and the result is the net level premium ($178.23) required for the five-year endowment contract.

$$NLP = NSP/TLAD$$
$$NLP = \frac{\$822.536}{4.615} = \$178.23$$

The net single premium for a 10-year endowment (30-year-old male) is equal to $678.14 (calculations are not shown). The TLAD for 10 years is equal to 8.368, and the level premium is $81.04. For comparison and instructional purposes, investigate why the 10-year endowment's net single premium and level premium are less than the 5-year endowment's net and level premiums. (Using the 1980 CSO and 4 percent, the NSP, TLAD and NLP are $822.53, 4.61407 and $178.2269 respectively for the five-year endowment policy issued to a male aged 30.)

Limited-Payment Plans

Limited-payment plans are generally associated with the whole life insurance product. These payment plans allow the insured to pay the life insurance company an amount equivalent to the net single premium in a shorter length of time than scheduled in ordinary life insurance. Purchasing a whole life insurance contract with a single premium is the most extreme case of a limited-payment plan. The single-pay life insurance contract pays a benefit when the insured event occurs, the promise extends over many years and the total premium is paid to the life insurance company with a single payment when the policy begins.

Individuals might require life insurance coverage but anticipate neither being able to nor wanting to pay a premium over the whole contract term. One example is an individual planning to retire at age 65. Because wage income is expected to cease upon retirement, the retiree may not want to continue premium payments. Such an insured might choose a limited-payment plan that allows for terminating insurance premiums at age 65. Upon death at any age, benefits still will be paid. Many such premium payment plans are available. Individuals may want to pay up their life insurance contract in one payment (single-pay), in five payments (five-pay), in ten payments (ten-pay) or in any practical length of time. A straight whole life insurance contract would not be included in this limited-pay category, because payments are made for all of one's life.

Mathematically, determining the periodic premium under a limited-payment plan is no different from leveling the net single premium over the entire potential life of the contract. The net single premium for the policy is the same regardless of the premium payment plan. The periodic payment must be calculated so that the life insurance company is indifferent to receiving the premium in one lump sum at the inception of the contract or to receiving a level periodic amount over the premium payment term. The main difference between leveling for the entire contract term and for a limited length of time is that in the limited-payment leveling calculation fewer periodic payments are used to determine the TLAD than the number of years benefits could possibly be paid.

Suppose a male aged 30 needs to purchase a whole life insurance contract that is paid up in 10 years instead of paying for the contract for all of his life. The net single premium for the whole life insurance contract, already calculated, is $209.185. To calculate the net level premium for paying the net single premium over 10 years, an appropriate temporary life annuity due must be determined. The new TLAD amount is calculated in Table 22.4.

Dividing the net single premium by the temporary life annuity due factor provides the level premium for the payment plan selected.

$$NLP = NSP/TLAD$$
$$NLP = \frac{\$209.185}{8.370} = \$24.99$$

The 30-year-old male will pay a net level premium equal to $24.99 for each $1,000 of whole life insurance. When 10 annual payments are made, the policy is said to be paid up, and the insured need not pay another premium. Of course, if the insured dies within the ten-year premium payment period, benefits will be paid, and further premiums will not be collected.

If the insured wants to pay up this whole life insurance contract in five years instead of ten, the annual installment should increase, because the new five-year TLAD is less than the ten-year TLAD. Dividing the same NSP by a smaller TLAD results in a larger net premium. The TLAD required is the same one calculated in Table 22.2. Notice that the TLAD (4.615) is equal to the sum of the first five lines in Table 22.4.

$$NLP = NSP/TLAD$$
$$NLP = \frac{\$209.185}{4.615} = \$45.33$$

The simplicity of this calculation allows other premium payment plans to be derived by adjusting the TLAD figure according to the number of desired payments.

Leveling Annuity Contracts

The process of determining a periodic payment to purchase an annuity contract is not the same one used to calculate the level premium for life insurance products.

Chapter 22 Leveling the Net Single Premium

Table 22.4
Temporary Life Annuity Due Calculation
(Male, age 30, 10 payments, 1980 CSO, 4 percent)

Year	Interest Factor	×	Probability of Survival	=	PVTLAD Factor
1	1.000		9,579,998/9,579,998		1.000
2	0.962		9,563,425/9,579,998		0.960
3	0.925		9,546,402/9,579,998		0.922
4	0.889		9,528,932/9,579,998		0.884
5	0.855		9,510,732/9,579,998		0.849
6	0.822		9,491,711/9,579,998		0.814
7	0.790		9,471,683/9,579,998		0.781
8	0.760		9,450,466/9,579,998		0.750
9	0.731		9,427,785/9,579,998		0.719
10	0.703		9,403,461/9,579,998		0.690
			Temporary life annuity due		8.370

Leveling the premium of a *deferred annuity* contract is also treated differently from an *immediate annuity* contract.

Immediate Annuity Contracts

A life annuity contract pays equal periodic installments to the annuitant for a specified length of time or "till death do us part." If the annuitant receives a rent payment on the next payment date after the contract is started, the annuity is referred to as an *immediate annuity*; otherwise a *deferred annuity* contract's rent starts after at least one payment date.

☐ **Example**

Rebecca Wade, who is age 60 and has no dependents or spouse, is concerned about allocating her savings over the remainder of her life. If Rebecca deposits all of her life savings in an immediate annuity contract, she would expect to receive the first monthly rent payment on the next payment date. If the contract is purchased on January 7, 1992, and all rent payments from the insurance company occur on the 15th, Rebecca will receive a rent payment on January 15, 1992. However, if a five-year deferred contract were purchased, Rebecca would have to survive until January 15, 1997, to receive any rent payments.

Because of the nature of the immediate annuity contract, accumulation of funds over a period of time or on an installment basis is not possible. The present value of the annuity contract (NSP) must be paid to the life insurance company at the inception of the contract, before rent payments begin; therefore it is not possible to level the payment for an immediate annuity.

Single-Premium Deferred Annuity Contracts

Deferred annuity contracts can be purchased on a lump-sum basis or through periodic installments. Consider the lump-sum purchase first.

Table 22.5 shows the NSP calculation for a ten-year temporary annuity deferred for five years. In this table the net single premium of $646.32 is the amount of money required by the life insurance company if the annuity contract is pur-

Table 22.5
10-Year Temporary Annuity
Age 65, Deferred 5 Years: Refund during Accumulation
(Male, 1983 Annuity Table, 4 percent)

Age	Year	Probability of Survival	×	$ Payment	×	Interest Factor	=	NSP
65	1	8,577,575/8,577,575		100		1.000		100.000
66	2	8,467,345/8,577,575		100		0.962		94.964
67	3	8,347,117/8,577,575		100		0.925		90.015
68	4	8,215,925/8,577,575		100		0.889		85.152
69	5	8,072,853/8,577,575		100		0.855		80.469
70	6	7,917,079/8,577,575		100		0.822		75.870
71	7	7,747,883/8,577,575		100		0.790		71.358
72	8	7,564,669/8,577,575		100		0.760		67.025
73	9	7,366,997/8,577,575		100		0.731		62.783
74	10	7,154,570/8,577,575		100		0.703		58.637

Temporary annuity benefit   786.274
Deferral factor   × 0.822
Deferred net single premium $646.317

chased on a single-premium deferred basis. The NSP of $646.32 is the result of discounting the NSP for an immediate ten-year temporary annuity for five years at 4 percent (0.822). (Instead of using the deferral factor of 0.822, the calculation may be made by adjusting the interest factor for the appropriate length of time.) During the accumulation period $646.32 will grow to $786.27 in five years at a 4 percent interest rate ($646.32 \times 1.04^5 = \$786.27$). To provide the $100 annuity for ten years, $786.27 is required when the distribution period begins. Thus the annuitant can pay $646.32 for a contract deferred five years or a larger amount if deferred for fewer years.

Level-Premium Deferred Annuity Contracts

In addition to purchasing the annuity contract with one deferred lump sum, the annuitant can purchase the contract by making installment payments. The amount of the net single premium and the net level premium is a function of two factors. The first factor is the discount rate, and the second is whether a refund provision exists during the accumulation period.

If the contract refunds savings during the accumulation period, no life contingencies are involved during the accumulation process. Thus, to calculate the annual installment to purchase the annuity contract, an annuity due payment needs to be calculated that will provide $786.27 to the life insurance company on the annuity's starting date.

$$FV = FVA_d \times PMT$$
$$PMT = \frac{\$786.27}{5.4162} = \$145.17$$

The future value amount ($786.27) is divided by the future value of an annuity due factor of 4 percent. If $145.17 is deposited at the beginning of each year for five years, $786.27 will be available when the fifth payment is made. The growth

Table 22.6
Accumulation Period:
Deferred Installment Contract

Year	Beginning Balance	Payment	Invested Funds	Interest Added	Ending Balance
1	$ 0.00	$145.17	$145.17	$ 5.81	$150.97
2	150.97	$145.17	$296.14	$11.85	$307.99
3	307.99	$145.17	$453.15	$18.13	$471.28
4	471.28	$145.17	$616.45	$24.66	$641.10
5	641.10	$145.17	$786.27		

of the installment payments with interest added is shown in Table 22.6. Notice that, in the accumulation process, payments are made at the beginning of the year and, as the last payment is made, the required NSP ($786.27) has been accumulated. The life insurance company then, on the next payment date, pays to the annuitant the first $100 rent payment.

When there is no refund during the accumulation period, the same options exist. The annuitant may purchase the contract on a deferred single-premium basis for $615.04. (Instead of using the deferral factor, the interest factor may be adjusted for the appropriate length of time.) Table 22.7 presents the single-premium, deferred calculation when there is no refund during accumulation. In addition to that option, the annuitant may purchase the contract on an installment basis. The calculation for the installment must consider the possibility of the annuitant's paying some (or all) of the premium payments and dying and forfeiting the accumulated amount before any rent payments begin. The periodic payment is calculated on the next page.

Table 22.7
10-Year Temporary Annuity
Age 65, Deferred 5 Years: No Refund during Accumulation
(Male, 1983 Annuity Table, 4 percent)

Age	Year	Probability of Survival	×	$ Payment	×	Interest Factor	=	NSP
65	1	8,577,575/9,013,785		100		1.000		95.161
66	2	8,467,345/9,013,785		100		0.962		90.368
67	3	8,347,117/9,013,785		100		0.925		85,659
68	4	8,215,925/9,013,785		100		0.889		81.031
69	5	8,072,853/9,013,785		100		0.855		76.575
70	6	7,917,079/9,013,785		100		0.822		72.199
71	7	7,747,883/9,013,785		100		0.790		67.905
72	8	7,564,669/9,013,785		100		0.760		63,782
73	9	7,366,997/9,013,785		100		0.731		59.745
74	10	7,154,570/9,013,785		100		0.703		55.800

Temporary annuity benefit	748.223
Deferral factor	× 0.822
Deferred net single premium	$615.040

Table 22.8
Future Value of a Temporary Annuity Due Calculation
Age 60, 4 Percent, 1983 Annuity Table

Age	Year	Probability of Survival	×	FVF	=	FV
0	1	9,013,785/9,013,785		1.217		1.217
1	2	8,938,628/9,013,785		1.170		1.160
2	3	8,858,332/9,013,785		1.125		1.106
3	4	8,772,052/9,013,785		1.082		1.053
4	5	8,678,805/9,013,785		1.040		1.001
		Future value of TLAD				5.537

$$FV = FVLAD \times PMT$$
$$PMT = \frac{FV}{FVLAD}$$

Table 22.8 shows the calculation of the future value of a temporary life annuity due. Notice that this calculation is similar to the PVTLAD used to level life insurance contracts. However, the numerator and denominator for the probability of survival are taken from the annuity table starting at age 60, the year the first payment is made, instead of the year of the first possible benefit. Also note that the time value factor is a future value factor. The factor for the first year is 1.04 to the fifth power (1.217), and in consecutive years the power is reduced by one.

Table 22.9 shows the process of collecting $135.15 (748.22/5.537) in premiums from 1,000 initial insureds who accumulate interest over the deferral period, resulting in an accumulation of $748.22 for each insured who started the accumulation period. Thus, for each insured starting the accumulation period, $748.22 is available at the beginning of the payment period when there is no refund during accumulation.

Table 22.9
Year-by-Year Analysis of Installment Payment:
No Refund

Year	Number of Insureds	Probability of Survival	Dollars Added	Beginning Balance	Interest	Ending Balance
1	1,000	1.000	135,152	135,152	5,406	140,558
2	1,000	0.992	134,025	274,583	10,983	285,567
3	1,000	0.983	132,821	418,388	16,736	435,123
4	1,000	0.973	131,527	566,651	22,666	589,317
5	1,000	0.963	130,129	719,446	28,778	748,224

$748,224/1,000 = $748.22

Note: Required installment = NSP/FVTLAD.
Premium = $748.223/5.537 = $135.15.
Dollars added = 1,000 × probability of surviving × $135.15.
Beginning balance = previous year's ending balance + dollars added.

Table 22.10
Year-by-Year Analysis of Distribution Period, $100 Payment

Year	Age	Number Living	Beginning Balance	× Number Alive	Invested Funds	Interest Added	Ending Balance
1	65	951.794	748,224	95,179	653,045	26,122	679,166
2	66	939.562	679,166	93,956	585,210	23,408	608,619
3	67	926.221	608,619	92,622	515,996	20,640	536,636
4	68	911.664	536,636	91,166	445,470	17,819	463,289
5	69	895.788	463,289	89,579	373,710	14,948	388,658
6	70	878.503	388,658	87,850	300,808	12,032	312,840
7	71	859.728	312,840	85,973	226,868	9,075	235,942
8	72	839.399	235,942	83,940	152,002	6,080	158,082
9	73	817.464	158,082	81,746	76,336	3,053	79,389
10	74	793.893	79,389	79,389	0	0	0

Numbers are rounded.
Number living is equal to the numbers surviving to receive a payment divided by the number starting at age 60 multiplied by 1,000 (the numbers starting the group).

To illustrate that the calculation is correct, Table 22.10 shows how the ending balance ($748,224) in Table 22.9 is distributed among the surviving annuitants. The probability of being alive at each age is calculated relative to the number of insureds starting the cohort at age 60. The beginning balance is reduced by the number of insureds who have survived, multiplied by the rent payment for each insured.

The rent payment, paid at the beginning of the year, reduces investable funds. The remaining funds are then invested at the assumed interest rate of 4 percent. Investment earnings are then added to the invested amount to equal the balance at the end of the year. Because the contract is a ten-year temporary annuity, only ten years of rent payments are possible. As the last rent payment is made to the surviving annuitants, the pool of funds is exhausted, and all obligations under the temporary annuity contract terminate.

Review Questions

1. Explain the term *present value of future benefits*. Use a mathematical example to demonstrate its calculation.

2. Explain what is meant by this statement: The leveling process compensates for missing premiums and missing interest.

3. Calculate the temporary life annuity due factor to level a ten-year term life insurance policy (1980 CSO Table, 6 percent, male aged 22).

4. Refer to question 3. Show the last five years of the calculation if a life annuity due amount is required to level a whole life contract for a male aged 22 (1980 CSO Table, 6 percent).

5. How does the calculation in question 3 change if the policy being leveled is a ten-year endowment?
6. What is meant by a limited-payment plan? At what point does the insurer consider the policy paid up?
7. Refer to the NSP calculations actually made in the review questions for Chapter 21. Calculate the level premiums required for the term and endowment contracts. Mathematically set up the leveling process for the whole life contracts.
8. Calculate the net single premium required to purchase (at age 55) a five-year temporary annuity with a refund during accumulation (1983 Annuity Table, 6 percent). What would the net single premium be if the contract promised deferred benefits (purchased at age 50, deferred five years)? Calculate the installments necessary to purchase the contract over the five-year accumulation period.
9. How does the calculation in question 8 change when no refund of accumulated amounts is allowed? Show all calculations.
10. What differences exist between calculating the level premium for a deferred temporary annuity and calculating it for a deferred life income annuity?

Bibliography

Batten, Robert W. *Mortality Table Construction*. Englewood Cliffs, N.J.: Prentice-Hall, 1978.

Harper, Floyd S., and Lewis C. Workman. *Fundamental Mathematics of Life Insurance*. Homewood, Ill.: Richard D. Irwin, 1970.

Huebner, S. S., and Kenneth Black, Jr. *Life Insurance*. 11th ed. Englewood Cliffs, N.J.: Prentice-Hall, 1987.

Jordan, C. W. *Life Contingencies*. 2d ed. Chicago: Society of Actuaries, 1967.

Pedoe, Arthur, and Colin E. Jack. *Life Insurance, Annuities and Pensions*. 3d ed. Toronto: University of Toronto Press, 1978.

Chapter 23 | Reserves, Nonforfeiture Values and Gross Premiums

Chapter Objectives

- Discuss the importance and calculation of the policyholder reserve
- Explore the nature of nonforfeiture values
- Investigate the components of the gross premium
- Demonstrate how the gross premium is tested for adequacy

Introduction

This discussion of life insurance mathematics would not be complete without elaborating on reserves, nonforfeiture values and the gross premium. The importance of reserves lies in the fact that a large portion of a life insurance company's assets is claimed by policyholders in the form of legal reserve liabilities. And, in order to remain solvent, assets must exceed all legal obligations. Life insurance policyholder reserves develop because of the leveling process. (Policyholder reserves also arise out of health and annuity contracts.) The excesses collected in the early years must be invested so that the life insurance company will be financially prepared to pay all future contractual obligations. Requiring minimum reserve (liability) amounts allows the company to maintain sufficient assets for the policy owners' protection.

Nonforfeiture values arise from the combination of the leveling process and the operation of nonforfeiture laws. Nonforfeiture laws guarantee that the insureds' cash value provided by the life insurance contract cannot be forfeited to the life insurance company. The laws also provide several methods of using these inherent values. In this chapter readers will notice the close relationship between the reserve amount (a statutory commitment) and the cash value amount (a contractual commitment). These two dollar amounts differ and need to be fully understood. The purpose of the reserve is to provide a conservative estimate of the present value of future obligations. The cash value, on the other hand, is a conservative estimate of the insureds' asset share.

The gross premium is the actual premium charged by the insurance company and is equal to the sum of the net premium, taxes, profits and a charge for overhead. The gross premium must be tested using asset share techniques to determine whether it will be adequate to provide funds for all of the needs of the life insurance company during the term of the contract. If the net premium is correct and the expenses, taxes and profits also are calculated correctly, the gross premium should meet the needs of the life insurance company. Asset share analysis, however, goes beyond testing the gross premium for cost adequacy. In addition, asset share analysis provides information regarding any changes in the capital and surplus position of the firm and information on the effect of policy lapses.

Reserves

Chapters 21 and 22 demonstrated the methods used to calculate the net single premium and the net level premium. The net single premium was leveled so the insured could maintain the life insurance contract with equal periodic premium payments. Because the leveling process overpays mortality costs in the early years and underpays mortality costs in the later years, the life insurance company must maintain the excess accumulations in the form of **legal reserves**. The reserve amount places the life insurance company in the position of being able to pay all future claims under existing contracts. Thus the reserve could be defined as a balance sheet liability representing the net present value of funds required to meet all future obligations to policyholders and beneficiaries called for by the contract. (The reserve should not be thought of as a pool of funds. It is an amount held on the balance sheet as a liability. An equal amount of assets may be in cash, securities or any other asset found on the asset side of the balance sheet.)

The importance of the reserve is illustrated by the magnitude of the dollars allocated to reserve accounts in one form or another. *The 1990 Life Insurance Fact Book* states that in 1989 U.S. life insurance companies' policy reserves totaled $1.083 trillion. Total assets for U.S. life insurance companies in 1989 were $1.299 trillion. Thus reserves were 83 percent of total assets. Table 23.1 provides data for selected years regarding policy reserves, total assets and reserves as a percent of total assets. This table shows that the reserve amount as a percent of assets has remained relatively constant over many years. The percentages in Table 23.1 are only averages. Life insurance companies selling a higher proportion of endowment and annuity contracts relative to the average have a higher ratio of reserves to assets. Life insurance companies emphasizing the sale of term contracts, on the other hand, have a lower percent of reserves to assets. This higher or lower amount results from differing contractual obligations and the resultant reserve for the respective policies.

Because reserves are held for the benefit of the policyholders, these amounts are shown as liabilities on the life insurance company's balance sheet. Policyholders and beneficiaries have a legal claim on the assets of the life insurance company, and this is why life insurance companies are called *legal reserve* companies. Because of the debtor-creditor relationship and the size of the reserve relative to the asset amounts of most life insurance companies, a careful analysis of the subject is warranted.

Reserve Valuation Timing

If the reserve amount is calculated at the beginning of the year, the amount is identified as *initial reserves*. If shown at the end of the year, the amount is identified as

Table 23.1
Reserves and Assets (000,000s)

Year	Policy Reserves*	Total Assets†	Reserves to Assets
1955	$ 75,359	$ 90,432	0.83
1965	127,620	158,884	0.80
1975	237,116	289,304	0.82
1980	390,339	479,210	0.81
1981	428,031	525,803	0.81
1982	479,360	588,163	0.82
1983	532,441	654,948	0.81
1984	584,193	722,979	0.81
1985	665,302	825,901	0.81
1986	761,924	937,551	0.81
1987	862,133	1,044,459	0.83
1988	968,963	1,166,870	0.83
1989	1,083,678	1,299,756	0.83

*Life, health, individual, group and supplementary contracts.
†Government securities, corporates, mortgages, real estate policy loans and miscellaneous assets.
Source: *1990 Life Insurance Fact Book* (Washington, D.C.: American Council of Life Insurance), pp. 73, 83.

terminal reserves. The terminal reserve for one year will be equal to the initial reserve of the following year. The *mean reserve* is the average of the initial and terminal reserves. The mean reserve is used when the insurer prepares its annual statement. The assumption is made that all policies are in their midyear and the mean reserve is representative of the reserve liabilities of the company. (This assumption is generally not true but is a good approximation relative to the magnitude of measuring the reserve of each and every policy.)

Calculation of Policyholders' Reserve

The policyholders' reserve amount can be calculated by using various techniques. For the purposes of discussion, a ten-year endowment policy will be used to illustrate three reserve calculation methods:

1. The year-by-year method (generally not in use but a valuable tool to demonstrate the reserve valuation process)
2. The retrospective method
3. The prospective method

To demonstrate these methods, the net single premium and net level premium amount first must be calculated for the hypothetical policy. These amounts for the ten-year endowment are based on a male aged 35, a 4 percent interest rate and the 1980 CSO Table.

The Year-by-Year Method

This method is used to show the cash flow associated with the group of insureds. It is also included to prove that the *retrospective* and the *prospective* methods result is the correct reserve amount. Based on the preceding assumptions, the net single premium for the ten-year endowment policy is equal to $679.01, and the net level premium is $81.36. Table 23.2 shows the expected year-by-year cash

Table 23.2
$1,000 10-Year Endowment: Year-by-Year Analysis*

Age	Number Alive	Number That Die	Beginning Balance	Premium Added	Total Funds	Interest (4 percent)	Claims	Ending Balance	Number Surviving	Terminal Reserve per Survivor
35	949.17	2.00	$0	$77,224	$77,224	$3,089	$2,003	$ 78,310	947.17	$ 82.68
36	947.17	2.12	78,310	77,061	155,372	6,215	2,122	159,465	945.05	168.74
37	945.05	2.27	159,465	76,889	236,353	9,454	2,268	243,539	942.78	258.32
38	942.78	2.43	243,539	76,704	320,243	12,810	2,432	330,621	940.35	351.59
39	940.35	2.62	330,621	76,506	407,127	16,285	2,624	420,788	937.72	448.73
40	937.72	2.83	420,788	76,293	497,081	19,883	2,832	514,132	934.89	549.94
41	934.89	3.08	514,132	76,062	590,195	23,608	3,076	610,727	931.81	655.42
42	931.81	3.32	610,727	75,812	686,539	27,462	3,317	710,683	928.50	765.41
43	928.50	3.59	710,683	75,542	786,225	31,449	3,593	814,081	924.90	880.18
44	924.90	3.88	814,081	75,250	889,331	35,573	3,875	921,029	921.03	1,000.00

Net single premium equals 679.01; TLAD equals 8.3457.
Net level premium equals 81.35958.
*Numbers are rounded: 1980 CSO, Male age 35, 4 percent.

flow for a group of insureds. The number of insureds starting at age 35 is arbitrary. Table 23.2 starts with 949.17 insureds because the 1980 CSO Table predicts that, out of each 1,000 lives that start the cohort at age zero, 949.17 insureds will have survived to age 35. The number of deaths in a given year is calculated by the probability of dying in that year given that 949.17 insureds started the group at age 35.

Following the cash flows projected in Table 23.2, each surviving insured at the beginning of each policy year pays a net level premium of $81.36 for each $1,000 of coverage. Interest at the rate of 4 percent is added to the sum of the previous year's balance and the new premiums paid. The predicted death claims are then subtracted at the end of each policy year. The fund's total amount available after the payment of the death claims, divided by the number of surviving insureds, equals the terminal reserve for each $1,000 of life insurance still in force at the end of each policy year. At the end of the ten-year period $1,000 is available for the endowment benefit. When $1,000 is finally paid to each surviving insured, all cash derived from premiums and interest will have been liquidated to meet all of the life insurance company's contractual obligations.

The year-by-year method is not the only way of determining terminal reserves. The *prospective* or *retrospective* methods may also be used to provide the same results. The prospective method looks forward in time from the valuation date and calculates the terminal reserve by subtracting the present value of future premiums from the present value of future benefits of the policy. The retrospective method looks back in time from the valuation date. The terminal reserve under this method is equal to the accumulated value of the net premiums received under the contract minus the accumulated cost of mortality. All of these methods result in the same reserve dollar amount.

Retrospective Terminal Reserve Calculation

The year-by-year method would be quite cumbersome if used to produce the terminal reserve amount for the 50th year of a whole life insurance policy. (The number of calculations needed to determine the reserve may be minimized by selecting the method demanding the fewest number of years for the procedure. The method selection should be based on the type of contract, the age of issue and the valuation date.) An alternative to the year-by-year method is the retrospective method, which looks back through time from the valuation date and determines the terminal reserve by using the following equation:

Reserve on the valuation date	=	Sum of the past net premiums with interest added Less: Sum of the past mortality cost with interest added

Using the ten-year endowment policy referred to in Table 23.2, the retrospective terminal reserve for the third policy year is determined by first calculating up to the valuation date the sum of the net premiums received with interest added. In this case the valuation date is the end of the third year. Second, the mortality cost with interest added is calculated up to the same valuation date, and the result is subtracted from the first amount.

The first part of the equation, the net premiums received with interest added, is calculated using the following formula:

$$\text{NLP} \times \frac{[l_{35} \times (1+i)^3] + [l_{36} \times (1+i)^2] + [l_{37} \times (1+i)^1]}{l_{38}}$$

$$\$81.3595 \times \frac{(949.17 \times 1.04^3) + (947.17 \times 1.04^2) + (945.05 \times 1.04^1)}{942.78}$$

$$\$81.3595 \times \frac{1067.68 + 1024.45 + 982.85}{942.78}$$

$$\$81.3595 \times 3.2616 = 265.3648$$

The net level premium ($81.3595) is multiplied by the number of insureds paying the premium installment. The result is increased by interest earnings at 4 percent $(1+i)^n$ for the appropriate length of time. This sum is then divided by the number of surviving insureds. The net level premium with interest added, according to the formula, is equal to $265.365 per surviving insured.

The second part of the equation, the mortality cost with interest added, is calculated next.

$$\$1,000 \times \frac{[d_{35} \times (1+i)^2] + [d_{36} \times (1+i)^1] + [d_{37} \times (1+i)^0]}{l_{38}}$$

$$\$1,000 \times \frac{(2.00 \times 1.04^2) + (2.12 \times 1.04^1) + (2.27 \times 1.04^0)}{942.78}$$

$$\$1,000 \times \frac{2.1632 + 2.2048 + 2.27}{942.78}$$

$$\$1,000 \times .00704 = 7.0408$$

$$\text{Terminal reserve} = 265.3648 - 7.0408 = \$258.32$$

The death benefit is multiplied by the number of insureds dying. This result is increased by interest earnings at 4 percent $(1+i)^n$ for the appropriate length of time. Notice that the future value exponent is one less for a given year than the exponent used to determine the accumulated value of premium payments. This difference arises from the fact that premium payments are made at the beginning of the year, whereas death payments are assumed to be paid at the end of each year. The number just calculated is then divided by the number of insureds surviving. The mortality cost with interest added is equal to $7.0408 per surviving insured.

The terminal reserve for the third year is equal to the net level premiums with interest added minus the mortality cost with interest added (265.3648 − 7.0408 = 258.32). The $258.32 reserve may be verified by inspecting the third terminal reserve calculated by the year-by-year analysis presented in Table 23.2.

Chapter 23 Reserves, Nonforfeiture Values and Gross Premiums

Prospective Terminal Reserve Calculation

The prospective method (more commonly used for reserve valuation) calculates yearly terminal reserves by looking forward in time. The following formula is used to calculate this amount:

$$\text{Reserve on the valuation date} = \text{Present value of future benefits under the contract} - \text{Present value of future premiums}$$

The prospective method determines the future obligations under the contract, adjusted for the time value of money and mortality, and subtracts the present value of the future premiums adjusted for the probability of surviving.

The terminal reserve should be the same for a given year regardless of the method used in calculating the number. It will be shown that the terminal reserve for the third year will be equal to $258.32, which is the amount calculated using the year-by-year method and the retrospective method. Again the ten-year endowment policy is used for the calculation.

The present value of future benefits to be provided by the endowment contract will be calculated first. The reader should remember from Chapter 21 that the net single premium is equal to the present value of the future benefits under the contract on the date of issue. For the first part of the terminal reserve calculation the present value of the future benefits under the contract is simply equal to the net single premium on the date of valuation. This is true because the net single premium is valued at the date of issue, whereas in the terminal reserve calculation the present value of future benefits is valued on the terminal reserve valuation date.

The net single premium on the valuation date is equal to present value of future premiums on the valuation date.

$$\$1{,}000 \times \frac{\left[\left(d_{38} \times \frac{1}{(1+i)^1}\right) + \left(d_{39} \times \frac{1}{(1+i)^2}\right) + \left(d_{40} \times \frac{1}{(1+i)^3}\right) + \left(d_{41} \times \frac{1}{(1+i)^4}\right) + \left(d_{42} \times \frac{1}{(1+i)^5}\right) + \left(d_{43} \times \frac{1}{(1+i)^6}\right) + \left(d_{44} \times \frac{1}{(1+i)^7}\right) + \left(l_{45} \times \frac{1}{(1+i)^7}\right)\right]}{l_{38}}$$

$$\$1{,}000 \times \frac{(2.43 \times .9615) + (2.62 \times .9245) + (2.83 \times .8889) + (3.08 \times .8548) + (3.32 \times .8219) + (3.59 \times .7903) + (3.88 \times .7599) + (921.02 \times .7599)}{942.78}$$

$$\$1{,}000 \times \frac{718.3044}{942.78} = 761.900$$

The death payment is multiplied by the probability of dying, and in the last year a survival calculation is added because the policy endows for survivors. This result is discounted at 4 percent $[1/(1+i)^n]$ for the appropriate length of time.

The present value of future premiums is the next part of the calculation. The annual net level premium calculated for the ten-year endowment policy is equal to $81.3595. Because payments are made at the beginning of each policy year, an annuity due factor is required to calculate the present value of the future premiums. Also, because some insureds will not survive to pay the premium, an adjustment for mortality must be made. Thus the temporary life annuity due is used to discount the premium for each year.

$$81.3595 \times \left[\left(\frac{l_{38}}{l_{38}} \times \frac{1}{(1+i)^0} \right) + \left(\frac{l_{39}}{l_{38}} \times \frac{1}{(1+i)^1} \right) + \left(\frac{l_{40}}{l_{38}} \times \frac{1}{(1+i)^2} \right) \right.$$
$$+ \left(\frac{l_{41}}{l_{38}} \times \frac{1}{(1+i)^3} \right) + \left(\frac{l_{42}}{l_{38}} \times \frac{1}{(1+i)^4} \right)$$
$$\left. + \left(\frac{l_{43}}{l_{38}} \times \frac{1}{(1+i)^5} \right) + \left(\frac{l_{44}}{l_{38}} \times \frac{1}{(1+i)^6} \right) \right]$$

$$81.3595 \times \left[\left(\frac{942.78}{942.78} \times 1.000 \right) + \left(\frac{940.35}{942.78} \times 0.9615 \right) \right.$$
$$+ \left(\frac{937.72}{942.78} \times 0.9245 \right) + \left(\frac{934.89}{942.78} \times 0.8889 \right)$$
$$+ \left(\frac{931.81}{942.78} \times 0.8548 \right) + \left(\frac{928.50}{942.78} \times 0.8219 \right)$$
$$\left. + \left(\frac{924.90}{942.78} \times 0.7903 \right) \right]$$

$81.3595 \times (1.00 + .95902 + .91953 + .88146 + .84485 + .80945 + .77531)$

$81.3595 \times 6.1896 = 503.58$

Third-year terminal reserve $= 761.900 - 503.58 = 258.32$

The net single premium is multiplied each year by the probability of surviving and then is discounted at 4 percent $[1/(1+i)^n]$ for the appropriate length of time. Notice that the prospective terminal reserve for the third year equals the terminal reserve for the third year under the year-by-year and the retrospective terminal reserve methods.

Regardless of the method used, the reserve amount will be exactly the same as long as the assumptions used to calculate the amounts are consistent. In addition, the total reserve for the insurer may be calculated on an individual basis or on a group basis. If the individual basis is used, the total reserve reported on the balance sheet is equal to the sum of the individual reserve amounts.

As a review, refer to Figures 23.1 and 23.2 for a graphic comparison of the retrospective and prospective methods of reserve valuation. The graphs are not drawn to scale and are not illustrative of the dollars involved or the rate of change

Chapter 23 Reserves, Nonforfeiture Values and Gross Premiums 517

**Figure 23.1
Prospective Reserve**

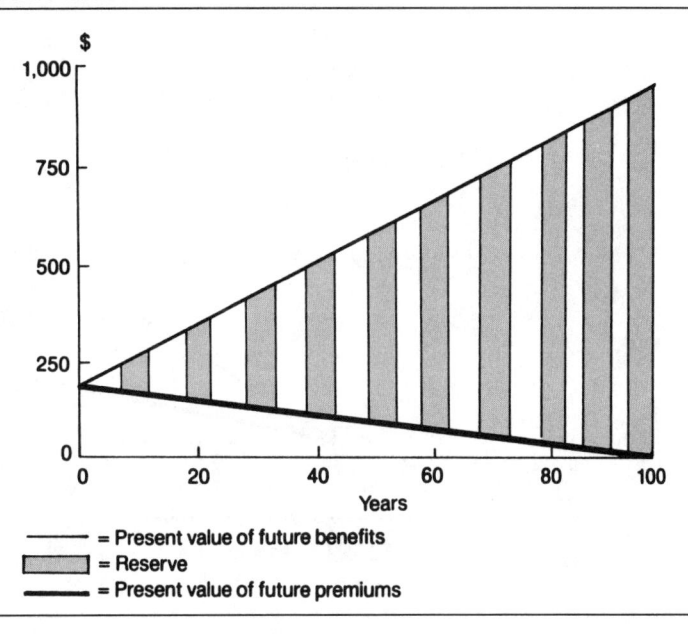

```
$
1,000

 750

 500

 250

   0
    0       20      40      60      80     100
                      Years
```
——— = Present value of future benefits
▨ = Reserve
▬▬ = Present value of future premiums

of the numbers plotted. The two figures are only representations of the prospective and retrospective methods of reserve computation for an arbitrary cash value policy. Notice that, regardless of the method used, the area between the two lines in both figures is the same; that is, the reserve amounts are equal at any given policy age. Study the figures, reconcile the differences and verify that equal results occur regardless of the reserve method used. (An alternative method [a reformulation of the above equation] for calculating the prospective reserve amount is: net level terminal reserve [at the age of valuation] = net single premium [at the age of valuation] − [net level premium (age of issue) × PVLAD factor], where PVLAD factor is for $1 for the remaining premium paying period.)

The Survivorship Benefit and the Net Amount at Risk

Additions to the policy reserve do not arise entirely from investment income on the previous year's reserve plus current year's premium. Also included is a survivor benefit. The following calculations illustrate this point.

If $81.3595 is the premium for the ten-year endowment policy discussed, investment income at a rate of 4 percent at the end of six years would provide only $561.217 as a terminal reserve amount. This number is calculated by multiplying 81.3595 (the yearly premium) by 6.898, the future value of an annuity due factor at 4 percent for six years. The difference between the terminal reserve (Table 23.2) for the sixth year ($549.94) and the future value of the annuity due ($561.217) is $11.28. This $11.28 is called the *survivorship benefit*. Members of the group who die during the policy term relinquish their asset share to the group, and in return the beneficiary receives the face amount of the contract.

Figure 23.2
Retrospective Reserve

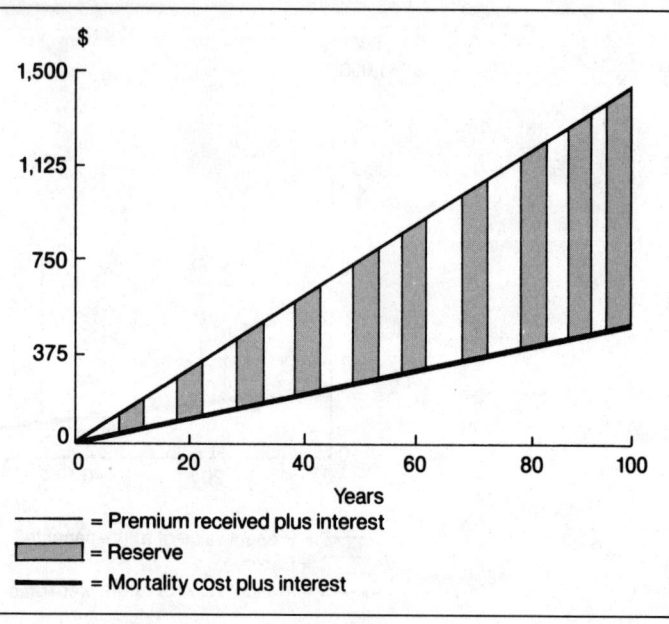

```
= Premium received plus interest
= Reserve
= Mortality cost plus interest
```

Consider the first year for an alternate view of the survivor benefit. An insured pays a net level premium of $81.3595 for the first year of the ten-year endowment policy. If this insured dies, the mortality expense was $2.11 (20,028/9,491,711) for this insured's contribution toward the death claim. The difference of $79.24 ($81.3595 − $2.11) is divided among the survivors, which increases their asset share of the pool by $0.084 ($79.24/947.17). Thus all those surviving participate in this survivor benefit, and their life insurance cost is effectively reduced by this participation.

When the face amount of the insurance policy is paid to the beneficiary, the death claim may be considered composed of the reserve amount plus an amount called the **net amount at risk**. The net amount at risk is equal to the face amount minus any reserve or cash value available. This is referred to as the *economic approach* to viewing the payment of a death claim.

An alternate view of the amount paid to the beneficiary uses a *survivorship approach*. Because the net single premium and net level premium calculations assume the death benefit to be $1,000, it would be inconsistent, in this context, to say that the amount of insurance declines with age. Upon death $1,000 is paid to the beneficiary. This amount is exactly what the premium calculations call for. The leveling process, in this context, is only a funding technique to overcome the problems of adverse selection (self-selection), lapses at older ages and unaffordable premiums. The reserve and cash values, produced by the leveling process, are only a consequence of that technique. The amount of the reserve required of, and accumulated by, the life insurance company depends on the type of policy issued, the age of issue and the number of years required for the policy to be paid up. (The reserve amount is also a function of the mortality table used [female, male, unisex] and whether a modified reserve technique is used.)

In term insurance contracts the life insurance company does not have to fund for a certain event because the contract is written to cover only part of one's life. For a young person the probability of surviving short periods of time is quite high; but for older individuals the probability of dying during short time periods is higher. Because of this fact, when term insurance is sold the company does not have to fund for a contingency that is certain to occur. The life insurance company need fund death claims on only a portion of the individuals starting the group. That portion is determined by the group's expected experience.

On the other hand, if whole life insurance contracts are sold, the life insurance company funds for a certain event. All insureds eventually die, so the face amount must be available to pay for each death claim regardless of when it occurs. Insureds withdrawing from the cohort or lapsing their contracts obviously will not be paid upon death unless a nonforfeiture option providing some form of a continuing death benefit was chosen. (When lapse occurs, the policy owner may also withdraw the cash value.)

In the endowment contract the life insurance company must also fund for a certain event. All insureds maintaining the policy throughout the term of the contract will have a claim paid. If death occurs during the policy term, a death benefit will be paid to the beneficiary, and if the insured survives the term of the policy, a survivor benefit will be paid to the insured.

The number of years until the policy is to be paid up also influences the rate of change of the reserve amount. All other factors being equal, the fewer number of planned installments to purchase the policy, the larger the overpayment will be in the early years so the insured can underpay the premium in the later years. Once the life insurance company is placed in the position of having the present value of the amount required to provide all future benefits under the contract, the insured need not pay the insurance company any more premiums, and the policy is termed *paid up*. The asset value required for the paid-up contract is equal to the net single premium of an equivalent contract starting on the date that the existing contract is to be fully paid.

The age of the insured also affects the rate of change of the reserve amount. If all other factors are the same, in whole life contracts the older the insured is when the contract is purchased, the faster the reserve needs to increase to accumulate $1,000 for each $1,000 of face amount.

Figure 23.3 shows the relative amount of reserve for each type of contract. By analyzing the graph, it should be possible to ascertain the relative amount of "protection" versus "savings" provided by the life insurance contract, the relative amount of yearly premium paid for the contract, the rate of change of the reserve amount and the number of payments to be made before the contract is paid up.

Referring to Figure 23.3, the reserve for the term contract increases and then decreases as the overpayments in the early years plus interest added are used to pay mortality expense. The rate of increase and decrease of the reserve amount depends on the portion of the mortality curve considered and the length of the contract. The reserve for the 20-year term contract increases from zero and then de-

**Figure 23.3
Comparison of Reserve Amounts**

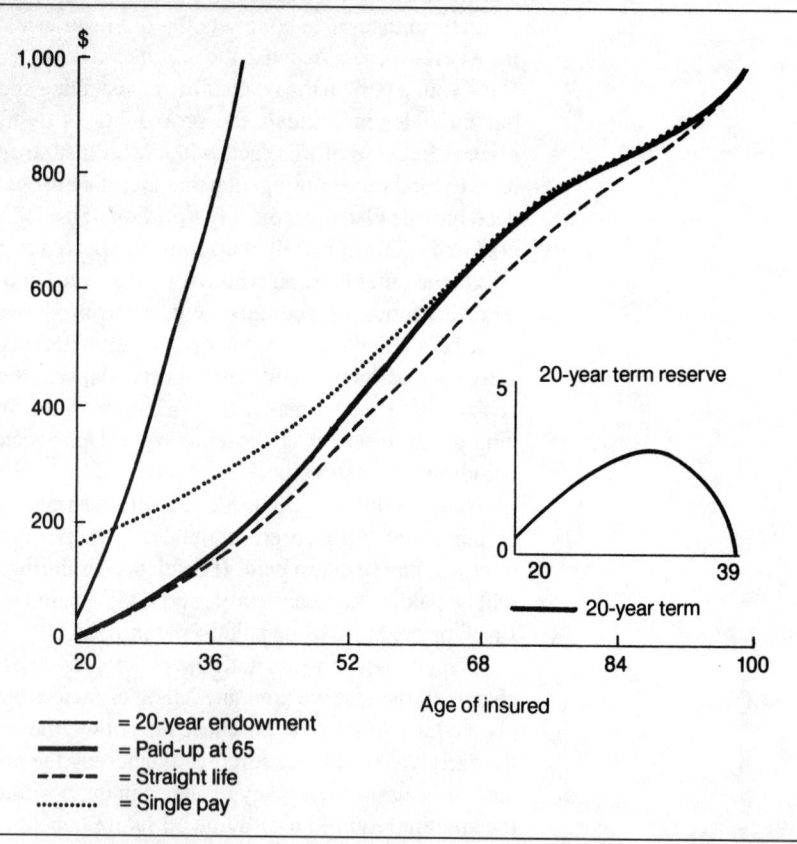

- ——— = 20-year endowment
- ——— = Paid-up at 65
- - - - - = Straight life
- ·········· = Single pay

Inset: 20-year term reserve (20 to 39)
——— = 20-year term

creases back to zero at the end of the 20th year. Overpayments in the early years plus interest added are liquidated to pay for higher mortality cost in the later years.

The single-pay whole life insurance contract accumulates a reserve amount starting at the net single premium of the policy at the age of issue and ending at $1,000 at age 100. The insured has overpaid the policy totally in the first year and will underpay the policy in the later years (paying nothing). This is an extreme case of the leveling process.

The reserve amount for the straight life insurance contract starts at zero and increases throughout the policy term until, at age 100, the reserve amount equals $1,000. The reserve amount for the whole life contract paid up at 65, on the other hand, starts at zero but increases faster than the reserve for the straight life contract because of a higher yearly premium. Once the reserve amount equals the present value of future benefits, the insured may stop paying premiums (the policy is paid up), and the reserve amount follows the reserve line of the net single premium contract until $1,000 is accumulated at age 100.

On the other hand, the reserve amount for the 20-year endowment policy also starts at zero but increases quite rapidly to $1,000 at the end of the 20th year. The

Figure 23.4
Group's Assets versus Individual's Asset Share

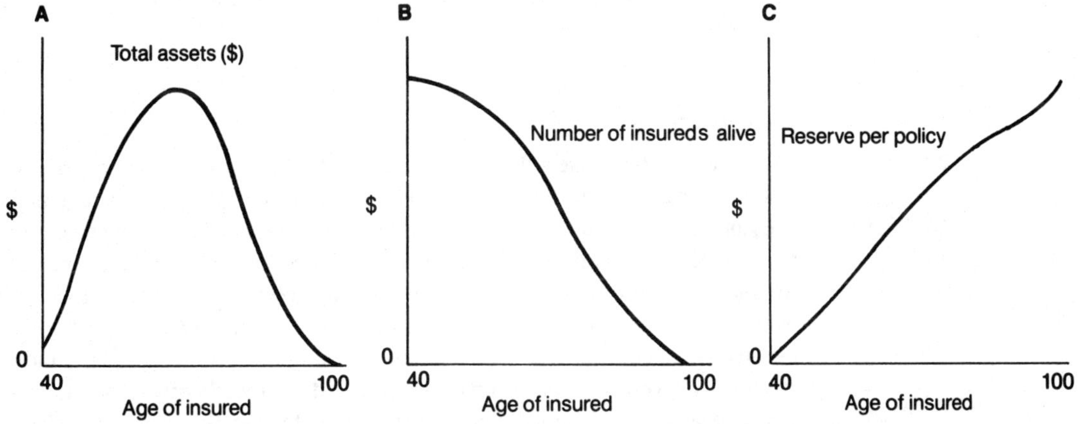

[Graph A: Total assets ($) vs Age of insured (40 to 100), bell-shaped curve]

[Graph B: Number of insureds alive vs Age of insured (40 to 100), decreasing curve]

[Graph C: Reserve per policy vs Age of insured (40 to 100), increasing curve]

reason for the rapid increase as well as terminating at $1,000 at the end of the 20th year is that the endowment contract anticipates that a claim will be paid for each insured. Whether the claim is a death claim or a survivor claim, funding must be available to pay all obligations.

How can the cash value provided by life insurance contracts continually increase for the individual policy throughout the contract period, when in the later years the underpayment of mortality expense should reduce the cash amount held for the insured? Refer to Figure 23.4, which presents three graphs.

Graphs A and B represent the total asset amount held for the cohort and the number of insureds remaining in the group. These two graphs show what is happening to the accumulated asset amount and number of insureds on a group basis over time. No insurance scheme can operate well without a large number of insureds in a pool, allowing the law of large numbers to operate.

If the ending year-by-year asset amount (Graph A) is divided by the number of survivors at the end of that year (Graph B), Graph C results, providing the asset share per surviving policy. Thus the group experience is translated into the individual policy on an asset share basis. This should explain the transition from the leveling process on a group basis to providing an increasing cash value for individual contracts.

Factors Affecting the Size of the Reserve

The size of the legal reserve is a function of the interest rate assumed, the mortality table selected and the type of reserve valuation method used. These factors are generally referred to as the *actuarial assumptions* for the reserve calculation.

Interest

When the reserve is calculated, the assumed interest rate can have a great impact on its dollar amount, especially over long periods of time. As the assumed interest rate increases, the reserve amount required decreases. This inverse relationship is readily understandable. As the interest rate increases, the discount factor used in the valuation procedure decreases, reducing the size of the required reserve. In other words, interest is being relied on to provide more of the life insurance company's funds.

Mortality Table

The mortality table used also has a significant impact on the reserve amount. As discussed earlier, the terminal reserve amount is approximately equal to the present value of future benefits minus the present value of future net premiums. If the mortality table predicts fewer deaths per thousand, then the present value of the future benefits should decrease and in turn lower the reserve amount. However, caution must be used in predicting changes in the direction of the reserve because of a decrease or increase in the mortality rate. A change in the mortality rate in any given year, or group of years, can dramatically affect the rate in other years because it is assumed that all insureds die by age 100. Thus over the life of the book of business the amount and the direction of change in the reserve are difficult to predict without actually calculating their impact for the term of the contract.

Reserve Method

Several reserve valuation methods besides those discussed so far are used. The preceding valuation methods calculate what is referred to as *full valuation reserves*, and regardless of the method used, the same dollar amount results. **Modified valuation reserve** methods also exist. Modified reserve methods are in use because the accounting for full valuation methods releases insufficient amounts of money to pay for all of the initial expenses occurring when the policy is written. These expenses arise from sales commissions, medical exams, the overhead of the insurance company and premium taxes. The reason for the use of modified terminal reserve calculation methods to modify accounting numbers can be explained best by an example.

☐ **Example**

Suppose that a whole life insurance contract was sold to a male age 30. The net level premium is $11.21 for each $1,000 of insurance. The gross premium, the amount that the life insurance company actually charges, is $18.25. The following expenses occur when the contract is issued:

Commission (55 percent of gross)	$10.04
Premium tax (2 percent of gross)	0.36
Overhead	12.00
Medical exam	15.00
Total	$37.40

If the life insurance company collects $18.25 from the insured and spends $37.40 to place the contract on the books, the deficit of $19.15 plus mortality expense of $1.73 for the first year must come from a reduction in the capital and surplus accounts of the company. The total reduction amounts to $20.88.

This accounting shrinkage may not pose a substantial problem for life insurance companies with large capital and surplus accounts, but small insurance companies may not be able to afford such a reduction. In addition, because of statutory accounting methods, the faster the insurance company sells insurance, even though in the long run the insurance may be highly profitable, the faster the capital and surplus accounts shrink. In other words, the addition to the capital accounts through profitable operations will be slower than the shrinkage due to growth. Eventually the capital accounts will recapture the reduction through later additions from operations. To reduce the impact of shrinkage in the capital accounts, several modified reserve valuation methods are used. Two of these methods, the *full preliminary term* method and the *NAIC Standard Valuation Law* or *commissioners valuation method,* will be discussed.

Full Preliminary Term Method

The full preliminary term reserve valuation method treats the reserve amount differently from the full valuation methods discussed. Regardless of the type of contract or the number of payments scheduled, the reserve for the first year is equal to zero under the full preliminary term method. In other words, the reserve amount is treated as if a one-year term insurance contract is written for the first year. In subsequent years the reserve amount is equal to the full valuation reserve for a policy with one less contract year, written for a person one year older, one year later. For example, if a 20-pay life insurance contract is written for a male aged 30, the reserve for the first year equals zero. The reserve for the following year equals the full valuation reserve of a 19-pay whole life contract, written for a male aged 31.

If the gross and level premiums are stated as above, the amount of loading (expenses) available under the full preliminary term valuation method will equal $16.52 ($18.25 − $1.73) for the first year. This amount is calculated by taking the gross premium and subtracting from it the net premium for the one-year term policy. For the next 19 years the amount of loading for expenses that will be available is equal to the gross premium minus the net level premium for the 19-pay contract written at age 31. If the net level premium for the 19-pay whole life contract is equal to $11.69, the amount of loading available for expenses is equal to $6.56 ($18.25 − $11.69).

Notice that the higher the gross premium, the more loading for expenses is freed in the first year. Contracts that have very high gross premiums can free more money than is required to pay expenses. Because of the problem of excess amounts being freed under certain circumstances (contracts with high initial premiums and relatively low expenses), other modified valuation methods have been developed. The National Association of Insurance Commissioners (NAIC) Standard Valuation Law (commonly referred to as the commissioners valuation method) is used to illustrate a second modified valuation method.

The NAIC Standard Valuation Law

The NAIC Standard Valuation Law (the commissioners reserve valuation method—CRVM) has been adopted almost unanimously throughout the United States. The commissioners method of calculating the reserve amount is quite complicated. It essentially sets a minimum valuation amount dependent on the contract issue date and the type of policy. After the issue date and type of policy are determined, the minimum reserve amount is calculated using the interest rate and mortality table mandated by the law.

With regard to life and endowment contracts, the commissioners method essentially splits these contracts into two groups. The first group includes all contracts in which the modified net level premium for the second and subsequent years is less than the net level premium for a 19-pay whole life contract issued one year later. The modified net level premium is the net level premium for the contract written for one less year, one year later. In this case the full preliminary term method is used, and

> reserves . . . shall be the excess, if any, of the present value, at the date of valuation, of such future guaranteed benefits provided for by such policies, over the then present value of any future modified net premiums therefor.[1]

If the modified net premium for the second and subsequent years is greater than the net level premium for a 19-pay whole life contract, then the

> net level annual premium shall not exceed the net level annual premium on the 19-year premium whole life plan for insurance of the same amount at an age one year higher than the age at issue of such policy.[2]

Therefore the reserve amount is equal to the present value of any guaranteed benefits minus the present value of the future net level annual premiums on a 19-pay whole life insurance policy written at an age one year older, one year later. These provisions, in essence, set a maximum amount that can be taken as loading in the first year of the contract and that, in turn, determines reserve amounts that can be deferred for later funding.

Other Reserves

Other reserves exist on the liability side of the balance sheet. *Deficiency reserves* are set up when improvements in the actuarial assumptions have brought the gross premium down below the valuation net premiums. When a valuation net level premium is used in the reserve formula that is larger than the gross level premium charged, the present value of future premiums is overstated, and therefore the reserve is understated. The deficiency reserve is an amount that adjusts for the difference and declines over the premium-paying period.

Substandard policy reserves are set up due to the anticipated additional mortality associated with individuals originally insured on a nonstandard basis. Companies vary as to the methods of setting these reserves. (In addition, state reserve laws generally require reserves to be set up for annuity contracts, accidental death benefits, waiver-of-premium benefits, adverse selection on group and term conversions and dividend accumulations among others. Voluntary reserves may be set up for various purposes.)

Nonforfeiture Values

Traditional life insurance contracts are required by law to contain a contractual provision making predetermined values available to the insured. (The state of Massachusetts enacted the first law on May 10, 1861 regulating the minimum amount to be returned to the policyholder upon surrender. All states enacted similar legislation by 1948.) These amounts, stipulated in the contract, are commonly referred to as *cash* or *surrender values*. Once the life insurance contract starts, these values may not be lowered. Nonforfeiture values arise from the operation of the leveling process. In the leveling process overpayments of the mortality cost in the early years plus interest added and a survivor benefit create an increasing amount of cash value in the life insurance contract, as illustrated in Chapter 22.

Nonforfeiture laws not only mandate the minimum values but also dictate the availability of alternative methods of using those inherent values. These alternatives are (1) the cash or loan value option, (2) the extended term option, and (3) a reduced-face-amount, paid-up insurance option. These options allow the insured to remove either all or some of the value in the contract. Also, the options provide for the continuation of some form of insurance even though premium payments may be discontinued. (Review the material in Chapter 10 that presents the legal aspects of the nonforfeiture options.)

Relationship Between the Reserve and the Surrender Value

When a policy owner surrendered a contract issued before 1948, many insurers returned the reserve amount less a surrender charge. The surrender charge allowed the insurer to recoup some of the expenses associated with selling the contract. Thus the reserve amount and the surrender amount were linked, arguably in an inequitable fashion. The reserve was designed to measure future liabilities of existing and continuing policies. On the other hand, nonforfeiture values are intended to measure an "equitable" settlement to those policy owners who either surrender their policy or stop paying premiums. This is the reason for uncoupling the reserve calculation and the nonforfeiture valuation.

Every state provides separate laws regulating the cash value or surrender value as well as the reserve amount of the life insurance contract. Reserve laws prescribe the interest rate, the mortality table and the reserving method used to generate minimum acceptable reserve liabilities.

In a similar manner nonforfeiture laws dictate the minimum cash value to be provided in life insurance contracts in an attempt to promote an equitable settlement. Nonforfeiture legislation specifies the maximum interest rate, the mortality table and the method to calculate the minimum cash value.

In the early years of the contract, life insurance companies are generally allowed to provide a cash value that is less than the reserve amount. The difference between the two amounts (reserve minus the cash value) is referred to as the *sur-*

render charge. In the later years of the contract the reserve and cash value are approximately equal. There are several reasons for providing nonforfeiture values that are less than the reserve amount in the early years: (1) the need to recapture expenses, (2) adverse mortality selection and (3) adverse financial selection.

The need to recapture expenses and make additions to surplus and to be compensated for adverse mortality selection and adverse financial selection all arise from the unilateral nature of the contract. Only one party to the contract must perform when a certain condition occurs: the life insurance company must pay a death benefit upon the death of the insured. However, the insured need not pay the premiums or perform any obligations unless continuance of the contract is desired. Thus there is considerable flexibility of action on the part of the policy owners, and they will tend to act to their advantage.

When the owner surrenders the contract, the life insurance company is at a disadvantage. Some expenses paid to produce and maintain the contract may never be recouped. From the point of view of equity the surrender charge contributes to the policy issuance and maintenance expenses that the life insurance company has not recaptured. Each life insurance contract, including those that lapse, should contribute to the surplus (profits) and costs of the life insurance company.

The life insurance company will also be at a disadvantage if the insureds select the periods to be insured. Individuals in good health who terminate their life insurance contract produce a cohort with higher than expected mortality cost. Thus the withdrawing policyholder should contribute to the expense of providing the insurance coverage to a pool of insureds that exhibit higher than expected mortality.

It is also argued that the surrender charge is justified on the basis of adverse financial selection. Adverse financial selection (called *disintermediation*) occurs when it is advantageous for the insureds to place life insurance premiums and/or cash value in an alternate investment. Instead of the life insurance company investing the funds at the highest available rates, the insureds do so; and the company forfeits investment earnings because its return is lowered to the policy loan rate. Also, if cash value is removed by the use of the cash or loan value option, the life insurance company may have to liquidate securities at depressed values to generate cash. For example, if interest rates are high, insureds could borrow the cash value at the low loan rate of interest and invest the money at a higher rate. If the life insurance company sells its fixed-dollar securities to create cash in a high-interest-rate environment, capital losses occur. (This process occurred frequently during the 1970s and was instrumental in the development of flexible loan rates and flexible-premium variable life insurance products.)

Laws Regulating Nonforfeiture Amounts

The NAIC Standard Nonforfeiture Law for Life Insurance has been adopted without significant changes in almost all states. The purpose of the nonforfeiture law is to force life insurance companies to include in applicable contracts nonforfeiture clauses at least as favorable as the ones contained in the legislation. Also, the nonforfeiture laws prescribe the method for calculating the minimum amount of cash value to be stated for each policy year. Part of Section 3 of the standard law states:

Chapter 23 Reserves, Nonforfeiture Values and Gross Premiums

Any cash surrender value under the policy . . . shall be an amount not less than the excess, if any, of the present value, on such anniversary, of the future guaranteed benefits which would have been provided for by the policy over the sum of (a) the then present value of the adjusted premiums . . . and (b) the amount of any indebtedness to the company on the policy.[3]

Thus, for life insurance, the minimum surrender (cash) value amount is calculated in two steps. In the first step the present value of the benefits provided by the contract on the anniversary date of valuation must be calculated. This number is equal to the net single premium for the contract in question on the valuation date. The mortality table and discount rate used in this calculation are prescribed by law, and these two factors depend on the contract's date of issue.

The second part of the calculation determines the present value of adjusted premiums. Section 5c of the Standard Nonforfeiture Law describes the method for calculating the adjusted premiums by the nonforfeiture net level premium method. The present value of the adjusted premiums is calculated in the same way as the net level premium except that the net single premium is increased by allowable expenses, and the sum is amortized over the term of the policy. The present value of the adjusted premiums is the sum of (1) the present value of the future benefits (NSP), (2) 1 percent of the uniform face amount and (3) 125 percent of the net level premium (maximum 4 percent of the amount of insurance). This sum is then leveled in a manner similar to the leveling process discussed earlier.

As a final step the present value of the future benefits on the valuation date is reduced by the present value of the adjusted level premiums on the valuation date. The result is the minimum surrender value to be provided by the contract for the year of valuation.

For example, if a $5,000 whole life insurance contract is sold to a male aged 30 (1980 CSO and 4 percent interest assumed), the minimum nonforfeiture value for the tenth year (valuation age 40) would be calculated as follows:

Step 1:
Present value future benefits (NSP), valuation date ($290.81 × 5) $1,454.05
Step 2:
Present value future benefits (NSP), date of issue ($209.18 × 5)   1,045.90
Allowable expense (.04 × 5,000 = $200.00 maximum)
    .01 × 5,000 = 50.00
    1.25 × 50.87 = 63.59

                                                                    113.59

Adjusted net single premium $1,159.49
Adjusted net level premium ($1,159.49 / 20.5611)   56.39
Present value of adjusted premiums, valuation date
(56.39 × 18.4389) $1,039.77

Nonforfeiture value ($1,454.05 − $1,039.77) $ 414.28

To review the calculation, the present value of future benefits on the valuation date is equal to the net single premium for the contract on the valuation date. The present value of future adjusted premiums was calculated in three steps. First, the adjusted single premium is calculated by adding allowable expenses to the net single premium. Second, the new adjusted single premium is leveled. This leveled amount amortizes the allowable expenses over the term of the contract. And third, the present value of the future adjusted level premiums is calculated by multiplying the adjusted level premium by the life annuity due factor calculated from age 40. The surrender value, or nonforfeiture value, for the 10th year is then equal to the present value of future benefits on the valuation date ($1,454.05) reduced by the present value of future adjusted premiums ($1,039.77).

Gross Premiums

The **gross premium** is the actual premium paid for the life insurance contract. The gross premium is derived after an analysis of the competition and of the life insurance company's cash needs. Besides paying for mortality costs, life insurance companies need money to pay for their overhead and taxes. Life insurance companies that are mutual companies also need to estimate dividends and expected amounts to be added to capital and surplus. Stock companies, on the other hand, need to pay dividends to stockholders and add to accumulated retained earnings.

Life insurance company expenses can be divided into three groups. The first group includes those expenses that occur when the policy is issued: (1) medical inspection costs, (2) commission expense, (3) premium tax and (4) underwriting. The second group of expenses arises out of the maintenance of the contract and includes (1) collection of premium, (2) record keeping, (3) contract changes and (4) policy loan activity. The third group of expenses occurs at maturity of the contract. The cost of settling the policy at the insured's death, or the cost of terminating the policy upon cash withdrawal, is included in this group. Clearly some expenses in these categories will vary according to the policy size, others will vary according to the length of the contract and still others will vary according to the number of specialized transactions that occur. Fixed expenses also exist regardless of the size, type, length or number of contracts written.

The expense amount to be added to the net premium in the form of loading can be determined in a variety of ways. Life insurance companies use techniques ranging from intensive study of the timing and amount of the expenses expected, resulting in complicated loading formulas, to the modification of existing rates to equal or beat competition. If the life insurance company uses the former, the process of calculating the gross premiums is similar to calculating the net single premium. The net single premium is equal to the present value of future benefits under the contract. And if the life insurance company estimates the timing and amount of the expense, the present value of the future expenses need only be added to the net single premium to derive the gross single premium. The result is leveled by the use of the leveling procedure.

If, on the other hand, the life insurance company simply modifies the current gross premiums, there must be a systematic determination of the actual costs to ascertain the financial impact of the change. If the new gross premium is inadequate to meet the cash needs of the firm, a redesign of the contract may be warranted.

Several changes can be made in insurance contracts as long as minimum or maximum requirements are not violated:

- The cash surrender amount can be lowered in earlier years as long as the amount is not less than specified by the nonforfeiture laws.
- The company can modify its actual investment philosophy and change the assumed investment rate of return.
- Underwriting criteria may be tightened, shifting the actual death rate of the group.
- Dividend or profit projections might be modified.

Regardless of the method used to determine the actual gross premium, the life insurance company must be assured that the premium paid by all insureds will generate sufficient funds to meet all the financial needs of the company, with excesses available to contribute to the surplus position.

Once the gross premium is tested for adequacy, the life insurance company may in the interest of equity modify the gross premium to allocate the expense burden among other policies. Because absolute equity in expense allocation is not possible, some life insurance companies charge a fixed policy fee (for example, $25) regardless of the size, type or length of the contract. This policy fee, paid only in the first year, is designed to partially compensate the insurance company for the fixed costs of underwriting and issuing the policy.

Life insurance companies also grade the premium according to the size of the contract. Many variable or nonfixed expenses do not increase proportionately to the face of the contract, such as the cost of the medical inspection, so quantity discounts are offered. The more life insurance purchased in one policy, the lower is the gross premium per $1,000 of coverage.

Asset Share Analysis Once the gross premium for a particular policy is calculated, the life insurance company must test the tentative gross premium to determine whether the premium generates sufficient cash flows for the company. **Asset share analysis** goes beyond merely investigating the adequacy of the cash flow to cover death claims. In addition, asset share techniques allow the life insurance company to analyze with relative ease changes in (1) assumed lapse rates, (2) investment assumptions, (3) mortality patterns, (4) participating dividends (in mutuals), (5) cash values (subject to statutory minimums) and (6) expense assumptions.

When the life insurance company develops and tests a gross premium, a balance must be struck between the company's realistic mortality, expense and investment assumptions and the conservative posture mandated by minimum reserve and nonforfeiture laws. Because of competitive pressure, the desire exists to provide low-premium, high-cash-value life insurance. A compromise must be made between the legal requirements (high liabilities) and lower premium amounts (low assets) to provide the "best" contract for the policyholder. In addition, changes in the capital and surplus position need attention because minimum capital and surplus requirements are imposed by the states to assure the continuance of the life insurance company by requiring a safety cushion of assets.

Asset share analysis provides the life insurance company with a method of "playing" with all of the variables individually or simultaneously to design a salable product and test its effect on the overall financial position of the company. Because of the repetitive yearly calculations made in this product analysis technique and because of the number of rows and columns required to perform the analysis, modern electronic spreadsheet programs can be utilized effectively. (Spreadsheet programs can be used efficiently to demonstrate the technique. Because of the number of plans and ages of issue, dedicated software is usually used for the analysis.)

The best way to discuss asset share analysis is to analyze a hypothetical life insurance policy using an electronic spreadsheet program. Table 23.3 presents the asset share analysis on a ten-year endowment policy. The tentative gross premium being tested is equal to $88.32 for each $1,000 of coverage. Because the purpose of this discussion is to demonstrate the use of this analytic tool, quantity discounts and other complicating factors will not be considered.

The number of insureds starting the group, the number of death claims expected to be paid and the number of insureds expected to surrender (lapse) the policy (columns B, C and D) must be estimated accurately.

The actual pattern of expenses to be attributable or charged to writing or selling the policy (column H) must also be estimated. One must consider the fixed costs associated with writing the policy, maintenance costs as a function of face amount and the costs associated with activity such as surrenders, beneficiary changes, premium collection and claims payment. The best estimate of the amount and the timing of these expenses is required for an accurate picture of the policy's impact on the finances of the company.

Dividend per $1,000 of face amount (column J) must be determined for each policy year only if the contract under consideration is participating; otherwise this amount is set at zero. Some mutual insurance companies publish illustrative dividend projections in promotional literature. If historic illustrations have underestimated or overestimated the dividend amount, an adjustment should be made for this fact.

The minimum legal nonforfeiture, surrender or cash value must be determined for each year of the proposed policy. Once this amount is determined, the contractual surrender value may be set at that level or may be increased, depending on the company's wishes.

The anticipated investment rate of return is selected. When this choice is made, statutory investment requirements must be considered along with the investment philosophy of the company. Regardless of the company's investment philosophy or the external statutory requirements influencing investment decisions, the analysis must reflect the best estimate of the rate of return. Life insurance companies tend to be conservative in their investments for many reasons. Among the reasons are statutory investment regulations and the need for safety of principal. Also, once the premium is contractually agreed to, it generally cannot be changed if

Chapter 23 Reserves, Nonforfeiture Values and Gross Premiums

Table 23.3
Asset Share Analysis: 10-Year Endowment, Male, Age 30

A Policy Year	B Beginning Number of Living Insureds	C Number of Deaths	D Number of Withdrawals	E Number of Insureds End of Year B − C − D	F Fund at Beginning of Year
1	948.00	2.00	90.00	856.00	$ 0.00
2	856.00	2.10	45.00	808.90	41,070.73
3	808.90	2.10	37.00	769.80	112,831.86
4	769.80	2.20	24.00	743.60	181,176.98
5	743.60	2.30	20.00	721.30	249,830.74
6	721.30	2.40	15.00	703.90	318,658.64
7	703.90	2.50	12.00	689.40	389,033.43
8	689.40	2.60	8.00	678.80	461,580.70
9	678.80	2.80	4.00	672.00	537,540.76
10	672.00	3.00	2.00	667.00	618,292.22

A Policy Year	G Premium Added: Premium × B	H Expenses per Insured	I Total Expenses B × H	J Dividend per Insured	K Total Dividend E × J
1	$83,727.36	$45.00	$42,660.00	$0.00	$ 0.00
2	75,601.92	3.00	2,568.00	1.07	865.52
3	71,442.05	3.00	2,426.70	1.09	839.08
4	67,988.74	3.00	2,309.40	1.11	825.40
5	65,674.75	3.00	2,230.80	1.14	822.28
6	63,705.22	3.00	2,163.90	1.16	816.52
7	62,168.45	3.00	2,111.70	1.18	813.49
8	60,887.81	3.00	2,068.20	1.20	814.56
9	59,951.62	3.00	2,036.40	1.23	826.56
10	59,351.04	3.00	2,016.00	1.25	833.75

A Policy Year	L Claims $1,000 × C	M Cash Value	N Dollars Paid from Withdrawals D × M	O Interest Earned .05 × [F + G − I − .5L]	P Balance End of year F − G − I − K − L − N + O
1	$2,000.00	$ 0.00	$ 0.00	$ 2,003.37	$ 41,070.73
2	2,100.00	88.00	3,960.00	5,652.73	112,831.86
3	2,100.00	183.00	6,771.00	9,039.86	181,176.98
4	2,200.00	262.00	6,288.00	12,287.82	249,830.74
5	2,300.00	355.00	7,100.00	15,606.23	318,658.64
6	2,400.00	460.00	6,900.00	18,950.00	389,033.43
7	2,500.00	549.00	6,588.00	22,392.01	461,580.70
8	2,600.00	675.00	5,400.00	25,955.02	537,540.76
9	2,800.00	810.00	3,240.00	29,702.80	618,292.22
10	3,000.00	890.00	1,780.00	33,706.36	703,719.87

Table 23.3 (continued)
Asset Share Analysis: 10-Year Endowment, Male, Age 30

A	Q	R	S	T
Policy Year	Asset Share P/E	Terminal Reserve	Surplus per Insured Q − R	Surrender Contribution per Insured Q − M
1	$ 47.98	$ 82.54	($34.56)	$ 47.98
2	139.49	168.51	(29.02)	51.49
3	235.36	258.07	(22.71)	52.36
4	335.97	351.38	(15.41)	73.97
5	441.78	448.61	(6.83)	86.78
6	552.68	549.91	2.77	92.68
7	669.54	655.49	14.05	120.54
8	791.90	765.54	26.36	116.90
9	920.08	880.30	39.78	110.08
10	1,055.05	1,000.00	55.05	165.05

Premium tested = 88.32 per thousand
The purpose of this analysis is to illustrate the technique. The numbers will vary depending on actuarial assumptions, the design of the policy and statutory requirements.

additional funds are required to make good on contractual promises. (Adjustments may be made within limits in current-assumption life and universal life types of policies. Dividends changes based partially on investment performance occur.) Because of this inability to raise premiums at will, the investment rate of return can be considered to be equal to the minimum rate of return expected on investments over the life of the contract (possibly 100 or more years). If any of the assumptions are incorrect, the cash flow projections will be faulty. The analysis is only as good as the accuracy of the assumptions made.

The reader should be aware that the cash value or surrender value amounts in column M are for illustrative purposes only and are not intended to be used for product comparison purposes.

Investment income flowing into the life insurance company is calculated in column O. Five percent is assumed to be earned on total assets held at the beginning of the year plus any premiums paid (F + G). This amount is reduced by any expenses paid at the beginning of the year (F + G − I) and also by one-half of the death claims (F + G − I − .5L). Investment income is earned on one-half of the claims amount because the timing of the payments is assumed to be distributed equally throughout the year. On the average, therefore, one-half of the claims amount will be available for investment for the whole year.

The asset share amount attributable to each surviving insured (Q) is calculated by dividing the end-of-year total asset balance (P) by the number of insureds persisting at the end of each year (E). Column R, the minimum legal reserve amount, is calculated and inserted in the column for each policy year. The reserve amount determined for each policy year is a function of the mortality table, the investment rate and the reserve method required by individual state statutes. The numbers provided in column R are for illustrative purposes only and should not be used for accurate ten-year endowment reserve amounts.

Additions or subtractions to the life insurance company's capital and surplus balance sheet accounts are determined in column S, surplus per insured. This amount is calculated by subtracting from the required reserve (R) the amount representing the asset share per person (Q). The life insurance company, in making the asset share analysis, finds it important to focus on this column, which summarizes the proposed policy's impact on the financial position of the firm.

In essence the surplus per insured (S) is equal to the amount of money on a yearly basis that is added to, or subtracted from, the capital and surplus position of the company. In designing the product, if the company feels that the reduction in capital for each policy written is too much, or that additions are being made too late, then the premium and/or assumptions may be changed to satisfy financial requirements. The life insurance company can also estimate the maximum number of policies (face amount) that can be written given the company's tolerance for capital shrinkage.

In addition to these points, the company can determine if the proposed policy will contribute to the overall value of the firm. If the sum of the additions is greater than the sum of the reductions (ignoring the time value of money), then the capital and surplus accounts will increase due to writing the contract. Otherwise the overall value of the firm will be reduced.

The final column, the contribution to surplus upon withdrawal (T), is calculated by taking the asset share per insured (Q) and subtracting the cash or surrender value amount (M). This column gives the life insurance company an indication of the amount of money that is "forfeited" by the insured when a surrender takes place. This column provides information on the dependency of withdrawals to provide cash for the group. If the numbers in this column are low, then the surrender charge is not contributing very much to the assets of the group, and any change in the withdrawal rate would not cause serious financial problems. On the other hand, if the numbers in this column are relatively large, the company is relying heavily on the assumed withdrawal rate to produce cash for the needs of the company. If the withdrawal rate is higher than expected, the value of the proposed contract to the company may be overstated, depending on the actual results.

By studying the preceding example and manipulating the assumptions employed in the spreadsheet, readers can develop an appreciation for the value of asset share analysis in determining the financial impact on a life insurer if the proposed policy is issued.

Review Questions

1. What is the policyholder reserve? Why must an insurer calculate the reserve amount and place it as a liability on the balance sheet?
2. Define how to calculate the terminal reserve amount on a retrospective basis and a prospective basis. Why do both of these methods result in the same amount of terminal reserve?

3. What is a survivorship benefit? How does it arise, and whom does it benefit?
4. Graph and compare the expected reserve patterns of the following policies: (1) ten-year term, (2) ten-year endowment, (3) continuous-premium whole life, (4) ten-pay whole life and (5) whole life paid up at age 65.
5. Explain how the reserve pattern for whole life insurance continually increases even while premiums are underpaying mortality expense in the later years.
6. List the factors affecting the size of the policyholder reserve amount.
7. What is the difference between full valuation reserves and modified reserves?
8. Why are modified reserve methods used in the valuation of policyholder reserves?
9. Explain the relationship between the policyholder reserve and the cash value amount provided as a nonforfeiture value.
10. What methods are used in determining the gross premium amount?
11. What is asset share analysis? Why must the insured use accurate estimates of death rates, lapse rates, dividend rates and interest earnings while testing a tentative gross premium? Which values used in the asset share analysis are set by law? How are gross life insurance rates regulated? (Hint: Which values are regulated by statute?)

Endnotes

[1] NAIC Standard Valuation Law, Model Regulation Service, April 1981, pp. 820–827.

[2] *Ibid*.

[3] NAIC Standard Nonforfeiture Law for Life Insurance, Model Regulation Service, April 1981, pp. 810–812.

Bibliography

Batten, Robert W. *Mortality Table Construction*, Englewood Cliffs, N.J.: Prentice-Hall, 1978.

Harper, Floyd S., and Lewis C. Workman. *Fundamental Mathematics of Life Insurance*. Homewood, Ill.: Richard D. Irwin, 1970.

Huebner, S.S., and Kenneth Black, Jr. *Life Insurance*. 11th ed. Englewood Cliffs, N.J.: Prentice-Hall, 1987.

Jordan, C.W. *Life Contingencies*. 2d ed. Chicago: Society of Actuaries, 1967.

Pedoe, Arthur, and Colin E. Jack. *Life Insurance, Annuities and Pensions*. 3d ed. Toronto: University of Toronto Press, 1978.

Chapter 24: Life Insurance Operations: Organization, Underwriting, Marketing and Reinsurance

Chapter Objectives

- Describe the methods used in organizing life insurance companies
- Provide an overview of the internal structure of life insurance companies
- Discuss how life insurance companies underwrite new business, distribute their product and compensate their agents
- Introduce the topic of reinsurance

Introduction

This chapter focuses on how insurance companies organize and how they operate in the areas of underwriting, product distribution and agent compensation. The different legal ways life insurance companies organize influence control, capital formation and the cost of the life insurance companies' products. Investigating company operations provides insight into how the organization provides products to consumers. The chapter also introduces the subject of reinsurance to describe how insurers handle unwanted risk.

Life Insurance Company Organization

Currently more than 2,300 companies sell life insurance in the United States.[1] Most of the companies organize as either **stock** or **mutual companies.** In addition, mutual savings banks, fraternal organizations, guarantee capital insurers and the U.S. government sell life insurance. (Guarantee capital life insurers provide a very small proportion of life insurance. New York Insurance Code Section 7310 describes the guarantee capital life insurer.) Table 24.1 presents the amount and relative proportion of life insurance in force in 1989 by source of coverage. Table 24.1 also presents the number of mutual and stock companies and their respective total assets. Note the number of mutual companies compared to the number of stock companies and the average life insurance face amount in force per company.

Table 24.1
Life Insurance Company Selected Data, 1989

Legal Reserve Type	Dollars (billions) in force	Percent of Total	Number Organized	Average in Force per Company ($ Billions)
Stock	6,347.5	60.1	2,188	2.90
Mutual	3,993.4	37.8	117	34.13
Fraternal	161.7			
Savings Bank:				
Connecticut	3.0	†		
Massachusetts	9.4	†		
New York	16.5	†		
Veterans Life*	26.8	†		
Total	10,558.3	100.0		

*Includes U.S. government Life Insurance (World War I), National Service Life Insurance (World War II and the Insurance Act of 1951).
†Less than 1%.

Stock and mutual insurance companies sell approximately 98 percent of the life insurance coverage in the United States. Fraternal organizations, mutual savings banks and the U.S. government (through various federal programs) provide the remaining 2 percent. Fraternal organizations are similar to mutual life insurance companies (discussed later). They employ a "lodge system" with current or historical ritualistic form, there is less state regulation and they enjoy a federal and state tax-free status. Savings bank life insurance (SBLI) exists currently in the states of Connecticut, Massachusetts and New York and provides limited amounts of individual life insurance. U.S. government sources of life insurance include coverage for veterans under U.S. government Life Insurance and National Service Life Insurance (World War I and II, respectively), Servicemen's Group Life Insurance (SGLI) for individuals currently in the uniformed services and Veterans' Group Life Insurance (VGLI).

Because of the small amount of life insurance written by fraternal organizations, mutual savings banks and the U.S. government, this discussion focuses mainly on the stock and mutual company forms.

Stock and Mutual Company Organization

Stock and mutual insurance companies are similar in many respects. Both are corporations, engage in essentially the same financial and investment activities and use the same distribution methods. They have different objectives, different paths of corporate control and different dividend distribution schemes.

Objectives

The stated objectives of stock and mutual life insurance companies differ. The objective of the stock company is to maximize the wealth of its stockholders, who own the company's capital stock. The stated objective of the mutual insurance company is to minimize the policyholders' cost and provide insurance on a not-for-profit basis. (Not-for-profit organizations are not necessarily charities enjoying favorable tax status. Mutual companies are not charities and do not enjoy a nontaxable status.)

Stock companies pursue the goal of maximizing the wealth of the stockholders by increasing earnings per share, dividends per share or the expected growth of the value of the stock. Mutuals pursue the goal of minimizing cost by paying to the policyholder dividend amounts based on the performance of the insurance company. Therefore, if mortality or overhead expenses decrease or investment performance increases, policyholder dividends will increase if the board of directors declares the dividend. The increase in policyholder dividends reduces the cost of the product to the owners. The opposite occurs if costs increase or investment returns decrease: policyholder costs increase.

Control

Mutual and stock insurance companies differ with respect to control. In a stock insurance company stockholders supply the initial capital and add to the capital base through retained earnings from operations (undistributed earnings). In return the stockholders receive a proportionate share of ownership, the right to receive dividends and the right to vote for the board of directors. The board in turn elects the officers of the corporation. Theoretical control and actual control of stock insurers may not be the same. Sufficient votes held by few shareholders, coupled with shareholders who fail to vote or who automatically return proxies favoring existing management, may produce sufficient leverage for a few individuals to control corporate activities.

In a mutual company policy owners contribute undivided earnings or surplus. These amounts are equivalent to undistributed policy owners' dividends. Policy owners vote for the board of directors, which in turn elects the officers of the company. Because of the low participation during annual meetings and the low rate of proxy return, mutual companies—like stock companies—can be controlled by a few people, who often are officers. For example, in a recent board of directors election of the Equitable Life Assurance Society, out of one million policyholders representing $250 billion of life insurance, 12,000 policy owners voted by mail and three people voted in person. One-third of the board was elected.[2]

Contributions to the company in the form of retained earnings and paid-in capital (stock) or in the form of undivided earnings or surplus (mutual) serve the same purpose. Regardless of the form of ownership or the title given to the net worth accounts of the company, this amount supplies a safety cushion for policy owners against adverse operating results. If assets shrink because of adverse operating results or through investment losses, the net worth gives policyholders a margin of safety before liabilities exceed assets.

Participating Versus Nonparticipating Contracts

Participating (par) contracts give policyholders the right to receive dividends. As noted in Chapter 6, the premium for a participating contract is usually higher than for a comparable **nonparticipating** (nonpar) policy. Companies issuing participating contracts charge conservative (higher) premiums as a measure of safety against adverse results. The insured receives the excess over the amount required to provide the insurance coverage as a year-end dividend. The participating dividend is not taxable income. All mutual insurance companies and a few stock insurance companies pay policyholders dividends based on the insurance company's experience with expenses, underwriting and investment. Stock insurance companies are more likely to sell indeterminate life or current-assumption life insurance contracts. The premiums for these contracts are adjusted periodically based on the current mortality and overhead expenses of the company and the expected investment performance. When a mutual converts to a stock form, participating dividends are still paid on the original participating policies. If expenses and losses are lower than expected or investment performance is better than expected, the board of directors may increase dividend amounts. The opposite will occur if expenses and losses exceed expectations or investment performance is poor. In addition, the dividend amount depends on the specific formula used to allocate the **divisible surplus.**

The Demutualization Issue

As noted in Chapter 1, many changes affecting the life insurance industry occurred in the past 20 years. The popularity of whole life insurance fell as the demand for term insurance, deferred annuities and other interest-sensitive life insurance products increased. Recent tax law changes encourage individuals to save through tax-advantaged investments. Federal income taxation of life insurance companies changed, placing a higher tax burden on the mutuals. And there is a growing awareness of the importance of financial planning in an increasingly uncertain environment. Some mutual insurers feel the challenges of the 1990s affect them more severely than stock insurance companies, because stock insurers often raise capital for corporate purposes through the sale of securities, while mutual insurers cannot.

A few mutuals have converted to the stock form, and others are considering converting to position the company for future competition. The following outline describes several advantages and disadvantages of **demutualization**—the process of changing a mutual insurance company to a stock insurance company.[3]

Advantages of Demutualization

1. Ability to Raise Venture Capital. Mutual insurance companies raise capital by borrowing, generating underwriting gains and realizing investment income. Stock insurance companies generate capital by these means and by selling equity securities or long-term debt issues. Equity securities include common and preferred stock. Because of the existence of stockholders and bondholders in the stock form, the financial market imposes discipline on the organization through market prices. (Many securities are privately placed and may not trade in an active and public financial market.) There is no direct financial market discipline through stock price with the mutual form. However, several rating organizations measure various aspects of claims-paying ability and financial strength of all insurers.

2. Improves Financial Statements. Stock insurance companies use generally accepted accounting principles (GAAP), while mutual insurance companies currently use statutory accounting principles. **Statutory accounting principles**

present a conservative picture of the insurance company's financial position and are used for reporting financial results to state regulators. GAAP accounting presents a more realistic picture of the performance and financial position of the life insurance company for investor purposes and is an additional statement required by the Securities and Exchange Commission.

3. Reduction of Federal Tax Burden. The Deficit Reduction Act of 1984 and subsequent tax changes have modified the manner in which life insurance companies are taxed. Through tax law changes the share of industry taxes on mutuals has increased. Previously stock insurance companies could not deduct dividends paid to shareholders, while mutuals deduct dividends paid to policyholders. This procedure gave mutuals a competitive advantage. Stock insurance companies still cannot deduct dividends. And through a complex formula mutuals must now reduce the amount of dividends deducted for tax purposes, thus increasing the amount of taxes paid. The 1984 act did not produce the expected amount of federal tax desired (expected $9.5 billion, paid $7.2 billion). The proportion of the tax paid by the stock and mutual companies also did not come out as expected (1985 and 1986 expected: mutuals, 55 percent, stocks, 45 percent; actual: mutuals, 39 percent, stocks 61 percent. Hearings were held on the subject of insurance company taxation before the Subcommittee on Select Revenue Measures of the Committee on Ways and Means on October 19, 1989.[4]

4. Availability of Stock Incentives. Stock insurance companies have an advantage in attracting and retaining key personnel because they may offer stock options and payroll-based stock ownership plans to officers, directors and employees.[5]

5. Corporate Expansion. Stock insurance companies have an advantage over mutuals because the purchase or sale of their stock facilitates growth through diversification or acquisition. In addition, stock insurance companies can create upstream or downstream holding companies, while mutual insurance companies may acquire other organizations only through exchange of money or notes. An upstream holding company enables expansion in other businesses without extensive regulation from state insurance departments.

Disadvantages of Demutualization

1. Cost of Demutualization. The cost of solving all the complex problems associated with changing the company's legal form is great. Calculating the policyholders' share of surplus, determining the manner of distribution and coping with legal, regulatory and tax problems are all difficult issues considering the vested interests or stakeholders involved.

2. Federal Regulation. Once the mutual insurance company changes to a stock company, it must comply with federal security laws. Compliance includes meeting the reporting and communication requirements of the SEC, including providing owners with annual and quarterly financial reports and shareholder proxy statements and making annual SEC reports. Mutuals are not subject to these SEC requirements.

3. Creates Takeover Target. Any stock company is a target for acquisition by the purchase of a controlling amount or a majority of available common stock through hostile or friendly means. (A hostile merger or acquisition occurs without the target company's board of director's consent.) Becoming a stock insurance company creates the risk of an unfriendly takeover. Life insurance companies may be a likely target of an acquisition to diversify operations, to expand an existing product line or merely to increase the organization's size.

The issues involved in demutualization are complex because actuarial, regulatory and tax issues must be addressed. Only a few states currently have statutory procedures for conversion. (Not only do mutual insurance companies change to stock insurance companies, but conversions occur between other types.)[6] Union Mutual filed a plan (January 2, 1985) with Maine's superintendent of insurance to start a two-year process of changing from a mutual to a stock insurance company. The resulting company is UNUM. As of this writing several mutual insurance companies are considering demutualization, including one of the largest mutual insurance companies, the Equitable Life Assurance Society.

Internal Structure of Life Insurance Companies

To operate successfully, the typical life and health insurance company must operate with the following functional areas:

- Actuarial
- Marketing
- Underwriting
- Policyholder Services and Claims
- Investments
- Legal

Additional areas may include human resources, information systems, accounting, finance, forecasting and shareholder services. All departments must efficiently coordinate their functions. The following paragraphs introduce the functional areas, then several are explored in more detail in this and the following chapter.

Actuarial. Actuaries develop and price products and establish surrender, nonforfeiture and loan values. The actuary tries to accurately estimate mortality and morbidity rates and patterns and develops classification schemes to rate exposures properly. In addition, actuaries assess the adequacy of reserves, calculate dividends and estimate the profitability of the insurer's product lines. In general, the actuary's responsibility is to make sure all insurance operations function on an actuarially or mathematically sound basis.

Marketing. Once the product and its prices are developed, the distribution process begins by marketing. The primary function of the marketing department is to build and maintain viable marketing and distribution channels for their products. Marketing department activities include but are not limited to:

- training, educating and motivating people in the distribution chain;
- collecting and analyzing market data;
- helping in the development or revision of products to meet identified needs; and
- developing promotional material or campaigns in support of the sales force.

Underwriting. The sales agents send the insurance applications to the home or branch office for proper underwriting. The underwriting department's responsibility is to classify all applicants correctly and charge rates appropriate to the given risk. That is, the underwriter collects all relevant information and makes an analysis of the factors that influence the applicant's expected mortality or morbidity. Modifications to the basic rate reflect the applicant's good and bad qualities, resulting in the rate charged. Underwriters also help to arrange reinsurance. (A more detailed discussion of underwriting and reinsurance follows.)

Policyholder Services and Claims. After the policy goes into effect, the policyholder services and claims department provides essential activities for beneficiaries (after the insured's death) and policy owners (before the policy matures as a death claim). The claims department does what is necessary to process death claims in a legal manner and in accordance with the contract's beneficiary designation or other contractual promise. The insurer is also involved in a variety of quality-of-care issues when paying health-related benefits. Insurers are becoming more involved in all aspects of managing health care. These activities include case management, utilization review, preauthorized admissions and the use of primary care physicians as coordinators of patient's health care. A necessary part of this function is to verify the validity of any claim and protect the company against fraud. If death occurs (in life insurance) within the contestable period, the underwriting department may be asked to review the application for a possible contest of the claim. (The insurance industry occasionally has been criticized for the practice of "post claim" underwriting. This criticism recently surfaced in the area of long-term care. Policies are sold without proper underwriting, then claims are contested after submission.) And, if the case goes to court, a claims administration representative may have to be present at any proceedings. Medical claims are scrutinized carefully for fraud and nonfraudulent overcharges.

The policyholder service department is responsible for any changes in the insurance policy during an insured's lifetime or the policy's term. For life insurance contracts these contract changes include administering policyholder loans and withdrawals, processing surrenders, changing the beneficiary designation, changing the ownership of the contract, adjusting the premium payment plan, changing dividend options and selecting nonforfeiture options.

Investments. Selling life, disability and health insurance contracts requires the collection of funds or reserves from many insureds in anticipation of future claims. The investment department is responsible for investing these funds consistent with the insurer's investment policy, state and federal laws and regulations. These funds and other assets are invested to generate positive rates of return consistent with the company's investment philosophy (risk, return, type and horizon) and projections for the need for liquid funds. Investing funds for future obligations allows insurers to reduce premium costs in anticipation of investment returns and provides a cushion against unexpected poor results. Investments are made in a variety of financial and hard assets including stocks, bonds, money market funds, real estate and mortgage loans. Various state regulations, in the interest of keeping companies solvent, greatly influence life insurance company investment decisions.

Legal. The legal department provides a variety of services to all the functional areas of the organization. The law is one of the "threads" that bind and border the activities of the actuarial, marketing, underwriting, policyholder services and claims and investment departments. Principally the legal department makes sure that all insurance operations comply with federal, state and local laws. Legal compliance by all the departments is essential. In addition, the legal department provides general counsel on corporate activities, human resource management, policyholder litigation and moral issues. The department also participates in the development of new products and monitors federal, state and local legislation.

Life Insurance Underwriting

Underwriting is the process of considering each insurance application, resulting in either rejecting or accepting the application or making a counteroffer. If the exposure is acceptable, the premium collected must fairly represent the cost of the coverage. The main goal of the underwriter is to accept a profitable pool of exposures; it is not to select only those applicants exhibiting the best characteristics of insurability. Thus the function of the underwriter is to classify and charge the applicant a fair premium based on predetermined statistics and judgment. If a large number of the applicants conform to the applied statistical assumptions, the total dollar amount of losses will approximate anticipated amounts, providing a profitable insurance pool.

It is important to make sure the company charges a "fair" premium because fair premiums tend to minimize selection against the insurer. If applicants perceive the contract as priced high compared to what other life insurance companies offer, they will seek coverage elsewhere. On the other hand, if the price is low, people will be attracted by it. An unsound financial position will result if the price is inadequate to cover all costs. Underwriters should be aware of whether the application was the result of an agent's solicitation. Unsolicited applications, as a whole, tend to exhibit higher than expected mortality. If applicants experiencing higher than expected mortality purchase insurance coverage at standard rates, the life insurance company will suffer underwriting losses.

Underwriting Criteria Life insurance underwriters decide on insurability and the rate charged based on predetermined patterns of mortality. The same is true for health insurance, except the contingency insured is morbidity. In annuity contracts the contingency is survival. Life insurance underwriters consider age, gender, health and occupation as prime determinants of loss expectancy. Other factors such as place of residence and travel plans, family history, financial position and the type of insurance plan sought are also relevant.

Age

Age is the primary rating criterion for life insurance. Groups of older applicants have greater death rates than groups of younger people. Many life insurance companies limit coverage to applicants over certain ages. (*See* Chapter 21 for a discussion of mortality table construction and interpretation.) For example, some life insurance companies will not write life insurance on infants until a short waiting period has elapsed. This practice avoids the high infant mortality rates in the first three to six months of life. In addition, some life insurance companies place limits on the insured's age for the purchase of term or whole life insurance. Because of the required high premium charged at advanced ages, underwriters try to identify people who cannot afford the coverage; they produce high lapse rates. Underwriters also try to eliminate people seeking coverage when they need it (adverse selection), even when they are willing to pay a high price. Though underwriters recognize these tendencies, some life insurance companies adjust the rates for the higher expected mortality and lapse rates and sell insurance to almost anybody requesting the coverage.

Gender

Gender is a determinant of mortality, morbidity and survival rates. Women live longer than men; thus the rate charged for life insurance should be lower and the rates charged for annuities higher for women. Women born in 1990 can expect to live about seven years longer than men. Underwriters impose the same underwriting rules on both women and men. There should be no sex discrimination that cannot be justified by sound statistical and actuarial practices. However, in pension plans sex discrimination is illegal, as explained in Chapter 19.[7] Several states—including Hawaii, North Carolina, Massachusetts and Michigan—require unisex rates for automobile coverage, while in Montana gender-based rates are not allowed for any coverage.[8] A few insurance companies for certain types of coverage (such as credit life and disability) have not used gender-based rates for many years, while some insurance companies have voluntarily shifted to unisex pricing in recent years.

Health

An individual's health and family history are predictive of future mortality and morbidity rates. An individual must be charged more or denied coverage when an illness or physical impairment exists that shortens the expected life span or significantly increases the chances that an accident may result in early death. Family history may provide valuable information concerning genetic predispositions. (Many insurers are currently investigating the ethics, accuracy and feasibility of genetic testing as an indicator of longevity.)

Besides writing life insurance based on medical reports, many life insurance companies issue coverage on a nonmedical basis. Underwriting rules generally limit *nonmedical life insurance* to certain ages and place limits on the amount of coverage sold.

Occupation

When an applicant engages in an occupation considered hazardous, life insurance companies charge higher premiums. Hazardous occupations include roofing, crop dusting and lumbering. Occupation not only affects the rate charged but also influences the availability and price of the disability income rider, the waiver-of-premium rider and accidental death benefits.

Besides occupation, an applicant's avocations are important. Auto racing, skydiving, skin diving, hang gliding and private aviation, among others activities, influence the applicant's expected mortality rate and are included in any underwriting consideration.

Other Factors

Underwriters also tend to consider the applicant's residence, financial position, any indication of bad morals and the type of insurance plan requested. (Private investigators or other investigative agencies may be used to report on these and other factors.) Quality of hygiene, health maintenance and the level of health care in the different areas of the world influence mortality and morbidity rates. Many insurance companies currently screen insureds for AIDS (acquired immunodeficiency syndrome). Where a person currently lives and any plans for future travel are important in determining life insurance rates.

An applicant's financial position provides insight into the motives for the insurance purchase. Underwriters make sure the total of owned insurance plus the amounts requested seem reasonable, considering the amount of income earned to support the premium and the need for the coverage. Moreover, the underwriter must be assured that a moral hazard is not being created by the issuance of unwarranted additional coverage.

Sources of Underwriting Information

The primary source of underwriting information is the application. The applicant and the life insurance agent both fill out or complete the application. Besides providing the insured's age, sex and other personal data, the application identifies the plan of insurance desired and beneficiary information. The application also may contain questions relating to the applicant's medical history. If the insurance requires a medical exam, a supplemental statement is provided by the professional performing the examination. Other sources of information include the agent's certification or statement, commercially available inspection reports and the Medical Information Bureau (discussed shortly).

The agent's statement provides information such as the length of time the agent has known the applicant; an opinion about the applicant's financial status, habits and character; and an estimate of the proportion of annual income spent on life insurance premiums.

Life insurance companies may hire independent commercial credit inspection companies to report on the character, habits, marital status and life-style of the applicant. Typically these reporting companies check their current records for historical information and contact the insured's friends, neighbors, relatives and employers for information.

Besides the sources of information provided by the medical examination, agent's report and inspection report, many life insurance companies belong to the **Medical Information Bureau, Inc. (MIB).** The MIB is a nonprofit association of life insurance companies formed in 1902 to exchange underwriting information among its member companies. The original and current purpose of this organization is to prevent fraud and misrepresentation against life insurance companies. Currently more than 750 life insurance companies belong to the MIB. These companies underwrite approximately 97 percent of the annual life insurance coverage sold in the United States and Canada.

MIB members report the results of any medical investigation on the applicant. Medical and nonmedical information is confidential and disclosed only to member companies. Member companies do not report the outcome of a company's underwriting process to the MIB, and therefore other member companies will not know whether the company issued the coverage requested or rated it above standard. Credit organizations, nonmembers and government agencies cannot access the information without authorization from the applicant or without a court order. Even member companies cannot request the information unless the applicant has provided written consent to release it.

Information obtained from the MIB and credit reporting services, the individual's application, the agent's certification and the medical report usually supply the underwriter with sufficient information to make proper selection and classification.

Privacy and Underwriting Information

The sensitive nature of underwriting information and the methods used for collecting information generate concern for protecting an individual's privacy. The need of underwriters to know relevant underwriting information must be balanced with an individual's right to privacy. Ideally life insurance applicants should allow legitimate information-gathering activities. In return for allowing the collection of private information, individuals must be allowed the opportunity to correct misinformation and know the data will be communicated to other parties only with their consent.

The Fair Credit Reporting Act of 1971 (FCRA) and the Federal Privacy Act of 1974 (FPA) were passed to protect an individual's right to privacy. The FCRA provides life insurance companies with guidelines and procedures for collecting underwriting information. Life insurance companies must inform the applicant that an investigation may be made into the applicant's health, character and other aspects of personal life. If any collected information results in declining the contract or causes it to be offered at a higher price, the source of the relevant data must be disclosed. The applicant then may inspect the file and go through the credit bureau's process to correct any misinformation.

The FPA set standards for federal agencies' information collection activities. Federal agencies are responsible for the relevance and accuracy of information collected. Further, federal agencies must allow citizens to inspect and correct any misinformation. Also, the FPA created the Privacy Protection Study Commission (PPSC). The PPSC conducted a two-year study into all abuses or violations (past, present and potential) of privacy in the private or public sectors. The study (completed in 1977) made many recommendations concerning the insurance industry. As a result a federal bill (the Fair Insurance Information Practices Act) was proposed to correct the many problems uncovered by the PPSC.[9] This legislation was never enacted.

Currently most of the states address the issue of privacy in the insurance industry through a version of the NAIC Insurance Information and Privacy Protection Model Act. This act requires that applicants for life insurance receive written notice disclosing the anticipated sources and methods of collecting information, the type of information sought and the people likely to receive the information. The type of information gathered must conform to the type spelled out in the written disclosure, and pretext interviews are generally not allowed. A pretext interview occurs when the information collector impersonates relatives or other individuals to get candid responses. Yet pretext interviews are considered fair when the investigation is looking into fraud. Under the model bill, when a rejection occurs or the policy is issued at substandard rates, the applicant must be informed of the reasons for the action and the source of the information causing the result. The applicant then has the right to inspect and correct any misinformation. Any information collected generally cannot be disclosed without the individual's consent.

Rating Life Insurance

Once the underwriter collects the appropriate data, proper classification of the insured results in an appropriate rate accurately reflecting expected mortality. Life insurance companies use a variety of rating methods, but *class* and *numerical rating* schemes are common. In a class rating scheme the underwriter bases the rates on an array of characteristics such as age, sex, normal weight and height and freedom from medical problems. When the insured meets underwriting rules, the company charges standard class rates. When the insured is not acceptable at the class rates, senior actuaries can be consulted to determine acceptability and price.

In a numerical rating system the applicant is initially assigned 100 points. Based on the life insurance company's experience, the underwriter will debit (add to) or credit (subtract from) the 100 points for good and bad characteristics. The debit or credit assigned reflects the percent of deviation from normal mortality. For example, if an applicant does not smoke, a credit of 15 results in a score of 85. This means that mortality experience is expected to be 85 percent of the company's norm. After the underwriter awards credits and debits for all relevant factors, the resulting score is compared to acceptable limits. If the numerical score is less than required for standard rates, the applicant is accepted as standard. Otherwise, substandard, extrahazard or rated policies may be written or the application may be declined.

Rating Substandard Lives

Life insurance companies use various methods to rate nonstandard applications. Extra (above-average) mortality can exhibit different patterns over a person's life. Underwriters must be aware of the different patterns and use a rating method that properly reflects the incidence of higher mortality. Three patterns of mortality increases are generally recognized. First, an additional constant mortality rate may be expected regardless of the insured's age. This would be the case if the applicant is a race car driver or a skydiver. The life insurance company may anticipate five extra deaths each year out of 1,000 insureds who engage in these activities. Second, mortality may temporarily increase, then decline over a short period until the expected approaches standard mortality. This might be the typical pattern for mortality after major surgery. Third, extra mortality may be anticipated with the mortality rate increasing with age. This pattern is characteristic of a person who has diabetes, is overweight or has chronic high blood pressure.

Among the techniques used to increase charges for substandard risks, insurance companies can add a flat additional premium, add years to the applicant's actual age, place the insured in a lower dividend class (if the policy is participating) or use extra premium tables.

Flat Additional Premium. A flat additional premium can be used to pay for a constant shift (increase) in the expected mortality of a group of applicants exhibiting a certain characteristic. For example, certain hazardous occupations, such as crop dusting and lumbering, experience increased mortality at a constant rate regardless of the applicant's age. The flat additional premium generally continues until the additional mortality exposure abates. The flat extra premium also may be used on a temporary basis where there is initial extra mortality but the rate approaches normal over a short period (e.g., surgery).

Though the flat additional premium approach is easy to understand, explain and administer, the mortality loading increases over time because the technique of adding a flat extra premium compensates for a decreasing net amount at risk (face amount minus cash value). Thus, to calculate the additional mortality loading accurately, a net level premium calculation as illustrated in Chapters 21 and 22 would have to be made based on the expected higher mortality rates.

Increased Rating Age. Increasing the applicant's age for rating purposes is another technique used to compensate for additional mortality. For example, if a male aged 35 has high blood pressure, a rate for a 45-year-old male may be charged. The result of this technique produces an increasing mortality charge as the insured ages. Because standard mortality tables tend to increase at an increasing rate, successive advances in age produce increasing margins in mortality. With this procedure, because of the artificial shift in age, actuarial considerations require policy values to be based on the rated age and not the actual age of the insured.

Lower Dividend Class. Placing the applicant in a special dividend class is an option used by life insurance companies issuing participating policies. Policies are issued at standard rates. As long as the gross premium is adequate to cover expected overhead costs, additions to surplus and the higher mortality, the insurer can lower or eliminate dividend payments and still sell the insurance coverage without incurring a loss.

Extra Premium Tables. Underwriters use extra premium or percent tables to price applicants when extra mortality tends to increase as a function of age.

Extra premium tables are developed based on the insurer's average increase in expected mortality. Table 24.2 reproduces a portion of extra premium tables labeled A, B and H for a participating whole life insurance plan. If the numerical rating system estimates that the expected mortality is between 115 and 139 percent of normal, Table A (125 percent average) would be used. For a male aged 20 with a numerical rating of 127 (percent range 115 to 139), an additional $.92 would be added to $14.72 for each $1,000 of life insurance. Note that the additional premium for a male aged 20 (Table A) is approximately 6 percent of the standard premium though the expected mortality is 125 percent of standard. This result occurs because the extra charge is based only on the increase in mortality and other expenses, such as commission and taxes, that vary directly with the premium. Other expenses not varying with the premium, such as the cost of medical exams and underwriting, do not increase the premium.

Marketing: Product Distribution and Agent Compensation

How to distribute life insurance products and how to compensate **agents** are two important operational considerations. Marketing may be done either through direct-response methods or by using sales agents. Direct-response methods contact prospects in a variety of ways, including the mail and mass media (such as newspapers and television). Characteristics of this form of sales method are that the consumer deals directly with the insurer and that no commissions are paid to sales agents. Insurers that use agents to distribute and market life insurance prod-

Table 24.2
Extra Premiums for Each $1,000
of Participating Whole Life Insurance: Male

Age	Standard Premium	A 125 percent*	B 150 percent**	H 350 percent†
20	$14.72	$ .92	$ 4.04	$ 29.07
30	18.21	1.13	5.01	35.98
40	29.25	1.82	8.04	57.78
50	43.75	2.73	12.03	86.40
60	67.29	4.20	18.50	132.91

*Expected mortality range = 115–139 percent.
**Expected mortality range = 140–164 percent.
†Expected mortality range = 340–364 percent; tables C through G not shown.

ucts, usually use as their distribution method a variation of either a *branch office system* or the *general agency system* or may receive applications from *brokers*.

In the branch office system the insurer hires employees to develop and manage the business written in a certain territory. These branch offices of the company are directly controlled by and responsible to the insurer. The company's responsibilities include providing expense allowances to pay overhead, providing the training and issuing the life insurance contracts. The branch managers oversee the agency staff and make sure they perform their sales function. Compensation for the branch manager typically is based on a salary plus a small commission. The commission portion is based on the volume of business sold by the supervised agents.

General agents have a contractual right to sell life insurance in a specific geographic area. The insurer agrees on a certain commission schedule for all sales processed through the agency. The commission typically is a large first-year commission with the amount declining in subsequent years. To cover the geographic territory, the general agent hires sales agents to actually solicit the business over which the company exercises considerable control. The general agent pays the sales agents a commission on each sale. The override commission—the difference between the commission received by the insurer and that paid to the sales agent—is kept by the general agent.

The main difference between the branch manager and the general agent is that the general agent pays all expenses such as training agents and overhead out of commission income. Any amount remaining after paying all expenses is profit for the general agent. The branch manager's overhead is typically paid by the insurer through expense allowances.

Many life insurance companies also accept applications from brokers. Brokers do not have a direct contractual relationship with the life insurance company or with a general agent. Insurance companies make it known through advertising or other means that applications may be submitted directly to the life insurance company.

Whatever the manner of distribution, the compensation system is an additional operational consideration and is important to customer satisfaction and the retention of insurance agents and contracts. For insurance companies licensed in the state of New York, the maximum first-year commission on a whole life contract is 55 percent. After the first year a lower percent is paid on renewal commissions. Life insurance companies not licensed in New York may pay higher rates. The high commission rate in the first year encourages initial sales. However, service to the policy owner in subsequent years may decrease, which in turn affects policy retention. Because of the commission differential, an incentive exists for agents to suggest replacing existing life insurance contracts with new ones to increase the agent's income.[10] However, ethical values and considerations argue against indiscriminate replacement activities.

Reinsurance

A **reinsurance** contract is created when one insurer purchases insurance from another insurer with the intent of transferring a portion of the issuing company's risk to the reinsurer. The company purchasing the insurance is called the *ceding company*. The company selling the coverage is the *reinsurer*. Life insurance companies use reinsurance to limit underwriting losses to a tolerable amount, called a *retention limit*. Large insurance companies with comfortable surplus amounts tend to have high retention limits, or they purchase no reinsurance. Small life insurance companies with commensurately small surplus positions have low retention limits. For example, if a small life insurance company sets the retention limit at $75,000 for each life insured, $50,000 would be reinsured (or ceded) on a $125,000 life insurance policy. The primary company issuing the coverage is responsible for paying the total claim, and the reinsurer reimburses the primary company based on the reinsured $50,000 if the loss occurs. Insureds do not know whether a reinsurance contract exists. If the reinsurer in turn reinsures the business, it is called *retrocession*.

There are several reasons why a life insurance company, after placing the business in force, would reinsure or cede the insurance coverage. First, reinsurance limits the impact on surplus. If 1,000 insureds purchase $100,000 policies, and ten insureds each purchase $1 million of coverage, the impact on total losses of a $1 million claim would be ten times that of a $100,000 claim. Thus, reinsuring the excess over $100,000 results in equal changes in financial condition regardless of which life insurance contract produces the loss.

Second, because limiting life insurance policy face amounts would reduce the efficiency of the sales process, life insurance companies generally allow the sale of any practical amount of insurance on any one insured (within underwriting limits). This creates the public appearance of good financial strength and capacity and reduces the agent's work in placing large amounts of life insurance coverage in force.

Third, the reinsurance transaction can help manage the company's problem of simultaneous loss caused by disasters or catastrophes. The company's loss from a random occurrence can be limited to an accident retention level. For example, if a factory explosion kills ten insureds each owning $100,000 of life insurance, the liability of the life insurance company will be $1 million. However, if the primary insurer purchased disaster reinsurance with a $5 million per accident limit with a $400,000 retention, all claims in excess of $400,000 for one accident, $600,000, would be paid by the reinsurer (up to $5 million).

Reinsurance companies provide other services to the industry. Reinsurance allows small insurance companies to compete, without limiting insurance amounts, with large ones. Small insurance companies use the expertise of reinsurers for underwriting and actuarial advice and guidance. If a life insurance company desires to eliminate a class of policies or terminate all policies in a territory, it can be handled through the reinsurance mechanism.

Arranging Reinsurance

Life insurance companies arrange reinsurance in three ways. First, the company may shop for reinsurance on a case-by-case basis, which is reserved for situations where no other prearranged reinsurance is available or the policy limits exceed treaty amounts. Shopping individually for reinsurance increases the time delay in issuing the policy. Insurers will not accept coverage when the price, terms and availability of reinsurance are unknown. Because of the delay, increased cost and volume of reinsurance contracts that would have to be negotiated individually, life insurance companies generally opt for the other two ways of arranging reinsurance: by prearranging **facultative** or **automatic reinsurance** treaties.

A facultative treaty is a contractual arrangement with a reinsurance company spelling out the terms, conditions, commission, premium and other duties and obligations of the parties affecting any transfer. Under the facultative treaty the primary company submits applications to the reinsurer. The primary company is under no obligation to submit all applications to the reinsurer, nor is the reinsurer obligated to accept the reinsurance. This method is similar to case-by-case negotiation in that the primary insurer does not know whether reinsurance will be accepted. However, the primary company may be confident of getting the required reinsurance because through previous dealings it learns the characteristics of acceptable exposures.

Under an automatic treaty all exposures meeting certain predetermined underwriting standards and characteristics are reinsured. The primary insurer cannot select the exposures to be submitted, nor can the reinsurer reject any applicants meeting the underwriting rules. This automatic arrangement eliminates the processing delay, and guarantees the primary insurer that reinsurance coverage exists for any business meeting the predetermined standards.

Types of Reinsurance

A life insurance company may either purchase **yearly renewable term (YRT)** reinsurance or engage in **coinsurance.** Under the YRT plan term insurance is purchased for the excess of the at-risk retention limit. The amount at risk is the difference between the face amount and the policy's terminal reserve. As the terminal reserve increases with the age of the policy, the amount at risk declines. For example, assume that five years ago a $500,000 whole life insurance policy was issued for a male then aged 32. Currently the terminal reserve is $20,000. If the primary insurer's retention limit is $100,000, then this year $380,000 ($500,000 − $20,000 − $100,000) of YRT reinsurance is purchased. The applicable rate for a 37-year-old male applies.

Under the coinsurance plan the primary carrier and the reinsurer share the life insurance premium and costs. For example, if a $500,000 life insurance contract is sold and there is a $100,000 retention, the reinsurer would receive four-fifths of the premium, less negotiated amounts for expenses and overhead. In return the reinsurer is responsible for the same fraction of the other contractual obligations, including the death claim, nonforfeiture values and dividends.

Review Questions

1. Describe the differences between the stock and mutual forms of organization. Comment about the organization, objective and control of each.
2. Explain the difference between a participating dividend paid to policyholders and a stockholder dividend paid by a stock insurer.

3. Discuss the advantages and disadvantages of a mutual insurance company converting to the stock form. Comment on this statement: if policyholders wanted a stock company, they would have purchased the contract from one. Do you think a mutual should be allowed to convert to the stock form?

4. In what ways do the underwriter and actuary coordinate their activities? What is the main job of the underwriter? Explain. What is meant by a "fair" premium?

5. Describe the main underwriting criteria for life and health insurance. Why is no medical exam required for annuities?

6. Where does an underwriter get information for proper underwriting? Why do underwriters need to be concerned about the confidentiality of information? Provide a few examples.

7. Describe the difference between a class rating scheme and a numerical rating scheme.

8. What methods are used to price coverage for people with impaired health? Explain three different methods, how they work and the mortality pattern implications.

9. Describe the branch office system and the general agency system as marketing or distribution methods for life insurance.

10. Why do life insurance companies engage in reinsurance transactions? Explain the following terms: retention limit, primary or ceding company, retrocession.

11. What is the difference between a facultative and an automatic treaty? Explain how yearly renewable term and coinsurance reinsurance plans work. Provide an example.

Endnotes

[1] The number of U.S. life insurance companies in business at the end of 1989 was 2,350. *1990 Life Insurance Fact Book,* (Washington, D.C.: American Council of Life Insurance), p. 103.

[2] *Wall Street Journal,* November 30, 1990, p. A10.

[3] Gregory E. Murray, "Demutualization of Insurance Companies—Advantages and Disadvantages," *Journal of the American Society of CLU,* January 1985, pp. 52–54.

[4] The Joint Committee on Taxation, *Taxation of Life Insurance Companies* (JCS-17-89), October 1989.

[5] New York Insurance Code Section 4230.

[6] New York Insurance Code Article 73.

[7] *City of Los Angeles, Department of Water and Power v. Marie Manhart,* 434 U.S. 815 (U.S. Supreme Court 1978).

[8] *See also* Donald W. Hardigree and Robert J. Carney, "Gender-Neutral Insurance Rating Issues," *The CPCU Journal* 43, No. 3, Sept. 1990, pp. 146–158; Robert J. Carney and Donald W. Hardigree, "The Impact of Gender-Neutral Insurance Rating on Women," *The Journal of Insurance Issues and Practices* XIII, No. 2, June 1990, pp. 1–23.

[9] For a discussion of the recommendations and concerns of the PPSC, *see* Harold D. Skipper, Jr., and Steven N. Weisbart, *Privacy and the Insurance Industry* (Atlanta: Publishing Services Division, College of Business Administration, Georgia State University, 1979).

[10]For a discussion of the compensation of life insurance agents, see Mark S. Dorfman, "Reformation in Life Insurance Agent's Compensation," *Journal of Risk and Insurance,* September 1976, pp. 447–461; David L. Schalow, "Compensation: Time for a Change?" *Journal of the American Society of CLU* 38, No. 4 (July 1984), pp. 56–62; and John S. Moyse, "Should the Life Insurance Agent Be Salaried?" *Journal of the American Society of CLU* 39, No. 2 (March 1985), pp. 74–77.

Bibliography

Benham, Barbara Tzivanis. "Rebating: Poultice or Poison." *Best's Review (Life/Health Edition).* September 1986, p. 38.

Ducharme, Guy N. "The Dark Side of Conversion." *Best's Review (Life/Health Edition),* July 1989, p. 34.

Galban, Leandro S. "The Unthinkable Option." *Best's Review (Life/Health Edition),* January 1989, p. 34.

George, Henry C. "Life Underwriting Medical Requirements in the 1980s . . . and Beyond." *Journal of American Society of CLU,* March 1985, p. 80.

Goodwin, Dennis W. *Life and Health Insurance Marketing.* Atlanta, Ga.: Life Office Management Institute, 1989.

Grossman, Eli A. *Life Reinsurance.* Atlanta, Ga.: Life Office Management Institute, 1980.

Huggins, Kenneth. *Operations of Life and Health Insurance Companies.* Atlanta, Ga.: Life Office Management Institute, 1988.

Ingram, David N. "Compensation for Value." *Best's Review (Life/Health Edition).* July 1987, p. 14.

MacDonald, Robert W. "Is the Future of the Agent About to Lapse?" *Best's Review (Life/Health Edition).* February 1988, p. 60.

Scully, John C. "The Case for Level Compensation." *Best's Review (Life/Health Edition).* January 1987, p. 22.

Stipp, David. "Genetic Testing May Mark Some People as Undesirable to Employees, Insurers." *Wall Street Journal.* July 9, 1990, p. B1.

Chapter 25 | Life Insurance Operations: Regulation, Financial Operations and Taxation

Chapter Objectives

- Outline the history of life insurance regulation and discuss the extent of current regulation
- Introduce topics related to insurance company financial operations
- Explore federal and state taxation of life insurance companies

Introduction

Chapter 24 examined the structural framework of insurance companies—how they are organized, how contracts are underwritten and how insurance products and services are marketed. This chapter delves more deeply into the workings of life insurance companies, focusing on three important aspects of day-to-day operations: regulation, finance and taxation. Insurers must conform to regulatory requirements imposed by federal and state governments. They must operate in a financially sound manner. And, life insurers must pay state and federal taxes.

The chapter begins with a brief history of insurance industry regulation to provide the background underlying the current controversy over Public Law 15, the McCarran-Ferguson Act. The **McCarran-Ferguson Act** exempts insurers from several federal laws if states regulate those areas. Some people feel the exemptions provided by the act are unnecessary. The federal government also influences the insurance industry through Federal Trade Commission (FTC) and Securities and Exchange Commission (SEC) regulations.

The next section in the chapter covers operational considerations—life insurance accounting, investments, dissolution and reorganization. Insurers follow various accounting rules to represent their financial picture accurately to regulators, stockholders and other interested parties. Accounting statements used for these diverse interests are different. Insurers make investments consistent with risk and return and cash flow needs. If financial distress occurs, state procedures govern the company's liquidation or reorganization. Regulators have some flexibility in deciding how to handle the continuation or dismantling of the company.

The final subject discussed is the taxation of life insurers. Life insurance companies pay taxes as do other industries. However, nontraditional life insurance products pose special problems when determining income and expenses. In addition, controversy exists over the amount of deductible policyholder dividends and the stock and mutual companies' respective share of the industry's tax payment.

Regulation of the Life Insurance Industry

Federal and state regulators oversee and regulate insurance industry activities. No other industry except banking has more regulation than insurance. A U.S. General Accounting Office (GAO) report cites three reasons for government regulation of insurance, all based in the failure of a competitive insurance marketing mechanism.[1] The first criticism concerns the unequal bargaining positions of the parties to the contract. All insurance contracts, including the life insurance contract, are technical documents that determine the rights, duties and obligations of the parties concerned. Because of the insurance transaction's legal complexity, state regulations address the parties' unequal knowledge and the inequity in their bargaining positions. Regulations also address the sales process and the inability of consumers to make product and price comparisons to encourage fair transactions.

The large number of people affected by the transaction provides another justification for regulation. Insurance transactions are allowed because it is "in the public interest." Because large numbers of people rely on the institution's integrity for payment after a loss, society would be greatly damaged if there were unregulated and unsecured transactions resulting in insurers defaulting on their obligations.

Finally, regulation exists because the insurance contract is a promise to pay future benefits. People pay money now in exchange for future payment. The date of payment may be many years from the contract's issue date. This places the insurance company in a creditor capacity because the insured trusts the insurance company to deliver contractual promises. Regulation tries to assure that society's trust is not violated.

States primarily regulate the insurance transaction because insurance is specifically exempt from many federal regulations. Several legislators currently question the right and desirability of the states to regulate insurance.[2] Challenges to state insurance regulation have been frequent during the past century, and future challenges could result in exclusive federal regulation. The following paragraphs provide a brief history of the struggle between the state and federal authorities over which body should regulate the insurance industry. This description not only provides a historical review but gives insight into the barriers that must be removed before federal control of insurance is complete.[3]

A Brief History of Insurance Regulation

Formal recognition of state regulation of insurance began with the Tenth Amendment to the U.S. Constitution, which states:

The powers not delegated to the United States by the Constitution, nor prohibited by it to the States, are reserved to the States respectively, or to the people.

Article I, Section 8, of the U.S. Constitution empowers the federal government to regulate commerce between the states. Because insurance was not "commerce," in 1851 the state of Massachusetts passed legislation to regulate the insurance transaction. Many states followed and passed statutes to regulate the insurance business within their boundaries.

Two bills introduced into Congress in 1866 and 1868 failed to create federal regulation. Proponents of federal regulation then attempted to have the insurance transaction classified as "commerce" so that Article I, Section 8, of the Constitution would apply, resulting in federal regulation.

The landmark case of *Paul v. Virginia* in 1869 tested the applicability of the commerce clause.[4] The U.S. Supreme Court upheld a Virginia statute requiring foreign (out-of-state) companies and their agents to be licensed in the state. Samuel Paul, an agent representing several New York insurance companies in Virginia, refused to meet the licensing requirements imposed by the state of Virginia. He argued that insurance, when sold across state lines, is "commerce" and could not be regulated by the state of Virginia. The U.S. Supreme Court upheld the Virginia statute and declared that insurance was not commerce even when conducted between states and affirmed the right of the states to continue regulating insurance.

Between the *Paul v. Virginia* decision in 1869 and 1944 there were no changes in regulatory authority. Many cases affirmed the states' right to regulate insurance. In 1871, 17 states sent representatives to the organizational meeting of the National Convention of Insurance Commissioners (the forerunner of today's National Association of Insurance Commissioners), demonstrating a serious intent to subject the insurance transaction to state regulation.

The need for regulation became apparent in the late 1800s and early 1900s. Tontine contracts, which promised to pay large dividends only if the insured survived as opposed to the practice of paying yearly participating (policy owner) dividends, were sold. Twisting, misrepresentation, rebating and other questionable transactions were common. Because of mismanagement, poor practices and ignoring the public interest, the New York legislature in 1905 established a committee (known as the Armstrong Committee) to investigate the practices of that state's life insurers.[5]

The Armstrong Committee investigated the state's regulatory powers, life insurance company investments and expenses and dividend calculation and payment practices. The committee uncovered many abusive practices violating the public trust. The resulting legislation was the New York Insurance Code of 1906. This body of law included most of the recommendations made by the Armstrong Report. The New York Insurance Code of 1906 set the model for many other states.

The states' right to regulate insurance as expressed in *Paul v. Virginia* was upheld for 75 years until the Justice Department acted against the South-Eastern Underwriters Association (SEUA) in 1941 for violation of the Sherman Antitrust Act. Though cooperation between insurance companies was permissible for pooling statistics, the SEUA allegedly conspired to fix rates arbitrarily to maintain a noncompetitive market among its 200 members in the states of Alabama, Florida, Georgia, North Carolina, South Carolina and Virginia. In defense of its activities the SEUA argued (based on *Paul*) that insurance was not interstate commerce and not subject to the Sherman Antitrust Act. The federal district court upheld the *Paul* doctrine. On appeal (1944) the Supreme Court reversed the lower court's decision, in a divided action, declaring that insurance is interstate commerce.[6]

The SEUA decision created the possibility of duplicative regulation and other jurisdictional problems. Federal regulation would control insurance across state lines, while state regulation would control intrastate insurance. The decision created many complex problems. Many federal and state laws now applied to the transaction. After the SEUA decision it was uncertain whether states continued to have the right to regulate the insurance transaction.

To resolve these jurisdictional problems Congress enacted the McCarran-Ferguson Act (**Public Law 15**) in 1945. (*See* Figure 25.1). Congress decided it was in the public's best interest to allow the states to continue to regulate the insurance business. The act declared that Congress would not override the states' authority to regulate insurance unless Congress specifically expanded control. Further, the act exempted the insurance business from the Clayton Act, the Federal Trade Commission Act and the Sherman Antitrust Act (except the parts addressing boycott, intimidation and coercion). When the exemptions expired (after 1948), federal regulation would apply only if the states did not regulate the exempted areas.

The importance of Public Law 15 lies in the fact that it allows the states to regulate insurance at the convenience of the federal government, because ultimate control of interstate transactions rests with Congress. In response to the federal government's action to prompt the states to enact laws regulating insurance, by 1948 an All-Industry Committee worked with the National Association of Insurance Commissioners to develop the necessary state laws. During the decade following the SEUA decision each state enacted laws meeting the requirements outlined in the McCarran-Ferguson Act.

Activities of the FTC

The Federal Trade Commission (FTC) directly challenged state regulation several times following the passage of the McCarran-Ferguson Act. The first challenge focused on health insurance company advertising in 1954 and 1955. The FTC challenged Public Law 15, alleging that the advertising of several insurers misrepresented the health insurance product's coverage, price, termination provisions and insurability standards. The Supreme Court affirmed the states' right to regulate advertising and denied the FTC jurisdiction over these deceptive practices.[7] Yet the FTC's authority to regulate unauthorized advertising through the mail and other mass media was upheld.[8] *The Guides for Mail-Order Insurance*, published by the FTC in 1964, provides federal guidelines for unlicensed mail solicitation in an attempt to reduce and eliminate misleading advertising.

The FTC's second critical look at the insurance transaction occurred in 1979, when it issued a report on life insurance cost and cost disclosure (*see* Chapter 10). One result of the controversy following the FTC report was an increased aware-

Figure 25.1
Title 15—Commerce and Trade
Chapter 20. Regulations of Insurance 15 USCS (1990)

Sec. 1011. Declaration of policy

The Congress hereby declares that the continued regulation and taxation by the several States of the business of insurance is in the public interest and that silence on the part of the Congress shall not be construed to impose any barrier to the regulation or taxation of such business by the several States.

Sec. 1012. Regulation by State law; Federal law relating specifically to insurance; applicability of certain Federal laws after June 30, 1948.

(a) State regulation. The business of insurance and every person engaged therein, shall be subject to the laws of the several states which relate to the regulation or taxation of such business.

(b) Federal regulation. No Act of Congress shall be construed to invalidate, impair or supersede any law enacted by any State for the purpose of regulating the business of insurance or which imposes a fee or tax upon such business, unless such Act specifically relates to the business of insurance: Provided, That after June 30, 1948, the Act of July 2, 1890, as amended, known as the Sherman Act and the Act of October 15, 1914, as amended, known as the Clayton Act and the Act of Septmber 26, 1914, known as the Federal Trade Commission Act, as amended, shall be applicable to the business of insurance to the extent that such business is not regulated by State law.

Sec. 1013. Suspension until June 30, 1948, of application of certain Federal laws; Sherman Act applicable to agreements to or acts of, boycott, coercion or intimidation

(a) Until June 30, 1949, the Act of July 2, 1890, as amended, known as the Sherman Act and the Act of October 15, 1914, as amended, known as the Clayton Act and the Act of September 26, 1914, known as the Federal Trade Commission Act, as amended and the Act of June 19, 1936, known as the Robinson-Patman Antidiscrimination Act, shall not apply to the business of insurance or to acts in the conduct thereof.

(b) Nothing contained in this Act shall render the said Sherman Act inapplicable to any agreement to boycott, coerce or intimidate or act of boycott, coercion or intimidation.

Sec. 1014. Applicability of National Labor Relations Act and the Fair Labor Standards Act of 1938

Nothing contained in this Act shall be construed to affect in any manner the application to the business of insurance of the Act of July 5, 1935, as amended, known as the National Labor Relations Act or the Act of June 25, 1938, as amended, known as the Fair Labor Standards Act of 1938 or the Act of June 5, 1920, known as the Merchant Marine Act, 1920.

Sec. 1015. Definition of "State"
As used in this Act, the term "State" includes the several States, Alaska, Hawaii, Puerto Rico, Guam and the District of Columbia.

Other provisions:

Separability clause. If any provision of this Act or the application of such provision to any person or circumstances, shall be held invalid, the remainder of the Act and the application of such provision to persons or circumstances other than those as to which it is held invalid, shall not be affected.

ness of the difficulty of accurately disclosing cost to consumers. With the current development of products such as universal life, variable life and indeterminate life insurance, whose benefits and costs relate directly to future economic conditions, quoting the cost of life insurance at the time of the sale is more difficult than before. Legislators passed the Federal Trade Commission Improvements Act (1980) limiting the FTC's power to investigate the insurance industry because of the controversy following the independent investigation.

Activities of the SEC

The SEC has the power to regulate all interstate security transactions through the *Securities Act of 1933* and the *Investment Company Act of 1940*. Because of the SEC's jurisdiction and the McCarran-Ferguson Act's specific exemption of insurance transactions from SEC regulation, the gray area of variable annuity regulation had to be litigated. Because variable annuity benefits depend on the investment performance of an underlying portfolio of securities, the SEC challenged the states' right to regulate these contracts.

In the case of *SEC v. Variable Annuity Life Insurance Co. of America et al.*,[9] the U.S. Supreme Court held that federal security acts apply to the issuance of variable contracts and to products whose benefits are a function of a portfolio of securities. This conclusion resulted because variable annuities typically have no substantial mortality guarantee during the accumulation phase and therefore closely resembled mutual funds. Because of this decision, agents selling variable products must be licensed by the National Association of Securities Dealers. Furthermore, sales of equity-based products involve meeting SEC reporting requirements and acquisition expense limitations.

Current Areas of Regulation

Regulation of the insurance business remains primarily the responsibility of the states. Because the products of the life insurance industry are changing rapidly, regulated competition is replacing strict and comprehensive regulation. Some states have reduced replacement disclosure requirements, and some cost disclosure model bills recognize that costs and future performance cannot be known. The prospective policyholder cannot be protected from all risk arising out of the purchase or replacement of life insurance products. What regulators are working for is a fair representation of the products' provisions and a reasonable estimate of costs so the consumer may make informed decisions about the purchase.

The National Association of Insurance Commissioners (NAIC) and the states' regulatory bodies do much to provide the environment for this fair representation. The chief insurance regulator of each state is a member of the NAIC. The main purpose of the NAIC is to promote uniform state regulation and develop model insurance regulation for state consideration. The chief state insurance official, on the other hand, is responsible for the proper operation of the insurance industry within the state to protect the consuming public. The areas regulated by the states include:

- organizational forms of insurance companies;
- requirements for licensing of companies and agents;
- insurance policy provisions and their rates;

- expenses;
- reserve, surplus and dividend calculations;
- advertising and marketing;
- financial reporting and investment activity; and
- dissolution and reorganization.

All of these areas are discussed in the following paragraphs. The last two are covered in depth in the next major section.

Insurance Company Organization

Several facts justify state regulatory control over how life insurance companies organize. First, the insuring organization needs to survive the insured to complete the contractual agreement. The long length of some insurance contracts and the need for continuity impose a long-term commitment. Thus states require newly formed entities selling life insurance to be corporations. Second, before the insurance company may operate, sufficient funds must exist to protect policyholders from adverse underwriting or investment results. For stock companies capital and surplus must be adequate. For mutuals a minimum dollar amount of premium must be deposited and a minimum number of applications taken for insurance. Policyholders in newly formed insurers sometimes need to be protected from founders unjustly benefiting from the initial accumulation of cash. Regulatory bodies impose on new organizations other requirements not ordinarily imposed on other businesses, such as minimum capital requirements, to reduce the probability of a corporate failure.

State requirements for organization of a stock or a mutual insurer include (1) approval of the name, address and type of business; (2) approval of the corporation's proposed charter; and (3) approval to issue securities and accumulate capital (stock) or receive a minimum number of applications for insurance (mutual). Once all requirements are met and the license is approved, the company receives authorization to sell insurance in that state.[10] Several mutual insurance companies are currently investigating the possibility of converting to the stock form. A discussion of the issue and complexity of the conversion process is found in Chapter 24.

The minimum amount of capital and surplus required to license an insurer varies by state. In New York the minimum paid-in capital amount is $2 million and the minimum paid-in initial surplus is $4 million.[11] Other states have lower capital and surplus requirements.

Licensing of Companies and Agents

Once the life insurance company organizes, a license to operate must be issued. The state issues licenses to regulate, monitor and control the company. Licenses will generally not be issued if a proposed founder or director "has been convicted of any crime involving fraud, dishonesty or like moral turpitude or is an untrustworthy person."[12] The NAIC has developed a national database to share information about owners, operators or agents of insurance companies to stop unscrupulous operators from repeating dishonest or undesirable activities in another state. After operations begin, if the insurance commissioner believes the life insurance company is not financially sound, is engaging in unauthorized, deceptive or fraudulent practices or refuses to submit to examination, its license may be revoked. If the state revokes a license and the company wants to continue to operate, the burden of proving the revocation was unwarranted lies with the insurer.

Life insurance agents must qualify to receive a license. Qualification requirements vary by state, but many impose stricter standards than in the past. In most states applicants must pass an examination after taking approved courses. Maintaining the license may require participation in continuing education programs. Regulators issue the sales license when an insurer consents to allow the person to sell insurance coverage. Besides meeting official licensing regulations, many agents have voluntarily earned professional designations, including the CLU (Chartered Life Underwriter), ChFC (Chartered Financial Consultant) and CFP (Certified Financial Planner).

Regulation of agent qualification and license requirements assures the public, the insurance companies and the regulators that licensed agents have a basic knowledge of the function and appropriate use of life insurance products. State insurance regulators may revoke or refuse to renew an agent's license if a hearing concludes there has been a violation of the state's insurance code. If the agent violated the law with respect to the agency; materially misrepresented facts in the application for the license; is guilty of fraud, dishonesty, twisting or rebating (where illegal); or is incompetent or untrustworthy, the license will be revoked or denied.[13]

Policy Provisions and Rates

Life insurance policies can be complicated, and many people do not understand the contract or their contractual rights. Most states require the insurer to submit the contract for approval before it can be issued. In other states the contract must be filed with the insurance commissioner's office. Once filed, the contract may be used if the state does not reject its wording within a short period.

Regardless of the mechanics of policy approval, the states typically prescribe a set of mandatory provisions, optional provisions and prohibited provisions. The contract's language must meet the minimum intent of the law. Both consumerists and regulators are encouraging complete product information and cost disclosure as well as simplified policy language.

Rates charged for life insurance are not directly regulated by state insurance departments as are rates in the property and casualty side of the insurance business. Rates, however, must be adequate, not excessive and not unfairly discriminatory. State regulations partially meet these goals by indirectly controlling rates by imposing legal reserve requirements. These reserve requirements prescribe how to calculate legal reserve amounts, a balance sheet liability. Practical minimum rates are set because premiums collected need to cover reserves and other cash needs of the company. Competitive pressures limit how high rates can go. Whether competition reduces life insurance rates is the subject of much debate.

Besides indirect rate regulation, life insurance companies are subject to other state insurance code requirements. Rates must not be unfairly discriminatory. That is, the same rate must be charged similar exposures (except quantity discounts). In the future, states may prohibit the use of gender to price all insurance coverage, as it is in the few states requiring unisex mortality tables.

Expense Limitations

New York Insurance Code Sections 4228 and 4230 impose limitations on life insurance company acquisition expenses.[14] Section 4228 places a limit on the amount of field expenses that can be incurred in a calendar year:

> No domestic life insurance company and no foreign or alien life insurance company doing business in this state shall make or incur in any calendar year total field expenses . . . in excess of . . . .

Field expenses include commissions on first-year premiums; compensation, salaries and expenses of the home office; advertising; and renewal commissions. The same section states:

> No such company shall pay . . . to an agent, a first-year's commission in excess of 55 per centum of the premium.

The section also imposes a 60 percent limit on the total commission amount paid to both the general agent and the soliciting agent. Though very few states limit expenses by statute, the extraterritorial nature of the New York Insurance Code imposes the same limitations on companies operating both within and outside the state. Because most of the large U.S. life insurance companies have a New York license, the majority of life insurance transactions are subject to New York law. Section 4230 limits salaries and pensions by the following provision:

> No domestic life insurance company shall pay any salary, compensation or emolument in any amount to any officer, trustee or director thereof or amounting in any year to more than $40,000 to any person, firm or corporation, unless such payment be first authorized by a vote of the board of directors of such company.

Reserve, Surplus and Dividend Calculations

Regulations also apply to amounts designated as policyholders' reserve and surplus. Insurers calculate policyholders' reserve amounts according to prescribed interest rates and mortality, annuity or morbidity tables reflecting conservative actuarial assumptions. These reserves provide a claim on assets to assure future contractual obligations (*see* Chapter 23).

Regulations apply to surplus to avoid large accumulations of undistributed earnings. Annual surplus distribution avoids the appearance of a tontine. New York Insurance Code Section 4219 allows mutual companies to accumulate a maximum of 10 percent of policy reserves and liabilities as surplus. Concerning the distribution of policyowner dividends, life insurance companies must annually:

> ascertain and distribute . . . the proportion of any surplus accruing upon every participating insurance policy . . . entitled . . . to share within . . .[14]

Advertising and Deceptive Practices

Article 24 of the New York Insurance Code specifically prohibits any unfair method of competition and any deceptive act or practice. The law lists all acts or practices violating Article 24. Any act considered deceptive or unfair can be declared a violation of Article 24 by the superintendent of insurance.

Unfair or deceptive practices include:

- unfairly discriminating between individuals in the same underwriting class,
- misrepresenting any product's benefits or price,
- disseminating misleading information concerning the nonguaranteed nature and future amount of dividends,
- misrepresenting the financial condition of the insurer and
- providing incomplete product comparisons for the purpose of inducing lapse, surrender or replacement.[15]

Financial Operations

Life insurance companies typically maintain several sets of financial records. The insurer maintains each for a particular need. The *annual blank* must be filed with state regulatory bodies. Financial statements must be prepared for presentation to the public. Books must be kept for federal tax purposes. And companies need useful financial information for internal operational control. The first part of this section concerns only the reports required for regulatory purposes. Other financial operation issues—investments and dissolution and reorganization—are discussed later in the section.

Financial Reporting

Each insurance company files the **annual statement blank** in each state in which it is operating. Standardization of the annual statement blank and the ability to file by computer now eases the task. State authorities use the annual blank as the primary source of their information for regulating insurers. All states use the blank (originally developed in 1872 by the NAIC, known then as the National Convention of Insurance Commissioners). Though each state requires the use of the blank, there may be discrepancies in reported values due to the difference in statutory definitions and requirements found in each state.

The annual statement contains many tables and schedules describing the operations of the life insurance company. The annual statement blank requires disclosure of:

- financial statements, including the balance sheet, income statement and statement of changes in financial position;
- a detailed analysis of operations by line of business, reserves, premiums and annuity considerations, capital gains and losses, investment income, expenses, claims and dividends;

- information concerning real estate bought and sold, mortgages, long-term invested assets and owned bonds and stocks;
- data on dividends (illustrated and paid), reinsurance ceded, development of incurred losses and nonadmitted assets; and
- answers to general interrogatories concerning the firm's operation.

The assets and liabilities life insurers report on the annual statement are similar in many respects to those for noninsurance businesses. However, because of the conservative nature of the financial reporting, important differences exist. Several differences arise from the types of assets included for statement purposes and in the valuation of investments. With respect to liabilities, life insurers must show several different types of reserves, and in the owner's equity section of mutual companies surplus is split into several classes.

Assets

Assets of life insurance companies are identified as **admitted** and **nonadmitted**. Admitted assets are those allowed to be shown on the company's financial statements. Nonadmitted assets are not shown on the balance sheet because they cannot be used to satisfy the obligations of the life insurance company under normal circumstances (i.e., not in liquidation). Examples of nonadmitted assets include supplies, furniture, fixtures, treasury stock, past-due or uncollectible interest income and uncollectible premiums. A balance sheet composed only of admitted assets produces a conservative financial picture.

Beyond the types of assets included for reporting purposes, life insurance companies make investments similar to those of other businesses. The types of assets appearing on the balance sheet include cash, loans outstanding, real estate, corporate bonds and stocks and government securities. Asset valuation for life insurance company reporting differs from manufacturing concerns.

For valuation purposes most states separate securities into *amortizable* and *nonamortizable* categories. Amortizable securities include bonds that are not in default and have sufficient security. These include bonds backed by the U.S. government, highly rated corporate bonds, highly rated bonds of municipal, city and state divisions and bonds approved by the NAIC Committee on Valuation of Securities. The value of amortizable securities is found by systematically increasing or decreasing the book value until the security equals its maturity value. This technique eliminates wide swings in valuation that occur with the use of current market values.

Securities considered nonamortizable include all common stocks (because they do not mature), bonds in default (normally amortizable) and bonds considered insufficiently secured. The value of these securities equals their market price as determined on December 31 of each year by the NAIC Committee on Valuation of Securities. Preferred stock poses a special problem because it is a hybrid security. Preferred stock pays a fixed dividend payment similar to a bond and lacks a maturity date like stock. Currently most states value preferred stock at cost instead of fair market value.

Liabilities

Beyond the liabilities noninsurance businesses incur (such as mortgage loans or other borrowed funds, employee benefits and taxes), insurers incur special obligations (liabilities) because of the nature of the business. Regulators require life insurance companies to set up liability reserves to meet future obligations and to present a complete picture of the company's financial strength. Reserves reported on the balance sheet include:

- reserves for policy proceeds (including interest and dividends) paid under settlement options;
- cash values on policies in default, canceled or paid under the automatic premium loan option;
- unpaid reported claims;
- an estimate of unreported and unpaid claims;
- dividends payable but not paid; and
- a mandatory securities valuation reserve (MSVR).

The MSVR is an amount designated as a cushion for any large changes in the valuation of investments held by the life insurance company. The MSVR helps reduce the impact of fluctuations in asset valuation.

Net Worth

Regardless of whether the company is a mutual or a stock, additions to the **net worth** section come from several sources. First, changes in net worth arise from the gain or loss from insurance underwriting and investment operations. Second, net worth reflects reserve changes. If mortality is lower, investment income higher or expenses lower than expected, net worth will increase. If reserves increase, net worth will decrease. In summary, the change in net worth is equal to gross premiums and other considerations, plus investment income, less actual mortality and operating expenses (including reinsurance premiums) and any increase (decrease) in reserve amounts.

Mutual companies' net worth is composed of surplus, while stock insurers' net worth is composed of both capital and surplus. Stock insurers' capital and surplus is equal to amounts representing ownership interest by stockholders as the par amount, any amounts paid in excess of par and amounts added to retained earnings through operations. Mutual insurance companies' balancing entry is *unassigned surplus* because the policyholders own the company. After identifying this amount, the company must decide how much of the unassigned surplus is to be transferred to divisible surplus (the amount to be paid to policyholders) and how to allocate divisible surplus among all policyholders.

Accounting Practices: GAAP Versus Statutory

Because investors, policyholders and state regulators have different information needs, different accounting procedures are employed for each group. A life insurance company's annual report to state officials is based on statutory reporting requirements. Stock companies have an additional reporting need. Statutory reporting paints a conservative financial picture, so investors require a different financial statement to analyze the company's financial position. To this end, in 1972 the American Institute of Certified Public Accountants (AICPA) issued a standards guide for auditing stock life insurers. The guide, entitled *Audits of Stock Life Insurance Companies*, provides standards of generally accepted principles (GAAP) for stock insurers.[16] Because of several perceived deficiencies, the Statement of Financial Accounting Standards (SFAS) No. 60 was issued in 1982 to set standards for treating all stock insurers (property, liability and life) similarly, based on the short-term or long-term nature of the insurance contract.[17]

The main differences between *GAAP* and *statutory accounting methods* include the treatment of expenses, the assumptions used in reserving methods, the treatment of nonadmitted assets and policyholder dividends.[18]

Expense Treatment. GAAP methods require that all expenses associated with the production of new business be amortized to match revenues and costs. These expenses can either vary directly with or independent of the sales process. For example, though claims can occur many years after the sale, GAAP requires insurers to accrue a liability for settlement costs. This procedure is substantially different from statutory methods in that all costs are recognized when they occur. Statutory accounting results in larger expense figures for new insurance contracts, while GAAP spreads the expense over the contract's life and allows a more realistic recognition and allocation of these expenses in an attempt to match revenues with costs.

Reserve Assumptions. Besides requiring an attempt to match revenues with costs, GAAP requires the use of mortality, interest and lapse assumptions that are more realistic and in line with actual company experience.

Nonadmitted Assets. GAAP financial statements, which include both nonadmitted and admitted assets, provide financial statements that can be compared more directly with the statements of noninsurance companies.

Policyholder Dividends. GAAP requires an insurance company to recognize dividend payments even though the board of directors has not authorized the distribution. In statutory accounting methods dividends cannot be recognized until the board of directors declares the dividend amount and the date of payment.

FASB 97. Stock as well as mutual companies must conform to new rules required by the Financial Accounting Standards Board. The new rules outlined in FASB statement number 97 restructure and change how stock insurance companies report their financial results to stockholders beginning in 1989.[19] FASB 97 does not change the financial reports required for statutory financial reporting. However, the new accounting rules change the amount of federal tax and cause some insurers to be subject to the alternative minimum tax (AMT).

The complicated rules outlined in FASB 97 clear up accounting procedures for universal life, limited-payment products and other investment-oriented products, including annuities. FASB 97 mandates the following changes:

- The recognition of insurers' earnings on the newer types of life insurance products that do not provide substantial mortality or morbidity risk is delayed.
- Policy charges are to be earned when assessed from cash value amounts. Policy charges assessed on limited-payment plans will be partially deferred as unearned because those charges pay for future services.
- Universal life insurance contracts must use the retrospective deposit method for accounting. Although difficult to calculate, the contract's value under the retrospective deposit method is equal to its gross account balance before deduction for surrender charges with an adjustment for deferred revenues.

Life Insurance Company Investments

The nature of the life insurance transaction requires pooling sums of money in anticipation of future claim payments. One-year term insurance contracts require small premiums in anticipation of claim payments occurring in the current policy year. Longer-term contracts, such as multiyear term policies, whole life, universal life, annuities, disability income and health contracts, require sufficient premiums in the early years to offset higher costs in the later years. Some contracts require prefunding to a greater extent than others.

Other sources of investment dollars include investment earnings from the sale of securities, capital gains, dividends and interest, earnings from insurance operations not reinvested in other assets and undistributed policy owners' earnings (mutual).

Life insurance companies make investments to accumulate funds for future obligations, to enhance earnings and to provide a cushion for adverse operating results. As illustrated in Chapters 21 through 23, insurers use time-value-of-money calculations and discount the premium payment in anticipation of investing the funds and generating investment income. Insurers' investment earnings offset the interest discount inherent in rate and premium calculations. Deposits made into various pension plans anticipate investment income to pay defined benefits, thus reducing funding requirements. Defined contribution plans also depend on investment income to enhance pension payments and to keep up with inflation's eroding effects. Investing the insurer's cash assets enhances earnings and provides a cushion for adverse operating results. Any investment earnings after tax add to the company's net worth and can offset unfavorable operating results.

Table 25.1 provides data for 1989 showing the dollar amount of investments by type made by U.S. life insurance companies. When selecting the individual investment, insurers include such factors as the world's general economic conditions, the security's expected rate of return, safety, liquidity, timing of income, meeting state regulations, tax laws and diversification (portfolio performance). Insurers must take the nature of the obligation into account. Insurers sell traditional life insurance products as well as investment-oriented products and are becoming more sensitive to asset management techniques—the coordination of investment strategy with the purpose of the investment.

Dissolution and Reorganization

Insurance regulators must protect the public from financially unsound life insurance companies. Regulators have the power to discontinue impaired insurers by

Table 25.1
U.S. Life Insurance Company Assets—1989

Source	$ Amount (000,000)	Percent
Corporate bonds	538,063	41.39
Mortgages	254,215	19.56
Government securities	178,141	13.70
Corporate stocks	125,614	9.67
Policy loans	57,439	4.42
Real estate	39,908	3.08
Other*	106,376	8.18
Total	1,299,756	100.00

*Other assets include cash, due and deferred premiums, due and accrued investment income and other miscellaneous assets.
Source: *1990 Life Insurance Fact Book Update*. American Council of Life Insurance, Washington, D.C., p. 83.

revoking their insurance license. If the company is financially distressed, the state will order the *rehabilitation, liquidation or conservation* of the insurer. Under rehabilitation, regulators take control of the insurer until it is back in good financial health. *Liquidation* refers to the orderly termination of the insurer to minimize the financial impact on policyholders; it is usually an act of last resort. Conservation keeps assets of foreign or alien insurers in the state so that they can be used to satisfy any claims. (A **foreign** insurer is domiciled in another state. An **alien** insurer is domiciled outside the United States.)

Insurance regulators receive financial and operating information on insurers in several ways. First, insurers file the NAIC blank, disclosing much financial and operating information. Second, the life insurance company is subject to a department on-site inspection at least once every three years. Third, other evaluative information is available, including Standard and Poor's ratings, Best's ratings and the results of the NAIC Insurance Regulatory Information System (discussed in the following section).

Most states follow the NAIC Model Insurers Supervision, Rehabilitation and Liquidation Act (1977) in handling rehabilitations or liquidations. For example, Article 74 of the New York Insurance Code cites many reasons why a company may be placed in rehabilitation, liquidation or conservation. These reasons include insolvency, refusal to submit financial documents or other material to the state, reinsuring the entire book of business or trying to merge without general authorization, cases where further continuance would not be in the best interest of policyholders, violation of the insurer's charter or laws of the state and officer(s)' refusing to be examined under oath.

The commissioner may seek (based on the reasons cited) a court order to take possession of the insurer and to operate it either in its own name or in the name of the court. The insurer may protest, and if the court finds the commissioner acted without cause, then control reverts back to the original owners.

To protect policyholders further, most states have **guarantee funds**. A guarantee fund is a nonprofit corporation that raises funds by assessing companies operating in the state in proportion to their admitted assets. Under Article 75 of the New York Insurance Code the guarantee fund has the power to assume, reinsure or guarantee insurance policies; to borrow money; and to collect by legal proceedings any assessments due but not paid.

NAIC Insurance Regulatory Information System (IRIS)

The National Association of Insurance Commissioners continues to show concern about protecting the public from insolvent insurers. In the early 1970s the NAIC monitored the financial condition of life insurance companies through an "early warning system." Composed of financial ratios, the system assisted state insurance departments in overseeing the financial position of life insurance companies operating in their territory. The system helped monitor the financial condition of insurers without the need for annual department inspections. The early warning system ratios identified unusual changes in financial conditions requiring more attention by the regulators. Over the years the effectiveness of the ratios has improved, and the early warning system evolved into the *Insurance Regulatory Information System (IRIS)*[20]. The information and ratios comprising IRIS identify life insurance companies likely to experience financial difficulty. The numerical results are public information. The NAIC reports a company ranking to state regulators based on the number of ratios that have unusual results. The companies with the highest numbers of ratios falling outside normal ranges require attention first.

Although IRIS provides the means for solvency surveillance, there are operational limitations in its use. First, submission to IRIS scrutiny is voluntary. There is no requirement for life insurance companies to submit annual data to the NAIC for inclusion in the report. Second, the accuracy of the information is based on standardization of the annual statements, the information-coding process and the honesty behind filing the statements. Third, unusual changes over time or in ratio amounts do not necessarily indicate financial difficulty. Individual state insurance departments still need to inspect life insurance companies individually when the ratios warrant further investigation.

Figure 25.2 provides the **IRIS ratios** used by the NAIC in 1989 for the first part, the statistical phase, of its analysis. Also included in the table is a brief description of each ratio. These ratios are modified occasionally when more accurate ratios are found to assess the insurer's financial well-being.

The second phase of the IRIS analysis, the analytical phase, occurs at NAIC headquarters in Kansas City, where teams from various state insurance departments meet to discuss individual companies' ratio results and their annual statements. Insurers are then classified by priority. High-priority companies require immediate regulatory assessment, while ones with a lower priority do not receive the same level of concern. Companies not prioritized are subject to the state's regular review process. In 1990, 1,926 life insurers submitted their financial information for analysis. Some states require submission of the data, while others do not. Out of the 1,926 insurance companies, 482 had four or more ratio results identified as outside the usual IRIS ranges.[21]

Figure 25.2
1989 Life and Health Insurance IRIS Ratios†

Ratio 1: Net Change in Capital and Surplus

$$= \frac{\text{Change in capital and surplus*}}{\text{Capital and surplus prior year}}$$

Ratio 1A: Gross Change in Capital and Surplus

$$= \frac{\text{Change in capital and surplus**}}{\text{Capital and surplus prior year}}$$

*Capital and surplus in the current year minus capital changes paid in minus surplus adjustments paid in minus capital and surplus in the prior year.
**Capital and surplus in the current year minus capital and surplus in prior year.

Ratios 1 and 1A measure the improvement or deterioration of a company's financial position during the year. The first takes into account amounts paid in. The second focuses on performance based solely on operations. Unusual values are over 50 or under −10 percent.

Ratio 2: Net Gain to Total Income

$$= \frac{\text{Net gain from operations}}{\text{Total income}}$$

Measures the profitability of operations. No capital gains and losses are included. Unusual values are under 0 percent.

Ratio 3: Commissions and Expenses to Premiums and Deposits

$$= \frac{\text{Commissions and expenses}}{\text{Direct and assumed premiums collected and annuity and other fund deposits}}$$

Measures the extent of commissions and expenses relative to premium and other considerations. Unusual values are over 60 percent.

Ratio 4: Adequacy of Investment Income

$$= \frac{\text{Net investment income}}{\text{Interest required}}$$

Measures whether the amount of interest income is adequate to meet interest obligations. Unusual values are over 900 and less than 125 percent.

Ratio 5: Nonadmitted to Admitted Assets

$$= \frac{\text{Nonadmitted assets}}{\text{Admitted assets}}$$

Measures the extent of assets not normally used to settle claims relative to assets available to settle claims. Unusual values are over 10 percent.

**Figure 25.2 (continued)
1989 Life and Health Insurance IRIS Ratios**

Ratio 6: Real Estate to Capital and Surplus

$$= \frac{\text{Real estate}}{\text{Capital and surplus}}$$

Measures the percent of capital and surplus invested in real estate. Unusual values for companies with capital and surplus over $5 million are over 200 percent. For companies with $5 million or less of capital and surplus an unusual value is greater than 100 percent.

Ratio 7: Investments in Affiliations to Capital and Surplus

$$= \frac{\text{Investments in affiliations}}{\text{Capital and surplus}}$$

Measures all investments held of parent, subsidiary and affiliate organizations relative to capital and surplus. Unusual values are over 100 percent.

Ratio 8: Surplus Relief

$$= \frac{\text{Net commissions and expense allowances received on reinsurance}}{\text{Capital and surplus}}$$

This ratio calculates the net amount of commissions and expenses received through reinsurance transactions relative to the capital and surplus amount. A small positive value indicates some reinsurance ceded. A negative value indicates net reinsurance assumed. Unusual values for companies with capital and surplus over $5 million are over 30 or under −99 percent. For companies with $5 million or less of capital and surplus an unusual value is greater than 10 or under −10 percent.

Ratio 9: Change in Premium

$$= \frac{\text{Change in premium}}{\text{Total premiums in the prior year}}$$

Measures the percentage change in current year's premium from the prior year. Unusual values are over 50 or under −10 percent.

**Ratio 10: Change in Product Mix
Ratio 11: Change in Asset Mix**

These ratios are complicated to calculate and provide an indication of how rapidly the product mix or asset mix is changing. Unusual results are over 5.0 on a scale from 0 to 9.9.

†*Using the NAIC Insurance Regulatory Information System (Life and Health Edition 1989.* (Kansas City, Mo.: National Association of Insurance Commissioners, 1990.)

Taxation of Life Insurers

As are other business entities, life insurers are subject to state and federal taxes. State tax regulations vary. *The Tax Reform Act of 1984* currently governs the federal income taxation of life insurers.

State Taxation

Many states impose an insurance premium tax (or sales tax) to fund regulatory activities. However, because the amount of state tax spent on insurance regulation is small relative to the amounts collected, states use the tax collected for other purposes.

The amount of the tax, the tax base and "in lieu of" provisions vary from state to state. These factors determine the amount of state tax paid. The most common rate imposed is 2 percent of the tax base (usually net premium income). The tax base, however, depends on the treatment of the different insurance contracts, the treatment of policyholders' dividends and whether other taxes exist. In addition, the tax may be a substitution for or "in lieu of" other taxes imposed by the state. Ohio's law relating to premium taxes is as follows:

> The superintendent shall compute a tax at the rate of two and one-half percent, and in case of fire insurance an additional one-half of one percent fire marshal tax, on the balance of such gross amount of premiums or deposits, after deducting premiums and deposits returned and credited and considerations received for reinsurance.[22]

One controversial feature of state taxation concerns tax retaliation. Some states impose a retaliatory tax on out-of-state insurers writing insurance in the state when the other state imposes a higher tax on in-state insurers.[23]

Retaliatory laws originated when states began to impose a higher tax on out-of-state insurers than on domestic insurers to protect domestic insurers' market share. Consider life insurance company A from state A (with a 2 percent tax) selling life insurance in state B (with a 3 percent tax). If company A crosses the state line and sells life insurance in state B, it pays a 3 percent premium tax. When company B (from state B) sells insurance in state A, B will have to pay 3 percent (not 2 percent) in retaliation for state B's imposing a higher tax rate on company A.[24] Here is part of Ohio's retaliatory provision as an example of one state's wording:

> When the laws of any other state, district, territory, or nation impose any taxes, fines, penalties, license fees, deposits of money, securities, or other obligation or prohibitions on insurance companies of this state doing business in such state, district, territory, or nation, or upon their agents therein, the same obligations and prohibitions shall be imposed upon insurance companies of such other state, district, or nation doing business in this state and upon their agents.[25]

Federal Taxation

Federal taxation of life insurance companies began with the proposal of the 16th Amendment to the Constitution in 1909. From 1909 to 1913 (due to the Excise Tax Act of 1909) all corporations paid a 1 percent excise tax for the privilege of incorporation. After 1913, because of the unique characteristics of the life insurance business, various taxing schemes have been used to tax the life insurance transaction.

From 1913 to 1920 life insurance companies were taxed like other companies. Taxable income was based on the total-income concept. From the sum of gross premiums, investment income and capital gains, ordinary expenses were sub-

Figure 25.3
The Structure of Life Insurance Company Taxation

	Life insurance company gross income:
	  Premiums
	  Investment income
	  Capital gains
	  Reserve decreases
	  All other income

Less	

	Life insurance company deductions:
	  General corporate expenses
	  Deductions peculiar to life insurance companies

Equals	Tentative LICTI
Less	
	Special life insurance deduction Small life insurance deduction
Equals	
	Life insurance company taxable income (LICTI)

tracted. Life insurance companies were allowed deductions for reserves, claims and rent payments under annuity policies.

In 1921 the scheme for taxing the life insurance industry changed from a total-income to an investment-income-base approach. Federal tax was levied on investment income plus interest on policy reserves less investment expenses. A deduction was allowed for interest required to meet contractual obligations. However, the deduction amount was the subject of much controversy. During 1947 and 1948 many life insurance companies paid no federal income tax because the interest deduction exceeded net investment income. Many stopgap tax measures were applied until the Life Insurance Company Income Tax Act of 1959 passed.

The *Life Insurance Company Income Tax Act of 1959* was supposed to be a permanent tax solution to the problem of life insurance company taxation, and a switch was made back to the total-income base approach. The 1959 act calculated the tax base using three phases, which included amounts based on investment income, underwriting gain and deferred underwriting gain. The 1959 act was modified in 1982 by the *Tax Equity and Fiscal Responsibility Act (TEFRA)*. The 1959 act and its modifications were replaced with the 1984 act (part of the Tax Reform Act of 1984).

The 1984 act again changed the tax base to a single-phase, total-income approach. Thus, life insurance companies pay federal tax on a basis similar to other taxable entities. However, the act recognizes special deductions and adjustments to gross income because of the special characteristics of the life insurance business. Figure 25.3 provides an outline of how to calculate *life insurance company taxable income (LICTI)*.[26]

Gross Income

Life insurance company gross income includes premiums (all considerations made for contracts), investment income (dividends and interest income from investments), capital gains (gains or losses from the sale of capital assets), decreases in reserves (a net reduction in insurance reserves) and all income not included under the other categories.

Life Insurance Company Deductions

Life insurance companies deduct amounts from gross income equal to general corporate deductions, deductions unique to the insurance business, a special life insurance company deduction and a small life insurance company deduction. The result of subtracting deductions from gross income is the life insurance company taxable income (LICTI).

General corporate deductions include 85 percent of dividends received from other entities besides subsidiaries (80 percent or more owned), losses from operations (carrybacks and carryovers) and operations expense (overhead). Deductions unique to life insurance companies include death benefits and claims, insurance operation reserves, costs of reinsurance and policyholder dividends. Stock insurance companies can deduct all policyholder dividends. To place 55 percent of the life insurance industry tax burden on mutual insurance companies, policyholder dividends of mutuals are subject to limited deductibility under Section 809 of the act. Because the 1984 act did not produce the expected amount of federal tax (expected $9.5 billion, paid $7.2 billion) and the proportion of the tax paid by the stock and mutual companies was not as expected (1985 and 1986 expected: mutuals 55 percent, stocks 45 percent; actual: mutuals 39 percent, stocks 61 percent), hearings on the taxation of life insurance companies were held before the Subcommittee on Select Revenue Measures of the Committee on Ways and Means on October 19, 1989.[27]

Included in the tax law are the *small* and *special life insurance company deductions*. The small and special life insurance company deductions reduce the impact of an increased tax burden on life insurance companies by other changes in the tax law. The small life insurance company deduction maximum is equal to 60 percent of the tentative LICTI (maximum $3 million) or $1,800,000. In addition, if the tentative LICTI exceeds $3 million, the deduction declines by 15 percent of the excess.

For example, if tentative LICTI is equal to $1,500,000, the small life insurance company deduction is equal to $900,000 (0.60 × $1,500,000). However, if tentative LICTI equals $6 million, the deduction would be calculated as follows:

0.60 × $3,000,000 (maximum allowed)	$1,800,000
Less: ($6,000,000 − $3,000,000) × .15	450,000
Small life insurance company deduction	$1,350,000

The special life insurance company deduction is equal to 20 percent of the excess of the tentative LICTI over the small life insurance company deduction. For example, if the small life insurance company deduction is $1,350,000 and the tentative LICTI is $6 million, the special deduction is $930,000 ([$6,000,000 − $1,350,000] × .20).

After all the deductions are subtracted from gross income, normal corporate tax rates apply to the resulting amount of LICTI.

Review Questions

1. Give several reasons for regulation of the insurance transaction. Describe which aspects of the insurance transaction are regulated.
2. What role do the state and federal governments play in regulating the insurance industry?
3. What is the importance of the McCarran-Ferguson Act as it relates to insurance regulation?
4. What do you think will happen if the McCarran-Ferguson Act is repealed completely?
5. Describe the current role of the SEC and FTC in regulating insurance transactions.
6. Explain the major differences between GAAP and statutory accounting methods.
7. Describe the difference between a nonadmitted asset and an admitted asset. Explain the difference between an amortizable and a nonamortizable security.
8. How are common stocks, preferred stocks and bonds valued for statutory reporting purposes?
9. Where does the money for life insurance capital and surplus come from?
10. Describe the terms *rehabilitation, liquidation* and *conservation*.
11. What is a life insurance guarantee fund? How does it work?
12. Discuss the purpose of the Insurance Regulatory Information System (IRIS). Which of the ratios do you think are more important in identifying insurers in financial distress?
13. How does federal taxation of life insurance differ from federal taxation of other businesses?

Endnotes

[1] U.S. General Accounting Office, *Issues and Needed Improvements in State Regulation of the Insurance Business*, October 9, 1979, p. 9.

[2] Geisel, Jerry, "McCarran Floor Vote in House Possible." *Business Insurance,* September 3, 1990, pp. 1, 85. *See also,* "Some Risk Managers Give Support to Repeal of McCarran: Survey," *Business Insurance*, September 3, 1990, pp. 84, 85.

[3] Bradford, Michael, "Spotlight Report: Insurance Regulation," *Business Insurance*, December 3, 1990, pp. 3–32.

[4] *Paul v. Virginia*, 8 Wall, 1968, 183 (1869).

[5] For an in-depth analysis of the history of life insurance in the United States, *see* Terence O'Donnell, *History of Life Insurance in Its Formative Years* (Chicago: American Conservation Company, 1936).

[6] *United States v. South-Eastern Underwriters Association et al.*, 64 S. Ct. 1162 (1944).

[7] *Federal Trade Commission v. National Casualty Co.*, 357 U.S. 560 (1958).

[8] *Travelers Health Association v. Federal Trade Commission*, 262 F.2d 241 (1959), 362 U.S. 293 (1960), 298 F.2d. 820 (1962).

[9] *Securities and Exchange Commission, Petitioner v. Variable Annuity Life Insurance Company of America and the Equity Annuity Life Insurance Company*, 19 U.S. Supreme Court Bulletin 821 (CCH, March 23, 1959).

[10] *See* Article 12 of the New York Insurance Code, which covers 58 pages, for the complete requirements for incorporating as a stock or mutual company in New York.

[11] New York Insurance Code Section 4202.

[12] New York Insurance Code Section 1102 (4).

[13] New York Insurance Code Section 2110.

[14] New York Insurance Code Section 4231.

[15] New York Insurance Code Section 4224.

[16] *Audits of Stock Life Insurance Companies* (New York: American Institute of Certified Public Accountants, 1972), p. 72.

[17] Financial Accounting Standards Board, *Statement of Financial Accounting Standards No. 60—Accounting and Reporting by Insurance Enterprises* (Stamford, Conn.: FASB, 1982).

[18] *See* Robert W. Strain, ed., *Life Insurance Accounting* (Santa Monica, Calif.: Merritt, 1977), for a more complete discussion on the difference between GAAP and statutory accounting methods.

[19] Jones, David, C., "FASB 97 Implementation: Major Accounting Expense," *National Underwriter (Life/Health Edition)*, June 6, 1988, p. 9. *See also* Mark V. Sever and Brian Zell, "FASB 97 'Daunting' Work for Insurers," *National Underwriter (Life/Health Edition)*, March 21, 1988, p. 5.

[20] *Using the NAIC Insurance Regulatory Information System (Life and Health Edition, 1989)*, (Kansas City, Mo.: National Association of Insurance Commissioners, 1990).

[21] Joseph M. Belth, *The Insurance Forum* 17, No. 9, September 1990, pp. 143–156.

[22] Ohio Revised Code Section 3931.07.

[23] For a further analysis of state premium taxation and retaliation, *see* Robert D. Goshey, "Net Income as a Base for Life Insurance Company Taxation in California: Implications," *Journal of Risk and Insurance* 43, No. 1 (March 1976), pp. 17–41; and Jerry J. Bodily, "The Effects of Retaliation on State Taxation of Life Insurers," *Journal of Risk and Insurance* 44, No. 1 (March 1977), pp. 21–36.

[24] *See Indemnity Ins. Co. of North America, v. Stowell*, 172 Ohio St. 167; 174 N.E.2d 536; 15 Ohio Op. 2d 321, April 26, 1961.

[25] Ohio Revised Code Section 3905.41.

[26] *See Life Insurance Tax Provisions—Tax Reform Act of 1984: Law Committee Reports—Explanation* (Chicago: Commerce Clearing House), for the complete text of the Tax Reform Act of 1984 applying to life insurance companies.

[27] The Joint Committee on Taxation, Taxation of Life Insurance Companies (JCS-17-89), October, 1989.

Bibliography

Harman, William Jr. "The Structure of Life Insurance Taxation—The New Pattern Under the 1984 Act—Part I." *Journal of American Society of CLU*, March 1985, p. 56.

Harman, William Jr. "The Structure of Life Insurance Taxation—The New Pattern Under the 1984 Act—Part II." *Journal of American Society of CLU*, May 1985, p. 76.

Huggins, Kenneth. *Operations of Life and Health Insurance Companies*, Atlanta, Ga.: Life Office Management Institute, 1986.

_____. Joint Committee on Taxation. *Taxation of Life Insurance Companies* (JCS-17-89). October 16, 1989.

Palmer, John J., and Douglas N. Hertz. "That Thorny Tax Dispute—The Stock Company Perspective and the Mutual Company Perspective." *Best's Review (Life/Health Edition)*, January 1990, pp. 34ff.

Sever, Mark V., and Brian Zell. "FASB 97 Means 'Daunting' Work for Insurers." *National Underwriter*, March 21, 1988, p. 5.

_____. *Using the NAIC Insurance Regulatory Information System (Life and Health Edition 1989)*. Kansas City, Mo.: National Association of Insurance Commissioners, 1990.

Zucconi, Paul J. *Accounting in Life and Health Insurance Companies*, Atlanta, Ga.: Office Management Institute, 1987.

Appendix A: Formulas for Compound Interest Tables[1]

Future Value of $1

$$FVF = (1 + i)^n$$

Present Value of $1

$$PVF = \frac{1}{(1 + i)^n}$$

Future Value of an Ordinary Annuity

$$FVA = \frac{(1 + i)^n - 1}{i}$$

Present Value of an Ordinary Annuity

$$PVA = \frac{1 - (1 + i)^{-n}}{i}$$

Future Value of an Annuity Due

$$FVAD = (1 + i)\left[\frac{(1 + i)^n - 1}{i}\right]$$

Present Value of an Annuity Due

$$PVAD = (1 + i)\left[\frac{1 - (1 + i)^{-n}}{i}\right]$$

i = interest rate for time period n
n = number of periods for the calculation
FVF = future value factor
PVF = present value factor
FVA = future value of an ordinary annuity factor
$FVAD$ = future value annuity due factor
$PVAD$ = present value annuity due factor

Endnotes

[1] For an excellent treatment of the mathematics of the time value of money, see Elbert B. Greynolds, Jr., Julius S. Aronofsky, and Robert J. Frame, *Financial Analysis Using Calculators: Time Value of Money* (New York: McGraw-Hill, 1980).

Glossary

A

accelerated benefits Early payment of all or part of a life insurance policy's death benefit when the insured is diagnosed as having a specified disease or being terminally ill.

acceptance A required act in the formation of a contract. Acceptance of a contractual offer means complete agreement with the proposed terms.

accidental bodily injury Accident policies cover the insured on either an accidental injury or accidental means basis. An accidental injury occurs if the result (the injury) was sudden and unexpected. *See* accidental means.

accidental death and dismemberment benefits A provision of a life insurance or health insurance contract requiring payment of the principal sum if the insured dies or has a defined dismemberment caused by an accident. Not all accidents are covered, and the policy may pay a multiple of the face amount.

accidental means Accident policies cover the insured on either an accidental means or an accidental injury basis. An accidental means insuring agreement covers the insured if the means to the injury was sudden and unexpected. *See* accidental bodily injury.

actuary The person professionally trained to apply probability and statistics to help in underwriting, rating, financial forecasting and reserving among other tasks.

adhesion A characteristic of an insurance contract. A contract of adhesion is interpreted against the writer of the contract when there are ambiguous terms.

administrative service only (ASO) An arrangement in which an insurance company or an independent organization handles administrative details of a self-insured group for a fee.

admitted assets Those assets the state allows an insurer to use in meeting tests of solvency. Typically these assets can be easily realized as cash and used to pay claims. Nonadmitted assets are those such as home office furniture that ordinarily could not be used to satisfy insureds' claims.

adverse selection Selection against the insurer. The tendency of less desirable exposures to loss, such as people in poor health, to try to purchase insurance protection at standard (average) rates.

Age Discrimination in Employment Act (ADEA) The ADEA prohibits discrimination against employees in the protected age group (ages 40 to 70). ADEA prevents employers from forcing employees to retire before age 70.

agent A person authorized to act for another person known as a *principal*. In the typical insurance transaction the individual dealing with the consumer is an agent acting for the insurer, the principal.

aleatory contract A contract in which both parties know from the inception that the monetary value exchanged will not be equal. Insurance is an aleatory contract in which the insured can receive more or less than the premium paid for the coverage.

alien insurance company An insurer from another country. A foreign insurance company is one doing business in a state other than the one in which it is incorporated. An Ohio-based insurer doing business in Indiana is a *foreign* insurer in Indiana. A Canadian insurer doing business in Indiana is an *alien* insurer.

allocated funding When an employer purchases an annuity or a life insurance policy identified for each employee to fund a pension plan.

ambulatory care Medical services provided out of the hospital or on an outpatient basis. These services include diagnostic treatment, outpatient surgery and rehabilitation services.

amount at risk The amount of the insurer's exposure to loss. This amount may be different from the face amount of insurance in cash value life insurance contracts because some death benefits received by the beneficiary may be considered as arising from the savings value of the contract. Thus the amount at risk ($700) is the difference between the face amount of insurance ($1,000) and the cash value ($300).

annual statement blank The annual report supplied to state insurance departments disclosing statutory financial data.

annuity A regular series of payments. If payments are made for a lifetime, the contract is called *a pure annuity* or a *straight life annuity*. If payments are guaranteed for a specified period, regardless of the annuitant's survival or death, the arrangement is called an *annuity certain*. If payments are guaranteed for a lifetime or a certain period, whichever event is last, the arrangement is called a *life annuity, period certain*. Annuities covering two or more lives are called *joint life annuities* if payments end at the first death. If payments end at the second of two deaths, the contract is called a *joint-and-last-survivor annuity*. Contracts calling for a refund when the total amount of rent received by the annuitant (for example, $25,000) is less than the premium paid for the contract (for example, $60,000) are called *refund annuities*. If the refund is made in lump sum ($35,000 in this example), the contract is called a *cash refund annuity*. If the refund is made by continuing the regular installment payments (for example, $6,000 a year until the $35,000 refund is paid) to contingent beneficiaries, the contract is called an *installment refund annuity*.

annuity due Equal or unequal money amounts paid or received at the beginning of each period.

annuity table A statistical table providing historical or projected patterns of survival rates for a large number of insured people based on factors such as age and sex.

apparent authority One method of receiving authority to sell life insurance. Apparent authority occurs when the public believes because of actions of the agent and the principal that an agency relationship exists.

Appleton Rule A New York law that states insurance companies licensed in New York must apply New York State insurance regulations wherever they sell insurance, thus imposing New York State law beyond the state.

asset share analysis A method used to project financial results and test the statistical and other assumptions used in designing life insurance contracts.

assignment The legal transfer of contractual rights and duties from one party to another. Assignment may or may not involve consideration. Assignment of insurance contracts is governed by policy language. Assignment of fire insurance policies is possible only with the consent of the insurer. Assignment of life insurance policies requires only the proper notification of the insurer.

assignment payment system Under Social Security Medicare, if a provider of health care services accepts assignment, the amount paid by Medicare is considered full payment except for deductibles and copayments owed by the patient. The provider may not bill the patient for the excess amount not paid by Medicare.

automatic premium plan (APL) An optional contractual feature of cash value life insurance policies. The insurer agrees to make a loan equal to any missed premiums to keep a policy in force. The total amount of loans made, plus interest thereon, must be supported by the available cash values of the contract.

automatic reinsurance A type of reinsurance arrangement where all contracts meeting specified underwriting characteristics are automatically reinsured. The primary company cannot select exposures to offer, and the reinsurer may not reject exposures. *See* reinsurance.

B

backdating The practice of dating an application or other forms prior to the actual day of signing. Backdating can reduce the insured's age for underwriting purposes.

Belth's single-year method A method used to calculate the net amount at risk's annual cost of life insurance.

beneficiary The person who is designated to receive the proceeds of a life insurance policy.

Best's rating The financial rating assigned an insurance company by the A. M. Best Company. The A. M. Best Company rates an insurance company's quality and safety for policy owners based on financial considerations and the quality of management.

binder An oral or written statement spelling out the particulars or terms of an insurance contract. Binders can be used as evidence of an existing contract before the actual policy is delivered.

binding receipt A written statement spelling out the terms for acceptance of a life insurance contract after an offer is made. Binding receipts provide insurance until the company accepts or rejects the application. *See* conditional receipt.

Blue Cross and Blue Shield An independent, nonprofit corporation providing health care on a service basis in a limited geographic area. Blue Cross provides hospital benefits. Blue Shield provides medical and surgical benefits.

broker An agent of the applicant for insurance. The broker may be authorized to design coverages or shop for insurance coverage.

business life insurance A term used to describe life insurance and disability products used for business purposes such as to fund business continuation plans and provide supplemental insurance benefits.

buy-and-sell agreement An arrangement made to allow the continuation of a business after the death of one of the owners. The agreement sets the price at which the sale will be made. It also forces the owners or estate to sell and the buyers to buy the property at this price. Such an agreement is often accompanied by the purchase of life insurance, which provides the funds to complete the transaction.

buy term and invest the difference (BTID) Instead of purchasing whole life insurance, some people purchase term insurance and invest the premium difference between a whole life plan and the term policy. This strategy attempts to duplicate the life insurance and savings of a whole life insurance contract.

C

callable provision A provision found in some securities that allows the issuer to retire them before their maturity date.

cancelable A contract that can be terminated by the insurance company at any time.

capacity The legal ability to make a binding contract.

cash surrender value The amount of money returned to the policy owner when a cash value contract is surrendered or terminated.

Civil Rights Act of 1964 This act prevents employers from discriminating in pension plan benefits based on gender or race.

claim A demand for payment made for a covered loss by an insured or beneficiary on an insurer.

coinsurance reinsurance A form of reinsurance where the insurer reinsures the policy amount that is excess of its retention level for the life of the contract. The reinsurer receives a proportionate amount of the premium less an allowance for expenses and is responsible for the same fraction of any claims. For example, a $100,000 policy is sold by an insurer with a $75,000 retention. The reinsurer receives one-quarter of the premium less an allowance for expenses and is responsible for one-quarter of the nonforfeiture values, dividends and the claim ($25,000). *See also* reinsurance and yearly renewable term reinsurance.

combination whole life Policies combining decreasing term insurance with a participating whole life policy. The contract requires reinvesting the annual dividends in the policy. The dividends purchase amounts of paid-up whole life insurance exactly offsetting the decreasing term portion of the contract.

common disaster A common disaster occurs when an insured and a primary beneficiary to a life insurance contract die as a result of the same accident. Problems may arise if it is unknown who died first. Various techniques are used to preplan for this event and direct policy proceeds based on the policy owner's wishes.

concealment Silence when obligated to speak. A duty is imposed on applicants for insurance to reveal all material facts even if specific information is not requested by the insurer. Typically there must be an element of deception. Neglect of this duty is called *concealment*.

conditionally renewable A type of renewability clause found in health and disability contracts. Renewal is not guaranteed, nor is the premium. Renewal is based on the contract's wording.

conditional receipt An arrangement used in life insurance that can provide coverage to an applicant before an actual contract can be issued. These agreements typically require the applicant to submit the first premium payment and are conditioned on the insured meeting all the requirements for acceptance by the insurer, including passing a medical examination.

consideration The amount of economic value given up in making a valid contract.

Consolidated Omnibus Budget Reconciliation Act of 1985 (COBRA) A federal law requiring employers to allow workers leaving their job, spouses of deceased employees and divorced spouses to continue group health insurance coverage for up to 36 months after a "qualifying event," such as separation from work, death or divorce.

consumer price index (CPI) A measure of price inflation calculated and published by the Bureau of Labor Statistics, U.S. Department of Labor. The CPI measures the price changes of a constant market basket of goods and services over time.

continuing care retirement community A group living arrangement for the elderly with independent living units and a nursing facility. Admission usually involves a large front-end fee.

continuous-premium whole life insurance Continuous-premium whole life insurance is the most popular form of whole life. To maintain the policy, the insureds must pay the same annual premium until they die or reach age 100. Insurers also call these policies *ordinary life, level-premium whole life* and *straight life*.

contract A legally enforceable agreement between two or more parties. Legal contracts require legality, capacity, offer and acceptance and consideration to be valid.

convertible term life insurance A term insurance policy allowing the insured to convert to a permanent form of insurance without providing evidence of insurability.

copayment A policy provision frequently found in major medical insurance contracts and Medicare. The insured and the insurer share in the covered expenses in a specified ratio—typically 20 percent by the insured and 80 percent by the insurer.

corporate bonds A long-term debt issued by a corporation paying a coupon rate of interest for the use of the funds. Bonds may be callable and convertible.

corporation An artificial entity recognized by state law. The Internal Revenue Code recognizes two major types of corporations: regular corporations, called *C corporations,* and corporations electing to have their income taxed to their shareholders, called *S corporations.*

cost-of-living adjustment (COLA) Automatic Social Security benefit increases made annually whenever the consumer price index rises above a certain percent.

credit life insurance Group insurance taken out to cover all the debtors of one creditor. The purpose of the insurance is to repay outstanding loan balances at the death of the debtor. Typical groups purchasing credit life insurance are the debtors of a merchant and people purchasing a car on credit from a finance company.

credit shelter bypass trust A trust set up for the purpose of allowing each spouse to use the $192,800 uniform transfer tax credit.

cross-purchase plan or agreement A form of buy-and-sell agreement forcing the estate of a deceased owner to sell and a purchaser to buy at a prearranged price. Cross-purchase agreements typically use life insurance to fund the purchase.

custodial care Care for the activities of daily living (bathing, dressing and toileting, for example). There is no expectation this care will improve a person's health. It is designed to maintain a person at his or her current level. Providing this care requires no medical training.

D

debit life insurance Also known as *home service life insurance* and *burial life insurance*. A form of life insurance typically sold in amounts of less than $1,000, with premiums collected at the insured's home on a weekly or monthly basis.

deductible The amount paid by the insured before any payment is made by an insurance company. Insurance companies pay the excess over the deductible to eliminate frequent small claims.

default risk The possibility that invested principal will not be returned. The possibility that creditors or businesses will fail and the investment will be lost. People assume no default risk with federally insured bank deposits or when they invest in U.S. Treasury securities.

deferred annuity A contract in which payments to the annuitant begin sometime after the premium payments to the insurer have ended. Thus a person aged 40 who purchases an annuity with payments to begin on his or her 65th birthday has purchased a deferred annuity.

deferred compensation plan A nonqualified compensation plan used as a fringe benefit for select employees in which compensation is reduced or forgone until some future date, such as at retirement.

defined benefit plans Defined benefit pension plans use a formula to determine the employee's pension benefit. Determining the projected pension benefit simultaneously establishes the employer's funding obligations.

defined contribution plans Defined contribution plans fix the employer's dollar cost; the employees' pension benefit remains undetermined until retirement.

demutualization The process of turning the legal form of an insurance organization from a mutual to a stock company.

diagnosis-related groups (DRG) A system of reimbursing for health care and all related services with one fixed amount based on a standard principal diagnosis category.

disability income insurance A form of health insurance that replaces lost income when a person is disabled on a total or partial basis. Payments are made for various lengths of time based on the definition of disability.

disability income rider Additional coverage attached to another type of policy providing disability income coverage. *See* disability income insurance.

disability (total) This term is subject to different definitions by different insurers and in different policies. One of the strictest definitions is "the inability to engage in any gainful employment." A more liberal definition would be "inability to engage in the employment one is trained for."

disintermediation A process in which people withdraw their money from a financial intermediary to invest at a higher yield. With respect to life insurance companies the process involves policy owners borrowing some or all of the cash values accumulated in a permanent form of life insurance and investing these funds at higher rates than the insurer charges as interest on the loan.

dividend An amount paid to the owners of a corporation. When dividends are paid to policyholders of mutual insurers, the dividends represent a nontaxable return. Dividends are also paid to owners of stock insurers; such dividends are a taxable return on their investment.

divisible surplus The amount identified by the board of directors of a mutual insurance company to be divided among policyholders in the form of participating dividends.

double indemnity An option on some life insurance contracts causing the insurer to pay twice the face of the policy if death is caused by a specified circumstance such as an accident.

E

Employment Retirement Income Security Act of 1974 (ERISA) Federal legislation designed to guarantee certain aspects of pension plans of private employers.

endowment life insurance A contract promising to pay proceeds to a beneficiary if the insured dies before the end of the endowment period or to pay the insured if the insured survives the specified period. A pure endowment promises payment only if the insured survives the specified period.

entire-contract clause A mandatory provision in life and health insurance making the entire policy and attached applications the agreement between the contract's parties.

entity purchase plan A form of buy-and-sell agreement forcing the estate of a deceased owner to sell and a purchaser to buy at a prearranged price. Entity purchase agreements use life insurance to fund the purchase. The business organization purchases the life insurance and is the beneficiary of each policy on the business owners.

equivalent level annual dividend A mathematical computation providing an index of the importance of the illustrated dividend distribution in reducing a participating life insurance policy's cost. This index is used with the surrender cost index and the net payment index.

errors and omissions insurance Liability coverage designed to protect professionals, such as accountants or insurance agents, from claims that their professional actions resulted in losses to their clients.

estate planning The development of a financial plan designed to cover the liquidation and disposal of assets before and at a person's death. Such a plan may involve living considerations (gifts), death considerations (identifying in a will which people will receive property) and tax considerations (including the federal unified transfer tax).

estate tax A tax imposed by the federal government when property is transferred at death.

estoppel A common law doctrine preventing a person from asserting a known right when such an assertion is inconsistent with the person's past actions. For example, if an insurer issues a policy knowing that the insured is ineligible for the coverage, it may be estopped from denying a claim because of the initial ineligibility.

evidence of insurability In life insurance, whatever evidence an applicant for insurance must provide to induce an insurer to offer a life insurance contract. The term includes, but is not limited to, good health.

exclusion A clause in an insurance policy in which the insurer specifies losses (circumstances, types of property, ineligible people, etc.) not covered by the policy.

expense ratio The ratio of all the expenses (such as sales commissions or credit investigations but not the costs of covered losses) incurred in writing insurance, divided by the premiums earned from selling the insurance.

experience rating A retroactive approach to group insurance pricing. Experience rating allows a particular group's premiums to reflect that group's costs, rather than the pooled costs of all insured groups.

extended term option A nonforfeiture option allowing the exchange of the cash surrender value for a term policy with the same face amount for a length of time. At the end of the period, no insurance exists.

F

face amount The initial amount of life insurance scheduled to be paid at the insured's death. The face amount may not be the amount received by the beneficiary because of outstanding loans at the time of the insured's death (which decreases the death benefit) or because of the inclusion of paid-up additions in the proceeds (which increases the death benefit).

fiduciary A person who acts on behalf of another person. A fiduciary is held by law to the highest standards of ethical conduct. Examples of fiduciaries are trustees and executors.

financial planning The process of integrating all financial transactions into an efficient, clearly directed, likely-to-succeed strategy.

fixed-amount option A settlement option directing the insurance company to pay the principal and accumulated interest to the beneficiary or owner. A fixed amount is paid until the principal and interest are exhausted.

fixed-benefit annuities With these contracts, once the annuitant begins the liquidation phase of the annuity, the guaranteed amount of the liquidation payments does not change.

fixed-period option A settlement option directing the insurance company to pay the principal and accumulated interest to the beneficiary or owner. A fixed period is selected, and the principal and interest are distributed over the period.

flexible-premium deferred annuity (FPDA) An annuity contract allowing the owner to make an uneven series of deposits before liquidation begins. Deposits earn compound interest at a minimum guaranteed rate, and this interest accrues on a tax-deferred basis until liquidation.

foreign insurance company *See* alien insurance company.

fortuitous Occurring by chance.

fraud An act, such as lying or other deception, designed to cheat an insurer. Fraud against an insurer generally allows the insurer to avoid the insurance contract.

front-end load A charge levied against the amount of money deposited or paid into a savings or insurance plan. *See also* rear-end load.

funded trust A trust with property in it. A trust with no present property but with the right to receive property (such as life insurance proceeds) in the future is an unfunded trust.

G

general partnership A form of partnership in which all partners are personally responsible for all partnership debts.

gift A transfer from one party to another for less than fair market value.

grace period A limited period of time, such as 30 days, in which an insured can pay a past-due life insurance premium without having to go through the formalities of reinstating the policy. Benefits are available during the grace period.

grantor trust A living trust where the income is available to the wealth owner during his or her lifetime. No tax advantages accrue to the grantor trust as all income is taxed to the donor.

gross premium The total amount of premium paid by a policy owner to an insurance company. The gross premium includes overhead expenses, taxes and loss estimates among other expenses.

group deferred annuities Annuities purchased by employers to fund pension plan obligations.

group insurance Insurance provided to groups of people usually through employee groups. One master contract is issued while individual certificates are given to the members.

guaranteed funds State-run organizations used to guarantee promises made by insurance companies if they fail. Insurance companies are generally assessed amounts based on the percent of business written in the state.

guaranteed insurability rider An agreement found in insurance contracts shifting the risk of insurability to the insurance company.

guaranteed renewable A contract provision found in health insurance stating that the insurer must renew and that premiums may not be changed for individual insureds until a certain age, usually 65. Premiums may be changed for the whole class of insureds.

H

health insurance A broad category of insurance that pays for various losses due to sickness, accidents or various levels of care.

health maintenance organization (HMO) A medical organization that typically allows subscribers (usually members of employee groups) to pay one annual fee (capitation payment) in exchange for the right to all needed health care services. HMOs stress preventive care.

home health care Health care or custodial care delivered in the home. These services are less expensive if delivered in the home instead of a hospital.

home office The headquarters of an insurance company. The home office of an insurer determines the state in which it is domiciled.

hospice A facility caring for the terminally ill.

hospitalization policy A basic form of health insurance providing benefits while an insured is hospitalized. Some policies extend benefits to emergency care and outpatient services.

human capital The investment people make in themselves to improve their productivity.

human life value The economic value of a person's future earnings less taxes paid and funds needed to support the wage earner. One measure of the loss incurred by a person's heirs or survivors.

I

immediate annuity A contract in which the first payment occurs on the next payment date after the contract is purchased.

incontestable clause A part of the life insurance contract preventing the insurer from denying a claim for alleged fraud occurring at the policy's inception. The insurer has a limited period of time to discover any such fraud, after which time there can be no defense for nonpayment by the insurer. This means the insurer must pay even if fraud can be proved.

increasing-benefit annuity An annuity in which liquidation payments in the early years are smaller than the actuarially determined amount. Starting from the reduced base, liquidation payments increase in each successive period.

indemnity A payment by the insurer to the insured that leaves the insured in the same financial position enjoyed before the covered loss took place.

indemnity contract A contract that attempts to return the insured to his or her original financial position, such as fire, inland marine and health insurance contracts. *See also* valued contract.

indemnity plan A form of medical insurance in which the insured is paid stated dollar amounts for certain losses.

individual life insurance Life insurance purchased by individuals as opposed to group insurance or business insurance.

individual retirement account (IRA) IRAs are designed to encourage people to save for retirement. Tax laws allow qualified people to make limited tax-deductible contributions and allow IRA accounts to earn tax-deferred investment income. Congress passed the original IRA provisions as part of the *Employment Retirement Income Security Act of 1974 (ERISA)*. Eligibility rules were broadened in 1982 and then restricted by the *Tax Reform Act of 1986* for tax years after December 31, 1986. Tax rules current in 1991 distinguish between deductible and nondeductible IRA contributions.

industrial life insurance *See* debit life insurance.

injury A wrong done to another, including damaging a person's body, property, reputation or rights.

inpatient Receiving hospital services while staying in a hospital.

insolvency (guaranty) funds *See* guaranteed funds.

installment or cash refund annuity. *See* annuity.

insurable interest The ability to demonstrate that the insured event is capable of causing a financial loss to the person owning the insurance. To collect from a property insurance contract the insurable interest must be demonstrated at the time of the loss. In life insurance the insurable interest must exist when the policy begins.

insurance (1) A contractual relationship between two parties in which one party, the insurer, is paid a premium by the other party, the insured. In return for the premium the insurer promises to pay the insured in the event of a covered loss. (2) A money transfer scheme in which those exposed to a loss voluntarily put money into a pool from which losses are paid to those pool members experiencing loss.

insuring agreement That part of the insurance contract describing the insurer's duty to pay dollar amounts to the insured.

integrated plans Pension or disability group insurance plans that consider Social Security benefits when determining benefits.

interest-adjusted methods Cost comparison techniques using time-value-of-money techniques to adjust for the timing of paying and receiving value.

interest option A settlement option in life insurance. Interest is paid on principal amounts. The owner or beneficiary may withdraw principal amounts at will unless restricted.

interest rate risk Changes in interest rates affect the market value of securities, including U.S. Treasury issues. Investors experience losses in market value when interest rates rise. The longer the term of the security, the greater the loss. The opposite result occurs when interest rates decline; people experience gains.

intermediate care Occasional nursing and rehabilitative care, ordered by a physician. This level of care is performed under the supervision of skilled medical personnel.

interpleader The process of paying policy proceeds into the court system for final distribution. Interpleader is used when various kinds of disputes exist.

intestacy (intestate) Dying without a valid will.

IRA rollover A rollover occurs when money from an IRA or other retirement plan is placed with a new trustee. Rollovers may occur when an employee switches jobs and takes vested retirement benefits from a pension plan or when an employer terminates a pension plan and makes payments of vested benefits to individual employees. If the employee takes the vested benefits and places them in an IRA, this transaction is considered a rollover. A rollover also would occur if a person switched from one investment medium to another, such as from a mutual fund to a bank.

IRIS ratios Insurance Regulatory Information System ratios. A series of ratios calculated from statutory information supplied to the NAIC for solvency testing and surveillance purposes.

J

joint-and-last-survivor annuity *See* annuity.

juvenile life insurance Life insurance designed specifically for children. Jumping juvenile policies provide for the face of the policy to increase, often to five times the initial amount, at the child's 18th birthday.

K

Keogh plans Also called *H.R.-10 plans,* Keogh plans allow self-employed people to take a deduction from their adjusted gross income for money contributed to a retirement fund. Keogh plans are available to sole proprietors or active partners in a partnership.

key employee An employee-nonowner whose death or disability would cause substantial financial loss to the business firm.

kiddie tax Internal Revenue Code rules taxing nonwage income in excess of $1,000 of children younger than age 14 at their parents' marginal bracket.

L

lapse The expiration of a life insurance policy because of nonpayment of the premium.

lapse ratio The number of policies lapsed in a year divided by the number of policies in force at the beginning of the year.

law of large numbers When an event based on chance is observed, the larger the number of observations, the more likely is the actual result to coincide with the expected result.

legal reserve The reserve (liability) required by state law to promote the solvency of life insurers. The reserve may be calculated on a prospective or retrospective basis and is a function of the insurer's contractual liabilities under the policies it has written.

level-premium whole life insurance *See* continuous-premium whole life insurance

life annuity option A settlement option found in life insurance and annuity policies paying rent until the death of the annuitant.

life insurance An insurance contract that pays amounts upon the death of an insured to a beneficiary.

Life Insurance Marketing and Research Association (LIMRA) An industry trade association preparing sales and marketing statistics and analysis.

Life Office Management Association (LOMA) An industry trade association providing education, research and other services for insurance company management.

limited partnership A form of partnership in which there is at least one general partner, who is personally responsible for partnership debts, and any number of limited partners, who may not actively engage in the management of the business.

limited-payment whole life insurance A form of cash value life insurance in which the number of scheduled premium payments is limited, such as 20 payments, or by the age of the insured, such as "paid up at 65."

Linton yield The rate of return equating the growth of life insurance cash value to a side fund giving consideration to mortality costs.

liquidity The ability to turn assets into cash quickly.

living or *inter vivos* trust A trust established during the grantor's lifetime.

long-term care coverage A form of insurance coverage providing various levels of custodial care.

loss An unexpected and unintentional reduction in economic wealth or value.

M

major medical health insurance A medical expense contract typified by a large upper limit of coverage (such as $50,000), a participation provision (causing the insured to pay some percentage of the claim, such as 20 percent) and a deductible provision (such as $500).

managed care Health care systems that integrate the financing and delivery of care. Managed care includes comprehensive care, standards of care, quality assurance and financial incentives to use the providers and to follow procedures.

material fact A fact is material if its disclosure would have caused the insurer's underwriters to issue the contract with a different premium or different wording (compared to standard) or to not accept the application (the offer).

McCarran-Ferguson Act See Public Law 15.

Medicaid A federal program established under the Social Security Act providing health-related benefits to people with low resources and income.

Medicaid qualifying trust A trust set up to receive a person's property to qualify for Medicaid benefits. Medicaid imposes a 30-month waiting period, and the trust cannot pay for expenses normally paid by Medicaid.

Medical Information Bureau (MIB) A nonprofit trade association of 750 life insurance companies formed to conduct a confidential interchange of underwriting information. The purpose of the MIB is to prevent fraud.

medical price index An index providing information about the rate of change and the level of health care costs.

medical selection effect A term to describe a mortality and morbidity pattern phenomenon. The mortality and morbidity rate is less in the early years of a contract than for someone the same age but insured for a number of years.

Medicare A part of the Social Security program providing health insurance to those receiving retirement benefits. See Medigap insurance, OASDI.

Medigap insurance Private insurance designed to supplement Medicare, filling in some of the Medicare limitations and participation features.

misrepresentation A false oral or written statement made to induce a party to enter a contract. Misrepresentations must be material to avoid the contract.

misstatement of age A mandatory provision of a life insurance contract. When an insured's age is misstated in the application, the policy proceeds are adjusted to an amount of insurance the actual premium would have purchased.

modified endowment contract (MEC) The IRS labels any life insurance policy failing a "seven-pay" test a MEC. To avoid being labeled a MEC and losing the advantage of tax-free policy loans, premiums cannot be paid more rapidly than necessary to provide the paid-up death benefits that seven level annual payments can purchase.

modified valuation reserve A reserve valuation technique that reduces reserve requirements for the first year of a contract so as to release more funds to pay first-year expenses.

modified whole life insurance Policies having level premiums rising in stair steps. The first step is below that of continuous-premium whole life, while the last step is above the comparable level premium.

morale hazard A person's indifference to loss because of the purchase of insurance, thus causing the chance of loss to increase. The difference between the moral hazard and the morale hazard is seen in the difference between the arsonist who intentionally destroys property to defraud an insurer (moral hazard) and the individual who does little or nothing to protect property before a loss or to conserve property after a loss, thinking the insurance will cover the loss.

moral hazard A person who deliberately causes a loss or exaggerates the size of a claim to defraud an insurer.

mortality charge The charge paid by the policy owner to compensate the insurer for death claims.

mortality table A numerical table showing the pattern of death based on a set of assumptions such as age and sex.

mutual company A method of organizing a company. In mutual insurance companies there are no stockholders. The policyholders own the company and are eligible to receive participating dividends.

N

National Association of Insurance Commissioners (NAIC) The association comprised of the state insurance commissioners formed to promote the uniform regulation of insurance.

national health insurance (NHI) A plan to finance and provide various levels of medical services to the entire population.

needs-based approach An approach to determine if a person needs life insurance and how much to buy. The needs approach calculates the present value of all future needs and subtracts amounts available to meet those needs. The remaining amount, if any, is the amount of life insurance needed to make up the deficit.

negatively correlated The tendency for two trends to move in opposite directions. A negatively correlated portfolio of two stocks would tend to stabilize total value as the market changes.

net amount at risk The difference between the face amount and the cash value of a life insurance contract.

net payments cost index (NPI) A technique used to calculate a life insurance cost index. This index assumes the insured survives the elected period of the calculation and then dies. This index is an interest-adjusted index.

net single premium (NSP) The onetime charge required to pay all future benefits under an insurance contract without paying any additional premiums. *Net* means there is no loading for expenses other than mortality and time-value-of-money considerations.

net worth A section of the balance sheet representing the owner's claim on the asset side of the balance sheet. Total assets must equal liabilities plus net worth.

nonadmitted assets Assets that are not allowed to be presented on the statutory balance sheet of an insurance company. Nonadmitted assets are ones that cannot be used to satisfy claim obligations.

noncancelable A type of cancellation provision. A noncancelable contract's premium cannot be changed nor can it be canceled by the insurer.

nonforfeiture options A provision in life insurance that specifies how the policy owner may receive the policy's cash value. Typically, the policy owner may receive the cash value in a lump sum or may continue life insurance by selecting either the extended term or paid-up life insurance option.

nonforfeiture value The amount to which the insured is entitled upon surrender of a cash value life insurance policy. The nonforfeiture options include a lump sum of cash (the cash surrender value), extended term insurance or a reduced amount of paid-up whole life insurance.

nonparticipating (nonpar) insurance A profit making insurance scheme that does not provide for dividend payments to policyholders. Nonpar insurance uses more realistic projections of losses and expenses than does participating insurance; thus initial premiums for nonpar insurance are typically lower than participating premiums. *See* participating insurance.

nonqualified pension plans Plans not meeting the IRC requirements for qualification or receiving special tax advantages. *See* qualified pension plans.

normal retirement age The earliest age at which a full pension benefit can be taken.

O

occupational illness (disease) Sickness arising out of employment. Some occupational diseases have long been recognized, such as black-lung disease. Stress-related complaints are a newer form of occupational illness recognized in some states.

Old Age, Survivors, Disability and Hospital Insurance (OASDI). Better known as *Social Security*. A federal insurance program, begun in 1935, providing death, retirement, survivors' and disability benefits to qualified recipients. Health insurance also is provided under the program.

optionally renewable A health insurance contract cancellation provision where the insured reserves the right to cancel the contract on an anniversary date. The insurer cannot cancel the contract between anniversary dates.

ordinary life insurance *See* continuous-premium whole life insurance.

P

paid-up insurance option A nonforfeiture option providing an insured with a paid-up policy with a lower face amount than the original policy.

paid-up policy A policy on which no further premiums are due but the insured is entitled to all present and future policy benefits.

partial disability A sickness or an accident that prevents the insured from performing one or more (not all) functions of his or her job.

participating insurance An insurance scheme allowing the policyholder to share in the favorable or unfavorable operating results of the insurance company. The policyholder-owner is entitled to an annual distribution of dividends based on the company's operating results. Typically, unrealistically high initial estimates are made of expected losses and expenses; when actual results are more favorable than the initial estimates, dividends are paid to the policyholders.

partnership A form of business organization. Two or more people enter a business relationship where individual assets are inseparable from business assets.

peril A contingency that causes a loss.

period certain annuity *See* annuity.

permanent coverage An insurance policy lasting until the insured's death, regardless of age. This policy type includes contracts building cash surrender values such as whole life insurance, universal life insurance and variable life insurance.

permanent needs Permanent needs for life insurance are not a function of time. These needs, such as the need for cash to pay for funeral arrangements, are present despite the insured's age at death. Permanent needs are met with permanent life insurance contracts.

policy loan The amount of money removed from the cash surrender value as a loan. Interest accrues on the borrowed amount, and the loan may be repaid at any time.

powers of appointment A general power of appointment means the holder can distribute the property to himself, his estate, his creditors or other eligible parties. A limited power of appointment means the holder cannot appoint the property for his or her benefit.

preexisting condition A medical condition treated or existing before making an application for insurance.

preferred provider organization (PPO) A health care financing and delivery system where a third party contracts with medical providers who furnish services at lower than usual fees in return for prompt payment and assurance of a certain number of patients.

present value of future benefits The probability of loss multiplied by the benefit payment adjusted for the time value of money. The present value of future benefits is the sum of each periodic calculation.

price-to-earnings ratio (P/E) The ratio of a stock's current price to its most recent year's earnings.

private annuities Annuities involving a series of payments made by one person to another in exchange for something of value. Private annuities typically involve the transfer of assets among family members.

probate A court proceeding used to pass the title of the decedent's property to parties named in a will or, in cases where no valid will exists, to distribute the property under the state laws of intestacy.

prospective payment system (PPS) A system used for compensating providers of health care under Medicare. Providers know how much they will receive based on the DRG classification. *See* diagnosis-related groups (DRG).

Public Law 15 (PL-15) Also known as the McCarran-Ferguson Act. A federal law that authorizes the continuation of state regulation of insurance, so long as state regulation continues to be held in the public interest.

purchasing power risk The change of purchasing power caused by inflation or deflation and taxes. People who postpone consumption and save are financially worse off when inflation and taxation more than offset the investment return on their savings.

pure annuity *See* annuity.

Q

qualified pension plans Plans meeting the requirements of the Internal Revenue Code Sections (IRC) 401(a) and 403(a). These plans receive significant tax advantages.

qualified terminable interest property (QTIP) Property to be enjoyed by a surviving spouse during his or her lifetime, but at the death of the second spouse the property is distributed by designation of the first spouse to die.

R

rated policy An insurance contract with an increased premium increased usually due to health-related problems.

rear-end load A charge levied against the amount of money removed or paid out of a savings or insurance plan. *See* front-end load.

rebating The act of returning to the policy owner part of the agent's commission income, usually to induce the person to purchase an insurance contract.

reentry term life insurance A type of term policy requiring insureds to pass regular medical examinations to qualify for significantly lower rates. This policy causes the insured to bear the risk of impaired health.

refund annuity *See* annuity.

regular medical contract A type of medical expense reimbursement contract paying for doctors' visits in and out of the hospital.

rehabilitation The restoration of a disabled person's health to enable him or her to regain previous abilities. Some long-term disability income contracts also have a rehabilitation benefit that continues benefits while a person is attempting to return to full productive employment.

reinstatement The right of a life insurance policyholder to return a lapsed contract to its original terms. Reinstatement must occur within the specified time limits provided in the policy. Reinstatement requires evidence of insurability and the payment of all policy financial obligations such as outstanding loan balances and missed premium payments. *See* lapse, evidence of insurability.

reinsurance The purchase of insurance on some portion of a covered exposure by an insurance company. The company purchasing the insurance is called the *primary insurer* or *ceding company*; the company providing the insurance is called the *reinsurer*. Two typical reinsurance arrangements are pro rata reinsurance (both the premiums and losses are shared on a proportional basis) and excess-of-loss reinsurance (the reinsurer pays only when covered losses exceed some predetermined amount and then only the excess above this amount).

renewable term life insurance A policy the insured can renew until a certain age without presenting evidence of insurability.

replacement The exchange of one insurance contract for another.

replacement ratio Calculated as retirement income/preretirement income. Typically, when designing pension plans, employers consider pension income combined with Social Security retirement benefits and other sources of employee retirement income when calculating the replacement ratio.

representation A statement made by an applicant in an insurance application. The insurer relies on the truth of the applicant's representations in underwriting the policy. A material misrepresentation generally allows the insurer to avoid the contract. *See* misrepresentation, material fact.

reserves *See* legal reserve.

residual disability benefits A provision of a disability contract that provides a proportion of full benefits relative to the reduction in earning capacity. This is also referred to as *proportionate benefits* and is designed to compensate for partial disability.

respite care Temporary care for the terminally ill to provide relief to individuals regularly providing care.

revocable The right to remove, change or cancel a previously designated decision.

revocable trust A trust allowing the grantor to change the terms of the trust or terminate the agreement. If the terms of the trust cannot be altered by the grantor, the trust is an irrevocable trust.

risk The inability to predict. Uncertainty surrounding an outcome.

risk management The process of choosing intelligently among all of the various alternatives to dealing with risk.

S

salary continuation plan A noninsured disability plan providing salary payments while the employee is sick or disabled.

savings bonds U.S. Savings bonds, called *Series EE bonds,* are sold by banks and savings and loan associations. These bonds sell at a discount. That is, the purchaser pays one-half the face value of the bonds and earns income when the bonds are redeemed at face value.

Section [IRC] 125 cafeteria plans The plans also are called *flexible-benefit* plans. Employee benefit plans allowing eligible employees some choice in the type and amount of their fringe benefits.

Section [IRC] 401(k) cash or deferred arrangements A 401(k) plan is a profit-sharing plan allowing an employee a choice between taking income in cash or putting the income in a qualified retirement plan.

Section [IRC] 403(b) plans, tax-deferred annuities (TDAs). Retirement plan for the employees of nonprofit organizations such as schools, hospitals and museums.

Section [IRC] 1035 exchange Under IRC Section 1035, if one life insurance policy is exchanged for another, no gain or loss is recognized unless the value of the new contract, plus any cash received, exceeds the cash basis of the old policy.

Section [IRC] 2503 (b) or (c) trust A trust allowing property to be held for minors, while allowing the $10,000 annual gift tax exclusion to be available for a gift of a future interest.

self-insurance A program by which the policy-owning group pays for all of its incurred eligible expenses rather than purchasing coverage from a carrier. Often self-insurance is administered by a third party.

settlement options The various options provided by an insurer in the contract to distribute the cash value to the policy owner before the insured dies or the death benefits to the beneficiary after the insured's death.

simplified employee pensions (SEPs) Some employers operate an employer IRA, also known as *simplified employee pension plans*. Employees participating in these plans receive immediate vesting of all sums contributed and may have some flexibility in directing the underlying investments.

single-premium deferred annuity (SPDA) If a single premium is paid more than one period before the initial receipt of benefits, the contract is called a *single-premium deferred annuity contract*. Deposits earn compound interest at a minimum guaranteed rate, and this interest accrues on a tax-deferred basis until liquidation.

single-premium whole life A type of whole life insurance requiring only one premium payment to secure all present and future benefits. This policy type emphasizes savings values and is categorized as a modified endowment contract by the Internal Revenue Service.

skilled care Daily nursing and rehabilitative care ordered by a physician. This level of care is performed under the supervision of skilled medical personnel.

skilled nursing facility A state-licensed facility providing skilled nursing care.

Social Security *See* Old Age, Survivors and Disability and Hospital Insurance (OASDI).

specified amount The initial amount of life insurance purchased in a universal or variable-universal life insurance contract.

spend-down The process of divesting assets to qualify for Medicaid benefits.

spendthrift trust provision A trust provision written into a beneficiary designation protecting policy proceeds from the beneficiary's creditors.

split-dollar life insurance A life insurance financing arrangement usually connected with business purchases of life insurance. The costs and benefits of the life insurance contract are split between the insured and the other entity.

statement of opinion An oral or written statement that is believed to be accurate. There is no intent to deceive even if the statement is technically false.

statute of limitations A law defining a specific period of time during which a lawsuit can be brought. For example, the law may allow an injured party three years from the time an injury was discovered to file suit. If the injured party does not begin the lawsuit within the specified period, the right to bring the suit is lost.

statutory accounting principles (SAP) Accounting procedures and principles imposed by the various states.

stepped-up basis The new owner's cost basis for property inherited at the original owner's death is the property's date-of-death value, not the original owner's cost basis.

stock insurance company An insurer organized as a profit-making venture, with owners who are not necessarily policyholders.

stock redemption plan A business continuation plan to purchase the outstanding stock of a deceased owner.

straight life annuity *See* annuity.

straight life insurance *See* continuous-premium whole life insurance.

stress Excessive external force acting on a person.

supplemental executive retirement program (SERP) A nonqualified deferred compensation plan that usually provides certain employees with additional retirement benefits in excess of any qualified plan. *See also* nonqualified pension plans.

surgical policy A contract providing the service or paying for the cost of surgical procedures.

surrender cost index (SCI) A life insurance cost estimating procedure. The SCI calculates an interest-adjusted cost index that assumes the person maintains the contract for a period of time and then surrenders the contract.

survivor or second-death life insurance policies Life insurance policies that pay only after the second of two deaths. These policies are frequently recommended in estate planning cases to pay estate taxes when the second spouse dies.

survivorship benefit A benefit received by living insureds or annuitants when the cash values (account balances) of deceased insureds (annuitants) are distributed to the living insureds (annuitants).

T

tax-deferral Delayed payment of taxes. This strategy involves two advantages. First, the individual earns money with dollars that otherwise would be paid in taxes. Second, the income can be recognized when tax conditions are relatively favorable. Tax deferral explains the tax advantage of such things as individual retirement accounts (IRAs), cash value life insurance, deferred annuities, some governmental savings bonds and some (qualified) pension plans.

tax-free Income to which no federal income tax applies. Examples include the receipt of life insurance death benefits and income on most state and municipal securities.

temporary coverage Insurance coverage protecting a portion of one's life. A person can outlive a temporary life insurance contract. *See* permanent coverage.

temporary life annuity An annuity arrangement in which payments from the insurer end at the death of the annuitant or at the end of the designated period, whichever event occurs first. For example, a ten-year temporary life annuity pays annuitants for ten years only if they live ten or more years. This contract pays only for the period of survival if it is less than ten years.

temporary needs Temporary needs diminish over time and ultimately disappear. For example, the need to repay a loan ends once the loan has been repaid. Temporary needs may be met with term life insurance.

terminable interest The right to use, give away or enjoy the property ends at the donee's death, remarriage or any other predetermined event.

term insurance A type of life insurance ending at a predetermined time. This type of coverage does not involve savings and has a relatively low initial premium that typically increases with the insured's age. Term life insurance is appropriately used for temporary needs or where the need for protection is great and premium dollars are limited.

testamentary trust A trust established in a will at death.

third-party administrator (TPA) The administration of a group insurance plan by someone other than the policy owner or insurer.

time limit on certain defenses A clause that provides a period of two or three years after the beginning of the contract during which the contract cannot be contested except for fraudulent misstatements.

tontine A money transfer scheme, now illegal in the U.S., where all money transferred to a pool is given to the last survivor(s) of the pool.

traditional life insurance Term, whole life insurance and endowment contract types sold by life insurance companies.

traditional net cost approach A cost disclosure approach in life insurance that generally provides incorrect information. Total dividends and the surrender cash value are subtracted from total premiums paid over a period of time. This approach ignores the time value of money and can show life insurance pays for itself or is costless.

transfer for value A transaction occurring when the current owner sells an existing life insurance policy to another person. The new owner must include the death benefits in taxable income when the insured dies, but may exclude the amount paid for the policy and any subsequent premiums paid.

treasury securities Debt instruments issued by the U.S. Treasury. U.S. Treasury securities are said to be risk-free due to the lack of default risk.

trust A legal entity that receives property from a donor and is controlled by a trustee (subject to the trust document) for the benefit of a beneficiary.

trustee An individual responsible for the proper accounting, management, distribution and operation of a trust.

twisting An illegal practice of insurance agents in an attempt to persuade policy owners to drop their current policy and purchase a new one. Twisting results from incomplete information, incorrect or incomplete comparisons, misrepresentations and transmitting false rumors.

U

unauthorized practice of law The practice of law, including giving legal advice or creating legal documents, by a person not admitted to the bar in the jurisdiction where the offense occurred.

underwriting The process of selecting and rating (calculating a premium) applicants for insurance.

unearned premium The portion of any paid premium that has not been earned by the insurer.

unified credit Each person is allowed one lifetime credit of $192,800 against his or her combined gift or estate tax liability.

unified transfer tax The federal estate tax applies to property transferred at death. The federal gift tax applies to lifetime property transfers. The federal estate tax and the federal gift tax are unified. Both taxes have identical tax rates and one unified credit.

Uniform Gifts to Minors Act (UGMA) Some states have passed a broader version called the Uniform Transfer to Minors Act (UTMA). Model legislation passed by states allowing adults to transfer property to children during their minority. The law allows adults (parents or guardians) to manage the property until the child reaches age 18. The UGMA is relatively easy and inexpensive to use.

Uniform Simultaneous Death Act Most states have passed these rules as part of their probate code. The laws provide that, if one spouse does not survive the other by at least 120 hours after a common disaster, it is assumed the property owner survived the other spouse.

unilateral contract A contract where only one party must perform. In bilateral contracts both parties must perform. Insurance contracts are unilateral because only the insurance company must perform if the policy owner wants it to do so.

universal life insurance A type of life insurance policy allowing the insured flexibility in choosing premium payments and death benefits during the contract period.

utilization review A technique used by health care providers to determine after the fact if health care was appropriate and effective.

V

valued contract A contract that agrees to pay a specific amount when the agreed-on contingency occurs. *See also* indemnity contracts.

vanishing-premium life A life insurance contract requiring large premium payments in the early years of the contract so that premiums may decline and stop earlier.

variable annuity An annuity designed to maintain constant purchasing power. The variable annuity does not guarantee purchasing power; rather, it arranges to deliver payments based on the performance of an underlying portfolio of equity investments.

variable life insurance A type of cash value life insurance policy giving the insured flexibility in choosing the underlying investment media.

variable universal life A type of cash value life insurance policy giving the insured flexibility in choosing the underlying investment media and providing much flexibility in premium payments.

W

waiting period A form of deductible found in medical expense and disability income contracts. Benefits are not paid during the waiting period.

waiver Giving up a known contractual right.

waiver of premium A policy provision waiving premium payment requirements during the time the premium payer is disabled.

warranty A condition of a contract. If the condition is breached (breach of a warranty), the contract will not pay the claim regardless of materiality. All warranties in life insurance contracts are treated as representations.

whole life insurance A contract promising payment whenever death occurs, or at age 100. Whole life contracts involve savings and are often called permanent insurance.

will A legally enforceable declaration by a testator of how he or she wants his or her property distributed upon death.

Y

yearly renewable term reinsurance A form of reinsurance where the insurer reinsures the net amount at risk in excess of its retention limit. For example, if the terminal reserve is $10,000 on a $100,000 life insurance policy, $90,000 is the net amount at risk. If the insurer's retention level is $25,000, $65,000 is reinsured. The reinsurance premium for the year is based on the amount reinsured and the insured's attained age. *See also* reinsurance and coinsurance reinsurance.

yield curve A graphical or numerical representation of interest rates paid or received based on the years to maturity. Yield curves often graph U.S. Treasury securities.

Z

zero-coupon bonds Corporate and municipal bonds sold at a discount. They pay no annual interest but are redeemable at face amount at maturity. Each year the difference between the market value and the face value of these bonds decreases. At maturity the market and face value are equal.

Index

A

Absolute assignment, 221
Absolute irrevocable beneficiaries, 224
A-B trust arrangement, 383, 384
Accelerated death benefits, 59
Acceptance, 187
Accident, 152
Accident policies, 143
Accidental bodily injury, 152
Accidental death and disability, 77, 80, 113, 143
Accidental death and dismemberment policy, 408
Accidental means, 152
Accountant, 439
Accounting practices, 554, 565–567
Accumulated earnings tax, 443
Acquired immuno deficiency syndrome (AIDS), 59, 544
Activities of daily living (ADL), 174
Actual delivery, 189
Actuarial assumptions, 521
Actuarial present value, 491
Actuaries, 467, 540
Additional purchase rider, 158
Adhesion, 190
Administrative services only (ASO), 135
Administrator, 447
Admitted assets, 564, 566
Adverse financial and mortality selection, 526
Adverse selection, 36, 154, 490, 518, 526, 543
Advertising, 563
After-tax rate, 279
Age, 467, 543
Age Discrimination in Employment Act (ADEA), 287, 288, 348, 422, 425
Agency agreement, 196
Agent compensation, 67, 535
Agents, 193, 548
Aging society, 343, 344, 374
Aid to Families with Dependent Children, 133, 170
Aleatory contract, 3, 191
Alien insurer, 568

Alternative minimum tax (AMT), 443
American Agency Life Insurance Company v. Russell, 188
American Bankers Association (ABA) assignment form, 222
American Hospital Association, 139
American Institute of Certified Public Accountants (AICPA), 566
American Medical Association (AMA), 139, 177
Amortizable assets, 564
Amount at risk, 41, 71
Annual gift tax exclusion, 252, 257
Annual statement blank, 563
Annuities, 5, 6, 86–107, 478
 age and, 94
 annuity certain, 96
 benefit calculations, 93–97
 cash refund, 97
 classifications, 90–101
 compared as an investment, 100–105
 deferred, 91–93, 343, 363–367
 defined, 86, 236
 due, 91
 estate tax, 249
 exclusion ratio, 103–105
 fixed dollar, 97, 98
 flexible premium, 92, 93
 gender and, 94
 group, 88, 431, 432
 guaranteed payments, 95–97
 immediate, 90
 increasing benefit, 98, 99
 individual, 88
 installment refund, 97
 insurance principle and, 90
 insured private, 89, 90
 investment alternative, 101–105
 joint-and-last-survivor, 95
 life, period certain, 96
 life insurance conversion, 88, 89
 lives covered, 94, 95
 mortality tables, 468, 471
 net single premiums, 491–492
 participating, 97
 payout table, 96
 pension benefit, 88

 period certain, 96
 premature distributions, 239, 240
 premium payment, 90–93
 private, 89
 pure, 95
 purpose of, 86, 87
 refund features, 97
 setback approach, 94
 single premium deferred (SPDA), 91
 single premium immediate, 91
 straight, 95
 survivor's benefit, 90
 taxation, 102–105, 238–240
 temporary life, 95
 variable, 98–100
 whole life insurance conversion, 88, 89
Annuity certain, 95, 480
Annuity due, 91, 265
Annuity immediate, 90
Annuity table(s), 94, 96, 239, 37, 468, 471
 payout, 94, 96, 371
 tax, 239
Apparent authority, 196
Appleton Rule, 202
Application, 187, 544–545
Arm's-length agreement, 450
Armstrong Committee, 217, 556
Asset share analysis, 509, 521, 529–533
Asset valuation, 564
Assignment, 221
Assignment payment method, 166
Attained age conversion, 45
Attained age reinstatement, 213
Attribution rules, 456
Audits of Stock Life Insurance Companies, 566
Automatic premium loan (APL), 198, 206, 211
Automatic reinsurance, 551
Average indexed monthly earnings formula (AIME), 299–301

B

Backdating, 190
Bankruptcy, 197
Basic medical expense plans, 144

597

Index

Bear market, 271
Becker, Ernest, 32, 33, 377
Begley v. Prudential Insurance Company of America, 221
Belth single-year method, 123
Beneficiary, 2, 182, 211, 222-224
Beneficiary designation changes, 541
Best's Flitcraft Compend, 122
Best's Insurance Reports (Life/Health Edition), 114
Bilateral contract, 191
Binding receipts, 188-189
Blackout period, 290
Blue Cross and Blue Shield, 6, 139, 411
Bonds, 233-235, 262, 542
   corporate, 234
   U.S. savings (EE), 233, 234
   zero-coupon, 235
Branch managers, 549
Branch office system, 549
Breach of warranty, 193
Broker, 195, 549
Building blocks of life insurance policies, 37-42
Bull market, 271
Burial life insurance, 61
Business continuation, 439, 447
Business life insurance, 22-24, 10, 439
Business overhead insurance, 445
Business valuation, 443
Buy-and-sell agreement, 24, 446, 450, 452
Buy-term-and-invest-the-difference (BTID), 109, 124

C

Cafeteria (Section 125) plans, 434, 435
Cancelable, 147
Cancellation, 147-148
Capacity, 186
Capital and surplus, 560
Capital gains, 276, 279
Capital requirements, 560
Case management, 138, 541
Cash balance plan, 427
Cash dividend option, 218
Cash refund income option, 97, 217
Cash surrender option, 207
Cash value, 8, 69, 492, 525
Cash value accumulation test, 8, 67, 73-76
Cash value life insurance, 37, 343; *see also* Whole life insurance; Universal life insurance
   college funding use, 319, 320
   source of savings, 39-40
C corporation, 445
City of Los Angeles v. Manhart, 422
Ceding company, 550
Certificates of deposit, 269
Certified Financial Planner (CFP), 561

Change in occupation, 150
Change of beneficiary, 150
Change of plan, 226
Chartered Financial Consultant, (ChFC), 561
Chartered Life Underwriter (CLU), 561
Civil Rights Act of 1964, 94, 422
Civilian Health and Medical Program for the Uniformed Services (CHAMPUS), 133
Claims, 149, 541
Class rating, 546
Clayton Act, 557
Close corporation, 454
Closed-panel HMO, 141
Coinsurance percentage, 137
Coinsurance reinsurance, 551
Collateral, 443
Collateral assignment, 221
Collateral split dollar, 461
Collectibles, 262
College education, 234, 318-321
   savings bonds and, 234
Combination policies, 55-56
Commission, 528, 549
Commissioners reserve valuation method (CRVM), 523-524
Commissioners Standard Ordinary Table 1980 (CSO), 468
Common disasters, 225
Community property, 247
Community rating, 140
Commutative, 191
Company evaluation, 322
   sources of information, 322
Company operations, 540
Compensation, 548-549
Compound interest, 263
Concealment, 192
Condition precedent, 187, 189
Condition subsequent, 187
Conditional contract, 191
Conditional probability, 477
Conditional receipts, 187, 189
Conditionally renewable, 148, 154
Conservation, 567
Consideration, 190
Consolidated Omnibus Budget Reconciliation Act of 1985 (COBRA), 413
Constructive delivery, 189
Consumer Price Index (CPI), 295, 310-311
Consumer Reports, 86
Contract, 182
Contract law, 4
Convertible term insurance, 45
Coordination of benefits, 137
Copayment, 166
Corporate control, 537
Corporations, C and S, 231-233, 445

Cost containment, 137, 140, 161, 414
Cost disclosure, 108, 115
Cost of life insurance, 116
Cost of living adjustments (COLAs), 158, 295
Cost of living rider, 47, 173
Cost-shifting, 137
Counteroffer, 187
Credit disability insurance, 11
Credit enhancement, 442
Credit life insurance, 11
Credit shelter bypass trust, 383, 384
Creditors' rights, 50
Creditors' rights in life insurance, 197-200
Cross purchase plan, 452-453, 455
Crummey trust, 256
Current assumption life, 65, 66, 115
Current yield, 273, 277
Custodial care, 163, 172

D

Death, 31
Death fund, 16
Debit life insurance, 11, 61
Deceptive practices, 563
Decreasing term insurance, 46
Deductibles, 137, 145
Default on premium, 210, 211
Deferred annuity, 91-93, 363-367, 480, 482
Deferred compensation plan, 419-421, 439, 458, 480
Deficiency reserves, 524
Deficit Reduction Act of 1984, 8, 60, 539
Defined benefit pension plan, 425, 426, 428
Defined contribution pension plan, 426-428
Deflation, 262
Delivery and effective date, 189
Demographic data, 18-24
   age cohorts, 24
   birthrate, 21
   family, 20
   life expectancies, 467, 474, 522
   marital status, 21
Demutualization, 538
Dental care, 146-147, 151
Dependents' support fund, 17
Depression, 28
Diagnosis related groups (DRGs), 165
Direct losses, 4
Direct response marketing, 549
Disability
   additional purchase rider, 158
   benefits (OASDI), 290, 291
   cost-of-living adjustment (COLA), 158
   data, 152

Index

definitions, 155, 410
income, 7, 111, 113, 151, 409–411, 438
income rider, 77, 80, 151, 227, 455, 460
partial disability, 156
planning, 316
presumptive total disability, 156
proportionate benefits, 156
recurrent disability, 157
rehabilitation benefits, 158
residual disability benefits, 156
transition benefits, 158
waiver-of-premium, 158
Discretionary trust, 199
Disintermediation, 65, 210, 312, 526
Dissolution, 554, 567
Diversification, 110
Dividend calculations, 562
Dividends, 51, 52, 238
actual v. illustrated, 51, 52
class, 548
income, 235
options, 218, 541
terminal, 116
Divisible surplus, 217, 538, 565
Dix, Dorthea, 176
Double indemnity riders, 226
Dual choice, 141
Duff & Phelps, 115

E

Early warning system, 569
Earnings test (OASDI), 292–294
Earnings-to-price ratio (E/P), 277
Economic approach to death claim, 518
Economic behavior, 24–26
Economic theory and life insurance, 24–27
Education fund, 17, 318–321
Effective date, 189
Ego, 30
Elimination periods, 173
Emergency fund, 16
Employee benefits, 397–437
accidental death and dismemberment, 408
data, 397
defined, 397
employees and, 401–403
employers and, 399–401
government and, 398, 399
group disability insurance, 409–411
group health insurance, 411–414
group life insurance, 405–408
group underwriting, 403–405
multiemployer trusts (METS), 403
pension plans, 417–437
post-retirement life insurance, 408, 409
supplementary life insurance, 407

Employee Retirement Income Security Act (ERISA), 421, 422
Employee stock ownership plan (ESOP), 434
Endorsement split dollar, 461
Endowment insurance, 8, 61, 235, 238, 478, 519
Entire contract clause, 148, 203
Entity purchase plan, 452–453
Equal outlay method, 125–126
Equalizing bequests, 385, 386
Equivalent level annual dividend, 120
Estate planning; *see also* Federal estate tax
A-B trust, 383
annual gift tax exclusion, 252
case study, 389–391
community property, 247
credit shelter bypass trust, 383, 384
Crummey trust, 256
definition of, 375
equalizing bequests, 385, 386
federal income tax, 232, 233
generation skipping transfer tax, 259
gifts, 248, 256, 257, 377, 378
hypothetical probate, 379
joint interests, 247, 380
life insurance and objectives, 16, 384–388
marital deduction, 382–384
objectives, 377–379
postmortem planning, 384
powers of appointment, 247, 248, 383
probate, 380
process, 376–380
professional skills required, 375
QTIP election, 250, 384
simultaneous deaths, 378
survivor life insurance, 388
trusts, 381, 382, 386–388
unauthorized practice of law, 375
wills, 381
Event-specific techniques, 116
Excess interest, 52–53, 70, 81
Exchange privilege, 81, 240
Excise Tax Act of 1909, 572
Execution, 186
Executor, 447
Expected retirement periods, 347
Expenses in life insurance policies, 37–39, 69, 528, 562
acquisition cost, 38–39
administrative, 39
limitations, 562
loading, 69
mortality charges, 37
Experience rating, 135, 140
Experimental surgery, 144, 151
Express authority, 196
Extended care, 138, 151, 163

Extended term option, 58, 128, 206, 209, 211
Extra premium tables, 548

F

Face amount, 2
Facultative reinsurance, 551
Fair Credit Reporting Act of 1971 (FCRA), 545
Fair Insurance Information Practices Act, 546
Family demographics, 18–20
Family health plans, 135
Family life insurance policies, 61
Family term coverage, 77, 80
FASB 97, 566
Federal bankruptcy, 197
Federal estate tax, 245–261
adjusted taxable gifts, 251
alternative valuation date, 249
annuities, 249
calculation outlined, 249
charitable gifts, 257
community property, 247
computation of tax, 379
credits, 252
deductions, 250, 251
gross estate, 247, 249
joint interests, 247
life insurance, 247, 249, 254, 255
marital deduction, 250
nonterminable interest, 250
pensions, 249
power of appointment, 247, 248
procedure outlined, 246
purposes of, 246
QTIP, 250
rates, 253
state death taxes, 252
stepped-up basis, 257
unified tax credit, 253, 383
Federal Gift Tax, 255–259
annual exclusion, 251, 256
calculation, 258
Crummey trust, 256
Federal income tax, 230–244; *see also* Internal Revenue Code
annuity income, 102–105, 238–240
corporations 231–233
dividends, 235
endowment life insurance, 61, 238
Form 1040, 231
health insurance premiums, 236, 237
life insurance, 235–240
defined, 235, 236
dividends, 238
exchanges, 240
loans, 240
premiums, 240
proceeds, 237
surrender, 237

partnerships, 233
pension plans, 239
premature distributions, 239, 240
table of rates, 232
taxable entities, 231–233
transfer for value rule, 237
trusts and estates, 233
U.S. savings bonds, 233, 234
Federal Privacy Act of 1974, 545
Federal taxation, 572
Federal Trade Commission, 554
  Act, 557
  Improvements Act (1980), 559
Financial operations, 563–569
Financial planning, 304–396
  case studies
    early adult years, 324–336
    later adult years, 374–396
    preretirement years, 342–372
  checklist, 315
  defined, 304–306
  estate planning and, 259, 260, 374–396
  expertise needed, 306, 307
  goals, 315, 316
  group life insurance and, 407
  inflation and, 310–312
  life insurance and, 321–323
  personal values, 307, 308
  process outlined, 312–318, 344, 345, 376–380
  risk tolerance, 307, 308
  Social Security and, 282, 295
  statements needed, 313, 314
  strategies, 316, 317
  Uniform Gifts to Minors Act, 320
  written reports, 318
Financial reporting, 563
First Executive Corporation, 49
Fixed-amount option, 128, 216, 466, 480
Fixed-dollar annuity, 97, 98
Fixed-period option, 128, 215, 466
Flexible premium deferred annuity, 92, 93
Flexible premium variable life insurance, 64
Forced sale, 447
Foreign insurer, 568
Fraternal organizations, 535, 536
Fraud, 545
Free-look exchange provision, 81
Freud, Sigmund, 30
Friedman v. Prudential Life Insurance Company, 192
Front-end load, 39, 69
Fuchs v. Old Line Life Insurance Company, 193
Full preliminary term reserves, 523
Full valuation reserves, 522
Funded plan, 458

Funding deferred compensation plans, 459
Future value of $1, 263

G
Gender, 543
General agency system, 549
General agents, 194, 549
General partnership, 451
Generally accepted accounting principles (GAAP), 113, 538–539, 565–566
Generation skipping transfer tax, 259
Generic drugs, 138
Genetic testing, 543
Geometric rate of return, 278
Gerontology, 348
Gifts, 251, 255–259, 377, 378
  charitable, 257
  to children, 257
  definition of, 255
  disadvantages, 257, 378
  interspousal, 256, 377
  taxes and, 251, 255–259
Going concern value, 442, 447
Grace period, 149, 206
Graduation, 468
Gross estate, 223
Gross income, 573
Gross premiums, 509, 528
Group annuities, 88
Group disability insurance, 409–411
  benefits, 410
  exclusions, 410
  long-term, 410
  short-term, 409
  taxation, 411
  underwriting, 410
Group health insurance, 133, 135, 142, 411–414
  basic medical, 412
  contract provisions, 413, 414
  contracts, 412, 413
  major medical, 412
  providers, 411
Group insurance, 10
Group life insurance, 405–408
  accidental death benefits, 408
  beneficiaries, 405, 406
  benefits, 405
  financial planning and, 407
  supplemental, 407
  taxation, 406
  universal, 409
Group model HMO, 141
Group pension plans, 480
Group-average techniques, 116
Growth potential, 273
Guarantee funds, 568
Guaranteed insurability, 77, 80, 113, 227

Guaranteed interest, 70, 81
Guaranteed renewable, 148
Guardian, 378
Guertin, Alfred N., 207
Guertin legislation, 207
Guideline premium/cash value corridor test, 8, 67, 73–76
Guides for Mail-Order Insurance, 557

H
Hazardous occupations, 467
Health, 467, 563
Health insurance, 6, 131, 142
  accident coverage, 143
  basic medical expense plans, 144
  cancelable, 147
  cancellation, 147–148
  coordination of benefits, 414
  cost containment 414
  covered losses, 143
  dental, 146–147, 151
  disability income, 7, 111, 113, 151, 409–411, 438
  group coverage, 133, 135, 142, 411–414; *see also* Group health insurance
  guaranteed renewable, 148
  hospice care, 136, 146–147, 163, 164
  hospitalization, 144
  major medical, 145
  medical expense, 7
  Medicare gap filling coverage, 146–147, 161, 168–170
  national health insurance, 176
  noncancelable, 148, 154
  nursing home care, 146–147, 151
  perils covered, 143
  preexisting condition, 148, 151, 154
  premiums, 236, 237
  prescription drug plan, 146–147
  reasonable and customary, 144
  regular medical, 145
  sickness coverage, 154
  surgical contracts, 144–145
  taxation, 236, 237
  vision care, 146–147, 151
Health Insurance Association of America (HIAA), 178
Health Maintenance Act of 1973, 141
Health maintenance organizations (HMOs), 140, 141, 411
  types
    closed-panel, 141
    dual choice, 141
    group model, 141
    independent practice association, 142
    individual model, 141, 142
    network model, 141
    open-ended, 142
    point-of-service, 141
    staff model, 141

Index

Hedges against inflation, 270
Hobbies, 467
Holding period return (HPR), 278
Holding period yield (HPY), 278
Home health care, 138, 163
Home service life insurance, 11, 42
Hospice care, 136, 146–147, 163, 164, 165
Hospital insurance (Part A), 162
Hospitalization contracts, 144
Hostile merger, 540
Huebner, S. S., 26
Human capital, 26
Human life value, 26, 443

I

Illegal activities, 184
Illegal occupation, 150
Illustrative dividends, 51, 52, 127
Immediate annuity contracts, 90, 480, 503
Immediate participation guarantee, 430
Impersonation, 205
Implied authority, 196
Incidence of ownership, 223, 249
Income tax; *see* Federal income tax
Incontestable clause, 127, 149, 204
Incorporation by reference, 203
Increasing term insurance, 46
Indemnity, 3
  contracts, 191
  payments, 143
  plans, 136, 139, 144
Independent Practice Association, 142
Indeterminate-premium life, 65, 112, 115
Index information; sources, 122
Indian Health Services, 133
Indirect losses, 4
Individual health plans, 135, 142
Individual life insurance, 10
Individual model HMO, 141, 142
Individual retirement accounts (IRAs), 350–353, 480
  eligibility, 351
  investments, 352
  rollovers, 352
  taxation, 352
Industrial life insurance, 11, 61
Inflation, 64, 98–100, 214, 262, 270, 310–312, 428, 429, 567
  Consumer Price Index, 295, 311
  pensions and, 428, 429
Initial reserves, 510
Insanity, 186
Inside build-up, 241
Installment or cash refund annuity contracts, 217, 487
Installment refund annuity, 97
Insurability, 127, 213, 542
Insurable interest, 3, 182, 205, 222, 445

Insurance Regulatory Information System (IRIS), 569–571
Insurance, definition of, 2
Insured, 182
Insurers, 540–569
  cost of operations, 540
  evaluation of, 569–571
  financial strength, 322, 563–569
  investments, 40, 541–542, 554, 565, 567
  net worth, 115, 565
Intentional injury, 151
Interest, 522
Interest adjusted methods, 118
Interest dividend option, 219
Interest option, 214
Interest rate risk, 270–271
Intermediate care, 172
Internal rate of return (IRR), 278
Internal Revenue Code (IRC), 198; *see also* Federal Income Tax Section
  171 (b) (1), 354
  401(k) plans, 433
  403(b) plans, 353, 354, 434
  415, 354, 425, 426
  501 (c) (3), 354
  1035 definitions, 235
  1035 exchange, 91, 240
  2036(c), 390
  2503(b) and (c) trusts, 321
International Congress of Actuaries, 468
Interpleader, 222, 224
Interspousal gifts, 256
Intestacy, 376
Intoxication, 150, 186
Investing, 269
Investment, 40, 541–542, 554, 567
  annuities, 101–105
  common stock, 262, 542
  decisions, 262
  liquidity, 269
  operations, 565
  rates, 477
  real estate, 269, 542
  retirement, 408–409
  risk, 79
  strategy, 269
IRAs, 110, 274; *see also* Individual retirement accounts
Irrevocable beneficiary, 211, 223–224
Issue-specific risk, 270, 273

J

Joint interests, 247, 380
Joint life annuity, 95, 480
Joint-and-last-survivor annuity, 95
Jones v. All American Life Insurance Company, 185
Juvenile life insurance, 62

K

Keogh plans, 353, 434
Key employee, 438
  insurance, 439–447
Key person indemnification, 442
Keynes, John Maynard, 24

L

Lamb et al. v. Northwestern National Life Insurance Company, 184
Lapse, 39, 493, 510, 518
Law of agency, 193
Law of large numbers, 466
Legal actions, 150
Legal counsel, 439
Legal department, 542
Legal reserve liabilities, 509
Legality, 182
Level premium, 489, 490
Level premium life insurance, 40, 54
  endowment, 61
  figure, 40
  term, 46, 476, 496–498
  whole life, 54, 499
Level-premium deferred annuities, 504
Leveling annuity contracts, 502
Leveling process, 494, 510
Leveling the whole life insurance contract, 499
Liabilities, 565
Liability reserves, 565
Licensing agents, 560
Licensing companies, 560
Life annuity, 95
  contracts, 216
  due, 91, 496
  installment or cash refund, 97
  option, 96–97, 128, 216–217, 460, 466, 480
  period certain, 6, 96
Life cycle hypothesis, 25–26
Life insurance, 7; *see also* Life insurance contract; Life insurers
  advantages as savings medium, 49, 50
  agent, 439
  buy term and invest the difference comparison, 109, 124
  charitable gifts of, 257
  comparison of policy costs, 60, 108–118
  creditors' rights, 50
  data, 42, 43
  death and, 31
  definition, 1–2, 235, 236
  disadvantages as a savings medium, 50
  dividends, 238
  equity-linked product, 98–100
  estate planning and, 248, 249, 254, 255, 384–388
  exchanges, 240

family, 61
financial ratings companies, 322
group; *see* Group life insurance
incidents of ownership, 223, 249
industrial, 11, 61
juvenile, 62
legality, 182
mathematics, 466
par/nonpar policies, 51–53, 109, 113, 537
pensions and, 430–432
policy comparison chart, 60
post retirement policies, 408
premium computation, 466–467, 494–510
premiums, 39, 240
psychological theories and, 27–33
retirement income policy, 432
retirement planning and, 349, 350
second death policies, 388
split dollar, 241
survivor policies, 388
taxation of exchanges, 240
taxation of proceeds, 237
temporary versus permanent protection, 15
term, 42–48, 385
trusts, 386–388
whole, 48–59, 385
Life Insurance Company Income Tax Act of 1959, 573
Life insurance company taxable income (LICTI), 573
Life insurance contract
 adhesion, 190
 apportionment of divisible surplus, 217, 538, 565
 assignment, 221
 automatic premium loan, 198, 206, 211
 backdating, 190
 beneficiary designations, 2, 182, 211, 222, 541
 capacity, 186
 common disasters, 225
 concealment, 192
 conditional, 191
 conditional receipt, 187, 189
 consideration, 190
 delivery actual and constructive, 189
 dividend options, 218, 541
 divisible surplus, 217, 538, 565
 effective date of policy, 189
 entire contract clause, 189
 execution of insured, 186
 grace period, 149, 206
 incontestable clause, 127, 149, 204
 incorporation by reference, 203
 inspection receipt, 190
 insurable interest, 3, 182, 205, 222, 445

 legal capacity, 186
 loans, 57, 210, 240
 misstatement of age, 150, 205
 misstatement of sex, 150
 murder of insured, 184, 205
 nonforfeiture options, 57, 58
 offer and acceptance, 187
 premium payment, 2, 67, 466–467
 processing delay, 189
 reinstatement, 45, 58, 149, 212
 replacement of, 108, 126, 197, 559
 representations and warranties, 192
 settlement options, 213, 466, 480
 spendthrift clause, 199
 surrender, 199
 suicide clause, 127, 220
 taxation, 237–241
 and replacement, 240
 trial application, 187
 unilateral, 191, 526
 utmost good faith, 192
 valued, 191
 warranty, 193
Life Insurance Marketing and Research Association (LIMRA), 18, 87, 388
Life insurers
 agency, 193, 549
 agent compensation, 67, 535
 financial strength, 322, 563–569
 investment management, 49, 262, 565
 organization, 560
 product distribution, 535
 reinsurance, 541, 549–551
 regulation, 555–563
 taxation of traditionally large, 554, 569–574
 underwriting, 535, 528, 541, 565
Life Rates & Data, 122
Life style, 467
Lifetime reserve days, 164
Limited partnerships, 451
Limited payment plans, 501
Limited payment whole life insurance, 54, 55
Linton yield, 124
Liquidating trustees, 452
Liquidation, 567
Liquidation Act (1977), 568
Liquidation value, 447
Liquidity, 269
Liquidity enhancement, 442
Living benefits, 172
Living trust, 382
Loans
 automatic premium loan (APL), 198, 206, 211
 policy, 57, 210, 540
Long-term care (LTC), 6, 147, 162, 172
Lost policy receipt, 209
Lotus Development Corp., 263
Lotus 1-2-3, 263

Lump-sum settlement, 214

M
Major medical, 145
Managed care, 136
Mandatory securities valuation reserve (MSVR), 565
Manhart case, 422
Market risk, 270–271
Marketing, 540, 548–549
Maslow, Abraham, 30
Matching principle, 112
Material fact, 192
Mathematics of life insurance, 466
Maximum family benefit (OASDI), 289, 291, 292
McCarran-Ferguson Act (P.L. 15), 554, 557, 558
Mean reserves, 511
Medicaid, 133, 162
Medicaid qualifying trust, 171
Medical expense insurance, 7
Medical Information Bureau (MIB), 545
Medical inspection costs, 528
Medical insurance (Part B), 162, 166–168
Medical price index, 166
Medical reports, 544
Medical selection effect, 467
Medical underwriting, 142
Medicare, 133, 161–168
 Catastrophic Coverage Act of 1988, 171
 gap filler coverage, 146–147, 161, 168–170
 supplement policy, 168
Medicare-Participating Physician/Supplier Directory, 166
Medigap, 161
Mental health contracts, 147
Minimum premium deposit plan, 220
Minors, 186
Misrepresentation, 192, 545, 556
Misstatement of age, 150, 205
Mitford, J., 32
Modified endowment contract (MEC), 53, 67, 236
Modified valuation reserves, 522
Modified whole life insurance, 55
Modigliani, F., 25
Money market funds, 542
Money purchase plan, 426, 427
Moody's, 115
Moral hazard, 544
Mortality cost, 71
Mortality table, 128, 467, 474, 522
Mortgage balance calculator, 268
Mortgage loans, 542
Mortgages
 calculation of balances, 268
 protection coverage, 17

Index

Multiple-indemnity riders, 226
Murder, 184, 205
Mutual Benefit Life Insurance Company, 49
Mutual companies, 109, 113, 114, 535–540, 565
Mutual funds, 79, 235
Mutual savings bank, 535

N

Narcotics, 150
National Association of Insurance Commissioners (NAIC), 82, 148, 169, 172, 556, 557, 559, 563
　annual statement blank, 568
　Committee on Valuation of Securities, 564
　Insurance Information and Privacy Protection Model Act, 546
　Model Insurers' Supervision, Rehabilitation and Liquidation Act, 568
　Standard Nonforfeiture Law, 526
　Standard Valuation Law, 523
National Association of Securities Dealers (NASD), 78, 559
National Convention of Insurance Commissioners, 556
National health insurance (NHI), 176
National Service Life Insurance, 536
Needs-based life insurance purchase, 15–18, 191
Net amount at risk, 517, 518
Net payments cost index (NPI), 119
Net single premium, 75, 219, 465, 467, 475, 489, 491–492
Net worth, 115, 565
Network model HMO, 141
New money rates, 40
New York Insurance Code of 1906, 556
Nonadmitted assets, 564, 566
Nonamortizable assets, 564
Noncancelable, 148, 154
Nonforfeiture options, 127, 206, 509, 540
Nonforfeiture value, 121, 492, 525,
Nonlife insurance, 4
Nonmedical life insurance, 10, 142, 544
Nonparticipating life insurance, 51–53, 109, 113, 537
Nonpayment of premium, 204
Nonqualified plan, 419–421, 438, 458
Nonstandard applications, 547
Nonterminable interest, 250, 251
Nontraditional life insurance, 7, 110
Norris case, 422
Northern National Life Insurance Company v. Lacy J. Miller Machine Company, Inc., 195
Numerical rating, 546
Nursing home care, 146–147, 151

O

Occupational Safety and Health Administration (OSHA), 133
Offer and acceptance, 187
Old Age and Survivors' Disability Insurance (OASDI) 282–303; *see also* Social Security
　average indexed monthly earnings (AIME), 299–301
　benefits, 286–294
　case study, 296–298
　cost of living adjustments (COLAs), 295
　currently insured status, 284
　death benefit, 289
　delayed retirement, 287
　dependent children, 288
　dependent's benefits, 288
　disability insured status, 285, 290, 291
　divorce, 289
　early retirement, 287
　earnings test, 292–294
　eligibility, 283
　Federal Insurance Contributions Act (FICA), 283
　financial planning and, 282, 295
　fully insured status, 284
　maximum family benefit, 289, 291, 292
　Medicare, 133, 161–168
　normal retirement age, 286
　primary insurance amount (PIA), 286, 299–301
　quarters of coverage, 284
　replacement ratio, 301
　retirement benefits, 286–289
　retirement earnings test, 292–294
　spouse's benefits, 288
　survivor benefits, 289, 290
　taxation of benefits, 284
　workers' compensation and, 291
Olsen v. Federal Kemper Life Assurance Company, 188
Omnibus Budget Reconciliation Act, 169
One-year term insurance, 219
Open-ended HMO, 142
Optionally renewable, 148
Ordinary annuity, 265
Ordinary life insurance, 54
Organization, 560
Organ transplants, 144, 151
Original-age conversion, 45
Original-age reinstatement, 212
Outpatient surgery, 138
Ownership changes, 541

P

P.S. 58 Rate Table, 461–462
Paid-in capital, 560
Paid-up additions, 219
Paid-up insurance, 53, 206, 211, 219, 519
Partial disability, 156
Participating (par) life insurance, 51, 52, 113, 537
Participating dividends, 111, 116, 217
Participation payments, 145
Partnerships, 451
Paul v. Virginia, 556
Pavlov, Ivan, 30
Payroll-based stock ownership plan, 539
Pensions, 6, 417–437
　benefits, 425–428
　contributions, 421
　eligibility, 424
　estate taxation, 249
　401(k) plan, 433
　403(b) plan, 434
　free enterprise and, 418, 419
　income taxation, 239
　inflation and, 428, 429
　life insurance and, 430–432
　nonqualified, 419–421
　profit sharing plan, 433
　qualified, 419
　reasons for, 417, 418
　replacement ratio, 418
　retirement age, 424
　vesting, 429
Pepper Commission, 177
Per capita distribution, 224
Per stirpes distribution, 224
Period certain life income option, 217
Permanent dependents, 16
Permanent needs for life insurance, 15, 16
Personal computers, 263
Physical exam and autopsy, 150
Place-of-making rule, 204
Plans A and B, 71, 81
Point-of-service HMO, 141
Policy comparison chart, 60
Policyholder dividends, 566
Policyholder loans, 57, 541
Policyholder reserve calculation, 511
Policyholder services, 541
Policy inspection receipt, 190
Policy lapse, 190
Policy loans, 210
Policy owner, 182
Policy provisions, 202
Portfolio diversification, 110
Portfolio management fees, 79
Post-claim underwriting, 174
Postmortem planning, 250, 251, 384
Pour-ins, 78
Power of appointment, 247, 248, 383
Preadmission testing, 138
Preauthorized admissions, 541
Predeath arrangements, 450

Predisability arrangements, 450
Preexisting conditions, 148, 151, 154
Preferred provider organizations (PPOs), 140, 142, 411
Preferred stock, 564
Premium, 2, 39, 466–467
Premium default, 210
Premium leveling process, 8, 494–510
Premium payments, 67
Premium tax, 569, 528
Premium waiver rider, 113, 451, 455, 460
Prescription drug reimbursement, 146–147
Present value of $1, 264
Present value of annuity, 266
Present value of annuity due, 266
Present value of future benefits, 219, 476, 491–492, 515, 520
Presumptive total disability, 156, 227
Pretext interviews, 546
Price-to-earnings (P/E) ratio, 277
Primary beneficiary, 224
Primary care physicians, 541
Principal sum, 143
Privacy and underwriting, 545–546
Privacy Protection Study Commission (PPSC), 546
Private annuity, 89
Private insurance companies, 140
Private investigators, 544
Probability of death, 468
Probate, 16, 222, 257, 376, 379, 380, 423
Processing delay, 189
Product distribution, 535
Projected annuity tables, 474
Promissory notes, 190
Proportionate benefits, 156
Prospective payment system (PPS), 165
Prospective terminal reserve calculation, 513, 515
Protection, 108
Proxy, 537
Psychological factors, 27–33, 346, 347, 377
Public Law 15 (P.L. 15), 554
Publicly traded securities, 269
Purchasing power risk, 270; *see also* Inflation
Pure annuity, 6

Q

Qualified pension plan, 419, 420, 458
Qualified terminable interest property (QTIP), 250, 251, 384
Quality-of-care, 541

R

Rabbi trust, 420, 459
Radix, 468
Rate of return, 275

Rated policies, 187, 211, 546–547
Ratification, 196
Rating age, 548
Rating life insurance, 546–548; *see also* Underwriting
Readjustment fund, 16
Real estate, 269, 542
Reallocating consumption, 268
Rear-end load, 39, 52, 69
Reasonable and customary, 137, 144
Reasonable expectations, 152
Rebating, 197, 556
Recurrent disability, 157
Reduced paid-up insurance option, 209
Reduced-age statutes, 186
Reentry term life insurance, 43–45
Refund annuity, 6
Refund features, 487
Regular medical, 145
Regulation of insurers, 555–563
Regulation of provisions, 561
Regulation of rates, 561
Rehabilitation benefits, 158, 567
Reinstatement, 58, 149, 212–213
 advantages and disadvantages, 212
 attained age, 45
 effect on suicide and incontestable clauses, 213
 insurability, 212
 original age, 45
Reinsurance, 541, 549–551
Reinsurer, 550
Renewability, 147–148
Renewable term life insurance, 44, 45
Rent, 480
Reorganization, 554, 567
Replacement, 108, 126, 197, 559
 tax considerations, 127
Replacement ratio, 301, 349, 418
Representations, 192
Reserve, 490, 492, 509–525
 adequacy, 540, 541
 amount, 519
 calculations, 562
 methods, 522
 requirements, 561
 and surrender values, 525
Residual disability benefits, 156
Resource-based relative value scale, 167
Respite care, 164, 165
Retention limit, 550
Retired lives reserves, 408, 409
Retirement, 347, 348, 424, 425
Retirement earnings test (OASDI), 292
Retirement Equity Act of 1984 (REA), 423
Retirement income life insurance, 432
Retirement planning, 342–372
 budget, 356
 case study, 358–367
 defined benefit plans, 357

defined contribution plans, 357
 developing goals for, 344, 345
 family considerations, 348
 financial considerations, 348, 349
 403(b) plans, 353, 354
 individual retirement accounts (IRAs), 350–353
 Keogh plans, 353
 physical factors, 346
 psychological factors, 346, 347
 replacement ratio, 349
 sources of income, 355
Retrocession, 550
Retrospective review, 138
Retrospective terminal reserve calculation, 513–514
Return of cash value rider, 47
Return of premium rider, 47
Revocable beneficiaries, 223
Risk, 270
Risk tolerance, 308–310
Rollover IRAs, 352

S

Safety, 269
Salary continuation plan, 458
Savings, 108
Savings bank life insurance (SBLI), 306, 536
Savings need for life insurance, 17, 18
Schelberger v. Eastern Savings Bank, 220
S corporation, 445
SEC v. Variable Life Insurance Company of America et al., 559
Second death policies, 388
Second opinions, 138
Secondary financial market, 269
Section 302 stock redemption, 456–457
Section 303 stock redemption, 456–457
Section 401(k) plans, 274, 433
Section 403(b) plans, 110, 274, 353, 354, 434
Secular trust, 458
Securities and Exchange Commission (SEC), 78, 539, 554
Select mortality tables, 474
Self-insurance, 135
Self-selection, 490, 518
Separate account, 78, 81
Servicemen's Group Life Insurance, 536
Set-back rating, 94
Settlement, 127, 128
Settlement options, 213, 466, 480
Sex, 467, 543
Sherman Antitrust Act, 556
Sickness, 154
Simplified Employee Pensions (SEPs), 352
Simplified policy language, 561

Index

Single life annuities, 480
Single premium annuities, 90, 91, 503
Single premium deferred annuities, 503
Single premium whole life insurance, 53, 236, 501, 520
Sinking fund, 457
Skilled nursing care, 138, 163–164, 172
Skinner, B. F., 30
Small life insurance company deduction, 574
Social Security Act of 1965, 133, 155, 161, 169
Social Security, 282–303, 418; *see also* Old Age Survivors' and Disability Insurance
  blackout period, 290
  integration with retirement plans, 418
  1983 Amendments, 283
  surpluses, 343
  taxation of benefits, 294
Sole proprietorship, 447
Soliciting offers, 187
South-Eastern Underwriters Association (SEUA), 556
Special agent, 194
Special life insurance company deduction, 574
Specified amount, 71
Spell of illness, 164
Spendthrift trust provision, 199
Split dollar life insurance, 241, 460
Spreadsheet software, 263
Staff model HMO, 141
Standard & Poor's, 115
State premium tax, 69
State taxation, 569
Statement of Financial Accounting Standards Board (SFAS) No. 60, 566
Statement of opinion, 193
Statutory accounting, 114
Statutory accounting principles (SAP), 538–539, 565–566
Stepped-up basis, 257, 378
Stock insurance companies, 113, 535–540, 560, 565
Stock options, 539
Stock redemption agreement, 454–455
Stocks, 262, 542
Straight life annuity, 6
Straight whole life, 501
Stress, 28, 29
Subcommittee on Select Revenue Measures of the Committee on Ways and Means, 539
Subrogation, 191
Substance abuse, 151
Substandard policies, 547
Substandard policy reserves, 524
Suicide, 127, 220

Supplemental Executive Retirement Program, 420
Supplemental life insurance plans, 407
Supplemental Social Security (SSI), 170
Surgical contracts, 144–145
Surplus, 537, 560
Surplus calculations, 562
Surrender, 77, 210, 540
Surrender charge, 39, 525–526
Surrender cost index (SCI), 118–119
Surrender value, 525
Survivor life insurance, 388
Survivorship approach to death claim, 518
Survivorship benefits, 41, 90, 517

T

Table of guaranteed policy values, 69, 207
T-account, 42
Target benefit plan, 427
Tax deferral, 401, 402
Tax Equity and Fiscal Responsibility Act (TEFRA) of 1982, 73, 168, 573
Tax lien, 198
Tax Reform Act of 1984, 67, 73, 569, 573
Tax Reform Act of 1986, 53, 139, 320, 408, 423, 433
Tax retaliation, 572
Tax-deferred annuity, 353, 354, 434
Tax-deferred investments, 273
Tax-free investments, 273
Taxation of
  403(b) plans 355
  group disability insurance, 411
  group life insurance, 406
  IRAs, 352
  life insurers, 554, 569–574
  Social Security, 294
  ULI, 77
  VLI, 80
Technical and Miscellaneous Revenue Act of 1988, 236
Temporary annuities, 481
Temporary life annuity due factor, 496
Temporary needs for life insurance, 17
Ten-day examination period, 148, 190
Term life insurance, 8, 42–48, 385, 443, 476, 519
  convertible, 45
  definition, 42
  level, increasing and decreasing, 46
  limitations of, 47
  reentry, 43–45
  renewable, 43–45
  uses, 47
Terminal dividends, 116
Terminal reserves, 511
Testamentary trust, 381
Third-party administrator (TPA), 135

Time limit on certain defenses, 149
Time value of money, 262, 466, 467
Tonti, Lorenzo, 218
Tontine, 218, 556, 562
Total interest adjusted cost (TIAC), 118
Total return, 273
Traditional net cost (NC), 116–118
Transfer for value, 237, 446
Transition benefits, 158
Trial application, 187
Trust officer, 439
Trusts, 455
  children and, 321
  credit shelter bypass, 383, 384
  Crummey, 256
  estate planning and, 381, 382, 386–388
  funded, 381
  grantor, 382
  irrevocable, 381
  life insurance, 386
  living, 382
  multiemployer, 403
  rabbi, 420
  revocable, 381
  taxation of, 232, 233
  testamentary, 381
  unfunded, 382
Twisting, 196, 556

U

Ultimate mortality tables, 475
Unassigned surplus, 565
Unauthorized practice of law, 197, 375
Underwriting, 528, 535, 541, 565
  adverse selection, 36, 154, 490, 518, 526, 543
  age, 467, 543, 548
  application, 187, 544
  class rating, 546
  criteria, 542, 544–545
  extra premium tables, 548
  group, 403–405, 410
  health, 467, 563
  increased rating age, 547
  lower dividend class, 547–548
  numerical rating, 546
  privacy of information, 545
  sex, 467, 543
  substandard rating, 547
  unisex tables, 206, 543
Undivided earnings, 537
Unearned premium, 225
Unfriendly takeover, 540
Unfunded plan, 458
Unified Transfer tax, 246
Uniform Gifts to Minors Act, 320
Uniform Individual Accident and Sickness Policy Provisions, 148
Uniform Simultaneous Death Act, 225
Unilateral contract, 191, 526

Unisex mortality and tables, 206, 543
U.S. government Life Insurance, 536
U.S. Treasury securities, 262
Universal life, 9, 64, 66, 112
Unpaid premiums, 150
Usual, customary and reasonable (UCR), 139
Utilization review, 138, 541
Utmost good faith, 192

V

Valuation, 443
Valued contracts, 191
Vanishing-premium ULI, 68
Variable annuity, 98–100
    example, 100
    mechanics, 99
    theory of, 98
Variable life insurance, 64, 78
Variable universal life, 9, 64, 81

Vending machines, 189
Vesting, 429
Veterans' Administration, 133
Veterans' benefits, 151
Veterans' Group Life Insurance, 536
Vision care, 146–147, 151
Void ab initio, 205

W-Y-Z

Waiting period, 144, 154
Waiver of premiums, 58, 77, 80, 111, 143, 151, 158, 227
War exclusions, 226
Warranty, 193
Welch v. Provident Life and Accident Insurance Company, 205
Whole life insurance, 8, 48–59, 484, 478, 519
    combination, 56
    continuous premium, 54
    definition, 48
    flexibility, 56–59
    limited premium, 54, 55
    modified, 55
    nonforfeiture options, 57
    nonparticipating, 50–53
    participating premiums, 51, 52
    savings vehicle, 48–53
    uses, 56
Will, 222, 381
Workers' compensation, 133, 151, 155
Wrongful death, 191

Yearly rate of return (YROR), 124–125
Yearly renewable term (YRT) reinsurance, 551
Yield to maturity, 278

Zero-coupon bonds, 325